The International Legal Order's Colour Line

The International Legal Order's Colour Line

Racism, Racial Discrimination, and the Making of International Law

WILLIAM A. SCHABAS

Oxford University Press is a department of the University of Oxford.
It furthers the University's objective of excellence in research, scholarship,
and education by publishing worldwide. Oxford is a registered trade mark of
Oxford University Press in the UK and certain other countries.

Published in the United States of America by Oxford University Press
198 Madison Avenue, New York, NY 10016, United States of America.

© Oxford University Press 2023

All rights reserved. No part of this publication may be reproduced, stored in a retrieval system, or transmitted, in any form or by any means, without the prior permission in writing of Oxford University Press, or as expressly permitted by law, by license, or under terms agreed with the appropriate reproduction rights organization. Inquiries concerning reproduction outside the scope of the above should be sent to the Rights Department, Oxford University Press, at the address above.

You must not circulate this work in any other form
and you must impose this same condition on any acquirer.

CIP data is on file at the Library of Congress

ISBN 978-0-19-774447-5

DOI: 10.1093/oso/9780197744475.001.0001

Note to Readers
This publication is designed to provide accurate and authoritative information in regard to the subject matter covered. It is based upon sources believed to be accurate and reliable and is intended to be current as of the time it was written. It is sold with the understanding that the publisher is not engaged in rendering legal, accounting, or other professional services. If legal advice or other expert assistance is required, the services of a competent professional person should be sought. Also, to confirm that the information has not been affected or changed by recent developments, traditional legal research techniques should be used, including checking primary sources where appropriate.

*(Based on the Declaration of Principles jointly adopted by a Committee of the
American Bar Association and a Committee of Publishers and Associations.)*

> You may order this or any other Oxford University Press publication
> by visiting the Oxford University Press website at www.oup.com.

Acknowledgements

Special thanks are due to Itaf Al-Awawdeh, Elizabeth Borgwardt, Roger Clark, Chile Eboe Osuji, Ndubuisi Idejiora-Kalu, Mohamed Kotby, Claus Kreß, Dareen Abou Naga, Malick Sow, Dire Tladi, and Mohamed Zeidy, all of whom answered questions promptly and with great courtesy. I was also assisted by librarians at the UNESCO archives in Paris (Alexandre Coutelle), the Dag Hammarskjöld Library in New York (Susan Kurtas), and the United Nations archives in Geneva (Jacques Oberson). My gratitude extends to Robert Cavooris, the commissioning editor at Oxford University Press, and all of those at the Press who have been involved in the production of this book. As always, the constant encouragement of Penelope Soteriou hastened the process and ensured the project was completed. She also provided great insights as I wrestled with some of the conceptual problems, and she read and corrected the final manuscript.

William A. Schabas
Paris
4 January 2023

Contents

List of Abbreviations	ix
1. 'Civilized Nations' and the Colour Line	1
2. The Great War and the Fragile Peace	25
3. Mandates, Minorities, and the League of Nations	52
4. The United Nations Charter	90
5. Early Years of the United Nations	106
6. The International Bill of Rights	137
7. UNESCO: Fighting the Doctrine of Racial Inequality	169
8. Colonialism and Neo-colonialism at the United Nations	198
9. The International Convention on the Elimination of All Forms of Racial Discrimination	244
10. Apartheid	287
11. Racial Discrimination as a Crime against Humanity	313
12. Days, Years, Decades, and Conferences on Racial Discrimination	351
13. The Colour Line's Long Twentieth Century	383
Bibliography	415
Index	457

Abbreviations

ECOSOC	Economic and Social Council
FMAE	Archives of the French Foreign Ministry
FRUS	Foreign Relations of the United States
LNA	League of Nations Archives
LNTS	League of Nations Treaty Series
NAACP	National Association for the Advancement of Colored People
NAC	National Archives of Canada
OP	operative paragraph
PP	preambular paragraph
TNA	National Archives (United Kingdom)
UN	United Nations
UNA	United Nations Archives
UNCIO	United Nations Conference on International Organization
UNESCO	United Nations Educational, Scientific and Cultural Organization
UNTS	United Nations Treaty Series
USNA	National Archives (United States)

1

'Civilized Nations' and the Colour Line

'The problem of the twentieth century'

'The problem of the twentieth century is the problem of the colour line – the relation of the darker to the lighter races of men in Asia and Africa, in America and the islands of the sea', wrote W.E.B. Du Bois, the great African-American intellectual and activist, in his magnum opus, *The Souls of Black Folk*, first published in 1904.[1] Du Bois actively participated in two of the century's great international law-making events, the 1919 Paris Peace Conference and the 1945 San Francisco Conference on International Organisation. At both of these he campaigned for condemnation of the odious scourge of racial discrimination. He died in 1963, the year the United Nations General Assembly adopted the Declaration on the Elimination of All Forms of Racial Discrimination. His contribution to the progressive development of international law and international organizations did much to address 'the problem of the colour line'. But the struggles of the twentieth century were not enough. The colour line persists well into the twenty-first century.

International law is and has always been characterized by a colour line. Its origins are known today principally through the writings of the great publicists of the sixteenth, seventeenth, and eighteenth centuries. These white Europeans endeavoured to bring order to the relations between the 'civilized nations'. International law also ensured the protection of their wealth-generating activities elsewhere in the world, which prospered on the basis of colonialism and the slave trade in people of colour. The victims of racial discrimination were entirely excluded from the process of international law-making. Martti Koskenniemi has described an international legal order premised on a 'logic of exclusion-inclusion' whereby some non-European peoples could participate in the obligations but were excluded from full rights of membership.[2] According to Georges Abi-Saab, the countries inhabited by people of colour were, by and

---

[1] W.E.B. Du Bois, 'Of the Dawn of Freedom', in Eric Foner and Henry Louis Gates Jr., eds., *W.E.B. Du Bois, Black Reconstruction and Other Writings*, New York: Library of America, 2021, pp. 887–905, at p. 887. The phrase had been used since the time of reconstruction following the Civil War. See, for example, Frederick Douglass, 'The Color Line' (1881) 132 *The North American Review* 567.

[2] Martti Koskenniemi, *The Gentle Civilizer of Nations: The Rise and Fall of International Law, 1870–1960*, New York: Cambridge University Press, 2001, pp. 127–31.

The International Legal Order's Colour Line. William A. Schabas, Oxford University Press.
© Oxford University Press 2023. DOI: 10.1093/oso/9780197744475.003.0001

2 'CIVILIZED NATIONS' AND THE COLOUR LINE

large, 'objects' of international law rather than its 'subjects'.[3] In the words of Judge Mohamed Shahabuddeen of the International Court of Justice, international law 'was both fashioned and administered by leading members of a select community [at a time] when that community, by itself called the international community, bore little resemblance to the world as it then stood, and even less to the world as it stands today'.[4]

A year after Du Bois made his famous comment about the 'colour line', Lassa Oppenheim of the London School of Economics published a seminal textbook. He explained how the history of international law had been marked by 'the successive entrances of various States into the Family of Nations'. The original members of this 'Family' were 'the old Christian States of Europe'. To this select club were gradually added the 'Christian States that grew up outside Europe', principally in the western hemisphere.[5] Oppenheim conceded that the 'Christian Negro Republic of Liberia in West Africa and of Haiti on the island of San Domingo belong to this group'. He also included the Congo Free State, a personal fiefdom of the King of Belgium.[6] Oppenheim failed to mention the Hawai'an Kingdom, then occupied by the United States for several years and purportedly annexed by it in 1898. The 'Family of Nations' ceased being reserved to Christian States with the admission of the Ottoman or Turkish Empire and Japan, during the nineteenth century, although Oppenheim thought inclusion of Persia, Siam, China, Korea, Abyssinia, 'and the like' to be doubtful.[7] It was a somewhat conservative assessment, because China, Persia, and Siam had already been among the 26 invitees at the first Hague Peace Conference, convened by the Russian Emperor in 1899. Forty-seven States were invited to attend the second Hague Peace Conference of 1907. The list included five Asian States: China, Japan, Korea, Persia, and Siam. Africa was represented by Ethiopia and by Haiti, a country of African descent.[8]

Some of international law's celebrated publicists have been singled out for their quite explicitly racist views and statements. A recent symposium about the legacy of James Lorimer, the Scottish international lawyer of the late nineteenth century, drew attention to his racist perspective but at the same time encouraged

---

[3] Georges Abi-Saab, 'The Newly Independent States and the Rules of International Law: An Outline' (1962) 8 *Howard Law Journal* 95, at pp. 97–8.

[4] *Territorial Dispute (Libyan Arab Jamahiriya/Chad)*, Judgment, I.C.J. Reports 1994, p. 6, Separate Opinion of Judge Shahabuddeen, p. 42.

[5] Lassa Oppenheim, *International Law, Vol. I, Peace*, London: Longmans, Green, 1905, pp. 30–1.

[6] William Roger Louis, 'Roger Casement and the Congo' (1964) 5 *Journal of African History* 99; Adam Hochschild, *King Leopold's Ghost: A Story of Greed, Terror, and Heroism in Colonial Africa*, Boston: Houghton Mifflin, 1998.

[7] Lassa Oppenheim, *International Law, Vol. I, Peace*, London: Longmans, Green, 1905, pp. 32–3.

[8] 'List of States Invited to Participate in the Labours of the Second Conference of the Hague', in James Brown Scott, *The Hague Peace Conferences, 1899-1907*, Baltimore: Johns Hopkins Press, 1909, pp. 179–80.

the view that this was somewhat of an aberration, uncharacteristic of the views of the liberal mainstream that prevailed in the Institut de droit international.[9] But as Christopher Gevers has pointed out, the focus on those who were candid enough to express obnoxious views about racial superiority has tended to conceal the centrality of race in the outlook of the international legal community. 'For Lorimer's nineteenth century contemporaries, then, racist views also went without thinking, as their common racial contract was not just political, moral, cultural, and economic, it was epistemological, setting the terms upon which its signatories interpreted, or misinterpreted, the world.'[10]

There is no great difficulty identifying manifestations of racism in the early centuries of the discipline. From the very beginning, the victims resisted. But their struggle did not take place within the structures and institutions of international law, from which they were entirely excluded. Until the twentieth century, that is, the century of the colour line, any objection to racism and racial discrimination within international law was half-hearted, patronizing, and paternalistic. This began to change as States of what we today call the Global South were able to participate in debates about the orientation and development of international law. Their leaders came to the negotiating tables with several major concerns, including racial equality. They fought against white supremacy, politely but resolutely. The battles would not have taken place had they not been there. This is still true today.

'Civilized' Nations

Like the increasingly embarrassing statues and monuments in the cities of Europe and North America that honour men whose lives, reputations, and fortunes were built on a foundation of racial discrimination, the fundamental texts of international law still bear the traces of its inglorious past. Several important treaties that remain in force make reference to 'civilized nations',[11] 'civilized peoples',[12] and the 'civilized

---

[9] Martti Koskenniemi, 'Race, Hierarchy and International Law: Lorimer's Legal Science' (2016) 27 *European Journal of International Law* 415.

[10] Christopher Gevers, 'Unwhitening the World, Rethinking Race and International Law' (2021) 67 *UCLA Law Review* 1652, at p. 1661.

[11] Statute of the International Court of Justice, art. 38(1)(c); European Convention on Human Rights (1953) 213 UNTS 222, art. 7(2).

[12] Convention for the Amelioration of the Condition of the Wounded and Sick in Armed Forces in the Field (1950) 75 UNTS 31, arts. 3(1)(d), 63; Convention for the Amelioration of the Condition of Wounded, Sick and Shipwrecked Members of Armed Forces at Sea (1950) 75 UNTS 85, arts. 3(1)(d), 62; Convention Relative to the Treatment of Prisoners of War (1950) 75 UNTS 135, arts. 3(1)(d), 142; Convention Relative to the Protection of Civilian Persons in Time of War (1950) 75 UNTS 287, arts. 3(1)(d), 158.

4 'CIVILIZED NATIONS' AND THE COLOUR LINE

world,[13] notions derived from ideas of European and white supremacy.[14] Theses archaic term originate in early multilateral treaties,[15] including the two Hague Conventions on the laws and customs of war: 'the usages established between civilised nations, from the laws of humanity, and the requirements of the public conscience.'[16] In our contemporary understanding of the term 'civilized', these States were hardly qualified. The law of 'civilized' peoples in which international law found its roots was entirely comfortable with the most barbaric manifestations of slavery, the slave trade, and even genocide.

Nineteenth century publicists such as William Edward Hall defined international law as 'certain rules of conduct in which modern civilised states regard as being binding on them in their relations with one another.'[17] For Hall, international law was 'a product of the special civilisation of modern Europe.'[18] Fyodor de Martens said international law was 'l'expression des lois communes aux nations civilisées.'[19] A prominent international lawyer of the period, James Lorimer, used pseudo-scientific racist theories to account for the hegemony of European international law.[20] John Westlake, the Whewell professor of international law at Cambridge University in the late nineteenth century, spoke of civilization as a feature of the 'European race' and referred to international law as 'the rules that are universally recognised by white men.'[21] A few decades later, his views had evolved, but only slightly: 'As English law is the law of England and French law that of France, so international law is that of a certain part of the world, which comprises if it is not exclusively composed of Europe, all nations outside Europe but of European blood, and Japan.'[22] Jan Hendrik Willem Verzijl wrote: 'Now

[13] Convention on the Prevention and Punishment of the Crime of Genocide (1951) 78 UNTS 277, PP 1.

[14] See generally Jean Allain, 'Slavery and the League of Nations: Ethiopia as a Civilised Nation' (2006) 8 *Journal of the History of International Law* 213; Brett Bowden, 'The Colonial Origins of International Law. European Expansion and the Classic Standard of Civilization' (2005) 7 *Journal of the History of International Law* 1.

[15] Declaration Renouncing the Use, in Time of War, of certain Explosive Projectiles. Saint Petersburg, 29 November–11 December 1868, PP 1; Pacific Settlement of International Disputes (Hague I), 1907, I Bevans 577, PP 3.

[16] Hague Convention (IV) respecting the Laws and Customs of War on Land, 1907, 100 BFSP 338, preamble.

[17] William Edward Hall, *A Treatise on International Law*, 3rd ed., Oxford: Clarendon Press, 1890, p. 1.

[18] Ibid., p. 42.

[19] Fyodor Fedorovič de Martens, *Traité de droit international*, Vol. I, Paris: Maresq, 1883, p. 1.

[20] Martti Koskenniemi, *The Gentle Civilizer of Nations: The Rise and Fall of International Law, 1870–1960*, New York: Cambridge University Press, 2001, at pp. 70–1. Also Martti Koskenniemi, 'Race, Hierarchy and International Law: Lorimer's Legal Science' (2016) 27 *European Journal of International Law* 447; Karen Knop, 'Lorimer's Private Citizens of the World' (2016) 27 *European Journal of International Law* 415.

[21] John Westlake, *Chapters on International Law*, Cambridge: Cambridge University Press, 1894, pp. 141, 143. See Antony Anghie on the 'racialisation of sovereignty', Antony Anghie, *Imperialism, Sovereignty and the Making of International Law*, Cambridge: Cambridge University Press, 2004, pp. 100–7.

[22] John Westlake, 'Native States of India' (1910) 24 *Law Quarterly Review* 312, at p. 313.

there is one truth that is not open to denial or even to doubt, namely, that the actual body of international law, as it stands today, is not only the product of the conscious activity of the European mind, but has also drawn its vital essence from a common source of European beliefs, and in both of these aspects it is mainly of Western European origin.'[23]

The Statute of the International Court of Justice, adopted in 1945 at the San Francisco Conference, refers to 'general principles of law recognised by civilised nations'. Use of the term 'civilized nations' does not appear to have provoked any objection at the time. But shortly afterwards, a reference to 'civilized nations' in an early draft of the Universal Declaration of Human Rights was removed following objections from India and the Soviet Union.[24] The Commission on Human Rights reverted to it in 1950 in the draft human rights covenant.[25] The United Kingdom persisted in its attachment to the term.[26] At its insistence, a reference to 'general principles of law recognised by civilised nations' was incorporated into the European Convention on Human Rights, adopted in November 1950.[27] When the Commission on Human Rights considered the expression in 1952, Britain's representative, Samuel Hoare, offered the pathetic explanation that it 'had not been proposed in a colonialist spirit'.[28] René Cassin's suggestion to replace the term with 'the community of nations'[29] was adopted by nine votes to none, but with eight abstentions![30] In 2021, the International Law Commission finally proposed that the term 'community of nations' used in article 15 of the International Covenant on Civil and Political Rights replace 'civilized nations' in references to 'general principles of law'.[31]

There was also a debate about using the term 'civilized' when Brazil, Colombia, and Senegal proposed an additional paragraph for the preamble of the International Convention on the Elimination of All Forms of Racial

---

[23] Jan Hendrik Willem Verzijl, 'Western European Influence on the Foundations of International Law' (1956) 1 *International Relations* 187, cited by R.P. Anand, 'Attitude of the Asian-African States toward Certain Problems of International Law' (1966) 15 *International and Comparative Law Quarterly* 55, at p. 57.

[24] Communication Received from India, 4 May 1948, E/CN.4/82/Add.7; Summary record, Drafting Committee, 19 May 1948, E/CN.4/AC.1/SR.39, p. 3; Summary record, Commission on Human Rights, 2 June 1948, E/CN.4/SR.56, p. 5.

[25] Summary record, Commission on Human Rights, 18 April 1950, E/CN.4/SR.159, para. 96.

[26] United Kingdom, Proposals on Certain Articles, 16 May 1949, E/CN.4/188; Comments of the Government of the United Kingdom, 7 January 1950, E/CN.4/353/Add.2.

[27] Comments of Governments on the draft International Covenant on Human Rights and Measures of Implementation [UN Doc. E/CN.4/353/Add.1-3], Doc. A 770, Collected Edition of the '*Travaux préparatoires*' of the European Convention on Human Rights, Vol. III, pp. 156–79, at p. 162.

[28] Summary record, Commission on Human Rights, 5 June 1952, E/CN.4/SR.324, p. 7.

[29] Ibid., p. 11.

[30] Ibid., p. 17.

[31] Report of the International Law Commission, Seventy-second session (26 April–4 June and 5 July–6 August 2021), A/76/10, p. 162. See also Sixth Committee Begins International Law Commission Third Cluster Review, Debating General Principles of Law, Replacement Language for 'Civilized Nations', 23 November 2021, GA/L/3649.

6 'CIVILIZED NATIONS' AND THE COLOUR LINE

Discrimination: 'Convinced that the existence of racial barriers is repugnant to the ideals of any civilized society.'[32] Clearly, they meant use of the term 'civilized' in a more modern sense, not one that implied European superiority but rather the opposite. The Senegalese representative in the Third Committee of the General Assembly explained that it meant 'any normative society guided by an ethical outlook whose fundamental general principles were laid down in the Universal Declaration of Human Rights; its opposite was savage society, which was dominated by the idea of might is right.'[33] But objections to the word 'civilized' prevailed and the sponsors agreed to replace it with 'human.'[34]

To many the term 'civilized' sounds amusingly quaint and perhaps innocuous, but the distinction between 'civilized peoples' and others was quite fundamental to early international law. Moreover, it was imbued with racist perspectives. Lurking behind the reference to 'civilized peoples' in the famous Martens clause of the 1899 and 1907 Hague Conventions was the implication that the laws and customs of war did not apply universally. One of the classic norms of this body of law was the prohibition of so-called dum-dum or hollow tipped bullets. At the 1899 Hague Conference, the British opposed a prohibition on such ammunition, which had been developed in colonial India to stop 'fanatical tribesmen'. Major-General Sir John Ardagh told the Conference that while in 'civilized war' a soldier hit by a bullet withdraws from the battlefield, '[i]t is very different with a savage' who 'continues on, and before anyone has time to explain to him that he is flagrantly violating the decisions of the Hague Conference, he cuts off your head.'[35] Some legal commentators contended that it was contrary to the international law of armed conflict to employ 'savages' in European wars.[36] During the First World War, Germany protested that use by the Allies of 'coloured troops' was contrary to the progressive development of international law.[37] According to the 1914 British military manual, 'the rules of International Law apply only to warfare between civilised nations ... They do not apply in wars with uncivilised States and tribes.'[38] These words were endorsed in 1927 in an article entitled

---

[32] Colombia and Senegal: amendments to the provisions of the draft international convention on the elimination of all forms of racial discrimination adopted by the Commission on Human Rights (A/5921, annex), 11 October 1965, A/C.3/L.1217.

[33] Summary record, Sixth Committee, 12 October 1965, A/C.3/SR.1301, para. 63.

[34] Summary record, Sixth Committee, 12 October 1965, A/C.3/SR.1302, para. 1.

[35] Third meeting, 31 May 1899, in James Brown Scott, ed., *The Proceedings of the Hague Peace Conferences, The Conference of 1899*, New York: Oxford University Press, 1920, p. 343.

[36] Rotem Giladi, 'The Phoenix of Colonial War: Race, the Laws of War, and the "Horror on the Rhine"' (2017) 30 *Leiden Journal of International Law* 847, at pp. 854–8.

[37] *Employment, contrary to International Law, of Colored Troops upon the European Arena of War by England and France*, [Berlin]: Foreign Office, 1915.

[38] James Edward Edmonds and Lassa Oppenheim, *Land Warfare: An Exposition of the Laws and Usages of War on Land, for the Guidance of Officers of His Majesty's Army*, London: HMSO, 1914, para. 7, cited in Frédéric Mégret, 'From "savages" to "unlawful combatants": A Postcolonial Look at International Law's "other"', in Anne Orford, ed., *International Law and its Others*, Cambridge: Cambridge University Press, 2009, pp. 265–317.

'How to Fight Savage Tribes' published in the *American Journal of International Law*. '[T]his is a different kind of war, this which is waged by native tribes, than that which might be waged between advanced nations of western culture', wrote Elbridge Colby in the prestigious academic publication.[39] Rotem Giladi has traced the prohibition in article 22(5) of the Covenant of the League of Nations of 'military training of the natives for other than police purposes' to this rejection of 'uncivilized' combatants.[40]

Antony Anghie has explained that the notion of 'civilized peoples' was 'a fundamental tenet of positivist epistemology and thus profoundly shaped the concepts constituting the positivist framework. The racialisation of positivist law followed inevitably from these premises as demonstrated, for example, by the argument that law was the creation of unique, civilised, and social institutions and that only states possessing such institutions could be members of "international society".[41] Those who were not 'civilied', essentially all of them non-Europeans, were excluded from the system. They were characterized as 'barbaric' and 'backward', to be 'civilised, redeemed, developed, pacified. Race has played a crucially important role in constructing and defining the other.'[42] This distinction, rooted in international law from its beginnings in the sixteenth and seventeenth centuries, and affirmed explicitly in the heyday of colonialism, led inexorably to racial discrimination. In James Gathii's words, 'deeply racialized discourses presumed the West was superior and civilized but were also predicated on assumptions of White supremacy, in which White was pure, neutral, and rational while the others were impure, abnormal, and degenerate.'[43] It was a world premised on inequality, of domination by a small number of countries. The planet was divided in two: in geographic terms, by the equator, in political terms, by the 'colour line'.

International law is often credited with bringing an end to slavery and the slave trade. But in earlier times, it protected these appalling practices. The great John Marshall, Chief Justice of the United States Supreme Court, ruled that while the slave trade might be 'contrary to the law of nature', it could not be considered 'contrary to the law of nations which was authorised and protected by the laws of all commercial nations'. Marshall wrote that international law 'is decided in

---

[39] Elbridge Colby, 'How to Fight Savage Tribes' (1927) 21 *American Journal of International Law* 279, at p. 287.

[40] Ibid., p. 871.

[41] Antony Anghie, 'Finding the Peripheries: Sovereignty and Colonialism in Nineteenth-Century International Law' (1999) 40 *Harvard International Law Journal* 1, at p. 25.

[42] Antony Anghie and B.S. Chimni, 'Third World Approaches to International Law and Individual Responsibility in Internal Conflicts' (2003) 2 Chinese *Journal of International Law* 77, at p. 85. See also the discussion in Patrick Thornberry, *The International Convention on the Elimination of All Forms of Racial Discrimination*, Oxford: Oxford University Press, 2016, pp. 9–12.

[43] James T. Gathii, 'Writing Race and Identity in a Global Context: What CRT and TWAIL Can Learn from Each Other' (2021) 67 *UCLA Law Review* 1610, at p. 1641.

8 'CIVILIZED NATIONS' AND THE COLOUR LINE

favour of the slave trade'. A consequence of his decision was the *refoulement* of nearly 100 African slaves to their 'owners'.[44] In an English judgment of about the same time, Justice William Scott rejected the legal significance of the anti-slavery declaration made by European leaders at the Congress of Vienna in 1815, upholding 'the established course of the general law of nations' that permitted the slave trade and protected its conduct. Scott held that it would be 'deemed a most extravagant assumption in any Court of the Law of Nations, to pronounce that this practice, the tolerated, the approved, the encouraged object of law, ever since man became subject to law, was prohibited by that law, and was legally criminal'.[45]

In the famous *Lotus* case, the Permanent Court of International Justice stated that international law 'governs relations between independent States . . . in order to regulate the relations between these co-existing independent communities or with a view to the achievement of common aims'.[46] In his seminal article in the *American Journal of International Law*, which has been cited in the academic literature nearly 2,000 times, Prosper Weil wrote that international law has always borne 'the stamp of an end that has never changed: to ensure the coexistence – in peace, if possible; in war, if necessary – and the cooperation of basically disparate entities composing a fundamentally pluralistic society'.[47] But these benign visions of international law only tell part of the story. International law is also a battleground, where the main protagonists are those seeking to ensure their dominance and those who confront and challenge it. The peoples of the Global South had to fight their way into the club of 'civilized nations'. Once there, they used international law to challenge the racist premises of the existing legal order.

The dialectic is apparent in the Charter of the United Nations, an instrument that codified important progressive developments but that also entrenched a world order premised upon the domination of 'great powers'.[48] The fundamental equality of members is affirmed by their participation in the General Assembly while their corresponding inequality underpins the status of the five permanent members of the Security Council. Human rights are acknowledged in a number of provisions of the Charter yet there is also a firewall in article 2(7) preventing the United Nations from interfering in matters of domestic jurisdiction. Article 1(2) proclaims the 'principle of equal rights and self-determination of peoples' while article 73 of the Charter, like an enduring scar, refers euphemistically to 'non-self-governing territories'. It provides a constant reminder that when the

---

[44] *The Antelope*, 23 U.S. 66 (1825).

[45] *Le Louis* (1817) 12 Dods 210, 165 E.R. 1464, at p. 1477.

[46] *The case of the S.S. Lotus*, P.C.I.J., Series A, No. 10, p. 18.

[47] Prosper Weil, 'Towards Relative Normativity in International Law?' (1983) 77 *American Journal of International Law* 413, at p. 418.

[48] Mark Mazower, *No Enchanted Palace: The End of Empire and the Ideological Origins of the United Nations*, Princeton, NJ: Princeton University Press, 2009.

'CIVILIZED' NATIONS 9

Charter was drafted much of the world still remained occupied and exploited by a handful of wealthy European States.

A similar distasteful reference to the existence of 'non-self-governing territories' appears, most ironically, in the second sentence of article 2 of the Universal Declaration of Human Rights, which sets out the right to equality and non-discrimination. Yet while acknowledging the reality of colonialism, the Universal Declaration also confirms that the will of the people is to be expressed in periodic and genuine elections by universal and equal suffrage. How could these two notions coexist? At best, the Universal Declaration was a 'common standard of achievement', to cite the words of its preamble, because many of the rights proclaimed in the Declaration were completely inaccessible to the indigenous peoples of the European colonial empires.

Critical race theorists Francisco Valdes and Sumi Cho explain, 'as it was in the beginning, international law today continues to be a racial and material project of the (white-identified) Global North and West in which the (coloured) Global South is the object of material control and political rule'.[49] But although international law may have originated in a system that facilitated the control of the southern portion of the planet by some 'Christian nations' of Europe and the western hemisphere, it was also the scene for confrontation as the victims of this profoundly unfair system fought back. This book is about one facet of this tension in international law. Its subject is racial discrimination or, if one prefers, racial equality. The study attempts to describe the conflict, essentially over the course of the twentieth century and the first decades of the twenty-first, but also to relate the often-neglected contribution made by individuals, groups, peoples, and nations of what is sometimes called the 'Global South' to the progressive development of international law.

Several terms are relevant to this analysis: 'race', 'people of colour', 'Global South', 'Third World', 'developing', 'underdeveloped', 'non-aligned'. They cannot be used interchangeably, but they often overlap to a large degree. There is no attempt here at precise definition and delineation. Ruth Gordon has noted that 'the southern, developing Third World is for the most part the coloured world. . . it is marginalised, disproportionately poor and relatively powerless'.[50] Prabhakar Singh has explained that the term 'Third World' can constitute 'a new currency for identifying the deprived of both the North and the South' providing 'a unified category of the famished of both the First and the Third World'.[51] In

---

[49] Francisco Valdes and Sumi Cho, 'Critical Race Materialism: Theorizing Justice in the Wake of Global Neoliberalism' (2011) 43 *Connecticut Law Review* 1513, at p. 1569.

[50] Ruth Gordon, 'Critical Race Theory and International Law: Convergence and Divergence' (2000) 45 *Villanova Law Review* 827, at pp. 830–1.

[51] Prabhakar Singh, 'Indian International Law: From a Colonised Apologist to a Subaltern Protagonist' (2010) 23 *Leiden Journal of International Law* 79, at pp. 97, 102. See also, on use of the term 'Third World', James T. Gathii, 'Writing Race and Identity in a Global Context: What CRT and TWAIL Can Learn from Each Other' (2021) 67 *UCLA Law Review* 1610, at pp. 1638–9.

10 'CIVILIZED NATIONS' AND THE COLOUR LINE

the 1947 submission to the United Nations of the National Association for the Advancement of Colored People, W.E.B. Du Bois described the complaint as being directed at 'a discrimination based mainly on colour of skin'.[52] For the purpose of this study, 'colour' is ultimately the common denominator, although without losing sight of the phenomenon of racism and racial discrimination involving peoples where differences in skin pigmentation are not the defining factor.

Probably the first appearance of the term 'race' in international treaty law was in the post-First World War treaties adopted in Paris in 1919. Pursuant to the Treaty of Versailles, Czechoslovakia and Poland agreed 'to protect the interests of their inhabitants who differ from the majority of the population in race, language or religion'.[53] These commitments were reaffirmed in separate treaties proclaiming a right to equal treatment 'without distinction of birth, nationality, language, race or religion'.[54] The 1922 treaty between Britain and Iraq recognizing the latter's independence provided 'that no discrimination of any kind shall be made between the inhabitants of Iraq on the ground of race, religion or language'.[55] The term 'race' was also used in the 1929 Geneva Prisoner of War Convention whose parties agreed 'so far as possible, [to] avoid assembling in a single camp prisoners of different races or nationalities'.[56] After the Second World War, 'race' regularly appeared in enumerations of prohibited grounds of discrimination. The term 'race' was never defined. Those who drafted these instruments often meant 'race' to refer to what would today be termed 'ethnicity'. For example, when the Universal Declaration of Human Rights was being drafted, a Lebanese representative said 'his country represented a harmonious amalgam of many racial groups'.[57] During drafting of the Genocide Convention, Henri Donnedieu de Vabres, who had been a judge at the International Military Tribunal, spoke of the Jewish racial group.[58]

The idea that race was a scientifically objective concept rather than a 'social construct' was debunked by UNESCO in a series of declarations.[59] Nevertheless, this does not mean that the term 'race' is obsolete or devoid of

---

[52] W.E.B. Du Bois, ed., *An Appeal to the World: A Statement on the Denial of Human Rights to Minorities in the Case of Citizens of the United States of America and an Appeal to the United Nations for Redress*, National New York, Association for the Advancement of Colored People, 1947.

[53] Treaty of Peace between the Allied and Associated Powers and Germany ('Treaty of Versailles') (1919) TS 4, arts. 86, 93.

[54] For example, Treaty between the Principal Allied and Associated Powers and Poland (1919) 112 BSP 232.

[55] Treaty between His Britannic Majesty and His Majesty the King of Iraq, 10 October 1922, art. 3.

[56] Convention relative to the Treatment of Prisoners of War (1929) 118 LNTS 343, art. 9. See the discussion of this issue, *infra*, p. 54.

[57] Summary record, Economic and Social Council, 12 February 1948, E/SR.139, p. 142.

[58] Summary record, Committee on the Progressive Development of International Law and its Codification, 13 June 1948, A/AC.10/SR.28, p. 13.

[59] See *infra*, pp. 174–189.

utility. Commenting on an initiative in Sweden to delete reference to 'race' in domestic legislation, the United Nations Working Group of Experts on People of African Descent said this 'may be a way to ignore, minimise or obscure the reality of the specifically "racial" racism faced by a part of the Swedish population'. According to the Working Group, '[r]ace may not be a biologically meaningful category, but it still is a socially salient category. And anti-discrimination law, and by extension politics, needs to be able to address this reality in unequivocal terms.'[60] The Committee on the Elimination of Racial Discrimination warned Sweden that the measure 'may lead to difficulties with the qualification and processing of complaints of racial discrimination thus hindering the access to justice for victims.'[61] Tendayi Achiume has written that deleting the word 'does little to erase the social meaning invested in this concept over centuries. Instead, it diverts attention from the urgent legal and other interventions necessary to remedy persisting racial inequality and discrimination, and keeps discriminatory structures and institutions alive and well.'[62] Achiume has defined 'race' as 'the historically contingent social systems of meaning that attach to elements of morphology and ancestry', explaining that '[i]t is centrally about the legal social, political and economic meaning of being categorised as Black, White, Brown or any other racial designation.'[63]

The 1948 Convention on the Prevention and Punishment of the Crime of Genocide refers to a 'racial . . . group'. Case law based upon provisions of the Convention has never defined the notion of 'racial group'. An early judgment of a Trial Chamber of the International Criminal Tribunal for Rwanda defined 'racial group', but without citing any authority, as being 'based on the hereditary physical traits often identified with a geographical region, irrespective of linguistic, cultural, national or religious factors.'[64] Another judgment referred to 'hereditary physical traits often identified with geography'.[65] The 1973 International Convention on the Suppression and Punishment of the Crime of Apartheid refers to 'inhuman acts committed for the purpose of establishing and maintaining domination by one racial group of persons over any other racial group of persons.'[66] The term 'racial group' may have been used in the Apartheid Convention because of its presence in South African legislation of the time.

---

[60] Report of the Working Group of Experts on People of African Descent on its sixteenth session, Addendum, Mission to Sweden, 25 August 2015, A/HRC/30/56/Add.2, paras. 22, 24.

[61] Concluding observations, Sweden, 23 September 2013, CERD/C/SWE/CO/19-21, para. 6.

[62] E. Tendayi Achiume, 'Putting Racial Equality onto the Global Human Rights Agenda' (2018) 28 *SUR – International Journal on Human Rights* 141, at p. 144.

[63] E. Tendayi Achiume, 'Race, Refugees, and International Law', in Cathryn Costello, Michelle Foster, and Jane McAdam eds., *The Oxford Handbook of International Refugee Law*, Oxford: Oxford University Press, 2021, pp. 43–59, at p. 44.

[64] *Prosecutor v. Akayesu* (ICTR-96-4-T), Judgment, 2 September 1998, para. 514.

[65] *Prosecutor v. Kayishema et al.* (ICTR-95-1-T), Judgment, 21 May 1999, para. 98.

[66] International Convention on the Suppression and Punishment of the Crime of Apartheid (1976) 1015 UNTS 243, art. II.

12 'CIVILIZED NATIONS' AND THE COLOUR LINE

In the early years of the United Nations, there was a tendency to use the word 'racialism' although by the 1960s it was replaced with 'racism'.[67] According to the Oxford English Dictionary, racialism is 'belief in the superiority of a particular race leading to prejudice and antagonism towards people of other races'. The Dictionary defines 'racism' as '[t]he theory that distinctive human characteristics and abilities are determined by race', overlooking the pejorative dimension of the term. At the same time, it views 'racialism' and 'racism' as synonyms. Albert Memmi defined racism for the *Encyclopaedia Universalis* as 'la valorisation, généralisée et définitive, de différences réelles ou imaginaires, au profit de l'accusateur et au détriment de sa victime, afin de justifier une agression'.[68] The International Convention on the Elimination of All Forms of Racial Discrimination does not define 'racism' but it does set out a meaning to be given to 'racial discrimination': 'any distinction, exclusion, restriction or preference based on race, colour, descent, or national or ethnic origin which has the purpose or effect of nullifying or impairing the recognition, enjoyment or exercise, on an equal footing, of human rights and fundamental freedoms in the political, economic, social, cultural or any other field of public life'.[69]

The Vienna Declaration and Programme of Action of 1993 confirmed that '[a]ll human rights are universal, indivisible and interdependent and interrelated'.[70] The pronouncement was directly addressed to the phenomenon of 'cultural relativism' which focussed on differences in values with historic and sometimes religious origins. That debate tended to mask the differences in emphasis on the importance of particular areas of human rights, one that had a geographic dimension. The burning issues of human rights were simply not the same in all parts of the world. For the Western states, which with the collapse of the Soviet Union were mutating into the 'Global North', the focus was on civil and political rights such as the prohibition of torture, the right to a fair trial, and freedom of expression. For the 'non-aligned', or the 'Global South', the priorities tended towards economic, social, and cultural rights, including people's rights such as development and self-determination. But first and foremost, the South was concerned with racial discrimination. The North, haunted by its own history, has invariably preferred that human rights be focussed elsewhere, and that the issues

---

[67] Implementation of the Declaration on the Granting of Independence to Colonial Countries and Peoples, 13 December 1966, A/RES/2189 (XXI), PP 7; Implementation of the Declaration on the Granting of Independence to Colonial Countries and Peoples, 16 December 1967, A/RES/2326 (XXII), PP 9; Measures to be taken against nazism and racial intolerance', 19 December 1968, A/RES/2438 (XXIII).

[68] Albert Memmi, *Le racisme*, Paris: Gallimard, 1982, p. 198.

[69] International Convention on the Elimination of All Forms of Racial Discrimination (1969) 660 UNTS 195, art. 1(1).

[70] Vienna Declaration and Programme of Action, A/CONF.157/23, para. 5.

'CIVILIZED' NATIONS   13

of racism racial discrimination be relegated to the margins. These differences in priorities have characterized human rights within the United Nations from its beginnings. Moreover, resistance of the Global North to addressing racial discrimination can be traced to even earlier days of international organization at the Paris Peace Conference in 1919.

If the fight against racial discrimination is seen as a central theme in human rights rather than something on its periphery, then international human rights have been driven forward as much if not more by the South than by the North. During the very first year of the United Nations, while Western intellectuals debated the semantics of the International Bill of Rights, countries from the South pushed racial discrimination to the centre of the agenda. The first standard-setting resolutions of the General Assembly, adopted during the second part of the 1946 session, dealt with racial discrimination including its most extreme form, genocide. There were also efforts to confront the quintessential racist regime, South Africa. These initiatives were proposed and promoted by Egypt, India, Cuba, Panama, Saudi Arabia, and other relative newcomers to the international scene.[71] If the list seems short, it is because the Global South was rather unrepresented at the time. Of the 51 founding members of the United Nations, 11 were from Africa and Asia, although even then those two continents accounted for more than half of the world's population.

Civil society has also made an important contribution to the development of human rights. Today, many of the major human rights organizations active on the international scene are headquartered in the capital cities of Europe and North America. These organizations did not exist in the 1940s. Then, it was African American organizations that took the lead in bringing human rights petitions and campaigns to the doors of the United Nations. Their submissions dealt with racial discrimination in the United States as well as elsewhere in the world, especially in colonized Africa.[72] The first human rights treaties adopted by the General Assembly – the Convention on the Prevention and Punishment of the Crime of Genocide[73] and the International Convention on the Elimination of All Forms of Racial Discrimination[74] – were proposed by States of the South, not the North. Their focus was on racism and racial discrimination. Histories of human rights within the United Nations rarely provide adequate recognition of this contribution.

The United States, together with other countries of the Global North, many with colonialist histories, has consistently resisted the progressive development

[71] See *infra*, pp. 110–115.
[72] See *infra*, pp. 122–131.
[73] See *infra*, p. 117.
[74] See *infra*, pp. 260–268.

14 'CIVILIZED NATIONS' AND THE COLOUR LINE

of international human rights law in this area. When African and Asian States struggled to advance the issue of racial discrimination within the organs of the United Nations, the Western bloc tried to weaken the texts through negotiation, only then to cast negative votes or abstain. Members of the Security Council who proposed intervention in situations involving racial discrimination in southern Africa found their efforts blocked by the 'triple veto' of France, the United Kingdom, and the United States. In 1978, at the time when the United States was purportedly showing its leadership in international human rights, it completely boycotted one of the major events in international human rights, the first World Conference on Racism and the International Decade with which it was linked. The only other State to do so was Israel. American indifference to this central issue of modern human rights persisted at the second World Conference, in 1983, and the third, in Durban in 2001. Its attempt to obstruct the anti-racism agenda continues to the present day. The thesis of the paramountcy of the American contribution is undermined by Washington's lack of genuine engagement over several decades with one of the central aspects of international human rights. There is of course a quite simple and obvious explanation for the relative absence of the United States from the global campaigns against racial discrimination, one that is rooted in its appalling history of slavery, prejudice, lynching, and Jim Crow.

Slavery, the Slave Trade, and Colonialism

International law as we know it can be traced to the midpoint of the second millennium of the modern era, corresponding to the period of 'discovery' when European trading nations began to venture beyond their continent to the Western hemisphere, Africa and Asia. International law governed the bilateral relationships between these 'Christian States' of Europe. It also provided a regulatory framework for their dealings with the 'uncivilized' peoples whom they encountered. Soon, the slave trade became an important feature of global commerce, greatly enriching the European States that profited not only from the sale of human beings but also the exploitation of their labour. For example, the Treaty of Utrecht between Spain and Great Britain secured the latter's right to import African slaves into Spain's colonies in the Western hemisphere: 'The Catholic King doth furthermore hereby give and grant to her Britannic Majesty, and to the company of her subjects appointed for that purpose, as well the subjects of Spain, as all others, being excluded, the contract for introducing negroes into several parts of the dominions of his Catholic Majesty in America, commonly called El Pacto de el Assiento de Negros, for the space of thirty years successively, beginning from the first day of the month of May, in the year 1713. . . and that the said negroes may be there kept in safety till they are sold.'[75] Slavery itself was not a new phenomenon. It was a feature of human society since antiquity although it had never before been carried out on such a scale. Paul Gordon Lauren has explained that although slavery had existed for centuries, '[i]n terms of total numbers, focus upon a particular race, creation of a justifying ideology, and tragic brutality' the African slave trade had no parallel in human history.'[76] Besides pouring wealth into the hands of Europeans, slavery and the slave trade greatly contributed to the economic development associated with settler colonialism. European migration also involved attacks on the indigenous peoples of what was being called the 'new world'.[77]

The slave trade was largely suppressed during the nineteenth century. Henry Wheaton explained that the 'African slave trade, once considered not only a lawful but desirable branch of commerce, a participation in which was made the object of wars, negotiations, and treaties between different European States, is now denounced as an odious crime, by the almost universal consent of nations'.[78] Nevertheless, a century later, Hugo Fischer wrote, in the prestigious *International Law Quarterly*, that 'it can be said that in customary international law slave-holding is not unlawful'.[79] Well-intentioned reformers made their contribution to slavery's abolition,[80] but the demise of slave labour was also the outcome of economic development. What Karl Marx called 'wage slavery' was simply more cost effective than ownership, which brought with it obligations of care, nutrition, and upkeep.[81] Philip Alston has explained that imperialism was also central to the international efforts directed at the suppression of slavery and the slave trade.[82] It provided a pretext for Britannia to confirm that it 'ruled the waves'.

---

[75] Peace and Friendship Treaty of Utrecht between Spain and Great Britain, 28 Consol. TS 325, art. XII.

[76] Paul Gordon Lauren, *Power and Prejudice, The Politics and Diplomacy of Racial Discrimination*, Boulder: Westview Press, 1996, p. 14.

[77] Matthew Craven, 'Colonialism and Domination', in Bardo Fassbender and Ann Peters, eds., *The Oxford Handbook of the History of International Law*, Oxford: Oxford University Press, 2012, pp. 862–89, at p. 863.

[78] Henry Wheaton, *Elements of International Law*, 6th ed., Boston: Little Brown, 1855, p. 186.

[79] Hugo H. Fischer, 'The Suppression of Slavery in International Law' (1950) 3 *International Law Quarterly* 28, at p. 41.

[80] Jenny S. Martinez, *The Slave Trade and the Origins of International Human Rights Law*, Oxford: Oxford University Press, 2012; Suzanne Miers, 'Slavery and the Slave Trade as International Issues 1890–1939' (1998) 19 *Slavery and Abolition* 16; Hugo H. Fischer, 'The Suppression of Slavery in International Law' (1950) 3 *International Law Quarterly* 28; Chaim D. Kaufmann and Robert A. Pape, 'Explaining Costly International Moral Action: Britain's Sixty-year Campaign Against the Atlantic Slave Trade' (1999) 53 *International Organization* 631.

[81] Eric Williams, *Capitalism and Slavery*, Chappell Hill: University of North Carolina Press, 1943.

[82] Philip Alston, 'Does the Past Matter? On the Origins of Human Rights, An Analysis of Competing Histories of the Origins of International Human Rights Law' (2013) 126 *Harvard Law Review* 2043, at pp. 2059–60.

16 'CIVILIZED NATIONS' AND THE COLOUR LINE

As slavery and the slave trade lost momentum, colonialism became increasingly important to European States.[83] According to W.E.B. Du Bois, '[t]he imperialist nations of Europe first used their African colonies as reservoirs from which to import slaves. But in the nineteenth century they began exploiting their African subjects on a large scale in the development of Africa itself.'[84] Eric Hobsbawm described this 'long nineteenth century' as the 'Age of Empire'.[85] In 1884, plenipotentiaries of all European States except Switzerland met in Berlin to divide virtually all of Africa amongst themselves. Attempts to participate by the Sultanate of Zanzibar, which governed a significant part of East Africa including much of modern-day Kenya, were rebuffed. The Congress was watched with anxiety from the continent that it victimized. The *Lagos Observer* wrote that 'the world had, perhaps, never witnessed a robbery on so large a scale'. Antony Anghie has pointed out that while 'European powers justified their expansion and occupation of Africa on the grounds that they were furthering civilisation and ending the slave trade', the agreements reached at Berlin in 1884 and 1885 authorized King Leopold's transformation of the Congo 'into the scene of massive atrocities as thousands of African laborers were killed by Belgians intent on exploiting the rich resources of that region'.[86] Leopold II subsequently hosted a conference, in Brussels in 1890, that proclaimed an end 'aux crimes et aux dévastations qu'engendre la traite des esclaves africains, afin de protéger efficacement les populations aborigènes de l'Afrique et d'assurer à ce vaste continent les bienfaits de la paix et de la civilisation'.[87] It was hailed as 'the most comprehensive treaty against the slave-trade'.[88] But this was no more than window-dressing for one of history's most noxious racist colonial regimes.[89]

Racism directed against people of colour was a phenomenon intricately associated with slavery, the slave trade, and above all with colonialism. Racism was, according to Basil Davidson, 'the conscious and systematic weapon of domination, of exploitation, which first saw its demonic rise with the onset of the trans-Atlantic trade in African captives sold into slavery, and which, later, led on to the

---

[83] Antony Anghie, 'Finding the Peripheries: Sovereignty and Colonialism in Nineteenth-Century International Law' (1999) 40 *Harvard International Law Journal* 1, at pp. 1–2.

[84] W.E.B. Du Bois, 'Inter-Racial Implications of the Ethiopian Crisis: A Negro View' (1935) 19 *Foreign Affairs* 82, at pp. 83–4.

[85] Eric Hobsbawm, *The Age of Empire, 1875–1914*, New York: Pantheon Books, 1987.

[86] Antony Anghie, 'Slavery and International Law: The Jurisprudence of Henry Richardson' (2017) 31 *Temple International and Comparative Law Journal* 11, at p. 20.

[87] Acte général de Bruxelles, 2 July 1890, 27 Stat. 886, Treaty Series 383.

[88] Hugo Fischer, 'The Suppression of Slavery in International Law' (1950) 3 *International Law Quarterly* 28, at p. 49.

[89] Adam Hochschild, *King Leopold's Ghost*, Boston: Houghton Mifflin, 1998; Visit to Belgium, Report of the Working Group of Experts on People of African Descent, 14 August 2019, A/HRC/42/59/Add.1, paras. 8–10, 32.

imperialist colonialism of our yesterdays'.[90] For Eric Williams, 'slavery was not born of racism, racism was the consequence of slavery'.[91] Alfred Métraux, who directed UNESCO's work against racism in the 1950s, wrote that racism was 'a relatively new myth, dating back to only two or three centuries ago. . . Before the colonial expansion of the European powers, men despised or hated one another for cultural or religious differences, but did not claim to be superior to one another because of the colour of their skin or the shape of their skull or their nose'.[92] Asbjørn Eide, in his 1989 report to the United Nations Sub-Commission on the Prevention of Discrimination and the Protection of Minorities, wrote:

> While ethnocentrism is a world-wide phenomenon, probably as old as the existence of ethnic groups, racism is a European invention dating less than 300 years back. It coincided with the European explorations of other continents of the world, and their encounter with peoples which differed from themselves both in appearance and in culture. Gradually, Europeans developed theories about biological links between appearance and culture. The foundation of racism was thereby established.[93]

Racism provided a rationale, a justification, an excuse for colonialism. 'Europeans, it was explained, colonised portions of Africa or Asia in order to preserve the indigenous peoples from barbarism, to convert them to Christianity, or to bring to them the "benefits" of civilisation', explained Hernán Santa Cruz with a dose of irony. 'Regrets were frequently expressed that the "natives" were so incapable of self-government, so far from being ready for independence, so thoroughly unable to manage the machinery of modern technology.'[94] It was 'the white man's burden' to bring civilization to the 'new-caught, sullen peoples, Half devil and half child' wrote imperialism's poet laureate, Rudyard Kipling, who was awarded the Nobel Prize for literature in 1907. The connection between colonialism and racism was affirmed in the 2001 Durban Declaration: 'We recognise that colonialism has led to racism, racial discrimination, xenophobia and related intolerance, and that Africans and people of African descent, and people of Asian descent and indigenous peoples were victims of colonialism and continue to be victims of its consequences.'[95]

---

[90] Basil Davidson, *African Civilisation Revisited: From Antiquity to Modern Times*, Trenton, NJ: World Press, 1991, p. 3.

[91] Eric Williams, *Capitalism and Slavery*, Chappell Hill: University of North Carolina Press, 1943, p. 7.

[92] Alfred Métraux, 'Race and Civilisation', 21 November 1950, UNESCO Archives 323.12 A 102.

[93] Study on the achievements made and obstacles encountered during the Decades to Combat Racism and Racial Discrimination, 7 November 1989, E/CN.4/Sub.2/1989/8 and Add.1, para. 257.

[94] Hernán Santa Cruz, *Racial Discrimination*, New York: United Nations, 1977, para. 40.

[95] Declaration, A/CONF.189/12, pp. 5–26, para. 14. See Anthony Anghie, 'Whose Utopia? Human Rights, Development, and the Third World' (2013) 22 *Qui Parle* 63.

18 'CIVILIZED NATIONS' AND THE COLOUR LINE

The Universal Races Congress

The Universal Races Congress, which met in London in 1911, marked an important development towards universalism and internationalism. Its object was 'to discuss, in the light of science and the modern conscience, the general relations subsisting between the peoples of the West and those of the East, between so-called white and so-called coloured peoples, with a view to encouraging between them a fuller understanding'.[96] W.E.B. Du Bois, who attended as a representative of the National Association for the Advancement of Coloured People, wrote that '[o]f the two thousand international meetings that have taken place in the last seventy-five years there have been few that have so touched the imagination as the Universal Races Congress'.[97] Among the more than 2,000 participants were François Denys Légitime, the former president of Haiti, Franz Boas, Mohandas Gandhi, Annie Besant, H.G. Wells, J.A. Hobson, and Emile Durkheim.[98] Resolutions adopted by the Congress emphasized that differences in civilization do not connote either inferiority or superiority, affirmed the absurdity of the belief prevalent among peoples of the world that 'their customs, their civilisation, and their physique are superior' to those of other peoples, and challenging the looseness in use of the term 'race'.[99]

Walther Schücking, who would later serve as Germany's judge at the Permanent Court of International Justice, was among the many international lawyers in attendance at the Universal Races Congress. His paper explained how international law had initially been confined to the 'Christian states of Europe', and that 'the inhabitants of the other countries of the world were only comprised in this international range, in so far as they were subject to the domination of the colonising Powers of Europe'.[100] Schücking noted the gradual expansion of international law throughout the world, to a point where 'the three races of men are already represented among the 43 states of the international commonwealth',

---

[96] Gustav Spiller, ed., *Papers on Inter-Racial Problems Communicated to the First Universal Races Congress*, London: P.S. King, 1911, p. v.; Marilyn Lake, 'Universal Races Congress', in Akira Iriye and Pierre-Yves Saunier, eds., *Palgrave Dictionary of Transnational History*, Basingstoke: Palgrave, 2009, pp. 1079–80.

[97] W.E.B. Du Bois, 'The First Universal Races Congress. Presented in 1911 at a conference in London', in Phil Zuckerman, ed., *The Social Theory of W. E. B. Du Bois*, London: Sage, 2005, p. 26.

[98] Robert John Holton, 'Cosmopolitanism or cosmopolitanisms? The Universal Races Congress of 1911' (2002) 2 *Global Networks* 153, at p. 158.

[99] Ulysses G. Weatherly, 'The First Universal Races Congress' (1911) 17 *American Journal of Sociology* 315, at p. 316 (emphasis in the original). Also Michael D. Biddiss, 'The Universal Races Congress of 1911' (1971) 13 *Race* 37; Robert Gregg and Madhavi Kale, 'The Negro and the Dark Princess: Two Legacies of the Universal Races Congress' (2005) 92 *Radical History Review* 134; Marilyn Lake and Henry Reynolds, *Drawing the Global Colour Line, White Men's Countries and the International Challenge of Racial Equality*, Cambridge: Cambridge University Press, 2008, pp. 251–8.

[100] Walther Schücking, 'International Law, Treaties, Conferences, and the Hague Tribunal', in Gustav Spiller, ed., *Papers on Inter-Racia! Problems Communicated to the First Universal Races Congress*, London: P.S. King, 1911, pp. 387–98, at p. 387.

a situation that he viewed as being profoundly positive.[101] He observed that China, Persia, and Siam had been represented at the Hague Conferences of 1899 and 1907 and said the question had been raised whether they 'ought not to be regarded as subject to international public law'.[102] He also anticipated the arrival of 'semi-civilized States', giving as examples Abyssinia, Morocco, and Liberia.[103] Schücking pointed to the participation of States like China, Siam, Persia, Turkey, and Egypt in international organizations such as the Universal Postal Union, and other treaty-based systems. He thought it desirable that membership in international organizations that were still confined to Europe be extended to include 'the States of alien races'.[104]

The other important paper on international law presented at the Conference was entitled 'International Law and Subject Races'. Sir John Macdonell, professor of law at the University of London, pointed to grievances of races that were non-dominant, giving as examples the circumstances of Jews in Russia and Poland, Armenians in Turkey, and East Indians in South Africa. He thought that such issues could not be addressed by international law, 'at all events for the time'. Macdonell said that one way to breach 'the walls of prejudice' might be 'by a clearer recognition of duties to subject races than now exists'.[105] 'One universally recognised duty is that, chiefly in the interest of inferior or backward races, the slave trade, dependent necessarily upon supplies from such races, should be put down and should be treated as a heinous crime', said Macdonell.[106]

The aftermath of the First World War brought with it early confirmation of Du Bois's prediction about the twentieth century and the problem of the colour line. As the victorious European States schemed to divide up Germany's overseas empire, dissonant voices were raised by those representing the indigenous peoples of the territories in question, including African Americans, like W.E.B. Du Bois and Marcus Garvey, who saw themselves as advocates not only for their own grievances but also as a voice for colonized peoples. After some initial efforts at the 1919 Paris Peace Conference, they campaigned in Geneva in the early years of the League of Nations.

One of the highlights of the 1919 Paris Peace Conference was the attempt by Japan to secure a clause proclaiming racial equality in the Covenant of the League of Nations. Its efforts were squelched by the American President, Woodrow Wilson, whose white supremacist outlook was notorious.[107] Treaties

---

[101] Ibid., p. 388.
[102] Ibid.
[103] Ibid.
[104] Ibid., p. 392.
[105] John Macdonell, 'International Law and Subject Races', in Gustav Spiller, ed., *Papers on Inter-Racial Problems Communicated to the First Universal Races Congress*, London: P.S. King, 1911, pp. 398–409, at p. 399.
[106] Ibid., p. 402.
[107] See *infra*, pp. 30–37.

20   'CIVILIZED NATIONS' AND THE COLOUR LINE

adopted at the Paris Peace Conference and in the years that followed affirmed a right to equality but one confined to the newly independent states of Central and Eastern Europe. Protection against racial discrimination was not extended to the metropolitan territories of the victor nations nor to the lands they controlled throughout the world.

The voices of people of colour were louder at San Francisco in 1945 than they had been in Paris, 26 years earlier, although the Charter of the United Nations did not include an explicit denunciation of racial discrimination. As mentioned earlier in this chapter, the main resolutions dealing with human rights adopted at the first session of the United Nations General Assembly were all related to racial discrimination. Within a few years, the struggle against apartheid became a central theme of United Nations activity in the field of human rights. The first major studies of human rights by a commission of inquiry, on the subject of apartheid in South Africa, were produced in the early 1950s under the leadership of the Chilean, Hernán Santa Cruz, pursuant to a mandate from the General Assembly. The collapse of colonialism in the late 1950s and early 1960s transformed the United Nations and ensured that racial discrimination would dominate human rights initiatives for many years. In the 1960s, what had begun as a modest effort at a General Assembly declaration on racial discrimination promoted by the Sub-Commission of the Commission of Human Rights suddenly mutated into a full-blown treaty, the International Convention on the Elimination of All Forms of Racial Discrimination. The impetus came from Africa, from States that had only just joined the United Nations. The Convention was adopted by the General Assembly in 1965, a year before the completion of the International Bill of Rights on which United Nations organs had been labouring for nearly two decades.[108] The presence of the new States in Africa and Asia was like an injection of steroids into the anaemic human rights activity that had characterized the United Nations during the early years of the Cold War.

UNESCO took an important initiative in 1950 when it convened an expert panel that condemned so-called race 'science', as practised by the Nazi regime, although it was hardly alone in promoting theories of racial inequality. The 1950 statement produced with the endorsement of a prestigious United Nations body was hugely influential. It was followed by a series of expert reports in the 1950s and 1960s and, in 1978, a political declaration on the subject.[109] The UNESCO statements on race were very effective, establishing a bulwark that largely constrained and entirely discredited the efforts of racists within the academy.

There were also some dark clouds. A series of advisory opinions of the International Court of Justice directed at South Africa's unlawful regime in

---

[108] See *infra*, pp. 267–280.
[109] See *infra*, pp. 189–193.

Namibia stumbled in 1966 when conservative judges at the International Court of Justice rejected a challenge by Ethiopia and Liberia. The astonishing decision, reached by a tie-breaking second vote of the Court's Australian president, reversed a judgment of only a few years. A slate of more progressive judges was elected within a matter of months.[110] The Court soon recovered its balance in the 1971 advisory opinion on South West Africa.

The dynamism of the new States from the darker side of the colour line also brought new vigour to United Nations initiatives in the area of international criminal law. Intense activity following the Second World War marked by the creation of international tribunals, the adoption of new treaties, and proposals for a permanent court was brought to a standstill by the General Assembly in 1954. But in the early 1960s, when the Assembly's composition had changed with the arrival of new African and Asian States, the language of international criminal law was revived in order to characterize racial discrimination and apartheid in southern Africa. General Assembly resolutions began to speak of crimes against humanity, over the objections of States from Europe who were resistant to attempts to push the precedents of Nuremberg to the next level. By defining apartheid as a crime against humanity, the war nexus restriction imposed by the International Military Tribunal was lifted, an important progressive development in international criminal law that was only entrenched nearly three decades later in a celebrated judgment of the International Criminal Tribunal for the former Yugoslavia. Moreover, a further step was taken in 1973 with the adoption of the International Convention on the Prevention and Suppression of the Crime of Apartheid. Besides defining the crime, the treaty explicitly called for establishment of an international criminal court and recognised the exercise of universal jurisdiction.[111]

During the 1970s and 1980s the anti-apartheid campaign's momentum continued to grow. One by one, the erstwhile Western friends of the South African white supremacist regime rallied to the anti-racist cause until the system finally collapsed. Meanwhile, there were many important activities within the United Nations directed not only at apartheid but at racial discrimination more generally: the work of the Committee on the Elimination of Racial Discrimination, the Decades devoted to the right against racism and racial discrimination, and the World conferences, held in 1978, 1983, and 2001. The third of these three meetings was the most controversial but also the most influential. The United States and Israel boycotted all three conferences, protesting charges that Israel's conduct towards its Arab population as well as that of the occupied Palestinian territories fell within the definition of racial discrimination. Some other Western

---

[110] See *infra*, pp. 227–234.
[111] See *infra*, pp. 329–332.

22 'CIVILIZED NATIONS' AND THE COLOUR LINE

States expressed sympathy with the position taken by Israel and the United States. But the Durban Declaration and Programme of Action of 2001 was adopted by consensus. It remains the defining statement on racial discrimination of the United Nations although important questions, including reparations for slavery and colonialism, have been left without clear answers as a result of the compromises reached at Durban.[112]

The unfinished campaign against racial discrimination revived dramatically in 2020, in the midst of the COVID 19 pandemic, when a Minneapolis policeman murdered George Floyd, a Black man who was being apprehended for allegedly using a counterfeit $20 bill to make a retail purchase. The 'Black Lives Matter' slogan reverberated around the world as the issue of racial discrimination became, once again, one of the pillars of the global human rights movement. Special procedures mandate holders of the Human Rights Council took the unprecedented step of condemning the conduct of the President of the United States.

Racial discrimination has been 'a neglected topic within international legal scholarship', Anna Spain Bradley has explained.[113] Writing of the convergence of Third World Approaches and Critical Race Theory, James Gathii has pointed to 'mainstream international lawyers' who 'ignore or underplay international law's role in past and continuing racial discrimination as well as the continuing effects of this discrimination'.[114] One of the great pioneers in this area, Henry Richardson, has described this as 'the scrubbing of evidence of racial manipulation out of the writing of international and national legal history'.[115] For Christopher Gevers, 'race remains largely unspoken about within the centerground of international law'.[116]

If they address racial discrimination at all, textbooks of public international law give short shrift to the subject, consisting of perfunctory references to the notion of equality in a general sense or isolated mention of apartheid.[117] The same observation applies to manuals for the teaching of international human rights law.[118] Although the struggle against racial discrimination has played a very

---

[112] See *infra*, pp. 372–80.

[113] Anna Spain Bradley, 'Human Rights Racism' (2019) 32 *Harvard Human Rights Journal* 1, at p. 53.

[114] James Thuo Gathii, 'Writing Race and Identity in a Global Context: What CRT and TWAIL Can Learn from Each Other' (2021) 67 *UCLA Law Review* 1610, at pp. 1616–17.

[115] Henry J. Richardson III, 'Excluding Race Strategies from International Legal History: The Self-Executing Treaty Doctrine and the Southern Africa Tripartite Agreement' (2000) 45 *Villanova Law Review* 1091, at p. 1133.

[116] Christopher Gevers, 'Unwhitening the World, Rethinking Race and International Law' (2021) 67 *UCLA Law Review* 1652, at p. 1657.

[117] For example, James Crawford, *Brownlie's Principles of Public International Law*, Oxford: Oxford University Press, 2012, pp. 645–6.

[118] For example, Ilias Bantekas and Lutz Oette, *International Human Rights Law and Practice*, Cambridge: Cambridge University Press, 2020, with eight pages out of 941 devoted to the issue (pp. 222–4, 581–5). Also Olivier De Schutter, International Human Rights Law, Cases, Materials,

THE UNIVERSAL RACES CONGRESS 23

important role in the progressive development of international law, and especially international human rights law, the contribution of this issue is very often
ignored in favour of a Western-centred narrative. For example, Jack Donnelly
has stated bluntly that '[a]s a matter of historical fact, the concept of human
rights is an artifact of modern Western civilisation'.[119] Samuel Moyn has spoken
of 'the first-world geography of the birth of human rights in the 1970s'.[120] Aryeh
Neier seemed to agree with Moyn, at least with respect to the importance of the
1970s as the 'beginning' of human rights.[121] Brian Simpson's massive account
of Britain's engagement with international human rights in the 1940s and 1950s
barely mentions the issue of racial discrimination.[122]

Derrick Nault has explained in a recent study that '[a] common thread uniting
most approaches to human rights history is an emphasis on Western civilisation,
political figures or intellectuals as the main impetus behind human rights
thought.'[123] When the issue of racial discrimination is given more significance,
the historical development looks rather different. Then, the major contributors to
human rights law are individuals and countries of the Global South. By ignoring
this dimension, a kind of human rights evangelism driven from the 'civilized'
North and directed at the 'uncivilized' South is reinforced. Among scholars of
international law, a new impetus has come from an epistemological community
situated at the conjunction of the schools known as Third World Approaches to
International Law and Critical Race Theory.[124] The emphasis of the Third World
Approaches has been on the role colonialism played in the development of international law. Critical Race Theory has been largely addressed to racial discrimination within the United States.

Commentary, Cambridge: Cambridge University Press, 2019, where discrimination on various
grounds is discussed but where race is not among them (pp. 689–713) and where there are only a
few isolated references to the International Convention on the elimination of All Forms of Racial
Discrimination (pp. 19, 190. 685, 713, 742, 745).

[119] Jack Donnelly, 'Human Rights and Human Dignity: An Analytic Critique of Non-Western
Conceptions of Human Rights' (1982) 76 *American Political Science Review* 303, at p. 303.
[120] Samuel Moyn, *The Last Utopia, Human Rights in History*, Cambridge, MA and London: Belknap
Press, 2010, p. 114.
[121] Aryeh Neier, *The International Human Rights Movement, A History*, Princeton and
Oxford: Princeton University Press, 2012, at pp. 3–4.
[122] A.W. Brian Simpson, *Human Rights and the End of Empire, Britain and the Genesis of the
European Convention*, Oxford: Oxford University Press, 2001, pp. 317–18.
[123] Derrick M. Nault, *Africa and the Shaping of Human Rights*, Oxford: Oxford University Press,
2020, p. 4.
[124] James T. Gathii, 'Writing Race and Identity in a Global Context: What CRT and TWAIL Can
Learn from Each Other' (2021) 67 *UCLA Law Review* 1610; Ruth Gordon, 'Critical Race Theory
and International Law: Convergence and Divergence' (2000) 45 *Villanova Law Review* 827; Makau
Mutua, 'Critical Race Theory and International Law: The View of an Insider-Outsider' (2000) 54
Villanova Law Review 841.

W.E.B. Du Bois was clairvoyant in his prediction that the twentieth century would be the century of the colour line. Many of his dreams came to fruition, including the effective end of colonialism and the elevation of persons of African descent to the status of global statesmen, such as Nelson Mandela, Kofi Annan, Kamala Harris, and Barack Obama, to name a few. Within the United States, he would have welcomed the demise of Jim Crow and the end of lynching. But he would also have been heartbroken to learn that black women and men continue to live with the terror of violence at the hands of those who are supposed to enforce the law, and to know that more than half of the mammoth prison population in the United States consists of persons of colour. Racial discrimination continues to haunt the planet. This long twentieth century of the colour line has yet to conclude.

2

The Great War and the Fragile Peace

Paris Peace Conference

The world was transformed by the Great War of 1914–1918. It brought the end to three of the great empires of previous centuries. The Russian Empire was replaced by an ambitious social experiment. The Austrian and Ottoman Empires fractured into pieces, some of which became new independent States while others were shared among the victors as mandates under the League of Nations. The entry of the United States into the war had tipped the balance against Germany. The conditions for peace were dictated by the two remaining European empires, Britain and France, and the upstart from across the ocean.

Accompanying the redrawing of the global map were major changes to international law and international organizations. The League of Nations was brought into existence. Although its Covenant made no explicit reference, the beginnings of the modern day international human rights legal framework appeared, manifested in the creation of new institutions, the International Labour Organisation and the High Commissioner for Refugees. The system was hardly comprehensive but it was certainly a beginning. Included in the post-war law making were the first attempts to place racism and racial discrimination on the international agenda. At the Paris Peace Conference, in 1919, Japan made a dramatic but ultimately unsuccessful attempt to place a clause within the Covenant of the League of Nations affirming racial equality. The Conference also took the first steps to enforce international criminal justice, including the adoption of treaty provisions directed at prosecuting the perpetrators of the genocide of the Armenians. Texts adopted to ensure the protection of minorities and ensure their right to equal treatment are the forerunners of provisions in modern day human rights treaties.

Within weeks of the end of the Great War, the Preliminary Peace Conference convened in Paris at the invitation of the five 'Great Powers', France, Britain, the United States, Italy, and Japan. Over the course of nearly six months, three major treaties were negotiated. The first, known generally as the Treaty of Versailles, dictated the terms of peace with Germany. Nestled within the Treaty of Versailles was a second treaty, the Covenant of the League of Nations, setting out the basic rules and framework for this novel international organization. The third, often called the 'little Treaty of Versailles', set out conditions for recognition of the

The International Legal Order's Colour Line. William A. Schabas, Oxford University Press.
© Oxford University Press 2023. DOI: 10.1093/oso/9780197744475.003.0002

26   THE GREAT WAR AND THE FRAGILE PEACE

independent State of Poland and provided a template for similar treaties with other so-called 'new states'. These texts were signed in the Palace of Versailles on 28 June 1919. The Conference continued, in different forms, for another year as agreements with other vanquished States were hammered out.

The Peace Conference was dominated by the United States, France, and Britain who used it to entrench and consolidate their global hegemony which had been built upon a foundation of colonialism and racial supremacy. The Peace Conference also drew delegates from many smaller States who hoped to seize the opportunity to promote a more egalitarian global order based upon legal norms rather than military might. Liberia was one of the States invited to attend the Paris Peace Conference. In the plenary it sat between Panama and the Hedjaz, the ancestor of Saudi Arabia. Haiti, too, had a delegation, placed between Peru and Greece.[1] Asian delegations attended from Japan, China, Siam, and the Hedjaz.

Woodrow Wilson was very much the dominant personality. A southern Democrat who was first elected President of the United States in 1912, Wilson encouraged racial segregation within the federal civil service. His racist leanings were no secret. 'One of the most baffling contradictions in American history is that the advent on the Washington scene of liberal, caused the most abrupt descent of the Negro's status in Woodrow Wilson, a man proclaimed as a great intellectual the District of Columbia', wrote Walter White of the National Association for the Advancement of Colored People.[2] Notoriously, Wilson hosted a showing in the White House of *The Birth of a Nation*, a film that glorifies lynching and the Ku Klux Klan,[3] as we are reminded by Harry Belafonte in Spike Lee's 2018 film *BlacKkKlansman*. The host and President of the Peace Conference was the French prime minister, Georges Clemenceau. A man of liberal views, Clemenceau had campaigned against the anti-Semitism associated with the wrongful conviction of Alfred Dreyfus that roiled France at the turn of the century. Zola's famous 'J'accuse' was published in Clemenceau's newspaper, *L'Aurore*.

Representatives of colonized peoples haunted the corridors of the Conference, inspired by Woodrow Wilson's hollow pledge to recognize 'self-determination'. The Council of Four insisted upon hearing the objections of the Aborigines

---

[1] Seating plan of Paris Peace Conference, Faith Hunter Dodge papers 2014.34.35, National WWI Museum and Memorial, Kansas City.

[2] Walter White, *How Far the Promised Land?*, New York: Viking Press, 1955, p. 179.

[3] Lloyd E. Ambrosius, 'Woodrow Wilson and the Birth of a Nation: American Democracy and International Relations' (2007) 18 *Diplomacy and Statecraft* 689, at p. 709. Also Kenneth O'Reilly, 'The Jim Crow Policies of Woodrow Wilson' (1997) 17 *Journal of Blacks in Higher Education* 117; Marilyn Lake and Henry Reynolds, *Drawing the Global Colour Line, White Men's Countries and the International Challenge of Racial Equality*, Cambridge: Cambridge University Press, 2008, p. 292; Eric S. Yellin, *Racism in the Nation's Service: Government Workers and the Color Line in Woodrow Wilson's America*, Chapel Hill: University of North Carolina Press, 2013.

Protection Society,[4] a British non-governmental organization, but not of course the Africans themselves,[5] when it came to decide whether Belgium could be entrusted with Germany's colonies in East Africa, modern-day Rwanda and Burundi, given its abysmal record in the Congo. In the United States, African American activists seized the opportunity provided by the Peace Conference. One of President Wilson's close advisors, Ray Stannard Baker, explained: 'We had at Paris the representatives of several powerful race groups, all asserting a new racial dignity, all working for the recognition of a new equality. Not only were there the powerful Japanese and Chinese, but there was a Jewish group and a Negro group.' According to Baker, 'no problems raised at Paris struck fire sooner than these: the hostility of the Poles to the Jews, the feeling of the Australians toward the Japanese, and so on.'[6] He might well have added Jim Crow, whose spirit animated many members of the American delegation, including its leader.

In December 1918, the National Equal Rights League designated a delegation of African Americans to travel to Paris and participate in the Peace Conference. Passports for the delegates were refused by the Department of State. The League's Secretary, William Monroe Trotter, remained determined to attend the Conference. He disguised himself as a ship's cook, arriving in Paris in early May where he lobbied and campaigned. Meanwhile, the National Equal Rights League telegraphed a petition addressed to the Conference's Commission on the League of Nations: 'Fourteen million coloured Americans, soldiers and civilians who helped win the war, through National Equal Rights League in National Convention, December, petition peace conference in fulfilment of war promises of democracy for everyone to incorporate in League covenant following clause: Real democracy for world being avowed aim of nations, establishing League of Nations, high contracting powers agree to grant their citizens respectfully full liberty, rights of democracy, protection of life without distinction based on race, colour or previous condition.'[7] In the final days of the Conference, Trotter wrote to the Conference protesting the fact that the treaties then being adopted would protect minorities in Eastern and Central Europe but not those in the United States.[8]

---

[4] Charles Swaisland, 'The Aborigines Protection Society, 1837–1909' (2000) 21 *Slavery and Abolition* 265.

[5] Notes of a Meeting Held at President Wilson's House in the Place des États-Unis, on Friday, 27 June 1919, at 4 p.m., FRUS PPC VI, pp. 723–32, at p. 728–9.

[6] Ray Stannard Baker, *Woodrow Wilson and World Settlement*, Vol. II, Garden City and New York: Doubleday, Page, 1922, p. 232.

[7] Charles H. Wesley, 'International Aspects of the Negro's Status in the United States' (1948) 11 *Negro History Bulletin* 108.

[8] 'Asks Rights for Negroes, Race Plea to Paris Conference Recites Terms to Enemy Minorities', *New York Times*, 23 June 1919, p. 4. See also 'Blacks Want Equal Rights, Send Petition to Peace Delegates to Insert Clause in League', *New York Times*, 13 June 1919, p. 4.

28 THE GREAT WAR AND THE FRAGILE PEACE

The International League for Darker People, an umbrella organization of groups affiliated with Marcus Garvey, attempted to send a delegation to Paris composed of Ida B. Wells and A. Philip Randolph, who were prominent African American activists. Wells and Randolph were denied visas and could not travel overseas. In their place, a Haitian, Eleizer Cadet, travelled to Paris in late-February 1919 but had little success in contacting delegates. Cadet promoted Marcus Garvey's proposal that the German colonies in Africa be returned to African control, with a role for the African diaspora.[9] Cadet met with Charles D.B. King of Liberia, who refused to support the campaign. Garvey and Cadet claimed the efforts had been undermined by W.E.B. Du Bois.[10]

Garvey's organizations had also sent a telegram to the Peace Conference calling for a clause to be incorporated into the Covenant of the League of Nations requiring members to 'grant their citizens respectively full liberty, rights of democracy, and protection of life without distinction based on race, colour or previous condition.[11] It was buried in the files of the Conference and never circulated or considered. The petition came to light in early July 1919 when it was referred to in a submission by the Delegation of Race Petitioners of the National Coloured World Democracy Congress. Eric Drummond, who was to become the Secretary-General of the League of Nations, had minuted the file asking for an inquiry into the fate of the original proposal. This was the answer: 'Cable was rec'd March 24th – more than a month after the Commission had carefully considered and definitely rejected a racial equality provision (February 18th); therefore it was never brought to the attention of the Commission.[12] It was an incorrect and misleading answer to Drummond's query, although accurate in noting that a provision on racial equality had been considered by the Commission on the League of Nations during the drafting of the Covenant. The proposal remained an active agenda item until April 1919.

Among those who made the pilgrimage to Paris in 1919 was W.E.B. Du Bois. 'I went to Paris because today the destinies of mankind centre there', he wrote in *The Crisis*.[13] He had been asked by the National Association for the Advancement

---

[9] Steven H. Hobbs and Frank H. Fitch II, 'The Marcus Garvey Case: A Law and Power Theory Analysis of Political Suppression of Human Dignity' (1991) 2 *George Mason University Civil Rights Law Journal* 15, at p. 38.

[10] Colin Grant, *Negro With a Hat. The Rise and Fall of Marcus Garvey*, Oxford: Oxford University Press, 2008, pp. 176–83. On rivalry between the two men, see Frank Chalk, 'Du Bois and Garvey Confront Liberia: Two Incidents of the Coolidge Years' (1967) 1 *Canadian Journal of African Studies / Revue Canadienne des Études Africaines* 135.

[11] Telegram from Shaw et al. to the Commission on the League of Nations, Paris Peace Conference, 24 March 1919, LNA R1568/40/78/151. The text in the telegram is somewhat garbled. The version cited is from a subsequent reference to the clause in a petition submitted to the League of Nations in July 1919, LNA R1568/40/78/151.

[12] Amendment to the League of Nations, minutes, 10 July 1919, R1568/40/78/151.

[13] W.E.B. Du Bois, 'Opinion' (1919) 18 *The Crisis* 7.

of Colored People to travel to France for the purpose of investigating the treatment of Black soldiers and documenting their involvement in the War. Du Bois understood the significance of the Peace Conference, where 'the problems of Africa were going to be discussed' and where 'the question of the colour bar was coming up' but with 'no provision, so far as we could see, to allow the Negro to speak for himself'.[14] With the help of Blaise Diagne, who represented Senegal in the French Assemblée nationale, and with 'the American Secret Service at my heels',[15] Du Bois obtained Georges Clemenceau's consent to convene the Pan African Congress in Paris while the Peace Conference was underway. Du Bois also credited the support and assistance of Madame Paul Calmann-Lévy, widow of a major French publisher.[16] In a memorandum to Daigne, Du Bois set out the objectives of the Congress, including '[t]he making of strong representations to the Peace Conference sitting in Paris in behalf of both voice in and protection for 250,000,000 Negroes and Negroids in the League of Nations'.[17]

The Congress, held on 19–21 February 1919, was attended by delegates from 15 countries, including the United States, France, and Belgium as well as from Africa and the Caribbean. The American Government refused passports to some of those who sought to participate, falsely claiming that France did not think it was propitious to hold the gathering.[18] American agents kept a 'weary eye on us', Du Bois said.[19] He thought the results of the meeting were small but not without influence. The Congress adopted resolutions calling for gradual self-government in Africa, a role in monitoring for the League of Nations, and mass education for Africans. Under the heading 'Civilised Negroes' it urged recognition of equal rights with other citizens where 'persons of African descent are civilised and able to meet the tests of surrounding culture. . . [T]hey shall not be denied on account of race or colour a voice in their own government, justice before the courts, and economic and social equality.' The Congress requested the League of Nations to provide '[g]reater security of life and property' for the protection of 'Native workers' by international labour legislation, and sought 'equitable representation

---

[14] W.E.B. Du Bois, *Dusk of Dawn*, in W.E.B. Du Bois, *Writings*, New York: New American Library, 1986, pp. 549–802, at p. 745.

[15] W.E.B. Du Bois, 'Opinion' (1919) 18 *The Crisis* 7, at p. 8.

[16] There is handwritten invitation from Mme Calmann-Levy in the David Graham Du Bois Trust archives at the University of Massachusetts in Amherst.

[17] 'Memorandum to M. Daigne and others on a Pan-African Congress to be held in Paris in February, 1919, 1 January 1919' (1919) 17 *The Crisis* 224.

[18] Sarah Claire Dunstan, 'Conflicts of Interest: The 1919 Pan African Congress and the Wilsonian Moment' (2016) 39 *Callaloo* 133. See also Paul Otlet, 'Les Noirs et la Société des Nations', *La Patrie Belge*, 19 January 1919; Mona L. Siegel, *Peace on Our Terms, The Global Battle for Women's Rights After the First World War*, New York, Columbia University Press, 2020, pp. 70–75; Charles Flint Kellogg, *NAACP, A History of the National Association for the Advancement of Colored People*, Vol. I, 1909–1920, Baltimore and London: Johns Hopkins University Press, 1967, pp. 279–284.

[19] W.E.B. Du Bois, 'The early beginnings of the Pan-African movement, June 20, 1958', W.E.B. Du Bois Papers (MS 312).

30 THE GREAT WAR AND THE FRAGILE PEACE

in all the international institutions of the League of Nations'. It said 'the participation of the Blacks themselves in every domain of endeavour shall be encouraged in accordance with the declared object of Article 19 of the League of Nations', which governed the mandated territories. The Congress concluded: 'Whenever it is proven that African Natives are not receiving just treatment at the hands of any State or that any State deliberately excludes its civilised citizens or subjects of Negro descent from its body politic and cultural, it shall be the duty of the League of Nations to bring the matter to the attention of the civilised world.'[20] Manifestly, the Congress was seeking League of Nations engagement not only with Africans in the mandated territories but more broadly, and this would obviously include those in colonies of the British, the French, the Spanish, the Portuguese, and the Italians.

Du Bois lobbied unsuccessfully to present a report to the Peace Conference. He managed to meet with some prominent delegates, including Colonel House, Wilson's right-hand man, and David Lloyd George, the British Prime Minister, and 'a number of lower officials among the French, English and Portuguese'.[21]

Japan's Proposal on Racial Discrimination

Negotiation of the Covenant of the League of Nations was the setting for an important confrontation on the issue of racial discrimination. This took place mainly within the Commission on the League of Nations in which, besides representatives of the five major powers, the United States, the United Kingdom, France, Italy, and Japan, nine other countries participated: Belgium, Brazil, China, Czechoslovakia, Greece, Poland, Portugal, Romania, and Serbia. The American President, Woodrow Wilson, presided. The Commission was the most prestigious of the Conference's subsidiary bodies, as the presence of Woodrow Wilson, who chaired the proceedings, confirmed. The other American delegate was Colonel House, Wilson's confidante. In private conference, the two referred to the Japanese delegates as 'the Japs'.[22]

Japan proposed that a clause on racial equality be included in the Covenant of the League of Nations: 'The equality of nations being a basic principle of the League of Nations, the High Contracting Parties agree to, as soon as possible, to all alien nationals of States members of the League, equal and just treatment in

---

[20] Pan African Congress. Resolutions, February 1919, W.E.B. Du Bois Papers (MS 312); W.E.B. Du Bois, 'The Pan-African Congress' (1919) 17 *The Crisis* 271, at p. 274.

[21] Clarence G. Contee, 'Du Bois, the NAACP, and the Pan-African Congress of 1919' (1972) 57 *Journal of Negro History* 13, at pp. 20, 25–6.

[22] 'Colonel House to the President, Paris, 24 January 1919', in Charles Seymour, *The Intimate Papers of Colonel House, Vol. IV, The Ending of the War*, London: Ernest Benn: London, 1928, p. 315.

every respect, making no distinction either in law or fact, on account of their race or nationality.'[23] The clause was the subject of 'long and difficult discussions', according to the British representative, Lord Robert Cecil.[24] Japan's initiative was followed with great attention by people of colour throughout the world. In the United States, Marcus Garvey said that Africans and peoples of African descent 'hope Japan will succeed in impressing upon her White brothers at the Peace Conference the essentiality of abolishing racial discrimination'.[25]

There were high expectations within Japan. When the delegation departed for Paris, the country's leading newspaper, the *Asahi*, stated: 'Above all our Peace envoy must not forget to persuade the Conference to agree to the relinquishment of the principle of racial discrimination, which if allowed to exist would continue to be a menace to the future peace of the world. Fairness and equality must be security for the coloured races who form 62 per cent of the whole of mankind.'[26] Japan's intentions on this point was sufficiently significant to attract the notice of the US Ambassador, Roland Morris, who informed Washington that it was hoped 'the organisation of a League of Nations will offer an opportunity to assert the quality of the yellow race, a question which underlies all discussions on the subject'.[27]

Baron Makino Nobuaki and Viscount Chinda Sutemi were the two Japanese delegates to the Peace Conference. Both had 'painful personal experiences' in 1913 relating to controversy over the Californian Alien Land Law. Makino was then the foreign minister and Chinda was ambassador to Washington.[28] Known as the Webb–Haney Act, it prohibited ownership or long-term leases of agricultural land by 'aliens ineligible for citizenship'. The legislation was directed primarily at Japanese migrants in California. It was a source of considerable tension between the governments of Japan and the United States.[29] At one point,

---

[23] Tenth Meeting of the Commission on the League of Nations, 13 February 1919, USNA FW 181.1101/10; David Hunter Miller, *The Drafting of the Covenant*, New York: GB Putnam's Sons, 1928, pp. 316–35, at p. 324.

[24] Tenth Meeting of the Commission on the League of Nations, 13 February 1919, USNA FW 181.1101/10; David Hunter Miller, *The Drafting of the Covenant*, New York: GB Putnam's Sons, 1928, pp. 98–105, at p. 105.

[25] Marcus Garvey, 'Race Discrimination Must Go', *Negro World*, 30 November 1918, in Robert A. Hill, ed., *The Marcus Garvey and Universal Negro Improvement Association Papers*, Vol. I, Berkeley: University of California Press, 1983, p. 3. See also David Wright, 'The Use of Race and Racial Perceptions among Asians and Blacks: The Case of the Japanese and African Americans' (1998) 30 *Hitotsubashi Journal of Social Studies* 135, at pp. 139–40.

[26] Cited in Paul Gordon Lauren, 'Human Rights in History: Diplomacy and Racial Equality at the Paris Peace Conference' (1978) 2 *Diplomatic History* 257, at p. 262.

[27] Ambassador (Morris) to Secretary of State, Tokyo, 15 November 1918, FRUS PPC Vol. 1, p. 490.

[28] Mr Chinda to Mr Bryant, 10 June 1914, FRUS 1914, p. 426; Mr Chinda to Mr Bryant, 25 November 1914, ibid., p. 428. Also Naoko Shimazu, *Japan, Race and Equality: The Racial Equality Proposal of 1919*, London: Routledge, 2002.

[29] Marilyn Lake and Henry Reynolds, *Drawing the Global Colour Line, White Men's Countries and the International Challenge of Racial Equality*, Cambridge: Cambridge University Press, 2008, pp. 263–73.

32   THE GREAT WAR AND THE FRAGILE PEACE

President Wilson intervened, claiming that such '[i]nvidious discrimination' might conflict with treaty obligations. He registered his 'very earnest and respectful protest against discrimination in this case'.[30] A challenge to its constitutionality on the basis of the fourteenth amendment was dismissed by the United States Supreme Court in 1923.[31]

The Japanese text was meant as an addition to a draft provision on freedom of religion that had originally been put forward by President Wilson.[32] Wilson's proposal took on more modest proportions at the first session of the Commission on the League of Nations: 'The High Contracting Parties agree that they will make no law prohibiting or interfering with the free exercise of religion, and that they will in no way discriminate, either in law or in fact, against those who practice any particular creed, religion, or belief whose practices are not inconsistent with public order or public morals'.[33] The provision went through a number of revisions, none of them meeting with general approval or satisfying Wilson himself. Eventually, the Drafting Committee reported that 'in view of the complications of this question' it was in favour of omitting the text altogether.[34] The 'complications', it seems, were related to the Japanese proposal.

When the Japanese delegates consulted Colonel House about their initiative, he advised them to prepare two resolutions, one that they preferred and the other that they would be willing to accept. In his diary entry for 4 February, House said he told them 'how much I deprecated race, religious, or other kinds of prejudices'. His words might well have been taken as encouragement by the two Japanese diplomats.[35] According to House's diary, the Japanese provided him with two drafts that he then shared with the President. Wilson rejected the first but thought the second 'might do by making a slight change' which he then inserted with his own handwriting. House showed the revised wording to

---

[30] Raymond Leslie Buell, 'The Development of Anti-Japanese Agitation in the United States' (1923) 38 *Political Science Quarterly* 57, at p. 63. The Supreme Court of the United States subsequently ruled that the California statute did not conflict with treaty obligations: *Terrace v. Thompson*, 263 US 197 (1923).

[31] *Porterfield v. Webb*, 263 US 225 (1923). See Thomas Reed Powell, 'Alien Land Cases in United States Supreme Court' (1924) 12 *California Law Review* 259; Edwin E. Ferguson, 'The California Alien Land Law and the Fourteenth Amendment' (1947) 35 *California Law Review* 61.

[32] Wilson's Third Draft or Second Paris Draft, 20 January 1919, in David Hunter Miller, *The Drafting of the Covenant*, New York: GB Putnam's Sons, 1928, pp. 98–105, at p. 105. It was repeated without change in Cecil-Miller Draft, 27 January 1919, ibid., pp. 131–41, at p. 141; Wilson's Fourth Draft or Third Paris Draft, 2 February 1919, ibid., pp. 145–54, at p. 154.

[33] First Meeting of the Commission on the League of Nations, 3 February 1919, USNA FW 181.1101/1, Annex 1, art. 19; David Hunter Miller, *The Drafting of the Covenant*, Vol. II, New York: GB Putnam's Sons, 1928, pp. 229–55, at p. 237.

[34] Seventh Meeting of the Commission on the League of Nations, 13 February 1919, Annex 1, USNA FW 181.1101/9; David Hunter Miller, *The Drafting of the Covenant*, Vol. II, New York: GB Putnam's Sons, 1928, pp. 298–316, at p. 307. Also David Hunter Miller, *The Drafting of the Covenant*, Vol. I, New York: GB Putnam's Sons, 1928, p. 221.

[35] Charles Seymour, *The Intimate Papers of Colonel House, Vol. IV, The Ending of the War*, London: Ernest Benn: London, 1928, pp. 320–1.

Chinda who 'seemed to think it would be satisfactory', but said he needed to discuss it with his colleagues.[36] A few days later, Chinda explained to House that his colleagues thought the text to be 'practically meaningless'. He had a new proposal but House believed it would not be acceptable 'either by our people or the British Colonies'.[37] Chinda told House that Japan would proceed with a text that was 'more drastic' than what Wilson had said he would accept, and that 'while it will not be adopted it will be an explanation' for the Japanese public.[38]

House discussed the Japanese initiative with Lord Balfour. The British aristocrat said the suggestion that 'all men are created equal' was 'an eighteenth century proposition which he did not believe was true. He believed that it was true in a certain sense that all men of a particular nation were created equal, but not that a man in Central Africa was created equal to a European.'[39] At House's request, David Hunter Miller prepared an alternative to the Japanese text that he appeared to acknowledge was entirely cosmetic in nature and without any legal consequence. Miller said he was unhappy with his own version 'because while I do not think it binds any country to anything, it makes the general subject a matter of international cognizance, and I doubt very much if that result is or should be acceptable'.[40]

On 13 February 1919, the Commission on the League of Nations took up Wilson's 'religious article'. The President was represented by Colonel House, who began the discussion by declaring that 'Wilson strongly desires the inclusion of this article in the text'. Fernand Larnaude of France explained that the provision had vexed the Drafting Committee which concluded it was better to omit the provision.[41] Apparently Wilson was especially concerned about anti-Semitism in Eastern Europe. Portugal's Jaime Batalha Reis said he had lived in Russia for six years, where '[m]any Israelites have submitted to baptism and become orthodox. Without wishing to offend the race, from certain points of view this race is inferior and is struggling against a superior race.'[42] Lord Robert Cecil, who was in the chair, repeated that Wilson 'especially desires' the inclusion of the article in the Covenant and said 'in principle, I think it cannot be omitted'.

At this point, Baron Makino formally presented Japan's amendment. 'That race discrimination still exists, in law and in fact, is undeniable, and it is enough here to simply state the fact of its existence', he said. Makino explained that 'the question of race prejudice is a very delicate and complicated matter, involving

---

[36] Ibid., p. 322 (diary entry of 5 February 1919).
[37] Ibid., p. 323 (diary entry of 6 February 1919).
[38] Ibid., p. 324 (diary entry of 12 February 1919).
[39] David Hunter Miller, *The Drafting of the Covenant*, Vol. I, New York: GB Putnam's Sons, 1928, p. 183.
[40] Ibid., p. 184.
[41] Ibid., p. 267.
[42] Ibid., p. 268.

34   THE GREAT WAR AND THE FRAGILE PEACE

play of deep human passion, and therefore requiring careful management'. The proposed clause enunciated 'the principle of equality', leaving implementation to the governments of the League's members, he noted. 'In this war, to attain the common cause, different races have fought together on the battlefield, in the trenches, on the high seas, and they have helped each other and brought succour to the disabled, and have saved the lives of their fellow men irrespective of racial differences, and a common thread of sympathy and gratitude has been established to an extent never before experienced. I think it only just that after this common suffering and deliverance the principle at least of equality among men should be admitted and be made the basis of future intercourse', Makino concluded.[43] In this way, racial discrimination was placed on the international agenda where it has remained ever since.

In response, Lord Cecil said 'it would be wiser for the moment' to postpone examination of the amendment which, he explained, 'had raised extremely serious problems within the British Empire'. He said the amendment was 'a matter of a highly controversial character' although he acknowledged 'the nobility of thought which inspired Baron Makino'. The Chinese delegate, Wellington Koo, manifesting an exceedingly rare solidarity of his country with Japan, said his Government was 'deeply interested' in the question raised by Japan and that 'he was naturally in full sympathy with the spirit of the proposed amendment'. However, he wished to reserve his position pending instructions. Others, including Eleftherios Venizelos of Greece, thought it better not to deal with 'questions of race and religion'. The minutes record that several members agreed. Colonel House, who was chairing the session, said he would inform President Wilson of the discussion.[44] When House reported to Wilson on the meeting, the President agreed to withdrawal of the religious freedom clause.[45] The chief legal advisor to the American delegation, David Hunter Miller, was himself pleased to see the end of Wilson's religious freedom clause. From his standpoint, the Japanese proposal 'served a good purpose for it helped to make impossible any article on religious liberty in any form: any such article in the Covenant would have been most dangerous and perhaps fatal to the League: the subject was never again considered'.[46]

---

[43] Tenth Meeting of the Commission on the League of Nations, 13 February 1919, USNA FW 181.1101/10; David Hunter Miller, *The Drafting of the Covenant*, Vol. II, New York: GB Putnam's Sons, 1928, pp. 316–35, at pp. 324–5.

[44] Tenth Meeting of the Commission on the League of Nations, 13 February 1919, USNA FW 181.1101/10; David Hunter Miller, *The Drafting of the Covenant*, Vol. II, New York: GB Putnam's Sons, 1928, pp. 316–35, at p. 325. Charles Seymour, *The Intimate Papers of Colonel House, Vol. IV, The Ending of the War*, London: Ernest Benn: London, 1928, p. 325 (diary entry of 13 February 1919).

[45] Ibid., p. 326 (diary entry of 13 February 1919).

[46] David Hunter Miller, *The Drafting of the Covenant*, Vol I, New York: GB Putnam's Sons, 1928, p. 269.

The Commission on the League of Nations did not meet for several weeks while its chairman, Woodrow Wilson, returned briefly to the United States. During this hiatus, Japan pursued attempts to revive its proposal on equality and racial discrimination. In an interview with the *New York Herald*, Baron Makino said 'all people must be prepared to do a little hard courage to part with many prejudices we have among which are racial prejudices'.[47] The Japanese ambassador to the United States, Viscount Ishii, made a 'strong plea' to include the clause as part of a speech at the annual dinner of the Japan Society, in New York. Britain's ambassador, Lord Reading, reported to London that the issue seemed focussed on Japanese immigration to the United States. He warned that Ishii's remarks would be 'seized upon' by opponents of the League as well as labour federations.[48]

Apparently on the advice of Colonel House, the Japanese reformulated their proposal as an addition to the preamble rather than a substantive provision of the Covenant. It was understood that the principal opposition came from the British Empire delegation and, more specifically, from William 'Billy' Hughes, Australia's Prime Minister, whom he described as the 'stumbling block'. H.W.V. Temperley wrote that Hughes was 'immovable' in his belief that the 'White Australia' policy of his Government was as entitled to recognition as was the Monroe Doctrine of the Americans, which was endorsed in the Covenant itself.[49] Hughes threatened the British that Australia would oppose the League of Nations altogether if the racial discrimination clause was included in the Covenant.[50] Colonel House had thought that the rest of the British Empire delegation would have found Chinda's original proposal, as amended by Wilson, to be acceptable.[51] However, Hughes appears to have been only the most rabid of the British Empire delegation. The racist policies of the other Dominions were quite similar to Australia's. In an interview with a Japanese journalist after the proposal had been decisively reject, Hughes said that blaming Australia was an 'absurd insinuation'.[52] The other members of the British Empire, including Britain itself, were merely more polite and less demagogic than the Australian.[53] The same could be said of Wilson himself.[54]

---

[47] 'Time to Give Up Race Prejudice: Japanese View', *New York Herald*, 17 February 1919.

[48] Racial discrimination and the League of Nations, 19 March 1919, TNA FO 608/243.

[49] H.W.V. Temperley, ed., *A History of the Peace Conference of Paris*, Vol. VI, London: Henry Frowde and Hodder and Stoughton, 1924, p. 352.

[50] Paul Gordon Lauren, *Power and Prejudice: The Politics and Diplomacy of Racial Discrimination*, Boulder: Westview Press, 1996, p. 94.

[51] Charles Seymour, *The Intimate Papers of Colonel House*, Vol. IV, *The Ending of the War*, London: Ernest Benn: London, 1928, p. 325 (diary entry of 13 February 1919).

[52] 'Hughes discusses racial amendment', *Japan Advertiser*, April 1919, in LNA R544/11/268/268.

[53] Naoko Shimazu, 'The Japanese attempt to secure racial equality in 1919' (1989) 1 *Japan Forum* 93, at pp. 95–6.

[54] Kristofer Allerfeldt, 'Wilsonian Pragmatism? Woodrow Wilson, Japanese Immigration, and the Paris Peace Conference' (2004) 15 *Diplomacy and Statecraft* 545.

36   THE GREAT WAR AND THE FRAGILE PEACE

The Japanese ambassador in Washington warned Wilson, prior to his return to Europe in mid-March, of the importance his country attached to the principle of racial equality: 'In view of the fundamental spirit of the League of Nations the Japanese Government regards as of first importance the establishment of the principle that the difference of race should in no case constitute a basis for discriminatory treatment under the law of any country.' The ambassador indicated that Japan would not insist upon its earlier proposal and that it would welcome suggestions from the American President.[55]

When the Commission on the League of Nations reconvened, Japan submitted a watered-down version of the text put forward in February. Japan's proposal was to add the words 'by the endorsement of the principle of the equality of Nations and the just treatment of their nationals' to the preamble of the Covenant. Baron Makino acknowledged that the proposal did not fully meet Japan's expectations. Some members of his own delegation had been furious about the 'miserable compromise'.[56] Makino explained to the Commission that '[i]n close connection with grievances of the oppressed nationalities, there exist the wrongs of racial discrimination which was, and is, the subject of deep resentment on the part of a large portion of the human race. The feeling of being slighted has long been a standing grievance with certain peoples.' This was the only explicit reference to racial discrimination in Makino's remarks. Subsequently, Viscount Chinda claimed that Japan 'had not broached the question of race or of immigration'.[57]

In his statement to the Commission, Baron Makino described the League as 'a world instrument for enforcing righteousness and defeating force'. He said the League was 'an attempt to regulate the conduct of nations and peoples towards one another according to a higher moral standard than has obtained in the past, and to administer fairer justice throughout the world. . . It has given birth to hopes and aspirations, and strengthened the sense of legitimate claims' that 'different peoples scattered over the five continents . . . consider as their due'. He emphasized the proposal's importance for the credibility of the League, stating that 'the announcement of the principle of justice for peoples and nationalities as the basis of the future international relationship has so heightened their legitimate aspirations, that they consider it their right that this wrong should be redressed'. Failure to recognize equality might contribute to unwillingness to carry out the obligations imposed by the Covenant, he warned.

---

[55] Cited in Ray Stannard Baker, *Woodrow Wilson and World Settlement*, Vol. II, Garden City and New York: Doubleday, Page, 1922, p. 236.

[56] Paul Gordon Lauren, 'Human Rights in History: Diplomacy and Racial Equality at the Paris Peace Conference' (1978) 2 *Diplomatic History* 257, at p. 269.

[57] Fifteenth Meeting of the Commission on the League of Nations, 11 April 1919, USNA FW 181.1101/15; David Hunter Miller, *The Drafting of the Covenant*, Vol. II, New York: GB Putnam's Sons, 1928, pp. 375–94, at p. 389.

JAPAN'S PROPOSAL ON RACIAL DISCRIMINATION 37

Makino's eloquent presentation visibly affected many members of the Commission who found it to be 'a persuasive, moving performance'.[58] Japan's proposal met with considerable support, including that of both France and Italy.[59] Delegates from China, Czechoslovakia, and Poland also endorsed the Japanese text. The Greek President said he had been largely responsible for removing a clause about religious freedom from the draft Covenant and that this had helped to rationalize the removal of a clause relating to racial equality.[60] He said that the new Japanese proposal was not about equality of races but rather about equality of nations and just treatment of their nationals.[61]

Two delegations, those of Britain and the United States, remained opposed. Replying to Makino, Cecil said that while he was personally in accord with the idea advanced by the Japanese proposal he could not vote in favour. 'The British Government realised the importance of the racial question, but its solution could not be attempted by the Commission without encroaching upon the sovereignty of States members of the League', he said. Cecil foresaw 'serious controversy' were the text to be adopted. He said that Japan would be a permanent member of the League's Executive Council where 'it would always be possible for her to raise the question of equality of races and of nations'. Woodrow Wilson, who chaired the session of the Commission, had the last word. Just before he spoke, House handed him a note: 'The trouble is that if this commission should pass it, it would surely raise the race issue throughout the world.'[62] Wilson spoke of 'controversies which would be bound to take place outside the Commission' were the reference to be included in the Preamble, and said 'it would perhaps be wise not to insert such a provision in the Preamble'. Wilson said 'the proposed clause would raise objections in the United States and thought it would be better not to insist upon it'.[63]

A vote was taken with 11 of 17 in favour. The minutes do not record whether there were negative votes or abstentions. Wilson then proclaimed that the Japanese amendment was not adopted given that it had failed to obtain unanimous approval of the Commission. It was a bit of chicanery, because in an earlier vote on an amendment supported by the United States but opposed by France Wilson had not insisted on consensus. The French representative, Ferdinand

---

[58] Paul Gordon Lauren, 'Human Rights in History: Diplomacy and Racial Equality at the Paris Peace Conference' (1978) 2 *Diplomatic History* 257, at p. 270.

[59] Fifteenth Meeting of the Commission on the League of Nations, 11 April 1919, in David Hunter Miller, *The Drafting of the Covenant*, Vol. II, New York: GB Putnam's Sons, 1928, pp. 375–94, at p. 390.

[60] Ibid.

[61] Ibid., p. 391.

[62] Paul Gordon Lauren, 'Human Rights in History: Diplomacy and Racial Equality at the Paris Peace Conference' (1978) 2 *Diplomatic History* 257, at p. 271, citing David Hunter Miller.

[63] Fifteenth Meeting of the Commission on the League of Nations, 11 April 1919, in David Hunter Miller, *The Drafting of the Covenant*, Vol. II, New York: GB Putnam's Sons, 1928, pp. 375–94, at pp. 391–2.

38   THE GREAT WAR AND THE FRAGILE PEACE

Larnaude, objected to Wilson's ruling, and said he reserved his country's position.[64]

Undaunted, the Japanese delegation made yet a third attempt at the 28 April 1919 plenary session of the Conference, when the report of the Commission on the League of Nations was discussed and adopted. Presumably, the Japanese understood that they could not succeed but nevertheless felt it important to put their position on record again. Some British Foreign Office officials thought it an 'innocuous amendment', warning that by failing to support the Japanese proposal they had 'made trouble for the future'.[65] After Woodrow Wilson had presented the draft Covenant for approval by the Plenary, Baron Makino took the floor. He recapitulated the history of the Japanese proposals in the Commission on the League of Nations. Makino recalled how he had pointed to 'the race question' as 'a standing grievance which might become acute and dangerous at any moment'. He said he had made it 'unmistakably clear' that given the 'very delicate and complicated nature, involving the play of a deep human passion' of the issue, Japan had sought 'the immediate realisation of the ideal of equality'. The proposed clause 'enunciated the principle only, and left the actual working of it in the hands of the different Governments concerned'. Makino recalled how Japan had attempted to reconcile conflicting views by submitting a more restrained text for inclusion in the Preamble, but with no greater success. Thus, said Makino, it was putting the original proposal to include a substantive provision on equality in the Covenant, one that referred explicitly to 'race and nationality'. In conclusion, he noted, 'the Japanese Government and people feel poignant regret at the failure to the Commission to approve of their just demand for laying down a principle aiming at the adjustment of this long-standing grievance'.[66]

Japan returned to the issue of racial discrimination once the League became operational. At the first session of the League Assembly, Viscount Ishii recalled how 'Japan had an opportunity, when the Covenant of the League of Nations was originally formulated, to declare her firm belief that equality before the law should be assured to all men irrespective of their nationality, race or religion'. The Japanese diplomat said that 'it was to the poignant regret of the Japanese Government and people that the original framers of the Covenant found themselves unable to accept the Japanese proposal in this matter, and the Japanese delegates declared that they would continue in their insistence for the adoption of their just demand by the League in the future'. However, he said that at present Japan would refrain from making any concrete proposal, 'and will patiently bide her time until the opportune moment will present itself'.[67]

[64] Ibid., p. 392.
[65] Minutes by Baker, Mackay, 2 and 3 May 1919, TNA FO 608/243.
[66] Plenary Session, 28 April 1919, USNA FW 180.0201/5, pp. 8–10.
[67] Verbatim record of the 11th plenary meeting of the Assembly of the League of Nations, 30 November 1920, LNA R1361/26/8399/8399, p. 9.

War Crimes and Crimes against Humanity

International criminal law, including the establishment of an international criminal court, was studied in detail at the Paris Peace Conference. The victorious allied powers proposed trial of German combatants, including generals and admirals, for violations of the laws and customs of war. They also entertained the prospect of prosecuting the German Emperor, Kaiser Wilhelm II, for starting the War. Article 227 of the Treaty of Versailles charged Wilhelm II with 'a supreme offence against international morality and the sanctity of treaties' and declared that he would be tried before an international tribunal. But the fallen Kaiser had obtained asylum in the Netherlands which refused to surrender him. The trial never took place.[68] Provisions of the Treaty of Versailles and of the other conventions with the defeated Central Powers created a basis for war crimes trials although only a few prosecutions actually took place.[69]

That Germans and their allies would be held to account for war crimes had been seriously considered from the earliest days of the First World War. The focus of the British, the French, and the Belgians was on atrocities perpetrated in the territories occupied by Germany on the Western Front, that is, most of Belgium and part of northeast France. The British were also seriously concerned with submarine warfare. In 1916, the British published a 'Blue Book' devoted to German war crimes in Africa. It contained detailed descriptions of attacks directed at civilian non-combatants by German soldiers, many of whom were of African origin, perpetrated in Cameroon, East Africa and South West Africa. Reports made reference to various war crimes including the use of hollow tipped bullets, poisoning of wells, and attacks on medical units bearing the red cross emblem. The British Blue Book also reproduced reports from the French about German conduct in Africa.[70] At the Paris Peace Conference, reports of German war crimes and other atrocities were studied by the Commission on Responsibilities. It requested the various Allied governments to provide details. The British and the French both submitted extensive information to the Commission. However, the reports on atrocities in Africa were entirely overlooked.[71] When Germany

---

[68] William Schabas, *The Trial of the Kaiser*, Oxford: Oxford University Press, 2018.

[69] James F. Willis, *Prologue to Nuremburg, The Politics and Diplomacy of Punishing War Criminals of the First World War*, Westport, CT and London: Greenwood Press, 1982; Gerd Henkel, *Die Leipziger Prozesse: Deutsche Kriegsverbrechen und ihre strafrechtliche Verfolgung nach dem Ersten Weltkrieg*, Hamburg: Hamburger Institute, 2003; United Nations War Crimes Commission, *History of the United Nations War Crimes Commission and the Development of the Laws of War*, London: His Majesty's Stationery Office, 1948, pp. 46–51; Gerd Henkel, *The Leipzig Trials, German War Crimes and their Legal Consequences after 1921*, Dordrecht: Republic of Letters, 2014.

[70] *Papers relating to German atrocities and breaches of the rules of war, in Africa*, London: His Majesty's Stationery Office, 1916.

[71] Christopher Gevers, 'The "Africa Blue Books" at Versailles: World War I, Narrative and Unthinkable Histories of International Criminal Law', in Immi Tallgren and Thomas Skouteris, eds., *The New Histories of International Criminal Law*, Oxford: Oxford University Press, 2019, pp. 145–66;

objected to the confiscation of its colonies, including those in Africa, the Allied Council of Four invoked 'Germany's dereliction in the sphere of colonial civilisation'. It noted 'the cruel methods of repression, the arbitrary requisition and the various forms of forced labour which resulted in the depopulation of vast expanses of territory in German East Africa and the Cameroons, not to mention the tragic fate of the Hereros in South West Africa, which is well known to all'.[72]

Nevertheless, war crimes committed against Africans were the subject of international litigation, but not criminal prosecution, in arbitration proceedings taken pursuant to provisions of the Treaty of Versailles. Portugal claimed damages against Germany for its 1914 attack on a fort in Angola at a time when Portugal was still neutral. Portugal claimed that the German action provoked a 'révolte des noirs' that it was necessary for the coloniser to suppress.[73] Germany declined responsibility, arguing that any damage to Portugal was a consequence not of its military activity but of 'la révolte des n . . . s', and that it had actually tried to assist Portugal in its suppression.[74] The arbitrators made a rather vague finding of responsibility against Germany given that 'en elle-même l'agression allemande était de nature à amener des troubles, dans la population indigène, qu'il était dans l'ordre naturel des choses que les noirs, soumis depuis bien peu d'années, en profitassent pour se révolter'.[75]

Britain, France, and Belgium 'reprimanded' Portugal for including the number of Africans killed during the war in its damage claim against Germany. While the British charged the Portuguese for not having understood 'the exact scope of the reparation provisions of the Treaty', Afonso Costa 'denied that loss of life in the colonies, mostly of civilians, fell outside the scope of the reparations'.[76] According to the Germans, only 'nationals' were entitled to claim reparations.

Christopher Gevers, 'Africa and International Criminal Law', in Kevin J. Heller Frederic Megret, Sarah Nouwen, Jens Ohlin, and Darryl Robinson, eds., *The Oxford Handbook of International Criminal Law*, Oxford: Oxford University Press, 2020, pp. 154–93.

[72] Conclusion of the Committee on the Political Clauses of the Treaty Relating to Countries Outside Europe, FRUS PPC VI, pp. 360–3, at p. 361.

[73] *Responsabilité de l'Allemagne à raison des dommages causés dans les colonies portugaises du sud de l'Afrique (sentence sur le principe de la responsabilité) (Portugal contre Allemagne)*, 31 July 1928 (2006) II RIAA 1011, at p. 1015. There is an unofficial English translation of the decision in Eric Heinze and Malgosia Fitzmaurice, eds., *Landmark Cases in International Law*, London, Kluwer Law International, 1998, pp. 1266–85.

[74] Ibid., pp. 1029–30.

[75] Ibid., p. 1032.

[76] Jakob Zollmann, *Naulilaa 1914. World War I in Angola and International Law, A Study in (Post-) Colonial Border Regimes and Interstate Arbitration*, Baden-Baden: Nomos, 2016, p. 324. See also 'Affaire Naulilaa entre le Portugal et l'Allemagne, 1914–1933: Reflexions sur l'Histoire Politique d'une Sentence Arbitrale Internationale' (2013) 15 *Journal of the History of International Law* 201; Jakob Zollmann, 'Unforeseen combat at Naulilaa. German South West Africa, Angola, and the First World War in 1914–1917' (2016) 20 *Journal of Namibian Studies* 79.

WAR CRIMES AND CRIMES AGAINST HUMANITY   41

A draft spoke of 'white' or 'European' nationals, although the reference was removed in the final version. According to legal historian Jakob Zollman, it seemed 'simply incomprehensible' that there could be claims by non-Europeans based upon destruction of their property. 'The Germans considered themselves to be the more "modern", more strict colonial administrators adhering to the "positivist view that uncivilised peoples were not legal entities" and had no concept of property and had no legal standing. "The native" was supposed to be invisible, he had to have no name – and if so it was conferred upon him (as a kind of joke) by his master', Zollmann has explained.[77]

During the War, British officials prepared other materials about the abusive treatment by Germany of the indigenous population in its African colonies.[78] These reports were directed at justifying the seizure of overseas territories rather than any accountability for war crimes and other atrocities. They concerned a range of pre-war abuses that were apparently investigated after the territories fell under British control during the conflict. In particular, the first major genocide of the twentieth century, that of the Herero in South West Africa, was described. A report prepared by the Foreign Office described in detail the attempted extermination of the group. It included a reference to a lecture by a German scholar, Prof. Moritz Bonn, of Munich, to the Royal Colonial Institute in London, more than seven months before the outbreak of the war with an astonishingly frank admission of genocidal intent:

> We wanted to build up on African soil a new Germany and create daughter States. We carried this idea to its bitter end. We tried it in South West Africa, and produced a huge native rising, causing the loss of much treasure and many lives. We tried to assume to ourselves the functions of Providence, and *we tried to exterminate a native race*, whom our lack of wisdom had goaded into rebellion. We succeeded in breaking up the native tribes, but we have not yet succeeded in creating a new Germany.[79]

---

[77] Jakob Zollmann, *Naulila 1914. World War I in Angola and International Law, A Study in (Post-) Colonial Border Regimes and Interstate Arbitration*, Baden-Baden: Nomos, 2016, p. 327.

[78] *Report on the Natives of South-West Africa and Their Treatment by Germany*, London: His Majesty's Stationery Office, 1918; *Treatment of Natives in the German Colonies*, London: His Majesty's Stationery Office, 1920; *South West Africa*, London: His Majesty's Stationery Office, 1920. See also Jeremy Silvester and Jan-Bart Gewald, *Words Cannot be Found. German Colonial Rule in Namibia: An Annotated Report of the 1918 Blue Book*, Leiden and Boston: Brill, 2003. In 1919, the German government published an answer to the British Blue Book: *The treatment of natives and other populations in the colonial possessions of Germany and England: an answer to the English blue book of August 1918: 'Report on the natives of Southwest Africa and their treatment by Germany'*, Berlin: German Colonial Office, 1919.

[79] *Treatment of Natives in the German Colonies*, London: His Majesty's Stationery Office, 1920, p. 1 (emphasis added).

42 THE GREAT WAR AND THE FRAGILE PEACE

Greater attention was devoted to what is today referred to as the genocide of the Armenians. The killing of up to 1.5 million Armenians who lived within what is modern day Turkey stands as one of the great crimes of racial discrimination of the twentieth century. Atrocities directed against the Armenian minority in the Ottoman Empire had taken place over many years but the scale of the attacks that began in April 1915 was without precedent. In May 1915, Britain, France, and Russia sent a declaration to the government of the Ottoman Empire referring to recent reports of massacres of the Armenian population, an important minority living for centuries within its own borders. The three Powers denounced 'these new crimes of Turkey against humanity and civilisation'.[80] Although the term 'crimes against humanity' had been employed previously by journalists and politicians, this is the first known occurrence of it in an official government document. Moreover, the declaration by the three Allied Powers announced that individuals, including leaders, would be held criminally responsible.

Intervention by Europeans on behalf of Christian populations in the Middle East had been going on since the time of the Crusades. Indeed, an early draft of the May 1915 declaration spoke of crimes against 'Christianity and civilisation'.[81] The British Ambassador to Paris thought it wise to remove the word 'Christianity'.[82] After this was agreed, the French proposed it be replaced with the word 'humanity'.[83] But the change came too late for the British, who had already issued the statement and organised its publication in *The Times*.[84] The French version referring to 'nouveaux crimes contre l'humanité et civilisation' was communicated to the Ottoman Government by the American Ambassador in Constantinople, acting at the request of the French Government.[85]

When the concept of laws and customs of war was first discussed in the Commission on Responsibilities at the Paris Peace Conference, the Greek representative, Nikolaos Politis, argued for a broad approach so as to deal with 'reprehensible acts' and not only 'those which the penal laws characterise as criminal and punish as such. I think we all agree that the expression should be understood in a general sense.' By way of illustration, he referred to the massacres of the Armenians perpetrated by the Ottoman Turkish regime. Politis explained that the acts of the Turks 'technically do not fall within any provision of the Penal

---

[80] Sharp to Secretary of State, Paris, 28 May 1915, FRUS 1915, Supplement, The World War, p. 981.

[81] Bertie to Delcassé, 19 May 1915, TNA FO 146/1574, FMAE Guerre, 1914–1918, Turquie, Vol. 887, 105–6.

[82] Bertie to Grey, 19 May 1915, TNA FO 371/2488; Delcassé to Bertie, 20 May 1915, FMAE Guerre, 1914–1918, Turquie, Vol. 887, 117; Bertie to Delcassé, 21 May 1915, FMAE Guerre, 1914–1918, Turquie, Vol. 887, 121–2.

[83] Bertie to Grey, 24 May 1915, TNA FO 371/2488.

[84] Press Release, 23 May 1915, TNA FO 146/4471; 'Allies Stern Warning to Turkey', *The Times*, 25 May 1915.

[85] Sharp to Secretary of State, 28 May 1915, FRUS 1915 Supplement, The World War, p. 981; Morgenthau to Secretary of State, 18 June 1915, FRUS 1915 Supplement, The World War, p. 982.

Code, and it is evident within the conscience of every civilised man that there is something in this a great deal more serious than the mere acts themselves that made up their programme'. Politis described such acts as being in violation of 'what one might call human or moral law'.[86]

When the penalty provisions of the treaty between the Allies and Turkey were being discussed, in 1920, the initial draft called for them to be adapted from the treaties that had already been finalized with Austria, Hungary, and Bulgaria.[87] But when this was discussed by the Allied Council, George Curzon, who was then the British Foreign Minister, said those clauses 'were not sufficiently wide, and would not, in the case of Turkey, cover the massacre of the Armenians'.[88] The following clause was drafted: 'The Turkish Government undertakes to hand over to the Allied Powers the persons considered to be responsible for the massacres committed during the continuance of the state of war on territory which formed part of the Turkish Empire on August 1, 1914'.[89] It became Article 230 of the Treaty of Sèvres, an instrument that was signed but never ratified by the Turkish Government, and pursuant to which no prosecutions were ever held.

Equality Clauses in Treaties with the New States

Although a general clause on racial discrimination was excluded from the Covenant of the League of Nations, the Paris Peace Conference did produce treaty provisions recognizing a right to equality. Adopted at the same time as the treaty with Germany, the 'little Treaty of Versailles' imposed an obligation upon Poland 'to assure full and complete protection of life and liberty to all inhabitants of Poland without distinction of birth, nationality, language, race or religion'.[90] The provision gave effect to article 93 of the Treaty of Versailles by which Poland agreed 'to embody in a Treaty with the Principal Allied and Associated Powers

---

[86] Second Meeting of the Commission on Responsibilities, 7 February 1919, Minutes: USNA FW 181.1201/16, pp. 19–25, at p. 19; USNA FW 181.1201/2 (M 820, Roll 140, 641–62), p. 2; USNA FW 181.1201/2 (M 820, Roll 140, 712–33), p. 3; Conférence de la Paix 1919–1920, *Recueil des actes de la Conférence, Partie IV B (2), Commission des responsabilités des auteurs de la guerre et sanctions*, Paris: Imprimerie nationale, 1922, pp. 31–7, at p. 31; Alfred Geouffre de Lapradelle, ed., *La Paix de Versailles, Responsabilité des auteurs de la guerre et des sanctions*, Vol. III, Paris: Éditions internationales, 1930, pp. 16–29, at p. 17.

[87] Draft Synopsis of Treaty of Peace with Turkey, in E.L. Woodward and Rohan Butler, eds., *Documents on British Foreign Policy*, First series, London: Her Majesty's Stationery Office, 1947–1960, Vol. VII, pp. 125–8, at p. 127.

[88] Notes of an Allied Conference, 10 Downing Street, 21 February 1920, 5 p.m., in E.L. Woodward and Rohan Butler, eds., *Documents on British Foreign Policy*, First series, London: Her Majesty's Stationery Office, 1947–1960, Vol. VII, pp. 189–94, at p. 191.

[89] Cambon to Lloyd George, 11 March 1920, TNA CAB 24/101; Hankey to Chairman, Drafting Committee of the Peace Conference, 30 March 1920, TNA CAB 24/101.

[90] Treaty between the Principal Allied and Associated Powers and Poland (1919) 112 BSP 232.

44 THE GREAT WAR AND THE FRAGILE PEACE

such provisions as may be deemed necessary by the said Powers to protect the interests of inhabitants of Poland who differ from the majority of the population in race, language or religion'.[91] These were the first clauses in any multilateral treaty to proclaim racial equality.

President Woodrow Wilson's early draft of the Covenant of the League of Nations contained provisions relating to the recognition of 'new states', to be created from the remnants of the old empires. In his 'Second Draft', dated 10 January 1919, Wilson specified that all new States would be required 'to bind themselves as a condition precedent to their recognition as independent or autonomous States, to accord to all racial or national minorities within their several jurisdictions exactly the same treatment and security, both in law and in fact, that is accorded the racial or national majority of their people'.[92] The British thought the issue of treatment of minorities was better left to separate agreements.[93] Minority protection in new States was set aside and no longer figured in negotiations of the draft Covenant.[94]

The issue of the 'new States' was eventually taken up by the Council of Four. Comprised of the leaders of the United States, the United Kingdom, France, and Italy, its meetings were shrouded in confidentiality. This was where most of the major issues of the Peace Conference were decided. In fact, on this matter the Italian member did not initially participate, and the body was therefore referred to as the Council of Three. At the 1 May meeting of the Council, Wilson told his colleagues that 'it had been brought to his attention that the Jews were somewhat inhospitably regarded in Poland'. He proposed the following clause: 'The State of . . . covenants and agrees that it will accord to all racial or national minorities within its jurisdiction exactly the same treatment and security, alike in law and in fact, that it accorded the racial or national majority of its people'.[95] Lloyd George thought that in Poland 'the Jews had themselves to blame to a considerable extent'. Wilson answered that their unpopularity might be explained by the fact that 'Jews were really more efficient men of business than the Poles'.[96] The Council of Four agreed to set up a Committee on New States for the purpose

---

[91] Treaty of Versailles, [1919] UKTS 4, art. 93.

[92] 'Wilson's Second Draft or First Paris Draft, January 20, 1919, with Comments and Suggestions by D.H.M.', in David Hunter Miller, *The Drafting of the Covenant*, New York: GB Putnam's Sons, 1928, pp. 65–93, at p. 91. See also 'Wilson's Third Draft or Second Paris Draft, 20 January 1919', in David Hunter Miller, ibid., pp. 98–105, at p. 105.

[93] 'Amalgamation of Wilson's Second Paris Draft and British Draft Suggested by Lord Eustace Perry', in David Hunter Miller, *The Drafting of the Covenant*, New York: GB Putnam's Sons, 1928, pp. 117–30, at pp. 129–30.

[94] David Hunter Miller, *The Drafting of the Covenant*, New York: GB Putnam's Sons, 1928, p. 70.

[95] Minutes of a meeting of the Council of Four, 1 May 1919, p. 7, para. 3, USNA FW 185.6/3. More detailed draft clauses on the protection of the Jewish minority are annexed to the minutes of the meeting.

[96] Ibid.

of drafting the relevant treaties. Its members were Philippe Berthelot of France, James Headlam-Morley of Britain, and David Hunter Miller of the United States.

Basing itself on texts prepared by Miller,[97] the Committee provided the Council with an initial draft of the treaty with Poland guaranteeing 'equal civil and political rights without distinction as to birth, race, nationality, language or religion' to citizens of Poland. It also imposed an obligation respecting 'inhabitants' of Poland to protect 'life and liberty, to religious freedoms, to the use of 'any language', and prohibiting discrimination 'on account of birth, race, nationality, language, or religion'. The Council understood that although the clauses were of general application, they were primarily directed at protection of the Jewish minority of Poland, which then numbered about 3 million, approximately 10 percent of the total population. Although the Committee's original proposals were destined for the treaty with Poland, it considered that the issues it was addressing concerning the protection of minorities were also relevant to Czechoslovakia and Yugoslavia, and that they were also important with respect to the status of Jews in Romania and Muslims in northern Greece.[98]

The Committee adopted a draft treaty containing several articles on the protection of minorities. Article 6 guaranteed to all inhabitants of Poland the protection of life and liberty, without distinction as to 'birth, race, nationality, language or religion'.[99] It also declared they were entitled to 'the free exercise, whether public or private, of any creed, religion, or belief, whose practices are not inconsistent with public order or public morals'. Article 7 stated that '[a]ll citizens of Poland shall be equal before the law and shall enjoy the same civil and political rights without distinction as to race, language or religion'. Distinctions based upon religious creed or confession were not to prejudice Polish citizens 'in matters relating to the enjoyment of civil or political rights as for instance admission to public employments, functions and honours, or the exercise of the various professions and industries'. No restriction was to 'be imposed on the free use by any citizen of Poland of any language in private intercourse, in commerce, in religion, in the press or published works or at public meetings'. Notwithstanding establishment of Polish as an official language, 'reasonable facilities shall be given to Polish citizens of non-Polish speech for the use of their language, either orally or in writing, before the Courts'. Pursuant to Article 8, 'Polish citizens who belong to racial, religious, or linguistic minorities' were to be accorded the same treatment and security in law and in fact as the other citizens of Poland, 'and in particular shall have an equal right to establish, manage and control at their

---

[97] Miller to House, 29 April 1919, Appendix I, USNA FW 185.6/3.

[98] Berthelot to Hankey, 5 May 1919, USNA FW 185.6/8.

[99] Second Report of the Committee on New States, 16 May 1919, Annex A, p. 7, USNA FW 185.6/16. The first draft referred to 'birth, language, race or religion' (Report on the Third Meeting of the Committee on New States, 7 May 1919, USNA FW 185.6/10).

own expense charitable, religious, and social institutions, schools and other educational establishments, with the free use in them of their own language and religion'. These provisions were placed 'under the protection of the League of Nations' with consent of the League's Council being necessary for any modification.[100] Robert Cecil proposed that individuals and groups contemplated by the minority rights provisions have a direct right of access to the future permanent international court in order to secure enforcement of their rights.[101] This prescient suggestion, which was rejected by the Council of Four when it decided only States should have access to the Court,[102] anticipated the right of individual access to the European Court of Human Rights, adopted in the 1990s.

Specific provision was made for administration of Jewish schools by the minority itself and respect for the Jewish sabbath.[103] The Committee said it had attempted to address concerns about the rights of Jews in Poland with general provisions. Describing the Jews as 'both a religious and a racial minority', the Committee observed that they required specific attention because unlike other national minorities, which tended to be concentrated in specific parts of the country, Jews were dispersed throughout the country. It also wrote that it was 'necessary to take into account the existence of the strong anti-Semitic feeling in Poland, which is not denied even by the Poles themselves, and there is strong evidence of a deliberate purpose to submit them to a cruel and calculated moral and physical persecution. This throws upon the Allies an obligation to provide safeguards which, it is hoped, will not be necessary for the other minorities.'[104] Britain's Headlam-Morley explained to the Council of Four that the provisions on the Jews had been drafted in consultation with their representatives. President Wilson commented that 'he not only had a friendly feeling towards the Jews, but he thought it was perfectly clear that one of the most dangerous elements of ferment arose from the treatment of the Jews. The fact that the Bolshevist movement had been led by the Jews was partly due to the fact that they had been treated largely as outlaws.'[105]

The French Minister in Warsaw was instructed to communicate the draft treaty to the Polish Government, but not the Report of the Committee, 'which contains remarks and observations whose communication might have certain disadvantages'.[106] On 7 June, the Polish Diet adopted a resolution insisting

---

[100] Second Report of the Committee on New States, 16 May 1919, Annex A, pp. 7–8, USNA FW 185.6/16.

[101] Proposition of Lord Robert Cecil, Annex C to Fifteenth Meeting, 31 May 1919, USNA FW 185.6/24.

[102] Council of Four, Minutes, 17 June 1919, USNA FW 185.6/39.

[103] Second Report of the Committee on New States, 16 May 1919, Annex A, pp. 7–8, USNA FW 185.6/16.

[104] Second Report of the Committee on New States, 16 May 1919, p. 3, USNA FW 185.6/16.

[105] Minutes of the Council of Four, 17 May 1919, USNA 185.6/17.

[106] Berthelot to Hankey, 19 May 1919, USNA FW 185.6/19; Draft telegram, 21 May 1919, USNA FW 185.6/21.

that Poland was hardly a 'new state', and that it had always treated its minorities properly. It condemned the imposition of international supervision regarding 'just claims of minorities, claims which Poland has always admitted', and said this was 'resented by the whole Polish nation and an unhappy restriction placed on the sovereign rights of the Republic'.[107] The Polish delegation to the Peace Conference produced a detailed critique of the minority rights provisions in the draft treaty. It spoke of a benign relationship historically between Poles and Jews, who had fled persecution in Germany, but said that '[t]he present discord is caused by the attitude adopted by the Jews who, considering the Polish cause as being a lost one, on many occasions sided with Poland's enemies. This policy of the Jews called forth a change of public opinion against them.' The document also warned that the minority rights provisions should not apply to the substantial German-speaking population within Poland. It spoke of 'one-sided obligations' that violated the sovereignty of the Polish State.[108] The Polish president, Jan Paderewski, also objected in a statement that largely echoed that of the Diet.[109]

Lloyd George thought Paderewski's letter to be a 'fundamental challenge' to the entire policy concerning minority protection in what he called 'Small States'.[110] Wilson seemed to agree, referring to Paderewski's argument that Poland was being asked to do more in its treatment of Germans than Germany was in its treatment of Poles. The Council of Four decided that a reply should be provided to Paderewski. A note to the Council of Four was prepared for the Committee on New States by the French representative, Philippe Berthelot.[111] He explained that it was 'in harmony with the practice of public law in Europe' in treaties concluded with 'New States' to include guarantees 'as has already been done in former times for Greece, Romania, Serbia'. Berthelot said 'Poland can the less refuse to conform in that she owes her liberation to the efforts and sacrifices of the Powers'.[112] After the Council endorsed Berthelot's letter, it instructed the Committee to prepare, for its approval, a draft letter to be sent to Paderewski together with the treaty itself.[113] The task fell to the British member of the Committee, James Headlam-Morley. His draft was accepted by the Committee on 21 June,[114] approved by the Council of Four two days

---

[107] Motion passed unanimously by the Polish Diet on 7 June 1919, USNA 185.6/31.

[108] Observations of the Polish Delegation, 15 June 1919, USNA FW 185.6/34.

[109] 'Memorandum by M. Paderewski', 15 June 1919, USNA FW 185.6/40, FRUS PPC VI, pp. 535–40.

[110] Notes of a Meeting Held at President Wilson's House in the Place des États-Unis, on Tuesday, 17 June 1919, at 4 p.m., FRUS PPC VI, pp. 529–35, at p. 529. At the time, the 'Small State' of Poland had a population of about 30 million whereas Britain had a population of about 40 million.

[111] Annex (B) to Twenty-fourth meeting, 19 June 1919, USNA FW 181.23201/24.

[112] Ibid.; Berthelot to Hankey, 19 June 1919, FRUS PPC VI, pp. 570–3.

[113] Notes of a Meeting Held at President Wilson's House in the Place des États-Unis, on 21 June 1919, FRUS PPC VI, pp. 569–70, at p. 569.

[114] Meeting of the Committee on New States, 21 June 1919, USNA FW 181.23201/26.

48 THE GREAT WAR AND THE FRAGILE PEACE

later,[115] and then sent to the Polish President under the signature of the President of the Conference, Georges Clemenceau.

The lengthy letter to Paderewski sought to explain the rationale for the inclusion of the minority protection clauses in the treaty, setting out the historical, oral, legal and social arguments.[116] It stated that this was 'no fresh departure', and that '[i]t has for long been the established procedure of the public law of Europe that when a state is created, or even when large accessions of territory are made to an established state, the joint and formal recognition by the great Powers should be accompanied by the requirement that such state should, in the form of a binding international convention, undertake to comply with certain principles of government'. The letter described the text as guaranteeing 'those elementary rights, which are, as a matter of fact, secured in every civilised State'.[117] Although insisting that there are 'numerous other precedents', the letter focussed on the example it considered 'most explicit'.

When the Congress of Berlin in 1878 recognised the sovereignty and independence of Serbia,[118] Lord Salisbury had affirmed 'the great principle of religious liberty'. Bismarck declared that Germany would admit the independence of Serbia, 'but on condition that religious liberty will be recognised'. Bismarck instructed the drafting committee to link the proclamation of Serbian independence and the recognition of religious liberty.[119] The Treaty of Berlin specified that '[t]he freedom, and outward exercise of all forms of worship shall be assured to all persons belonging to Servia, as well as to foreigners, and no hindrance shall be offered either to the hierarchical organisation of the different communions, or to their relations with their spiritual chiefs'.[120] Such provisions, said the letter, had become 'an established tradition', and the Allies 'would be false to the responsibility which rests upon them if on this occasion they departed' from it.

The Polish treaty provided that '[a]ll inhabitants of Poland shall be entitled to the free exercise, whether public or private, of any creed, religion or belief, whose practices are not inconsistent with public order or public morals', and

[115] Notes of a Meeting Held at President Wilson's House in the Place des États-Unis, on Monday, 23 June 1919, at 12:10 p.m., FRUS PPC VI, pp. 624–8.

[116] Jacob Robinson, Oscar Karbach, Max. M. Laserson, Nehemiah Robinson and Marc Vichniak, *Were the Minorities Treaties a Failure?*, New York: Institute of Jewish Affairs, 1943, p. 21.

[117] Draft of the Covering Letter to be Addressed to M. Paderewski in Transmitting to Him the Treaty to be Signed by Poland under Article 93 of the Treaty of Peace with Germany, FRUS PPC VI, p. 629 (1919) 13 *American Journal of International Law* (supplement) 416.

[118] Draft of the Covering Letter to be Addressed to M. Paderewski in Transmitting to Him the Treaty to be Signed by Poland under Article 93 of the Treaty of Peace with Germany, FRUS PPC VI, p. 629 (1919) 13 *American Journal of International Law* (supplement) 416, at pp. 417–18.

[119] Protocol No. 8, 28 June 1878 (1877–1878) 69 BFSP 946; Edward Hertslet, *The Map of Europe by Treaty*, Vol. IV, London: HMSO, No. 528, p. 2743.

[120] Treaty between Great Britain, Austria-Hungary, France, Germany, Italy, Russia, and Turkey, for the Settlement of the Affairs of the East, signed at Berlin, 13 July 1878 (1877–1878) 69 BFSP 749; Edward Hertslet, *The Map of Europe by Treaty*, Vol. IV, London: HMSO, No. 530, p. 2759, art. XXXV.

to that extent was consistent with the 1878 treaty to which the letter addressed to Paderewski referred. But it was itself little more than a developed version of clauses on religious freedom that had been included in treaties since the seventeenth century. The Polish treaty was a great innovation because it went much further. Poland undertook 'to assure full and complete protection of life and liberty to all inhabitants of Poland without distinction of birth, nationality, language, race or religion'.[121] This was a text addressing discrimination broadly, including racial discrimination. The language should sound familiar to modern day human rights practitioners. The text is the ancestor of provisions in the Universal Declaration of Human Rights and the treaties that it inspired.

The Treaty was signed by Poland and by the Allied Powers on 28 June 1919 at the Palace of Versailles. Treaties with similar provisions were soon adopted with Czechoslovakia, Yugoslavia, Greece, and Romania. Unilateral declarations along similar line were made by Albania, Latvia, Lithuania, Bulgaria, and Greece. The Treaties made the protection of minorities subject to a degree of judicial supervision by the Permanent Court of International Justice.

Although the minorities treaties did not appear to have any direct application to the issue of discrimination against people of colour, the recognition of equality that they contained did not escape the attention of those concerned. Within days of the adoption of the 'little Treaty of Versailles', an African American activist, Monroe Trotter, invoked the recognition of equality rights in a petition to the nascent League of Nations.[122] Eric Drummond, who was already acting head of the League of Nations, indicated that he would be pleased to meet with Trotter, but only after he had checked this with the Americans.[123] A few days later, Trotter submitted a petition addressed to the Council of the League of Nations on behalf of the Delegation of Race Petitioners of the National Equal Rights League that called for an amendment to the Covenant. The petition noted the contribution to the War made by people of colour in all of the Allied and Associated countries, and stated: 'Whereas neither in the Covenant of the League of Nations, nor in the Treaty of Peace itself, that with Germany, nor in the treaty with Austria nor in any of the conventions of the Conference of world Peace is there any word or clause giving or designed to give full liberty, democracy or humanity to the Coloured citizens of the Allied or associated nations . . . ' The petition made a detailed argument that invoked a range of legal developments associated with the Peace Conference including the clauses in the minorities treaties and the letter of explanation sent by Clemenceau to Paderewski justifying inclusion of equality rights in the treaty with Poland. 'The peace of the world has not been made

---

[121] Treaty between the Principal Allied and Associated Powers and Poland (1919) 112 BSP 232.

[122] Petition for an Amendment to the League of Nations, 4 July 1919, R1568/40/78/151.

[123] Trotter to Drummond, 30 June 1919, LNA R1568/40/78/78; Walters to Auchincloss, 7 June 1919, ibid.; Drummond to Trotter, 9 July 1919, ibid.

50 THE GREAT WAR AND THE FRAGILE PEACE

secure unless and until the union of the civilised governments declare for identity of public rights and protection of life without distinction of race and colour.
Coloured America, as yet confident in the ultimate ascendency of the Right over
Might, calmly waits upon the League of Nations.'[124] Submission of the petition
was reported in the *New York Times*.[125] Another petition, dated 30 October
1919, came from the World Alliance for Promoting International Friendship,
a religious organization, and urged the League of Nations to 'devise means for
ensuring equality of race treatment by all nations in the League'.[126]

W.E.B. Du Bois thought it was not at all clear that the treatment of Blacks
could fall within the scope of the League's Minorities Commission. He noted
that where Blacks were victims of discrimination, they were not often a minority
within the country. In 'the most conspicuous case (that of the United States),
where the Negro forms a minority which is discriminated against', the country
was not a member of the League. 'If, in the future', the United States should elect
to come into the League the question is, would it be asked to assent to the treaties
for the protection of minorities as other entering nations are now being asked?
And would the likelihood of its being required to make such promises militate
against the possibility of its ever entering the League of Nations?'[127] The United
States never did join the League of Nations.

The comments of Trotter and Du Bois only underscore the hypocrisy of the
major powers at the Paris Peace Conference. They were willing enough to impose
non-discrimination obligations on new States in Central and Eastern Europe.
But in no way would they recognise similar obligations applicable to themselves
and particularly, in the case of the British and French, to their colonial empires.

* * *

The year 1919 was a turning point in many ways. It brought the emergence of
several components of the international legal order in the field of human rights.
Two elements of particular relevance to the issue of racial discrimination are the
development of the minorities protection regime and the international criminalization of 'massacres' directed against racial or ethnic groups. These were only
beginnings, of course, but taken as a whole they meant that racial equality and
non-discrimination had found its place on the international agenda.

The great disappointment was the failed Japanese effort at a clause on racial
equality in the Covenant of the League of Nations. Wilson's veto of the equality

---

[124] Petition for an Amendment to the League of Nations, 4 July 1919, LNA R1568/40/78/151.
[125] 'Negroes Appeal to League, Want Clauses Inserted in Covenant to Guarantee "Full Liberty"',
New York Times, 7 July 1919, p. 12.
[126] Letter from the World Alliance for Promoting International Friendship, 30 October 1919, LNA
R1572/40/1827/1827.
[127] The Negro and the League of Nations, ca. 1921, W.E.B. Du Bois Papers (MS 312).

clause was not easily forgotten. In the 1940s, when policy makers in the United States Department of State began preparing the legal framework for the United Nations, they not only undertook a study of the 1919 debate but shared their observations with the British. The failed efforts of Japan in 1919 cast a dark shadow over the San Francisco Conference in 1945. New Zealand's diplomats alerted London of their concern 'that the Chinese will press for formal recognition of the principle of racial equality at the Peace Conference, or before, in the same way as did the Japanese at Versailles'. A Foreign Office official minuted that it 'seems likely that the racial equality question will come up again in some form in the postwar settlement'.[128] Several veterans of 1919 were involved, including Wellington Koo of China, who had voted in support of the Japanese proposal, Jan Smuts of South Africa, who had opposed it, and W.E.B. Du Bois of the United States, who had watched the Paris Peace Conference from the wings. Even a century later, in 2021, Judge Iwasawa of the International Court of Justice made reference in a dissenting opinion to the failed Japanese efforts at the Paris Peace Conference.[129]

Essentially, the opposition to the Japanese proposal came from the United States and the United Kingdom. No explanation for their reluctance to condemn racial discrimination is really required. This was a theme that would repeat itself over the century. The main point is that the battle for equality was now launched. Racial discrimination was an issue in international law. It was firmly placed on the global agenda. The efforts at Paris, by the Japanese but also by African Americans and their friends, would be pursued at the League of Nations after it began its work in 1920.

---

[128] Day to Bennett, 17 February 1945, TNA FO 371/46324.
[129] *Application of the International Convention on the Elimination of All Forms of Racial Discrimination (Qatar v. United Arab Emirates), Preliminary Objections, Judgment, I.C.J. Reports 2021*, p. 71, Separate Opinion of Judge Iwasawa, para. 5.

3

Mandates, Minorities, and the League of Nations

African Troops in a European War

The First World War was unprecedented in many respects. Never before in human history had there been armies of such size, nor had there been casualties on such a scale. One of the features of colonialism was the resort by European powers to the recruitment of troops from the territories that they controlled and their deployment in the European theatres. France took the lead, with 172,800 soldiers from Algeria, 134,300 from West Africa, 60,000 from Tunisia, 37,300 from Morocco, 34,400 from Madagascar, and 2,100 from the Somali Coast. Indochina contributed a contingent of about 44,000 soldiers.[1] The British recruited huge numbers of colonial troops, including about 1.5 million from India alone. The British troops of colour were deployed in combat in Africa and Asia but not, apparently, in Europe. The United States had nearly 400,000 African Americans in uniform, of whom about half served in Europe.

Travelling in France when the War was over, W.E.B. Du Bois inquired into the conditions of African American soldiers. 'American white officers fought more valiantly against Negroes than they did against the Germans', he wrote.[2] Discrimination against those who sacrificed their lives was perpetuated in memorialization. Although the Commonwealth War Graves Commission has insisted that it makes no distinction based upon 'race and creed', in Africa, where there were more than 200,000 deaths, 'the Imperial War Graves Commission developed a policy of conserving what it called the "white graves", while allowing "native" graves to revert to nature. The occupants of the latter were commemorated on memorials rather than given headstones . . .'[3]

---

[1] Albert Sarraut, *La mise en valeur des Colonies françaises*, Paris: Payot, 1923, p. 44, cited in Christian Koller, 'The Recruitment of Colonial Troops in Africa and Asia and their Deployment in Europe during the First World War' (2008) 26 *Immigrants & Minorities* 111, at p. 114. Also Richard Fogarty, *Race and War in France: Colonial Subjects in the French Army, 1914-1918*, Baltimore: Johns Hopkins University Press, 2008.

[2] W.E.B. Du Bois, 'Dusk of Dawn', in W.E.B. Du Bois, *Writings*, New York: New American Library, 1986, pp. 549–802, at p. 746. See also his essay, 'An Essay Toward a History of the Black Man in the Civil War', in ibid., pp. 879–922.

[3] Michèle Barrett, 'Subalterns at War' (2007) 9 *Interventions* 451, at p. 455. Also Michèle Barrett, '"White Graves" and Natives: The Imperial War Graves Commission in East and West Africa,

Following signature of the Treaty of Versailles in June 1919, parts of the eastern bank of the Rhine were occupied by France, in accordance with provisions of the Treaty. France sent troops of colour, from Senegal, Indochina, and Madagascar, over the objections of Woodrow Wilson and David Lloyd George and a specific protest from the Germans themselves.[4] The Treaty of Versailles was enough of a humiliation; that it should be enforced upon 'a great people of culture' by 'coloured men of low and lowest standard of culture', in the words of a petition submitted to the League of Nations from the *Deutscher Volksbund 'Rettet die ehre'*, seemed too much to bear.[5] The African troops of the French army were accused of widespread sexual and gender-based violence against German women and girls. These were fabricated charges rooted in racist stereotypes, pushed by right-wing German propagandists but with considerable resonance in other European countries and in the United States, where the campaign was picked up by socialists, trade unionists, and feminists.[6] A letter distributed to the League of Nations Council from the Netherlands Women's Association for the Improvement of Morals protested the presence of the troops as 'an outrage to Germany and an insult to our civilisation', adding that 'they outrage in the grossest fashion women, young girls, children and even boys, but we are faced by the fact that they spread the worst forms of venereal diseases'.[7]

In the occupied territories themselves, the French troops of colour were generally much appreciated for their professionalism and lack of arrogance or contempt for the Germans, which could not always be said of the soldiers from the *Hexagone*.[8] Some of the submissions to the League of Nations treated the African troops as victims of French colonialism. A meeting of the British branch of the pacifist Women's International League for Peace and Freedom in April

1918–1939', in Paul Cornish and Nicholas J. Saunders, eds., *Bodies in Conflict: Corporeality, Materiality, and Transformation*, London: Routledge, 2013, pp. 80–90.

[4] Keith Nelson, 'The "Black Horror on the Rhine": Race as a Factor in Post-World War I Diplomacy' (1970) 42 *Journal of Modern History* 606; Ernest Müller-Meiningen, *'Who Are the Huns?', The Law of Nations and its Breakers*, Berlin: George Reimer, 1915, pp. 57–60.

[5] Deutscher Volksbund 'Rettet die ehre', To the League of Nations at Geneva, LNA R572/11/4150/9047.

[6] Robert Reinders, 'Racialism on the Left: E.D. Morel and the "Black Horror on the Rhine"' (1968) 13 *International Review of Social History* 1; Peter Campbell, 'The "Black Horror on the Rhine": Idealism, Pacifism, and Racism in Feminism and the Left in the Aftermath of the First World War' (2014) 49 *Histoire sociale/Social History* 471; Iris Wigger, '"Against the Laws of Civilisation": Race, Gender and Nation in the International Racist Campaign Against the "Black Shame"' (2002) 46 *Berkeley Journal of Sociology* 113; Rotem Giladi, 'The Phoenix of Colonial War: Race, the Laws of War, and the "Horror on the Rhine"' (2017) 30 *Leiden Journal of International Law* 847.

[7] The Employment of Coloured Troops in the Rhine Provinces, Letter, dated 1 February 1921, from the Netherlands Women's Association for the Improvement of Morlas (De Nederlandsche Vrowenbund tot verhooging van het zedelyk bewustzyn), LNA R572/11/4150/10698.

[8] Sally Marks, 'Black Watch on the Rhine. A Study in Propaganda, Prejudice and Prurience' (1983) 13 *European Studies Review* 297, at pp. 299–300.

1920 called on the League of Nations to prohibit 'the importation into Europe for warlike purposes of troops belonging to primitive peoples'.[9] A letter along similar lines from the Committee of the Society of Friends in Great Britain, albeit couched in patronizing language, was circulated to the League Assembly in October 1920.[10] An inquiry by the United States military concluded that allegations of 'wholesale atrocities by French negro Colonial troops' were 'false and intended for political propaganda'.[11] An official French report published in 1921 reached a similar conclusion.[12]

The participation of troops from Africa and Asia on European battlefields had provoked concerns when they were taken prisoner.[13] Because the fighting units were segregated, it was contended that this should continue in POW camps. After the war, British international lawyers contemplated new legal norms for the treatment of prisoners of war. In one proposal, George G. Phillimore proposed that '[p]risoners of different nationalities or races or colours shall not be confined together'.[14] It may have inspired a provision in the 1929 Geneva Convention along these lines, based upon an American proposal: 'Belligerents shall, so far as possible, avoid assembling in a single camp prisoners of different races or nationalities'.[15] The 1949 version of the Convention, which is still in force, specifies that prisoners should be detained 'according to their nationality, language and customs'.[16] The Commentary on the 1949 Convention issued by the International Committee of the Red Cross explains that reference to 'race' was removed 'mainly because of the derogatory implication which this term has acquired as a result of certain persecutions'.[17]

---

[9] Women's International League to Drummond, 3 May 1920, LNA R572/11/4150/4150.

[10] Letter, dated 1 October 1920, from the Committee of the Society of Friends in Great Britain, LNA R572/11/4150/7550.

[11] 'Finds Negro Troops Orderly on Rhine', *New York Times*, 19 February 1920.

[12] *La campagne allemande contre les troupes noirs, Rapport du Capitaine Bouriand surs ses missions en pays rhénans*, Paris: Gauthier Villars, 1922. There is a copy in the League of Nations archives: LNA R572/11/19750/4150.

[13] Timothy L. Schroer, 'Racial Mixing of Prisoners of War in the First World War', in James E. Kitchen, Alisa Miller, and Laura Rowe, eds., *Other Combatants, Other Fronts: Competing Histories of the First World War*, Newcastle upon Tyne: Cambridge Scholars, 2011, pp. 177–98.

[14] George G. Phillimore, 'Some Suggestions for a Draft Code for the Treatment of Prisoners of War' (1920) 6 *Transactions of the Grotius Society* 25, at p. 27.

[15] Convention relative to the Treatment of Prisoners of War (1929) 118 LNTS 343, art. 9. See Timothy L. Schroer, 'The Emergence and Early Demise of Codified Racial Segregation of Prisoners of War under the Geneva Conventions of 1929 and 1949' (2013) 15 *Journal of the History of International Law* 53.

[16] Geneva Convention Relative to the Treatment of Prisoners of War of 12 August 1949 (1950) 75 UNTS 134, art. 22.

[17] Jean de Preux, ed., *Commentary, Geneva Convention Relative to the Treatment of Prisoners of War*, Geneva: International Committee of the Red Cross, 1960, p. 184.

Petitioning the League

The League of Nations formally began in January 1920 following the entry into force of the Treaty of Versailles. The Covenant of the League of Nations was part I of the Treaty. There were 42 founding members, the vast majority countries of Europe or countries ruled by persons of European descent. The League had four founding members from Asia: China, Japan, Persia, and Siam. Besides South Africa, which was a dominion of the British Empire, Liberia was the only African founding member. Haiti was the other founding member state that could be described as one of African descent. In 1920, it was under American military occupation and would remain so for many years.[18] Abyssinia joined the League in 1923. Afghanistan, Egypt, and Iraq became members during the 1930s. At its heart, the League was a European organization with an important focus on the management of the consequences of the First World War. Within Europe, the League dealt with the new States and the new borders, addressing issues related to the rights of minorities. Outside Europe, it was concerned with the remnants of the German and Ottoman Empires, which had been divided among the victors under the Mandate System provided for in article 22 of the Covenant. Issues of racial discrimination arose in both of these contexts.

The Pan-African Congress, which had met in Paris in 1919 while the Peace Conference was underway, convened again in London in 1921. It addressed three requests to the League of Nations, describing it as 'the greatest international body in the world', and noting that it 'must sooner or later turn its attention to the great racial problem as it today affects persons of Negro descent'. First, the Congress asked the International Labour Office to set aside a section charged with dealing 'particularly and in detail with the conditions and needs of Native Negro Labour especially in Africa and in the Islands of the Seas'. The International Labour Office was a component of the International Labour Organisation created under part XIII of the Treaty of Versailles and itself related to the League of Nations. The Congress petition said that the labour problems of the world 'could not be understood or properly settled so long as coloured and especially Negro labour is enslaved and neglected and that a first step toward the world emancipation of labour would be through investigation of Native labour'. Second, the Congress said that the mandates, 'peopled as they are so largely by black folk, have a right to ask that a man of Negro descent, properly fitted in character and training be appointed a member of the Mandates Commission as soon as a vacancy occurs'.[19]

---

[18] Musab Younis, 'Race, the World and Time: Haiti, Liberia and Ethiopia (1914–1945)' (2018) 46 *Millennium: Journal of International Studies* 352, at pp. 358–60; Robert Knox, 'Haiti at the League of Nations: Racialisation, Accumulation and Representation' (2020) 21 *Melbourne Journal of International Law* 245.

[19] Pan African Congress. Letter from Pan-African Congress to League of Nations, ca. September 1921. W.E.B. Du Bois Papers (MS 312); W.E.B. Du Bois, 'Manifesto to the League of Nations' (1921)

56 MANDATES, MINORITIES, AND THE LEAGUE OF NATIONS

Finally, the Congress asked the League to address 'the condition of civilised persons of Negro descent throughout the world'. It said that

> [c]onsciously and unconsciously there is in the world today a widespread and growing feeling that it is permissible to treat civilised men as uncivilised if they are coloured and more especially of Negro descent. The result of this attitude and many consequent laws, customs and conventions is that a bitter feeling of resentment, personal insult and despair is widespread in the world among those very persons whose rise is the hope of the Negro race.

The Congress said it was aware that the League had little direct power, but that it had 'the vast moral power of public world opinion and of a body conceived to promote peace and justice among men'. For this reason, it said the League should 'take a firm stand on the absolute equality of races' and suggested that the colonial powers connected with the League create an international institute for the study of the Negro Problem, and for the Evolution and Protection of the Negro Race.[20]

Edouard Junod, Secretary of the Swiss-based Bureau international pour la défense des indigènes, wrote to Eric Drummond, Secretary-General of the League, saying he had received a request from the 'black gentlemen' of the Congress to circulate its resolutions. He asked whether this was appropriate and whether there was a time limit for submission.[21] William Rappard, head of the Mandates Section, promptly replied that the resolutions of the Congress could be made available to the League Assembly if their character justified this.[22] Days later, the League Secretariat received a telegram from the World Confederation of Negroes, whose leader was Marcus Garvey, charging that Du Bois and the 'so-called Pan African Congress and those associated with him are not representative of the struggling Negro peoples of the world of their intention and have no mandate from the said people to call a congress in their name'.[23] Garvey also submitted a resolution adopted in New York on 31 August 1921 by the International Convention of Negroes protesting against 'the distribution of the

---

23 *The Crisis* 18. See also: '1921 Pan-African Congress, London Manifesto' (2015) 8 *Journal of Pan African Studies* 117.

20 Pan African Congress. Letter from Pan-African Congress to League of Nations, ca. September 1921.

21 Junod to Drummond, 8 July 1921, LNA R39/1/13940/13940.

22 Rappard to Junod, 12 July 1921, LNA R39/1/13940/13940.

23 Telegram from The Secretary, World Congress of Negroes to Drummond, 1 August 1921, LNA R39/1/13940/13940. Also Telegram from Garvey to Drummond, 7 September 1921, LNA R39/1/13940/13940.

lands of Africa by the Supreme Council and the League of Nations among the white nations of the world'.[24]

Gratien Candace, a French parliamentarian from Guadeloupe, also wrote to the League with copies of the Congress resolutions. Candace was particularly keen on a proposal to create an international institute charged with studying problems relating to the protection of the Black race, which seems to have been his own paraphrase of the Congress resolution directed at the International Labour Organisation.[25]

Du Bois travelled to Geneva to present the views of the Pan-African Congress to the League. According to an account by him written in the late 1940s, Du Bois actually submitted the resolutions of the Congress to Eric Drummond.[26] In the eyes of Du Bois, the League of Nations was 'absolutely necessary to the salvation of the Negro race. Unless we have some supernational power to curb the anti-Negro policy of the United States and South Africa, we are doomed eventually to *fight* for our rights'.[27] He asked Drummond to distribute the Pan-African Congress petition to members of the Council of the Assembly as well as various commissions.[28]

The Secretary-General circulated officially an address by Du Bois setting out the contents of the Congress resolutions, accompanied by a supportive letter from Junod.[29] Du Bois also met with representatives of civil society: René-Édouard Claparède of the Bureau international pour la défense des indigènes,[30] John H. Harris of the Aborigines Protection Society, and Leif Jones, a British politician and activist. Du Bois obtained the support of William Rappard for the proposal to name a Black member to the Permanent Mandates Commission.[31]

On his first day in Geneva, Du Bois attended a session of the League of Nations Assembly. By coincidence, he was present when one of India's representatives, V.S. Srinavasa Sastri, took the floor with a warning about South Africa's mandate over German South West Africa. Sastri said that its laws and regulations, and 'habits of administration', imposed a 'colour bar' and made 'invidious distinctions between white and coloured populations'. He said that in general South Africa

---

[24] Garvey to Drummond, 2 September 1921, LNA R41/1/15345/15345.

[25] Candace to League of Nations, 12 October 1921, LNA R39/1/13940/13940.

[26] W.E.B. Du Bois, 'The American Negro before the United Nations [fragment], December 1947', W.E.B. Du Bois Papers (MS 312). See Letter from Du Bois to Drummond, 16 September 1921, LNA R39/1/13940/13940.

[27] W.E.B. Du Bois, 'The League of Nations' (1919) 18 *The Crisis* 10 (emphasis in the original).

[28] Du Bois to Drummond, 16 September 1921, LNA R391/15865/13940, W.E.B. Du Bois Papers (MS 312).

[29] Second Pan-African Congress, August/September 1921, LNA R39/1/13940/15865, LNA R39/1/13940/13940.

[30] Du Bois to Claparède, 18 June 1921, W.E.B. Du Bois Papers (MS 312).

[31] W.E.B. Du Bois, The American Negro before the United Nations [fragment], December, 1947, W.E.B. Du Bois Papers (MS 312).

might not hesitate 'to subject coloured populations . . . to certain hardships and, I am sorry to add, even indignities'. He said he had no evidence that this had yet occurred, but said it would be a source of 'great pain and grief, . . . a matter of great uneasiness and searching of heart' were India's representatives to come to the Assembly and say 'We are worse off under the trustees of the League than we were under the Germans'. The Record of the meeting says that Sastri, who was renowned for his eloquence, ended his remarks to 'loud and prolonged applause'.[32]

Du Bois enlisted the support of Gilbert Murray, an Oxford academic who was a strong supporter of the League of Nations, and of Henri La Fontaine, a Belgian senator and Nobel Peace Prize laureate.[33] Ironically, Murray attended the Assembly as a representative of South Africa, described by Du Bois as 'the worst Negro-hating country in the world'. But Du Bois respected him as a 'liberal-minded Englishman' and thought him particularly well placed to raise the issue. Murray wrote to Du Bois telling him the resolutions were 'too late to be profitably referred to a Committee for discussion' but that he had also suggested to Dantès Bellegarde that the second request, concerning a Black member of the Mandates Commission, be put to the Assembly during its debates. Bellegarde, who had been honorary president of the second Pan African Congress, had been appointed by Haiti's president, Philippe-Sudre Dartiguenave, to represent Haiti at the League.[34] He was apparently then the only Black person to participate in the League Assembly. Bellegarde first refused, insisting that Du Bois had chosen Murray because of his great influence and because he thought it better for a white man to make the case. But Murray said Bellegarde had the ear of the Assembly and that the appeal would be more effective coming from him.[35] Bellegarde presented the proposal as a 'principle' rather than an amendment to the report of the Committee. 'A day will come when the League of Nations will have to concern itself with the race problem', he said, 'when it will have to work for the disappearance of racial differences, differences marked by ill-treatment meted out to particular races and resulting in a menace to universal peace'.[36] Murray reported that Bellegarde's speech was 'quite a remarkable success', and he thought that next year it might be quite suitable to put this in the form of a resolution.[37] Assessing these efforts, Du Bois considered that it was 'a small beginning toward

---

[32] Record of the 9th Plenary meeting of the Second Assembly of the League of Nations, 12 September 1921, *Records of the Second Assembly, Plenary Meetings*, pp. 216–17.

[33] Du Bois to Murray, ca. September 1921, W.E.B. Du Bois Papers (MS 312).

[34] Patrick Bellegarde-Smith, 'International Relations/Social Theory in a Small State: An Analysis of the Thought of Dantès Bellegarde' (1982) 39 *The Americas* 167; Patrick Bellegarde-Smith, *In the Shadow of Powers: Dantes Bellegarde in Haitian Social Thought*, Atlantic Highlands, NJ: Humanities Press International, 1985; Robert Knox, 'Haiti at the League of Nations: Racialisation, Accumulation and Representation' (2020) 21 *Melbourne Journal of International Law* 245.

[35] Mercer Cook, 'Dantès Bellegarde' (1940) 1 *Phylon* 125, at pp. 129–30.

[36] Dantès Bellegarde, 'Haiti and the Rights of Man' (1950) 14 *Negro History Bulletin* 41.

[37] Murray to Du Bois, 23 September 1921, W.E.B. Du Bois Papers (MS 312).

bringing Africa into the centre of the international movement of the world, but it is an important beginning, and if pushed in the future may mean a revolution for the Negro race, particularly if the League of Nations survives to fulfil its present promise.[38] In the course of its 19-year history, membership in the Permanent Mandates Commission never went beyond the Member States of Europe with the exception of Japan. Moreover, other than representatives from Norway, Switzerland, and, latterly, Germany, they were all nationals of colonial powers. It was, as Susan Pedersen has described, 'very much an imperialists' club'.[39]

While in Geneva, Du Bois also called on the International Labour Office. He presented the Pan-African Congress petition to Albert Thomas, its first director, and to Gustav Spiller, a senior official who had attended the International Races Congress in 1911.[40] Du Bois thought Thomas 'showed much interest, pointed out that some attention had already been given to this matter and intimated that further steps might be taken'.[41] Thomas later sent a detailed reply to Du Bois, who published it in *The Crisis*, the journal of the National Association for the Advancement of Colored People. Thomas wrote that he had learned of the Congress resolution 'with the utmost interest because it set before the International Bureau of Labour the entire problem of the protection of native labourers and especially of Negro labourers. This matter of protection indeed has been one of the principal preoccupations of this institution ever since its inception.' He said the Office considered it had a duty to protect workers 'without making any race distinction and indeed that its protection ought to extend especially to those men who are subjected to the most inhuman conditions of labour, as is the case of a large number of native peoples, particularly of black peoples'. Thomas pointed to the 'principle of the equality of races', citing the preamble and article 427 of the Treaty of Versailles. It was a generous, and quite progressive, reading of the relevant provisions of the Covenant of the League of Nations that does not, in fact, contain any explicit reference to racial equality. Thomas recognized that the Office could 'interfere only with the greatest difficulty' on such issues, and that its main weapon was recourse to public opinion. He noted that it could solicit reports concerning implementation of treaties, and that it had requested one from Britain. Thomas said that his enthusiasm for these issues had been revived by the Pan-African Congress. He planned to establish a section of Native Labour. In the meantime an official of the Scientific Division would be

---

[38] The Negro and the League of Nations, ca. 1921, W.E.B. Du Bois Papers (MS 312).

[39] Susan Pedersen, *The League of Nations and the Crisis of Empire*, Oxford: Oxford University Press, 2017, p. 61.

[40] Memoranda of Monsieur Thomas, ca. 1921, W.E.B. Du Bois Papers (MS 312).

[41] W.E.B. Du Bois, 'The Negro and the League of Nations', ca. 1921, W.E.B. Du Bois Papers (MS 312).

60 MANDATES, MINORITIES, AND THE LEAGUE OF NATIONS

charged with 'following up the conditions of native, and particularly of Negro labour'.[42]

In May 1922, Marcus Garvey, president of the militant US-based Universal Negro Improvement Association, wrote to League of Nations Secretary-General Eric Drummond seeking a meeting.[43] Garvey's failed efforts of the previous year to undermine the work of Du Bois must have taught him that he needed to engage directly with the League. G.H.F. Abraham, a member of the League Secretariat, advised caution:

> As the presence of a negro delegation will be a novelty, it will be referred to by the Press—especially the American Press—and it might antagonise many of our friends in America, who might think that the League was meddling in the negro question in the States, where this question is a very burning one.[44]

Drummond's reply to Garvey referred to the upcoming Assembly session in September, noting that these were open to the public but that 'the rules of procedure do not provide for the hearing of delegations other than those officially representing such States Members'.[45] In September, Drummond apologized to the delegation for his failure to meet personally, attributing this to a busy schedule, but said he had assigned senior officials to represent him and that he had reserved seats for them in the Assembly hall.[46] 'They have a real case which we cannot totally ignore and should not greatly encourage', minuted a League official.

The Universal Negro Improvement Association presented the League of Nations with a petition on behalf of 'the 400 million Negroes Indigenes of Africa, the British Subjects in the West Indies South and Central America, and the Citizens, and other Negro inhabitants of the United States of America and those of Asia and Europe'. The petition noted that 'fully 2 millions of us' had fought on behalf of various allied powers during the War. 'Your petitioners were told, as a race, that all peoples who contributed to the war would be considered at its conclusion', it said, referring to the 'restoration of Palestine to the Jew', independence for Ireland and Egypt, and 'a great consideration for India'. The petition said that '[w]ith the sacrifice we have given in blood, labour and money, we have not been

---

[42] Thomas to Du Bois, ca. October 1921, W.E.B. Du Bois Papers (MS 312) (there are versions of the letter in both English and French); Albert Thomas, 'The International Bureau of Labour of the League of Nations' (1921) 23 *The Crisis* 69.

[43] Garvey to Drummond, 23 May 1922, LNA R60/1/21159/21159. Also Garvey to League Council, 23 May 1922, LNA R60/1/21159/21159.

[44] Minute of Abraham, 15 June 1922, LNA R60/1/21159/21159.

[45] Drummond to Garvey, 20 June 1922, LNA R60/1/21159/21159. See Arnulf Becker Lorca, 'Petitioning the International: A "Pre-history" of Self-determination' (2014) 25 *European Journal of International Law* 497, at p. 511.

[46] Drummond to Marke, 15 September 1922, LNA R60/1/21159/21159.

justly considered by the League of Nations nor by the individual Governments under whom we live and who are members of your august body'. The League of Nations was asked to designate the former German colonies in east and south west Africa as a 'national home' for the 'Negro race'.[47]

William Rappard explained that the League was not in a position to assign the German colonies. He told the Association representatives that, pursuant to the Treaty of Versailles, Germany had ceded the rights to her overseas possessions to the Allied powers who were administering them under mandates as provided for in article 22 of the Covenant of the League.[48] The petition was circulated to members of the League Assembly following a request from the head of the Persian delegation.[49] A representative of the Universal Negro Improvement Association returned to Geneva for the fourth session of the League Assembly in 1923. Garvey described him as a 'delegate' who would present his 'credentials' to the Secretary-General.[50] In 1924, Marcus Garvey sent a telegram to Eric Drummond repeating the claim that the former German colonies be developed as 'independent negro nations'.[51] Garvey renewed the petition four years later, expanding upon the arguments, especially with regard to South Africa. The 1928 submission noted that the earlier petition was 'referred to a special committee for action, but up to the present time we have received no notification of any action, other than to observe that at a subsequent meeting you carried a resolution that all nationals who had grievances should present them through their respective governments'.[52]

Garvey travelled to Geneva in 1931, where he met with Peter Anker of the Mandates Section.[53] Petitions continued to be filed throughout the 1930s. In 1938, the United Africa Front requested the 'Secretary of State' of the League of Nations to 'give Africa to the Black People, who are the rightful owners of that land'. Its petition noted that Marcus Garvey had been denied the right to be heard by the League of Nations 'for some unknown reason to him as well as to the people he represented'. A note in the file by Edouard De Haller proposed that there be no acknowledgement of receipt of the petition.[54]

Indigenous peoples also campaigned at the League of Nations. In 1923, the leader of the Six Nations of the Iroquois (or Haudenosaunee), Levi General

---

[47] Petition of the Universal Negro Improvement Association and African Communities League, 26 July 1922, LNA R60/1/21159/21159, LNA R2344/6A/7158/7158/Jacket 1.

[48] Drummond to Marke, 16 September 1922, LNA R60/1/21159/21159.

[49] Arfa-ed-Dowleh to Drummond, 28 September 1922, LNA R60/1/21159/21159; Drummond to Arfa-ed-Dowleh, 3 October 1922, LNA R60/1/21159/21159.

[50] Garvey to Drummond, 14 August 1923, LNA R60/1/30405/21159.

[51] Garvey to Drummond, 4 August 1924, LNA R60/1/37672/21159.

[52] See, for example, Renewal of Petition of United Negro Improvement Association and African Communities League to League of Nations, September 1928, LNA R2344/6A/7158/7158/Jacket 1.

[53] Anker to Catastini, 22 August 1931, LNA R2344/6A/7158/7158/Jacket 1.

[54] Ajai Ben Rama to Drummond, 2 May 1938, LNA R4123/6A/3628/3628/20.

62 MANDATES, MINORITIES, AND THE LEAGUE OF NATIONS

Deskaheh, went to Geneva to present a petition entitled 'The Redman's Appeal for Justice'. The title might suggest an emphasis on racial discrimination although the submission was focussed on the 'independent right of home rule'. It alleged that Canada and the British Empire had breached treaties.[55] The Six Nations based their application on article 17 of the Covenant of the League of Nations which governed disputes between a Member of the League and a State which was not a member. Ireland, Estonia, Panama, and Persia addressed Hjalmar Branting, the President of the League's Council, citing the universal interest in 'la conservation de l'antique race des Indiens Peaux-Rouges'. They suggested that the application of article 17 to the Six Nations might be examined by the Permanent Court of International Justice.[56]

The Netherlands made a formal request that the matter be placed on the Council's agenda.[57] Canada complained to Drummond that the Netherlands had promoted an issue that was entirely internal in nature.[58] Drummond let it be known that he felt the matter should be 'buried'.[59] The subject wasn't addressed by the Council in 1923 but the four Member States renewed their efforts in early January with a letter from the Persian envoy explaining that the objective was 'to give a small nation a chance of at least being heard'.[60] Eventually the Canadian Government prepared a paragraph-by-paragraph rebuttal of the submission by the Six Nations. It was published in the *Official Journal* of the League.[61] In a handwritten post-script to a letter addressed to Drummond, the British Foreign

---

[55] 'The Red Man's Appeal to Justice', 6 August 1923, LNA R612/11/2807530626. Several copies of an earlier version, in both English and French, may be found in LNA R612/11/28075/28075. See Ronald Niezen, 'Recognizing Indigenism: Canadian Unity and the International Movement of Indigenous Peoples' (2000) 42 *Comparative Studies in Society and History* 119; Ronald Niezen, *The Origins of Indigenism: Human Rights and the Politics of Identity*, Berkeley: University of California, 2003; Grace Li Xiu Woo, 'Canada's Forgotten Founders: The Modern Significance of the Haudenosaunee (Iroquois) Application for Membership of the League of Nations' [2003] *Law, Social Justice and Global Development* 1; Richard Veatch, *Canada and the League of Nations*, Toronto: University of Toronto Press, 1975; Yale D. Belanger, 'The Six Nations of Grand River Territory's Attempts at Renewing International Political Relationships, 1921–1924' (2007) 13 *Canadian Foreign Policy Journal* 29; Laurence M. Hauptman, *The Iroquois Struggle for Survival: World War II to Red Power*, Syracuse: Syracuse University Press, 1986; Joëlle Rostkowski, 'The Redman's Appeal for Justice: Deskaheh and the League of Nations', in Christian F. Feest, ed., *Indians and Europe: An Interdisciplinary Collection of Essays*, Lincoln: University of Nebraska Press, 1999, pp. 435–53; Joëlle Rostkowski, 'Deskaheh's Shadow: Indians on the International Scene' (1995) 9 *European Review of Native American Studies* 1; Amar Bhatia, 'The South of the North: Building on Critical Approaches 137 to International Law with Lessons from the Fourth World' (2012) 14 *Oregon Review of International Law* 131.

[56] MacNeill et al. to Branting, 27 September 1923, LNA R612/11/28075/31340, LNA R612/11/28075/32700.

[57] Van Panhuys to Drummond, 26 April 1923, LNA R612/11/28075/28075.

[58] Pope to Drummond, 25 May 1923, LNA R612/11/28075/29185.

[59] Abraham to Van Hamel, 31 July 1923, LNA R612/11/28075/29540.

[60] Arfa-ed-Dowleh to Branting, 13 December 1923, LNA R612/11/28075/32700; Arfa-ed-Dowleh to Branting, 8 January 1924, LNA R612/11/28075/32700.

[61] Statement respecting the Six Nations' Appeal to the League of Nations, 27 December 1923, *Official Journal*, June 1924, pp. 829–42.

Secretary, Alexander Cadogan, objected to describing the matter as a 'dispute between Canada and Six Nations of the Grand River', saying it would be better to call it 'an impertinent and frivolous complaint'.[62] At the end of 1924, the Canadian Government sent multiple copies of the report of an investigation into 'the affairs of the Six Nations Indians' for use of members of the Council of the League.[63]

No sooner had Deskaheh returned to Canada than a delegation of Maori, led by spiritual leader T.W. Ratana, arrived in Geneva from New Zealand to protest their treatment. There they had two meetings, one with Paul Mantoux and the other with J.V. Wilson, who was himself a national of New Zealand. They told Mantoux that in New Zealand Maori were not treated as equals. In a minute to the file, Drummond described the case as 'very similar' to that of the Six Nations.[64] Much later, in August 1938, the Secretary of the Australian Aborigines Progressive Association, Pearl Gibbs, reported to the League of Nations protesting 'the ill treatment of the aborigines throughout Australia in the past' as well as recent events involving a racist judge. A League bureaucrat minuted the file with the words 'I don't think any action is possible or desirable'.[65]

As the League was entering its twilight years, several organizations wrote to the Permanent Mandates Commission about the demands by Nazi Germany for the return of the mandated territories. The London-based Negro Welfare Association, submitting a resolution adopted at public meeting under its auspices, wrote:

The Negro peoples cannot forget the extermination of the Hereros in South West Africa and the massacre of tens of thousands of East Africans under former German rule, while in Germany itself the Hitler regime has committed the most atrocious crimes, mass torture, murdering of the German toilers, the destruction of all workers' organisations, the most abominable persecution of the Jew and other non-Aryan people ... As Hitler bases his idea of Government on the racial question and in view of his openly expressed race prejudice, this meeting sees clearly the hell that awaits people of the colonies if subjected to Fascist rule, under which the struggle of the native people and of Negroes

---

[62] Cadogan to Drummond, 5 April 1924, LNA R612/11/28075/35296.

[63] Walker to Drummond, 31 December 1924, LNA R612/11/28075/40899.

[64] Claims of the Maori People with regard to the tenure of land in New Zealand, LNA R618/38827/38827.

[65] Gibbs to the President of the League of Nations, 4 July 1938, LNA R3690/1/34895/34895. See Marilyn Lake, 'Women's International leadership', in Joy Damousi, Kim Rubenstein, and Mary Tomsic, eds., *Diversity in Leadership Australian women, past and present*, Canberra: ANU Press, 2014, pp. 71–90, at p. 84; Sophie Rigney, 'On Hearing Well and Being Well Heard: Indigenous International Law at the League of Nations' (2021) 2 *TWAIL Review* 122, at pp. 133–34.

64   MANDATES, MINORITIES, AND THE LEAGUE OF NATIONS

everywhere for National emancipation would receive a tremendous setback and the colonial slave system would be further entrenched.[66]

Minorities Treaties, the Permanent Court, and the League Council

The Permanent Court of International Justice, known colloquially as the 'World Court', was one of the new institutions established following the First World War. Previously, legal disputes between States might have been settled by arbitration, in effect, by an ad hoc tribunal following an agreement by the parties. The 1899 Hague Convention had established a Permanent Court of Arbitration but it was not really a tribunal as such, rather a panel from which States involved in disputes could select arbitrators. Prior to the First World War, the Peace Palace in The Hague was built as a home for the Permanent Court of Arbitration. During July 1914, there were unsuccessful efforts to bring Austria's dispute with Serbia to the Court at the Peace Palace.

The new Permanent Court of International Justice was established in 1920. It was authorized to deal with interstate disputes, providing that the two parties consented, but it could also deliver an 'advisory opinion' upon request from the Council of the League of Nations. In this way, a number of issues concerning the minority rights treaties were adjudicated, including those relating to the equality and non-discrimination provisions. None of them dealt with race in the sense of colour. Nevertheless, they did address matters of racial discrimination taken in its broad sense.

The *German Settlers in Poland* advisory opinion of 1923 was the first dispute resulting from the 'little Treaty of Versailles', by which the Allied and Associated Powers recognized Poland. The case resulted from an initiative of the German League for the Protection of the Rights of Minorities in Poland (*Deutschtumsbund zur Wahrung der Minderheitsrechte in Polen*) of Bydgoszcz.[67] It involved German residents of territory in Upper Silesia that had become part of Poland. Leases consented by Germany prior to 11 November 1918 were revoked by the Polish government when it assumed sovereignty over the territory. The leases had been granted by Prussia in order to promote the Germanization of the region. The German League, representing several thousand of those who had seen their leases cancelled, contended that this was a violation of the provisions of what the Court referred to as the 'Minorities Treaty'. After a Committee of Jurists of the

---

[66] Resolution on Germany's demand for colonies, 4 April 1937, LNA R4137/6A/27984/27984.
[67] Letter and Memorandum from the German Association in Poland, 28 June 1920, LNA R1639/41/6180/6180.

MINORITIES TREATIES, PERMANENT COURT, LEAGUE COUNCIL 65

League of Nations had ruled in favour of the German settlers, the Council decided to seek the views of the Court.

In its Advisory Opinion, the Court recalled article 2 of the Treaty, protecting 'life and liberty to all inhabitants of Poland without distinction of birth, nationality, language, race or religion'; article 7, granting all Polish nationals equality before the law without distinction as to 'race, language or religion'; and article 8, which ensured equal treatment to 'Polish nationals who belong to racial, religious or linguistic minorities'. The Court described the issue as one of 'racial discrimination' (the French version of the opinion uses the expression 'distinction expresse de race') and spoke of the settlers who had lost their rights under the leases as members of the 'German race'. It said that

> [t]he fact that no racial discrimination appears in the text of the law of July 14th, 1920, and that in a few instances the law applies to non-German Polish nationals who took as purchasers from original holders of German race, make no substantial difference... There must be equality in fact as well as ostensible legal equality in the sense of the absence of discrimination in the words of the law.[58]

Deciding in favour of the settlers and against the Polish government, the Court said that the intent of the Minorities Treaty was 'to eliminate a dangerous source of oppression, recrimination and dispute, to prevent racial and religious hatreds from having free play and to protect the situations established upon its conclusion, by placing existing minorities under the impartial protection of the League of Nations'.[69]

The Permanent Court returned to the issue of discrimination and equal treatment a decade later. The *Treatment of Polish Nationals* case concerned the application of provisions similar to those in the Treaty with Poland that applied to the Free City of Danzig, where Germans were in the majority. A special provision in the Treaty of Versailles was also relevant. It required the constitution of the Free City of Danzig 'to provide against any discrimination within the Free City to the detriment of citizens of Poland and other persons of Polish origin or speech'.[70] At issue were various legal provisions under the laws of Danzig that discriminated against Polish nationals in the areas of education, labour, acquisition of land, and police registration. The Court explained that '[a]n unsympathetic or even hostile attitude in a community towards a group of persons merely because of their possessing a particular attribute, e.g. nationality, origin, race or religion, is not

---

[68] *German Settlers in Poland, Advisory Opinion*, PCIJ, Series B, No. 6, 10 September 1923, p. 24.
[69] Ibid., p. 25.
[70] Treaty of Versailles [1919] UKTS 4, art. 104(5).

66 MANDATES, MINORITIES, AND THE LEAGUE OF NATIONS

without precedent'.[71] For this reason, the Treaty of Versailles made provision to prohibit discrimination against Polish nationals and other persons of Polish origin or speech in Danzig. Returning to the point it had made in the case of the German settlers, the Court held that

> the prohibition against discrimination, in order to be effective, must ensure the absence of discrimination in fact as well as in law. A measure which in terms is of general application, but in fact is directed against Polish nationals and other persons of Polish origin or speech, constitutes a violation of the prohibition.[72]

The Court also noted that the protection provided to minorities varied depending upon whether they were citizens.[73]

When the borders of Poland and Germany were being considered at the Paris Peace Conference, the Upper Silesia region was in dispute. Following a decision by the Council of the League of Nations, Poland and Germany agreed to a division of the territory. The treaty between Germany and Poland provided for various remedies including a direct petition to the League of Nations as well as recourse to a Mixed Commission. When the Nazis took power in Germany in March 1933, they applied anti-Semitic legal measures to the German part of Upper Silesia as well as encouraging 'unofficial actions' that included a boycott of Jewish merchants and professionals. The President of the Mixed Commission promptly issued an opinion prohibiting the boycott but its application was obstructed by the local courts. On 12 May 1933, Franz Bernheim, a German Jewish Upper Silesian who had been dismissed from his job pursuant to the racist legislation, applied to the Council of the League of Nations.[74] Bernheim's petition listed a range of grievances concerning the anti-Semitic measures, and was in reality a kind of *actio popularis*. Bernheim annexed a letter from his employer, the Deutsches Familien Kaufhaus GMBH, where he worked as an assistant, announcing his dismissal effective 30 April 1933. When the petition became public, some German Jews wrote to the League protesting Bernheim's right to speak on their behalf, claiming he represented 'germanophobe elements'.[75]

Following a recommendation from the head of the Minorities Section, Pablo de Azcárate, Secretary-General Eric Drummond decided that he 'cannot but

---

[71] *Treatment of Polish Nationals and Other Persons of Polish Origin or Speech in Danzig Territory, Advisory Opinion*, PCIJ, Series A./B., No. 44, 4 February 1932, p. 28.

[72] Ibid.

[73] Ibid., p. 39.

[74] Petition des Franz Bernheim dentseher Reichsangehoriger aus Gleiwitz, Deutsch-Oberschlesien, im Sinne des Artikels 147 des deutsch-polnisehen Abkommens über Oberschlesien vom 15.Mai 1922 in Bezug auf die Bestimmungen des III.Teiles dieses Abkommens, 12 May 1933, LNA R3928/4/3634/4150.

[75] Naumann and Siegmann to Drummond, 23 May 1933, LNA R3928/4/3634/4150.

MINORITIES TREATIES, PERMANENT COURT, LEAGUE COUNCIL   67

apply the urgent procedure' to Bernheim's petition.[76] After consulting with three legal experts, Max Huber, Maurice Bourquin, and Manuel Pedroso,[77] Seán Lester of Ireland presented his draft report to the League Council on 30 May 1933.[78] It concluded that the German legislation was obviously inconsistent with international obligations under the treaty with Poland. It pointed out that Germany had acknowledged the pre-eminence of the treaty, stating that if it had been infringed this was a result of mistaken interpretation of the law by local officials. Lester wrote:

> I propose that the Council take note of these declarations by the German Government, which imply that persons who, because they belong to the minority, have lost their employment or found themselves unable to practise their trade or profession in consequence of the application of these laws, will be reinstated in their normal position without delay.

Because Germany objected to the admissibility of the petition, Lester prepared a revised draft of the report addressing the issue, again based upon consultation with the three expert jurists.[79] The report was approved by the League Council on 6 June 1933, with Germany and Italy abstaining in the vote.[80] The previous evening, the German representative had assured Lester that he would not vote against the resolution although he would formulate some reservations.[81] The Alliance Israelite Universelle wrote Seán Lester to thank him for 'son intervention généreuse en faveur des isréalites allemands de la Haute Silésie devant la Société des Nations'.[82]

Bernheim's victory at the League Council resulted in his prompt reinstatement. Many other Jews in Upper Silesia were able to invoke the precedent.[83] In September 1933, the German representative in Geneva wrote Lester to inform him that the German Government had ordered cities in Upper Silesia 'to abstain from any economic or other discrimination against the Jewish population'.[84] Jews also met with some success in blocking the anti-Semitic media.

---

[76] Minute from Drummond to 18 May 1933, LNA R3928/4/3634/4150.

[77] Avis du Comité de juristes, 30 May 1933, R3928/4/3643/4470.

[78] Report by the Representative of the Irish Free State, LNA R3928/4/3643/4207; Seventy-third session of the Council of the League of Nations, Minutes, Sixth meeting (Public), 30 May 1933, p. 1; 'Irish Delegate and the Jews', *Irish Times*, 31 May 1933.

[79] Opinion of the Committee of Jurists, 2 June 1933, R3928/4/3643/4470.

[80] Seventy-third session of the Council of the League of Nations, Minutes, Seventh meeting (Public), 6 June 1933, p. 5.

[81] Lester to Department of Foreign Affairs, 6 June 1933, LNA 47279/SLP/1933/Jun.6/VD2.

[82] Lévy to Lester, 2 June 1933, LNA 47273/SLP/1933/Jun.2/VD.

[83] See the report of the President of the Mixed Commission, Felix Calonder, to the League of Nations: 'Pétitions juives /art. 149/ de la Haute-Silésie allemande', 13 August 1934, LNA R3928/4/3643/3643.

[84] Von Keller to Lester, 30 September 1933, LNA R3929/4/3643/6857.

68 MANDATES, MINORITIES, AND THE LEAGUE OF NATIONS

A decision by the Mixed Commission resulted in a prohibition of *Der Stürmer* within German Upper Silesia. The 1922 treaty between Germany and Poland expired after 15 years, bringing an end to this period when the Jews of Upper Silesia enjoyed a degree of legal protection that was denied to Jews elsewhere in the country.[85] The League declined to act on a petition filed by Paul Chrzanowski because the applicable treaty was no longer in force.[86] Yet, as Brendan Karch has observed, '[t]he lives of many hundreds or even thousands of Jews were improved significantly by League-enforced civil rights'.[87] Although the respite for the Jews of German Upper Silesia was only temporary, it shows that international mechanisms directed at racial discrimination, and in particular those of the League of Nations, sometimes delivered concrete protection.

The Mandates System, Colonialism by Another Name

The mandates system was devised for the administration of colonies that were governed by Germany and the Ottoman Empire prior to the First World War. It also extended to three European territories, Saar, Danzig, and Memel. According to article 22 of the Covenant of the League of Nations, the mandates applied to 'colonies and territories . . . which are inhabited by peoples not yet able to stand by themselves under the strenuous conditions of the modern world', the implication being that the situation was only temporary in nature. The Covenant said that 'the best method of giving practical effect to this principle is that the tutelage of such peoples should be entrusted to advanced nations who by reason of their resources, their experience or their geographical position can best undertake this responsibility'. It all sounded very benevolent. In reality, though, this was little more than a division of the spoils of war. Germany's colonies in Africa were doled out to Belgium, Britain, France, and South Africa. In the Pacific region, the beneficiaries were Japan, Australia, and New Zealand. Parts of the former Ottoman Empire in the Middle East were apportioned to Britain and France. Mark Mazower has described the scheme as 'an ingenious way of squaring the

---

[85] Georges Kaeckenbeeck, *The International Experiment of Upper Silesia: A Study in the Working of the Upper Silesian Settlement 1922–1937*, Oxford: Oxford University Press, 1942, pp. 261–66; Philipp Graf, *Die Bernheim Petition 1933: Jüdische Politik in der Zwischenkriegzeit*, Götttingen: Vanderhoeck and Ruprecht, 2008; J.W. Brugel, 'The Bernheim petition: A Challenge to Nazi Germany in 1933' (1983) 17(3) *Patterns of Prejudice* 17; Jody M. Prescott, 'Litigating Genocide: A Consideration of the Criminal Court in Light of the German Jews' Legal Response to Nazi Persecution, 1933–1941' (1999) 51 *Maine Law Review* 297; Dorothy V. Jones, 'The League of Nations Experiment in International Protection' (1994) 8 *Ethics and International Affairs* 77.

[86] Petition from Paul Chrzanowski, 16 June 1937, LNA R3929/4/3643/29898.

[87] Brendan Karch, 'A Jewish "Nature Preserve": League of Nations Minority Protections in Nazi Upper Silesia, 1933–1937' (2013) 46 *Central European History* 124, at p. 126.

THE MANDATES SYSTEM, COLONIALISM BY ANOTHER NAME   69

circle between the British Dominions' demand to annex former German colonies and the need to pay lip service to Wilsonian idealism.[88]

The original draft of the Covenant did not explicitly envisage the mandate system. Article 17 of the draft addressed the subject of territories 'which formerly belonged to the German Empire or to Turkey, and which are inhabited by peoples unable at present to secure for themselves the benefit of a stable administration'. It said their well-being was 'a sacred trust for civilisation' and specified that Member States of the League of Nations had an 'obligation to render help and guidance in the development of the administration'.[89] At the sixth meeting of the Commission on the League of Nations, Jan Smuts of South Africa, representing the British Empire, made a detailed proposal whereby 'the tutelage of such peoples should be entrusted to advanced nations' acting as 'mandatories on behalf of the League'.[90] Smuts is credited with proposing the mandate system although his conception of it was confined to the remnants of the Russian, Austrian, and Ottoman Empires, and he did not envisage its application to Germany's colonies in Africa and elsewhere.[91] It identified different categories of territories to be subject to the mandates. During the debate on Smuts' proposal, the French delegate insisted upon distinguishing between 'backward countries like certain African colonies' and those territories with 'a very ancient and very complete civilisation, but which have been oppressed by foreign domination'.[92] The amendment specified that some of those peoples, 'especially those of Central Africa, are at such a stage that the mandatory must be responsible for the administration of the territory, subject to conditions which will guarantee freedom of conscience or religion, subject only to the maintenance of public order and morals, the prohibition of abuses, such as the slave trade . . . '.[93] The British text was approved[94] and eventually adopted as article 22 of the Covenant. Australia and New Zealand, concerned about Japanese migration, insisted that they would only agree if they could prohibit or restrict non-white settlers, as they had done in their own countries.

---

[88] Mark Mazower, *No Enchanted Palace: The End of Empire and the Ideological Origins of the United Nations*, Princeton: Princeton University Press, 2009, p. 45.

[89] First Meeting, 3 February 1919, USNA FW 181.1101/1, Annex 1, art. 17; David Hunter Miller, *The Drafting of the Covenant*, Vol. II, New York: GB Putnam's Sons, 1928, pp. 229–55, at pp. 236–37.

[90] Sixth Meeting, 7 February 1919, USNA FW 181.1101/6, Annex 1; David Hunter Miller, *The Drafting of the Covenant*, Vol. II, New York: GB Putnam's Sons, 1928, pp. 271–77, at pp. 274–75.

[91] 'The Smuts Plan', in David Hunter Miller, *The Drafting of the Covenant*, Vol. II, New York: GB Putnam's Sons, 1928, pp. 23–60, at pp. 29–33.

[92] Sixth Meeting, 7 February 1919, USNA FW 181.1101/6; David Hunter Miller, *The Drafting of the Covenant*, Vol. II, New York: GB Putnam's Sons, 1928, pp. 271–77, at p. 273.

[93] Sixth Meeting, 7 February 1919, USNA FW 181.1101/6, Annex 1, art. 17; David Hunter Miller, *The Drafting of the Covenant*, Vol. II, New York: GB Putnam's Sons, 1928, pp. 271–77, at pp. 274–75.

[94] Seventh Meeting, 10 February 1919, USNA FW 181.1101/7, Annex 3, art. 17; David Hunter Miller, *The Drafting of the Covenant*, Vol. II, New York: GB Putnam's Sons, 1928, pp. 277–87, at p. 282.

70 MANDATES, MINORITIES, AND THE LEAGUE OF NATIONS

There were three categories of mandate, labelled A, B, and C, meant to reflect the level of economic and political development and their relative proximity to full autonomy. According to Eyre Crowe of the British Foreign Office, the 'C' mandates, which were on the lowest rung, were 'specially designed to enable [the southern Dominions] to apply their protective tariffs and their legislation for excluding coloured immigrants'.[95] When Tokyo objected, Australia's Governor-General wrote to the Colonial Secretary in London that 'Japanese Government is endeavouring to amend conditions of mandate to introduce thin end of wedge of racial equality', an allusion to Japan's failed effort to obtain a non-discrimination clause in the Covenant of the League of Nations.[96] At the time of ratification of the Covenant, Japan formulated a declaration with respect to the 'C' mandates affirming that it did not 'acquiesce' in the 'submission of Japanese subjects to a discriminatory and disadvantageous treatment in the mandated territories'.

Alongside the euphemistic words of the Covenant, it is useful to consider the patronizing and often racist language of the bureaucrats in European governments. For example, in Britain, when consideration was being given as to whether the flag of the mandate should be that of the mandate holder or of the League of Nations, Colonial Office officials objected that this would have 'a confusing effect on the primitive natives of Tropical Africa', and that 'the result on the natives of the Tropical African Mandated territories will be to form the opinion that (in the expressive lingo of the West Coast) "British flag, no dam good Sar!"'.[97] In correspondence about the French hope that it could conscript indigenous troops within its African mandates, L.S. Amery, who was Undersecretary at the Colonial Office, wrote that the French 'want n . . . r conscripts'.[98] If nothing else, the use of such language in official records suggests not only that there were no people of colour working in the Colonial Office but also that it was unthinkable that there would ever be any.

Unlike colonies, the mandated territories were subject to a degree of international supervision, a situation that was quite unprecedented. This took the form of the League of Nations Permanent Mandates Commission, a body of nine, later ten, members who met once or twice each year to receive and examine annual reports from the mandatories. The members were defined as independent experts rather than representatives of their countries, although their

[95] Minute by Eyre Crowe, 8 September 1921, TNA FO 371/7051. See also Luther Harris Evans, 'Are "C" Mandates Veiled Annexations?' (1927) 7 *Southwestern Political and Social Science Quarterly* 381.
[96] Governor-General of Australia to Colonial Secretary (paraphrase copy), 15 November 1920, TNA FO 371/4787, cited in William Roger Louis, 'The United Kingdom and the Beginning of the Mandates System, 1919–1922' (1969) 23 *International Organisation* 73, at pp. 78–79.
[97] Minutes by H.J. Read and Charles Strachey, 5 March 1919, TNA FO 608/242/6.
[98] Minute by L.S. Amery, 2 February 1920, TNA CO 640/84, cited in William Roger Louis, 'The United Kingdom and the Beginning of the Mandates System, 1919–1922' (1969) 23 *International Organisation* 73, at p. 84.

appointment was in practice negotiated at the diplomatic level. Most of them had acquired their expertise through work as senior administrators in colonial systems. Nationals of Belgium, Britain, France, and Japan were permanent members of the Commission. At various times throughout its life, members were designated from other States, all of them European. Britain's representative on the Commission from 1922 to 1936, Frederick Lugard, had served in a range of functions in the colonial administration of Hong Kong and Nigeria. He sympathized with concerns about racial miscegenation, which he feared might lead to 'deterioration'.[99]

As a general proposition, the members of the Commission essentially shared the same racist outlook that was a *leitmotif* of colonialism, albeit with a somewhat benign and paternalistic veneer. Educational policy provides an example, where the Permanent Mandates Commission looked to the segregated school system in the United States as a model for Africa. This was driven by one of the members of the Commission, Anna Wicksell, a Swedish feminist and one of the very few women delegates to participate in the League Assembly. Wicksell urged the Commission to promote education that was 'more practical', with an emphasis on 'more effective agriculture, a more careful animal husbandry, better ways of exercising the local industries and arts and crafts', suggesting that schools for African Americans in the United States provided a model.[100] This resulted in a resolution of the Commission asking the Council of the League 'to call the attention of all the mandatory powers to this system of education as being in its opinion particularly suitable to the conditions of life of backward peoples'.[101]

In early 1927, Wicksell visited a number of educational institutions in the United States, including Morehouse College and the Tuskegee Institute, as well as primary and secondary schools that were available to African Americans. Her report was translated into French and annexed to the minutes of the Commission. The premise of her study, and its perceived relevance to the work of the Special Mandates Commission, seems to have been the view that segregated schools in the United States provided useful guidance for education of the indigenous population in African territories subject to League mandates.[102] She might well have

[99] Frederick D. Lugard, 'The Colour Problem', *The Edinburgh Review*, April 1921, p. 268.

[100] Note by Madame Bugge-Wicksell on Education Policy, CPM 151, Annexes to the Minutes of the 4th session of the Permanent Mandates Commission, 24 June to 8 July 1924, Annex 12, LNA R44/1/36857/16466/J4.

[101] Report on the Work of the Fourth Session of the Commission, 16 July 1924, A.15.1924.VI, LNA R45/1/37086/16466, p. 3. See J.M. Barrington, 'The Permanent Mandates Commission and Educational Policy in Trust Territories' (1976) 22 *International Review of Education* 88, at p. 90.

[102] Some coloured schools in the United States, by Mrs. A. Wicksell, LNA R81/1/61775; also Permanent Mandates Commission—Working Papers, LNA S1676/2/69/7. See Susan Pedersen, 'Metaphors of the Schoolroom: Women Working the Mandates System of the League of Nations' (2008) 66 *History Workshop Journal* 188; Edward H. Berman, 'American Influence on African Education: The Role of the Phelps-Stokes Fund's Education Commissions' (1970) 15 *Comparative Education Review* 132.

72 MANDATES, MINORITIES, AND THE LEAGUE OF NATIONS

asked about the rationale behind separate schools for Black and white students in the United States, which had nothing to do with pedagogy and learning, and everything to do with racial discrimination. Wicksell's successor on the Commission, Valentine Dannevig, maintained the same patronizing approach to education. In 1938, she produced a statement for the Commission that lamented the slow progress in education, which she attributed to a number of factors. 'To my mind, however', she wrote, 'native education for the masses does not principally mean teaching them the three Rs in the vernacular, but involves first of all instruction in better methods of domestic life, better care of their own and their children's health, more efficient agricultural methods, development of arts and crafts and native trade, and a better understanding of their own traditions and native customs, as well as of the changed conditions of life which will become more and more unavoidable as the strenuous conditions of modern times extend into hitherto primitive native areas, for instance, through the growing recruiting of native workers by Europeans.'[103]

In 1932, the fifteenth plenary congress of the International Federation of League of Nations Societies adopted a resolution expressing its concern about the influence of cinema on what it labelled 'peoples referred to in article 22 of the Covenant'. Correspondence on the subject abbreviated this to 'backward races'. The issue was 'the possible effects of the indiscriminate showing of western-made films' and the belief that 'the moral effects of such exhibitions are deleterious'. The Secretary of the League of Nations Union reported that he had discussed the matter with Lord Lugard, who agreed about 'the immense danger of the indiscriminate showing of Western-made films to primitive people'. The resolution said this was an issue for the Permanent Mandates Commission but it appears that the dossier was passed to the International Committee of Intellectual Cooperation, the ancestor of UNESCO.[104]

The States with mandates were required to provide annual reports to the Permanent Mandates Commission. These addressed issues like administrative organization, the persistence of slavery, working conditions, policing, traffic in arms, liquor and narcotic drugs, material, moral, and social welfare, public finance, and education. In its 1923 consideration of the report from South West Africa, the Commission said it was 'a matter of painful surprise' when it learned 'that the inhabitants of South West Africa were generally animated by hostile sentiments towards the natives'. It said it was 'all the more conscious of its responsibilities towards the latter' and that it would watch the efforts of the

---

[103] General Statement regarding Native education and social Services in African and South Sea Mandated Territories. Memorandum by Mademoiselle Dannevig. (14 June 1938), C.P.M. 2073, LNA R4138/6A/34351/34351.

[104] Effect of the cinema on backward races, LNA R2349/6A/33439/32641; Effect of the cinema on backward races, LNA R2349/6A/32641/32641.

mandatory power 'to ameliorate a moral situation which is essentially contrary to the spirit of article 22 of the Covenant'.[105] In reality, the expectations were low. For example, South Africa responded to concerns from the Commission about high mortality rates in the alluvial diamond mines of South West Africa. The issue had also arisen at the International Labour Office. The South African representative acknowledged the problem, noting that the annual death rate of indigenous mine workers had been 120 per 1,000, but that with significant efforts it had been reduced to 'only' 28 per 1,000 over an eight-month period.[106]

Brutal Suppression of Namibians by South Africa

The Permanent Mandates Commission had barely begun its work when it was confronted with reports of brutal conduct of the South African authorities within the former German colony of South West Africa. In a punitive mission intended to quell unrest among indigenous peoples within the mandate territory related to the imposition of onerous new taxes, disproportionate attacks using armed force, including aircraft, resulted in the killing of about 100 Nama. The South Africans lost two or three soldiers. Known as the Bondelzwarts rising, it took place in late May and early June 1922 and soon garnered attention throughout the world after a correspondent of *The Times* picked up the story.[107] Ruth First would later describe it as 'the Sharpeville of the 1920s', an allusion to the notorious attack of 21 March 1960 on peaceful demonstrators by South African police.[108]

The confrontation between international law and what would later emerge as the apartheid regime had begun. The matter came before the League of Nations Assembly in September 1922 when the South African representative, Edgar Walton, attempted to immunize his government against negative repercussions of the attack. He tabled copies of a preliminary report on the rising[109] and announced that a 'Special Commission of investigation and inquiry' had been appointed by the South African Government. Noting the attention to the events in the international media, he said he hoped 'judgment will at any rate be suspended until this Report is published and at the disposal of the Members of the

---

[105] Permanent Mandates Commission, South West Africa, C.P.M. 80, LNA S268/1/59/1.

[106] Note sur la mortalité dans les champs de diamants du Sud-Ouest africain, communiquée par le représentant du Bureau international du Travail, 7th session of the Permanent Mandates Commission (1925), LNA S267/1/58/2.

[107] 'Hottentot Rising. Rebels Bombed', *The Times*, 31 May 1922, p. 9. The best account of the Bondelzwarts rising and the League of Nations is in Susan Pedersen, *The Guardians, The League of Nations and the Crisis of Empire*, Oxford: Oxford University Press, 2015, pp. 112–41.

[108] Ruth First, *South West Africa*, Baltimore: Penguin, 1963, p. 101. On the Sharpeville massacre of 1960, see *infra*, p. 296.

[109] *Report of the Administrator of South West Africa on the Bondelswarts Uprising, 1922*, Cape Town: Cape Times Government Printers, 1922.

74 MANDATES, MINORITIES, AND THE LEAGUE OF NATIONS

Assembly'.[110] But this did not prevent a reaction within the Assembly, rather the contrary. A few days later, Dantès Bellegarde of Haiti took the floor to condemn the massacre. This, too, was the start of a pattern, with delegations from the Global South leading the battle at the international level against racial discrimination. Bellegarde described the events as of 'special gravity', noting that they had been provoked by imposition of new taxes. 'Taxation is the usual form in which civilisation makes its appearances to savages', he quipped, to the amusement of members of the Assembly. He said that although there was no act of rebellion and there were no attempts against life, 'an expedition was undertaken with all the materials of modern warfare—machine-guns, artillery, and aeroplanes. The natives, who were practically unarmed, were massacred, and as there can be no choice of victims in an air attack, it appears that women and children were killed in great numbers.' Bellegarde concluded: 'That women and children should have been massacred in the name of the League of Nations and under its protection is an abominable outrage which we cannot suffer', he said. The verbatim record notes that his remarks were followed by 'loud and prolonged applause'.[111]

A resolution on the subject proposed by Bellegarde was examined by the Sub-Committee on Mandates and Slavery of the Sixth Committee of the Assembly. Robert Cecil, who led the South African delegation, invited him to withdraw the proposal given South Africa's commitment to undertaking an inquiry. Bellegarde replied that his text was not meant as an 'indictment' of South Africa. It was intended to underscore the importance of providing assistance to the victims. Outmanoeuvred, Cecil conceded that Bellegarde's explanation was satisfactory. The Sub-Committee adopted the resolution, taking note of South Africa's announcement that there would be 'a full and impartial inquiry' into the events, expressing its 'profound satisfaction' that 'the mandatory power will make every effort to relieve the sufferings of the victims, particularly the women and children, and that it will ensure protection and restitution of the remaining livestock, and, in general, the restoration of the economic life in the Bondelzwarts district'.[112] The resolution was subsequently adopted by the Sixth Committee[113] and by the plenary Assembly.[114]

---

[110] Verbatim record of the 4th plenary meeting of the Third Assembly, 5 September 1922, LNA R1375/26/23218/23218, pp. 4–5.

[111] Verbatim record of the 7th plenary meeting of the Third Assembly, 8 September 1922, LNA R1375/26/23218/23218, p. 13.

[112] Minutes of the 3rd meeting of the Sub-Committee on Mandates and Slavery of the Sixth Committee, 14 September 1922, LNA R1375/26/23443/23165, pp. 1–3.

[113] Minutes of the 6th meeting of the Sixth Committee, 16 September 1922, LNA R1375/26/23293/23165, pp. 11–12.

[114] Verbatim record of the 12th plenary meeting of the Third Assembly, 20 September 1922, LNA R1375/26/23218/23218, p. 17; 'Mandats', Resolutions and Recommendations Adopted on the Reports of the Sixth Committee, *Official Journal*, Special Supplement No. 9, October 1922, p. 36.

The Anti-Slavery and Aborigines Protection Society led a campaign on the issue. It made a submission to the Permanent Mandates Commission even before a petition procedure had been agreed and implemented. The Anti-Slavery and Aborigines Protection Society had been formed in 1909 from the merger of two human rights organizations with origins in the early nineteenth century, the Anti-Slavery Society and the Aborigines' Protection Society.[115] The Society was in frequent communication with the Permanent Mandates Commission, principally through its President, John Harris, described as a 'benevolent paternalist of the old school' who believed in racial segregation in order to protect indigenous Africans from white settlers.[116] Although a progressive body in a general sense, it was willing to tolerate forms of segregation including legislation making a distinction between lands available for indigenous Africans and those reserved for white settlers. In a 1922 statement to the Commission, the Society recommended that there be 'native reservations' where only Africans could obtain title to land. The Society said it was 'averse from the adoption of any form of legalized industrial and social segregation of races inhabiting mandated areas' but that it also recognized 'the practical difficulties which occur where white and native farms adjoin each other'.[117]

Another non-governmental organization, the League of Nations Union, wrote to the Secretary-General saying that South Africa should be congratulated for deciding to conduct an inquiry even before being asked to do so by the League Assembly but also noting that the inquiry was not in fact public, contrary to the Assembly's wishes. The League of Nations Union said that 'no punitive expedition should in future be permitted to take place in Mandated Territory without the prior consent and directions of the Mandatory Government'.[118] But insisting on prior approval from the South African regime before an armed attack on the indigenous population was hardly the way to address the situation.

South Africa's report noted that the Bondelzwarts people 'considered themselves the equals of white men, and were unwilling to accept the position of a servile race'. According to the report, '[w]ith such people the only hope of a sound and peaceful administration lay in a well-considered Native policy, sympathetically but firmly administered with no resentment or vacillation, and

---

[115] Charles Swaisland, 'The Aborigines Protection Society, 1837–1909' (2000) 21 *Slavery and Abolition* 265; Brian Willan, 'The Anti-Slavery and Aborigines' Protection Society and the South African Natives' Land Act of 1913' (1979) 20 *Journal of African History* 83; James Heartfield, *The Aborigines' Protection Society, Humanitarian Imperialism in Australia, New Zealand, Fiji, Canada, South Africa, and the Congo, 1837–1909*, London: Hurst, 2011; James Heartfield, *The British and Foreign Anti-Slavery Society, 1838–1956, A History*, London: Hurst, 2016.

[116] Paul B. Rich, 'Philanthropic racism in Britain: The Liverpool university settlement, the anti-slavery society and the issue of 'half-caste' children, 1919–51' (1984) 3 *Immigrants & Minorities* 69, at p. 75

[117] Harris to Rappard, with annex, 15 March 1922, LNA S265/1/56/1.

[118] Murray to Drummond, 12 July 1923, LNA S265/1/59/1.

76 MANDATES, MINORITIES, AND THE LEAGUE OF NATIONS

under the local direction of a strong personality'.[119] Behind these euphemisms sat the rationale for what was in reality a brutal punishment attack, described by the South African report as a response to 'rebellion'. The report observed that 'the Bondelzwarts have never easily adjusted themselves to a position subordinate to the white man'. It suggested that dissatisfaction among the Bondelzwarts might be explained by their expectations of an improvement in their conditions when the British took over from the Germans, hopes that were not fulfilled. 'The change from the strictness of the German regime to the personal freedom of the British rule was probably too great and too sudden', it concluded.[120] The Anti-Slavery and Aborigines' Protection Society was harshly critical of South Africa's report. The Society questioned whether it was accurate to describe the situation as a 'rebellion' rather than simple resistance by indigenous peoples to repressive policies of the mandate authority.[121]

At its third session, in July 1923, the Permanent Mandates Commission prepared a list of detailed questions for the South African government,[122] to which South Africa responded with a lengthy reply.[123] South Africa's representatives explained that the report that had been submitted had not been endorsed by the government, and that they were without instructions on the matter.[124] The Commission then proceeded to question Major Herbst, who was one of the South African administrators in the mandate territory. It was a one-sided inquiry and Herbst's claims about various issues, including the number of civilian casualties and the necessity of using force altogether, went unchallenged. A few days later, after the Commission had begun drafting its report, Major Herbst returned before it with a plea to make further submissions. He said that he had not previously considered that it was possible for the Commission to rule against South Africa, and that he had taken the matter rather too lightly. Herbst spoke of the danger to the country's white population if it did not respond promptly and

---

[119] *Report of the Commission Appointed to Enquire into the Rebellion of the Bondelzwarts*, Cape Town: Cape Times Limited, 1923, p. 2. There is a copy in the United Kingdom archives: TNA CO 633/168.

[120] Ibid., p. 29.

[121] Harris to Rappard, with annex, 13 July 1923, LNA S265/1/56/1; Letter dated 23 July 1923, from the Anti-Slavery and Aborigines Protection Society to the Secretary-General of the League, Annexes to the Minutes of the 3rd session of the Permanent Mandates Commission, 20 July to 10 August 1923, Annex 8, LNA R43/1/16466/29735/J6.

[122] Questionnaire concerning the remedial measures, 28 July 1923, CPM 70 and 70(1), LNA S265/1/59/1. Also Bondelzwarts rebellion, General questions adopted by the Commission, CPM 69, LNA S265/1/59/1; Annexes to the Minutes of the Third Session of the Permanent Mandates Commission, 20 July to 10 August 1923, Annex 8a, LNA R43/1/16466/29735/J6.

[123] Memorandum on the Bondelzwarts Rising and its suppression, CPM 73, LNA S265/1/59/1.

[124] Minutes of the 18th meeting (Private) of the Special Mandates Commission, 31 July 1923, LNA R43/1/16466/29735/J6, pp. 113–14.

effectively to resistance from the indigenous Africans. 'We still have natives there who are only impressed by show of force', he said.[125]

The conclusions of the draft report prepared by two members of the Commission recommended adoption by South Africa of 'a policy and an administrative practice tending to diminish the force of these racial prejudices which, in these territories, have always been the fundamental cause of the hostility between whites and natives'. It said the Bondelzwarts affair was typical of colonial administration in Africa both in the past and 'for a long time to come'.[126] Mandates were not colonies, the draft report noted. It said there should be a 'gradation of interests' where 'the interests of the natives' take priority, while those of 'the whites' were to be considered in light of the fulfilment of their duties under the mandate. In the Bondelzwarts case, the draft report said that the South African administration 'appears to have been concerned chiefly to assert its own authority in defence of the interests of the white minority'.[127]

The militant tone of the draft report was not appreciated by some of the other members of the Commission. Lord Lugard of the United Kingdom resented the aspersions it cast upon other States with African colonies.[128] Portugal's Alfreido Freire D'Andrade, a former governor of Mozambique, was sympathetic to the South Africans and dissociated himself from the report of the majority. It became clear that Alberto Theodoli, of Italy, who was the Chairman of the Commission, had drafted the most controversial paragraphs. In the absence of more information in the form of diaries or letters, it is very difficult to assess the scale of the crisis in the Commission. Clearly, though, there was considerable discord. Theodoli, with a very progressive view of the philosophy behind mandates, was apparently in the minority, isolated and unable to rally his colleagues. He suddenly announced he was stepping down as chairman and, claiming exhaustion, said he was leaving Geneva.

Theodoli produced his own personal statement containing the radical statements in the draft that referred to 'racial prejudice' and the general practice of colonialists. 'First in importance come the interests of the natives, secondly the interests of the whites', he wrote, in an attempt to contrast the approach under mandates with that of traditional colonial regimes.[129] Theodoli had struck at the heart of the conceit of the Permanent Mandates Commission, namely, whether

---

[125] Minutes of the 27th meeting (Private) of the Special Mandates Commission, 7 August 1923, LNA R43/1/16466/29735/J6, pp. 183–87.

[126] Draft report by the Permanent Mandates Commission on the Bondelzwarts rebellion, LNA S268/1/59/1.

[127] Ibid.

[128] Minutes of the 31st meeting (Private) of the Special Mandates Commission, 8 August 1923, LNA R43/1/16466/29735/J6, p. 203.

[129] Minutes of the 32nd meeting (Private) of the Special Mandates Commission, 9 August 1923, LNA R43/1/16466/29735/J6, pp. 205–06.

78 MANDATES, MINORITIES, AND THE LEAGUE OF NATIONS

to perpetuate colonialist perspectives with some humanitarian overtones or to condemn them by implication and set out a vision premised on the best interests of the indigenous population. Therein lay the rub. If the latter perspective were adopted, it would make the mandates system a genuine rival to colonialism rather than its adjunct. As Theodoli had requested, his declaration was appended to the report adopted by the Commission under the title 'Statement made by the Chairman, Marquis Alberto Theodoli'.

The Commission's report highlighted the significance of the colour line: 'The causes which led to the rising appear to the majority of the Commission to be due primarily to the unfortunate feelings of distrust which, it has been informed, characterised the attitude towards each other of the white and black races. In South-West Africa even the educated classes, the Commission was told, regarded the natives as existing chiefly for the purpose of labour for whites.' It expressed the frustration of the Commission in obtaining information about the events, and noted the absence of a formal report from the mandatory power itself. 'By failing to pronounce on this matter, the mandatory Power rendered it impossible for the Mandates Commission to decide which of the contradictory versions which had been supplied was the one which should be regarded as exactly describing the course of events and the measures of the administration', it said.[130]

After presentation of the Commission's report, the League Council adopted a resolution noting 'with satisfaction the renewed assurances given by the representative of the Mandatory Power of its desire to take all practical steps to restore the prosperity of the Bondelzwarts people and to re-start them in the peaceful occupation of their lands'.[131] The League Assembly had not been so sanguine. Its resolution on the Commission report, proposed by Fridtjof Nansen who was speaking for a unanimous Sixth Committee, expressed 'regret' that the Permanent Mandates Commission 'has not been able to report that satisfactory conditions have as yet been re-established in the Bondelzwarts district'.[132]

Although neither the Covenant itself nor the mandates negotiated by the League provided explicitly for petitions, the Council established a procedure for this in 1923, at the same session in which it examined the Bondelzwarts issue. The procedure never provided a very useful mechanism to the inhabitants of the mandates to litigate grievances related to racial discrimination. As Susan

---

[130] Permanent Mandates Commission: The Bondelzwarts Rebellion, Report of the Commission submitted to the Council of the League of Nations on 31 August 1923, Annex 548(b), *Official Journal* November 1923, pp. 1396–402. Also Annexes to the Minutes of the Third Session of the Permanent Mandates Commission, 20 July to 10 August 1923, Annex 8(b).

[131] Verbatim record of the 5th meeting (public) of the Council of the League of Nations, 13 December 1924, *Official Journal* February 1923, p. 341.

[132] Verbatim record of the 14th plenary meeting of the Assembly of the League of Nations, 26 September 1923, *Official Journal* Special Supplement 13 (1923), pp. 92–93.

Pedersen has explained, '[i]n its handling of petitions, the Mandates Commission articulated and acted out the authoritarian if paternalistic principles on which the system was based.[133] This 'reflected and instantiated the racial hierarchies and authoritarian structures that lay at the system's heart.[134] The vast majority of petitions originated in the 'A' mandates of the Middle East, principally Syria and Palestine, while little more than a handful came from Tanganyika, Ruanda-Urundi, French Cameroon, French Togo, and South West Africa. For example, in her 1927 report on petitions respecting French Togo, Anna Wicksell included a sub-heading entitled 'atrocities' where she described the alleged beating to death of an African chauffeur by French policemen 'because of some futile offence'. The French government offered a simple denial, noting that '[l]es indigènes ne cessent de reconnaître, au contraire, la bienveillance des pouvoirs publics qu'ils jugent même parfois exagérés'.[135] Wicksell said she accepted the explanations as 'in the main satisfactory' although she would have preferred 'further information about the alleged death'.[136]

In many cases petitions originated in the settler communities, generally of European origin, where there were individuals who felt the privileged status they had enjoyed under the Germans was now threatened. Several of the petitions concerning South West Africa came from a single German settler, E.J.H. Lange, who claimed he had not received adequate compensation following the confiscation of his farm in 1917.[137] Individuals of European descent also attempted to litigate a range of issues relating to their dealings with the local administration.[138] Yet another was filed by an aggrieved German mining company whose lands had been expropriated under South African legislation adopted in 1920, prior to the mandate.[139] A petition concerning determination of the border between South

---

[133] Susan Pedersen, 'Samoa on the World Stage: Petitions and Peoples before the Mandates Commission of the League of Nations' (2012) 40 *Journal of Imperial and Commonwealth History* 231, at p. 250.

[134] Ibid., p. 233.

[135] Service français de la Société des Nations, 1 April 1927, LNA R37/1/32095/12226.

[136] Report by Mrs. A. Wicksell, 11 June 1927, CPM 573, LNA R37/1/32095/12226, pp. 4–5.

[137] For example, Petition from Mr. E.J.E. Lange relating to the Confiscation of his Property in South West Africa, Minutes of the 17th meeting of the 4th session Permanent Mandates Commission, 3 July 1924, LNA R44/1/36857/16466/J4; Petition filed by Mr E.J.E. Lange concerning the alleged confiscation of his property in South West Africa, 25 May 1925, CPM 96(b), LNA S268/1/59/2; Letter from South Africa transmitting petitions, 7 December 1932, LNA R2289/A/443/443.

[138] Petition from Mr. John Robertson relating to the so-called Wilmer Concessions in South West Africa, Minutes of the 17th meeting of the 4th session Permanent Mandates Commission, 3 July 1924 and Minutes of the 19th meeting of the 4th session Permanent Mandates Commission, 4 July 1924, LNA R44/1/36857/16466/J4; Petition by Mr Frank Gramowsky, Report by Mrs A. Wickel, 30 May 1925, CPM 233, LNA S268/1/59/2.

[139] Petition of the Kaoko Land und Minen Gesellschaft, 4 February 1926, LNA R12/1/49370/1347; Kaoko-Land Petition, Note by Lord Lugard, 18 November 1929, LNA R2290/6A/6070/443.

80 MANDATES, MINORITIES, AND THE LEAGUE OF NATIONS

West Africa and Angola was considered by the Commission because of the impact on lands of indigenous peoples.[140]

The Rehoboth minority in South West Africa submitted a number of petitions although they did not really speak to issues relating to racial discrimination. They were essentially concerned with issues of autonomy and independence, and of title to territory. One of them was directed at the determination of the boundaries of their lands by the Germans. The Commission considered that the matter had been dealt with by Germany and that this was confirmed in a subsequent agreement in 1923.[141] A second petition amounted to a claim for independence.[142] The Rehoboths persisted for many years in their petitions to the League.[143] In his report to the Commission, Lugard described them as 'extremely vague protests that the action of the Administration and the Proclamations enacted regarding the Rehoboths are unjust and ultra vires and that they are innocent of any opposition to the law'.[144] The Commission held that the petitions were not well-founded, and recommended to the Rehoboths that they 'abandon their internal dissensions and, as a united community, to work in harmony with the Administration'.[145]

The Tanganyika Indian Association petitioned the Commission about various forms of discriminatory treatment in matters of education, medical care, and mobility rights. At the same time, the Indian population in Tanganyika was opposed to British plans for a federation of territories in East Africa, as this would weaken the protection against discrimination that they felt was provided by the mandate.[146] The British reply spoke to allegations of racial discrimination, insisting they were 'unfounded'. With respect to grievances about medical care, the British explained that they had inherited two hospitals from the Germans, one for Europeans and the other for Africans. They said that 'Goans

---

[140] Petition dated 24 May 1926 from Mr Will Stuart, LNA R12/1/54271/1347; Frontier between South-West Africa and Angola: Petition of Mr. Stuart, Minutes of the 2nd meeting of the 10th session of the Permanent Mandates Commission, 4 November 1926, LNA R53/1/55200/16466/J4.

[141] Petition of Mr. P. Drew, 9 August 1928, Report by Lord Lugard, 1 June 1929, LNA R2289/6A/1194/443. Also LNA R2289/6A/2180/443. See Tilman Dedering, 'Petitioning Geneva: Transnational Aspects of Protest and Resistance in South West Africa/Namibia after the First World War' (2009) 35 *Journal of Southern African Studies* 785, at pp. 794–800; Andries M. Fokkens, 'The Suppression of Internal Unrest in South West Africa (Namibia) 1921–1933' (2012) 40 *Scientia Militaria* 109.

[142] Examination of the Petition from the Rehoboth Community of South-West Africa, Minutes of the 10th meeting of the 6th session of the Permanent Mandates Commission, 1 July 1925, LNA R47/1/44915/16466/J4.

[143] Petition from burghers of the Rehoboth Community, 5 Mary 1925, CPM 227, LNA S268/1/59/2; Petition from members the Rehoboth Community, Report by Sir Frederick Lugard, 30 May 1925, CPM 234, LNA S268/1/59/2; Petition of 26 November 1926 of the Rehoboth Community, CPM 559(I), LNA R55/1/60241/16466.

[144] New petitions from certain members of the Rehoboth community, Reports by Lord Lugard, 15 May 1930, CPM 1012, LNA R2300/6A/20536/486.

[145] Report, 18th session of the Commission, 18 June–1 July 1930, p. 8, LNA R2300/6A/20726/486.

[146] Petition of the Indian Association, Tanganyika, 20 October 1930, CPM 1164, LNA R2313/6A/551/28334.

and Indian patients who have acquired a western mode of life' were admitted to the European hospital on a discretionary basis. However, the British reported to the Permanent Mandates Commission, '[i]t is not practicable, however, to open the Goan wards in the European hospital to Asiatics in general, and these Asiatic patients who still cleave to oriental habits are more suitably accommodated at the African hospital at Dar-es-Salaam' although, admittedly, 'the amenities at the native hospital at Dar-es-Salaam leave much to be desired by patients of all races'. They said that '[i]n a country like Tanganyika some measure of separation of races is not always avoidable in certain spheres'.[147] The Permanent Mandates Commission concluded that 'the local Government of Tanganyika has always sedulously endeavoured to avoid any unfair differentiation in the treatment of the Indian or of any other community in the territory and to extend even-handed justice to all, irrespective of race, class and creed'.[148]

Beginning in 1929, chiefs and other leaders of the indigenous population in French Cameroons presented a series of petitions to the League. The initial submission was in German. It addressed political and constitutional issues in a general sense, noting that the entire colonial policy, be it sovereign or mandated, and the proper education of the natives to independence are two opposites. The general colonial policy does not tolerate the national idea of independence on the part of the *niederen Rassen* ('lower races'), it said.[149] The French government replied that with respect to 'droits et libertés des indigènes', '[a]ucun fait précis n'est signalé par les pétitionnaires'. France boasted about its investment in education and claimed that there was equal access to justice.[150] The rapporteur of the Permanent Mandates Commission noted that many of the matters that were raised went beyond its authority, and that those complaints concerned with issues such as unequal justice, mixed marriages, and education of the indigenous population were not supported by concrete facts.[151] Subsequently, a body named Citoyens nègres camerounais submitted petitions that were more focused on the oppression of the indigenous peoples. One of them spoke of 'le système de civilisation' imposed under the mandate, protesting that it amounted to 'pillage, la spoliation des terres les plus fertiles des habitants, et le massacre des noirs sur les chantiers d'Ottelé, et une récente dépêche encore, datée du 3 août 1931,

---

[147] Observations of His Majesty's Government, CPM 1164, LNA R2313/6A/551/28334.

[148] Report, 18th session of the Commission (18 June–1 July 1930), p. 9, LNA R2300/6A/20726/486.

[149] Cameroun sous mandate français, Petition d'un groupe de personnes de Douala, 19 December 1929, CPM 1045, LNA R2339/6A/17643/3989.

[150] Cameroun sous mandate français, observations du gouvernement français, 17 October 1930, CPM 1082, LNA R2339/6A/17643/3989.

[151] Cameroun sous mandate français, Report by M. Palacios, 14 November 1930, CPM 1120, LNA R2339/6A/17643/3989.

82 MANDATES, MINORITIES, AND THE LEAGUE OF NATIONS

elle annonce une fusilade des femmes, inoffensives mères de famille'.[152] France insisted that the petitions, which called for the mandate to be rescinded, were manifestly inadmissible.[153] The objection was accepted by the Commission.[154]

Slavery in Africa

The prohibition of slavery was an important dimension of the human rights activity of the League of Nations. When the League began in 1920, much of the abhorrent practice of previous centuries had been eliminated, in part as a consequence of colonialism. European powers controlled the coast of Africa. Slavery was not necessarily unlawful, but applicable legislation made contracts for the buying and selling of human beings unenforceable by the courts.[155] The Treaty of St. Germain-en-Laye, adopted at the Paris Peace Conference on 10 September 1919, addressed the issue of slavery.[156] Article 11(1) was based on Article 6 of the 1885 Berlin Act. It provided that 'the signatory Powers exercising sovereign rights or authority in African territories will continue to watch over the preservation of the native population and to supervise the improvement of the conditions of their moral and material well-being. They will, in particular, endeavour to secure the complete suppression of slavery in all its forms and the slave-trade by land and sea'.[157] Provisions against slavery were contained in the B mandates. However, the C mandates provided only for the abolition of the slave trade.[158]

Slavery and the slave trade are closely related to racial discrimination for historic reasons. Racial discrimination developed as a justification or rationale for the trade in slaves, principally from Africa although other parts of the Global South were not untouched. The Berlin Act concerned the 'slave trade', and although it did not specify the colour or race of the slave, its scope was confined to West Africa.[159] The 1890 General Act of the Brussels Conference addressed the

[152] Petition from Citoyens nègres camerounais, 18 May 1931 and 14 August 1931, LNA R2339/6A/17643/3989.
[153] De Laboulaye to Drummond, 26 May 1930 and De Laboulaye to Drummond, 4 June 1931, LNA R2339/6A/17643/3989; De Laboulaye to Drummond, 13 May 1933, LNA R4124/6A/2836/2836.
[154] Report, 21st session of the Permanent Mandates Commission, 26 October–13 November 1931, p. 8, LNA R2302/6A/32645/486.
[155] Suzanne Miers, 'Slavery and the slave trade as international issues, 1890–1939' (1998) 19 *Slavery and Abolition* 16, at p. 22.
[156] Convention of Saint-Germain-En-Laye Revising the General Act of Berlin, 26 February 1885, and the General Act and Declaration of Brussels, 2 July 1890 (relating to Congo River Basin) (1922) 8 LNTS 26, art. 11.
[157] Hugo Fischer, 'The Suppression of Slavery in International Law (II)' (1950) 3 *International Law Quarterly* 508, at p. 504.
[158] Ibid., p. 505.
[159] General Act of the Berlin Conference on West Africa, 26 February 1885, art. 6.

'the slave-trade in the interior of Africa'.[160] Provisions in the Act imposed special rules relating to Black passengers and crew on seagoing vessels.[161] To facilitate that instrument, the Institut de droit international prepared a regulation for enforcement with respect to 'navires négriers', a term used to refer to slave ships.[162] These texts were consolidated and revised in the Treaty of St-Germain-en-Laye, adopted in September 1919 at the Paris Peace Conference. The term used in the official French version was 'la traite des noirs' although the English text, unofficially translated by the British Foreign Office and published in the League of Nations Treaty Series, referred to 'the slave trade'.[163]

Alongside the 'black slave trade' was another issue of international law known as the 'white slave trade' (in French treaty language, 'la traite des blanches'). The principal legal instruments were the 1904 International Agreement for the Suppression of the White Slave Traffic and the 1910 International Convention for the Suppression of the White Slave Traffic. The 'white slave trade' was defined by its purpose ('in order to gratify the passions of another person'), and by the gender ('a woman or girl under age') rather than the colour or race of its victims.[164] Jean Allain has observed that 'much like the phrase "general principles of law recognized by civilised nations", "White Slave Traffic" is a window onto a very different world of the early twentieth century, one dominated by a Euro-centrism of overt racism, at the height of its colonial conquest'.[165] Indeed, like the phrase 'civilised nations', traces of the 'white slave traffic' remain in international law to the present day. Chapter VII of the United Nations Treaty Collection, entitled 'Traffic in Persons', lists the 'International Convention for the Suppression of the White Slave Traffic, signed at Paris on 4 May 1910, amended by the Protocol signed at Lake Success, New York, 4 May 1949'.[166]

Discomfort with the term 'white slave traffic' was evident at the 1921 League of Nations Conference 'on traffic in women and children'. The Final Act referred to the 1904 and 1910 texts without even mentioning 'white slave traffic',

---

[160] General Act of the Brussels Conference relating to the African Slave Trade between Austria-Hungary, Belgium, Congo, Denmark, France, Germany, Great Britain, Italy, the Netherlands, Persia, Portugal, Russia, Spain, Sweden-Norway, Turkey, the United States, and Zanzibar, signed 2 July 1890, I Bevans 134, XVI de Martens 2nd ser. 3, art. I.

[161] Ibid., arts. XXXV, XXXVI, XXXVIII, XLI.

[162] Projet de règlement sur la police des navires négriers, Paris, 1894, *Annuaire de l'Institut de droit international*, pp. 47–49, 335–46.

[163] Convention of Saint-Germain-En-Laye Revising the General Act of Berlin, February 26,1885, and the General Act and Declaration of Brussels, 2 July 1890 (relating to Congo River Basin) (1922) 8 LNTS 27, art. 11.

[164] International Convention for the Suppression of the White Slave Traffic, 1910, 211 Consol. T.S. 45, 1912 GR. Brit. T.S. No. 20, art. 1.

[165] Jean Allain, 'White Slave Traffic in International Law' (2017) 1 *Journal of Trafficking and Human Exploitation* 1, at p. 1.

[166] International Convention for the Suppression of the White Slave Traffic, signed at Paris on 4 May 1910, and as amended by the Protocol signed at Lake Success, New York, 4 May 1949 (1951) 98 UNTS 101.

84 MANDATES, MINORITIES, AND THE LEAGUE OF NATIONS

as if the expression was anathema. The President of the 1921 Conference, Michel Levie, drew attention to the change in terminology noting that it was more precise and more adequate, although a modification 'de pure forme'.[167] Based on a proposal from the United Kingdom's representative,[168] Article XIII of the Final Act stated: 'The Conference recommends that the words "White Slave Traffic" should be replaced in the texts of international instruments by the words "Traffic in Women and Children"'. Moreover, the Final Act specified its intention 'to provide for the protection of women and children, whatever their race or colour'.[169] Nevertheless, the file containing the Final Act of the Conference in the League of Nations archives is entitled 'International Conference on White Slave Traffic'. In the aftermath of the Conference, Edouard Junod of the Bureau international pour la défense des indigènes wrote to the League to signal the importance of studying the traffic in women and girls of colour, indicating that the subject had been 'si peu étudié'.[170]

The first initiatives concerning slavery in the League of Nations were closely related to the situation in Ethiopia, an independent African country ruled by Africans, albeit one hemmed in by British, French, and Italian colonies. An influential memorandum on Ethiopia by Frederick Lugard, who was Britain's representative on the Permanent Mandates Commission, described Ethiopia as 'immensely rich' and 'capable of great wealth and prosperity'. Nevertheless, he wrote, 'the Abyssinians are an ignorant, turbulent and very conceited people, suspicious of and hostile to Europeans'. The Ethiopian government had outlawed slavery but appeared unable to implement fully the prohibition. There were reports of traffic in slaves on the Red Sea, from Ethiopia to markets in Saudi Arabia. European legations in Ethiopia were alleged to have slaves. Lugard proposed a form of intervention under the auspices of the League of Nations that, he said 'would be little different in principle from the B class of mandates'. He thought that the League might be justified, 'acting on the general principles of the Covenant, in notifying a small State like Abyssinia their disapproval of conduct in violation of the principles of humanity, and their intention to put a stop to it'.[171] This was, in effect, the 'responsibility to protect' *avant la*

---

[167] Opening Speech by the President, LNA R654/12/13722/13722, p. b.

[168] International Conference on Traffic in Women and Children, Provisional verbatim report, 5th plenary meeting, 4 July 1921, LNA R656/12/14010/14010, p. 99. Also International Conference on Traffic in Women and Children, Provisional verbatim report, 4th plenary meeting, 2 July 1921, LNA R656/12/14010/14010, p. 55.

[169] International Conference on Traffic in Women and Children, 30 June 1921, Final Act, LNA R655/12/13895/13895, art. II.

[170] Junod to Crowdy, 7 April 1922, LNA R658/12/20050/20050. On 'white slavery' in 'black Africa', see Saheed Aderinto, '"The Problem of Nigeria is Slavery, not White Slave Traffic": Globalization and the Politicization of prostitution in Southern Nigeria, 1921–1955' (2012) 46 *Canadian Journal of African Studies / La Revue canadienne des études africaines* 1.

[171] Slavery in Abyssinia, LNA R61/1/24628/23252. The memorandum was submitted to Eric Drummond under cover of a letter from Lugard dated 10 November 1922.

lettre.[172] Lugard's initiative was reinforced by the work of the Bureau international pour la défense des indigènes. Its Secretary-General, Édouard Junod, lobbied with the director of the Mandates Section for League initiatives concerning slavery to be focussed on only one or two regions, proposing Ethiopia as a candidate.[173]

Understandably suspicious of British initiatives, Ethiopia responded by applying for membership in the League.[174] As a condition for its admission, Ethiopia was required to adhere to the anti-slavery obligations in the Treaty of St-Germain-en-Laye of 1919 and the Brussels Declaration of 1890, and to provide reports on its implementation upon request from the League.[175] It was the only Member State subjected to such a requirement.

Following Ethiopia's admission, League activity was directed towards standard-setting generally, although it was widely understood that the independent African State of Ethiopia remained the main target. In 1924 the League established the Temporary Slavery Commission. It had eight members, six of whom were either serving or former colonial officials of Britain, France, Portugal, Italy, Belgium, and the Netherlands.[176] A representative of the International Labour Organisation sat as the seventh member. The eighth member was Dantès Bellegarde, of Haiti. Later, a Committee of Experts on Slavery took its place. It was followed by an Advisory Committee of Experts on Slavery. This activity generated the Slavery Convention, adopted by the League in 1926.[177] It also provided momentum that resulted in the Forced Labour Convention, adopted by the International Labour Organisation in 1930.[178]

Liberia, one of the founding members of the League of Nations, soon became the other target of activities concerning slavery and the slave trade. In 1925, the International Labour Organisation's representative on the Temporary Slavery Commission, Harold A. Grimshaw, presented a report on the general situation. In Africa, he said, everywhere that European powers were in charge of territory the slave trade had virtually disappeared. The situation was not the same, however, in the two states that were not subject to 'European control', namely Ethiopia and Liberia. He attributed the practice to indigenous tribes in the interior who were

---

[172] World Summit Outcome, 16 September 2005, A/RES/60/1, OP 139.

[173] Junod to Rappard, 26 February 1923, LNA R62/1/26925/23252.

[174] Antoinette Iadarola, 'Ethiopia's Admission into the League of Nations: An Assessment of Motives' (1975) 8 *International Journal of African Historical Studies* 601, at p. 614; Jean Allain, 'Slavery and the League of Nations: Ethiopia as a Civilised Nation' (2006) 8 *Journal of the History of International Law* 213, at pp. 220–21.

[175] Abyssinia's application for membership in the League, Report of the second sub-committee, 20 September 1923, *Official Journal*, 1923, Annex 5.

[176] Suzanne Miers, 'Slavery and the Slave Trade as International Issues, 1890–1939' (1998) 19 *Slavery and Abolition* 16, at pp. 25–26.

[177] Slavery Convention (1927) 60 LNTS 253.

[178] Forced Labour Convention, 1929 (No. 30).

86 MANDATES, MINORITIES, AND THE LEAGUE OF NATIONS

not fully subject to the central government although adding that even in territory that was under control 'the trade was not unknown'.[179] Adom Getachew has pointed to the hypocrisy of the obsession of the League of Nations with slavery within Africa's independent States, noting that other related forms of oppression, such as forced labour, were common practice in colonies, yet they did not attract the same attention. This helps to explain why forced labour was excluded from the 1926 Slavery Convention adopted by the League. 'That the charge of slavery became the idiom through which black self-government would be undermined should strike us as deeply perverse not only because of Europe's central role in the transatlantic slave trade and slavery in the Americas but also because of the labour practices that characterised colonial Africa in the twentieth century', Getachew has observed.[180] These words echo those of W.E.B. Du Bois, writing in the early 1930s.[181] 'Liberia is not faultless', wrote Du Bois in *Foreign Affairs*. 'But her chief crime is to be black and poor in a rich, white world; and in precisely that portion of the world where colour is ruthlessly exploited as a foundation for American and European wealth.'[182]

An initiative from the United States in 1929 resulted in an International Commission of Inquiry into slavery in Liberia chaired by Cuthbert Christy, an English scientist and 'explorer'. It found that there was extensive use of unpaid labour in the country as well as forms of forced labour conducted with official tolerance.[183] In a communication to the League of Nations, Liberia said it accepted the recommendations and conclusions of the Commission.[184] The League of Nations subsequently set up its own inquiry. The League did not respect Liberia's request that its members not be drawn from countries with colonies. The report devoted most of its attention to economic matters and the country's contract with the Firestone rubber company. On the slavery issue, it said that 'the experts on their arrival in Monrovia found that the Liberian government had already passed laws on slavery and forced labour, and actually the experts found that the exportation of forced labour had been suppressed'.[185]

* * *

[179] Mémoire de M. H.A. Grimshaw, 15 April 1925, LNA R66/1/44564/23252.

[180] Adom Getachew, *Worldmaking after Empire, The Rise and Fall of Self-Determination*, Princeton: Princeton University Press, 2019, p. 59. This comes from Pedersen.

[181] Frank Chalk, 'Du Bois and Garvey Confront Liberia: Two Incidents of the Coolidge Years' (1967) 1 *Canadian Journal of African Studies/Revue Canadienne des Études Africaines* 135.

[182] W.E.B. Du Bois, 'Liberia, the League and the United States' (1933) 11 *Foreign Affairs* 682, at p. 695.

[183] Report of the International Commission of Enquiry into the Existence of Slavery and Forced Labour in the republic of Liberia, Monrovia, Liberia, August 1930, Washington: United States Government Printing Office, 1931. A copy is filed in LNA R2356/6B/24718/14352/Jacket1. See also 'The 1930 Enquiry Commission to Liberia' (1931) 30 *Journal of the Royal African Society* 277.

[184] Communication from the Liberian government, 9 January 1931, LNA R2356/6B/24718/14352/Jacket1.

[185] League of Nations *Official Journal*, March 1932, Part II, p. 525.

Two systems of the League of Nations, concerning minorities and mandates, exemplified the contradictions that were inherent in a world divided by race. In effect, there was a colour line within the League itself. The minorities system was essentially concerned with white Europeans. Their entitlement to equal treatment regardless of religion, language, or ethnicity (although the texts spoke of 'race' rather than 'ethnicity'), was affirmed as a guiding principle. There was an understanding that the maintenance of peace required ensuring that there was no discrimination against minorities. Mechanisms were put in place to enforce the rights of members of minority groups. Sometimes, they were even effective to a degree, as in the case of the Bernheim litigation in Upper Silesia. Yet the system was incomplete because it did not apply to the Great Powers and their allies, where inequality was as rampant as it was in the 'new States' upon whom the minority rights instruments were imposed.

The mandates system, on the other hand, was essentially concerned with people of colour. There was even a form of discrimination within the mandates system, with the 'A' mandates being mainly for Arab peoples of the Middle East while the 'B' and 'C' mandates were reserved for Africa and Asia. There was nothing equivalent to the recognition of equality based upon race, religion, and language when the mandates were concerned. Rather, they were essentially premised on the racial inequality of colonialism, admittedly a form under a modest degree of international supervision. In the area of education, for example, the minorities system was premised on ensuring full rights to equal education whereas the mandates system reinforced and entrenched an approach that was profoundly unequal, with modern schools of high quality for Europeans and inadequate, impoverished institutions for the indigenous peoples. The League looked to segregated schools in the United States as a model for education of indigenous Africans. It may be that in some territories the mandatory powers behaved with greater respect for the indigenous peoples than they did in their colonies. Even if this might have been the case for Britain and France, it cannot be said of Belgium, which ruled Rwanda and Burundi in much the same brutal fashion as it had the Congo. As for South Africa, it had no colonies with which to make a comparison. But the peoples of Namibia certainly fared no better than did non-whites in South Africa.

African Americans seemed to grasp the paradox within the League of Nations. They pointed to the hypocrisy of the United States and its European allies imposing racial equality on new States in Central and Eastern Europe while denying the same to minorities within their own borders. They also saw themselves as spokespersons for people of the South, especially Africans. Some of them took the view that the German colonies in Africa should be returned to Africans, including those of the diaspora.

88 MANDATES, MINORITIES, AND THE LEAGUE OF NATIONS

One of the League's signal failures as its role became increasingly irrelevant was its inadequate reaction to the Italian invasion of Ethiopia that began in 1935. Mussolini's regime indulged in one of the final gasps of colonial conquest as it sought to expand its small African empire. '[T]he black world knows this is the last great effort of white Europe to secure the subjection of black men', wrote W.E.B. Du Bois.[186] The tactics were as brutal as any that had been employed by the other European colonial regimes, and included the use of poison gas and dum-dum bullets. Wholesale massacres of civilians took place.[187] Around the world people of colour showed great solidarity with the Ethiopians, campaigning for the League to intervene against Italian aggression. It was 'the story of the year for the black press'.[188] Petitions to the League were sent by the Negro Welfare and Cultural Association of Trinidad and Tobago, the Ligue haïtienne pour la défense du people éthiopien, the British Guiana Labour Union, the 'Negros of Panama', the Columbus City Federation of Colored Women's Clubs, the Continuation Committee for All Harlem Independent Political Action, the Colored Welfare Association, the Conférence Internationale des Noires et des Arabes, the League of Coloured Peoples, the National Negro Congress, Jeunesses antiracistes, amongst many others.[189]

When the United Nations War Crimes Commission was convened in London during the Second World War, Ethiopia questioned why it had not been invited to participate. Bureaucrats in the British Foreign Office contrived various explanations, none of them very convincing, in answers to parliamentary questions on the subject.[190] After the Second World War, Ethiopia campaigned for the United Nations War Crimes Commission to investigate the Italian atrocities. In an effort to persuade the Commission to take up the Ethiopian cases, its representative recalled that 'Ethiopia did not get much help in those days and years when she was suffering from the oppression of one of the

---

[186] W.E.B. Du Bois, 'Inter-Racial Implications of the Ethiopian Crisis: A Negro View' (1935) 19 Foreign Affairs 82, at p. 88.

[187] Richard Pankhurst, 'Italian Fascist War Crimes in Ethiopia: A History of Their Discussion, from the League of Nations to the United Nations (1936–1949)' (1999) 6 n.s. Northeast African Studies 83.

[188] John Munro, 'Ethiopia Stretches Forth Across the Atlantic: African American Anticolonialism during the Interwar Period' (2008) 13(2) Left History 37, at p. 47.

[189] See, for example, LNA R3649/1/15227/15227/J21, LNA R3648/1/15227/15227/J16, LNA R3649/1/15227/15227/J21/20(1). Also William Randolph Scott, The Sons of Sheba's Race: African-Americans and the Italo-Ethiopian War, 1935–1941, Bloomington: Indiana University Press, 1993; William Randolph Scott, 'Black nationalism and the Italo-Ethiopian conflict, 1934–1936' (1978) 63 Journal of Negro History 118; Robert G. Weisbord, 'British West Indian Reaction to the Italian-Ethiopian War: An Episode in Pan-Africanism' (1970) 10 Caribbean Studies 34; Cedric Robinson, 'The African Diaspora and the Italo-Ethiopian crisis' (1985) 27 Race and Class 51; Arlena Buelli, 'The Hands Off Ethiopia Campaign, Racial Solidarities and Intercolonial antifascism in South Asia (1935–36)' [2022] Journal of Global History 1.

[190] See 'Exclusion of Ethiopia from War Crimes Commission', 8 November 1943, TNA 371/34378. Also 'War criminals: Marshall Badoglio', 5 August 1943, TNA 371/34370.

European nations.[191] Initially deciding not to consider the Ethiopian cases, the Commission reversed itself and reached preliminary conclusions about the international criminal responsibility of two of the Italian leaders.[192]

The League of Nations was only formally dissolved in 1946 although most of its activities came to a halt with the outbreak of the Second World War. The modest engagement of the League in the area of racial discrimination was paused, only to resume in a much more robust form under the aegis of the United Nations. The war itself brought perhaps the most intense paroxysm of racism and racial discrimination that the world had ever known.

[191] Minutes of the Meeting of the UN War Crimes Commission, 24 September 1947, M.130, p. 4.
[192] Summary Minutes of the Meeting of Committee I of the UN War Crimes Commission, 4 March 1948, pp. 2–10.

4

The United Nations Charter

The Atlantic Charter

Speaking in 2020 in response to the global rise of the Black Lives Matter movement, United Nations Secretary-General António Guterres said that '[t]he position of the United Nations on racism is crystal clear: this scourge violates the United Nations Charter and debases our core values'. The Charter of the United Nations has often been cited in this way for its condemnation of racial discrimination. In the years following its adoption, the Charter was invoked as authority in national judicial decisions for this reason, albeit not to great effect.[1] But while the Charter speaks of respect for equal rights 'without distinction as to race, sex, language, or religion', it directs no particular attention to the phenomenon of racial discrimination. The Preamble to the Charter affirms 'equal rights of men and women and of nations large and small' but presents nothing similar on the issue of racism. The Charter was also ambiguous on the subject of racism's evil twin, colonialism.

Almost immediately following adoption of the Charter in June 1945, victims of racial discrimination in various parts of the world began to submit petitions and communications seeking the protection that they believed had been promised by the new international organization. The answer from the United Nations, at least in those early years, was a polite reference to article 2(7) of the Charter, which prohibits intervention by the United Nations in 'matters which are essentially within the domestic jurisdiction of any state'. For decades, this phrase was invoked by the paradigmatic racist regime, South Africa, as well as by its allies in Europe and North America. As for the other classic example of institutionalized and lawful racial discrimination at the time the Charter was adopted, the United States of America remained relatively sheltered from condemnation by United Nations organs until very recently.

Early in the Second World War, even before the United States had officially joined the conflict, Franklin D. Roosevelt and Winston Churchill met aboard a

---

[1] In the United States, see for example *Kemp v. Rubin* (1947) 69 NYS 2d. 680; *Sipes v. McGhee* (1947) 316 Mich. 614. Also Bert B. Lockwood Jr, 'The United Nations Charter and United States Civil Rights Litigation: 1946–1955' (1984) 69 *Iowa Law Review* 901. In Canada, see *Re Drummond Wren* [1945] 4 DLR 674 (Ont. HC).

The International Legal Order's Colour Line. William A. Schabas, Oxford University Press.
© Oxford University Press 2023. DOI: 10.1093/osc/9780197744475.003.0004

THE ATLANTIC CHARTER 91

ship off the coast of Newfoundland and adopted the Atlantic Charter. It affirmed 'the right of all peoples to choose the form of government under which they will live' and pledged that following the 'final destruction of the Nazi tyranny, they aspired to a peace which will afford to all nations the means of dwelling in safety within their own boundaries, and which will afford assurance that all the men in all the lands may live out their lives in freedom from fear and want'.[2] The Atlantic Charter echoes the 'four freedoms' proclaimed by Roosevelt in a speech to Congress earlier in 1941.[3] But while the 'four freedoms' in many respects constitute an eloquent capsule version of modern human rights – freedom of expression and belief, freedom from fear and want – they are deficient in addressing racial discrimination. Neither the 'four freedoms' nor the Atlantic Charter recognize equality as a fundamental right.

Prior to the issuance of the Atlantic Charter, officials in Britain's Foreign Office considered whether relations with Japan might be improved by issuance of 'some statement making it clear that the white races and the dark races are not unequal'. One senior official, Ashley Clarke, wrote that 'it is impossible for discrimination to be allowed to exist in the world as it stands today'. But the suggestion found no support, principally because of concerns about upsetting the Americans and some of the governments of the British Dominions. Clarke warned that 'any premature injection of the racial issue into existing controversies might have unfortunate results on the cause of aid for Britain'.[4]

With its implied promises, the Atlantic Charter seemed to galvanize victims of racial discrimination around the world.[5] In his memoirs, Nelson Mandela observed that '[s]ome in the West saw the Charter as empty promises, but not those of us in Africa. . . We hoped that the government and ordinary South Africans would see that the principles they were fighting for in Europe were the

[2] 'Joint Statement by President Roosevelt and Prime Minister Churchill, 14 August 1941', FRUS 1941 I, pp. 367–9. See also Elizabeth Borgwardt, *A New Deal for the World, America's Vision for Human Rights*, Cambridge, MA and London: Harvard University Press, 2005; Marika Sherwood, '"Diplomatic Platitudes": The Atlantic charter, The United Nations and Colonial Independence' (1996) 15 *Immigrants & Minorities* 135; Edward A. Laing, 'The Contribution of the Atlantic Charter to Human Rights Law and Humanitarian Universalism' (1989) 26 *Willamette Law Review* 113; Bonny Ibhawoh, 'Testing the Atlantic Charter: Linking Anticolonialism, Self-determination and Universal Human Rights' (2014) 18 *International Journal of Human Rights* 842; M.S. Venkataramani, 'The United States, the Colonial Issue, and the Atlantic Charter Hoax' (1974) 13 *International Studies* 1.

[3] Congressional Record, 1941, Vol. 87, Pt. I.

[4] Advisability on a Statement on Relaxation of Racial Discrimination in Far East, 3–12 March 1941, TNA FO 371/27889.

[5] Penny M. Von Eschen, *Race against Empire: Black Americans and Anticolonialism, 1937–1957*, Ithaca: Cornell University Press, 1997, pp. 25–8; Carol Anderson, *Eyes Off the Prize, The United Nations and the African American Struggle for Human Rights, 1944–1955*, Cambridge: Cambridge University Press, 2003, pp. 16–17; Marika Sherwood, 'Diplomatic Platitudes': The Atlantic Charter, The United Nations and Colonial Independence' (1996) 15 *Immigrants and Minorities* 135; Bonny Ibhawoh, 'Testing the Atlantic Charter: Linking Anticolonialism, Self-determination and Universal Human Rights' (2014) 18 *International Journal of Human Rights* 842.

92 THE UNITED NATIONS CHARTER

same ones we were advocating at home.'[6] At the San Francisco Conference, in June 1945, the Philippine leader Carlos Rómulo spoke of 'the flame of hope that swept the Far East when the Atlantic Charter was made known to the world'. He said that everywhere people asked: 'Is it for one side of the world, and not the other? For one race only and not for them too?'[7]

Not everyone was taken in. In a letter to Roosevelt, Mohandas Gandhi wrote that the claim the Allies were fighting 'to make the world safe for freedom of the individual and for democracy sounds hollow, so long as India, and for that matter, Africa are exploited by Great Britain, and America has the Negro problem in her own home'.[8] Upon his return to London, Churchill told the House of Commons that the Atlantic Charter did not apply to regions whose people owe allegiance to the British Crown'.[9] In November 1942 he explained to an adoring audience in London that he had not become Prime Minister 'to preside over the liquidation of the British Empire'.[10] An editorial in the Chicago Defender, one of the principal African American newspapers, answered: 'Black America is truly shocked by the bold and brazen stand by Churchill. We have never known or believed him a friend but we hoped that he as well as the world is learning about democracy from the very "blood, sweat and tears" of war.'[11]

The role of human rights in the war aims of the Allies was broadened considerably on 1 January 1942 when 36 States, including the United States, the United Kingdom, the Soviet Union, China, Canada, Haiti, Cuba, India, New Zealand, and South Africa signed the 'Declaration of the United Nations'. It explicitly endorsed the Atlantic Charter and declared that 'complete victory over their enemies is essential to defend life, liberty, independence and religious freedom, and to preserve human rights and justice in their own lands'.[12] Racial discrimination was addressed more explicitly in a proclamation by the Soviet leader, Joseph Stalin, on the twenty-fifth anniversary of the Bolshevik revolution, on 6 November 1942. Stalin described the programme of the enemy, starting with 'race hatred'. He contrasted this with '[t]he programme of action of the Anglo-Soviet-American coalition' which was premised on 'abolition of racial exclusiveness'.[13]

---

[6] Nelson Mandela, A Long Walk to Freedom, Boston: Little Brown, 2000, pp. 82–3.
[7] Verbatim minutes of the 3rd meeting of Commission II, 20 June 1945, 1144 II/16, UNCIO VIII, p. 139.
[8] Gandhi to Roosevelt, 1 July 1942, FRUS 1942 I, pp. 677–8. See also Elizabeth Borgwardt, ' "When You State a Moral Principle, You Are Stuck with It": The 1941 Atlantic Charter as a Human Rights Instrument' (2005–2006) 46 Virginia Journal of International Law 501, at p. 545.
[9] HC Deb, 9 September 1941, vol 374, cc67-156.
[10] 'Great Design in Africa', The Times, 11 November 1942, p. 8.
[11] 'Danger from Overseas', Chicago Defender, 28 November 1942.
[12] Declaration by United Nations, FRUS 1942 I, pp. 25–6.
[13] Joseph V. Stalin, On the Great Patriotic War of the Soviet Union, Moscow: Foreign Languages Publishing House, 1954, pp. 87–8, 90–1.

In the United States, the Commission to Study the Organisation of Peace, an unofficial but influential body, released a report warning that there should be no repeat of Wilson's rejection of the Japanese proposal at the 1919 Paris Peace Conference, 'a rejection which embittered the Oriental world'. It stated that '[t]he Negro situation in our country and expressions of anti-Semitism, which foster enemy propaganda, are not to be passed over'. The Commission thought that '[t] hrough revulsion against Nazi doctrines, we may however speed up the process of bringing our own practices in each nation more in conformity with our professed ideals'[14] These were strong words, inconsistent with the general discourse about human rights in United States government circles that largely ignored the issue of racial discrimination.[15] The United States embassy in London shared with the British a confidential study that had been prepared on the Japanese initiatives in 1919.[16] Woodrow Wilson's rebuff at the Paris Peace Conference had certainly not been forgotten.

The Dumbarton Oaks Proposals

The principal stage in preparations for the post-war world order was the Dumbarton Oaks Conference, organized in Washington in August, September, and October 1944 by the United States and the United Kingdom, together with the Soviet Union and, later, China. W.E.B. Du Bois noted the irony of holding the sessions in an historic mansion that had been built in the time 'of that curious combination of Negro slavery and British imperialism when America was a colony of Britain and conceived of as primarily a matter of income and investment for British merchants and aristocrats'.[17] At the outset, the British made it clear to the Americans that they could not agree unconditionally to any promise of independence of self-government for dependent territories. London showed great reluctance even to discuss the issue.[18] The human rights language that had figured in the Atlantic Charter and the Declaration of the United Nations was

[14] 'International Safeguard of Human Rights: Statements of the Commission to Study the Organization of Peace' (1944) 22 *International Conciliation* 552, at pp. 569–70. This was toned down from an earlier version of the report, cited in Paul Gordon Lauren, 'First Principles of Racial Equality: History and the Politics and Diplomacy of Human Rights Provisions in the United Nations Charter' (1983) 5 *Human Rights Quarterly* 1, at p. 6. It speaks of the 'cancerous Negro situation in our country', noting that it 'gives fodder to enemy propaganda and makes our ideals stick like dry bread in the throat. In anti-Semitism we are a mirror of Nazi grimaces'.

[15] See, for example, Quincy Wright, 'Human Rights and the World Order' (1943) 21 *International Conciliation* 238.

[16] Japan and the issue of racial equality at Paris, 1919, 3 February 1943, TNA FO 371/35949.

[17] W.E.B. Du Bois, *The World and Africa and Color and Democracy*, Oxford: Oxford University Press, 2007, p. 245.

[18] Memorandum by Mr. Leo Pasvolsky, Special assistant to the Secretary of State, 15 March 1944, FRUS 1944 I, pp. 627–32, at p. 632.

94 THE UNITED NATIONS CHARTER

cast aside. Ultimately, there was only one perfunctory reference in the document that emerged: 'promote respect for human rights and fundamental freedoms'.[19] Now confident of military victory, these great powers were no longer as concerned as they had been a few years previously about the need to rally smaller countries and their populations, as well as minorities within their own borders, by means of promises of freedom, equality, and self-determination.

Writing about Dumbarton Oaks in *The Crisis*, the monthly publication of the National Association for the Advancement of Coloured People, Ernest Johnson observed that 'only one coloured group participated, the Chinese, and the equality and basic problems of Negroes and colonial coloured people were not on the agenda'.[20] China wasn't really a full participant and only joined in the final week of the meetings, which took more than a month overall. By the time China arrived, 'the Big Three (Britain, the Soviet Union, and the United States) already had agreed among themselves to bury any mention of human rights deep within the text and confine it to social and economic cooperation, and to completely eliminate all mention of racial equality'.[21] Officially, the bifurcation of the meeting was justified by the neutrality of the Soviet Union in the war with Japan, but this was more of a pretext to relegate China to the margins. Writing to Roosevelt accept the invitation to participate, President Chiang Kai-shek had warned that '[w]ithout the participation of Asiatic peoples, the conference will have no meaning for half of humanity'.[22]

In its preparations for the Dumbarton Oaks talks, China considered insisting upon inclusion of an anti-racial discrimination clause in the preamble of the draft charter. China was of course inspired by the Japanese effort in 1919 for incorporation of such a reference in the Covenant of the League of Nations. China's great diplomat, Koo Vi Kyuin, known at the international level as Wellington Koo, prepared a lengthy internal memorandum prior to Dumbarton Oaks entitled 'Notes on the Principle of the Equality of Races'. He wrote: 'As a means of promoting this ... it will be highly desirable to consecrate the principle of equality of races as of states in the fundamental instrument of the new institution. ... Reference to this principle ... in the preamble of the new charter will not only give moral satisfaction to the greater part of humanity, but will also go far to pave the way for the realisation of the ideal of universal brotherhood inseparable from the ideal of

---

[19] Proposals for the Establishment of a General International Organisation, FRUS 1944 I, pp. 890–900, at p. 898.

[20] Ernest Johnson, 'A Voice at the Peace Table?', *The Crisis*, November 1944, p. 345.

[21] Paul Gordon Lauren, *The Evolution of International Human Rights, Visions Seen*, Philadelphia: University of Pennsylvania Press, 2003, at p. 163; Carol Anderson, *Eyes Off the Prize, The United Nations and the African American Struggle for Human Rights, 1944-1955*, Cambridge: Cambridge University Press, 2003, pp. 36–7.

[22] 'The Chinese Ambassador (Wei) to the Secretary of State', 3 June 1944, FRUS 1944 I, p. 640.

THE DUMBARTON OAKS PROPOSALS   95

permanent world peace.'[23] Decades earlier, when Koo represented China at the Paris Peace Conference, he had expressed 'full sympathy' with the Japanese proposal, despite considerable tension between the two delegations.[24]

China prepared a list of 'essential points' to be included in the Charter of the new organization, of which the second affirmed that 'the principle of equality of all States and all races shall be upheld'.[25] The issue could hardly have been more prominent and the echo of 1919 more evident. China's paper was circulated to the other powers. It is cited in notes of their informal conversations.[26] A telegram from Viscount Halifax to the Foreign Office summarized the Chinese proposals, referring to 'Equality of races'.[27] Under Secretary of State Edward Stettinius, who headed the American delegates, thought a general statement on human rights might be included but he was not enthusiastic about China's very explicit attention to racial equality.[28] The British delegate, Alexander Cadogan, reported to the Foreign Office: 'Argument strongly advanced is that it would be against our interest and tradition as a liberal power to oppose the expression of a principle denial of which figures so predominantly in Nazi philosophy and is repugnant to the mass of British and foreign opinion. Such action would moreover prejudice British and American relations in a sphere of great delicacy by supplying ammunition to critics . . . ' Cadogan thought the principle could withstand any concrete application by the proviso that this was a matter of domestic jurisdiction.[29] A minute in one of the British files warned that '[a]ttention might possibly be drawn to the Chinese emphasis on "racial equality" (which may cause some trouble)'.[30] When the relevant ministries were consulted there were no objections to the approach proposed by Cadogan.[31] But the issue did not arise. Upon its arrival in Washington in early October, the Chinese delegation presented a list of

---

[23] 'Notes on the principle of the equality of races', Wellington Koo papers, Box 76, cited in Marilyn Lake, 'Chinese Colonists Assert their "Common Human Rights": Cosmopolitanism as Subject and Method of History' (2010) 21 *Journal of World History* 375, at pp. 389–91.

[24] Minutes of the Tenth Meeting of the Commission on the League of Nations, 13 February 1919, p. 64, USNA FW 181.1101/10, M820 Roll 140.

[25] 'Tentative Chinese Proposals for a General International Organisation', 23 August 1944, FRUS 1944 I, pp. 718–28, at p. 718; Chinese Government's memorandum on international organization, Communicated by Dr. Kung to Sir A. Cadogan at Dumbarton Oaks, Washington, D.C., 22 August 1944, TNA FO 371/40708.

[26] 'Extracts of the Personal Diary of the Under Secretary of State (Stettinius)', 29 August 1944, FRUS 1944 I, pp. 748–50, at p. 750.

[27] Telegram from Halifax to Foreign Office, 29 August 1944, TNA FO 371/40708.

[28] Paul Gordon Lauren, 'First Principles of Racial Equality: History and the Politics and Diplomacy of Human Rights Provisions in the United Nations Charter' (1983) 5 *Human Rights Quarterly* 1, at p. 10.

[29] Telegram from Halifax to Foreign Office, 29 September 1944, TNA FO 371/40716.

[30] Minute to memorandum of J.G. Wood, 3 October 1944, TNA FO 371/40708.

[31] Foreign Office to Washington, 4 October 1944, TNA FO 371/40716. Also Day to Sterndale Bennett, 17 February 1945, TNA FO 371/46324.

96 THE UNITED NATIONS CHARTER

seven issues of concern. Racial discrimination was no longer among them.[32] The Americans must have talked them out of it.

The original Chinese proposal was not officially made public at the time but its existence seems to have been well known. The October 1944 issue of *The Crisis* reported that 'the Chinese government is proposing formally that a declaration on the equality of races and nations be included in the peace treaty', warning that it was 'in for a stiff fight and past history indicates that she has little chance of winning her point'.[33] Early in 1945, Du Bois wrote that the 'proposed international declaration on racial equality' had been 'suppressed' but he didn't say by whom.[34]

More generally, the shortcomings of the Dumbarton Oaks proposals were strongly criticized by many countries that had not been involved but were expected to participate in the creation of the new organization.[35] Small and middle-sized States, including South Africa,[36] Panama,[37] and Cuba,[38] made proposals to insert provisions concerning human rights in the draft Charter. Dissatisfaction within Latin America was particularly apparent at the Inter-American Conference on Problems of War and Peace, convened at Chapultepec in Mexico City in February 1945.[39] Recalling that the participants at Chapultepec did not take part in the Dumbarton Oaks Conversations, the Conference adopted resolutions concerning the protection of human rights.[40] Resolution XLI affirmed that '[w]orld peace cannot be consolidated until men are able to

[32] Memorandum by the Under Secretary of State (Mr. Stettinius) to the Secretary of State, 3 October 1944, FRUS 1944 I, pp. 863–5; Memorandum by the Under Secretary of State (Mr. Stettinius) to the Secretary of State, 4 October 1944, FRUS 1944 I, pp. 865–7. See also Paul Gordon Lauren, *Power and Prejudice: The Politics and Diplomacy of Racial Discrimination*, Boulder: Westview Press, 1996, p. 160.

[33] 'Race Equality in the Peace' (1944) 51 *The Crisis* 312.

[34] W.E.B. Du Bois, *The World and Africa and Color and Democracy*, Oxford: Oxford University Press, 2007, p. 247.

[35] Paul Gordon Lauren, *The Evolution of International Human Rights, Visions Seen*, Philadelphia: University of Pennsylvania Press, 2003, at pp. 168–70.

[36] Verbatim Minutes of the 6th Plenary Session, UNCIO I, 55 P/13, pp. 416–55, at p. 425.

[37] Additional Amendments Proposed by the Delegation of the Republic of Panama concerning the Proposals for the Maintenance of Peace and Security agreed upon at the Conference of Dumbarton Oaks, UNCIO III, 2 G/7(g)(2), pp. 265–9.

[38] Seven Proposals on the Dumbarton Oaks Proposals Submitted by the Delegation of Cuba, UNCIO III, 2 G/14(g), pp. 493–509, at pp. 499–502.

[39] Kathryn Sikkink, 'Latin American Countries as Norm Protagonists of the Idea of International Human Rights' (2014) 20 *Global Governance* 389, at pp. 393–4. Also Mary Ann Glendon, 'The Forgotten Crucible: The Latin American Influence on the Universal Human Rights Idea' (2003) 16 *Harvard Human Rights Journal* 27; Manuel S. Canyes, 'The Inter-American System and the Conference of Chapultepec' (1945) 39 *American Journal of International Law* 504; Josef L. Kunz, 'The Inter-American Conference on Problems of War and Peace at Mexico City and the Problem of the Reorganization of the Inter-American System' (1945) 39 *American Journal of International Law* 527.

[40] Paul Gordon Lauren, *The Evolution of International Human Rights: Visions Seen*, Philadelphia: University of Pennsylvania Press, 1998, pp. 174–9; Kathryn Sikkink, 'Latin American Countries as Norm Protagonists of the Idea of International Human Rights' (2014) 20 *Global Governance* 389, at pp. 393–4.

exercise their basic rights without distinction as to race or religion.'[41] The formulation drew on a statement adopted at the Eighth International Conference of American States, in December 1938: 'That in accordance with the fundamental principle of equality before the Law, any persecution on account of racial or religious motives which makes it impossible for a group of human beings to live decently, is contrary to the political and juridical systems of America.'[42] A resolution on racial discrimination, proposed by Haiti, was also adopted, after revisions from the American delegation 'to avoid possible statements which would invite controversies'.[43]

The Dumbarton Oaks proposals were the focus of much criticism from victims of racial discrimination. The National Council of Negro Women wrote that '[t]he Dumbarton Oaks proposals do not give assurance to the non-white peoples, the dependent peoples, and the minority groups of the world that a new page of history affecting their welfare is about to be written.'[44] Roy Wilkins of the NAACP said the proposals manifested 'a total lack of consideration of colonial peoples and darker races'.[45] W.E.B. Du Bois described the proposals as 'a government of the world in which 800,000,000 white and yellow peoples will rule mankind. There will be 750,000,000 coloured and black folk inhabiting colonies owned by white nations, who will have no rights that the white people of the world are bound to respect.'[46] A declaration by the London-based League of Coloured Peoples noted the Dumbarton Oaks discussions and insisted that '[i]nternational cooperation demands the abolition of every kind of discrimination on account of colour, race and creed wherever such discrimination exists'.[47]

[41] Acta Final de la Conferencia Interamerican sobre Problemas de la Guerra y de la Paz, Ciudad de Mexico, 21 February to 8 May 1945, Washington: Pan American Union, pp. 96–7.

[42] 'Persecution for racial or religious motives, Resolution XXXVI' (1940) 34 *American Journal of International Law Supplement* 198.

[43] American Delegation to the Acting Secretary of State, 6 March 1945, FRUS 1945 IX, p. 144. Also Camille M. Cianfarra, 'Bias Ban Approved at Mexico Parlay, Committee Adopts Measure on Racial Discrimination', *New York Times*, 7 March 1945, p. 9. For the declaration, see Pan American Union, *Final Act of the Inter-American Conference on Problems of War and Peace, Mexico City, February–March 1945*, Washington, 1945.

[44] Cited in Elizabeth Borgwardt, 'Race, Rights and Nongovernmental Organisations at the UN San Francisco Conference', in Kevin M. Kruse and Stephen Tuck, eds., *The Fog of War: The Second World War and the Civil Rights Movement*, Oxford: Oxford University Press, 2012, pp. 188–207, at pp. 196–7.

[45] Wilkins to Eichelberger, telegram, 19 February 1945, cited in Carol Anderson, *Bourgeois Radicals, the NAACP and the Struggle for Colonial Liberation, 1941–1960*, Cambridge: Cambridge University Press, 2015, p. 62.

[46] W.E.B. Du Bois, *The World and Africa and Color and Democracy*, Oxford: Oxford University Press, 2007, pp. 245–9.

[47] 'League of Coloured Peoples, Manifesto on Africa in the Post-War World: for presentation to the United Nations Conference, San Francisco, April 1945', W.E.B. Du Bois Papers (MS 312).

98   THE UNITED NATIONS CHARTER

The Charter of the United Nations

The Charter of the United Nations was adopted at the San Francisco Conference, which convened in April 1945 and concluded on 26 June. The Charter makes four references to 'race', always as part of a larger enumeration of categories. Article 1(3) lists as one of the 'purposes' of the United Nations the achievement of 'international cooperation in solving international problems of an economic, social, cultural, or humanitarian character, and in promoting and encouraging respect for human rights and for fundamental freedoms for all without distinction as to race, sex, language, or religion'. The same formulation is used in three other provisions: article 13, on the authority of the General Assembly 'to initiate studies and make recommendations'; article 55, on the remit of the Economic and Social Council; and article 76, on the objectives of the international trusteeship system that replaced the League of Nations mandates.[48] These references were added to the draft Charter on the proposal of the four powers[49] and appear to have originated from the Soviet Union.[50] But while the package of amendments appeared to respond to the critics of the Dumbarton Oaks proposals, there was a catch to this concession. A new clause specified that '[n]othing contained in the present Charter shall authorise the United Nations to intervene in matters which are essentially within the domestic jurisdiction of any state'.[51] This was to become article 2(7) of the Charter.

John P. Humphrey, the Canadian academic who served as secretary to the Commission on Human Rights for more than two decades, wrote that the Charter of the United Nations would have had 'only a passing reference' to human rights were it not for the efforts of non-governmental organizations.[52] The United States stood out in this respect, associating representatives of 42 non-governmental

[48] On the human rights clauses of the Charter, see generally Farrokh Jhabvala, 'The Drafting of the Human Rights Provisions of the UN Charter' (1997) 44 *Netherlands International Law Review* 1; Edward R. Stettinius, 'Human Rights in the United Nations Charter' (1946) 243 *The Annals of the American Academy of Political and Social Science* 1; Benjamin V. Cohen, 'Human Rights under the United Nations Charter' (1949) 14 *Law and Contemporary Problems* 430.

[49] Amendments Proposed by the Governments of the United States, the United Kingdom, the Soviet Union, and China, 5 May 1945, 2 G/29, UNCIO III, pp. 622–8, at pp. 623, 626. The order of categories was slightly different: 'race, language, religion or sex'.

[50] Minutes of the First Four-Power Consultative Meeting on Charter Proposals, 5 May 1945, FRUS 1945 I, pp. 548–58, at p. 551; Verbatim Minutes of Second Meeting of Commission II, 11 June 1945, UNCIO VIII, pp. 52–64, at p. 56.

[51] Amendments Proposed by the Governments of the United States, the United Kingdom, the Soviet Union, and China, 5 May 1945, 2 G/29, UNCIO III, pp. 622–8, at p. 623. See Antonio Cançado Trindade, 'The Domestic Jurisdiction of States in the Practice of the United Nations and Regional Organisations' (1976) 25 *International and Comparative Law Quarterly* 715; Kawser Ahmed, 'The Domestic Jurisdiction Clause in the United Nations Charter: A Historical View' (2006) 10 *Singapore Yearbook of International Law* 175.

[52] John P. Humphrey, 'The UN Charter and the Universal Declaration of Human Rights', in Evan Luard, ed., *The International Protection of Human Rights*, London: Thames and Hudson, 1967, pp. 30–58, at pp. 39–40.

THE CHARTER OF THE UNITED NATIONS   99

organizations with its delegation as 'consultants'.[53] The British Government, on the other hand, rejected a proposal from Nigerian legislators to join their delegation, contending that 'observers' were not allowed and that in any case the interests of the colonies were adequately protected.[54] The American consultants included representatives of several trade unions, religious bodies, and service clubs like the Lions and Kiwanis. Five women's organizations were included in the delegation while others attended on their own initiative and without any official delegate status. Their significant presence undoubtedly contributed to the special mention of women's quality in the preamble of the Charter.[55] Of the 42 consultant organizations, only one focussed on the rights of African Americans, the National Association for the Advance of Colored People (NAACP). It was represented by Walter White, W.E.B. Du Bois, Mary McLeod Bethune, and Roy Wilkins.[56] Critics within the community protested that 'no purely Afro-American group' had been selected by the Department of State, alluding to the important role of whites in the creation and the leadership of the NAACP.[57]

The American consultants assembled prior to the beginning of the Conference for a briefing from the head of the delegation, former Secretary of State Edward Stettinius. Several organizations were concerned about the omission from the draft of the charter of a declaration of fundamental rights. O. Frederick Nolde of the Federal Council of Churches of Christ raised the issue with the support of Judge Joseph M. Proskauer, representing the American Jewish Committee. On behalf of the NAACP, Walter White insisted that a phrase in the draft charter pledging 'equality of opportunity' must include a reference to colonized and other dependent peoples. According to White's account of the meeting, 'Mr. Stettinius smiled somewhat embarrassedly and cryptically at this point'.[58]

Black American leaders viewed themselves as responsible not only for defending the rights of their own population but also the rights of the 750 million colonized peoples of Africa. They hoped that the Charter would point the way to independence and the end of colonialism. A new alignment of powerful nations,

---

[53] Dorothy B. Robins, *Experiment in Democracy: The Story of U.S. Citizen Organizations in Forging the Charter of the United Nations*, New York: Parkside Press, 1971.

[54] Marika Sherwood, '"There is no New Deal for the Blackman in San Francisco": African Attempts to Influence the Founding Conference of the United Nations April–July 1945' (1996) 29 *International Journal of African Historical Studies* 71, at pp. 81–2.

[55] Torild Skard, 'Getting Our History Right: How Were the Equal Rights of Women and Men Included in the Charter of the United Nations?' (2008) 35 *Forum for Development Studies* 37.

[56] United Nations Conference on International Organization list of consultants, ca. May 1945, W.E.B. Du Bois Papers (MS 312).

[57] Penny M. Von Eschen, *Race against Empire: Black Americans and Anticolonialism, 1937–1957*, Ithaca: Cornell University Press, 1997, pp. 79–80; Robert L. Harris Jr., 'Racial Equality and the United Nations Charter', in Armstead L. Robinson and Patricia Sullivan, eds., *New Directions in Civil Rights Studies*, Charlottesville: University of Virginia Press, 1991, pp. 126–45, at p. 136.

[58] Confidential memorandum from Walter White to W.E.B. Du Bois and Mary McLeod Bethune, 3 May 1945, W.E.B. Du Bois Papers (MS 312).

100   THE UNITED NATIONS CHARTER

where two countries without any colonial interests, the Soviet Union and China, had filled the empty chairs of the 'Great Powers', showed much promise. The international perspective enhanced the view that African Americans were themselves in a situation that was analogous to colonization. Mary McLeod Bethune told a meeting of Black organizations in New York that the creation of the United Nations had put into 'bold relief' the 'common bond' with colonized Africans and confirmed that the 'Negro in America' enjoyed 'little more than colonial status'.[59]

Like China's Wellington Koo and South Africa's Jan Smuts, who were both delegates in 1945, W.E.B. Du Bois had also been present in Paris in 1919. Du Bois felt strongly that African Americans, and in particular the NAACP, should speak for colonized Africans who had no voice at the United Nations.[60] In preparation for San Francisco, Du Bois convened a 'Colonial Conference', on 6 April 1945, that was attended by delegates from India, Puerto Rico, Indonesia, Jamaica, British Guiana, Burma, Uganda, the Gold Coast, and a number of missionary societies. It called for a representative International Mandates Commission in which colonized peoples participated directly, with robust powers. 'No state which practises legally sanctioned discrimination against anybody of its inhabitants because of race, creed, or colour should be regarded as qualified to serve as a mandatory power', stated the Conference Declaration.[61]

The NAACP delegation at San Francisco formulated its concerns about the so-called 'domestic jurisdiction clause'. In a telegram to the United States delegation, the NAACP noted: 'This means that the international organisation cannot interfere in colonial affairs, and it may also make impossible any attempt to safeguard the rights of groups in any nation; for instance, it could not combat the race and religious persecution of another Hitler.' It said the declaration of 'purposes' in article 1(3) was 'encouraging' in that it put the United Nations 'on the side of justice and non-discrimination'. However, it left out 'the mass of people living in colonies, against whom discrimination is customary and unjustifiable'. The NAACP wanted the Charter to lay down the principle of 'transition of all colonial peoples from colonial status to such autonomy as they desire'.[62]

---

[59] Statement of Mary McLeod Bethune, 23 June 1945, Mary McLeod Bethune Papers, Box 3, folder 17, Amistad Research Centre, New Orleans, quoted in Carol Anderson, 'From Hope to Disillusion: African Americans, the United Nations, and the Struggle for Human Rights, 1944–1947' (1996) 29 *Diplomatic History* 531, at p. 542.

[60] Memorandum from W.E.B. Du Bois to Walter White, 28 March 1946. W.E.B. Du Bois Papers (MS 312); A Suggested statement to the UNO, 28 March 1946, W.E.B. Du Bois Papers (MS 312).

[61] Colonial Conference resolution, April 1945, W.E.B. Du Bois Papers (MS 312); Carol Anderson, 'From Hope to Disillusion: African Americans, the United Nations, and the Struggle for Human Rights, 1944–1947' (1996) 20 *Diplomatic History* 531; Carol Anderson, *Bourgeois Radicals, the NAACP and the Struggle for Colonial Liberation, 1941–1960*, Cambridge: Cambridge University Press, 2015, pp. 57–9.

[62] Telegram from NAACP to United States Delegation to the United Nations Conference on International Organization, 7 May 1945, W.E.B. Du Bois Papers (MS 312).

THE CHARTER OF THE UNITED NATIONS   101

Du Bois called for issuance of a 'preliminary statement on the essential equality of all races, the same statement which the United States and Great Britain once refused to grant Japan; and identical with the suppressed proposal of the Chinese Delegation at Dumbarton Oaks'. He protested the attempt to recognize fundamental rights 'without any specific mention of the people living in colonies'. Du Bois said he spoke 'in the name of 13 million Americans who are blood brothers of these colonists'.[63] He called on the United States delegation to propose the following article for the Charter of the United Nations:

> The colonial system of government, however deeply rooted in history and custom, is today undemocratic, socially dangerous and a main cause of wars. The United Nations recognising democracy at the only just way of life for all peoples make it a first statute of international law that at the earliest practical moment no nation or group shall be deprived of effective voice in its own government and enjoyment of the four freedoms. An international colonial commission on which colonial peoples shall have representation will have power to investigate the facts and implement this declaration under the Security Council.[64]

Writing after the Charter's adoption, Hans Kelsen questioned why the Preamble referred to equality of men and women but did not refer to the other categories, including race.[65] The 'oversight' is easily explained. The man who is credited with drafting the Preamble, Jan Smuts of South Africa, was a dedicated proponent of racial discrimination and white supremacy.[66] Smuts espoused 'an international framework that reflected and supported notions of white rule so dear to the maintenance of power in Pretoria, western Europe, and the United States'.[67] His involvement cast an 'enigmatic shadow' over the San Francisco Conference, in the words of Mark Mazower.[68] Smuts's original draft did not refer to women's equality either but this was added in the revised version proposed by the South African delegation.[69] Committed to human rights at the international

[63] Memorandum from W.E.B. Du Bois to United States Delegation to the United Nations Conference on International Organization, 16 May 1945, W.E.B. Du Bois Papers (MS 312).

[64] Ibid.

[65] Hans Kelsen, 'The Preamble of the Charter--A Critical Analysis' (1946) 8 *The Journal of Politics* 134, at pp. 146–7.

[66] Noel Garson, 'Smuts and the Idea of Race' (2007) 57 *South African Historical Journal* 153.

[67] Caroline Elkins, *Legacy of Violence, A History of the British Empire*, London: Bodley Head, 2022, p. 91.

[68] Mark Mazower, *No Enchanted Palace: The End of Empire and the Ideological Origins of the United Nations*, Princeton, NJ: Princeton University Press, 2009, p. 19.

[69] Draft preamble to the Charter proposed by the Union of South Africa, 26 April 1945, 2 G/14 (d), UNCIO III, pp. 474–7. See Torild Skard, 'Getting Our History Right: How Were the Equal Rights of Women and Men Included in the Charter of the United Nations?' (2008) 35 *Forum for Development Studies* 37, at p. 50.

102   THE UNITED NATIONS CHARTER

level, Smuts denied them at home. He was blind to the role that racism and theories of racial superiority had played in bringing the world to the abyss.

Smuts first mooted the issue of the preamble at a meeting of Commonwealth leaders in London, in April 1945. Smuts thought the draft Charter that emerged from the Dumbarton Oaks meetings the previous year 'lacked something'. Explaining his view that the Second World War 'had at bottom been a religious war', he presented a draft text for the preamble that spoke of a 'common faith'. In public lectures, Smuts indicated his view that the Second World War was the result of 'something deeper and more sinister in human outlook and beliefs'.[70] Smuts pursued his campaign at San Francisco, stressing the importance of 'fundamental human rights' in the Charter although, as we know, he was firmly opposed to one of the most fundamental of them all.[71] Smuts alone cannot be blamed for the absence of any reference to racial discrimination in the Preamble. But the first draft of any document is likely to set the tone, leaving it to others to recognize oversights and then take initiatives to address them.

It is not as if there were no efforts from delegates to introduce a condemnation of racial discrimination in the Charter. The Haitian Government had criticized the Dumbarton Oaks proposals for failing to recognize that 'the actual world conflict' could be attributed to 'racial and religious discrimination'.[72] It submitted the following paragraph as a 'principle' of the United Nations: 'The Organisation is based on the principle of the sovereign equality of all States that love peace and exclude from their relations any racial or religious discrimination'.[73] The Philippines proposed the insertion, in article 1 on 'Principles', of the phrase 'and the spirit of brotherhood and racial equality' after the words 'To develop friendly relations . . .'[74] In the discussion of the former mandates and the trust territories, the Netherlands referred to 'the humiliation caused by the assertion of racial superiority' as one of the 'grievances which were felt by dependent peoples'. The American delegate responded that there was a 'moral obligation' to overcome this.[75] China said '[i]t was essential that the Conference got away from all ideas of racial superiority and racial inferiority if peace were to be achieved'.[76] Iraq's

---

[70] Christof Heyns, 'The Preamble of the United Nations Charter: The contribution of Jan Smuts' (1995) 7 *African Journal of International and Comparative Law* 329, at p. 344.

[71] Saul Dubow, 'Smuts, the United Nations and the Rhetoric of Race and Rights' (2008) 43 *Journal of Contemporary History* 43; Peter Marshall, 'Smuts and The Preamble to The UN Charter' (2000) 90 *The Round Table, the Commonwealth Journal of International Affairs* 55; Willem H. Gravett, 'The Smutsian Concept of Human Rights' (2016) 32 *South African Journal of Human Rights* 538.

[72] Verbatim minutes of the 6th plenary session, 1 May 1945, 55 P/13, UNCIO I, p. 443. See also Summary report of 4th meeting of Committee I/2, 10 May 1945, 242 I/2/11, UNCIO VII, p. 25.

[73] Haiti, 5 May 1945, G/7 (b) (1), UNCIO III, p. 52, UNCIO IV, p. 84, and UNCIO VI, pp. 563, 616.

[74] Philippines, 5 May 1945, G/14 (k), Vol, IV, pp. 757, 765, Vol. VI, p. 551.

[75] Summary report of the 15th meeting of Committee II/4, 18 June 1945, 1090 II/4/43, UNCIO X, pp. 563, 586.

[76] Summary report of the 11th meeting of Committee II/4, 31 May 1945, 712 II/4//30, UNCIO X, p. 497.

delegate said racial discrimination was 'a purely Nazi philosophy' that should be 'discarded forever'. Iraq considered that nations to whom trust territories were assigned should 'feel that the peoples of these territories are their brothers and that there is no superiority of any sort, national, racial, or religious'.[77] India proposed inclusion in Chapter I of a new paragraph 2: 'to promote recognition of fundamental human rights for all men and women, irrespective of race, colour or creed, in all nations . . . '[78] France wanted a purpose of the Organization to be 'to see to it that the essential liberties of all are respected without distinction of race, language, or creed'.[79]

After the Charter was adopted, Du Bois testified before the American Senate, which was then considering ratification: 'The proposed Charter should, therefore, make clear and unequivocal the straightforward stand of the civilised world for race equality, and the universal application of the democratic way of life, not simply as philanthropy and justice, but to save human civilisation from suicide. What was true of the United States in the past is true of world civilisation today – we cannot exist half slave and half free'.[80] Du Bois called for the United States to make the following declaration at the time of ratification: 'The main groups of mankind, commonly called races, are essentially equal in capability of progress and deserve equality of treatment, opportunity and respect. In the eyes of both science and religion, all men are brothers, with rights of freedom of belief and expression, freedom of domicile and communication; justice before the courts and equal civil, economic, political and social rights'.[81] He was less circumspect writing to a journalist with the *Chicago Defender*: '[W]e have conquered Germany but not their ideas. We still believe in white supremacy, keeping Negroes in their places and lying about democracy, when we mean imperial control of 750 million human beings in colonies'.[82] During the American congressional hearings on the Charter, Colorado Senator Eugene Millikan questioned whether racial discrimination would fall within the jurisdiction of the United Nations. Senator Vandenberg explained that the domestic jurisdiction clause

[77] Verbatim minutes of the 3rd meeting of Commission II, 20 June 1945, 1144 II/16, UNCIO VIII, p. 134.

[78] Documentation for meetings of Committee I/1, 11 May 1945, G/14/h, UNCIO VI, p. 542.

[79] Documentation for meetings of Committee I/1, 11 May 1945, G/7/o, UNCIO VI, p. 540.

[80] Statement of W.E.B. Du Bois, 11 July 1945, Senate Committee on Foreign Relations, The Charter of the United Nations: Hearings Before the Committee on Foreign Relations, 79th Cong., 1st Sess, July 1945, p. 218. See David Levering Lewis, *W.E.B. Du Bois, A Biography*, New York: Henry Holt, 2009, pp. 657–8.

[81] Testimony of W.E.B. Du Bois, ca. July 11, 1945, W.E.B. Du Bois Papers (MS 312). The Du Bois archives contain a somewhat longer version of this text, with his handwritten note saying he had tried to present it as a resolution or amendment but 'was unable to get anywhere'. See The American Negro before the United Nations [fragment], December 1947, W.E.B. Du Bois Papers (MS 312).

[82] Letter from W.E.B. Du Bois to *Chicago Defender*, 4 May 1945, W.E.B. Du Bois Papers (MS 312), cited in Carol Anderson, *Bourgeois Radicals, the NAACP and the Struggle for Colonial Liberation, 1941-1960*, Cambridge: Cambridge University Press, 2015, pp. 64–5.

104   THE UNITED NATIONS CHARTER

was an obstacle to United Nations intrusion into domestic measures of racial discrimination, and that in no manner could the Charter impact upon the conduct of the American states.[83] Needless to say, the American Senate did not make the declaration that Du Bois had proposed.

* * *

There is a piece missing in the Charter of the United Nations. It should contain a firm commitment to racial equality and a denunciation of racism and racial discrimination. Instead, these issues are swallowed up within more general commitments to equality based upon sex, language, and religion. The absence was no oversight. The proposal had been present from the earliest discussions of the new United Nations organization, and even before. Indeed, the entire process of establishing the United Nations seemed to be haunted by memories of the unsuccessful Japanese initiative at the Paris Peace Conference for specific recognition of racial equality.

Promises about the new world order that was to follow the defeat of Nazi Germany were made by Roosevelt and Churchill in the Atlantic Charter of August 1941, when the United States had not even entered the war. At the time, victory was far from assured. The Americans and the British understood that there was a *quid pro quo* if they were to broaden their appeal for support to oppressed peoples within their own jurisdiction and subject to their authority, as well as others. The pledges were vague and somewhat equivocal but they were understood to point to some recognition of racial equality and self-government for colonized peoples in the Global South.

Nevertheless, when the moment arrived for formal recognition of these ideas, the Great Powers stepped back. China made hesitant suggestions about including a racial equality clause in the legal framework of the United Nations. However, it did not push the point when faced with resistance from the United States. At the San Francisco Conference, the issue of racial discrimination lingered in the background. W.E.B. Du Bois and others recalled the Japanese proposal of 1919 but it was not picked up by the delegates themselves. The San Francisco Conference of 1945 was only a marginal improvement on the Paris Peace Conference of 1919 as far as representation of people of colour were concerned.

It took less than four months for the Charter to enter into force. This in turn set in motion the process of convening and preparing for the first session of the General Assembly, in January 1946. The Charter provided for six rather autonomous principal organs of the United Nations. In one way or another, they all depended upon the General Assembly for decisions about their composition.

---

[83] Senate Committee on Foreign Relations, The Charter of the United Nations, 79th congress, 1st session, 10 July 1945, p. 311.

Within a few weeks of the opening session of the General Assembly, members of the Security Council, the Economic and Social Council, and the Trusteeship Council had been elected. Once the Security Council was operational, elections of the Secretary-General and the judges of the International Court of Justice took place. Even before these organizational issues were fully resolved, the General Assembly began dealing with matters of substance. It immediately became clear that human rights would play an important role in the work of the United Nations, arguably more important than the Charter itself suggested and that those at San Francisco had anticipated. Furthermore, racial discrimination would immediately rise to the top of the human rights agenda.

5

Early Years of the United Nations

The General Assembly's First Session

Few who were present at San Francisco in June 1945 could have anticipated that inter-State disputes about racial discrimination would confront the new organization from the earliest days of its existence. The first session of the United Nations General Assembly opened in London's Central Hall, only steps from Westminster Abbey and the Houses of Parliament, on 10 January 1946. Less than a week later, Haiti's delegate, Léon Laleau, took the floor in the plenary General Assembly to lament the 'sorry record' of world history characterized by 'dictatorial oppression and discrimination of race and creed, in which even room to breathe was begrudged the smaller nations as well as the so-called inferior races'. He said that even before the law, 'there was no assurance of equality', and spoke of a 'new statute of humanity' that replaced 'foolish discriminations of colour and creed'.[1]

A few days after these inspiring remarks, shameless racism reared its head. George Heaton Nicholls, who was then South Africa's High Commissioner in the United Kingdom and head of delegation, took the floor to boast about the 'civilising mission' of South Africa at a time when '[t]he whole continent was steeped in primordial savagery'.[2] A white South African, born in England, Nicholls claimed he was the 'spokesman for Africa' in the General Assembly.[3] Other African Member States, Ethiopia and Egypt, took the floor in the following days but neither challenged Nicholls's outrageous assertion. France and Belgium boasted of their benign administration of African peoples.[4]

In the Fourth Committee of the General Assembly, Nicholls put forward the provocative proposal that South West Africa, the former German colony, should be annexed to his country and not merely converted from a League of Nations mandate into a United Nations trust territory.[5] Nicholls was immediately taken to task by Liberia's Secretary of State, Gabriel L. Dennis, who questioned 'why the

[1] Verbatim record, plenary General Assembly, 16 January 1946, A/PV.10, pp. 158–60.
[2] Verbatim record, plenary General Assembly, 17 January 1946, A/PV.12, p. 181.
[3] Ibid., p. 182.
[4] Verbatim record, plenary General Assembly, 18 January 1946, A/PV.15, p. 238; Verbatim record, plenary General Assembly, 19 January 1946, A/PV.16, p. 251.
[5] Summary record, Fourth Committee, 22 January 1946, A/C.4/4.

The International Legal Order's Colour Line. William A. Schabas, Oxford University Press.
© Oxford University Press 2023. DOI: 10.1093/oso/9780197744475.003.0005

THE GENERAL ASSEMBLY'S FIRST SESSION   107

allegedly backward peoples of Africa had not been given fair opportunities for advancement', adding that it was imperative that States holding mandates recognize 'the principle that the interests of the indigenous populations were paramount'.[6] It was Dennis, not Nicholls, who was the genuine 'spokesman for Africa'.

Human rights was only a marginal issue during the London phase of the first session of the General Assembly, which concluded in mid-February 1946 and was essentially concerned with organizational and administrative matters. While in London, the Assembly adopted a resolution on the apprehension of suspected war criminals[7] and another on refugees.[8] Cuba failed in its attempt to modify the agenda so as to include debate on a proposed human rights declaration.[9] The Executive Committee of the Preparatory Commission, which had met late in 1945, had proposed the establishment of several Commissions including a Commission on Human Rights although this was not strictly necessary because it was already specified in article 68 of the Charter. The Preparatory Commission said the Commission on Human Rights would 'promote human rights' through 'studies and recommendations' that would 'eliminate discrimination and other abuses'.[10] That it might also actually address violations of human rights in Member States does not seem to have been contemplated.

The Economic and Social Council, which also held its first session in London, voted to set up a 'nuclear Commission on Human Rights' pending establishment of the Commission, which was to wait until January 1947 to begin its work.[11] The nuclear Commission was composed of nine members, two from Asia, one from South America, and six from Europe and North America. This reflected the membership of the United Nations but it was hardly representative of the world's peoples. The nuclear Commission met in New York in May 1946 and discussed the proposed international bill of rights although it stayed well clear of possible violations or specific circumstances where human rights might have been breached.[12] The NAACP leaders, Walter White and W.E.B. Du Bois, with the encouragement of Ralph Bunche, had thought they might intervene before

---

[6] Summary record, Fourth Committee, 23 January 1946, A/C.4/5.

[7] Extradition and punishment of war criminals, 13 February 1946, A/RES/3 (I).

[8] Question of refugees, 29 January 1946, A/RES/7 (I).

[9] Supplementary List of Items for Inclusion in the Agenda of the First Part of the First Session of the General Assembly, 5 January 1946, A/3; Verbatim record, plenary General Assembly, 14 January 1946, A/PV.7, pp. 103–8.

[10] Report of the Preparatory Commission of the United Nations, 23 December 1945, PC/20, para. 15; Report by the Executive Committee to the Preparatory Commission of the United Nations, 12 November 1945, PC/EX/113/Rev.1, pp. 7, 51.

[11] Commission on Human Rights and Sub-Commission on the Status of Women, 15 February 1946, E/20.

[12] Commission on Human Rights, Report, 17 May 1946, E/38; Summary record, Economic and Social Council, 28 May 1946, E/2nd sess./SR.4, pp. 27–9.

108 EARLY YEARS OF THE UNITED NATIONS

the 'nuclear' Commission on behalf of the unrepresented peoples of Africa, but there was in fact no opportunity for them to participate in the sessions.[13]

Histories of human rights in the United Nations often focus on the nuclear Commission's preparatory work on the International Bill of Rights, quickly jumping from its May 1946 meetings to the first session of the Commission on Human Rights at the beginning of the following year. Moreover, they tend to treat this phase of the human rights activities of the United Nations as one of 'standard-setting' focussed on drafting of the components of the International Bill of Rights. The dominant actors in that work were intellectuals from Europe and North America. But alongside that narrative of the growth of human rights within the United Nations is another dimension, one that is often neglected. During the 'Second Part' of the 1946 session of the General Assembly, held in New York from October to December, Member States from the Global South took the lead in the promotion of important human rights initiatives.

By the time the Assembly reconvened in October, States from the Global South that had behaved with caution at San Francisco were showing their eagerness to exploit the new opportunities provided by the General Assembly, where all Member States were viewed as equals. 'Never before in the history of diplomacy had any international body so openly and directly confronted the issue of race', Paul Gordon Lauren observed.[14] Assessing the achievements of this Second Part of the 1946 General Assembly session at the opening session of the Commission on Human Rights, in January 1947, Henri Laugier of the Secretariat invited delegates to 'witness the strongly worded resolution which proclaimed genocide to be an international crime; the resolution calling upon Member States to put an end to religious and racial persecution and discrimination; and the resolution dealing with the treatment of Indians in the Union of South Africa'.[15] Along similar lines, a document prepared by the Secretariat for the first session of the Commission on Human Rights highlighted the same three resolutions as those 'having a bearing on human rights'.[16] The initiators of all of these human rights resolutions were Member States from the Global South: India, Cuba, Panama, and Egypt. Moreover, all three of the human rights resolutions adopted in the New York phase of the Assembly's first session were focussed on issues relating to racial discrimination.

[13] Memorandum from W.E.B. Du Bois to Walter White, 28 March 1946, W.E.B. Du Bois Papers (MS 312); A Suggested statement to the UNO, 28 March 1946, W.E.B. Du Bois Papers (MS 312); Memorandum from Ralph Bunche to Walter White, ca. 16 May 1946, W.E.B. Du Bois Papers (MS 312).

[14] Paul Gordon Lauren, *Power and Prejudice: The Politics and Diplomacy of Racial Discrimination*, Boulder: Westview Press, 1996, p. 181.

[15] Summary record, Commission on Human Rights, 27 January 1947, E/CN.4/SR.1, p. 2.

[16] Working Paper on an International Bill of Rights, 13 January 1947, E/CN.4/W.4, p. 8.

THE GENERAL ASSEMBLY'S FIRST SESSION 109

Even before the General Assembly reconvened in New York, a painfully direct confrontation with racism awaited the United Nations. The Secretariat had arranged for the delegations to be lodged at the Waldorf-Astoria Hotel in mid-town Manhattan and in apartments owned by the Metropolitan Life Insurance Company. Secretary-General Trygve Lie was stunned when his office was informed that the delegations from Ethiopia, Liberia, and Haiti would not be welcome at these establishments because of their strict 'Jim Crow' policies. The representative of Met Life told the State Department that 'no persons of other than the white race, and few, if any, Jews would be admitted'.[17] The previous year, the United Nations Relief and Rehabilitation Administration had been accused of lodging its African American employees at the Hotel Theresa, in Harlem, while white employees stayed at the Hotel Victoria, a grand establishment in midtown.[18] The famous *Green Book*, which was a tourist guide for African Americans directing them to establishments where they would be welcome, did not even bother listing hotels in Manhattan south of 110th Street, which was the southern limit of Harlem.[19] When Josephine Baker returned from Europe to New York after the War, she and her husband were refused service at 36 New York hotels.[20] United Nations Secretary-General Lie intervened personally with the chairman of the board of the Waldorf Astoria, obtaining the hotel's agreement to accept the African delegations, but not the Haitians. The American delegation to the United Nations was also involved, both in solving the problem as best it could and in ensuring that the matter was not publicized.[21]

At the first session of the General Assembly, in London, the General Assembly adopted a host state agreement as the basis of negotiations with the United States regarding the seat of the organization. The draft provided that in the 'zone of protection' where the headquarters buildings would be located 'no form of racial discrimination shall be permitted'.[22] In an internal memorandum, American

[17] Carol Anderson, *Eyes Off the Prize, African Americans, the United Nations and the Struggle for Human Rights, 1944–1955*, New York: Cambridge, 2002, p. 106. Also David Freeland, *American Hotel, The Waldorf-Astoria and the Making of a Century*, New Brunswick, NJ: Rutgers University Press, 2021, p. 9.

[18] Caustin to Howell, 27 March 1945, UNA S-1304-0000-0213-00001; Bough to Lehmann, 17 March 1945, ibid.

[19] *The Negro Motorist Green Book*, 1948 edition, p. 46.

[20] Mary L. Dudziak, 'Josephine Baker, Racial Protest, and the Cold War' (1994) 81 *Journal of American History* 543, at p. 548.

[21] Thomas F. Power, Jr., Memorandum to Samuel Palma, 20 June 1947, Records of the Foreign Service Posts of the Department of State, Record Group 84, United States Mission to the United Nations, 1945–1949, box 78, National Archives II, College Park, Maryland, cited in Cary Fraser, 'Crossing the Color Line in Little Rock: The Eisenhower Administration and the Dilemma of Race for U.S. Foreign Policy' (2000) 24 *Diplomatic History* 233, at p. 235.

[22] Resolution relating to negotiations with the competent authorities of the United States of America concerning the arrangements required as a result of the establishment of the seat of the United Nations in the United States of America, and text of a draft convention to be transmitted as a basis of discussion for these negotiations, 13 February 1946, A/RES/22 B (I), section 16.

110   EARLY YEARS OF THE UNITED NATIONS

negotiators expressed concern with the section in question because 'it would, in effect, have given the United Nations a blank check to set aside constitutional provisions or the civil or criminal law of the United States'.[23] In the final version, the provision read: 'It is agreed that no form of racial or religious discrimination shall be permitted within the headquarters district.'[24] The headquarters district consisted of about 7 hectares of land in the Turtle Bay neighbourhood of eastern Manhattan. Outside this small zone, persons of colour participating in activities of the new international organization would continue to suffer racist abuses and humiliations in the restaurants, shops, and hotels of the great city. In 1961, when the number of African diplomats increased dramatically as a result of decolonization, the Department of State established a special protocol service with the mandate to deal with the racism encountered by diplomats of colour upon posting in Washington or New York.[25]

Confronting the Domestic Jurisdiction Clause

During the interval between the two phases of the first General Assembly session, India submitted a request to address the treatment in South Africa of workers of Indian descent. India had achieved a degree of international recognition in 1919 as a signatory of the Treaty of Versailles and a founding member of the League of Nations although in 1946 it was still not fully sovereign.[26] At the San Francisco Conference, as *The Hindu* newspaper put it, India had been 'a good little boy', avoiding anything that might offend Britain and the other powers, 'meek and content to stand and wait, because that, too, is service. She has lost an opportunity which will never come again.'[27] But new challenges soon presented themselves and India rose to the occasion. India was about to become one of the leading voices of the Global South in the international battle against racial discrimination. Nearly five decades later, in his maiden speech in the General

---

[23] United States Delegation Working Paper, February 1946, FRUS 1946 I, pp. 67–71, at p. 70.

[24] Agreement between the United Nations and the United States of America regarding the headquarters of the United Nations (1947) 11 UNTS 12, section 19.

[25] Renee Romano, 'No Diplomatic Immunity: African Diplomats, the State Department, and Civil Rights, 1961–1964' (2000) 87 *Journal of American History* 546; Thomas Borstelmann, *The Cold War and the Color Line: American Race Relations in the Global Arena*, Cambridge, MA: Harvard University Press, 2001, pp. 164–5; Michael Kress, 'African Diplomats in Washington', in Brenda Gayle Plummer, ed., *Window on Freedom: Race, Civil Rights, and Foreign Affairs, 1945–1988*, Chapel Hill and London: University of North Carolina Press, 2003, pp. 163–80.

[26] Amritha V. Shenoy, 'The Centenary of the League of Nations: Colonial India and the Making of International Law' (2018) 24 *Asian Yearbook of International Law* 4; T.A. Keenleyside, 'The Indian Nationalist Movement and the League of Nations: Prologue to the United Nations' (1983) 39 *India Quarterly* 281.

[27] *The Hindu*, 27 June 1945, cited in R.P. Anand, 'The Formation of International Organizations and India: A Historical Study' (2010) 23 *Leiden Journal of International Law* 5, at p. 21.

CONFRONTING THE DOMESTIC JURISDICTION CLAUSE 111

Assembly, Nelson Mandela acknowledged India's contribution in putting the question of racism in South Africa on the Assembly's agenda.[28]

During the second half of the nineteenth century and into the early years of the twentieth, indentured workers had been brought from India to South Africa to work on sugar plantations. From the beginning, they experienced appalling racism at the hands of European settlers. By 1946, they constituted about 280,000 people, not quite 3% of the total population of South Africa. That year, the Asiatic Land Tenure and Indian Representation Act was adopted, imposing various discriminatory measures and prohibiting the purchase of land by persons of Indian origin in certain areas. The Indians labelled it the 'Ghetto Act'. For decades, India had struggled against South Africa's policies within the British Empire institutions, but without much success given their endemic racism. India seized the opportunity created by the creation of the United Nations to bring the issue to a new forum.[29] In so doing, 'India inscribed racial discrimination onto the international agenda'.[30] Days after adoption of the South African legislation, by a letter dated 22 June 1946, the Government of India submitted the issue to the General Assembly.[31]

The South Africans, and their friends in London and Washington, were confident that the Indian application was inadmissible in light of the 'domestic jurisdiction' clause of the Charter. Article 2(7) reads: 'Nothing contained in the present Charter shall authorise the United Nations to intervene in matters which are essentially within the domestic jurisdiction of any state or shall require the Members to submit such matters to settlement under the present Charter.' The clause had not been part of the Dumbarton Oaks proposals. It emerged at the San Francisco Conference where it was meant to be a counterweight to the modest human rights language that was being included in the Charter. The National Association for the Advancement of Colored People had lodged a protest about the clause with the American delegation: 'This means that the international organisation cannot interfere in colonial affairs, and it may also make impossible

---

[28] Verbatim record, plenary General Assembly, 3 October 1994, A/49/PV.14, p. 7.

[29] See India's detailed submission to the General Assembly: Memorandum on the Position of Indians in the Union of South Africa, 26 August 1946, A/68 and Add.1 and 2; Ronald Hyam and Peter Henshaw, *The Lion and the Springbok: Britain and South Africa since the Boer War*, Cambridge: Cambridge University Press, 2003, pp. 146–67; Lorna Lloyd, '"A family quarrel": The Development of the Dispute over Indians in South Africa' (1991) 34 *Historical Journal* 703; Mark Mazower, *No Enchanted Palace: The End of Empire and the Ideological Origins of the United Nations*, Princeton, NJ: Princeton University Press, 2009, pp. 171–80.

[30] Lorna Lloyd, '"A Most Auspicious Beginning": The 1946 United Nations General Assembly and the Question of the Treatment of Indians in South Africa' (1990) 16 *Review of International Studies* 131, at p. 132.

[31] Mudaliar to Lie, 22 June 1946, A/149.

112   EARLY YEARS OF THE UNITED NATIONS

any attempt to safeguard the rights of groups in any nation; for instance, it could not combat the race and religious persecution of another Hitler.'[32]

The British and the Americans schemed to defeat the Indian proposal, aware of their own vulnerabilities on the issue of racial discrimination. An American Senator, Arthur Vandenberg, admitted he could not distinguish between the situation of 'Indians in South Africa and negroes in Alabama'.[33] The General Committee ignored South Africa's objection to the item being added on the agenda, although it could not agree upon the appropriate organ of the General Assembly for consideration of the issue. The First and Sixth Committees jointly addressed India's complaint over several sessions in November 1946. India contended that South Africa had not only breached agreements between the two States but that it had also violated the Charter's human rights provisions including the prohibition of racial discrimination. The two Committees adopted a resolution that concluded 'the treatment of Indians in the Union should be in conformity with the international obligations under the agreements concluded between the two Governments *and the relevant provisions of the Charter*'.[34]

In the plenary General Assembly, the debate continued over two days. India was represented by the dynamic Vijaya Lakshmi Pandit, the sister of India's prime minister, Jawaharlal Nehru. 'It is too late now to argue that fundamental violations of the principles of the Charter are matters of domestic jurisdiction of Member States', she told the Assembly. 'If this were the case, the Charter would be a dead letter, and our professions about a free world, free from inequalities of race, free from want and free from fear, an empty mockery.'[35] Jan Smuts himself spoke for South Africa, arguing that the Assembly should seek an opinion from the International Court of Justice as to 'whether the matters referred to in the Indian application are, under Article 2, paragraph 7 of the Charter, essentially within the domestic jurisdiction of the Union'.[36] What followed was the first real debate about the role of human rights in general, and the prohibition of racism in particular, within the legal framework of the United Nations. The resolution adopted in the Committees was confirmed by the General Assembly in a vote that required a two-thirds majority.[37] It achieved precisely that, with 32

---

[32] Telegram from NAACP to United States Delegation to the United Nations Conference on International Organization, 7 May 1945, W.E.B. Du Bois Papers (MS 312).

[33] Carol Anderson, 'From Hope to Disillusion: African Americans, the United Nations, and the Struggle for Human Rights, 1944–1947' (1996) 29 *Diplomatic History* 531, at pp. 550–3.

[34] Treatment of Indians in the Union of South Africa, Report of the Joint First and Sixth Committee, 2 December 1946, A/205 (emphasis added).

[35] Verbatim record, plenary General Assembly, 7 December 1946, A/PV.50, p. 1016.

[36] Amendment Submitted by the Delegation of the Union of South Africa, 5 December 1946, A/205/Add.1.

[37] Treatment of Indians in the Union of South Africa, 8 December 1946, A/RES/44 (I).

CONFRONTING THE DOMESTIC JURISDICTION CLAUSE   113

in favour, 15 opposed and 7 abstentions. Among the nays were the United States, the United Kingdom, Belgium, Canada, the Netherlands, and New Zealand.[38]

It was a stinging defeat for South Africa and its supporters. Two years later, South Africa would be denounced in the General Assembly for its failure to implement the resolution.[39] During the 1946 debates in the General Assembly, several delegates spoke of Smuts with great respect, politely overlooking his white supremacist views while honouring his contribution to the Charter. Much later, Smuts described the 'bitter experience' and lamented: 'Here is the author of the great preamble of the Charter exposed as a hypocrite and a double-faced time server!'[40] Thus, in its first session, the United Nations General Assembly deemed it unnecessary to obtain legal guidance from the International Court of Justice in order to treat racial discrimination as a matter of international concern, immune from the 'domestic jurisdiction' exception in article 2(7) of the Charter. Henri Laugier described it as 'a precedent of fundamental significance in the field of international action'.[41] Hersch Lauterpacht wrote that the General Assembly resolution was based on the view 'that questions relating to human rights and freedoms are matters which by reason of their solemnly proclaimed international character are not essentially within the domestic jurisdiction of States in the full sense of Article 2, paragraph 7'.[42]

For several years India, soon joined by Pakistan, persisted with resolutions on the South African policies, obtaining increasingly significant majorities. When the question returned to the General Assembly in 1952, only six Member States, the United States, the United Kingdom, Australia, France, Belgium, and Luxembourg, sided with South Africa.[43] Haiti's Dantès Bellegarde, who had denounced South African racism in the Assembly of the League of Nations three decades previously,[44] took the floor in the plenary General Assembly to condemn the South African measures as a violation of the Charter of the United Nations. He said that while this might appear to be a dispute between India, Pakistan, and South Africa, 'the question at issue is the equality of races'. Bellegarde said that South African racism was 'derived directly from the hitlerite theory of the inequality of human races'. Responding to the Western delegates who clung to

---

[38]   Verbatim record, plenary General Assembly, 8 December 1946, A/PV.52, p. 1061.

[39]   Summary record, Third Committee, 13 October 1948, A/C.3/SR.101, p. 136.

[40]   Smuts to Gillett, 14 January 1947, cited in Saul Dubow, 'Smuts, the United Nations and the Rhetoric of Race and Rights' (2008) 43 *Journal of Contemporary History* 43, at p. 66. See also Mark Mazower, *No Enchanted Palace: The End of Empire and the Ideological Origins of the United Nations*, Princeton, NJ: Princeton University Press, 2009, pp. 182–3.

[41]   Summary record, Commission on Human Rights, 27 January 1947, E/CN.4/SR.1, p. 2.

[42]   Hersch Lauterpacht, *International Law and Human Rights*, London: Stevens and Sons, 1950, pp. 194–5.

[43]   Verbatim record, plenary General Assembly, 5 December 1952, A/PV.401, para. 80.

[44]   Verbatim record of the 7th plenary meeting of the Third Assembly, 8 September 1922, LNA R1375/26/23218/23218, p. 13.

114 EARLY YEARS OF THE UNITED NATIONS

article 2(7) of the Charter in denying support to the resolution, Bellegarde said 'we are not interfering in the domestic affairs of the Union of South Africa when we affirm that a certain act passed by that State is at variance with the principles of the Charter and that it should be repealed if the Government of the Union of South Africa intends to remain faithful to the obligations it undertook by signing and ratifying the Charter'.[45]

A General Declaration on Racial Discrimination

The second significant development concerning racial discrimination during the first session of the General Assembly resulted from an Egyptian proposal entitled 'Persecution and Discrimination'. Its adoption actually preceded the Indian resolution on South Africa by a few weeks. Indeed, when the Indian resolution was adopted, Egypt hailed it as an opportunity to 'reaffirm our stand against discriminatory treatment'.[46] Egypt was one of the four African Member States. Egypt's resolution consisted of a single paragraph: 'The General Assembly declares that it is in the higher interests of humanity to put an immediate end to religious and so-called racial persecution and discrimination, and calls on the Governments and responsible authorities to conform both to the letter and to the spirit of the Charter of the United Nations, and to take the most prompt and energetic steps to that end.'[47] Egypt's original proposal included a lengthy preamble that spoke of persecution and discrimination in 'several States of Central Europe' directed at 'citizens belonging to religious minorities'.[48] No other specifics were provided. Egypt was referring to the attacks on Jews reported in 1946 that took place in Poland, Hungary, Slovakia, and Romania.[49] Egypt dropped the preamble but this was not enough of a compromise to satisfy members of the General Committee, who voted against adding the item to the agenda, by three to three, with three abstentions.[50]

Egypt did not relent, however, and raised the matter in the plenary General Assembly, explaining that the resolution had been prompted by information

---

[45] Verbatim record, plenary General Assembly, 12 January 1952, A/PV.360, paras. 22–30.

[46] Verbatim record, plenary General Assembly, 8 December 1946, A/PV.51, p. 1037.

[47] Persecution and Discrimination, 19 November 1946, A/RES/103 (I); Verbatim record, plenary General Assembly, 19 November 1946, A/PV.48, p. 975.

[48] Resolution on Persecution and Discrimination, Request from the Delegation of Egypt for the inclusion of an Additional Item in the Agenda, 2 November 1946, A/BUR/51.

[49] David Bankier, *The Jews Are Coming Back: The Return of the Jews to Their Countries of Origin after WWII*, Jerusalem: Yad Vashem and Berghahn Books, 2005; Péter Apor, Tamás Kende, Michala Lôncíková, and Valentin Săndulescu, 'Post-World War II anti-Semitic pogroms in East and East Central Europe: collective violence and popular culture' (2019) 26 *European Review of History: Revue européenne d'histoire* 913.

[50] Report of the General Committee to the General Assembly, 7 November 1946, A/181, para. 8.

about racial and religious persecution and discrimination 'inherited from the Nazi regime' that was 'still widespread after the suppression of that regime'.[51] Saudi Arabia promptly endorsed the Egyptian initiative, explaining that the General Assembly 'should declare that it is in the higher interests of humanity to put an immediate end to religious and so-called racial persecution and discrimination, and call on the Governments and responsible authorities to conform both to the letter and to the spirit of the Charter of the United Nations'.[52] Support also came from India and from Haiti, which said 'such a vital problem as the crying evil of racial discrimination should not be glossed over or shirked'.[53] Poland directly addressed the issues that had prompted the Egyptian proposal, explaining that although all Governments in that part of Europe opposed any form of discrimination or persecution, 'it is true that in Europe – not only in Central Europe – and maybe in other parts of the world' there were remnants of the racist ideology associated with fascism.[54]

Adopted unanimously, without a vote, it was obvious that the Egyptian resolution lacked teeth, as Carlos Rómulo of the Philippines stated in the General Assembly.[55] The Egyptian resolution is best viewed as a complement to the Charter of the United Nations, an explicit condemnation of racial discrimination that is at best only implied in the Charter itself. This was the clause that Wellington Koo of China initially contemplated and then withdrew at Dumbarton Oaks. It was the clause that Jan Smuts had neglected to include in his draft of the Charter's preamble at San Francisco. It is the clause that W.E.B. Du Bois and his NAACP colleagues tried to sell to the American delegation at San Francisco. Egypt's removal of the reference to violations in Central and Eastern Europe made the resolution more palatable but also more universal. Yet here was the General Assembly, in the first months of its existence, addressing a specific manifestation of racism. The enthusiasm of both Egypt and Saudi Arabia in denouncing anti-Semitism is striking.

The Egyptian resolution was invoked in late 1947 at the first session of the Sub-Commission on the Prevention and Discrimination and the Protection of Minorities. Alexander P. Borisov of the Soviet Union said that a year had passed and that nothing had been done to give effect to the General Assembly's call for effective measures to address racial discrimination.[56] The resolution was also an important reference as the General Assembly began to address apartheid in South Africa. It was invoked in both preambular and operative references where it was

---

[51] Verbatim record, plenary General Assembly, 9 November 1946, A/PV.47, p. 955.
[52] Ibid., p. 956.
[53] Ibid., p. 958.
[54] Ibid., p. 950.
[55] Ibid., p. 972.
[56] Draft resolution proposed by A.P. Borisov, 1 December 1947, E/CN.4/Sub.2/24.

116 EARLY YEARS OF THE UNITED NATIONS

directly associated with the Charter itself: 'Recalling that the General Assembly declared in its resolution 103 (I) of 19 November 1946 that it is in the higher interests of humanity to put an end to religious and so-called racial persecution, and called upon all governments to conform both to the letter and to the spirit of the Charter and to take the most prompt and energetic steps to that end.'[57] The resolution was cited by the Commission on the Racial Situation in South Africa in its 1953 report to the General Assembly.[58] The resolution that was adopted subsequently 'reaffirmed' the Egyptian resolution of 1946.[59] Member States referred to Resolution 103 (I) during debates in the Fourth Committee about racial discrimination in non-self-governing territories.[60] The General Assembly again invoked the Egyptian resolution in 1971,[61] perhaps inspired to do so when the director of human rights referred to it as well as to the Universal Declaration of Human Rights to demonstrate that condemnation of racial discrimination was 'well-established doctrine of the United Nations'.[62] Ethiopia and Liberia referred to Resolution 103 (I) in submissions to the International Court of Justice in the mid-1960s.[63] At one point, Israel went on record opposing such references 'because it was aware of the real intentions of the sponsors of General Assembly resolution 103 (I)', but without offering further explanation.[64]

[57] The question of race conflict in South Africa resulting from the policies of apartheid of the Government of the Union of South Africa, 5 December 1952, A/RES 616 (VII) A, PP 3 and OP 1. Also: Treatment of people of Indian origin in the Union of South Africa, 2 December 1950, A/RES/395 (V), PP 3; Treatment of people of Indian origin in the Union of South Africa, 12 January 1952, A/RES/511 (VI), PP 4; The question of race conflict in South Africa resulting from the policies of apartheid of the Government of the Union of South Africa, 5 December 1952, A/RES 616 (VII) B, PP 3; The question of race conflict in South Africa resulting from the policies of apartheid of the Government of the Union of South Africa, 14 December 1954, A/RES/820 (IX), PP 2.

[58] Report of the United Nations Commission on the Racial Situation in South Africa, 1953, A/2505, paras. 105, 904(d).

[59] The question of race conflict in South Africa resulting from the policies of apartheid of the Government of the Union of South Africa, 8 December 1953, A/RES/721 (VIII), OP 1. Also: The question of race conflict in South Africa resulting from the policies of apartheid of the Government of the Union of South Africa, 14 December 1954, A/RES/820 (IX), PP 2; The question of race conflict in South Africa resulting from the policies of apartheid of the Government of the Union of South Africa, 6 December 1955, A/RES/917 (X), PP 3.

[60] Summary record, Fourth Committee, 28 October 1960, A/C.4/SR.1027, para. 45 (Bulgaria); Summary record, Fourth Committee, 28 October 1960, A/C.4/SR.1028, paras. 33 (Philippines), 37 (Bulgaria), 39 (Mali), 43 (Bolivia); Summary record, Fourth Committee, 16 November 1961, A/C.4/SR.1212, para. 19.

[61] Establishment of Bantustans, 29 November 1971, A/RES/2775 (XXVI), PP 1.

[62] Summary record, Third Committee, 21 October 1971, A/C.3/SR.1845, para. 4.

[63] Reply of the Governments of Ethiopia and Liberia, in *South West Africa Cases (Ethiopia v. Union of South Africa; Liberia v. South Africa)*, 1966, Memorials, Pleadings, Documents, Vol. IV, pp. 220–616, at p. 502.

[64] Summary record, Ad Hoc Political Committee, 18 November 1952, A/AC.61/SR.19, para. 6.

Genocide or Crimes against Humanity?

The third initiative dealing with racial discrimination at the first session of the General Assembly was the adoption of the resolution on the crime of genocide. Genocide is 'the ultimate expression of racism',[65] a crime defined as the intentional destruction of a national, ethnic, racial or religious group. On 11 December 1946 the Assembly unanimously approved a resolution entitled 'The Crime of Genocide'. The resolution described genocide as a crime 'which the civilised world condemns' and specified that its punishment 'is a matter of international concern'.[66] The resolution was proposed by Cuba, Panama, and India,[67] and its most significant amendment, which called for the drafting of a convention, came from Saudi Arabia.[68] Once again, issues of racial discrimination were being pushed in the General Assembly by countries of the Global South. When the resolution was being debated, the Soviet delegate described it as being 'in conformity with the principles of the Charter', adding that 'the General Assembly was therefore justified in attaching great importance to racial discrimination, and had just unanimously adopted an Egyptian resolution concerning that matter'.[69] China also linked the genocide resolution to the Egyptian-sponsored resolution on racial discrimination that had been adopted by the General Assembly a few weeks previously.[70]

The resolution on the crime of genocide was one of two resolutions in the area of international criminal law that were adopted at the same time, on 11 December 1946. The other resolution, originating in a proposal by President Truman,[71] confirmed the principles of the Charter of the International Military Tribunal and of the judgment, which had been issued on 30 September and 1 October 1946. When the genocide resolution was presented to the General Assembly, the Cuban delegate, Ernesto Dihigo, described it as a reaction to a shortcoming of the Nuremberg judgment. 'At the Nürnberg trials, it had not been possible to punish certain cases of genocide because they had been committed before the beginning of the war', Dihigo told the Sixth Committee of the General Assembly.[72] In other

---

[65] Kevin Boyle and Anneliese Baldaccini, 'A Critical Evaluation of International Human Rights Approaches to Racism', in Sandra Fredman, ed., *Discrimination and Human Rights: The Case of Racism*, Oxford: Oxford University Press, 2001, pp. 135–92, at p. 139.

[66] The Crime of Genocide, 11 December 1946, A/RES/96 (I).

[67] Draft resolution relating to the crime of genocide, proposed by the delegations of Cuba, India and Panama, 2 November 1946, A/BUR/50.

[68] Draft protocol for the prevention and punishment of the crime of genocide, proposed by the delegation of Saudi Arabia, 26 November 1946, A/C.6/86.

[69] Summary record, Sixth Committee, 22 November 1946, A/C.6/SR.22, pp. 103–4.

[70] Summary record, Sixth Committee, 29 November 1946, A/C.6/SR.24, p. 117.

[71] 'Text of Biddle's Report on Nuremberg and Truman's Reply', *New York Times*, 13 November 1946; United States Delegation Working Paper, Proposal regarding draft resolution on codification of international law, FRUS 1946 I, pp. 539–41.

[72] Summary record, Sixth Committee, 22 November 1946, A/C.6/SR.22, p. 101.

118   EARLY YEARS OF THE UNITED NATIONS

words, the American-sponsored resolution sought to affirm the Nuremberg principles while the resolution of Cuba, India, and Panama was aimed at filling a gap that they had left.

Dihigo's reference was to the interpretation given in the judgment of the International Military Tribunal to the scope of crimes against humanity. Despite abundant evidence of Nazi atrocities perpetrated prior to September 1939 that were very broadly associated with policies of racial discrimination, the Tribunal declined to convict the defendants for any acts perpetrated prior to the outbreak of the war. Nazi anti-Semitism was discussed in some detail in the judgment of the International Military Tribunal. It referred to the 1935 Nuremberg laws and other discriminatory measures adopted in the years following the seizure of power. However, the judges rejected the prosecution's argument that anti-Semitism was in some way connected with preparations for aggressive war. 'The Nazi persecution of Jews in Germany before the war, severe and repressive as it was, cannot compare, however, with the policy pursued during the war in the occupied territories', they wrote. The judgment explains that '[o]riginally the policy was similar to that which had been in force inside Germany. Jews were required to register, were forced to live in ghettos, to wear the yellow star, and were used as slave labourers.' This changed in the summer of 1941, following the invasion of the Soviet Union, when the 'final solution' emerged. 'This "final solution" meant the extermination of the Jews, which early in 1939 Hitler had threatened would be one of the consequences of an outbreak of war', according to the judgment.[73] In other words, the anti-Semitic measures of the Nazi regime prior to September 1939 were 'mere racial discrimination' that was not punishable under international law.

In their failure to convict the Nazi defendants for pre-war racist atrocities, the judges did no more than rigorously apply the definition of crimes against humanity in the Charter of the Tribunal. It had been adopted at the London Conference of June–August 1945 by the four major powers, Britain, France, the United States, and the Soviet Union, as the legal framework for the great trial. The American negotiator at the Conference, Supreme Court Justice Robert Jackson, insisted on defining crimes against humanity in such a way as to encompass Nazi persecution but at the same time exclude allegations that the Allies, including his own government, were guilty of the same crimes. In an allusion to lynching of African Americans and to Jim Crow segregation, Jackson admitted that '[w]e have some regrettable circumstances at times in our own country in which minorities are unfairly treated'. He said there was no other basis under international law for dealing with atrocities committed against Germans,

---

[73] *France et al. v. Göring et al.*, Judgment, 30 September–1 October 1946 (1947) 1 IMT 171, at pp. 248–9.

GENOCIDE OR CRIMES AGAINST HUMANITY? 119

regardless of whether they were in accordance with or even contrary to German law, unless they could be linked to aggressive war.[74] Jackson's comment reflected the concerns of American policy makers who feared establishing a legal principle by which States could be held responsible under international for racist crimes committed within their own territory.[75] The four powers agreed that Nazi atrocities perpetrated against civilians were punishable as crimes against humanity only to the extent that they were linked to the waging of a war of aggression. With no small measure of cynicism, this enabled them to condemn their enemies while at the same time sheltering themselves from liability under international criminal law for their own abuses directed against racial and ethnic minorities as well as colonized peoples. 'What Irony!' headlined the *Pittsburgh Courier*, an African American newspaper. 'U.S. Signs Agreement [under which] "Racial Persecutions" [are] a Crime Against International Society.'[76]

During the post-war trials at Nuremberg, German defence lawyers occasionally reminded American judges of the parallels between Nazi racism and the treatment of African Americans. In the *Ministries case*, counsel for Wilhelm Stuckart, a government bureaucrat, challenged the prosecution theory that those involved in restrictive measures against Jews were instigators of 'the horrors committed during the war by a handful of maniacs'. 'How could the members of a legislative body in one of the United States of America, who voted (unconstitutionally perhaps) for segregation and similar measures against coloured people in their state, be held responsible on these grounds for the lynching of a Negro which occurred later!', he said.[77] In the *RuSHA case*, SS official Otto Hofmann noted that states in the United States had legislation forbidding mixed-race marriage, which was punishable as a crime.[78] Hofmann submitted a German document dated 1937 with the heading 'Race Protection Laws of Other Countries' that had several examples drawn from American legislation.[79] There is also a subtle allusion to racial discrimination in the celebrated Stanley Kramer film

---

[74] Minutes of Conference Session, 23 July 1945, in *Report of Robert H. Jackson, United States Representative to the International Conference on Military Trials*, Washington: U.S. Government Printing Office, 1949, pp. 328–47, at p. 333.

[75] Guillaume Mouralis, *Le moment Nuremberg, Le procès international, les lawyers et la question raciale*, Paris: SciencesPo, 2019, pp. 114–20.

[76] *Pittsburgh Courier*, 29 September 1945, p. 1, cited in Guillaume Mouralis, 'Legal Imagination and Legal Realism, "Crimes against Humanity" and the US Racial Question in 1945', in Ornella Rovetta and Pieter Lagrou, ed., *Defeating Impunity: Attempts at International Justice in Europe since 1914*, New York: Berghahn, 2022, pp. 109–32, at p. 123.

[77] *United States of America v. Ernst von Weizsaecker et al.*, Extracts from Closing Statement for Defendant Stuckart, 17 November 1948 (1949) 14 TWC 226, at p. 242.

[78] *United States of America v. Griefeldt et al.*, Extract from the Closing Statement for Defendant Hofmann, 17 February 1948 (1949) 4 TWC 1156, at p. 1157.

[79] 'Extract from "Information Service of the Racial-Political Office of the NSDAP Reich Administration", 30 July 1937, concerning race protection laws of other countries' (1949) 4 TWC 1158–60.

120 EARLY YEARS OF THE UNITED NATIONS

Judgment at Nuremberg, released in 1961. The lead prosecutor, played by Richard Widmark, refers to the hanging of children in Buchenwald concentration camp. As he pronounces the word 'hanging', the camera lingers for several seconds on an American soldier standing guard in the courtroom. He is the only Black actor in the film.[80]

Raphaël Lemkin, who had first proposed the term 'genocide' in his 1944 book *Axis Rule in Occupied Europe*, was enraged by what he described as the refusal of the International Military Tribunal to acknowledge 'peacetime genocide'. Lemkin had been present at Nuremberg when the judgment was issued on 30 September and 1 October 1946. He was reported to have described the issuance of the judgment as 'the blackest day' of his life.[81] According to one of the American prosecutors, Henry King, who encountered Lemkin in the lobby of Nuremberg's Grand Hotel immediately after the judgment was issued:

> . . . he was unshaven, his clothing was in tatters. Lemkin was very upset. He was concerned that the decision of the International Military Tribunal (IMT) - the Nuremberg Court - did not go far enough in dealing with genocidal actions. This was because the IMT limited its judgment to wartime genocide and did not include peacetime genocide. At that time, Lemkin was very focussed on pushing his points.[82]

In the weeks that followed, Lemkin returned to New York City where he campaigned in the corridors of the General Assembly, convincing the Cuban Dihigo, and delegates from Panama and India, to sponsor a resolution condemning genocide as an international crime even when committed in time of peace.[83]

At first blush, the two 1946 resolutions on international criminal justice seem closely related, as if they are siblings, two peas in a pod. But Lemkin's temper tantrum in the Grand Hotel and Dihigo's speech in the Sixth Committee suggest that the two General Assembly resolutions adopted in December 1946 do not really complement one another. Resolution 95 (I) summarily endorses and confirms a vision of crimes against humanity involving persecution of racial and ethnic minorities that was bespoke, a perfect fit for the Nazis but at the same time the wrong size for the acts of the major powers. Not surprisingly, that resolution bears the fingerprints of the United States and was supported by its

---

[80] Guillaume Mouralis, *Le moment Nuremberg, Le procès international, les lawyers et la question raciale*, Paris: SciencesPo, 2019, p. 192. This is at the 108th minute in the film.

[81] William Korey, *An Epitaph for Raphael Lemkin*, New York: Jacob Blaustein Institute, 2001, p. 25.

[82] Henry T. King Jr, 'Origins of the Genocide Convention' (2008) 40 *Case Western Reserve Journal of International Law* 13, at p. 13.

[83] John Cooper, *Raphael Lemkin and the Struggle for the Genocide Convention*, Basingstoke, Palgrave Macmillan, 2008, pp. 78–87.

allies. Raphael Lemkin speculated that Resolution 95 (I) pursued an agenda that could be traced to the Romanian jurist Vespasian Pella. He called it the 'Pella-Vishinsky project', alluding to the Soviet official.[84] Resolution 96 (I), on the other hand, contemplates a crime under international law that involves attacks upon and destruction of racial and ethnic minorities but one that may be committed in peacetime as well as in time of war. It was proposed and supported by countries of the Global South who had no involvement in preparation of the legal framework for the post-Second World War international military tribunals.

The apparent friction between the two resolutions adopted by the General Assembly was addressed the following year in a memorandum by France, submitted in May 1947. The Secretariat was then in the midst of preparing the draft genocide convention in accordance with a mandate given by the Economic and Social Council. France referred to the two resolutions adopted the previous December by the General Assembly, noting that the General Assembly 'appears to desire to introduce important innovations' to the Charter of the International Military Tribunal and the judgment of the International Military Tribunal. 'Not only is the hitherto admitted expression "crime against humanity" replaced by a neologism, the term genocide, but the conception of the infringement is broadened', said France. It explained that the definition in article 6(c) of the Charter of the Tribunal provided a 'restrictive enumeration of acts constituting crimes against humanity'.[85]

Over the next several years, the International Law Commission debated whether to amend the definition of crimes against humanity in order to fill the enormous gap left by the Nuremberg trial. Nevertheless, in its codification of the Nuremberg principles, the Commission took the view that crimes against humanity must be in execution of or in connexion with any crime against peace or any war crime'.[86] In 1954, the Commission replaced the war nexus with a State policy requirement, specifying that crimes against humanity be perpetrated 'by the authorities of a State or by private individuals acting at the instigation or with the toleration of such authorities'.[87] Controversy persisted when the Commission returned to the issue of limitations upon crimes against humanity in the 1980s. In the meantime, countries of the Global South took up the campaign to broaden the scope of crimes against humanity so as to deal with racial discrimination in peacetime.[88]

---

[84] Untitled and undated document (c. 1951) in Lemkin archives, New York Public Library file 3, frames 307–12.

[85] Memorandum on the subject of genocide and crimes against humanity submitted by the representative of France, 19 May 1947, A/AC.10/29.

[86] Report of the International Law Commission covering its second session, 5 June–29 July 1950, A/1316, para. 119.

[87] Report of the International Law Commission covering the work of its sixth session, 3 June–28 July 1954, A/2693, para. 150.

[88] See *infra*, pp. 314–325.

122   EARLY YEARS OF THE UNITED NATIONS

Petitioning the United Nations

While Member States were struggling with the extent to which the Charter of the United Nations allowed the organization to intervene in human rights violations of its Member States, individuals and organizations around the world began submitting petitions expressing grievances with their own governments. Most of them were inspired by phrases in the Charter and the inspiring promises of world leaders that the war would be followed by a new world order. The Charter of the United Nations made no allowance for individuals to participate in the organization's work, other than authorizing the Economic and Social Council to 'make suitable arrangements for consultation with non-governmental organisations which are concerned with matters within its competence'.[89] But nor did the Charter explicitly exclude individuals from seeking justice from the organization. To many who suffered from persecution by their own governments, including those in colonies, appealing for help to an organization whose Charter pledged 'promoting and encouraging respect for human rights and for fundamental freedoms for all' seemed only logical.

Possibly the very first human rights petition to the United Nations was submitted in June 1946 by the National Negro Congress, an African American organization aligned with the Communist Party of the United States and associated with such personalities as Paul Robeson and William Paterson. The 16-page document briefly set out a claim that the Economic and Social Council had jurisdiction, citing relevant provisions of the Charter and documents generated at the first session of the Council in February 1946. This was followed by a factual portion authored by Marxist historian Herbert Aptheker. The covering letter to the Secretary-General of the United Nations, signed by Max Yergan, said the petition was submitted with 'profound regret', and that after seeking 'for almost a century since emancipation to solve [this vital issue] within the boundary of our country' the applicants considered themselves compelled to address 'this historic body'.[90] The petition received publicity around the world as well as support from a range of organizations in different countries, to the consternation of officials in the Department of State.[91] The National Negro Congress reported that it had been invited by United Nations officials to submit more evidence. It undertook

[89]   Charter of the United Nations, art. 71.
[90]   National Negro Congress, *A Petition to the United Nations on Behalf of 13 Million Oppressed Negro Citizens of the United States of America*, New York, 1946; Charles H. Martin, 'Internationalizing "The American Dilemma": The Civil Rights Congress and the 1951 Genocide Petition to the United Nations' (1997) 16(4) *Journal of American Ethnic History* 35, at p. 37; Charles P. Henry and Tunua Thrash, 'U.S. Human Rights Petitions Before the UN' (1996) 26 *The Black Scholar* 60, at pp. 62–3.
[91]   Carol Anderson, *Eyes Off the Prize, African Americans, the United Nations and the Struggle for Human Rights, 1944–1955*, New York: Cambridge, 2002, pp. 81–2; Carol Anderson, 'From Hope to Disillusion: African Americans, the United Nations, and the Struggle for Human Rights, 1944–1947' (1996) 29 *Diplomatic History* 531, at pp. 545–6.

PETITIONING THE UNITED NATIONS   123

a variety of campaigns in order to augment the June 1946 submission.[92] John Humphrey, head of the United Nations Division of Human Rights, sent polite notes of acknowledgement to those who wrote to support the petition.[93]

Leaders of the National Association for the Advancement of Colored People (NAACP), which was politically less radical, were impressed with the effectiveness of the National Negro Congress petition and made plans for their own submission. In August 1946, W.E.B. Du Bois began work preparing a substantial submission to the United Nations on behalf of the NAACP. The project took many months to complete. Du Bois campaigned successfully for support from African American organizations, the media, trade unions, and prominent personalities.[94] He met with Secretary-General Trygve Lie informing him of the organization's plans for a petition.[95] A version of the submission was sent to the United Nations in January 1947. Arthur Springarn signed the covering letter on behalf of the NAACP, addressing it to John Humphrey. The NAACP archives record its director attending the first meeting of the Commission on Human Rights, 'escorted by Dr. Ralph Bunche', although there is nothing in the official documents confirming this, perhaps because the organization had not obtained formal observer status. The NAACP archives also say that Humphrey 'promised to have the petition entered on the list of petitions received, if possible'. In February, after the Commission's session had concluded, Humphrey wrote to Springarn acknowledging receipt of the petition and expressing regrets that the Commission was powerless to take action regarding any complaints concerning human rights. He promised to 'bring your communication to the attention of the Commission at its next session'.[96]

A more complete and polished text was published by the NAACP in October 1947: *An Appeal to the World: A Statement on the Denial of Human Rights to Minorities in the Case of Citizens of the United States of America and an Appeal to the United Nations for Redress*. Authored by several prominent academics, including Du Bois, it provided detailed information about lynching and racial segregation, and about inequality with respect to education, housing, health care, and voting rights. Du Bois hoped to make a formal presentation of the report to the United Nations. He sought the assistance of Eleanor Roosevelt, who was the Chairman of the Commission on Human Rights, but she only referred him to the Secretary-General.[97] Du Bois complained about her 'vague and meagre

---

[92] Carol Anderson, *Eyes Off the Prize, African Americans, the United Nations and the Struggle for Human Rights, 1944–1955*, New York: Cambridge, 2002, pp. 88–92.
[93] Humphrey to Guinier, 9 July 1946, UNA S-0472-0070-0004-00001 UC.
[94] Gerald Horne, *Black and Red, W.E.B. Du Bois and the Afro-American Response to the Cold War, 1944–1963*, Albany: State University of New York Press, 1986, pp. 76–7.
[95] Chronology of NAACP petition to United Nations, 1948, W.E.B. Du Bois Papers (MS 312).
[96] Humphrey to Arthur, 19 February 1947, W.E.B. Du Bois Papers (MS 312).
[97] Roosevelt to Du Bois, 22 July 1946, W.E.B. Du Bois Papers (MS 312).

124　EARLY YEARS OF THE UNITED NATIONS

advice'. He said that Roosevelt was 'following orders' from a Department of State that was 'determined that American Negroes shall have no chance to state their grievances before the world'.[98]

On 9 October 1947, John Humphrey, the Secretary of the Commission on Human Rights, replied to a letter from Du Bois explaining that 'there does not exist at present any machinery which would enable the Secretariat to place the petition before either the General Assembly or the Economic and Social Council', unless a Member State were to take the initiative. Humphrey described the 'confidential procedure' for the handling of complaints about human rights that had been adopted by the Economic and Social Council two months earlier.[99] In August 1947, the Economic and Social Council had authorized the Commission on Human Rights to consider 'complaints concerning human rights'. In his memoirs, Humphrey dismissed the mechanism as an 'elaborate wastepaper basket'.[100] According to the Council's decision, the United Nations Secretariat was to provide the Commission with a confidential list of 'communications' received that could then be examined in 'private meeting'. Those submitting communications were to receive some acknowledgement they had been received along with, 'where necessary', an indication 'that the Commission has no power to take any action in regard to any complaint concerning human rights'.[101] Humphrey acknowledged petitions with a brief note explaining that the Commission 'has at present no power to take action on any complaint regarding human rights' but that the communication would be brought to the attention of the Commission at its next session'.[102] The United Nations archives also contain a file of postcards sent to the Organization referring to the Du Bois petition and protesting '[t]he illegal denial of the right to vote to minorities in this country'.[103]

Du Bois wrote again to Humphrey, but also to the Special Advisor to the Secretary-General, protesting the confidentiality and asking for an opportunity to present the petition publicly.[104] On 23 October 1947, Du Bois and Walter White formally delivered the petition to Henri Laugier and John Humphrey at United Nations headquarters, located then at Lake Success on Long Island, about 30 kilometres from Manhattan. The two petitioners explained that their submission was 'open and articulate, and not designed for confidential concealment in your archives', and that is was 'a frank and earnest appeal to all the world for

---

[98] Notes on human rights petition, 24 November 1947, W.E.B. Du Bois Papers (MS 312).

[99] Humphrey to Du Bois, 9 October 1947, W.E.B. Du Bois Papers (MS 312).

[100] John P. Humphrey, *Human Rights and the United Nations: A Great Adventure*, Ardsley, NY: Transnational Publishers, 1984, p. 28.

[101] Communications concerning human rights, 5 August 1947, E/RES/75 (V).

[102] See, for example, various letters in Human Rights Division, violations and complaints, UNA S-1472-0071-0002-00002.

[103] Human Rights Division, violations and complaints, UNA S-1472-0071-0003-00001.

[104] Du Bois to Stoneman, 16 October 1947, W.E.B. Du Bois Papers (MS 312); Du Bois to Humphrey, 16 October 1947, W.E.B. Du Bois Papers (MS 312).

elemental justice against the treatment which the United States has visited upon us for three centuries – we, who are an integral part of this land and ever as loyal as any other group of its citizens'.[105] Humphrey again acknowledged that he was without authority to take action on the complaint but suggested it could assist in drafting the international bill of rights. The presentation of the NAACP petition to the United Nations was reported in the *New York Times*.[106]

The NAACP petition provoked an intense debate at the first session of the Sub-Commission on the Prevention of Discrimination and the Protection of Minorities, one of three such subsidiary bodies of the Commission on Human Rights. The initial composition of the Sub-Commission on the Prevention of Discrimination and the Protection of Minorities consisted of experts from Australia, Belgium, China, Ecuador, France, Haiti, India, Iran, Sweden, Soviet Union, the United Kingdom, and the United States. A proposal from the American representative, Jonathan Daniels, to delegate the examination of petitions concerning discrimination to small committees was immediately attacked by Alexander Borisov of the Soviet Union who insisted upon examination of such communications by the plenary Sub-Commission. Borisov accused Daniels of attempting to 'bury the petitions made by National groups, such as the 15 million Negroes in the United States'.[107] Borisov said the NAACP petition 'had been left aside for two years without being discussed'.[108] He wanted the Sub-Commission to consider the petition.[109] In a rather feeble reply, Daniels 'admitted the existence of discrimination in the United States of America as well as in practically every other country'.[110] He said that he was aware of the problem of the Negroes in the United States of America, and that the President had himself authorized a comprehensive investigation of this problem.[111] Daniels was a journalist from North Carolina, one of the southern states, who had worked in the administrations of Presidents Roosevelt and Truman. He was not always so apologetic about racism in the United States. At a session of the Sub-Commission in 1951 he boasted about how 'a well-known Negro journalist had written recently

---

[105] The American Negro before the United Nations [fragment], December 1947, W.E.B. Du Bois Papers (MS 312).

[106] George Streator, 'Negroes to Bring Cause Before UN; Statement Charges that South Offers Greater US Threat than Soviet Activities', *New York Times*, 12 October 1947, o, 52.

[107] Summary record, Sub-Commission on Prevention of Discrimination and Protection of Minorities, 2 December 1947, E/CN.4/Sub.2/SR.12, p. 5.

[108] Ibid., p. 9.

[109] Summary record, Sub-Commission on Prevention of Discrimination and Protection of Minorities, 2 December 1947, E/CN.4/Sub.2/SR.13, p. 3.

[110] Summary record, Sub-Commission on Prevention of Discrimination and Protection of Minorities, 2 December 1947, E/CN.4/Sub.2/SR.12, p. 6; Summary record, Sub-Commission on Prevention of Discrimination and Protection of Minorities, Tuesday, 2 December 1947, E/CN.4/Sub.2/SR.13, p. 2.

[111] Summary record, Sub-Commission on Prevention of Discrimination and Protection of Minorities, 2 December 1947, E/CN.4/Sub.2/SR.13, p. 7.

126 EARLY YEARS OF THE UNITED NATIONS

that the Negroes were proud of their progress, which was certainly greater than that of any other population group'.[112]

A draft resolution calling on the Economic and Social Council to consider the NAACP petition was defeated by five votes to one, with five abstentions.[113] Then the Sub-Commission turned to Borisov's proposal 'to consider at its meetings the petition presented to the United Nations twice since 1946 by 15 million Negroes residing in the United States of America who are subjected to discrimination on racial grounds' as well as the establishment of a commission to study 'on the spot the facts of discrimination to which a native population is subjected in colonies on the groups of race, sex, language or religion'.[114] It was defeated by four votes to one, with seven abstentions. Several of the abstainers explained they thought it wrong 'to emphasise a petition from one particular group of coloured people'.[115] The draft report prepared by the Sub-Commission included the sub-heading 'Communications from the National Association for the Advancement of Coloured People',[116] but the Rapporteur told the Sub-Commission that this had been included by mistake.[117] The entire section was deleted in the final report submitted to the Commission on Human Rights.[118] The Commission held its second session immediately after the Sub-Commission had concluded its meetings. In December 1947, the Commission held two closed sessions in which it briefly considered a list of human rights communications, presumably including the NAACP petition. The records make isolated reference to certain situations, in Spain and Yugoslavia for example, but contain nothing precise about the conditions of African Americans in the United States.[119]

Evidence of petitions to the United Nations has also emerged from domestic archives where they became public following normal embargo periods. For example, the Canadian archives contain a petition submitted to the United Nations alleging that a traveller was informed by a hotel in Quebec that the clientele was restricted to Christians only.[120] There is also a complaint that the African American singer Paul Robeson had been prevented from leaving the United

[112] Summary record, Sub-Commission on Prevention of Discrimination and Protection of Minorities, 5 October 1951, E/CN.4/Sub.2/SR.71, p. 5.

[113] Summary record, Sub-Commission on Prevention of Discrimination and Protection of Minorities, 3 December 1947, E/CN.4/Sub.2/SR.14, p. 6.

[114] Draft resolution proposed by A.P. Borisov, 1 December 1947, E/CN.4/Sub.2/24.

[115] Ibid., p. 7.

[116] Report Submitted to the Commission on Human Rights (Draft), E/CN.4/Sub.2/38 (Continuation), 5 December 1947, pp. 1–2.

[117] Summary, Sub-Commission on Prevention of Discrimination and Protection of Minorities, 5 December 1947, E/CN.4/Sub.2/SR.18, p. 2.

[118] Report submitted to the Commission on Human Rights, 6 December 1947, E/CN.4/52.

[119] Summary record, Commission on Human Rights, 2 December 1947, E/CN.4/SR.24; Summary record, Commission on Human Rights, 3 December 1947, E/CN.4/26.

[120] 'Communication from Individuals', 'From United States of America. Letter dated 8 June 1949 addressed to the Director of the Division on Human Rights', NAC RG 25, Vol. 3690, 5475-W-4-40.

'WE CHARGE GENOCIDE'   127

States and coming to Canada, noting that this violated articles 13(2) and 19 of the Universal Declaration of Human Rights. A note from a Canadian official in the file says: 'I don't think we should reply. Perhaps [Royal Canadian Mounted Police] would like a copy of her letter.'[121] In October 1948, a non-governmental organization representing Canadians of Japanese descent petitioned the United Nations arguing that the deprivation of various fundamental rights imposed during the war and continued after it was over constituted racial discrimination.[122] Canadian officials sought guidance from Washington about how to respond. They were told that the policy of the United States was to ignore human rights petitions to the United Nations.[123]

W.E.B. Du Bois persisted in his efforts to advance the anti-racist cause within the human rights bodies of the United Nations. In 1949, he advised the National Committee to Free the Ingram Family on submitting a petition to United Nations in a case concerning an African American woman and two of her sons who were sentenced to death for resisting sexual assault by a white farmer.[124] In a letter to the Third Committee of the General Assembly dated 10 October 1957, he recalled the initiatives of 1947. 'This is not the first time that American Negroes have appealed to the United Nations for a hearing', he wrote, evoking the 'Appeal to the World!' submitted a decade earlier. 'We presented this to the Human Rights Commission which at first refused to receive it; then the Commission received it but refused to discuss it; then discussed it briefly, but refused to present it to the Assembly.'[125]

'We Charge Genocide'

It is often said that the Genocide Convention was a reaction to the racist ideology of the Nazi regime. Germany was responsible for the attempted extermination of an entire human group, described variously with the adjectives 'religious', 'ethnic' and, at the time of the Convention's adoption, 'racial'. Earlier in the century, German colonizers in South West Africa had tried to wipe out the Herero of Namibia. That example is cited as the first genocide of the twentieth

---

[121] 'Letter from Jean Carlson, Lake Cowichan Peace Council, Feb 6, 1952 to External Affairs Department', NAC RG 25, Vol. 3690, 5475-W-4-40.

[122] Memorandum for American and Far Eastern Division, concerning 'Complaints forwarded to Human Rights Commission by Residents of Canada', NAC RG 25, Vol. 3690, 5475-W-4-40, Part 1.

[123] Letter of G.L. Magann, 19 February 1949, NAC RG 25, Vol. 3690, 5475-W-4-40, Part 1.

[124] Letter from W. E. B. Du Bois to National Committee to Free the Ingram Family, 15 April 1949, W.E.B. Du Bois Papers (MS 312); Memorandum from W. E. B. Du Bois to National Committee to Free the Ingram Family, 10 June 1949, W.E.B. Du Bois Papers (MS 312).

[125] Letter from W. E. B. Du Bois to the Membership of the Third Committee, United National General Assembly, 10 October 1957, James Aronson-W.E.B. Du Bois Collection (MS 292).

128 EARLY YEARS OF THE UNITED NATIONS

century.[126] Nazi persecution of Jews in Germany and in the territories it occupied throughout Europe was the most acute manifestation of a phenomenon present in many countries of the world. It is just as plausible to maintain that the Genocide Convention was a reaction to forms of racial discrimination that were characterized by the ravages of colonialism and its predecessor, the African slave trade. This was the culture from which the Nazi ideology of racial superiority emerged.

Demonstrating the rationale underpinning an international instrument like the Genocide Convention is not a straightforward matter. More than 50 countries participated in the drafting of the text. In agreeing to the Convention, their views, which varied considerably, cannot be reduced to a simple formulation. Nevertheless, certain indications emerge from the language of the Convention. Article 2 defines genocide as one of five punishable acts 'committed with intent to destroy, in whole or in part, a national, ethnical, racial or religious group, as such'.[127] The 1946 General Assembly resolution gave a slightly larger scope to genocide, applying it to 'racial, religious, political and other groups'.[128] The broader language of the 1946 resolution was consistent with the approach taken by the International Military Tribunal, which prosecuted persecution as a crime against humanity 'on political, racial or religious grounds'.[129] The original draft of the resolution, apparently authored by Raphael Lemkin, referred to 'national, racial, ethnical or religious groups'.[130] The reference to political groups was added during the negotiations in the Sixth Committee but the records do not provide any indication of the source of the amendment.

The narrowing of the focus in the Convention by the removal of reference to political groups indicates an intent to address crimes rooted in racial discrimination. When the Convention was being drafted, a few delegations argued that political groups should be dropped because they were not 'permanent and stable', as opposed to national, ethnic, racial, and religious groups.[131] These were isolated statements, however. Uruguay, which proposed the deletion of political groups,[132] said that 'the concept of genocide was, indeed, the outcome of the Nazi

[126] Report of the Working Group of Experts on People of African Descent on its mission to Germany, 15 August 2017, A/HRC/36/60/Add.2, para. 7.
[127] Convention on the Prevention and Punishment of the Crime of Genocide (1951) 78 UNTS 277, art. 2.
[128] The Crime of Genocide, 11 December 1946, A/RES/96 (I), PP 2.
[129] Agreement for the Prosecution and Punishment of Major War Criminals of the European Axis, and Establishing the Charter of the International Military Tribunal (IMT), annex (1951) 82 UNTS 279, art. VI(c).
[130] Draft resolution relating to the crime of genocide, proposed by the delegations of Cuba, India and Panama, 2 November 1946, A/BUR/50, PP 1.
[131] Summary record, Economic and Social Council, 26 August 1948, E/SR.218 (Perez Perozo, Venezuela), p. 705; Summary record, Sixth Committee, 4 October 1948, A/C.6/SR.66 (Abdoh, Iran), p. 31; Summary record, Sixth Committee, 7 October 1948, A/C.6/SR.69 (Amado, Brazil), p. 57.
[132] Uruguay: amendments to the draft convention on genocide (E/794), 1 October 1948, A/C.6/209.

theories of race superiority which were at the basis of the Hitlerian ideology. If the scope of the convention were to be extended, some word other than "genocide" would have to be found.'[133] Iran also submitted an amendment to omit reference to political groups.[134] Its delegate distinguished racial groups from political groups, explaining that 'the destruction of the first type appeared most heinous in the light of the conscience of humanity'.[135] Although a Trial Chamber of the International Criminal Tribunal for Rwanda cited the *travaux préparatoires* as authority, and endorsed the thesis that political groups were excluded because they were not 'stable and permanent',[136] a more careful reading of the materials suggests something different.

Adopted by the General Assembly in 1948, the Genocide Convention confirmed, in article I, that the crime could be committed in time of peace as well as in wartime. This was its great improvement on the law of the Nuremberg Tribunal whereby crimes against humanity were saddled with the war nexus. President Truman signed the Genocide Convention two days after its adoption, confident that the definition of the crime was too narrow to be applicable to racial discrimination in the United States. Nevertheless, convincing truculent senators to authorize ratification was to take another 40 years. African Americans almost immediately understood that the adoption of the Genocide Convention offered a new angle for their campaigns against racial discrimination.

Of all of the initiatives taken by African American organizations in these early years of the United Nations, *We Charge Genocide* probably had the greatest impact and attracted the most international attention.[137] Eleanor Roosevelt told President Truman that the petition had 'hurt [the United States] in so many little ways'.[138] It has been described as 'the most damning human rights report on Jim Crow written during the Cold War'.[139] The petition emanated from the Civil Rights Congress, a body closely aligned with the American Communist Party

---

[133] Summary record, Sixth Committee, 14 October 1948, A/C.6/SR.74, p. 106.

[134] Iran: amendments to the draft convention on genocide (E/794) and draft resolution, 5 October 1948, A/C.6/218.

[135] Summary record, Sixth Committee, 14 October 1948, A/C.6/SR.74, p. 99.

[136] *Prosecutor v. Akayesu* (ICTR-96-4-T), Judgment, 2 September 1998, para. 515. Also *Prosecutor v. Rutaganda* (ICTR-96-3-T), Judgment and Sentence, 6 December 1999, para. 57; *Prosecutor v. Musema* (ICTR-96-13-T), Judgment and Sentence, 27 January 2000, para. 162.

[137] Gerald Horne, *Communist Front? The Civil Rights Congress, 1946–1956*, Rutherford, NJ: Fairleigh Dickinson University Press, 1988, p. 167; Carol Anderson, 'Bleached Souls and Red Negroes, The NAACP and Black Communists in the Early Cold War, 1948–1952', in Brenda Gayle Plummer, ed., *Window on Freedom: Race, Civil Rights, and Foreign Affairs, 1945–1988*, Chapel Hill and London: University of North Carolina Press, 2003, pp. 93–113, at pp. 95–100.

[138] Eleanor Roosevelt to Truman [fragment], 29 December 1951, cited in Carol Anderson, *Eyes Off the Prize, African-Americans, the United Nations and the Struggle for Human Rights, 1944–1955*, New York: Cambridge, 2002, p. 200, fn. 107.

[139] Erik S. McDuffie, '"I Wanted a Communist Philosophy, but I Wanted Us to Have a Chance to Organize Our People": The Diasporic Radicalism of Queen Mother Audley Moore and the Origins of Black Power' (2010) 3 *African and Black Diaspora: An International Journal* 185.

130   EARLY YEARS OF THE UNITED NATIONS

and a successor to the National Negro Congress. The submission, of more than 200 pages, contained detailed information about racially motivated killings and violent attacks as well as impoverished living conditions. It contended that these met the terms of the punishable acts in article II of the 1948 Convention. The report included a staggering list of police killings, of executions following unfair trials, and mob violence of which African Americans had been victim in recent years.[140] At the time, there had been no judicial application of the Genocide Convention by any court and academic writers had barely discussed the scope of this new international crime. *We Charge Genocide* adopted a very broad interpretation of the terms of the Convention.[141] It blurred the legalities of the application of treaties given that the United States was not a party to the Convention. But its claim that the General Assembly had the authority to address genocide was not legally incorrect, even if the source was the Charter and the 1946 General Assembly resolution rather than the Convention itself.

William L. Patterson travelled to Paris in December 1951 to present the report to United Nations officials during the sixth session of the General Assembly, held exceptionally in the French capital, as it had been three years earlier. At the same time, a delegation led by Paul Robeson, who was prevented from travelling abroad by the Department of State, delivered the petition to United Nations headquarters in New York City. Du Bois publicly endorsed the genocide petition, describing it as 'a very excellent effort'.[142] Journalist and pundit I.F. Stone wrote that he had been initially suspicious that the petition was a Communist ploy within the context of the Cold War but that the evidence cited was shameful, and that while it might not correspond to the technical definition in the Genocide Convention it focussed attention on the most serious of issues.[143]

The initiative was attacked by Eleanor Roosevelt, who praised the efforts of the United States in addressing racial discrimination, and by Raphael Lemkin, the man who had first proposed the term 'genocide'. Lemkin contended that the

---

[140] Gerald Horne, *Black Revolutionary: William Patterson and the Globalization of the African American Freedom Struggle*, Urbana, Chicago and Springfield: University of Illinois Press, 2013, pp. 125–40.

[141] Charles H. Martin, 'Internationalizing "The American Dilemma": The Civil Rights Congress and the 1951 Genocide Petition to the United Nations' (1997) 16 *Journal of American Ethnic History* 35; Stephen Leonard Jacobs, '"We Charge Genocide": A Historical Petition All but Forgotten and Unknown', in Scott W. Murray, *Understanding Atrocities: Remembering, Representing, and Teaching Genocide*, Calgary: University of Calgary Press, 2017, pp. 125–43; David Helps, '"We Charge Genocide": Revisiting black radicals' appeals to the world community' (2018) 1 *Radical Americas* 3; Lisa Guenther, '"We Charge Genocide", Anti-Black Racism in the United States as Genocidal Structural Violence', in Anne O'Byrne and Martin Shuster, eds., *Logics of Genocide, The Structures of Violence and the Contemporary World*, New York: Routledge, 2020, pp. 134–51; Benjamin Meiches, 'The Charge of Genocide: Racial Hierarchy, Political Discourse, and the Evolution of International Institutions' (2019) 13 *International Political Sociology* 20.

[142] Du Bois to Foreman, 21 February 1955, W.E.B. Du Bois Papers (MS 312).

[143] *New York Daily Compass*, 20 December 1951.

African American population was actually increasing and that racial violence was confined to an individual rather than a mass level.[144] Interviewed by the *New York Times*, Lemkin dismissed the petition as 'a manoeuvre to divert attention away from the crimes of genocide committed against Estonians, Latvians, Lithuanians, Poles and other Soviet subjugated peoples'. He described Patterson and Robeson as 'un-American' elements in service of 'a foreign power'.[145] In previous correspondence with Patterson, Lemkin had been vehement in his insistence that the Genocide Convention could have no application to the situation of people of colour in the United States.[146] Lemkin is often cited today for promoting a broad understanding of the notion of genocide. But he appears to have had a blind spot for racial discrimination in the United States, which had been his home since the early 1940s. His manuscript on historic genocides dealt with many manifestations of racial attacks on people of colour but omitted any discussion of the situation in the United States, as one of his enthusiastic commentators has noted.[147] Douglas Irvin-Erickson has concluded that Lemkin was 'so desperate to convince white political elites in the United States to ratify the UN Genocide Convention that he tried to make the treaty appeal to a white political establishment that wanted to maintain institutionalised racism and believed the UN and international law would be used by Jews and Communists to empower blacks'.[148]

Eleanor Roosevelt was caught between Scylla and Charybdis. When W.E.B. Du Bois pushed for racial discrimination in the United States to be addressed by the Commission on Human Rights, Roosevelt said this would put her in an unpleasant position and that she might even find it necessary to resign from the United States' delegation to the United Nations.[149] She said 'I had no answer' when challenged by the Soviet delegate to account for the lynching of African Americans in southern states. 'What do you say, standing before a committee of a World Organisation, when you are asked about the Ku Klux Klan?' she told listeners on one of her regular radio broadcasts.[150]

---

[144] 'U.S. Accused in U.N. of Negro Genocide', *New York Times*, 18 December 1951, p. 13.

[145] Ibid.

[146] William L. Patterson, *The Man Who Cried Genocide: An Autobiography*, New York: International Publishers, 1971, p. 179.

[147] Stephen Leonard Jacobs, ' "We Charge Genocide": A Historical Petition All but Forgotten and Unknown', in Scott W. Murray, *Understanding Atrocities: Remembering, Representing, and Teaching Genocide*, Calgary: University of Calgary Press, 2017, pp. 125–43, at pp. 132–3.

[148] Douglas Irvin-Erickson, *Raphael Lemkin and the Concept of Genocide*, Philadelphia: Penn, 2017, pp. 207–8. Also John Cooper, *Raphael Lemkin and the Struggle for the Genocide Convention*, Basingstoke: Palgrave Macmillan, 2008, pp. 224–5.

[149] 'W.E.B. Du Bois to Walter White, 1 July 1948', in Allida Black, ed., *The Eleanor Roosevelt Papers, Vol. I, The Human Rights Years, 1945–1948*, Charlottesville and London: University of Virginia Press, 2007, pp. 862–3.

[150] 'Eleanor and Anna Roosevelt Radio Program, 22 December 1948', in ibid., pp. 975–7.

132 EARLY YEARS OF THE UNITED NATIONS

Racial Discrimination and the Sub-Commission

The Sub-Commission on the Prevention of Discrimination and the Protection of Minorities was one of three subsidiary bodies established by Economic and Social Council established to assist the Commission on Human Rights. The Sub-Commission on the Status of Women met briefly but was almost immediately converted into a full-fledged Commission. The Sub-Commission on Freedom of Information and of the Press functioned for several years before being discontinued in 1952. That year, the Economic and Social Council, 'a conservative and unrepresentative body' in the words of John Humphrey,[151] had also resolved to suspend the work of the Sub-Commission on the Prevention of Discrimination and the Protection of Minorities.[152] The decision was reversed by the General Assembly,[153] 'where the representatives of the underprivileged peoples of the world have a strong and effective voice, reflect[ing] the deep feelings of the Asiatic and other coloured peoples in the matter of discrimination', wrote Humphrey.[154] Haiti proposed the resolution to reverse the decision of the Economic and Social Council and retain the Sub-Commission.[155] Australia, Belgium, Canada, Luxembourg, the Netherlands, New Zealand, Nicaragua, Sweden, the United Kingdom, and the United States all voted to shut it down.[156] The Sub-Commission on the Prevention of Discrimination and the Protection of Minorities survived until 2006 when the Commission itself came to an end. Over the decades, the Sub-Commission came to be a kind of think tank for the Commission where creative human rights initiatives where explored.

In 1947, the Sub-Commission briefly considered the petition submitted to the United Nations by the NAACP.[157] The Sub-Commission also prompted UNESCO to undertake the work that led to its statements on race. In 1951, a Sub-Commission resolution expressed satisfaction with UNESCO's statement on race, which the Sub-Commission mistakenly labelled the 'Statement by Experts on Problems of Race'.[158] The Sub-Commission also offered praise for the United Nations Conference of Non-governmental Organisations interested in prejudice

---

[151] John P. Humphrey, 'The United Nations Sub-Commission on the Prevention of Discrimination and the Protection of Minorities' (1968) 62 *American Journal of International Law* 869, at p. 876.

[152] Organisation and operation of the Council and its commissions, 18 September 1951, E/RES/414 (XII), OP 18(d).

[153] Sub-Commission on the Prevention of Discrimination and the Protection of Minorities, 4 February 1952, A/RES/532 B (VI).

[154] Ibid.

[155] Report of the Joint Second and Third Committee, 2 February 1952, A/2113, para. 16(c).

[156] Verbatim record, plenary General Assembly, 4 February 1952, A/PV.373, para. 9.

[157] *Supra* pp. 125–126.

[158] Report of the fourth session, Sub-Commission on Prevention of Discrimination and Protection of Minorities, 25 October 1951, E/CN.4/Sub.2/122, para. 38.

and discrimination, held in Geneva in March and April 1955.[159] The Conference was dominated by a range of NGOs from the Global North interested in various forms of discrimination with no particular focus on racism. Ralph Bunche complained to the Secretary-General about 'the question of poor representation of coloured peoples' at the Conference.[160] Until the 1960s, the Sub-Commission focussed on issues relating to religious groups, political rights, ex-nuptial children, migrants, education, and employment. It was almost as if racial discrimination was a taboo subject, guaranteed to make some of the members of the Sub-Commission uncomfortable about the practices of their own governments. This might be explained by the composition of the Sub-Commission which was largely dominated by delegates from Europe and the United States.

In what was an exception to the general neglect of the topic by the Sub-Commission in its early years, Special Rapporteur Charles Ammoun, of Lebanon, devoted considerable attention to racial discrimination in education in his report to the Sub-Commission, initially presented in 1956. Ammoun conceded that he had tried 'not to be aggressive' and that he had 'assumed that the authors of discriminatory measures themselves were acting in good faith'.[161] But even the benign descriptions in his report were further adulterated in the final version. Ammoun's draft report stated that discrimination in education based on race or colour was found in South Africa, in South West Africa, in 'certain' Trust or Non-Self-Governing Territories and 'to some extent in the United States of America'.[162] This reference to the United States met with strenuous objections from the American member, Philip Halpern.[163] He explained to the Sub-Commission that '[w]ith regard to discrimination against Negro students, . . . the stage at which there had been inequality of tangible factors for the white and coloured population had now been passed'.[164] In the final version, issued a few months before the Arkansas National Guard was called out to block African American children from attending Little Rock's Central High,[165]

---

[159] Report of the eighth session, Sub-Commission on Prevention of Discrimination and Protection of Minorities, E/CN.4/Sub.2/177, 31 January 1956, paras. 143–57.

[160] John Hobbins, ed., *On the Edge of Greatness, The Diaries of John Humphrey*, Vol. III, Montreal: McGill University Libraries, 1998, p. 124.

[161] Summary record, Sub-Commission on the Prevention of Discrimination and the Protection of Minorities, 4 January 1956, E/CN.4/Sub.2/SR.174, p. 7.

[162] Study of discrimination in education: Draft report drawn up by the Special Rapporteur (Mr. Charles Ammoun), 4 November 1955, E/CN.4/Sub.2/L.92, para. 94.

[163] Summary record, Sub-Commission on the Prevention of Discrimination and the Protection of Minorities, 5 January 1956, E/CN.4/Sub.2/SR.176, p. 5; Summary record, Sub-Commission on the Prevention of Discrimination and the Protection of Minorities, 10 January 1956, E/CN.4/Sub.2/SR.181, p. 7.

[164] Summary record, Sub-Commission on the Prevention of Discrimination and the Protection of Minorities, 10 January 1956, E/CN.4/Sub.2/SR.181, p. 11.

[165] Karen Anderson, *Little Rock: Race and Resistance at Central High School*, Princeton: Princeton University Press, 2010.

134   EARLY YEARS OF THE UNITED NATIONS

Ammoun replaced his rather tame comment and noted that unlike South Africa, the United States was 'in the process of eliminating discrimination in education by legislation, by court decisions, by administrative action and by the education of public opinion'.[166] Ammoun observed that African Americans constituted only 2.5 per cent of the medical school population yet they represented 10 per cent of the overall population. However, he said 'studies on the subject have indicated not only an absence of discrimination on the basis of statistical measurement but also a tendency in some cases to accept Negro applicants with lower qualifications than others'.[167]

Ammoun's report discussed the situation in South Africa and in the African colonies of Belgium and the United Kingdom at considerable length.[168] The approach was generally descriptive and uncritical. In discussing vocational education, rather than condemn the flagrant racism of the system he merely observed that 'the Native people consider this type of education to be inferior'.[169] On the Belgian Congo and Ruanda-Urundi, he spoke favourably of 'a policy of gradual integration has led to the progressive decrease in racial discrimination in the field of education'.[170] As for the Gold Coast, a British colony about to become independent Ghana, he noted that 'similar progress towards equality of educational opportunity is being made'.[171] For Kenya, he quoted lengthy passages from a British memorandum that attributed inequality in education to the country's poverty and the absurd claim that until recently there had hardly been any demand for education from Africans.[172]

Ammoun's grotesquely unrealistic assessment of discrimination in education based upon race and colour went largely unchallenged, according to the Sub-Commission's report. The British member, Richard Hiscocks, thought that Ammoun had actually overstated the significance of discrimination based upon race and colour.[173] Egypt's Mohamed Awad agreed and suggested that 'the problem throughout most of Africa was not, strictly speaking, one of racial discrimination, but rather of neglect of large sectors of the population by colonial

[166] Study of discrimination in education by Charles D. Ammoun, Special Rapporteur of the Sub-Commission on Prevention of Discrimination and Protection of Minorities, August 1957, E/CN.4/Sub.2/181/Rev.1, p. 11.
[167] Study of discrimination in education by Charles D. Ammoun, Special Rapporteur of the Sub-Commission on Prevention of Discrimination and Protection of Minorities, August 1957, E/CN.4/Sub.2/181/Rev.1, p. 16.
[168] Ibid., pp. 10–28.
[169] Ibid., p. 15.
[170] Ibid., pp. 21–3.
[171] Ibid., p. 23.
[172] Ibid., p. 27.
[173] Summary record, Sub-Commission on the Prevention of Discrimination and the Protection of Minorities, 5 January 1956, E/CN.4/Sub.2/SR.175, pp. 4–6; Summary record, Sub-Commission on the Prevention of Discrimination and the Protection of Minorities, 9 January 1956, E/CN.4/Sub.2/SR.180, pp. 10, 12.

RACIAL DISCRIMINATION AND THE SUB-COMMISSION 135

authorities, acquiesced in by the privileged group'.[174] Halpern bragged about the number of African Americans who went to university.[175] The only negative assessment came from the Soviet member, Andrei Andronovich Fomin, who politely criticized 'Ammoun's optimistic views regarding the racial discrimination situation in certain countries'.[176] Fomin said he thought Ammoun had been 'too optimistic in indicating that racial discrimination was on the decline; it was still rampant not only in colonial territories but even in some independent countries'. Fomin also quarrelled with Halpern, noting that 'existing statistics show that Negroes in the United States of America have far less access to institutions of higher learning than white citizens, which was proof of racial discrimination'.[177]

The Sub-Commission began to take a more direct interest in racial discrimination in 1960 in response to a wave of anti-Semitic vandalism known as the 'swastika epidemic'. It prepared the initial drafts of both the Declaration on racial discrimination and the International Convention on the Elimination of All Forms of Racial Discrimination, adopted by the General Assembly in 1963 and 1965 respectively.[178]

* * *

In its first years of activity, the United Nations gingerly explored the scope of its engagement with human rights. When the Charter was being debated, the thrust had been on standard-setting. The challenge, which met with only limited success, was to implant human rights within the text of the Charter itself. After the Charter entered into force, the relevant institutions sought to focus their efforts on negotiating the international bill of rights. In effect, they were filling the gap in the Charter which ideally should have had a catalogue of rights, as some of the Latin American delegations had desired. This could all have been anticipated at the San Francisco Conference. What was then far less obvious was the engagement of the United Nations in the monitoring of human rights within Member

[174] Summary record, Sub-Commission on the Prevention of Discrimination and the Protection of Minorities, 9 January 1956, E/CN.4/Sub.2/SR.180, p. 11.
[175] Summary record, Sub-Commission on the Prevention of Discrimination and the Protection of Minorities, 5 January 1956, E/CN.4/Sub.2/SR.176, pp. 5–6; Summary record, Sub-Commission on the Prevention of Discrimination and the Protection of Minorities, 19 February 1957, E/CN.4/Sub.2/ SR.199, p. 12; Report of the ninth session, Sub-Commission on Prevention of Discrimination and Protection of Minorities, 8 March 1957, E/CN.4/Sub.2/186, paras. 39–40.
[176] Summary record, Sub-Commission on the Prevention of Discrimination and the Protection of Minorities, 19 February 1957, E/CN.4/Sub.2/SR.198, p. 10; Summary record, Sub-Commission on the Prevention of Discrimination and the Protection of Minorities, 19 February 1957, E/CN.4/Sub.2/ SR.199, pp. 13–14.
[177] Report of the ninth session, Sub-Commission on Prevention of Discrimination and Protection of Minorities, 8 March 1957, E/CN.4/Sub.2/186, paras. 39–40; Summary record, Sub-Commission on the Prevention of Discrimination and the Protection of Minorities, 21 February 1957, E/CN.4/ Sub.2/SR.201, p. 6.
[178] See Chapter 9.

136 EARLY YEARS OF THE UNITED NATIONS

States. Many of the founding members believed this to be impossible because of the domestic jurisdiction clause contained in article 2(7).

The domestic jurisdiction clause succumbed to its first challenge at the initial session of the General Assembly, battered by the Indian initiative dealing with racial discrimination in South Africa. In 1946, India was not even yet fully independent. As one of the relatively few Member States of the Global South within the United Nations, it led the struggle for the General Assembly to confront violations of fundamental rights in general and racism in particular. Two other important initiatives at the first session of the General Assembly were also directed at racial discrimination, the Egyptian-sponsored resolution on persecution and discrimination and the resolution on genocide which was backed by India, Panama, and Cuba.

Petitions to the United Nations by African American organizations were blocked. Nevertheless, the three main petitions obtained significant publicity and generated debate within the United Nations. Eventually, the Economic and Social Council formalized a procedure to address human rights petitions. Adopted in 1967, ECOSOC resolution 1235 was entitled 'Question of the violation of human rights and fundamental freedoms, including policies of racial discrimination and segregation and of apartheid, in all countries . . . ' The resolution authorized the Commission on Human Rights and its Sub-Commission to 'examine information relevant to gross violations of human rights and fundamental freedoms, as exemplified by the policy of apartheid as practised by the Republic of South Africa. . . and racial discrimination as practised notably in Southern Rhodesia'.[179] The initiative came from African States, most of them Member States since 1960.[180]

Histories of the emergence of international human rights at the United Nations have not attached enough importance to these developments. Of course, the peoples of the Global South were grossly underrepresented in these early days of the United Nations. To the extent that they had a voice, it was eloquent, persuasive, and clearly aimed at the scourge of racial discrimination. The momentum would only build in subsequent years, strengthened as new States emerged from the yoke of colonialism. International law was being transformed.

---

[179] Question of the violation of human rights and fundamental freedoms, including policies of racial discrimination and segregation and of apartheid, in all countries, with particular reference to colonial and other dependent countries and territories, E/RES/1235 (XLII), OP 2.

[180] Kevin Boyle and Anneliese Baldaccini, 'A Critical Evaluation of International Human Rights Approaches to Racism', in Sandra Fredman, ed., *Discrimination and Human Rights: The Case of Racism*, Oxford: Oxford University Press, 2001, pp. 135–92, at p. 145.

6

The International Bill of Rights

All are Born Free and Equal

When the text of the Universal Declaration of Human Rights was being finalized by the United Nations General Assembly, meeting in Paris in late 1948, René Cassin felt that the draft preamble, 'while denouncing the dreadful acts of barbarism which the world had witnessed not long previously, hesitated to assign responsibility and did not denounce with proper vigour the racist and racial doctrines which had been the cause of the last war. He thought that more boldness might be shown in drafting the preamble.'[1] Twenty years later, Cassin was to receive the Nobel Peace Prize, largely for his contribution to the Declaration. In light of Cassin's remarks, the French delegation proposed the following addition to the second recital of the Declaration's preamble: 'whereas, particularly before and during the Second World War, *Nazism and Racialism engendered countless acts of barbarism* which outraged the conscience of mankind.'[2] But when he spoke in support of the amendment, Cassin failed to draw attention to the importance of the reference to racism.[3] There was no enthusiasm for the French amendment from other delegations and it was subsequently withdrawn.[4]

Like the Charter of the United Nations, the Universal Declaration of Human Rights gives no special attention to racial discrimination. The same is true for the two International Covenants adopted by the General Assembly in 1966. Taken together, the Universal Declaration and the two Covenants comprise the 'International Bill of Rights'. Like the Universal Declaration, the two Covenants deal with equality and non-discrimination in general in provisions that refer to 'race, colour, sex, language, religion, political or other opinion, national or social origin, property, birth or other status'. Other relevant articles of the Declaration deal with protection against discrimination, incitement of discrimination, equality in the workplace, the purposes of education, and the right to marry.

---

[1] Summary record, Third Committee, 2 October 1948, A/C.3/SR.92, pp. 61–2.
[2] France: Amendments, 15 November 1948, A/C.3/339 (emphasis in the original, to indicate the words added by the proposed amendment). The original French version reads: 'que, spécialement dans la période qui a précédé la Deuxième guerre mondiale et durant cette guerre, *le nazisme et le racisme ont été à l'origine d'actes de barbarie innombrables*, et révoltants pour la conscience humaine'.
[3] Summary record, Third Committee, 30 November 1948, A/C.3/SR.165, p. 760.
[4] Summary record, Third Committee, 30 November 1948, A/C.3/SR.166, p. 777.

The International Legal Order's Colour Line. William A. Schabas, Oxford University Press.
© Oxford University Press 2023. DOI: 10.1093/oso/9780197744475.003.0006

138 THE INTERNATIONAL BILL OF RIGHTS

The International Covenant on Civil and Political Rights requires that '[a]ny advocacy of national, racial or religious hatred that constitutes incitement to discrimination, hostility or violence shall be prohibited by law'.[5] The International Covenant on Economic, Social, and Cultural Rights declares that education shall promote 'understanding, tolerance and friendship among all nations and all racial, ethnic or religious groups'.[6]

The phrase 'international bill of rights' is traced to President Harry Truman's speech in the San Francisco Opera House on 26 June 1945, immediately following the adoption of the Charter of the United Nations. Despite the hopes of many of the founding members, as well as of global civil society, the human rights provisions of the Charter are insubstantial. They consist of rather perfunctory references to 'human rights and fundamental freedoms for all without distinction as to race, sex, language, or religion'. They provide little else in terms of the content of fundamental rights. Truman said:

> Under this document we have good reason to expect an international bill of rights, acceptable to all the nations involved. That bill of rights will be as much a part of international life as our own Bill of Rights is a part of our Constitution. The Charter is dedicated to the achievement and observance of human rights and fundamental freedoms. Unless we can attain those objectives for all men and women everywhere – without regard to race, language, or religion – we cannot have permanent peace and security in the world.[7]

The message was surely bittersweet for victims of racial discrimination. Truman's speech was preceded by remarks of representatives of several governments from different parts of the world: Brazil, Czechoslovakia, China, France, the Soviet Union, the United Kingdom, and Saudi Arabia. Africa's voice in the ceremony was provided by Jan Smuts, who spoke immediately prior to Truman. An avowed white supremacist and leader of one of the paradigmatic racist governments, Smuts made a patronizing reference to 'dependent peoples still unable to look after themselves' and he praised Britain as 'the greatest colonial world power'.[8]

Just as the Charter of the United Nations was inspired by the Atlantic Charter of August 1941, signed by Roosevelt and Churchill, the origins of the International Bill of Rights are often traced to the four freedoms speech of Franklin D. Roosevelt in January 1941. The preambles of the three main components of the International Bill of Rights all allude to Roosevelt's four freedoms. For example, the Preamble of the Universal Declaration of Human Rights

---

[5] International Covenant on Civil and Political Rights (1976) 999 UNTS 171, art. 20(2).
[6] International Covenant on Economic, Social and Cultural Rights (1976) 993 UNTS 3, art. 13(1).
[7] Verbatim minutes of the closing Plenary Session, 26 June 1945, UNCIO I, p. 683.
[8] Ibid., p. 678.

states that 'the advent of a world in which human beings shall enjoy freedom of speech and belief and freedom from fear and want has been proclaimed as the highest aspiration of the common people'. The absence in Roosevelt's formulation of any reference to racial equality is easily explained. It was not a priority for a president whose political party held power thanks to the support of political leaders in the 'deep South'. Credit for some of Roosevelt's initiatives in the promotion of racial equality are often attributed to the influence of his wife, Eleanor Roosevelt, who presided over the initial drafting of the International Bill of Rights as representative of the United States.

The Universal Declaration of Human Rights was adopted by the United Nations General Assembly on 10 December 1948. Although references to 'signatories' of the Declaration are not uncommon, it is in reality a resolution adopted by most of the Member States of the United Nations at the time. Eight States abstained and two did not vote. Countries that were not Member States at the time as well as countries that did not exist at the time cannot become 'signatories' of the Declaration. Nevertheless, there can be no serious doubt that the Declaration, a succinct statement comprising thirty articles and about 1,700 words, is accepted not only by those States that voted in favour in 1948 but by all current Member States of the United Nations as well as the handful of States that are not Members.

The two Covenants are international treaties. The texts of the Covenants were approved by the General Assembly in 1966. At present, the States Parties number slightly more than 170. The two Covenants are in many respects an expanded and more detailed version of the rights set out in the Universal Declaration. A few of the rights enshrined in the Covenants cannot be traced to the Universal Declaration and a few of them that are enshrined in the Declaration have no echo in the Covenants.

A distinction that is often made between the Universal Declaration and the two Covenants describes the former as 'non-binding' and the latter as 'binding'. This was no doubt the general understanding in the early years. It facilitated the rapid adoption of the Declaration and at the same time helps to account for the extraordinary delays in negotiation of the Covenants. Over time, however, the legal status of the Declaration has become more robust. When the Human Rights Council established the basis for the Universal Periodic Review, in 2007, it listed the Declaration as well as the human rights treaty obligations.[9] This provides the normative framework for the regular reports to the Council on their compliance with human rights. That the Universal Declaration set out norms that Member States were obliged to respect was an idea promoted by countries of the Global

---

[9] Institution-building of the United Nations Human Rights Council, 18 June 2007, A/HRC/RES/5/1, Annex, para. 1(b).

140   THE INTERNATIONAL BILL OF RIGHTS

South during the 1950s and 1960s. The developed countries persisted in their resistance to such an enhanced role for the Declaration.

This comprehensive codification of human rights and fundamental freedoms had been attempted by organizations and by individuals but never before had it been undertaken with the express purpose of defining enforceable rules of international law. Success meant achieving agreement amongst countries with very different visions, values, and sensitivities. When the process began within the United Nations, in 1946, the ideological differences between what would later be called the 'First World' and the 'Second World' were already apparent although the Cold War was only beginning. As the drafting of the Covenants proceeded, during the 1950s and the early 1960s, scores of States joined the United Nations and participated in the work. A large number were former colonies who quickly manifested their special concerns about racial discrimination. But the new reality of significant African membership in the General Assembly was not enough to transform documents that were already at an advanced stage, and that had been prepared in bodies dominated by countries of the Global North.

The International Bill of Rights had several predecessors prepared by non-governmental organizations and individuals. One of the earliest efforts at codification, the 1929 Declaration of the Institut de Droit International, proclaimed the full and entire protection of the 'equal right of every individual to life, liberty and property . . . without distinction as to nationality, sex, race, language, or religion'.[10] The preamble of the 1929 Declaration cited the 14th amendment to the American Constitution and an allegedly expansive interpretation it had been given by the United States Supreme Court. It was an odd reference given the reactionary approach of the Supreme Court's case law to the interpretation of the amendment that prevailed at the time.[11]

During the Second World War and in its aftermath a number of declarations of fundamental rights were proposed. A draft adopted by the London International Assembly in 1943 contained no right to equality although it recognized protection against deprivation of property, 'in particular because of the nationality, race, religion or political condition of the holder'.[12] The American Law Institute prepared a draft bill of rights that contained a clause on equal protection of the law: 'Every one has the right to protection against arbitrary discrimination in the

---

[10] Institut de Droit International, 'Declaration of the International Rights of Man' (1941) 35 *American Journal of International Law* 663. On the background to the Declaration, see Louis B. Sohn, 'How American International Lawyers Prepared for the San Francisco Bill of Rights' (1995) 89 *American Journal of International Law* 540.

[11] *Plessy v. Ferguson*, 163 U.S. 537 (1896). *Plessy* was reaffirmed by the Court in 1927, in *Lum v. Rice*, 275 U.S. 78 (1927), only two years before the Institute adopted its Declaration.

[12] London International Assembly, Report of the Third Commission (Legal Commission) on individual rights, TNA LNU 6/7, art. III.

provisions and application of the law because of race, religion, sex, or any other reason.'[13]

Much attention was given to a declaration proposed by the writer H.G. Wells. He listed several fundamental rights, including the right to privacy, to property, to education, and freedom of movement, but somehow overlooked the right to equality and the prohibition of racial discrimination.[14] Perhaps racial discrimination was not a particularly burning issue for Wells's readership, presumably middle-class intellectuals in Britain. Yet it bore the subheading 'What are we fighting for?' Racial discrimination was at the core of the enemy's world view. How curious that Wells did not bring any attention to bear on the racist dimension of the Nazi regime.

In December 1944, the American Jewish Committee produced a succinct single-page 'Declaration on Human Rights' that was focussed on 'the Hitler regime'.[15] The African American poet Langston Hughes was among the signatories. But when W.E.B. Du Bois's endorsement was solicited,[16] he replied that he was 'greatly disappointed', noting that it made an appeal for sympathy for persons driven from the land of their birth, 'but how about American Negroes, Africans and Indians who have not been driven from the land of their birth but nevertheless are deprived of their rights'. He described it as 'a very easily understood Declaration of Jewish Rights' that 'has apparently no thought of the rights of Negroes, Indians, South Sea Islanders. Why then call it the Declaration of Human Rights?'[17]

Professor Hersch Lauterpacht of Cambridge University published a draft bill of rights along with a detailed commentary. It affirmed that '[a]ll nationals of the State shall enjoy full equality before the law and equal treatment in all respects by the authorities of the State. In particular, there shall be no discrimination on account of religion, race, colour, language, or political creed.'[18] But Lauterpacht, who lost most of his family to Nazi genocide, contemplated an exception to this principle in the text he proposed on the right to participate in government: 'No State shall deprive its citizens of the effective right to choose their governments and legislators on a footing of equality, in accordance with the law of the State,

---

[13] Louis B. Sohn, 'How American International Lawyers Prepared for the San Francisco Bill of Rights' (1995) 89 *American Journal of International Law* 540, at pp. 550–3.

[14] Herbert G. Wells, *The Rights of Man; or, What Are We Fighting For?*, Harmondsworth: Penguin Books, 1940.

[15] The text is reproduced in James Loeffler, *Rooted Cosmopolitans, Jews and Human Rights in the Twentieth Century*, New Haven and London: Yale University Press, 2018, pp. 106–7.

[16] Letter from American Jewish Committee to W.E.B. Du Bois, 24 October 1944, W.E.B. Du Bois Papers (MS 312).

[17] Letter from W.E.B. Du Bois to American Jewish Committee, 14 November 1944. W.E.B. Du Bois Papers (MS 312).

[18] Hersch Lauterpacht, *An International Bill of the Rights of Man*, New York: Columbia University Press, 1945, p. 71.

142 THE INTERNATIONAL BILL OF RIGHTS

in free, secret, and periodic elections.'[19] Lauterpacht explained that the phrase 'in accordance with the law of the State' was intended to carve out an exception for States with racist laws denying the franchise to their own people. 'No Bill of Rights is likely to prove acceptable which in an inelastic or uncompromising fashion makes the question of the franchise of the Negro population in the United States or in South Africa a test of the democratic system of those countries or a matter of direct and immediate international concern', he wrote.[20] Writing in 1950, Lauterpacht considered that the Charter of the United Nations prevented States from imposing 'fresh discrimination', implying that he did not want to quarrel with the status quo.[21]

In the months following Truman's speech at the close of the San Francisco Conference, several draft bills of rights were submitted to the United Nations as a basis for the discussions. None of them addressed racial discrimination specifically, although each of them had a provision dealing with equality or discrimination. Cuba's proposal recognized a 'right to equality before the law without distinction as to race, religion, colour, class or sex'.[22] Panama put forward a 'statement of essential rights' prepared by the American Law Institute that included 'protection against arbitrary discrimination in the provisions and application of the law because of race, religion, sex, or any other reason'.[23] One commentator has noted that although race was mentioned in the equal protection clause, and, 'although some of the American advisers were attentive to racial discrimination, the advisers generally did not perceive this bill of rights as an instrument that aimed to end racial discrimination'.[24] Chile also provided a draft, prepared by the Inter-American Juridical Committee, with the following text: 'All persons shall be equal before the law in respect to the enjoyment of their fundamental rights'.[25] Finally, the American Federation of Labor text stated: 'All human beings have real security and are free from discrimination on account of race, colour, creed or difference of political belief from the government in control or the party in power'.[26] The United States government presented a document of proposals that comprised a summary list of categories of rights consisting of individual rights, procedural rights, social rights, and political rights, but with no mention

[19] Ibid., p. 134.
[20] Ibid., pp. 137–8.
[21] Hersch Lauterpacht, *International Law and Human Rights*, London: Stevens and Sons, 1950, p. 153.
[22] Draft Declaration on Human Rights, 12 February 1946, E/HR/1, para. 5.
[23] Statement of Essential Human Rights Presented by the Delegation of Panama, 26 April 1946, E/HR/3, art. 17.
[24] Hanne Hagtvedt Vik, 'Taming the states: the American Law Institute and the "Statement of essential human rights"' (2012) 7 *Journal of Global History* 461, at p. 482.
[25] Draft Declaration of the International Rights and Duties of Man, 22 April 1946, E/CN.4/2, art. XVIII.
[26] International Bill of Rights, 20 August 1946, E/CT.2/2, para. 12.

ALL ARE BORN FREE AND EQUAL   143

of equality or non-discrimination.[27] A United Kingdom draft contemplated provisions on non-discrimination but said this would not be attempted until the Commission on the Status of Women and the Sub-Commission on the Prevention of Discrimination and the Protection of Minorities had met.[28]

During 1947 and the first half of 1948, drafting of the International Bill was primarily the work of the Commission on Human Rights. The Commission was composed of representatives of 18 Member States. Five were from Asia (China, India, Iran, Lebanon, Philippines). Three were from South America (Chile, Panama, Uruguay). Egypt was the only member from Africa. The Commission soon divided the work into two separate texts, a manifesto or declaration and a treaty or covenant. Drafting of the Declaration moved more quickly than that of the Covenant. Some Member States insisted that adoption of the Declaration should wait until the Covenant was also ready, mainly because of concerns that the Covenant would be postponed indefinitely. Belgium pointed to the need for a treaty, giving as an example South Africa's failure to comply with the General Assembly resolution concerning Indians in South Africa.[29] However the Economic and Social Council decided to proceed on two tracks, allowing for adoption of the Declaration while postponing its decision on the Covenant, all the while 'recognising at the same time that the Bill of Rights was incomplete without the draft Covenant and measures for implementation'.[30]

The final text of the Universal Declaration of Human Rights was negotiated in the Third Committee of the General Assembly, in late 1948. After its adoption, attention shifted to the unfinished work on the Covenant. The General Assembly, emphasizing the interdependence of all categories of human rights, including economic, social, and cultural rights, called upon the Commission on Human Rights to prepare a single convention.[31] However, bowing to pressure from the United Kingdom and the United States the Assembly reversed itself the following year and decided to proceed with two Covenants, organized thematically.[32] In 1954, the Commission on Human Rights finalized drafts of the International Covenant on Civil and Political Rights and the International Covenant on Economic, Social and Cultural Rights.[33] Over the next 12 years, the General Assembly debated the texts, ultimately adopting them at its 1966

---

[27] United States Proposals Regarding an International Bill of Rights, 6 February 1947, E/CN.4/17.

[28] International Bill of Human Rights, 5 June 1947, E/CN.4/AC.1/4, p. 13.

[29] Summary record, Commission on Human Rights, 4 December 1947, E/CN.4/SR.28, p. 4.

[30] Report of the Economic and Social Council, 18 August 1947 to 29 August 1948, A/625, para. 116.

[31] Draft International Covenant on Human Rights and measures of implementation: future work of the Commission on Human Rights, 4 December 1950, A/RES/421 (V).

[32] Preparation of two Drafts International Covenants on Human Rights, 5 February 1952, A/RES/543 (VI). See also Annotation prepared by the Secretary-General, 1 July 1955, A/2929, pp. 22–4.

[33] For the text of the two drafts, see Report of the Tenth Session of the Commission on Human Rights, 23 February–16 April 1954, E/2573, Annex I.

144   THE INTERNATIONAL BILL OF RIGHTS

session.[34] The Covenants entered into force a decade later after obtaining 35 ratifications or accessions.[35]

Article 1 of the Universal Declaration of Human Rights begins with the phrase '[a]ll human beings are born free and equal in dignity and rights'. When the text was being discussed in the Third Committee, South Africa proposed amending the general statement so as to specify that this only applied to 'fundamental rights and freedoms'. The South African representative, Charles Te Water, explained that because 'there could be no universality in the concept of equality, there could not be, neither was there, any universal standard among the peoples of the world in their different concepts of human dignity, which were, surely, determined by the differences in religious and social systems, usages and customs'. He ducked the race issue – apartheid had been imposed several months previously – and instead focussed his attention on women who, he said 'would have different rights' than men. 'There were, for instance, marked divergences in the property rights as well as in the political rights of women', argued the South African.[36]

Yugoslavia's Vladimir Dedijer reacted immediately, saying the South African's speech 'had aroused his indignation'. A few days later, he attacked Te Water for having made 'a statement in which he defended his country's right to practise racial discrimination'.[37] South Africa abstained in the final vote on the Universal Declaration in the plenary General Assembly. South Africa's representative explained that the Declaration went too far, and that although formally not a binding legal document it was likely to be taken as an authoritative interpretation of the Charter of the United Nations. He insisted that South Africa was second to no State represented in the Assembly in ensuring fundamental rights to everyone 'without distinction of race, creed or sex'.[38] It was an outrageous claim.

Without Distinction based on Race or Colour

Article 2(1) of the Universal Declaration states that everyone is entitled to the rights and freedoms set forth in the Declaration 'without distinction of any kind, such as race, colour, sex, language, religion, political or other opinion, national or social origin, property, birth or other status'. Each of the two Covenants contains a clause based upon article 2(1) of the Universal Declaration, with some minor

[34] International Covenant on Economic, Social and Cultural Rights, International Covenant on Civil and Political Rights and Optional Protocol to the International Covenant on Civil and Political Rights, 16 December 1966, A/RES/2200 A (XXI).

[35] International Covenant on Economic, Social and Cultural Rights (1976) 993 UNTS 3; International Covenant on Civil and Political Rights (1976) 999 UNTS 171.

[36] Summary record, Third Committee, 6 October 1948, A/C.3/SR.95, p. 92.

[37] Summary record, Third Committee, 13 October 1948, A/C.3/SR.101, p. 136.

[38] Verbatim record, plenary General Assembly, 10 December 1948, A/PV.183, pp. 910–11.

differences. The International Covenant on Civil and Political Rights declares that States Parties undertake to respect and ensure rights 'without distinction of any kind, such as race, colour, sex, language, religion, political or other opinion, national or social origin, property, birth or other status'.[39] The Covenant on Economic, Social and Cultural Rights states that the rights it contains will be exercised 'without discrimination of any kind as to race, colour, sex, language, religion, political or other opinion, national or social origin, property, birth or other status'.[40]

All of these clauses on equality rights can be traced back to the Drafting Committee of the Commission on Human Rights which first met in June 1947. The Committee debated a 'draft outline' prepared by the Secretariat. Article 45 stated: 'No one shall suffer any discrimination whatsoever because of race, sex, language, religion, or political creed. There shall be full equality before the law in the enjoyment of the rights enunciated in this Bill of Rights.'[41] The phrase 'race, sex, language, religion' was clearly drawn from the provisions of the Charter of the United Nations. The Secretariat had added 'political creed' to the enumeration of prohibited grounds.

The Secretariat had devised its text from a compilation of various proposals that had been submitted as well as an analysis of the relevant provisions in national constitutions. It identified texts relevant to the right to equality and non-discrimination in the constitutional documents of Afghanistan, Argentina, Belgium, Bolivia, Brazil, Chile, China, Colombia, Costa Rica, Cuba, Czechoslovakia, Denmark, Ecuador, Egypt, El Salvador, France, Greece, Guatemala, Haiti, Honduras, Iceland, India, Iran, Iraq, Lebanon, Liberia, Luxembourg, Mexico, Nicaragua, Panama, Paraguay, Peru, Philippines, Poland, Siam, the Soviet Union, Syria, Turkey, the United States, Uruguay, and Yugoslavia. Those of Brazil, China, Czechoslovakia, Egypt, France, Guatemala, Iraq, Nicaragua, Panama, Siam, the Soviet Union, Syria, Turkey, the United States, and Yugoslavia referred explicitly to 'race'.[42]

The Drafting Committee did not endorse the Secretariat's addition of 'political creed'. The Committee's draft stated that '[e]veryone is entitled to the rights and freedoms set forth in this Declaration, without distinction as to race, sex, language, or religion.'[43] On the recommendation of the Drafting Committee, this text was then examined by the Sub-Commission on the Prevention of

---

[39] International Covenant on Civil and Political Rights (1976) 999 UNTS 171, art. 2(1).

[40] International Covenant on Economic, Social and Cultural Rights (1976) 993 UNTS 3, art. 2(2).

[41] Draft Outline of International Bill of Rights (prepared by the Division of Human Rights), 4 June 1947 E/CN.4/AC.1/3.

[42] International Bill of Rights Documented Outline, 11 June 1947, E/CN.4/AC.1/3/Add.1, pp. 360–79.

[43] Suggestions of the Drafting Committee for Articles of an International Declaration on Human Rights, 1 July 1947, E/CN.4/21, Annex F, p. 74.

146 THE INTERNATIONAL BILL OF RIGHTS

Discrimination and the Protection of Minorities where Minocher A. Masani of India proposed adding the term 'colour' after race, noting that it had been used in the American Federation of Labor draft.[44] There was a lively debate, with a range of views. Masani considered that 'race' and 'colour' were not entirely synonymous, giving as an example immigration to the United States and South Africa where distinctions were made between 'Caucasian immigrants of the fair type and those of a darker one'. The American member of the Sub-Commission, Jonathan Daniels, considered it best not to modify the list of four categories in the Charter of the United Nations. Others thought it preferable to specify colour so as to avoid any uncertainty about the scope of the term 'race'.[45] According to John Humphrey of the Secretariat, the Sub-Commission was concerned that were it to add the term 'colour' to the enumeration this might imply that the Charter of the United Nations had overlooked the question.[46] Many years later, when the General Assembly decided to prepare a declaration and convention on religious intolerance, it mistakenly referred to 'the equality of all men and all peoples without distinction as to race, colour or religion, as stated in the Charter of the United Nations'.[47] The Sub-Commission could reach no agreement and concluded by adopting this phrase: 'It being understood that the term "race" includes the idea of colour'.[48]

The members of the Commission on Human Rights were not as ambivalent. Charles Malik thought it important to add the term, saying he disagreed with the Sub-Commission: 'Scientifically there was a very clear distinction between persons of different races and of different colour'.[49] Malik formally moved an amendment to add 'colour'; it was adopted by the Working Group of the Commission by three votes with two abstentions.[50] In the plenary Commission, Hansa Mehta of India argued that she 'understood the term "race" to include colour, but if there was any doubt on the subject, she thought that the word "colour" should

---

[44] Summary record, Sub-Commission on Prevention of Discrimination and Protection of Minorities, 26 November 1947, E/CN.4/Sub.2/SR.4, p. 2. It was also used in the Cuban draft: Draft Declaration on Human Rights, E/HR/1, art. 5. For a detailed account of the *travaux préparatoires*, see Stephanie Farrior, 'Color in the Non-Discrimination Provisions of the Universal Declaration of Human Rights and the Two Covenants' (2015) 14 *Washington University Global Studies Law Review* 751.

[45] Summary record, Sub-Commission on Prevention of Discrimination and Protection of Minorities, 26 November 1947, E/CN.4/Sub.2/SR.4, pp. 2–5.

[46] Summary record, Working Group on the Convention, 10 December 1947, E/CN.4/AC.3/SR.8, p. 19.

[47] Preparation of a draft declaration and a draft convention on the elimination of all forms of religious intolerance, 7 December 1962, A/RES/1781 (XXVII), PP 1.

[48] Summary record, Sub-Commission on Prevention of Discrimination and Protection of Minorities, 26 November 1947, E/CN.4/Sub.2/SR.4, p. 5.

[49] Summary record, Working Group on the Convention, 10 December 1947, E/CN.4/WG.3/SR.8, p. 19.

[50] Ibid.

WITHOUT DISTINCTION BASED ON RACE OR COLOUR   147

be inserted in the Declaration'.[51] Mehta proposed the phrase 'race including colour',[52] but in a subsequent meeting suggested the words 'also colour'.[53] This became 'race, which includes colour' in the draft declaration adopted by the Commission[54] and then 'race (which includes colour)' in the text annexed to the Commission's December 1947 Report.[55] At its third session, in June 1948, the Commission finally settled on 'race, colour' . . .'[56] The issue did not lead to any discussion in the Third Committee of the General Assembly.

The first sentence of article 2 of the Universal Declaration states: 'Everyone is entitled to all the rights and freedoms set forth in this Declaration, without distinction of any kind, such as race, colour, sex, language, religion, political or other opinion, national or social origin, property, birth or other status.' The Commission on Human Rights adopted identical texts dealing with equality and non-discrimination for the two Covenants, replicating the language found in the Universal Declaration of Human Rights.[57] However, the final text of the International Covenant on Economic, Social and Cultural Rights adopted by the General Assembly in 1966 substitutes 'discrimination' for 'distinction'. The change can be traced to Italy's delegate, Francesco Capotorti, who thought it would make clearer the permissibility of temporary special measures and the pejorative or arbitrary element.[58] The text of article 2(1) of the Covenant on Economic, Social and Cultural Rights results from an amendment by Argentina, Italy, and Mexico, that made the change to 'discrimination'.[59] Several delegations noted that 'discrimination' had increasingly replaced 'distinction' in international usage. Use of the term 'discrimination' in article 26 of the draft International Covenant on Civil and Political Rights was also noted.[60] Article 2(1) of the International Covenant on Civil and Political Rights was discussed the following year by the Third Committee. Delegates proposed that the wording be the same as that of article 2(2) of the other Covenant, which had already been agreed.[61] But there

---

[51] Summary record, Commission on Human Rights, 12 December 1947, E/CN.4/SR.34, p. 10.

[52] Ibid.

[53] Summary record, Commission on Human Rights, 12 December 1947, E/CN.4/SR.35, p. 11.

[54] Draft International Declaration on Human Rights, 16 December 1947, E/CN.4/77/Annex A, art. 3.

[55] Draft International Declaration on Human Rights, 17 December 1947, E/600, Annex A, pp. 17–22, at p. 17.

[56] Draft International Declaration of Human Rights, 18 June 1948, E/CN.4/148/Add.1, art. 2.

[57] Draft covenant on economic, social and cultural rights, E/2573, Annex I, art. 2(2); Draft covenant on civil and political rights, E/2573, Annex I, art. 2(1).

[58] Summary record, Third Committee, 14 November 1962, A/C.3/SR.1183, paras. 16–18; Summary record, Third Committee, 16 November 1962, A/C.3/SR.1185, para. 15.

[59] Amendment to article 2 of the draft covenant on economic, social and cultural rights, 15 November 1962, A/C.3/L.1028 and Rev. 1 and Rev. 2; Summary record, Third Committee, 10 December 1962, A/C.3/SR.1206, para. 40.

[60] Report of the Third Committee, 17 December 1962, A/5365, paras. 55–7, 60.

[61] Summary record, Third Committee, 8 November 1963, A/C.3/SR.1257, paras. 11, 22, 23; Summary record, Third Committee, 8 November 1963, A/C.3/SR.1258, para. 27, 39.

148 THE INTERNATIONAL BILL OF RIGHTS

was no formal amendment when the text was put to a vote,[62] perhaps because it was assumed, mistakenly, that both Covenants would eventually be revised with a view to ensuring terminological consistency.

Equal Protection of the Law

Article 7 of the Universal Declaration states: 'All are equal before the law and are entitled without any discrimination to equal protection of the law. All are entitled to equal protection against any discrimination in violation of this Declaration and against any incitement to such discrimination.' The same idea is formulated in article 26 of the International Covenant on Civil and Political Rights: 'All persons are equal before the law and are entitled without any discrimination to the equal protection of the law. In this respect, the law shall prohibit any discrimination and guarantee to all persons equal and effective protection against discrimination on any ground such as race, colour, sex, language, religion, political or other opinion, national or social origin, property, birth or other status.' Article 26 has been described as 'a self-standing non-discrimination clause'.[63] The negotiations of both provisions proved complicated. Article 26 of the Covenant was opposed by many Western States. Credit for its inclusion is due to the growing influence of countries from the Global South during the final negotiations in the early 1960s.

The draft of article 7 of the Universal Declaration of Human Rights adopted by the Commission on Human Rights in June 1948 read as follows: 'All are equal before the law and are entitled without any discrimination to equal protection of the law against any discrimination in violation of this Declaration and against any incitement to such discrimination.'[64] In the Third Committee of the General Assembly, Cuba proposed that it be dropped and that article 2 be reworded as follows: 'All men are equal before the law and are entitled to the rights, and subject to the duties, laid down in this Declaration without distinction of race, birth, sex, language, religion, political opinion, or property or other status.'[65] Eleanor Roosevelt said the Cuban proposal did no more than reformulate the content of articles 2 and 7.[66] But others were less sanguine. Although in theory this was a debate about equality and discrimination in general, on a broad range of grounds, it

[62] Summary record, Third Committee, 11 November 1963, A/C.3/SR.1259, para. 30.
[63] *Application of the International Convention on the Elimination of All Forms of Racial Discrimination (Qatar v. United Arab Emirates), Preliminary Objections, Judgment, I.C.J. Reports 2021*, p. 71, Separate Opinion of Judge Iwasawa, para. 8.
[64] Draft International Declaration of Human Rights, 28 June 1948, A/800, Annex A, art. 6.
[65] Cuba: Amendments to the first nine Articles of the Draft Declaration, E/800, 6 October 1948, A/C.3/224.
[66] Summary record, Third Committee, 12 October 1948, A/C.3/SR.100, p. 128.

EQUAL PROTECTION OF THE LAW   149

is quite evident from the context that the central issue concerned racial discrimination and closely related phenomena such as discrimination based on national origin. René Cassin explained that the two provisions were similar but different, the first (article 2) setting forth the principle of non-discrimination while the second (article 7) protected the individual against discrimination.[67] Peng Chun Chang of China also opposed the Cuban proposal. He said he could not insist too much on 'the importance which the fight against discrimination of any kind had for vast sections of the world's population. It was essential for those peoples that they should not only be protected within their national legislation against discrimination, but that the principle of equality in respect of all the fundamental freedoms and rights of mankind should be solemnly proclaimed.'[68]

Alexey Pavlov of the Soviet Union warned that the Cuban amendment was 'not as innocent as it might appear at first sight'. By deleting article 7, the obligation upon States to decree legal sanctions against discriminatory measures would be removed, he said. He made one of the more dramatic interventions about racial discrimination during the entire drafting of the Universal Declaration. Pavlov began by citing the NAACP petition to the United Nations protesting racial discrimination in the United States.[69] 'President Truman himself had admitted that in the United States, coloured men and women were still suffering as regards their human dignity, that they were living in a state of constant moral and physical fear and could not fall back on the national conscience of the American people any more than on legislation', he said. 'A similar state of affairs was to be found in the Union of South Africa. In the province of Natal the Indians did not have a vote, and 80 per cent of their children could not attend school. Racial discrimination had become a veritable system.' He also referred to British colonies in the Gold Coast (Ghana) and Nigeria, as well as Southern Rhodesia (Zimbabwe) where '28 pounds sterling were assigned for the education of each European child and only four shillings for that of each Native child'.[70]

South Africa submitted a proposal that completely undermined article 7 of the Declaration: 'Delete the words "against any discrimination in violation of this Declaration and against any incitement to such discrimination".'[71] South Africa's amendment to article 7 provoked a fierce response, much of it directed at the country's racist policies. Poland asserted that 'approximately five-sevenths of the population of the Union of South Africa did not enjoy equal rights'.[72] Lakshmi

[67] Ibid., pp. 128–9, 131.
[68] Ibid., p. 130.
[69] See *supra*, pp. 123–126.
[70] Ibid., pp. 131–2.
[71] Union of South Africa: Amendments to the Draft Declaration (E/800), 6 October 1948, A/C.3/226.
[72] Summary record, Third Committee, 25 October 1948, A/C.3/SR.112, p. 231. See also ibid., p. 232 (Uruguay, Cuba), p. 234 (the Philippines).

150 THE INTERNATIONAL BILL OF RIGHTS

Menon of India condemned the South African proposal, recalling the discriminatory treatment accorded to Indians and other peoples in the Union of South Africa. Menon said the proposed deletion 'would defeat the purpose for which the declaration was being drawn up'. She acknowledged that India itself had practised discrimination in the past but was trying to eradicate it. Menon said that '[i]nstances of discrimination could be found both in the United States and in South Africa. It was the duty of the Assembly to see that such violations were abolished and not condoned.'[73] The Soviet Union's delegate spoke of the 'colour line', saying that in South Africa it was 'strictly drawn in theatres, parks, restaurants, cafés and railway trains. . . Millions of people paid in blood and tears for the policy of discrimination pursued by the Government of the Union of South Africa.'[74]

Yugoslavia called upon South Africa to withdraw the proposal but also to modify 'the policy which had inspired it'.[75] But Salomon Grumbach of the French delegation said he did not want the amendment to be withdrawn. He hoped for a decisive vote in order to leave no uncertainty about where the Third Committee stood. He thought rejection of the amendment might further the protection of human rights in the Union of South Africa. 'The fact that the policy of the Union of South Africa was one of segregation and racial discrimination was responsible for the mistrust with which the South African amendment had been greeted', said Grumbach.[76] The Soviet delegate, Alexey Pavlov, also sought a vote on the amendment. He would insist it be by a roll call, so that South Africa's supporters could be identified.[77] There was no doubt that South Africa had friends in the room. Some delegations, including those of the United States, the United Kingdom, New Zealand, and Australia, had not joined in the outpouring of condemnation, and made no comment about the South African proposal when they addressed the Committee that day. Greece actually complimented South Africa.[78] Eventually, South Africa ended the debate by withdrawing the proposal, as several delegates had urged. It said it was 'surprised and pained' at the acrimony provoked by its 'sincere effort'. South Africa's delegate, Charles Te Water, said the Committee had not properly appreciated '[t]he difficulty which European civilisation was facing in its struggle for survival in that country'.[79]

The relevant provision in the draft Covenant adopted by the Commission on Human Rights in December 1947 consisted of two sentences, the first prohibiting discrimination with respect to the guaranteed rights and freedoms

[73] Ibid., p. 232.
[74] Ibid., p. 236.
[75] Ibid., p. 235.
[76] Ibid., pp. 235–6.
[77] Ibid., p. 236.
[78] Ibid., p. 237.
[79] Ibid., p. 240.

and the second providing for 'equal protection under the law against any arbitrary discrimination or against any incitement to such discrimination'.[80] Arguing that the second sentence become a distinct article, Alexey Pavlov of the Soviet Union pointed to discriminatory legislation against Blacks in the United States and Indians in South Africa.[81] However, the Drafting Committee decided that a separate and general prohibition of discrimination was 'not necessary'. Chile, France, and the Soviet Union insisted that their support for a general prohibition of discrimination be noted.[82]

In its final draft, adopted in 1954, the Commission on Human Rights recognized equality before the law and required that the law prohibit discrimination by law and 'guarantee to all persons equal and effective protection against discrimination on any ground such as race, colour . . . '[83] Speaking against the text, Britain's Samuel Hoare said it was 'much too wide since it was interpreted as relating not to the administration of justice but to the content of particular laws, and it imposed on States obligations of equality throughout the whole field which they could not respect at the present stage of legislation'.[84] The provision adopted by the Commission was based upon a Yugoslav proposal that succeeded with the support of delegates from the socialist countries and from the South.[85] During the debate, reference was made to recent events in Cicero, a Chicago suburb, where a huge mob had attacked an African American family when it moved into an apartment building in a previously all-white neighbourhood. On the defensive, Eleanor Roosevelt argued rather unconvincingly that 'the events showed that legal provisions were not enough', adding that she regretted that 'all the examples quoted dealt exclusively with the racial prejudices that existed in the United States and wondered whether certain delegations could not refer to other types of discrimination'.[86]

The Third Committee of the General Assembly only considered the provision in 1961, when the membership of the General Assembly was being transformed by the influx of new Member States from Africa. The United Kingdom attempted to revive the arguments that it had made a decade earlier in the Commission on Human Rights.[87] Others, who had not been members of the United Nations in the early 1950s, felt differently. Tunisia said that while it was arguable that the issue was already addressed in article 2 of the Covenant, 'discrimination was so

---

[80] Draft International Covenant on Human Rights, 17 December 1947, E/600, Annex B, art. 20, p. 35.

[81] Summary record, Drafting Committee, 11 May 1948, E/CN.4/AC.1/SR.27, pp. 5–6.

[82] Ibid., p. 7.

[83] Draft Covenant on Civil and Political Rights, E/2573, Annex I(B), art. 24.

[84] Summary record, Commission on Human Rights, 9 June 1952, E/CN.4/SR.328, p. 4.

[85] Amendments to the' provisional text of the first eighteen articles of the Draft International Covenant on Human Rights, 27 April 1951, E/CN.4/573, art. 17.

[86] Ibid., p. 8.

[87] Summary record, Third Committee, 9 November 1961, A/C.3/SR.1097, paras. 25–32.

152 THE INTERNATIONAL BILL OF RIGHTS

detestable and was so strongly resented in African countries that they wished to see its abolition elevated to the level of a principle of law'.[88] Morocco's delegate said that 'at a time when the peoples of Algeria, Angola and South Africa were shedding their blood for the principles of the equality of peoples, their right to self-determination and the other human rights on which the United Nations was founded, there should be no compromise in the Committee on such matters'.[89] Mali characterized an amendment submitted by the United Kingdom and Greece[90] as 'a manoeuvre designed to weaken the text, if not indeed to divest it of its positive content'.[91] Haiti's delegate said he was 'astonished' that there was a proposal to limit the scope of the provision.[92]

The amendment proposed by the United Kingdom and Greece was actually quite weak and did not in fact eliminate the provision. Moreover, any impact it might have had was attenuated when the Third Committee adopted an amendment from India adding the phrase 'equal protection of the law'.[93] In the end, the British and Greek proposal, with the Indian amendment, prevailed by a very close vote of 36 to 30 with 11 abstentions in what was very much of a North/South split.[94] The impact of the countries of the South was decisive in the adoption of a text that has subsequently been interpreted as providing a substantive guarantee of equality, including an obligation upon States to enact legislation prohibiting discrimination.[95]

Incitement

According to article 7 of the Universal Declaration, '[a]ll are entitled to equal protection . . . against any incitement to such discrimination'. It has a counterpart in the International Covenant on Civil and Political Rights: 'Any advocacy of national, racial or religious hatred that constitutes incitement to discrimination, hostility or violence shall be prohibited by law'.[96] The prohibition of incitement has proven to be an issue of great difficulty, one where there were and remain considerable differences of view. While the Universal Declaration was being

---

[88] Ibid., para. 43.

[89] Summary record, Third Committee, 13 November 1961, A/C.3/SR.1102, para. 29.

[90] Greece and United Kingdom: amendment to art. 24 of the draft covenant on civil and political rights, 9 November 1961, A/C.3/L.946.

[91] Summary record, Third Committee, 10 November 1961, A/C.3/SR.1100, para. 35.

[92] Ibid., para. 34.

[93] India: amendment to art. 24 of the draft covenant on civil and political rights, 9 December 1961, A/C.3/L.945.

[94] Summary record, Third Committee, 13 November 1961, A/C.3/SR.1102, para. 63.

[95] General Comment No. 18: Non-discrimination, 10 November 1989, A/45/40, pp. 173–4, para. 12.

[96] International Covenant on Civil and Political Rights (1976) 999 UNTS 171, art. 20(2).

INCITEMENT   153

finalized, in the Third Committee of the General Assembly in late 1948, a parallel debate was underway in the Sixth Committee about the criminalization of 'direct and public incitement to commit genocide'. Many years later, when discussions about the incitement provision in the Covenant were underway, similar debates arose in the drafting of the International Convention on the Elimination of All Forms of Racial Discrimination.

There was no provision on incitement to racial hatred or discrimination in the draft bill of rights prepared by the Secretariat in June 1947 or in the other drafts submitted to the United Nations. Nor was there any mention of the subject in the articles for inclusion in a convention adopted by the Drafting Committee of the Commission on Human Rights at its second session in June 1947 although this was probably out of deference to the work of the Sub-Commission which was to meet later in the year.[97] The texts on incitement in both the Universal Declaration and the International Covenant can be traced to a proposal of the Soviet delegate in the Sub-Commission on the Prevention of Discrimination and the Protection of Minorities: 'Any advocacy of national, racial and religious hostility or of national exclusiveness or hatred and contempt, as well as any action establishing a privilege or a discrimination based on distinctions of race, nationality or religion, constitute a crime and shall be punishable under the law of the State.'[98]

When the American member of the Sub-Commission expressed concerns about possible encroachment on freedom of expression, Alexander P. Borisov retorted that he was not surprised because 'discrimination against the Negroes apparently existed in the United States'. He referred to 4,000 cases of lynching in the United States until 1927, and 40 since the end of the Second World War.[99] The components of Borisov's proposal were rejected in a series of votes that nevertheless manifested support for a provision on incitement. A new text, authored by the Australian and Chinese members of the Sub-Commission, reduced the scope to incitement to violence. It obtained ten votes with none against and one abstention: 'The Sub-Commission recommends to the Human Rights Commission the inclusion in the proposed Convention or in the Declaration or Rights, at appropriate places, of clauses condemning incitement to violence against any religious group, race, nation or minority.'[100] The nuances between Borisov's proposal

[97] Report of the Drafting Committee to the Commission on Human Rights, 1 July 1947, E/CN.4/21, paras. 85–6.
[98] Opinion of Mr. Borisov (USSR) on Article 6, 26 November 1947, E/CN.4/Sub.2/21.
[99] Summary record, Sub-Commission on the Prevention of Discrimination and the Protection of Minorities, 28 November 1947, E/CN.4/Sub.2/SR.7, pp. 7–8.
[100] Report, Sub-Commission on the Prevention of Discrimination and the Protection of Minorities, 5 December 1947, E/CN.4/Sub.2/38, p. 52; Summary record, Sub-Commission on the Prevention of Discrimination and the Protection of Minorities, 28 November 1947, E/CN.4/Sub.2/SR.8, p. 17.

154   THE INTERNATIONAL BILL OF RIGHTS

and the Sub-Commission's recommendation would persist. It was easy to reach agreement on incitement to violence, something that is in any rate covered by ordinary criminal legislation. It is altogether different to address 'hostility', 'hatred', and 'contempt'. Furthermore, Borisov's text required that such incitement be declared a crime.

Borisov's proposal requiring a broad criminalization of hate speech was revived by the Soviet delegate, Alexander E. Bogomolov, in the Working Group of the Commission on Human Rights on the draft declaration.[101] His amendment was endorsed by Alex Easterman of the World Jewish Congress.[102] However, it was rejected by a vote of two to two with two abstentions.[103] In the plenary Commission on Human Rights, in June 1948, the Soviets did not pursue the idea that incitement be expressly linked to criminal punishment. Even then, Britain and the United States remained unenthusiastic.[104] Nevertheless, the text adopted by the Commission on Human Rights in June 1948 incorporated a reference to incitement that did not limit it to violence: 'All are equal before the law and are entitled without any discrimination to equal protection of the law against any discrimination in violation of this Declaration and against any incitement to such discrimination.'[105] The draft Covenant on Civil and Political Rights adopted by the Commission on Human Rights in 1954 and submitted to the General Assembly stated: 'Any advocacy of national, racial or religious hostility that constitutes an incitement to hatred and violence shall be prohibited by the law of the State.'[106]

The debate in the Third Committee began with firm statements of opposition to the provision by the United States and the United Kingdom.[107] As momentum for the provision grew, the United States and the United Kingdom adjusted their stance and no longer insisted upon deletion of the provision.[108] Statements in support pointed to the importance of combatting racism, citing the conclusions of the Bandung Conference,[109] General Assembly resolution 1514 (XV), and the links with colonialism.[110] For nearly 15 years, the issue of prohibiting incitement to racism and racial hatred had been discussed by the Third Committee, the Commission on Human Rights and the Sub-Commission on the Prevention

---

[101] Summary record, Working Group on the Declaration, 10 December 1947, E/CN.4/AC.2/SR.9, pp. 6–8.

[102] Ibid., p. 9.

[103] Ibid., p. 11.

[104] Summary record, Commission on Human Rights, 28 May 1948, E/CN.4/SR.28, pp. 13–16.

[105] Report of the Third Session of the Commission on Human Rights, 24 May to 18 June 1948, E/800, p. 11.

[106] Draft Covenant on Civil and Political Rights, E/2573, Annex I B, pp. 63–72, at p. 69.

[107] Summary record, Third Committee, 19 October 1961, A/C.3/SR.1078, paras. 6, 17.

[108] Summary record, Third Committee, 23 October 1961, A/C.3/SR.1080, paras. 17–19.

[109] See *infra*, pp. 200–201.

[110] Summary record, Third Committee, 20 October 1961, A/C.3/SR.1079, paras. 17–19.

of Discrimination and the Protection of Minorities. But only now was the voice of Africa on the subject of the prevention of racial discrimination being heard. One after another African delegates took the floor to proclaim their enthusiasm for the text adopted by the Commission: Cameroon,[111] Congo (Leopoldville),[112] Ghana,[113] Liberia,[114] Mali,[115] and Tunisia.[116] The Third Committee voted on a revised text, presented by 16 countries, including Congo (Leopoldville), Ghana, Guinea, Mali, and Morocco.[117] It was adopted by 52 to 19 with 12 abstentions in a North/South split.[118]

According to the Human Rights Committee, the authoritative body for interpretation of the Civil Rights Covenant, article 20(2) 'provides protection for people as individuals and as members of groups against this type of discrimination'.[119] It is 'crafted narrowly in order to ensure that other equally fundamental Covenant rights, including freedom of expression under article 19, are not infringed'.[120] Article 20(2) of the Covenant, together with the case law of the Human Rights Committee on its application, was cited by a Trial Chamber of the International Criminal Tribunal for Rwanda as evidence that 'hate speech that expresses ethnic and other forms of discrimination violates the norm of customary international law prohibiting discrimination. Within this norm of customary law, the prohibition of advocacy of discrimination and incitement to violence is increasingly important as the power of the media to harm is increasingly acknowledged'.[121]

Equal Pay for Equal Work

Article 23(2) of the Universal Declaration states that '[e]veryone, without any discrimination, has the right to equal pay for equal work'. The International Covenant on Economic, Social and Cultural Rights guarantees '[f]air wages and

---

[111] Ibid., para. 33.
[112] Ibid., paras. 41–3, 63; Summary record, Third Committee, 23 October 1961, A/C.3/SR.1081, paras. 17–20.
[113] Summary record, Third Committee, 20 October 1961, A/C.3/SR.1079, paras. 53–8.
[114] Summary record, Third Committee, 19 October 1961, A/C.3/SR.1078, para. 20.
[115] Summary record, Third Committee, 23 October 1961, A/C.3/SR.1080, paras. 4–7.
[116] Ibid., para. 9.
[117] Brazil, Cambodia, Congo (Leopoldville), Ghana, Guinea, Indonesia, Iraq, Lebanon, Mali, Morocco, Philippines, Poland, Saudi Arabia, Thailand, United Arab Republic, and Yugoslavia: revised amendment to art. 26 of the draft covenant on civil and political rights, A/C.3/L.933.
[118] Summary record, Third Committee, 25 October 1961, A/C.3/SR.1083, para. 59.
[119] *Rabbae et al. v. the Netherlands*, no. 2124/2011, Views, 14 July 2016, CCPR/C/117/D/2124/2011, para. 9.7.
[120] Ibid., para. 10.4.
[121] *Prosecutor v. Nahimana et al.* (ICTR-99-52-T), Judgment and Sentence, 3 December 2003, para. 1076.

156 THE INTERNATIONAL BILL OF RIGHTS

equal remuneration for work of equal value without distinction of any kind, in particular women being guaranteed conditions of work not inferior to those enjoyed by men, with equal pay for equal work.'[122] Early drafts referred to this as a right of women. At the June 1948 session of the Commission, deletion of a specific reference to women was considered.[123] The Soviet delegate proposed that the equal pay provision apply 'regardless of race, nationality or sex', explaining that this 'would cover discrimination against women, and also discrimination against coloured workers as compared to white, colonial workers as compared to those of metropolitan Powers, etc.'[124] The Commission settled on the following: 'Everyone has the right to equal pay for equal work.'[125]

In the Third Committee of the General Assembly, the United States proposed that the text in the Universal Declaration be limited to '[m]en and women'.[126] Lakshmi Menon of India argued that 'in various parts of Asia and in countries elsewhere, as well as in Trust Territories and Non-Self-Governing Territories, there was still discrimination for reasons not only of sex, but of race and colour. India was opposed to discrimination which compelled women and certain coloured races to accept a lower standard of living than other groups and thought the declaration should clearly condemn that practice.'[127] The Ukrainian representative said that in South Africa 'the average wages of a white worker were about 12 times those of a coloured worker'. In the colonies the situation could be even graver, he said, and 'the wages of a white worker were often as much as 50 times higher than those of a coloured worker'.[128]

The draft article on the right to work in the Universal Declaration of Human Rights raised a number of issues but it seems that it was the equal pay question that proved the sticking point. The Soviet delegate charged that this was because 'colonial Powers did not wish to see in the declaration an article forbidding discrimination as to race, nationality or sex in connexion with work'.[129] In explanations of their votes, several delegates, including Fernand Dehousse of Belgium, René Cassin of France, and Eleanor Roosevelt of the United States, all claimed they were opposed to the troublesome paragraph because it was too narrow, pointing to the longer enumeration of prohibited grounds in article 2.[130]

---

[122] International Covenant on Economic, Social and Cultural Rights (1976) 993 UNTS 3, art. 7(a)(i).
[123] Summary record, Commission on Human Rights, 9 June 1948, pp. 5–11.
[124] Ibid., p. 9.
[125] Report of the Third Session of the Commission on Human Rights, 24 May to 18 June 1948, E/800, p. 13.
[126] United States of America: Amendments to the Draft Declaration of Human Rights, 5 October 1948, A/C.3/223.
[127] Summary record, Third Committee, 16 November 1948, A/C.3/SR.139, p. 519.
[128] Summary record, Third Committee, 16 November 1948, A/C.3/SR.140, p. 524.
[129] Summary record, Third Committee, 16 November 1948, A/C.3/SR.141, p. 541.
[130] Ibid., pp. 540, 542.

Lakshmi Menon charged that the 'true motives' behind the opposition to the wording proposed by the Soviets, with its reference to discrimination based on race and nationality, had been concealed. 'It was no doubt difficult for Powers accustomed to regarding some races as inferior to understand and share the feelings of those who for centuries had suffered from discrimination', she said.[131] A compromise text proposed by the Soviet Union and Ecuador, using the formulation 'without distinction as to race, nationality, sex, age or religion, etc', was rejected.[132] Then, the final wording, 'without any discrimination', was adopted by a near-unanimous vote.[133]

The text on equal pay in the International Covenant on Economic, Social and Cultural Rights is identical to one adopted in 1952 by the Commission on Human Rights.[134] The annotations to the draft covenants prepared by the Secretariat in 1955 explain that the provision is not limited to equal pay as between men and women workers, because it expressly excludes 'distinction of any kind'. The annotations point out that reference was made to the rights of people of different races and to equality as between nationals and non-nationals.[135] There was considerable debate in the Commission on Human Rights on whether specific reference should be made to 'men and women' in the provision on equal pay for equal work. The British argued that 'the question not only of men and women but also of people of different races, of nationals and non-nationals and of similar categories had to be taken into account'.[136] Initially, the Commission adopted a general provision on equal pay for equal work.[137] The reference to men and women in the final text was a response to a resolution adopted by the Commission on the Status of Women.[138] Its representative presented this to the Commission as requiring the words 'for men and women' to be added.[139] The Commission was also influenced by the International Labour Organisation which in 1951 adopted Convention (No. 100) concerning Equal Remuneration for Men and Women Workers for Work of Equal Value.

---

[131] Summary record, Third Committee, 25 November 1948, A/C.3/SR.157, pp. 674–82.
[132] Ibid., p. 687 (by 26 votes against to 18 in favour, with 4 abstentions).
[133] Ibid.
[134] Draft Covenant on Economic, Social and Cultural Rights, E/2256, Annex I(A), art. 8.
[135] Draft international covenants on human rights, annotation prepared by the Secretary-General, 1 July 1955, A/2929, p. 304.
[136] Summary record, Commission on Human Rights, 28 April 1951, E/CN.4/SR.218, p. 14.
[137] Summary record, Commission on Human Rights, 30 April 1951, E/CN.4/SR.220, p. 9.
[138] Equal pay for equal work (resolution adopted on 1 April 1952), E/CN.6/197.
[139] Summary record, Commission on Human Rights, 5 May 1952, E/CN.4/SR.279, p. 7.

158   THE INTERNATIONAL BILL OF RIGHTS

Education to Combat Racial Prejudice

The right to education is enshrined in article 26 of the Universal Declaration of Human Rights. It specifies that education is to be directed 'to the full development of the human personality and to the strengthening of respect for human rights and fundamental freedoms. It shall promote understanding, tolerance and friendship among all nations, racial or religious groups . . . ' The International Covenant on Economic, Social and Cultural Rights addresses the 'direction' of education in the context of affirming the right to education. According to article 13, States Parties agree that education shall ' . . . promote understanding, tolerance and friendship among all nations and all racial, ethnic or religious groups . . . '

These texts can be traced to a proposal from the World Jewish Congress.[140] Its representative, Alex Easterman, proposed the following in the Working Group of the Commission on Human Rights, in December 1947: 'This education shall be directed to the full development of the human personality to strengthening respect for human rights and fundamental freedoms, and shall combat the spirit of intolerance and hatred against other nations or racial or religious groups everywhere.' Easterman explained that the current draft provision contained nothing about 'the spirit governing education which was an essential element. Neglect of this principle in Germany had been the main cause of two catastrophic wars.'[141] René Cassin, who thought the World Jewish Congress text was too long, offered an alternative: 'Education should aim at the full development of the physical, spiritual and moral powers of the individual. It shall be founded on the respect for human rights and must banish racial, national, religious or other hatreds.'[142] With minor modifications, the World Jewish Congress proposal was adopted by the Commission on Human Rights in December 1947.[143]

The provision was debated at length within the Commission in June 1948. UNESCO's legal advisor, Pierre Lebar, argued vigorously that the provision be retained, referring to Germany under Hitler.[144] Nevertheless, there were attempts to weaken the strong language in the original text. Several proposals were targeted at removing the reference to 'racial and religious groups'.[145]

[140] List of communications received from non-governmental organizations granted category (b) or (c) consultative status, 26 November 1947, E/CN.4/Sub.2/19.
[141] Summary record, Working Group on the Declaration, 10 December 1947, E/CN.4/AC.2/SR.8, p. 4.
[142] Ibid., p. 5.
[143] Ibid., p. 6.
[144] Summary record, Commission on Human Rights, 10 June 1948, E/CN.4/SR.67, p. 11. See also the remarks of Franz R. Bienenfeld of the World Jewish Congress, ibid., p. 13, and of Alexei Petrov of the Soviet Union, Summary record, Commission on Human Rights, 11 June 1948, E/CN.4/SR.69, pp. 3–4.
[145] Summary record, Commission on Human Rights, 10 June 1948, E/CN.4/SR.67, p. 16; Summary record, Commission on Human Rights, 11 June 1948, E/CN.4/SR.69, p. 1; United

EDUCATION TO COMBAT RACIAL PREJUDICE   159

In the Third Committee of the General Assembly, the British and the Americans argued that other groups should not be omitted.[146] In an effort to reach consensus, the Soviets suggested adding 'etc.' to the text.[147] A proposal by the United States and Mexico in the Third Committee changed the tone of the text, replacing the reference to 'intolerance and hatred' with 'tolerance and friendship'.[148] When the Third Committee voted, it agreed by a strong majority to restore the more specific language of 'racial and religious groups'.[149] Then, the Committee took virtually unanimous votes in favour of the American/Mexican amendment.[150]

The corresponding text in the International Covenant on Economic, Social and Cultural Rights appeared in the earliest provisions on economic, social, and cultural rights adopted by the Commission on Human Rights in 1951, at a time when there was still only one draft Covenant. It specified that education was to 'encourage. . . the suppression of all incitement to racial and other hatred'.[151] Franz Rudolf Bienenfeld of the World Jewish Congress called upon the United States to reverse its call for deletion of the reference to the promotion of tolerance. He pointed to the importance of strengthening respect of human rights 'in contrast to the Nazi doctrine of the enslavement of inferior races' and of promoting tolerance 'particularly between racial and religious groups, in contrast to the Nazi doctrine of racial inequality and the Nazi practice of racial extermination'. Bienenfeld referred to the UNESCO Constitution which recognized the misuse of education for the dissemination of racial hatred as one of the main causes of the Second World War.[152] The United States said it agreed to include the text of paragraph 26(2) of the Universal Declaration in the right to education provision of the Covenant,[153] but the proposal it submitted contained no reference to racial discrimination, as a representative of UNESCO pointed out.[154]

It was Yugoslavia that proposed adding the phrase about suppression of incitement to racial hatred, as it was 'particularly anxious that some provision should

---

Kingdom: Amendment to Article 23 of the Draft Declaration (E/800), 19 November 1948, A/C.3/354; Mexico-United States: Joint Amendment to Article 23 of the Draft Declaration (E/800), 19 November 1948, A/C.3/356.

[146] Summary record, Third Committee, 19 November 1948, A/C.3/SR.147, p. 599; Summary record, Third Committee, 19 November 1948, A/C.3/SR.148, p. 600.
[147] Summary record, Third Committee, 19 November 1948, A/C.3/SR.148, p. 601.
[148] Mexico-United States: Joint Amendment to Article 23 of the Draft Declaration (E/800), 19 November 1948, A/C.3/356.
[149] Summary record, Third Committee, 19 November 1948, A/C.3/SR.148, p. 603.
[150] Ibid., p. 604.
[151] Draft International Covenant on Human Rights, E/1992 - E/CN.4/640, Annex I, art. 28.
[152] Summary record, Commission on Human Rights, 4 May 1951, E/CN.4/SR.226, pp. 18–20.
[153] Summary record, Commission on Human Rights, 4 May 1951, E/CN.4/SR.227, p. 14.
[154] Summary record, Commission on Human Rights, 7 May 1951, E/CN.4/SR.228, p. 13, referring to E/CN.4/593/Rev.2

160   THE INTERNATIONAL BILL OF RIGHTS

be made for the direct use of education as a means of abolishing racial hatred'.[155] Yugoslavia told the Commission on Human Rights that it favoured 'an explicit reference to the prevention of discriminatory teaching and to the fostering of racial hatred' because '[t]here were countries in the world where backward peoples were being led astray by those nefarious practices. It was essential, therefore, clearly and explicitly to state that racial theories and discriminatory propaganda be banned'.[156] Chile then incorporated Yugoslavia's suggestion in a comprehensive proposal on the right to education. Chile's draft included a phrase whereby education was to encourage 'the suppression of all incitement to racial and other hatred'.[157] After Eleanor Roosevelt requested a separate vote on this text, the Commission agreed to retain it. The phrase about promoting understanding tolerance and friendship among all nations, racial, ethnic or religious groups, drawn from the Universal Declaration of Human Rights, was also included.[158]

During the 1951 session of the Commission, France said it was wrong to speak of 'racial groups' and it proposed that the term be replaced with 'ethnic groups'.[159] The rationale was not entirely clear although France may have been influenced by the ongoing work of UNESCO on the fallacy of the very notion of race and its rejection by progressive scientists.[160] France's motivation appears to have been misunderstood by some delegates who thought it was an attempt to downplay the significance of racial discrimination.[161] The delegate of Ukraine seized on the debate to attack the United States: '[T]he whole of the United States educational system was so permeated – he would even say saturated – with the doctrine of the racial superiority of white Americans and the inferiority of other races, particularly the negro races... [A]ny American who expressed progressive ideas on racial issues was considered to have betrayed his country's ideals.'[162]

At the same session of the Commission, the Soviet Union's Alexander P. Morosov condemned 'the appalling situation of colonial and non-self-government peoples in respect of educational facilities'. Morozov turned on the Australian government, citing a 1949 report in a Sydney newspaper stating that aboriginal children had been prohibited from attending school by the Administrator of the Northern Territory. According to the Sydney *Sun Pictorial*,

---

[155] Ibid., p. 4.

[156] Ibid.

[157] Chile: Proposal on the right to education and cultural rights based on suggestions of UNESCO (E/CN.4/AC.14/2/Add.4 Section IV and E/CN.4/541/Rev.1), 7 May 1951, E/CN.4/613/Rev.1.

[158] Summary record, Commission on Human Rights, 7 May 1951, E/CN.4/SR.228, p. 23. Also Report on the seventh session of the Commission on Human Rights, 16 April to 19 May 1951, E/1992 - E/CN.4/640, para. 47.

[159] Summary record, Commission on Human Rights, 4 May 1951, E/CN.4/SR.227, p. 19.

[160] Summary record, Commission on Human Rights, 5 May 1951, E/CN.4/SR.228, pp. 13, 16–19, 21. On the UNESCO statements, see *infra*, pp. 175–189.

[161] Summary record, Commission on Human Rights, 4 May 1951, E/CN.4/SR.227, p. 22.

[162] Summary record, Commission on Human Rights, 5 May 1951, E/CN.4/SR.228, p. 9.

the Administrator had said the presence of aboriginal children in State schools was contrary to Australian Government policy. An official report stated that 'native children needed special education which could only be given by missionary or State schools for natives under the control of the Director for the Department of Native Affairs'. Morozov also condemned South Africa, where the Prime Minister, Daniël F. Malan, had said the education of natives would 'weaken' the position of the white population. Morozov noted that 'very much smaller sums were spent on native education than on education for whites'. These were 'nothing less than manifestations of unashamed racial discrimination, based on the theory of the superiority of the white peoples', he said.[163] Morozov's allegations provoked a lengthy response from Australia's representative, Fred Whitlam. In Australia 'the interests of the indigenous population were looked after by the Protector', said Whitlam. He acknowledged that 'the process of assimilation . . . was accompanied by occasional friction'. He said that '[e]very effort was being made . . . to help the aboriginal peoples to adjust themselves to modern civilisation. Special tribunals had been set up to deal with offences involving indigenous persons, at which their customs, beliefs and culture were given full weight.'[164] Today, many Australians would recognize that there was more truth to Morozov's critique than to Whitlam's denial. A recent report for the Secretariat of the United Nations Permanent Forum on Indigenous Issues confirms that until the 1950s, it was common to exclude indigenous children from state schools.[165]

In 1952, the Commission on Human Rights adopted a draft Covenant on Economic, Social and Cultural Rights. The references to the direction of education adopted the previous year, including the requirement that education encourage the suppression of racial hatred, were incorporated.[166] An American amendment to the right to education provision removed the reference to racial hatred but maintained the language about tolerance.[167] A British amendment removed everything related to the direction of education.[168] Explaining its view, the United Kingdom delegate said that although 'the intention was excellent', ideas concerning the content of education should remain implicit. A good system of education 'must necessarily teach the mischief of incitement to racial

---

[163] Ibid., pp. 21–3. See also Summary record, Commission on Human Rights, 7 May 1951, E/CN.4/SR.228, pp. 14–15.

[164] Summary record, Commission on Human Rights, 7 May 1951, E/CN.4/SR.228, pp. 6–8.

[165] Andrea Smith, *Indigenous Peoples and Boarding Schools: A Comparative Study*, New York: Secretariat of the United Nations Permanent Forum on Indigenous Issues, 2009, p. 13, citing Quentin Beresford and Gary Partington, eds., *Reform and Resistance in Aboriginal Education*, Crawley: University of West Australia Press, 2003, p. 45.

[166] Draft Covenant on Economic, Social and Cultural Rights, E/2256-E/CN.4/669, Annex IA, 14(1).

[167] United States of America: Amendment to article 28, 2 May 1952, E/CN.4/L.80.

[168] United Kingdom: Revised amendment to article 28, 12 May 1952, E/CN.4/L.85/Rev.1.

162   THE INTERNATIONAL BILL OF RIGHTS

and other hatred . . . but to state positively that education should be directed to those aims was to narrow the whole concept of education', said Samuel Hoare.[169]

Criticizing the British and American amendments, Maurice Perlzweig of the World Jewish Congress insisted that 'true education' be clearly distinguished from 'the kind of education that produced blind obedience and which had poisoned the minds of countless children under the Hitler regime with disastrous effects'.[170] Several delegations insisted upon including the reference to racial hatred.[171] Lebanon presented a new draft provision where the provision on racial hatred was absent although it only explained why this was done after being challenged to do so by the Soviet Union.[172] The Lebanese representative said the reference to incitement to racial hatred had been dropped 'because he felt the idea was adequately expressed, in a positive form, in the passage which called for promoting understanding, tolerance and friendship'.[173] A separate vote was taken on the phrase, which was adopted by 12 votes to 6 with no abstentions.[174]

The reference to incitement of racial hatred was dropped by the Third Committee of the General Assembly.[175] Some delegates insisted that the point was adequately covered without such a specific text that it was unnecessary to single out racial hatred as opposed to other forms, and that it had a negative tone.[176] Australia suggested that such a clause might justify censorship that would encroach upon freedom of expression although it acknowledged this might be 'a rather far-fetched interpretation'.[177] But Ceylon said it was a 'paradoxical truth' that 'racial bigotry had its ugliest manifestations in the educational field'. Ceylon said the reference should be retained 'as a reminder to all countries that if differences between nations were to be eliminated, divisions within nations must be eliminated first, through education'.[178] Malaysia thought the reference was necessary because 'discrimination remained undeniably a phenomenon in

---

[169] Summary record, Commission on Human Rights, 8 May 1952, E/CN.4/SR.285, p. 5.

[170] Ibid., p. 11.

[171] Summary record, Commission on Human Rights, 8 May 1952, E/CN.4/SR.286, p. 3 (Yugoslavia), p. 4 (India).

[172] Lebanon: amendment to the amendment submitted by the United Kingdom E/CN.4/L.85, 8 May 1952, E CN.4/L.96.

[173] Summary record, Commission on Human Rights, 12 May 1952, E/CN.4/SR.290, p. 4.

[174] Ibid., p. 11. In favour: Belgium, Chile, China, Egypt, France, Greece, Pakistan, Poland, Ukraine, Soviet Union, Uruguay, Yugoslavia; against: India, Lebanon, Sweden, United Kingdom, United States, Australia.

[175] Report of the Third Committee, A/3764, para. 40.

[176] Summary record, Third Committee, 14 October 1957, A/C.3/SR.780, para. 31; Summary record, Third Committee, 15 October 1957, A/C.3/SR.781, para. 6; Summary record, Third Committee, 16 October 1957, A/C.3/SR.782, paras. 27, 39; Summary record, Third Committee, 16 October 1957, A/C.3/SR.783, paras. 41, 48; Summary record, Third Committee, 21 October 1957, A/C.3/SR.785, paras. 4, 16, 17, 37, 50; Summary record, Third Committee, 22 October 1957, A/C.3/SR.786, paras. 4, 12, 27, 31, 34, 49.

[177] Summary record, Third Committee, 16 October 1957, A/C.3/SR.782, para. 41.

[178] Summary record, Third Committee, 15 October 1957, A/C.3/SR.781, para. 17.

the modern world'.[179] Costa Rica and Greece proposed an amendment to delete the phrase on incitement to racial hatred.[180] Given that speaker after speaker had called for its removal from the draft, the actual vote showed that there was significant support for its retention. The Third Committee voted, by 35 votes to 22, with 8 abstentions, to delete the phrase on incitement to racial hatred.[181]

The Covenant on Economic, Social and Cultural Rights does not contain a non-discrimination clause targeted specifically at the right to education. The initial draft article adopted by the Commission on Human Rights in 1951 contained the following: '2. That educational facilities shall be accessible to all in accordance with the principle of non-discrimination enunciated in paragraph 1 of Article 1 of this Covenant'.[182] In the Commission, some States insisted upon including such a clause. Venezuela argued that a specific reference was required given 'conditions prevailing in a number of countries with regard to measures of discrimination, in particular racial segregation in the field of education'. No names were mentioned. 'Even if governments gave everyone equal educational opportunity, racial segregation could nevertheless constitute a very definite form of discrimination and could give some races feelings of superiority over others.'[183] Many States contended that the provision was superfluous in light of the more general recognition of equality and non-discrimination applicable to the Covenant as a whole. They said it might even create confusion by giving the impression that the general non-discrimination clause only applied to rights where the principle was specifically repeated.[184] But the objections to the clause were not solely technical. Samuel Hoare of the United Kingdom was concerned about 'the immediacy of the obligation on States in the realm of non-discrimination'.[185] The final text of the Commission did not include a non-discrimination clause.[186] There were renewed calls for this in the Third Committee of the General Assembly.[187]

Reaffirming a right to equality and non-discrimination in the area of education would only have underscored the reality of discrimination in several member States, including some of the most powerful. During the debates, developed countries were frequently challenged about the adequacy of education for minorities and indigenous peoples within their own territory as well as those in

[179] Summary record, Third Committee, 22 October 1957, A/C.3/SR.786, para. 31.
[180] Costa Rica and Greece: amendment to the Working Party's text for Article 14 of the draft Covenant on Economic, Social and Cultural Rights (A/C.3/L.625), 22 October 1957, A/C.3 /L.628.
[181] Summary record, Third Committee, 22 October 1957, A/C.3/SR.787, para. 44.
[182] Draft International Covenant on Human Rights, E/1992 - E/CN.4/640, Annex I, art. 28.
[183] Summary record, Commission on Human Rights, 12 May 1952, E/CN.4/SR.289, p. 4.
[184] Report on the eighth session of the Commission on Human Rights, 14 April to 14 June 1952, E/2256, para. 119.
[185] Summary record, Commission on Human Rights, 12 May 1952, E/CN.4/SR.289, p. 10.
[186] Draft international covenants on human rights, annotation prepared by the Secretary-General, 1 July 1955, A/2929, p. 324.
[187] Summary record, Third Committee, 16 October 1957, A/C.3/SR.782, para. 14.

164 THE INTERNATIONAL BILL OF RIGHTS

their colonies or in territories over which they exercised mandates. Poland noted that the former United States Secretary of State, James Byrnes, had defended racial segregation in schools.[188] Poland said that in African colonies, only a small percentage of indigenous children attended school whereas European children in those countries had adequate facilities. Its delegate pointed to French Morocco where only 78,500 Moslem children out of a population of 8 million were enrolled in schools.[189] France replied to criticism by claiming that education in its overseas territories had undergone 'radical change', and that school attendance had doubled in some of them.[190] In the Third Committee, Bulgaria said that '[i]n colonies and dependent territories the situation was even less satisfactory. Indeed, it left something to be desired even in some industrial countries: it was common knowledge that many children had to endure racial discrimination in the United States of America.'[191]

The Right to Marry

The Universal Declaration of Human Rights also refers expressly to 'race' in article 16(1). The right to marry and to found a family is affirmed 'without any limitation due to race, nationality or religion'. The early drafts of the Declaration recognized an equal right of men and women to contract marriage, although they did not contemplate a right to marry as such and made no reference to 'race, nationality or religion'.[192] In August 1948, immediately prior to the General Assembly session, the Economic and Social Council adopted a resolution on 'mixed marriages' in which it '[d]eplores all legislative measures which forbid mixed marriages between persons differing as to colour, race, nationality, citizenship or religion, and in general such other legislative of administrative provisions as restrict the freedom to choose a spouse (with the exception of restrictions based on family relationships, age, the nature of the functions being exercised, or other similar reasons)...'[193]

The phrase 'without distinction as to race, nationality or religion' was added to the Universal Declaration of Human Rights by the Third Committee in response to a Mexican proposal.[194] Explaining the rationale, the Mexican delegate acknowledged that this was a repetition of article 2, but that repeating ideas again

---

[188] Summary record, Commission on Human Rights, 12 May 1952, E/CN.4/SR.290, p. 6. Byrnes was then Governor of South Carolina where he fought to retain school segregation.

[189] Ibid.

[190] Ibid., p. 5.

[191] Summary record, Third Committee, 16 October 1957, A/C.3/SR.782, para. 12.

[192] Draft International Declaration on Human Rights, E/600, Annex A, pp. 17–22, at p. 18.

[193] Report of the second session of the Commission on the Status of Women, 30 August 1948, E/RES/154 (VII) D.

[194] Mexico: Amendments to Articles 3, 6, 7, 14, 23 and 25 of the Draft Declaration (E/800), 12 October 1948, A/C.3/266. Also Comments of the Mexican Government of the Draft International

THE RIGHT TO MARRY   165

and again was not necessarily undesirable and would 'strengthen the article immeasurably in the eyes of the common man'. Pablo Campos Ortiz referred to 'notorious cases of discrimination in marriage, particularly by the Nazis'.[195] The Soviets endorsed the Mexican proposal as 'most opportune', noting that 'in certain parts of the United States, for example, mixed marriages were heavily penalised'.[196] The only overt objection to the Mexican proposal came from Pakistan, which said it completely disregarded the religious factor as a hindrance to marriage.[197] Mexico's amendment was adopted on a roll call vote, by 22 votes to 15, with 6 abstentions.[198]

Consideration of the mixed marriage issue by the Economic and Social Council, as well as by the Commission on the Status of Women, continued after the adoption of article 16 of the Universal Declaration. These were the early days of the Cold War. The Soviet Union was criticized by the British and the Americans because in some cases it denied the right to emigrate to Soviet nationals who married foreigners.[199] The Soviets reacted by insisting that the focus be placed on racial discrimination and the right to marriage. In the Commission on the Status of Women, the Soviet delegate claimed that in the United States 15 states prohibited mixed marriages, 10 prohibited marriage between whites and mulattoes and 5 prohibited marriage between whites and Indians. If a white man married a woman of colour in a state that authorized mixed marriage and then moved to a state where this was prohibited, the marriage would be declared null and void.[200]

The Secretary-General sought information from Member States about marriage legislation, including whether men and women had free choice in marriage regardless of nationality, race, religion, or political affiliation. Most replies indicated that there were no such restrictions. A few States indicated that there were prohibitions on marriage based upon religion (Egypt, Greece, Iran, Israel, Lebanon, Pakistan, Syria).[201] Only two Member States acknowledged racial discrimination in marriage legislation. South Africa reported that in the provinces of the Orange Free State and Transvaal existing legislation did not 'contemplate' marriage of persons of different races and that 'in these provinces they do not take place'.[202] South Africa filed a supplementary report in which it said there

---

Declaration on Human Rights and the Draft International Covenant on Human Rights, 16 April 1948, E/CN.4/82/Add.1, p. 4.

[195] Summary record, Third Committee, 6 November 1948, A/C.3/SR.124, p. 364.
[196] Ibid., p. 365.
[197] Summary record, Third Committee, 8 November 1948, A/C.3/SR.125, p. 374.
[198] Ibid., p. 375.
[199] Information Concerning Soviet Exit Visas, 16 June 1949, FRUS 1949 V, pp. 617–822, at p, 619.
[200] Summary record, Commission on the Status of Women, 25 March 1949, E/CN.6/SR.47, p. 6. See also the remarks in the Economic and Social Council: Summary record, Economic and Social Council, 1 August 1949, E/SR.316, p. 477.
[201] Civil liberties for women, 17 January 1951, E/CN.6/157 and Add 1 and 2.
[202] Ibid.

166　THE INTERNATIONAL BILL OF RIGHTS

was freedom of choice 'subject to the provisions of Act no. 55 of 1949'. South Africa did not bother to provide the title of the statute in question, which was 'The Prohibition of Mixed Marriages Act'.[203] The United States declared that this was a matter governed by the states, not the federal government. 'No statutory restrictions exist on the basis of nationality (apart from race) . . .', it reported.[204] At the time, 29 of the 48 states in the United States had relevant legislation on the subject, all of it prohibiting 'Negro-white marriages'.[205]

The right to marry is protected by article 23 of the International Covenant on Civil and Political Rights. The text of the provision is derived from article 16 of the Universal Declaration of Human Rights. But in contrast with the Declaration, the Covenant does not specify that the right to marry is 'without any limitation due to race, nationality or religion'. The Commission on the Status of Women proposed that article 23 be added to the draft Covenant.[206] A few delegates noted that the list of grounds in article 16 of the Declaration did not correspond to the longer enumeration found in article 2 of the Universal Declaration, but the curious result was to delete the clause altogether. The *travaux préparatoires* of the Commission on Human Rights are unclear, making it difficult to reach any legal conclusion about the significance of the removal of the reference to race, nationality or religion.[207] The suggestion returned in the Third Committee of the General Assembly, where the Venezuelan delegate said that while a reference to non-discrimination was legally necessary, 'discrimination had caused so much suffering, not only in countries which had recently emerged from colonial status, but also in more advanced nations, that he wondered whether a clause dealing with it should not be added. . . [T]he inclusion of such a clause would have some constructive effect, since it would be publicised through the information agencies of the United Nations.' He said he would support 'a strongly worded paragraph condemning religious and racial discrimination in marriage'.[208] Italy voiced support for the Venezuelan proposal but recognized that such a clause was not necessary in a legal sense given the general non-discrimination clause.[209] Bulgaria also endorsed the suggestion.[210] But there was also opposition to the reference, based upon the danger of confusion if some provisions of the

---

[203] Civil liberties for women, 4 August 1952, E/CN.6/157/Add.3. See Pierre L. van den Berghe, 'Miscegenation in South Africa' (1960) 1 *Cahiers d'Études Africaines* 68.

[204] Civil liberties for women, 17 January 1951, E/CN.6/157.

[205] James R. Browning, 'Anti-Miscegenation Laws in the United States' (1951) 1 *Duke Bar Journal* 26.

[206] Draft Covenant on Civil and Political Rights, 7 April 1953, E/CN.4/686.

[207] Summary record, Commission on Human Rights, 12 May 1953, E/CN.4/SR.384, especially pp. 23–4. See also Draft international covenants on human rights, annotation prepared by the Secretary-General, 1 July 1955, A/2929, p. 170.

[208] Summary record, Third Committee, 1 November 1961, A/C.3/SR.1090, para. 46.

[209] Summary record, Third Committee, 6 November 1961, A/C.3/SR.1093, para. 47.

[210] Summary record, Third Committee, 7 November 1961, A/C.3/SR.1094, para. 8.

THE RIGHT TO MARRY 167

Covenant had special non-discrimination clauses, and no formal proposal was ever submitted.[211]

* * *

The International Bill of Rights is the centrepiece of international human rights law. Its provisions were negotiated over a period spanning two decades. The early drafts did not accord any particular attention to racial discrimination. This can be explained by the composition of the bodies that were responsible for the subject. Only a small number of people of colour were involved during the initial stages. Furthermore, the drafting of these texts does not appear to have interested non-government organizations like the National Association for the Advancement of Colored People and prominent personalities associated with it. W.E.B. Du Bois thought it would be a 'waste of money and time' for the NAACP to be represented in Geneva for meetings of Sub-Commission on the Prevention of Discrimination. 'If Mrs Roosevelt or the Commission had wished our advice or opinion they have had a year to ask it. They have, on the contrary, discouraged us from action in every possible way', he wrote.[212] To the extent civil society was engaged in promoting the anti-discrimination agenda, this seems largely to have been the work of Jewish organizations.

Over time, the changing composition of the General Assembly influenced the two covenants. These were only finalized in 1966. By then African and Asian States had come to dominate the General Assembly. Their influence can be seen in provisions like article 26 of the International Covenant on Civil and Political Rights. Western States were never enthusiastic and might well have suppressed the provision entirely had it not been for the massive support from States of the Global South. The same can be said of article 20(2) dealing with incitement to racial discrimination.

The absence of any explicit condemnation of racial discrimination in the Universal Declaration of Human Rights never seems to have prevented reference to it, as well as to the Charter of the United Nations, as sources of international law prohibiting racism and apartheid. For many years after their adoption the two Covenants were of more limited application because of the modest rates of ratification. South Africa only ratified the two Covenants in the 1990s after apartheid had been dismantled.

The two Covenants have been applied to racial discrimination in the work of the Human Rights Committee and the Committee on Economic, Social and Cultural Rights. In application of the International Covenant on Civil and

---

[211] Summary record, Third Committee, 2 November 1961, A/C.3/SR.1091, paras. 14, 29; Report of the Third Committee, 5 December 1961, A/5000, para. 86.
[212] Notes on human rights petition, 24 November 1947, W.E.B. Du Bois Papers (MS 312).

168 THE INTERNATIONAL BILL OF RIGHTS

Political Rights, the Human Rights Committee has occasionally addressed issues of racial discrimination, for example in situations of police profiling[213] and where there has been racial bias in criminal trials.[214] In a case involving an African American who was challenging extradition from Canada to the United States where he was threatened with capital punishment, the Committee decided that there was no threat of 'systemic discrimination'.[215] The Committee found a violation of article 26 in an application by Senegalese veterans of the French army whose pension payments were much lower than those of their European counterparts.[216] When it examines periodic reports of States Parties, the Committee occasionally comments on manifestations of racial discrimination. For example, in its Concluding Observations on a report from the United States, it said it was 'concerned with reports that some 50 % of homeless people are African American although they constitute only 12 % of the United States population'. The Committee said the United States should 'bring an end to such de facto and historically generated racial discrimination'.[217] It concluded that in Australia migrants from African countries were being particularly targeted by discrimination and racial profiling.[218] One explanation for the relatively low level of engagement with these issues may be the existence of a specialized body with similar powers and authority, the Committee on the Elimination of Racial Discrimination, established pursuant to the International Convention on the Elimination of All Forms of Racial Discrimination.

---

[213] *Williams Lecraft v. Spain* (no. 1493/2006), Views, 27 July 2009, CCPR/C/96/D/1493/2006, para. 7.4.

[214] General Comment No. 32, Article 14: Right to equality before courts and tribunals and to a fair trial, 23 August 2007, CCPR/C/GC/32, para. 25.

[215] *Cox v. Canada* (no. 539/1993), Views, 9 December 1994, CCPR/C/52/D/539/19930, para. 16.7.

[216] *Ngeye et al. v. France* (no. 96/1985), Views, 3 April 1985, CCPR/C/35/D/196/1985, para. 9.5.

[217] Concluding Observations, United States of America, 18 December 2006, CCPR/C/USA/CO/3/Rev.1, para. 22.

[218] Concluding Observations, Australia, 1 December 2017, CCPR/C/AUS/CO/6, para. 19.

7

UNESCO

Fighting the Doctrine of Racial Inequality

'Scientific' Racism

Racial inequality was one of the hallmarks of the Nazi regime. In its judgment, the International Military Tribunal described how Chapter 2 of Book 1 of Hitler's *Mein Kampf* was 'dedicated to what may be called the "Master Race" theory, the doctrine of Aryan superiority over all other races, and the right of Germans in virtue of this superiority to dominate and use other peoples for their own ends'.[1] Many of those around the world who fought to defeat Hitler's regime were driven by their revulsion at the Nazi doctrines of racial supremacy that led inexorably to the unprecedented genocide of Europe's Jewish population. The racist ideology of the Nazis brought suffering and destruction to Roma and Sinti, to Poles, and to other ethnic groups within Germany and occupied Europe. The children fathered by the African troops who participated in French occupation of the Rhineland in 1919 and 1920 were not immune from persecution. But while Hitler's Germany marked the paroxysm of racist ideologies, the Nazis had no monopoly on the outlook in which it was rooted. Notions of racial inequality were widely held by academics in a range of disciplines, and not just in Germany.

So-called 'scientific' racism is said to have originated in the work of Arthur de Gobineau, who published a study on the 'inequality of human races' in France in the mid-1850s.[2] Gobineau identified three principal racial groups, described as white, yellow, and black, concluding that 'history springs only from contact with the white races'. The three racial groups were ranked: 'the negro, being hardly more than a mere brute, the yellow race committing none of the strange excesses so common among negroes but tending to mediocrity in everything, and at the top the white race gifted with energetic intelligence, perseverance, an instinct for order and a love of liberty'.[3] Gobineau viewed the Aryan race as

---

[1] *France et al. v. Goering et al.*, Judgment, 30 September–1 October 1946 (1948) 1 IMT 171, at p. 180. See Michael Burleigh and Wolfgang Wippermann, *The Racial State, Germany 1933–1945*, Cambridge: Cambridge University Press, 1991.

[2] Arthur de Gobineau, *Essai sur l'inégalité des races humaines*, Paris: Firmin Didot, 1853.

[3] Raymond J. Vincent, 'Race in International Relations' (1982) 58 *International Affairs* 658, at p. 660.

The International Legal Order's Colour Line. William A. Schabas, Oxford University Press.
© Oxford University Press 2023. DOI: 10.1093/oso/9780197744475.003.0007

170   UNESCO: FIGHTING THE DOCTRINE OF RACIAL INEQUALITY

the most developed and warned that race mixing would result in the 'downfall of civilisations'.[4] During the late nineteenth and the first half of the twentieth centuries, Gobineau's work inspired a range of scholarly initiatives premised upon racial inequality and white supremacy.[5]

The chapter in this volume on the establishment of the United Nations points to the failure of the Charter of the United Nations to direct special attention to the scourge of racial discrimination.[6] That woeful omission was to some extent rectified in the Constitution of the United Nations Education, Science and Culture Organisation (UNESCO), adopted in November 1945 at the Conference for the Establishment of UNESCO. The following paragraph appears in the preamble: 'That the great and terrible war which has now ended was a war made possible by the denial of the democratic principles of the dignity, equality and mutual respect of men, and by the propagation, in their place, through ignorance and prejudice, of *the doctrine of the inequality of men and races*'.[7]

The clause on racial inequality was not part of the initial draft of the Constitution prepared in the name of the Conference of Allied Ministers of Education.[8] The initial draft of the UNESCO Constitution was a product of the United States Department of State.[9] It contained a preamble but there was no reference to racial discrimination.[10] The draft went through significant revision at the London Conference in November 1945, where the organization was founded. According to a report on the Conference by the United States delegation, it was 'rewritten so as to take account of a wide-spread desire for a statement which would incorporate the highest aspirations of the peoples of the United Nations and would evoke a ready response from all who believe in the dignity of man and the validity of his striving toward knowledge and his search for truth'.[11]

The clause on racial inequality can be traced to the first sentence of the first recital in the French proposals for the preamble of the Constitution: 'Whereas the world war, in which civilisation and mankind itself have narrowly escaped

---

[4] Michael D. Biddiss, *Father of Racist Ideology: The Social and Political Thought of Count Gobineau*, London, Weidenfeld and Nicolson, 1970.

[5] Juan Comas, ' "Scientific" Racism Again?' (1961) 2 *Current Anthropology* 303.

[6] *Supra*, pp. 93–104.

[7] Constitution of the United Nations Educational, Scientific and Cultural Organisation (1947) 4 UNTS 275, Recital 3 (emphasis added).

[8] Conference of Allied Ministers of Education, Draft proposals for an educational and cultural organization of the United Nations, in Conference for the Establishment of the United Nations Educational, Scientific and Cultural Organisation, ECO/CONF/29, pp. 1–5. Also 'Draft Constitution' (1945) 23 *International Conciliation* 734; International Organisation for Education and Cultural Cooperation, 8 March 1945, in *Postwar Foreign Policy Preparation, 1939–1945*, Washington: Department of State, 1949, p. 649.

[9] Secretary of State to Winant, 11 April 1945, FRUS 1945 I, p. 1510.

[10] International Organisation for Education and Cultural Cooperation, 8 March 1945, in *Postwar Foreign Policy Preparation, 1939–1945*, Washington: Department of State, 1949, p. 649.

[11] Summary Report on the UNESCO Conference, 3 December 1945, FRUS 1945 I, pp. 1524–9, at p. 1526.

destruction, was rendered possible by the abandonment of democratic ideas the promulgation of doctrines glorifying violence and proclaiming the inequality of races . . . '[12] The Drafting Committee of the First Commission reformulated the two drafts, incorporating the French proposal about racial inequality in the concluding phrase of recital 3: ' . . . and by the propagation, in their place, of ignorance and prejudice and the doctrine of the inequality of men and races . . . '[13] This was adopted by the Commission, the only critical observation predictably coming from the delegate of South Africa, who noted the 'negative character' of the paragraph and the mistake of giving undue prominence to one among many causes of war.[14] It appears that the Central Drafting Committee made some slight changes to the wording, as can be seen in the final version contained in the report of the First Commission to the plenary Conference.[15] The preamble was then adopted unanimously and without any comment by the plenary.[16]

Race-related issues were not significant during the sessions of the London Conference. 'Lying and ill-informed propaganda about any country or race must not be allowed', said Rajkumari Amrit Kaur of India, in a statement that stands out because it is so isolated.[17] J.J. Moniz de Aragao of Brazil, who was one of the vice-presidents of the London Conference, expressed the desire of his Government 'that the projected organisation should give special attention to the problems originating from racial contacts, emphasising that education should bear such problems in mind and offer equal opportunities to all young people and adults without distinction of racial origin'.[18] In a puzzling statement that seems terribly out of place, at least by today's standards, he referred to Brazilian sociologists, 'who have affirmed the principle now defended by the Committee responsible for this Conference: that the inequality of races and biological inferiority of mixed blood, when it exists, are contingencies connected with the lowering of the standards of the social and cultural classes'.[19]

The ancestor of UNESCO was the International Committee of Intellectual Cooperation, set up by the League of Nations in September 1921. Its membership consisted of individuals, many of them very prominent intellectuals such as Albert Einstein, Marie Curie, Henri Bergson, Sarvepalli Radhakrishnan, Thomas

---

[12] French proposals for the Constitution of the United Nations Organisation of intellectual co-operation, ECO/CONF/29, pp. 5–9, at p. 5.

[13] Report of the Drafting Committee, ECO/CONF/Com.1/18, reproduced in ECO/CONF/29, pp. 107–8.

[14] Summary record of the fifth meeting of the First Commission, 12 November 1945, ECO/CONF/29, p. 101.

[15] Draft text of the Preamble and Article I of the Constitution, as adopted by the First Commission and revised by the Central Drafting Committee, 13 November 1945, ECO/CONF/12.

[16] Seventh plenary meeting, 14 November 1945, ECO/CONF/29, pp. 61–4, at p. 62.

[17] Third plenary meeting, 2 November 1945, ECO/CONF/29, pp. 28–39, at p. 33.

[18] Ibid., p. 29.

[19] Ibid.

172   UNESCO: FIGHTING THE DOCTRINE OF RACIAL INEQUALITY

Mann, and Paul Painlevé.[20] Three years later, the League Assembly welcomed the establishment of the International Institute of Intellectual Cooperation which was henceforth formally affiliated with the League of Nations. In 1928, there were initiatives to convene a second Universal Races Congress, similar in nature to the celebrated gathering in London in 1911.[21] However, the International Committee was wary and the project did not proceed.[22]

After the Nazis took power in 1933, Ignaz Zollschan, a Czech physician, undertook an international campaign against racist anthropology.[23] Zollschan was '[a]mong the first and most energetic anti-racist activists in Europe'.[24] He first obtained the backing of the government of Czechoslovakia. In 1933, the Czech Academy published a book on the scientific basis of the equality of races.[25] This led to support from Cardinal Pacelli, who would soon become Pope Pius XII. The Czechoslovak president, Edvard Beneš, proposed that the International Institute for Intellectual Cooperation organize 'a discussion on the doctrine of racial superiority'. Three sections of the International Congress on Anthropology, held in London in 1934, approved a resolution calling on the International Institute to undertake research on the subject, '[i]n view of the fallacious use of the term Aryan, increasingly prevalent at the present day, with the implied association of inherent mental aptitude and cultural achievements', although the resolution was then withheld by the Bureau of the Congress.[26] Senior officials of the International Institute of Intellectual Cooperation were favourable, including its president, Edouard Herriot, a former French Prime Minister, and its director, Henri Bonnet. However, as UNESCO officials were later to explain, '[i]n order to avoid giving offence to Germany, the League of Nations declined to consider convening an expert committee. The scientific facts which could so easily have been disclosed had to be concealed, lest Dr. Goebbels' feelings should be

---

[20] Jean-Jacques Renoliet, *L'UNESCO oubliée, la Société des Nations et la coopération intellectuelle (1919-1946)*, Paris: Publications de la Sorbonne, 1999.

[21] See *supra*, pp. 18–19.

[22] Daniel Laqua, 'Transnational Intellectual Cooperation, the League of Nations, and the Problem of Order' (2011) 6 *Journal of Global History* 223, at pp. 232–3.

[23] See his own publications: Ignaz Zollschan, *Le role du facteur racial dans les questions fondamentales de la morphologie culturelle*, Paris: Arthur Rousseau, 1934; Ignaz Zollschan, *The Significance of the Racial Factor as a Basis in Cultural Development*, London: Play House Press, 1934. On Zollschan, see also: Paul Weindling, 'The Evolution of Jewish Identity: Ignaz Zollschan between Jewish and Aryan Race Theories, 1910-1945', in: Geoffrey Cantor and Marc Swetlitz, eds., *Jewish Tradition and the Challenge of Darwinism*, Chicago: University of Chicago Press, 2006, pp. 116–36; Paul Weindling, 'Central Europe Confronts German Racial Hygiene: Friedrich Hertz, Hugo Iltis and Ignaz Zollschan as Critics of German Racial Hygiene', in: M. Turda and P. Weindling, eds., *Blood and Homeland: Eugenics and Racial Nationalism in Central Europe 1900-1940*, Budapest: Central European University Press, 2006, pp. 263–80.

[24] Elazar Barkan, *The Retreat of Scientific Racism: Changing Concepts of Race in Britain and the United States between the World Wars*, Cambridge, Cambridge University Press, 1992, p. 318.

[25] Ibid., p. 320, fn. 109.

[26] Question of the Factor of Race as a Basis in Cultural Development, LNA R4035/5B/13014/13014.

'SCIENTIFIC' RACISM   173

hurt, and fell victim in its turn to the spirit of Munich.'[27] This reticence of the International Institute for Intellectual Cooperation to address racism was consistent with the organization's general aloofness to political developments of the time.[28]

UNESCO's first director was Julian Huxley, a British biologist. Huxley was then described as a 'left-wing humanist'; perhaps today he might be called a 'progressive'. But his views on racism and discrimination don't always fit this profile. Writing about America's 'negro problem' in *The Spectator*, in 1924, Huxley said '[t]he negro mind is as different from the white mind as the negro from the white body', that '[t]hey are often childlike in their intellects', and that '[y]ou have only to go to a n . . . r camp meeting to see the African mind in operation.'[29] By the 1940s, Huxley was probably more careful in the way he spoke and wrote about people of African descent. Yet a letter to Alfred Métraux in 1950 referred to the 'the expansive and rhythm-loving Negro temperament', echoing his remarks of the early 1920s.[30] Although Huxley was a 'committed eugenicist', he was also a very public opponent of racism.[31]

Despite the preambular reference to racial inequality in its Constitution, race and racism did not figure in UNESCO's early priorities.[32] The push for its engagement came from the human rights organs of the United Nations. In December 1947, at its first session, the Sub-Commission on the Prevention of Discrimination and the Protection of Minorities requested that 'UNESCO consider, as a first step, the desirability of initiating and recommending the general adoption of a programme of disseminating scientific facts with regard to race.'[33] This was later reformulated more purposely in a resolution of the Economic and

---

[27] 'UNESCO launches major world campaign against racial discrimination', Background Paper 104, 19 July 1950, p. 3. Also Albert Métraux, 'UNESCO and the Racial Problem' (1950) 2 *International Social Science Bulletin* 384, at pp. 385–6.

[28] Jean-Jacques Renoliet, *L'UNESCO oubliée, la Société des Nations et la coopération intellectuelle (1919–1946)*, Paris: Publications de la Sorbonne, 1999, pp. 119–25

[29] Julian S. Huxley, 'America Revisited, III. The Negro Problem', *The Spectator*, 29 November 1924, p. 821.

[30] Huxley to Métraux, 26 January 1950, UNESCO Archives 323.12 A 102.

[31] Paul Weindling, 'Julian Huxley and the Continuity of Eugenics in Twentieth-century Britain' (2012) 10 *Journal of Modern European History* 480.

[32] 'Progress Report Prepared by UNESCO Secretariat, Paris, 26 March 1947' (1947) 25 *International Conciliation* 317, at pp. 319–21. Also 'Report of the Chairman of the Programme Coordinating Committee, Archibald, MacLeish, to the UNESCO General Conference, Paris, 9 December 1946' (1947) 25 *International Conciliation* 304; Howard E Wilson, 'The Development of UNESCO' (1947) 25 *International Conciliation* 295, at p. 297.

[33] Report submitted to the Commission on Human Rights, 6 December 1947, E/CN.4/52, p. 17. The proposal was endorsed without change by the Commission on Human Rights: Report of the Commission on Human Rights, Second Session, Geneva, 2 December to 17 December 1947, E/600, para. 35.

174 UNESCO: FIGHTING THE DOCTRINE OF RACIAL INEQUALITY

Social Council, the phrase 'with regard to race' replaced with 'designed to remove what is commonly known as racial prejudice'.[34]

In May 1949, UNESCO reported on implementation of the resolution, noting that 'recognised scientific authorities' in various parts of the world had made statements during the Second World War concerning Nazi racial theories, including Britain's Royal Anthropological Society, the American Anthropological Association, the Society for the Study of Social Issues, and the Brazilian Society of Anthropologists. UNESCO said a compilation and publication of such statements, with a suitable introduction, could be done almost immediately. It also referred to the work of individual anthropologists, whose work was not readily accessible to a broad public. Their materials could be organized around several themes, such as race from the standpoint of biology, anthropology, and psychology, the cultural contributions of 'the races of mankind', the 'irrational nature of race prejudice', its cost, 'successful experiments in race relations', and methods of combating race prejudice. The report said an expert group would be convened in July 1949 to issue a statement on 'racial problems and racial prejudice'.[35]

The ECOSOC resolution also requested the Secretariat to prepare a study of 'the main types of discrimination'. In early June 1949, the Secretary-General of the United Nations responded with a lengthy 'Report on the Prevention on Discrimination'. On the subject of race, the Secretary-General wrote that '[c]ontemporary science does not admit the concept of race as meaning a division of mankind into different parts, each of them characterised by a complex of special traits, both physical and mental. Anthropology has failed clearly to establish such a concept'.[36] The Report concluded that it was not possible to speak of races as 'distinct human groups'. It said use of the term 'race' to describe a definite human group was 'illegitimate from the scientific standpoint'.[37] The Secretary-General turned to the issue of 'prejudice' based upon race, offering at least in part an historical explanation. Following 'the Age of Discovery', traders sought to justify the use of cheap labour and slaves in 'newly discovered countries' with reference to 'a belief in the racial superiority of the exploiters and the racial inferiority of the colonized or controlled peoples'. When slavery or political submission ended, 'the interest in considering the peoples formerly subjugated as inferior did not disappear, but rather increased'.[38] The lengthy report was very

[34] Report of the Second Session of the Economic and Social Council, 1–2 March 1948, E/RES/116 (VI) B, para. B(iii).

[35] Note on implementation of Resolution E/RES/116 (VI) B, 9 May 1949, E/CN.4/173, pp. 4–6.

[36] Report on the Prevention of Discrimination, 7 June 1949, E/CN.4/Sub.2/40, para. 59. See also The Main Types and Causes of Discrimination, 7 June 1949, E/CN.4/Sub.2/40/Rev.1, which includes a lengthy bibliography.

[37] Ibid., para. 63.

[38] Ibid., para. 69.

thin on concrete examples. It never mentioned the apartheid system of South Africa, which had been formally introduced the year before, or the Jim Crow measures that were widespread in the United States.

UNESCO's 1950 Statement on 'The Race Question'

Before the proposed UNESCO meeting of experts was convened, the organization's General Conference instructed the Director-General to 'study and collect scientific materials concerning questions of race', to 'give wide diffusion to the scientific information collected' and to 'prepare an educational campaign based on this information'.[39] The reference to 'questions of race' was clearly more reserved than the language used in the ECOSOC resolution, which had spoken of 'racial prejudice'. Organisation of the expert gathering was the responsibility of UNESCO's head of social sciences, Arthur Ramos, who died suddenly only weeks before the meeting. Ramos had already set the tone with an article in UNESCO's journal, *Social Sciences*. '[T]he "racial" technique has led to one of the greatest states of disequilibrium that exist, namely war. The present century has just paid tribute in the shape of the European nations' Second Great War, of which there were many causes; but one cause was undoubtedly the philosophy of racial domination espoused by the racialists of our time, that is to say the Germans', he wrote. 'We see then, in the last analysis, that racialism is a direct result of Europeanisation and imperialism.'[40]

The Committee of Experts on Race Problems convened in Paris in December 1949. In preparation, UNESCO issued a detailed memorandum that appears to be the outline of a book, developing the themes that were identified in the report on implementation of the resolution earlier that year.[41] The Committee had eight members: E. Franklin Frazier, Ashley Montagu, Ernest Beaglehold, Juan Comas, L.A. Costa Pinto, Morris Ginsberg, Humayun Kabir, and Claude Levi-Strauss. Frazier, head of the sociology department at Howard University and the first Black president of the American Sociological Association, was elected chairman.[42] Montagu was designated as rapporteur.[43] It was 'an international

[39] Records of the General Conference of UNESCO, Fourth Session, 1949, p. 22.

[40] Arthur Ramos, 'The Question of Race and the Democratic World' (1949) 1(3–4) *International Social Science Bulletin* 1, at p. 10.

[41] Committee of Experts on Race Problems, Implementation of the Resolution of the Economic and Social Council, 7 December 1949, UNESCO/SS/Conf.1/2.

[42] See Frazier's magnum opus, *Black Bourgeoisie*, New York: Macmillan, 1962. Also Anthony M. Platt, *E. Franklin Frazier Reconsidered*, New Brunswick, N.J.: Rutgers, 1991. For a critical assessment of the individual views of the Committee's members, see Sebastián Gil-Riaño, 'Relocating anti-racist science: the 1950 UNESCO Statement on Race and economic development in the global South' (2018) 51 *British Journal for the History of Science* 281.

[43] UNESCO/SS/Conf.1/SR.1, p. 4.

176 UNESCO: FIGHTING THE DOCTRINE OF RACIAL INEQUALITY

dream team of scholars' assembled to draft 'the final rebuttal to Nazism and eugenicists worldwide'.[44]

Josep Xirau explained UNESCO's position to the participants, noting that it had been entrusted by the United Nations with the collection and dissemination of scientific information on race problems 'and of fighting racial prejudice'. He said a definition of race 'which would have prestige and would carry exceptional weight in the scientific world, would be most valuable to UNESCO'.[45] Claude Lévi-Strauss, the great French anthropologist, thought the experts agreed on 'the need to explain to men why they are not identical – and that entailed the need for a definition of race from the physical and biological points of view'.[46] Lévi-Strauss said that 'race had a purely historical, wholly relative and extremely fluid value, since the concentration of genes never reached a point of density and permanence sufficient to make the resulting character unchangeable and non-reversible. It was regrettable that excessive cautiousness had led scientists for more than half a century to leave such a delicate problem to less qualified people'.[47]

Edward Lawson represented the United Nations Secretariat as an observer. He explained that the Division of Human Rights had reached the conclusion that it was 'scientifically illegitimate' to attempt to define the concept of race. Lawson told the expert group that the Secretariat felt what was needed was 'a clear, concise statement of fact about race which could be disseminated all over the world and which would serve as a basis for eliminating false ideas about race'.[48] His words were echoed by the rapporteur, Ashley Montagu, who explained that genetical and social evidence from recent research showed 'race questions were not of a biological character'. Montagu said differences in genes among humans were insignificant, and that all belonged to the human race 'with superficial physical differences'. The real 'species character' common to humans was 'educability or plasticity'.[49] Montagu was himself somewhat of an *enfant terrible* on the subject. Trained in the United States by Ruth Benedict and Franz Boas, he had advanced his controversial positions in scholarly debates,[50] apparently 'with little humility and, probably as a result, little effect', according to Michelle Brattain.[51] Montagu

---

[44] Ibram X. Kendi, 'Reigning Assimilationists and Defiant Black Power: The Struggle to Define and Regulate Racist Ideas', in Keisha N. Blain, Christopher Cameron, and Ashley D. Farmer, eds., *New Perspectives on the Black Intellectual Tradition*, Chicago: Northwestern University Press, 2018, pp. 157–73, at p. 162.

[45] UNESCO/SS/Conf.1/SR.2, p. 7

[46] Ibid.

[47] Ibid., pp. 7–8.

[48] UNESCO/SS/Conf.1/SR.1, p. 7.

[49] Ibid., p. 8.

[50] For example, M.F. Ashley Montagu, 'The Genetical Theory of Race, and Anthropological Method' (1942) 44 (n.s.) *American Anthropologist* 369.

[51] Michelle Brattain, 'Race, Racism, and Antiracism: UNESCO and the Politics of Presenting Science to the Postwar Public' (2007) 112 *American Historical Review* 1386, at p. 1393. See also

UNESCO'S 1950 STATEMENT ON 'THE RACE QUESTION'   177

was the author of a best-selling monograph, *Man's Most Dangerous Myth: The Fallacy of Race*.[52]

Pressed to agree upon a definition of race, Montagu proposed the following: 'A race, in the commonly accepted sense, which has been confirmed by custom and tradition, is any group – or any members of a group – which anyone chooses to call a "race".' He said it would be better to reject a term 'which had become dangerously lacking in meaning', and to replace it with 'ethnic group' for which a definition might then be crafted.[53] Montagu presented the other experts with a draft text.[54] It underwent minor modifications following some debate,[55] and was further revised by Montagu after it had been shown to several other experts who were not present at the December meeting.[56] Theodosius Dobzhansky of Columbia University said he was 'wholeheartedly in agreement' with the Statement.[57] UNESCO's head of the Social Sciences Department, Robert C. Angell, wrote Montagu to report on the comments received. He said that only one of them, Julian Huxley, had been 'seriously critical' of the draft adopted in December. Angell thought Huxley to be 'severely genetic'. But Angell also observed that almost all of the experts felt 'you have gone too far in the direction of stating that we know that genetic factors have nothing to do with temperamental and mental characteristics, so far as racial groups are concerned'. He said that they seemed to feel it better to state the case negatively, in the sense that 'we have no scientific knowledge on the matter of intelligence which would support a race doctrine'.[58]

Montagu answered that he found most of the comments to be 'very helpful' and acknowledged that 'in the attempt to be positive we have been somewhat overpositive'. He agreed that it is 'better to understate than to overstate' and promised not only to revise the text but also to submit it for comments to a number of other experts. By then, said Montagu, 'it really ought to be bombproof', although he acknowledged that it would never satisfy everyone.[59] Julian Huxley proposed

---

Anthony Q. Hazard, 'A Racialized Deconstruction? Ashley Montagu and the 1950 UNESCO Statement on Race' (2011) 19 *Transforming Anthropology: Journal of the Association of Black Anthropologists* 174, and the chapter entitled 'Ashley Montagu: The Negro Question and the Myth of Race' in Anthony Q. Hazard, *Boasians at War*, New York: Palgrave Macmillan, 2020, pp. 59–100.

[52] Ashley Montagu, *Man's Most Dangerous Myth, The Fallacy of Race*, New York: Harper, 1942. For an assessment, see Anthony Q. Hazard, 'Ashley Montagu, the "Most Dangerous Myth," and the "Negro Question" during World War II' (2016) 72 *Journal of Anthropological Research* 289

[53] UNESCO/SS/Conf.1/SR.2, p. 9.

[54] UNESCO/SS/Conf.1/SR.3, pp. 2–5.

[55] UNESCO/SS/Conf.1/SR.5, pp. 3; UNESCO/SS/Conf.1/SR.6, pp. 3. The final text is UNESCO/SS/Conf.1/6.

[56] See, for example, Angell to Huxley, 5 January 1950, UNESCO Archives 323.12 A 102.

[57] Dobzhansky to Angell, 7 January 1950, UNESCO Archives 323.12 A 102.

[58] Angell to Montagu, 8 February 1950, UNESCO Archives 323.12 A 102.

[59] Montagu to Angel, 13 February 1950, UNESCO Archives 323.12 A 102.

178 UNESCO: FIGHTING THE DOCTRINE OF RACIAL INEQUALITY

a final round of changes, some of which were agreed to by Montagu.[60] Much later, Montagu denied being the statement's primary author.[61] The final version was formally issued on 18 July 1950.

Entitled 'The Race Question', the statement noted the relatively narrow use of the term by anthropologists, referring to the current usage of three major divisions, Mongoloid, Negroid, and Caucasoid. But it said '[t]o most people, a race is any group of people whom they choose to describe as a race'. It explained that Englishmen and Frenchmen were not a race, nor were Catholics, Protestants, Moslems, or Jews, or people who were 'culturally' Turkish or Chinese. The statement recommended that 'when the term "race" is used in popular parlance, it would be better when speaking of human races to drop the term "race" altogether and speak of ethnic groups'. The statement continued:

> For all practical social purposes 'race' is not so much a biological phenomenon as a social myth. The myth of 'race' has created an enormous amount of human and social damage. In recent years it has taken a heavy toll in human lives and caused untold suffering. It still prevents the normal development of millions of human beings and deprives civilisation of the effective co-operation of productive minds. The biological differences between ethnic groups should be disregarded from the standpoint of social acceptance and social action. The unity of mankind from both the biological and social viewpoints is the main thing. To recognise this and to act accordingly is the first requirement of modern man.[62]

The very specific issue of 'race mixture' was also confronted. Montagu's original draft contained a strong plea favouring the benefits of 'hybridisation'. He wrote that 'the evidence points unequivocally to the fact that race mixture is always biologically good in its effects. . . Race mixture is biologically one of the greatest of all powers for the creation of novel and desirable traits in man.'[63] But this was a step too far for some of the experts, and in the final version reference to any beneficial consequences of intermarriage were removed. Montagu's sentence about 'convincing evidence' was changed to state that there was nothing to indicate 'that race mixture of itself produces biologically bad effects. Statements that human hybrids frequently show undesirable traits, both physically and mentally, physical disharmonies and mental degeneracies are not supported by the facts.'

---

[60] Huxley to Montagu, 24 May 1950, UNESCO Archives 323.12 A 102; Angell to Lawson, 1 June 1950, UNESCO Archives 323.12 A 102.

[61] Ashley Montagu, 'UNESCO Statements on Race' (1961) 133 (n.s.) *Science* 1632.

[62] UNESCO/SS/Conf.1/SR.3, p. 4.

[63] Ibid.

UNESCO'S 1950 STATEMENT ON 'THE RACE QUESTION' 179

Consequently, said the UNESCO statement, there was 'no biological justification for prohibiting intermarriage between persons of different ethnic groups'.

The Statement also advanced the thesis of mutual aid amongst racial or ethnic groups, stating that 'the whole of human history shows that a cooperative spirit is not only natural to man, but more deeply rooted than any self-seeking tendencies'. It said that biological studies supported 'the ethic of universal brotherhood', and that man is 'a social being who can reach his fullest development only through interaction with his fellows'. In that sense, said the statement, 'every man is his brother's keeper. For every man is a piece of the continent, a part of the main, because he is involved in mankind.' This was a rebuke to social Darwinists who conceived of human evolution as a struggle amongst humans for the 'survival of the fittest'. It reflected ideas developed by Montagu in a book he was in the course of publishing, *On Being Human*.[64]

The UNESCO statement is given great credit for its positive impact on scientific discussion as well as on public opinion.[65] A headline on page 1 of the *New York Times* proclaimed 'No Scientific Basis for Race Bias Found by World Panel of Experts'.[66] After decades of debate among recognized scientists that ultimately did much to fuel the genocidal plans of the Nazis and their supporters, an authoritative international body backed by established scholars had radically changed the discussion, both within the academic community but also in public opinion generally. According to Elazar Barkan, the Statement 'highlighted the dramatic transformation in the scientific and public understanding of the race concept'.[67] UNESCO's press release described it as 'the most far-reaching and competent pronouncement of its kind ever made and provides a scientific foundation for some of the basic principles expressed in the Universal Declaration of Human Rights'.[68] Later in the year, Montagu published a detailed commentary on the 1950 statement.[69]

---

[64] Ashley Montagu, *On Being Human*, New York, Henry Schuman, 1950.

[65] For example, Adam Hochman, 'Against the New Racial Naturalism' (2013) 110 *Journal of Philosophy* 331, at p. 331.

[66] 'No Scientific Basis for Race Bias Found by World Panel of Experts', *New York Times*, 18 July 1950, p 1.

[67] Elazar Barkan, 'The Politics of the Science of Race: Ashley Montagu and UNESCO's Anti-racist Declarations', in Larry T. Reynolds and Leonard Lieberman, eds., *Racism and Other Misadventures, Essays in Honour of Ashley Montagu in his Ninetieth Year*, Dix Halls, NY: General Hall, 1996, pp. 97–105, at p. 97.

[68] 'No Biological Justification for Race Discrimination Say World Scientists', Press Release 328, 18 July 1950, UNESCO Archives 323.12 A 102; 'UNESCO on Race' (1950) 50 (Oct.) *Man* 138.

[69] Ashley Montagu, *Statement on Race: An Extended Discussion in Plain Language of the UNESCO Statement by Experts on Race Problems*, New York: Henry Schuman, 1951.

180   UNESCO: FIGHTING THE DOCTRINE OF RACIAL INEQUALITY

A *mise au point* in 1951

Ashley Montagu had been right in expecting the 1950 Statement would not please everyone, and he may have been too optimistic in thinking it was 'bombproof'. Within a week of its publication, a critical letter by William B. Fagg, writing on behalf of the Royal Anthropological Institute, was published in *The Times*. It claimed that several propositions in the Statement were 'distinctly controversial in the present state of our knowledge'. Fagg said the assertion that 'race is less a biological fact than a social myth' was 'too simplified'. As for the conclusion that humans are driven towards universal brotherhood and cooperation, Fagg said 'surely very few anthropologists anywhere would yet venture to commit themselves' to this.[70] In the months that followed, the Royal Anthropological Institute's journal, *Man*, published several letters from English academics that challenged the Statement on a variety of grounds.[71] At least one of the critics was known for holding quite racist views about 'interbreeding' and the positive consequences of competition between races.[72] The editor of *Man* referred to UNESCO's document as the 'Ashley Montagu Statement'.[73] A lengthy, mocking critique of the Statement appeared in the *Eugenics Review*.[74] Physical anthropologists and biologists grumbled that the expert panel had been dominated by social scientists, with the exception of Montagu, whom many regarded as a maverick. The journal of the Royal Anthropological Institute noted the views of prominent physical anthropologists who, while in 'cordial agreement with the purpose and essential thesis of the document' seemed to view it as simplistic.[75] Although England provided the core of the opposition to the UNESCO Statement, there were also a few critical comments from elsewhere including the United States.[76]

The Director-General of UNESCO himself, Jaime Torres Bodet, explained to one of those consulted on the 1950 statement that it had been widely distributed and well received. 'It has given hope and courage to many people', he said,

---

[70] William B. Fagg, Letter to the editor, *The Times*, 24 July 1950.

[71] For example, H.V. Vallois, 'UNESCO on Race' (1951) 51 *Man* 15. See also Michelle Brattain, 'Race, Racism, and Antiracism: UNESCO and the Politics of Presenting Science to the Postwar Public' (2007) 112 *American Historical Review* 1386, at p. 1398. On the prevalence of racist views within the Royal Anthropological Institute, see Bradley S. Hart 'Science, Politics, and Prejudice: The Dynamics and Significance of British Anthropology's Failure to Confront Nazi Racial Ideology' (2013) 43 *European History Quarterly* 301.

[72] W.C. Osman-Hill, 'UNESCO on Race' (1951) 51 *Man* 16, as was pointed out by Prof. Don J. Hager of Princeton University in a letter to Alfred Métraux, 21 January 1951, UNESCO Archives 323.12 A 102 (Part II). See also Hager's reply to the letters by Osman-Hill and Vallois, 'Race' (1951) 51 *Man* 53.

[73] 'Note' (1951) 51 *Man* 17.

[74] Cedric Dover, 'UNESCO on Race' (1950) 42 *Eugenics Review* 177.

[75] 'UNESCO on Race' (1950) 50 (Oct.) *Man* 138. See the assessment by Michael Banton, 'The Vertical and Horizontal Dimensions of the Word Race' (2010) 10 *Ethnicities* 127, at pp. 137–8.

[76] Thomas D. Stewart, 'Scientific Responsibility' (1951) 9 (n.s.) *American Journal of Physical Anthropology* 1.

and did not think that 'in the present state of science, the text of this document could be altered'. But he added that a new meeting of physical anthropologists and geneticists would be convened in early June 1951 'in order to show our scientific impartiality'.[77] There was a recognition that the findings of the 1950 meeting, which had been composed of sociologists and cultural anthropologists, needed to be reinforced by the views of physical anthropologists and geneticists. Alfred Métraux, who had only just been appointed head of UNESCO's Division for the Study of Race Problems, had the task of convening the second meeting. Métraux described his work as part of UNESCO's 'world-wide campaign against racial prejudice'.[78] Writing to one of the British anthropologists, Métraux said criticism of the 1950 Statement, 'especially in England', had prompted the Director-General to convene a new panel of experts 'to prepare a new statement which, let us hope, will meet with the approval of most men of science'. In a letter to the President of the American Association of Physical Anthropologists Métraux recognized that the 1950 Statement had been 'sharply criticised' and said he hoped that the new consultation would result in 'a few formulations which will meet greater favour than the previous text'.[79] To the great American anthropologist, Margaret Mead, Métraux confided that he was 'painfully conscious of the weak-point of the Statement'.[80]

Métraux spent weeks trying to recruit participants for the new meeting.[81] Invitation letters described the meeting's purpose as being 'to re-examine and discuss the definition of race and the question of ethnic differences as expressed in UNESCO's "Statement on Race"'.[82] Métraux was not impressed with Ashley Montagu's 'exhibitionistic demeanours'.[83] But in response to a request from Montagu, Métraux not only invited him to the meeting, he asked him to prepare the agenda so as 'to avoid the impression that the statement which resulted from [the 1949 meeting] is going to be disavowed'.[84] Métraux explained to Montagu that the objective was not a 'reversal' of the initial Statement but rather a '*mise-au-point*', and he cautioned that 'we must not forget that we are going to redefine the concept of race and not go into polemics or empty discussions'.[85] Experts from the United States, the United Kingdom, France, Sweden, Germany and the Netherlands participated: Leslie C. Dunn, Harry Shapiro, Ashley Montagu, Solly

---

[77] Bodet to Hager, 1 March 1951, UNESCO Archives 323.12 A 102 (Part II).
[78] Métraux to Mandelker, 17 August 1950, UNESCO Archives 323.12 A 102.
[79] Métraux to Steward, 9 February 1951, UNESCO Archives 323.12 A 102/064(44)"51".
[80] Métraux to Mead, 14 November 1950, UNESCO Archives 323.12 A 102.
[81] Métraux to Little, 7 November 1950, UNESCO Archives 323.12 A 102.
[82] For example, Myrdal to Dunn, 12 March 1951, UNESCO Archives 323.12 A 102 (Part II).
[83] Métraux to Mead, 14 November 1950, UNESCO Archives 323.12 A 102.
[84] Métraux to Montagu, 22 March 1951, UNESCO Archives 323.12 A 102 (Part II).
[85] Montagu to Métraux, 7 March 1951, UNESCO Archives 323.12 A 102 (Part II); Métraux to Montagu, 12 March 1951, UNESCO Archives 323.12 A 102 (Part II); Myrdal to Montagu, 12 March 1951, UNESCO Archives 323.12 A 102 (Part II).

182 UNESCO: FIGHTING THE DOCTRINE OF RACIAL INEQUALITY

Zuckerman, J.B.S. Haldane, A.E. Mourant, J.C. Trevor, Henri Vallois, Eugène Schreider, Hans Nachtscheim, Gunnar Dahlberg, Theodosius Dobzhansky, and R.A.M. Bergman. The editor of *Man* described the 1951 panel as being 'excellently balanced in point both of specialisms and of nationalities'.[86]

In preparation for the meeting, UNESCO produced a 'Working Paper' that began by noting the relative absence of experts from physical anthropology and genetics at the December 1949 meeting where the first Statement was adopted. The purpose of this new gathering was 'to state in clear and simple terms the conclusions which have been reached in the fields of physical anthropology and biology concerning the following aspects of the race problem: (a) race formation and the dynamic aspects of speciation; (b) transmission of psychological traits and race differences; (c) biological effects of racial mixture; (d) formation of new races; (e) definition of race; (f) suggestions of modifications or improvements on the *Race Statement*'. The Working Paper attempted to summarize the criticisms of the 1950 Statement. These included its rejection of polygenesis, substitution of the term 'ethnic' for 'race', the designation of 'race' as a 'social myth', the suggestion that mental capacity was the same for all races, and its rejection of harmful consequences of intermarriage. The 'most constant target for criticism', said the Working Paper, was the phrase 'man is born with drives toward co-operation', a proposition some thought belonged 'rather to philosophy than to the realm of pure science'. Annexed to the Working Paper were specific suggestions from J.B.S. Haldane and Julian Huxley.[87]

Some of the language in the 1951 Statement appears to draw upon the paper submitted by Julian Huxley prior to the meeting. Otherwise, the authorship of the draft is not known. In his report on the June 1951 meeting, Leslie C. Dunn of Columbia University wrote that '[i]n general, the chief conclusions of the first Statement were sustained, but with differences in emphasis and with some important deletions. There was no delay or hesitation or lack of unanimity in reaching the primary conclusion that there were no scientific grounds whatever for the racialist position regarding purity of race and the hierarchy of inferior and superior races to which this leads.' Dunn said that 'all of us believed that the biological differences found amongst human racial groups can in no case justify the views of racial inequality which have been based on ignorance and prejudice, and that all of the differences which we know can well be disregarded for all ethical human purposes'.[88]

---

[86] 'UNESCO's New Statement on Race' (1951) 51 *Man* 154.

[87] Working Paper, 15 May 1951, UNESCO/SS/RACE/Conf.2/2.

[88] Report on meeting of physical anthropologists and geneticists for a definition of the concept of race, held at UNESCO house, from 4 to 8 June 1951, by L.C. Dunn, Rapporteur', UNESCO Archives 323.12 A 102 (Part II); 'Professor Dunn's Report' (1951) 51 *Man* 155.

A *MISE AU POINT* IN 1951   183

The 1950 Statement had clearly discouraged use of the term race, which it said was often confused with that of ethnic group. Dunn's report explained that the 1951 meeting tried, but without success, to find a 'new word to express the same meaning of a biologically differentiated group'. The meeting agreed that the word 'race' could be reserved for 'anthropological classification of groups' based upon physical traits. Dunn also confirmed that there was no agreement on the cooperative nature of humans in general. On the issue of inter-marriage, the 1951 meeting concluded 'that race mixture in general did not lead to disadvantageous results', adding that many participants in the meeting 'thought it quite likely that hybridisation of different races could lead to biologically advantageous results, although there was insufficient evidence to support any conclusion'.[89] The 1950 Declaration had concluded: 'There is, therefore, no *biological* justification for prohibiting intermarriage between persons of different ethnic groups.' The word 'biological' was italicized, although the emphasis seems to have been dropped by UNESCO in subsequent publications. Writing to Métraux upon receipt of the 1951 Declaration, John Humphrey, director of human rights in the United Nations Secretariat, asked whether the intent of the phrase was to suggest that there might be another reason to prohibit marriage between persons of different races.[90]

Perrin Selcer has described the second statement's 'more matter-of-fact tone', basing itself on 'the rather esoteric argument that biological diversity must be understood through a population rather than a typological approach and more clearly hedged on the actual equality of races. Nevertheless, the second statement surprised even many of its own signatories with the strength of its anti-racism, and UNESCO successfully presented it as another weapon in the fight against racial prejudice.'[91] For Michelle Brattain, 'the second statement project revealed how much the categories, premises, empirical records, and authority of an older, supposedly discredited body of work once dedicated to measuring difference continued to influence the science of race'.[92] Métraux himself was enthusiastic about the June 1951 meeting. He had anticipated a 'great battle'[93] but ultimately felt the results were constructive. Far from 'invalidating' the 1950 Statement, he felt that the earlier document had been 'reinforced'.[94] Writing to his wife, he described 'une très bonne réunion. . . Ashley Montagu s'est comporté

---

[89] Report on meeting of physical anthropologists and geneticists for a definition of the concept of race, held at UNESCO house, from 4 to 8 June 1951, by L.C. Dunn, Rapporteur', UNESCO Archives 323.12 A 102 (Part II); 'Professor Dunn's Report' (1951) 51 *Man* 155.

[90] Humphrey to Métraux, 29 June 1951, UNESCO Archives 323.12 A 102 (Part II).

[91] Perrin Selcer, 'Beyond the Cephalic Index, Negotiating Politics to Produce UNESCO's Scientific Statements on Race' (2012) 53 *Current Anthropology* S173, at p. S174.

[92] Michelle Brattain, 'Race, Racism, and Antiracism: UNESCO and the Politics of Presenting Science to the Postwar Public' (2007) 112 *American Historical Review* 1386, at p. 1388.

[93] Métraux to Fagg, 29 May 1951, UNESCO Archives 323.12 A 102/064(44)"51".

[94] Métraux to Whyte, 18 July 1951, UNESCO Archives 323.12 A 102 (Part II).

184   UNESCO: FIGHTING THE DOCTRINE OF RACIAL INEQUALITY

mieux que prévu et, je dois le reconnaître, il a apporté beaucoup à la réunion en se présentant comme une cible'.[95]

The 1951 Statement was published the following year as the first chapter of a volume entitled *The Race Concept: Results of an Inquiry*. The six-page Statement was then followed by a review of comments and criticisms comprising nearly eighty pages, indicating a range of opinions on issues that had been raised. The 1950 Statement was an appendix. Initially, the report of the meeting, which was prepared by Leslie C. Dunn, had been made public but the draft Statement was not released pending further consultation to be undertaken by UNESCO with experts from around the world. The text adopted at the meeting went through a further consultation with a broad range of experts who were invited to pro-pose changes. A number of very minor changes were made at the suggestion of Huxley, Dunn, Dobzhansky, and others.

Ashley Montagu considered that the 1950 statement had mainly been the work of social scientists whereas the 1951 statement was drafted primarily by phys-ical anthropologists and geneticists. 'The difference is as between Tweedledum and Tweedledee', he wrote, in an effort to minimise suggestions that the second statement had been drafted in order to diminish the first.[96] One critic noted that a member of the committee that produced the 1950 statement, Juan Comas, reproduced only the 1951 statement in his textbook.[97] In a journal article on so-called 'scientific' racism published in the early 1960s, Comas described the 1951 statement as 'the conclusions at which modern science has arrived concerning race and the interpretation of racial differences' and made no mention of the re-port issued in 1950.[98]

To make its message accessible to young people. UNESCO published a pic-ture book entitled *What Is Race? Evidence from Scientists*.[99] It also undertook an investigation into the factors that 'produced in Brazil a spirit of tolerance and a degree of harmony in interracial relations in strong contrast with the morbid intransigence of other types of culture'. Short monographs, averaging about 50 pages each, were produced as part of a collection entitled 'The Race Question in Modern Science'.[100] *Race and Biology* was authored by Leslie C. Dunn, professor

---

[95] Cited in Harald Prins and Edgar Krebs, 'Vers un monde sans mal: Alfred Métraux, un anthropologue à l'UNESCO (1946–1962)', in *60 ans d'histoire de l'UNESCO*, Paris: UNESCO, 2007, pp. 115–25, at p. 121.

[96] Ashley Montagu, 'UNESCO Statements on Race' (1961) 133 (n.s.) *Science* 1632.

[97] Thomas D. Stewart, 'UNESCO Statements on Race' (1961) 133 (n.s.) *Science* 1634.

[98] Juan Comas, ' "Scientific" Racism Again?' (1961) 2 *Current Anthropology* 303, at p. 304.

[99] Jenny Bangham, '*What Is Race?* UNESCO, mass communication and human genetics in the early 1950s' (2015) 28 *History of the Human Sciences* 80.

[100] Alfred Métraux, 'UNESCO and Anthropology' (1951) 53 (n.s.) *American Anthopologist* 294. See Edgardo C. Krebs, 'Popularizing Anthropology, Combating Racism: Alfred Métraux at The UNESCO Courier', in Poul Duedahl, *The History of UNESCO, Global Actions and Impacts*, London: Palgrave Macmillan, 2016, pp. 29–48. On the Brazil study, see Marcos Chor Maio, 'UNESCO and the Study of Race Relations in Brazil: Regional or National Issue?' (2001) 36 *Latin American*

of biology at Columbia University.[101] Others included *Race and Culture*, by Michel Leiris of the Musée de l'Homme in Paris,[102] *Racial Myths* by Juan Comas, professor at the Mexican School of Anthropology,[103] *Race and Prejudice* by Arnold Rose, professor of sociology at the University of Minnesota,[104] and *Race and History* by Claude Lévi-Strauss.[105] A second series, published in 1953 and 1954, was entitled 'The Race Question and Modern Thought' and approached the issue from a religious perspective.[106] Some of UNESCO's efforts met with opposition from right-wing organizations.[107]

Propositions on the Biological Aspects of Race, 1964

Within a few years, however, UNESCO's anti-racism campaign seemed to lose some momentum. This was associated with the departure of Alva Myrdal, who left the organization to become Sweden's ambassador to India. Myrdal had been the head of UNESCO's social sciences section from 1950 to 1955. Alfred Métraux described huge cuts to the programme. 'La question raciale est en passe de disparaître de notre programme futur. Je ne le regrette pas parce que, avec la politique de l'UNESCO consistant à ne faire de peine à personne, je me sentais paralysé et je m'ennuyais', he wrote.[108] In 1960, in response to the 'swastika epidemic',[109] the Commission on Human Rights requested UNESCO to 'obtain any information or comments relevant to such manifestations and public reaction to them, the measures taken to combat them, and their causes or motivations'.[110] This prompted UNESCO's Department of Social Sciences to initiate a 'sociological and psychological inquiry', preparing a report for the Commission that would also take into account research by eminent specialists.[111] In 1963 the

---

Research Review 118; Marcos Chor Maio and Rosemary Galli, 'Florestan Fernandes, Oracy Nogueira, and the UNESCO Project on Race Relations in São Paulo' (2011) 38 *Latin American Perspectives* 136.

[101] Leslie C. Dunn, *Race and Biology*, Paris: UNESCO, 1951.

[102] Michel Leiris, *Race and Culture,* Paris: UNESCO, 1951.

[103] Juan Comas, *Racial Myths*, Paris: UNESCO, 1951.

[104] Arnold Rose, *Race and Prejudice*, Paris: UNESCO, 1951.

[105] Claude Lévi-Strauss, *Race and History*, Paris: UNESCO, 1952.

[106] 'The Activities of UNESCO in Combating Racial Prejudice and Discrimination' (1955) 7 *International Social Sciences Bulletin* 461, at p. 463.

[107] Randle J. Hart, 'The Greatest Subversive Plot in History? The American Radical Right and Anti-UNESCO Campaigning' (2014) 48 *Sociology* 554.

[108] Harald Prins et Edgar Krebs, 'Vers un monde sans mal: Alfred Métraux, un anthropologue à l'UNESCO (1946–1962)', in *60 ans d'histoire de l'UNESCO*, Paris: UNESCO, 2007, pp. 115–25, at p. 123.

[109] See *infra*, p. 245.

[110] Manifestations of Anti-Semitism and Other Forms of Racial Prejudice and Religious Intolerance of a Similar Nature, 16 March 1960, E/CN.4/RES/6 (XVI), para. 4.

[111] Report by the Director-General on the Activities of the Organisation, 1 January 1960–31 August 1960, 11 C/3, p. 26.

186 UNESCO: FIGHTING THE DOCTRINE OF RACIAL INEQUALITY

Director-General announced a draft programme for an international conference of specialists on race questions to be held the following year in the Soviet Union. Nearly 50 experts from various countries were consulted. Their replies showed 'very lively interest'. The Director-General said that the 1964 meeting 'might constitute the first stage towards formulating a new statement on race and race prejudice, to amplify the "Statement on Race" published in 1951'.[112]

Twenty-six experts, none of whom had been at the previous meetings in 1949 and 1951, met in Moscow in August 1964. The theme of the meeting was 'biological aspects of race'. Participants were to 'study the race question in the light of the scientific advances which have taken place since the first statement on the nature of race and race differences was drawn up in 1951'. A note prepared by the Secretariat prior to the meeting suggest that it should take into account the latest biological findings and 'enlarge its scope by means of encompassing in the new version a number of points not previously covered, dealing with the nature and forms of racial prejudice in inter-racial situations'.[113] The meeting lasted seven days. The programme consisted largely of presentations by the participants on elements of their own research and in that sense it resembled an academic conference. Discussion of a draft declaration was reserved for the final day only.[114]

The 1964 event was hardly more diverse in composition than the 1949 and 1951 meetings, with only one expert from Africa (Nigeria) and two from Asia (India and Japan). The others came from Canada, Poland, Mexico, Venezuela, the Soviet Union, Belgium, Germany, Brazil, Norway, and Czechoslovakia, in addition to the United States, the United Kingdom, and France. According to the Director-General of UNESCO, the meeting developed a set of proposals 'which stress the unitary character of the human species, thus providing the scientific elements for the refutation of racist theories'. He said a subsequent meeting was to be held in 1966 to examine 'social and ethnical aspects of the race question'. A new statement would then incorporate the conclusions of both meetings.[115]

The meeting adopted a statement entitled 'Proposals on the Biological Aspects of Race'. Explaining the conclusions of the meeting in the *UNESCO Courier*, its chairman, the Soviet academic Georghi F. Debetz, recalled earlier debates among anthropologists as to whether humans had one or several ancestors. 'Today, this question can be regarded as finally settled. It was not even raised during the 1964 Moscow meeting', he said. 'The declaration merely notes, as if to sum up earlier discussions, that "all living human beings belong to a single species, known as 'Homo Sapiens' and are derived from a common stock origin".'

---

[112] Report of the Director-General on the Activities of the Organisation in 1963, p. 70.
[113] UNESCO's actions in the field of race relations and the Statements on race, UNESCO/SS/Race/1, p. 3.
[114] Agenda, UNESCO/SS/Race/2.rev.
[115] Report of the Director-General on the Activities of the Organisation in 1964, p. 65.

Debetz also pointed to the conclusion that 'as entities defined by sets of distinctive traits, human races are at any time in a process of emergence and dissolution'. Still more important, he said, was the affirmation that 'certain physical characters have a universal biological value for the survival of the human species'. Debetz explained that the experts were divided about the utility of racial classifications. But despite differences of opinion about the importance of racial classifications, Debetz said there was general agreement that 'as entities defined by sets of distinctive traits, human races are at any time in a process of emergence and dissolution'. Still more important, he observed, was the declaration's conclusion that 'certain physical characters have a universal biological value for the survival of the human species Irrespective of the environment. The differences on which racial classifications are based do not affect these characters and therefore it is not possible from the biological point of view to speak in any way whatsoever of a general inferiority or superiority of this or that race'.[116]

The Proposals addressed the issue of 'interbreeding', noting that there was no proof that it had biological disadvantages for mankind as a whole. It even contemplated a positive dimension of intermarriage: 'On the contrary, it contributes to the maintenance of biological ties between human groups and thus to the unity of the species in its diversity'. The declaration concluded that the biological data 'stand in open contradiction to the tenets of racism. Racist theories can in no way pretend to have any scientific foundation and the anthropologists should endeavour to prevent the results of their researches from being used in such a biased way that they would serve non-scientific ends'. Apparently it is the first official document issued by UNESCO to use the word 'racism'.[117] Anthony Q. Hazard has observed that '[i]n lending support to the idea of "race mixing" in its statements, UNESCO actually reinforced the idea that biological "races" existed'.[118]

Statement on Race and Racial Prejudice, 1967

The second meeting was postponed to September 1967.[119] Eighteen experts participated in a conference convened at UNESCO headquarters in Paris. Representing the disciplines of genetics, anthropology, sociology, ethnology, history, and law, they came from 16 countries: Belgium, Brazil, Cuba, India, Israel,

---

[116] Georghi F. Debetz, 'Biology Looks at Race', *UNESCO Courier*, April 1965, pp. 4–7, at p. 5.

[117] Preliminary Study on the Legal and Technical Aspects of a Draft Declaration on Race and Racial Prejudice, 19 September 1974, UNESCO 18 C/3G, para. 4.

[118] Anthony Q. Hazard Jr., *Postwar Anti-racism, The United States, UNESCO, and 'Race', 1945–1968*, New York: Palgrave Macmillan, 2021, p. 154.

[119] Working Paper, 22 August 1967, SHC/CS/122/3,

188 UNESCO: FIGHTING THE DOCTRINE OF RACIAL INEQUALITY

Japan, Kenya, Poland, Senegal, Sudan, Trinidad and Tobago, the Soviet Union, the United Kingdom, the United States, and Yugoslavia. Adopted unanimously, the 'Statement on Race and Race Prejudice' began with the first sentence of article 1 of the French *Déclaration des droits de l'homme et du citoyen* of 1789: 'All men are born free and equal both in dignity and in rights.' That phrase had actually been amended slightly when it inspired the first sentence of article 1 of the Universal Declaration of Human Rights, where 'all men' was replaced by 'all human beings' on the proposal of Bodil Begtrup, who was representing the Commission on the Status of Women.[120] Curiously, in the French version of the 1967 Statement, which is translated from the English, the gender-neutral provision in the Universal Declaration is the one that is employed.[121] The explanation of this inconsistency may well lie in the exclusively masculine composition of the expert meeting and the fact that it was obviously working principally in English.

The 1967 Statement focussed not so much on race as on racism: 'Racism continues to haunt the world ... Racism stultifies the development of those who suffer from it, perverts those who apply it, divides nations within themselves, aggravates international conflict, and threatens world peace.' The Statement noted that racism is not a universal phenomenon, and that many of its forms arose 'out of the conditions of conquest, out of the justification of Negro slavery and its aftermath of racial inequality in the West, and out of the colonial relationship. Among other examples is that of antisemitism, which has played a particular role in history, with Jews being the chosen scapegoat to take the blame for problems and crises met by many societies.' According to the experts, '[t]he anticolonial revolution of the twentieth century has opened up new possibilities for eliminating the scourge of racism'. But it does not seem to have been easy for the meeting to reach a consensus on many points. It appeared to equate racism with 'prejudice', thereby obscuring the fundamental issue of unequal treatment and focussing on the attitudes and conduct of individuals. The 1967 Statement was in many respects a return to the militant position promoted by Ashley Montagu in 1950. It used the term 'race' in inverted commas, treating it as synonymous with 'ethnicity'. As Anthony Q. Hazard Jr. has observed, the 1967 panel 'echoes the sentiments of increasingly impatient and angry activists whose governments failed to embody the rhetorical antiracism that accompanied the Allies' victory at the end of World War II'.[122] The composition of the expert panel, where finally UNESCO had managed to achieve significant representation from Africa, may help to explain this.

---

[120] Suggestions made by the Commission on the Status of Women, 24 March 1948, E/CN.4/81.
[121] Déclaration sur la race et les préjugés raciaux, SHC/CS/122/4/Rev.
[122] Anthony Q. Hazard Jr., *Postwar Anti-racism, The United States, UNESCO, and 'Race', 1945–1968*, New York: Palgrave Macmillan, 2021, pp. 163–4.

THE 1978 DECLARATION ON RACE AND RACE PREJUDICE   189

UNESCO produced a detailed summary of the proceedings that referred rather cautiously to 'a considerable amount of agreement between participants'. Compared to the earlier Statements of 1950, 1951, and 1964, the summary said the 1967 document was written 'with a sense of the urgency of the problems of "race" in today's world'. It said historical and sociological considerations were uppermost, that racism was not innate but rather was 'a result of the society in which man exists'.[123]

UNESCO hosted an expert meeting in 1968 on educational methods designed to combat racial prejudice.[124] As part of the observance in 1971 of the International Year for Action to Combat Racism and Racial Discrimination, the United Nations Sub-Commission on the Prevention of Discrimination and the Protection of Minorities recommended that the 1967 UNESCO statement be distributed, 'with a view to eradicating once and for all false racial beliefs based upon a lack of scientific knowledge'.[125]

The 1978 Declaration on Race and Race Prejudice

In 1978, UNESCO's General Conference adopted the Declaration on Race and Race Prejudice. This was a political statement, negotiated by diplomats rather than scientific experts, and was meant as a comprehensive instrument that would deal with race and racism from UNESCO's multi-disciplinary perspective. Natan Lerner has explained that the Declaration goes beyond purely legal implications and deals with biological, sociological, cultural, economic, and political aspects of racism.[126] The Declaration was proposed at the seventeenth General Conference of UNESCO in 1972 in a resolution that noted 'the persistence of racialist ideas and conceptions'. It endorsed the 1967 Statement of the UNESCO experts, drawing attention to its recognition that '[a]ll men living today belong to the same species and descend from the same stock' and that '[t]he division of the human species into "races" is partly conventional and partly arbitrary and does not imply any hierarchy whatsoever'. It requested the Director-General of UNESCO to develop a programme for the United Nations Decade for Action to Combat Racism and Racial Discrimination. He was also invited to prepare a preliminary study on the legal and technical aspects of a draft declaration on the subject, using the 1967 Statement as a basis.[127]

---

[123] Final report, Meeting of Experts on Race and Racial Prejudice, SHC/CS/122/8, p. 5.
[124] Meeting of Experts on Educational Methods Designed to Combat Racial Prejudice, Final Report, 24 October 1968, ED/MD/4.
[125] Elimination of racial discrimination, 26 August 1970, E/CN.4/Sub.2/RES/4 (XXIII), OP 3.
[126] Natan Lerner, 'New Concepts in the UNESCO Declaration on Race and Racial Prejudice' (1981) 3 *Human Rights Quarterly* 48, at p. 49.
[127] UNESCO's contribution to peace and its tasks with respect to the elimination of colonialism and racialism, General Conference, 17th session, 1972, Resolution 10.1(II), paras. 9–14.

190 UNESCO: FIGHTING THE DOCTRINE OF RACIAL INEQUALITY

In 1973, UNESCO hosted an expert consultation to discuss possible changes to the 1967 Declaration. This produced a revised draft of the earlier document with additions underlined. The discussing of various social, economic, and political factors that contributed to racism as well as the role of education and the media in addressing it was developed somewhat.[128] The Director-General's report was issued in 1974. It referred to the Declaration and Convention on racial discrimination adopted by the United Nations General Assembly during the previous decade, observing that these dealt with the 'political aspect of the problem'. The 1967 UNESCO Statement, on the other hand, dealt with the 'scientific angle' within 'the very context of the social structure'. The Director-General proposed that the declaration be negotiated by an inter-governmental committee and that it be adopted at a session of the General Conference. He referred to an expert meeting held in May 1974 at UNESCO headquarters that agreed that it was not feelings or attitudes that were the determining factor in combating racism, but that the 'primary cause lies in the actual situation, that is to say in the economic, social and legal relations, the power relations between groups'. Under the heading 'biology and genetics', the report devoted specific intention to the debate around the significance of IQ scores.[129]

In preparation for the planned meeting of inter-governmental experts, the Director-General prepared a draft convention. It must have been UNESCO's hope that the next General Conference would be held in Africa because the draft referred to the Declaration's adoption 'on the soil of Africa, whose peoples have paid and are still paying the heavy price of racism'.[130] Apparently because Member States lacked diligence in working on the subject, the inter-governmental meeting did not take place. At the time, there was considerable tension related to the General Assembly resolution of the previous year equating Zionism and racism,[131] and this may have weighed in the decision to cancel the meeting. Instead, the draft of the Director-General was submitted to the 1976 General Conference along with the substantive comments that had been received from a handful of States.[132] At the 1976 General Conference, several delegations sought something more extensive that could be aimed at a broader public. It was to consist of a concise, clearly written statement of principles accompanied by

[128] Results of an expert consultation on possible changes in the 1967 Statement on Race and Racial Prejudice (Paris, 9 to 13 July 1973), SHC-76/CONF.207/COL.4.
[129] Preliminary study of the legal and technical aspects of a draft declaration on race and racial prejudice, 19 September 1974, 18 C/3G; Analysis and evaluation of results obtained by utilization of education and information to combat racism and racial discrimination, 10 July 1974, SHC/74/wS/16.
[130] Preliminary draft of a Declaration on race and racial prejudice, 14 June 1976, SHC/MD/33.
[131] See infra, pp. 356–359.
[132] Preparation of a draft declaration on race and racial prejudice: Report of the Director-General on the implementation of the relevant provisions of 18 C/Resolution 5.11 and recommendations of the Executive Board concerning the measures to be taken in order to complete the elaboration of the draft to be submitted to the General Conference, 1 November 1976, 19 C/95.

THE 1978 DECLARATION ON RACE AND RACE PREJUDICE   191

'indications' of the actions necessary for implementation, followed by a second part providing the basic natural and social science evidence and ethical ideas from which the principles are derived.[133] The General Conference approved of the draft's 'concepts and general substance' but said further work was necessary. The Declaration should 'address itself to a wide public opinion all over the world', 'serve as a major document for the definition and analysis of socio-economic situations marked by, or leading to, manifestations of racialism', and 'constitute a powerful instrument for the mobilisation of people, organisations and governments to enable them to take appropriate social and legal action to eradicate the causes and effects of all forms and manifestations of racialism and racial prejudice'.[134]

UNESCO held an expert consultation on the draft declaration in 1977. Mohamed Bedjaoui, Manfred Lachs, Clarence Clyde Ferguson, and Seán MacBride were among the 'eminent specialists on human rights' who attended. This was a group of lawyers, with no particular expertise in anthropology, sociology, or psychology. It was the first significant engagement of international law in the debate about race since UNESCO began its activities in the area in 1949. On the basis of advice from this consultation, a Working Paper was prepared for the inter-governmental conference. The new draft was significantly shorter than the earlier versions.[135] Some 100 States were represented at the Conference, held in March 1978 at UNESCO headquarters in Paris, including the experts who had been consulted in 1977.[136] The negotiations appear to have largely concerned peripheral and even tangential issues, such as describing apartheid as a crime against humanity and references to United Nations resolutions that might be viewed as endorsing the view that Zionism was racist.

The text of the Declaration, together with a separate resolution on its implementation and an explanatory report,[137] was presented to the General Conference in 1978 where it was adopted without alteration. The Declaration consists of a preamble and 10 articles. The preamble begins by reprising the recital in the UNESCO Constitution referring to 'the doctrine of the inequality of men and races'. It refers to 'the process of decolonisation and other historical changes which have led most of the peoples formerly under foreign rule to recover their sovereignty, making the international community a universal and

---

[133] Draft amendment submitted by a Working Group established by the Chairman of the Commission and consisting of Algeria, Australia, Cuba, India, Iran (Chairman of the Working Group), Kenya, Nigeria, Portugal and USSR to the draft resolution proposed in document 19 C/ 95 'Preparation of a draft declaration on race and racial prejudice', 6 November 1976, 19 C/PRG III/ DR.4, para. 3.

[134] Human rights and peace, General Conference, 19th session, 1976, Resolution 3.173.

[135] Working paper, 18 August 1977, SS-77/CONF.201/1.

[136] Draft final report, 20 March 1978, SS-78/CONF.201/6.

[137] Draft Declaration on Race and Racial Prejudice, 25 September 1978, 20 C/18.

192 UNESCO: FIGHTING THE DOCTRINE OF RACIAL INEQUALITY

diversified whole and creating new opportunities of eradicating the scourge of racism and of putting an end to its odious manifestations in all aspects of social and political life, both nationally and internationally'. The preamble notes that 'the essential unity of the human race and consequently the fundamental equality of all human beings and all peoples, recognised in the loftiest expressions of philosophy, morality and religion, reflect an ideal towards which ethics and science are converging today'. The preamble cites several international treaties and declarations and, of course, the four statements on the race question adopted by experts convened by UNESCO.

The operative provisions of the UNESCO Declaration commence with the affirmation that '[a]ll human beings belong to a single species and are descended from a common stock'.[138] This formulation is drawn from the four expert statements issued over the previous three decades. The 1950 Statement had said that everyone was 'probably' descended from a common stock, but the word was dropped in the 1964 Statement. Referring to the opening words of the 1978 Declaration in a statement at the 2001 Durban Conference, the European Union said: 'This is fundamental. Doctrines that asserted the contrary were used to justify some of the most appalling and disgraceful tragedies in human history, including the Holocaust and also apartheid.'[139]

In what is an entirely original contribution to human rights law, the Declaration then affirms the right of all individuals and groups 'to be different, to consider themselves as different and to be regarded as such'. It adds that 'the diversity of life styles and the right to be different may not, in any circumstances, serve as a pretext for racial prejudice; they may not justify either in law or in fact any discriminatory practice whatsoever, nor provide a ground for the policy of apartheid, which is the extreme form of racism'. The 'right to be different' emerged from the text adopted by the legal experts in 1977: 'Identity of origin in no way affects the fact that human beings can and may live differently, or the right of individuals and groups to be different, to consider themselves as different and to be regarded as such.'[140] Although the text in the draft did not refer explicitly to a 'right to be different', this formulation was used in the explanatory report.[141] According to one commentator, it was a 'principe alors en vogue dans les milieux antiracistes'.[142] Natan Lerner explained that it is related to the right not to be forced to assimilate, an idea that is touched upon in the preamble.[143] The

[138] UNESCO Declaration on Race and Racial Prejudice, art. 1.1.
[139] Report of the World Conference against Racism, Racial Discrimination, Xenophobia and Related Intolerance, Durban, 31 August–8 September 2001, A/CONF/189/12, p. 118.
[140] Working paper, 18 August 1977, SS-77/CONF.201/1, p. 10.
[141] Ibid., p. 14.
[142] Yvan Gastaut, 'L'UNESCO, les « races » et le racisme', in 60 ans d'histoire de l'UNESCO, Paris: UNESCO, 2007, pp. 197–210, at p. 205.
[143] Natan Lerner, 'New Concepts in the UNESCO Declaration on Race and Racial Prejudice' (1981) 3 Human Rights Quarterly 48, at p. 53.

explanatory report notes that it ensures the right of individuals and groups 'to lead their lives without abandoning their essential identity'.[144] It also claims that the right to be different is recognized 'for the first time at the international level' in the UNESCO Declaration. And the last, it would seem. There appear to be no echoes of this 'right' in subsequent treaties or declarations dealing with racial discrimination. Moreover, at its heart, racial discrimination is not about individuals being denied the right to choose their identity but rather about persecution and prejudice relating to features that are innate and that are not chosen.

Article 1 of the 1978 Declaration also contains a paragraph affirming that '[t]he differences between the achievements of the different peoples are entirely attributable to geographical, historical, political, economic, social and cultural factors. Such differences can in no case serve as a pretext for any rank-ordered classification of nations or peoples.' An early draft prepared by UNESCO made reference to 'certain psychological tests in current use', explaining that their application provided no support for the conclusion that differences exist 'in the hereditary endowments of human groups', noting that no test yet devised was completely free of cultural bias.[145] The language survived, but only in the explanatory report.[146]

The Declaration suggests a definition with the formulation '[a]ny distinction, exclusion, restriction or preference based on race, colour, ethnic or national origin or religious intolerance motivated by racist considerations'.[147] The text is slightly different from that of article 1 of the International Convention on the Elimination of All Forms of Racial Discrimination in its omission of the term 'descent'. Moreover, the International Convention does not refer to religious intolerance, probably because at the time of its adoption in 1965 there were plans to draft a corresponding treaty on religion-based discrimination. It seems that the phrase 'motivated by racist considerations' is only meant to refer to 'religious intolerance'; this is clearer in the French version. The Declaration is directed not only at the obligations of States but also those of individuals, who have 'duties towards their fellows, towards the society in which they live and towards the international community. They are accordingly under an obligation to promote harmony among the peoples, to combat racism and racial prejudice and to assist by every means available to them in eradicating racial discrimination in all its forms.'[148]

The European Union invoked the 1978 UNESCO Declaration in a statement at the conclusion of the 2001 Durban Conference. Referring to the words

---

[144] Draft Declaration on Race and Racial Prejudice, 25 September 1978, 20 C/18, Annex, p. 1.
[145] Preliminary draft of a Declaration on race and racial prejudice, 14 June 1976, SHC/MD/33.
[146] Draft Declaration on Race and Racial Prejudice, 25 September 1978, 20 C/18, Annex, p. 2.
[147] UNESCO Declaration on Race and Racial Prejudice, art. 3.
[148] Ibid., art. 8(1).

194 UNESCO: FIGHTING THE DOCTRINE OF RACIAL INEQUALITY

'All human beings belong to a single species', it said 'this is fundamental'. The European Union expressed concern that use of the terms 'race' or 'racial' might indicate implicit acceptance of theories or doctrines of racial superiority.[149] There have been several initiatives, mainly in European countries, to remove reference to race in human rights legislation containing enumerations of prohibited grounds for discrimination.[150] Germany referred to the 2001 statement when it explained to the Committee on the Elimination of Racial Discrimination that its use of the term 'racial discrimination' does not in any way mean that it supports theories or doctrines which claim that there are different human races'.[151] Norway does not include 'race' as a prohibited ground in its Anti-Discrimination Act. When challenged about this by the Committee on the Elimination of Racial Discrimination, Norway explained that the 'concept of race' was based upon 'theories that have no justifiable scientific basis or content' and, moreover, has 'strong negative connotations'.[152] The Committee has urged Norway to reconsider, noting that 'this term is widely used by the public and in social media'.[153] The French National Assembly even voted to remove the term from article 1 of the constitution although this amendment never entered into force.[154] Sweden explained to the Working Group of Experts on People of African Descent that its legislation did not use the word 'race' because 'the law assumes that all people belong to the human race'.[155]

Some international human rights bodies appear embarrassed by the term 'race'. The Inter-American Commission on Human Rights said it used the term 'not because it adheres to theories claiming the existence of different races in the human species, but rather in line with the nomenclature of Article 1 of the American Convention on Human Rights'.[156] Similarly, the Committee on Economic, Social and Cultural Rights has insisted that use of the term 'race' in the International Covenant and in its own general comments 'does not imply

---

[149] Report of the World Conference against Racism, Racial Discrimination, Xenophobia and Related Intolerance, A/CONF.189/12, paras. 117–18.

[150] Richard Lappin, 'Should CERD Repudiate the Notion of Race?' (2016) 28 *Peace Review* 393.

[151] Eighteenth periodic reports of States parties due in 2006, Addendum, Germany, 16 January 2007, CERD/C/DEU/18, p. 7, fn. 1.

[152] Combined 23rd and 24th periodic reports of Norway, 20 September 2017, CERD/C/497/Add.1, para. 10. CERD/C/NOR/23-24, para. 85.

[153] Concluding observations on the combined 23rd and 24th periodic reports of Norway, 2 January 2019, CERD/C/NOR/CO/23-24, para. 7; also Summary record of the 2695th meeting, 5 December 2018, CERD/C/SR.2695, para. 10.

[154] 'L'Assemblée supprime de la Constitution le mot « race » et interdit la « distinction de sexe »', *Le Monde*, 12 July 2018.

[155] Report of the Working Group of Experts on People of African Descent on its sixteenth session, Addendum, Mission to Sweden, 25 August 2015, A/HRC/30/56/Add.2, para. 22.

[156] The situation of people of African descent in the Americas, 5 December 2011, OEA Ser.L/V/II. Doc.62, p. 6.

THE 1978 DECLARATION ON RACE AND RACE PREJUDICE 195

the acceptance of theories which attempt to determine the existence of separate human races'.[157]

The French *Code pénal* was recently amended to refer to 'prétendue race', which in English might be translated as 'so-called race', so as 'to avoid giving the impression that the legislator supports the idea that human races exist'.[158] Another manifestation of this linguistic discomfort is the term 'racialized group', apparently used as a substitute for 'racial group'. According to the Advisory Committee of the United Nations Human Rights Council, '[t]he term "racialized group" is used to explain the process by which perceived patterns of physical difference (e.g. skin colour or eye shape) are used to differentiate groups of people (racialization)'.[159]

* * *

Beginning with the 1950 Statement and concluding with the 1978 Declaration, UNESCO nailed the coffin shut on pseudo-scientific theories that have been used to bolster racial discrimination. Until the Second World War, racist 'science' was widespread in academic circles throughout the developed world. The forerunner of UNESCO found itself blocked when it attempted to confront the issue during the 1930s. The reaction to the 1950 Statement managed to draw out some of those who were still clinging to racist theories, but they were largely neutralized by the 1951 Statement.

UNESCO's activity in the field of international human rights has always been somewhat limited in scope, confined to the mandate of the organization in the areas of education, science, and culture. That it would even take up the issue of racial discrimination was surely a surprise to some. Its engagement went through spurts of activity accompanied by significant periods of inaction. After the first two statements were adopted in 1950 and 1951, UNESCO's interest waned for several years. The revival in the 1960s is explained by the general significance of the racial discrimination issue at that time and the pressure to deal with it as the membership of the organization swelled, a result of decolonization.

UNESCO was serious engaged in activities directed against apartheid, producing studies and analyses documenting the history of political and economic domination of people in south Africa and Namibia.[160] It also conducted

---

[157] General Comment 20, Non-discrimination in economic, social and cultural rights (art. 2, para. 2, of the International Covenant on Economic, Social and Cultural Rights), 2 July 2009, E/C.12/GC/20, para. 19.

[158] Combined 22nd and 23rd periodic reports submitted by France under article 9 of the Convention, due in 2017, 9 May 2019, CERD/C/FRA/22-23, para. 68.

[159] Moving towards racial equality: study of the Advisory Committee on appropriate ways and means of assessing the situation, 16 August 2021, A/HRC/48/72, para. 9, fn. 6.

[160] Study on the achievements made and obstacles encountered during the Decades to Combat Racism and Racial Discrimination, 7 November 1989, E/CN.4/Sub.2/1989/8 and Add.1, paras. 119–24.

196 UNESCO: FIGHTING THE DOCTRINE OF RACIAL INEQUALITY

training programmes for members of national liberation movements. UNESCO published several books on the subject, including *Race, Class and the Apartheid State* by Harold Wolpe[161] and *Verrouillage ethnique en Afrique du Sud* by Claude Meillassoux.[162]

The *UNESCO Courier* devoted a special issue to racism in 2001, in conjunction with the Durban Conference on racism and racial discrimination. The short chapter by Prof. George Frederickson entitled 'The rise and fall of the laboratory racist' refers to 'the scientific racism that had been respectable and influential in the United States and Europe before World War II' but inexplicably made no mention of the four UNESCO statements on race.[163] Indeed, they are not cited anywhere in the 22-page special issue. The UNESCO declarations on race are also almost entirely neglected in its 700-page history of the organization's contribution to science, including the social sciences.[164] A sidebar to the Frederickson article refers to UNESCO's Universal Declaration on the Human Genome and on Human Rights, adopted in 1997,[165] stating that it 'disclaims once and for all the pseudo-scientific foundations of racism'. Adopted by UNESCO's General Conference, the Declaration on the Human Genome repeats the line from the UNESCO Constitution condemning the doctrine of the inequality of men and races. It also cites the 1978 Declaration on Race and Racial Prejudice, but within rather lengthy list of legal instruments. Otherwise, there is nothing specific on the 'pseudo-scientific foundations of racism' in the Declaration on the Human Genome.

The notion of the human genome was not part of the conversation when Ashley Montagu and others developed the UNESCO statements on race. The human genome is a sequence of DNA, itself a concept that was unknown until the 1950s. The identification of the components of the human genome has demonstrated the irrelevance of race as an explanation for human diversity. Rather, 'DNA is the best evidence of our shared complex and global ancestry',

---

[161] Harold Wolpe, *Race, Class and the Apartheid State*, London: James Currey, Addis Ababa: Organisation of African Unity, Paris: UNESCO, 1988.

[162] Claude Meillassoux, *Verrouillage ethnique en Afrique du Sud*, Addis Ababa: Organisation of African Unity, Paris: UNESCO, 1988.

[163] George M. Frederickson, 'The rise and fall of the laboratory racist', *UNESCO Courier*, September 2001, pp. 21–3.

[164] Patrick Petitjean, Vladimir Zharov, Gisbert Glaser, Jacques Richardson, Bruno de Padirac, and Gail Archibald, eds., *Sixty Years of Science at UNESCO 1945–2005*, Paris: UNESCO, 2006. There is a perfunctory reference in a single sentence on p. 523.

[165] UNESCO, Records of the General Conference, 29th Session, Vol. I, Resolutions, resolution 16. The Declaration was endorsed by the United Nations General Assembly: The human genome and human rights, 10 March 1999, A/RES/53/152. See Shawn H. E. Harmon, 'The Significance of UNESCO's Universal Declaration on the Human Genome and Human Rights' (2005) 2 *SCRIPTed* 20; Noëlle Lenoir, 'Universal Declaration on the Human Genome and Human Rights: The First Legal and Ethical Framework at the Global Level' (1999) 30 *Columbia Human Rights Law Review* 537.

THE 1978 DECLARATION ON RACE AND RACE PREJUDICE   197

as Anna Spain Bradley has written.[166] Nevertheless, with its ability to suggest components of 'ancestry', research on the human genome has spawned a new wave of pseudo-science. Perhaps it is time for UNESCO to refresh its great historic statements on race in light of modern-day science as well as its perversions.

Since the 1970s, UNESCO has been active in both research and commemoration of the African slave trade. In January-February 1978, UNESCO organized an expert meeting on the slave trade in Port-au-Prince. In 1994, UNESCO launched the 'Slave Route' Project at a meeting in Benin. Its object has been to bring universal attention to the issue of the transatlantic slave trade but also the slave trade in the Indian Ocean and the Mediterranean region. The project is ongoing. In 2021, UNESCO hosted the first Global Forum against Racism and Discrimination. 'Fighting racism is part of UNESCO's DNA. Its history', the organization's Secretary-General, Audrey Azoulay, told the Forum.

---

[166] Anna Spain Bradley, 'Human Rights Racism' (2019) 32 *Harvard Human Rights Journal* 1, at p. 55.

8

Colonialism and Neo-colonialism at the United Nations

Addressing Colonialism in the Charter

Fifty-one Member States belonged to the United Nations when the General Assembly first convened in January 1946. Nineteen years later, when the International Convention on the Elimination of All Forms of Racial Discrimination was adopted by the General Assembly, the organization had grown to 117 members. One-third of the Member States in 1965 had been either colonies or League of Nations mandates when the United Nations was established. Of these, most were African. Only four African States were founding members of the United Nations: Egypt, Ethiopia, Liberia, and South Africa. By 1965, there were 36 African Member States, comprising slightly more than one-third of the membership.

The League of Nations did not meddle in the affairs of the colonial empires except for those territories subject to the Permanent Mandates Commission. The Dumbarton Oaks conference took no decisions about colonies or mandates although it was understood that these issues would eventually have to be confronted. The future of the mandates regime was discussed by the Soviet Union, the United States, and the United Kingdom at the Yalta conference, in February 1945. The three powers agreed on a trusteeship scheme for the territories held under League of Nations mandates, to territories that would be taken from Japan and Italy as a result of the war, and territories that States voluntarily placed within the system.[1] Pursuant to the Charter of the United Nations, the League mandates were repackaged as 'Trust Territories'. The mandate holders were monitored by the Trusteeship Council, a principal organ of the United Nations, in what amounted to a more robust version of the League's Permanent Mandates Commission.[2] Over the two decades following entry into force of the Charter, most of the Trust Territories became fully independent with the

---

[1] Huntington Gilchrist, 'Colonial Questions at the San Francisco Conference' (1945) 39 *American Political Science Review* 982.

[2] On the Trusteeship Council, see Sherman S. Hayden, 'The Trusteeship Council: Its First Three Years' (1951) 66 *Political Science Quarterly* 226.

The International Legal Order's Colour Line. William A. Schabas, Oxford University Press.
© Oxford University Press 2023. DOI: 10.1093/oso/9780197744475.003.0008

notorious exception of South West Africa, which had been assigned to South Africa at the Paris Peace Conference. South Africa refused to adopt a trusteeship agreement. In fact if not in law, the territory of modern-day Namibia was annexed by South Africa and its people subjected to the racist regime that would soon be labelled 'apartheid'.

The Charter of the United Nations also contemplated 'non-self-governing territories', a concept that was unknown under the Covenant of the League of Nations. This had not been discussed at Dumbarton Oaks or at Yalta. That the United Nations might have some monitoring role over colonies was anathema to the United Kingdom, the only one of the 'big three' with a significant interest in the survival of the colonial system. Since the time of Woodrow Wilson, the United States had taken an anti-colonial posture although it was not without some territories in a situation analogous to colonization.[3]

Chapter XI of the Charter of the United Nations, consisting of articles 73 and 74, is entitled 'Declaration regarding non-self-governing territories'. It applies to 'Members of the United Nations which have or assume responsibilities for the administration of territories whose peoples have not yet attained a full measure of self-government', a euphemism for colonial powers. In the Declaration, they 'recognise the principle that the interests of the inhabitants of these territories are paramount, and accept as a sacred trust the obligation to promote to the utmost, within the system of international peace and security established by the present Charter, the well-being of the inhabitants of these territories'. The declaration contains echoes of the General Act of Berlin of 1885 and of the Covenant of the League of Nations. At San Francisco, a representative of Australia described it as 'the most important and far-reaching joint declaration of colonial policy in history' whose 'significance for the future could scarcely be exaggerated'.[4] Among the obligations assumed by the colonial powers was the regular transmission to the United Nations 'for information purposes' of 'statistical and other information of a technical nature relating to economic, social, and educational conditions in the territories for which they are respectively responsible'.[5]

Whether they were trust territories or non-self-governing territories, the reality amounted to people of colour being ruled by Europeans or by countries controlled by people of European descent. Inevitably, there were many manifestations of racial discrimination. The link between colonialism and racial

---

[3] Jon M. Van Dyke, Carmen Di Amore-Siah, and Gerald W. Berkley-Coats, 'Self-Determination for Nonself-Governing Peoples and for Indigenous Peoples: The Cases of Guam and Hawai'i' (1996) 18 *University of Hawai'i Law Review* 623; Jose Alberto Axtmayer, 'Non-Self-Governing Territories and the Constitutive Process of the United Nations: A General Analysis and the Case Study of Puerto Rico' (1976) 45 *Revista Jurídica de la Universidad de Puerto Rico* 211.

[4] Verbatim minutes of third meeting of Commission II, 20 June 1945, 1144 II/16, UNCIO VIII, p. 135.

[5] See Non-self-governing peoples, 9 February 1946, A/RES/9 (I).

200 COLONIALISM AND NEO-COLONIALISM AT THE UNITED NATIONS

discrimination is affirmed in many General Assembly resolutions[6] as well as in article 15 of the International Convention on the Elimination of All Forms of Racial Discrimination. Despite claims to the contrary by the colonial powers, the entire system was pervaded with and premised upon racial discrimination. There were separate schools for the children of the colonizers and those of the colonized, to the extent that there were schools at all for the latter. There were separate hospitals for the colonizers and for the colonized, to the extent that advanced medical care in any form was available to the latter. Labour legislation, including rules on the minimum wage, applied differently depending upon the ethnicity of the worker. Consequently and inexorably, issues of racial discrimination were on the agenda of the relevant United Nations bodies, in particular the Fourth Committee of the General Assembly and the Trusteeship Council.

Although the United Nations was the primary forum for the struggle against colonialism at the international level, no account is complete without some reference to the Bandung Conference, in Indonesia. It was convened in 1955 by India, Pakistan, Ceylon, Burma, and Indonesia. Of the 29 States that were represented, the great majority were Asian. Six were from Africa: Egypt, Ethiopia, Liberia, Libya, the Gold Coast (Ghana), and the Anglo-Egyptian Sudan. The superpowers were not invited. The Bandung Conference 'ushered in a new era of international relations as nations of colour began a sustained campaign to end colonial rule in the non-European world and its corollary of white supremacy. It was the first major conference of non-European states and led to the creation of the non-aligned movement.'[7]

Bandung was a meeting with a colour line, but unlike any other. There were antecedents for international meetings of people of colour, like the Pan African Congress organized by W.E.B Du Bois and others in Paris in 1919, but this was the first gathering where the delegates were governments. President Sukarno of Indonesia, when he opened the Conference, described it as 'the first intercontinental conference of coloured peoples in the history of mankind'. Du Bois was prevented from attending the Bandung Conference by the Department of State, which would not give him a passport. He sent a message to the delegates: 'We coloured folk of America have long lived with you Yellow, Brown and Black folk of the world under the intolerable arrogance and assumptions of the White race. . . We beg you to close ranks against men of America, Britain,

---

[6] For example, Declaration on the granting of independence to colonial countries and peoples, 14 December 1960, A/RES/1514 (XV), PP 8.

[7] Cary Fraser, 'An American Dilemma: Race and Realpolitik in the American Response to the Bandung Conference, 1955', in Brenda Gayle Plummer, ed., *Window on Freedom: Race, Civil Rights, and Foreign Affairs, 1945–1988*, Chapel Hill and London: University of North Carolina Press, 2003, pp. 116–40, at p. 115.

ADDRESSING COLONIALISM IN THE CHARTER   201

France, Spain, Belgium and the Netherlands as long as they fight and scheme for the colonial system, for colour caste and class exploitation.'[8]

Richard Wright, the great African American novelist, was among those who attended in their personal capacity. He later published a book-length account of the Conference. Wright explained how he learned of it:

> Idly, I picked up the evening's newspaper that lay folded near me upon a table and began thumbing through it. Then I was staring at a news item that baffled me. I bend forward and read the item a second time. *Twenty-nine free and independent nations of Asia and Africa are meeting in Bandung, Indonesia, to discuss 'racialism and colonialism'*... What is this? I scanned the list of nations involved: China, India, Indonesia, Japan, Burma, Egypt, Turkey, the Philippines, Ethiopia, Gold Coast, etc. My god! I began a rapid calculation of the populations of the nations listed and, when my total topped the billion mark, I stopped, pulled off my glasses and tried to think. A stream of realisations claimed my mind: these people were ex-colonial subjects, people whom the white West called 'coloured' peoples... Almost all of the nations mentioned had been, in some form or other, under the domination of Western Europe; some had been subjected for a few decades and others had been ruled for 350 years... And most of the leaders of these nations had been political prisoners, men who had lived lonely lives in exile, men to whom secret political activity had been a routine matter, men to whom sacrifice and suffering had been daily companions...[9]

Harlem politician Adam Clayton Powell Jr., a member of the House of Representatives, failed to persuade the Department of State to send a truly representative observer delegation so he went with a press badge on behalf of the *New York Age Defender*.[10] Malcolm X, a leading African-American activist in the 1950s and 1960s, would later describe Bandung as the 'first unity meeting in centuries of black people'.[11] Western diplomats got the message. In a telephone conversation with American Secretary of State John Foster Dulles, an American official described the participants as 'practically all coloured'.[12] Australia's

---

[8] 'To the peoples of Asia and Africa meeting at Bandung, April 1955, W.E.B. Du Bois Papers (MS 312).

[9] Richard Wright, *The Color Curtain: A Report on the Bandung Conference*, New York: World, 1956, pp. 11–12 (emphasis in the original).

[10] Matthew Jones, 'A "Segregated" Asia?: Race, the Bandung Conference, and Pan-Asianist Fears in American Thought and Policy, 1954–1955' (2005) 29 *Diplomatic History* 841, at p. 863.

[11] George Breitman, ed., *Malcolm X Speaks: Selected Speeches and Statements*, New York: Grove Press, 1965), pp. 5–6.

[12] Dulles-Robertson telephone conversation, 31 December 1954, cited in Matthew Jones, 'A "Segregated" Asia?: Race, the Bandung Conference, and Pan-Asianist Fears in American Thought and Policy, 1954–1955' (2005) 29 *Diplomatic History* 841, at p. 853.

202   COLONIALISM AND NEO-COLONIALISM AT THE UNITED NATIONS

minister of external affairs wrote in his diary that Bandung was 'a "colour" in-spired conference, with anti-colonialism as its apparent objective'.[13]

Racism in Non-Self-Governing Territories

Of the founding members of the United Nations, eight were responsible for non-self-governing territories: Australia, Belgium, Denmark, France, the Netherlands, New Zealand, the United Kingdom, and the United States. Spain and Portugal, with colonies in Africa and elsewhere, joined the United Nations in 1955 as part of a more general expansion of the membership. At its first session, the General Assembly established an 'ad hoc Committee' composed of the eight colonial powers and an equal number of other countries. Brazil, China, Cuba, Egypt, India, Philippines, the Soviet Union, and Uruguay were elected by the General Assembly to the Committee.[14] In 1947, the General Assembly replaced the ad hoc committee with a 'Special Committee on Information'.[15] The Committee issued its first report in 1948.[16]

The General Assembly adopted a 'Standard Form' for the guidance of the colonial States in compiling and submitting information on non-self-governing territories. The initial version included a rubric entitled 'human rights' followed by this heading: 'Civil rights protected by law', although this was in an optional part of the Form. Elsewhere the Form contained a rubric on 'social conditions' that included a heading on 'Social problems of race and cultural relations, including laws safeguarding the indigenous population from discrimination'.[17] In 1950, the General Assembly recommended that information on human rights cease to be an optional category for the reporting.[18] A General Assembly resolution invited Member States with non-self-governing territories to include in the information

[13] Entry for 30 December 1954, T.B. Miller, ed., *Australian Foreign Minister: The Diaries of R.G. Casey, 1951–60*, London: Harper Collins, 1972, p. 197.
[14] Transmission of information under Article 73e of the Charter, 14 December 1946, A/RES/66 (1).
[15] Creation of a special committee on information transmitted under Article 73 e of the Charter, 3 November 1947, A/RES/146 (II). See Usha Sud, 'Committee on Information from Non-Self-Governing Territories: Its Role in the Promotion of Self-Determination of Colonial Peoples' (1965) 7 *International Studies* 311; Yassin El-Ayouty, *The United Nations and Decolonization: The Role of Afro-Asia*, The Hague: Martinus Nijhoff, 1971, pp. 67–88; Usha Sud, *United Nations and Non-Self-Governing Territories*, Delhi: University Publishers, 1965; Sergio Armanda Frazão, 'International Responsibility for Non-self-governing Peoples' (1954) 296 *Annals of the American Academy of Political and Social Science* 56.
[16] Report of the Special Committee on Information transmitted under Article 73 e of the Charter (2–29 September 1948), A/593.
[17] Standard form for the guidance of Members in the preparation of information to be transmitted under Article 73 e of the Charter, 3 November 1947, A/RES/142 (II), Annex.
[18] Voluntary transmission of information under part I of the Standard Form concerning Non-Self-Governing Territories, 2 December 1949, A/RES/327 (IV), OP 1.

they submitted 'a summary of the extent to which the Universal Declaration of Human Rights is implemented in the Non Self-Governing Territories under their administration'[19] The Standard Form was revised to specify, under the heading 'human rights', information about how human rights 'in accordance with the principles set forth in the Universal Declaration of Human Rights, are protected by law, particularly in respect of: (a) Legal principles and procedures; (b) Basic legislation and its application; (c) Anti-discrimination legislation'[20]

Racial discrimination soon became an important subject at the annual meetings of the Special Committee and, subsequently, the Fourth Committee of the General Assembly. Colonial powers were grilled, not always politely, about their governance. The responses were often little more than pathetic rationales for colonialism, replete with paternalistic language as well as transparent justifications for the racial discrimination that was deeply entrenched in their world view. During the 1948 session of the Special Committee, when the Soviet Union made allegations of racial discrimination in the non-self-governing territories, France replied that in its territories 'racial discrimination was unknown'[21] In its 1949 report, the Special Committee described as 'incomplete and vague' the information on racial discrimination submitted by the 'Administering Members', as the colonialists were called. The Committee said information transmitted on Kenya admitted there was no legal protection from racial discrimination and 'made the unsatisfactory statement that discriminatory laws had recently been repealed wherever possible'[22]

The Special Committee proposed that the General Assembly adopt a resolution on 'equal treatment in matters relating to education'. It invited the Administering Members 'to take steps, where necessary, to establish equal treatment in matters related to education between inhabitants of the Non-Self Governing Territories under their administration, whether they be indigenous or not'[23] In the Fourth Committee, Cuba proposed an additional paragraph: 'Invites the Administering Members, in cases where for exceptional reasons educational facilities of a separate character are provided for different communities, to include in the information transmitted under Article 73 e of the Charter full data on the costs and methods of financing the separate groups of educational institutions'[24] The resolution did not explicitly refer to racial discrimination, but this was implied.

[19] Information on human rights in Non-Self-Governing Territories, 12 December 1950, A/RES/ 446 (V), OP 1.
[20] Report of the Special Committee on Information transmitted under Article 73 e of the Charter (2–27 October 1951), A/1836, p. 15.
[21] Report of the Special Committee on Information transmitted under Article 73 e of the Charter (2–29 September 1948), A/593, p. 5.
[22] Report of the Special Committee on Information transmitted under Article 73 e of the Charter (25 August–12 September 1949), A/923, para. 55.
[23] Ibid., Annex II, p. 16.
[24] Report of the Fourth Committee, 29 November 1949, A/1159, para. 8.

204   COLONIALISM AND NEO-COLONIALISM AT THE UNITED NATIONS

Years later, the Secretary-General referred to the resolution as the first manifestation of the General Assembly's engagement with the issue of racial discrimination in non-self-governing territories.[25] That the resolution struck a nerve can be seen from the voting record. Cuba's amendment was adopted by 34 votes to 1 (Belgium), with 12 abstentions (Australia, Canada, Chile, Denmark, France, Greece, New Zealand, Norway, Sweden, South Africa, United States, United Kingdom). The Netherlands and Israel were the only Western States to vote in favour. The resolution as amended was adopted by 42 to 1 (United Kingdom) with 4 abstentions (Belgium, Canada, Greece, South Africa).[26]

In 1950, the United Kingdom responded to concerns by insisting that its 'declared policy' was removal of 'any vestiges of racial discrimination'.[27] Pakistan 'expressed the hope' that the United Kingdom would implement this policy.[28] Pakistan observed that despite the General Assembly's recommendation that information on compliance with the Universal Declaration of Human Rights be furnished, very few of the States concerned had done this. 'There was reason to believe that racial discrimination existed in some territories', said Mian Ziauddin. 'Domination by a foreign Power, however benevolent, was a heavy burden, and the addition of racial discrimination meant real oppression'.[29] Iraq's delegate to the Fourth Committee, giving Morocco as an example, said that '[i]n some Non-Self-Governing Territories there was flagrant discrimination between the European and the indigenous inhabitants'.[30] Ukraine's representative charged that in Swaziland 'a policy of racial discrimination was being openly practised . . . where the wages of African agricultural workers were one-seventh of those of European workmen doing the same work'.[31]

The debate intensified during the 1952 session of the Special Committee. Four of the eight non-colonial States, India, Egypt, Indonesia, and Pakistan, each of them bearing the scars of colonialism, proposed a resolution on racial discrimination.[32] The proposers noted that similar resolutions condemning racial discrimination in the Trust Territories had been adopted. The General Assembly could not do less than confirm the same principle, which derived from the Charter and the Universal Declaration of Human Rights.[33] The resolution was opposed by several of the colonial powers. Belgium, France, and the United Kingdom argued that racial discrimination was being addressed elsewhere in the

---

[25] Racial discrimination in non-self-governing territories, 2 October 1962, A/5249, para. 2.
[26] Report of the Fourth Committee, 29 November 1949, A/1159, paras. 9–10.
[27] Yearbook of the United Nations, 1950, p. 690.
[28] Ibid., p. 691.
[29] Summary record, Fourth Committee, 22 November 1951, A/C.4/SR.208, para. 15.
[30] Summary record, Fourth Committee, 22 November 1951, A/C.4/SR.209, para. 13.
[31] Ibid., para. 68.
[32] Summary record, Committee on Information, 3 October 1952, A/AC.35/SR.70, p. 4.
[33] Ibid., p. 5.

United Nations and that it was unnecessary to consider the subject within the specific context of non-self-governing territories. The Soviet Union, on the other hand, pointed to the absence of indigenous peoples in government institutions in the colonies, exclusion of colonized peoples from education and medical care, and the infliction of corporal punishment. After the resolution was adopted by the Special Committee it was again debated within the plenary Fourth Committee, where the same arguments were made.[34] France protested that it was wrong to examine racial discrimination only in the context of such territories. This would ultimately lead, it said, 'to the astonishingly simple deduction that colonisation was tantamount to racial discrimination'.[35] The French representative criticized his Haitian colleague for suggesting that there was a 'relationship of cause and effect between colonisation and racial discrimination', warning of the danger of 'discrimination in reverse'.[36] Belgium complained that the resolution only imposed obligations on colonial powers, and that it would abstain on the resolution rather than compromise its view that racial discrimination should be eradicated throughout the world.[37] Adopted by the General Assembly, it bore the blunt title: 'Racial discrimination in Non-Self-Governing Territories'. The resolution consisted of a series of recommendations to States responsible for such territories to abolish discriminatory laws and practices contrary to the principles of the Charter and the Universal Declaration of Human Rights, to make public facilities accessible without discrimination based upon race, and to examine laws that were allegedly for the purpose of protecting sections of the population to ensure that the 'protective aspect is still predominant'.[38]

In 1958, the subject of racial discrimination in non-self-governing territories returned to the Fourth Committee of the General Assembly. Introducing the subject, the Venezuelan representative said that despite the provisions of the Charter and the Universal Declaration of Human Rights, 'it remained a fact that in the African continent as a whole and in the Non-Self Governing Territories in particular discrimination was rife in all spheres, and especially with respect to trade-union organisation, administration, the judiciary and education'.[39] Venezuela was among the 10 sponsors of a draft resolution that referenced the 1952 resolution, observing that since its adoption and 'the progress made in certain Territories towards the removal of practices and the abolition of laws based on racial grounds has been limited'.[40] During the debate, the French

---

[34] Report of the Fourth Committee, 8 December 1952, A/2296, paras. 6–14.
[35] Summary record, Fourth Committee, 31 October 1952, A/C.4/SR.260, para. 32.
[36] Ibid., paras. 40–1.
[37] Ibid., para. 43.
[38] Racial discrimination in Non-Self-Governing Territories, 10 December 1952, A/RES/644 (VII).
[39] Summary record, Fourth Committee, 3 December 1958, A/C.4/SR.827, para. 1.
[40] Racial discrimination in Non-Self-Governing Territories, 12 December 1958, A/RES/1328 (XIII), PP 3. The original draft used the phrase 'limited progress has been made in certain Territories towards the removal of practices and the abolition of laws based on racial grounds'

206 COLONIALISM AND NEO-COLONIALISM AT THE UNITED NATIONS

representative boasted that his country had 'always been in the vanguard of those who championed the cause of racial equality' but then said 'he could not vote affirmatively because the text did not reflect the real situation'.[41] The United Kingdom's representative said his country was 'committed to the progressive removal of all restrictions based upon race as soon as it might be practicable'.[42] Former colonies were unimpressed. Indonesia's representative said that the slow rate of political development in some Non-Self-Governing Territories was attributable 'to the subordination, on racial grounds, of the interests of the indigenous inhabitants to those of the administering Powers'. He said the reluctance of Administering Powers to provide information revealed 'the incompatibility of their racial policies with contemporary standards of national and international life'.[43]

The preamble of the 1960 Declaration on the granting of independence to colonial countries and peoples made the link between ending colonialism 'and all practices of segregation and discrimination associated therewith'.[44] That year, the report of the Committee on Information from Non-Self-Governing Territories concluded that discrimination on grounds of race or colour continued to exist in some Non-Self-Governing Territories, being most acute in Africa where 'immigrant communities' were present. It noted that in such territories, the indigenous inhabitants constituted the vast majority of the population, while the 'European group' was extremely small in number yet with special political, social, and economic privileges. 'Not only was inferior treatment accorded in varying degrees to indigenous inhabitants in the field of human rights and fundamental freedoms, but in the economic and educational fields and in the exercise of political rights also, their role was restricted', the report said. 'In some cases, discriminatory practices survived because of personal or group attitudes; in others they were reinforced by law and regulation.'[45] The Report stated that the Members of the Committee 'expressed their satisfaction' that there was no racial discrimination in the territories administered by France, New Zealand, and the United States.[46]

(Racial discrimination in non-self-governing territories, Ceylon, Czechoslovakia, Ghana, Greece, India, Indonesia, Libya, Panama, Venezuela and Yemen: draft resolution, 2 December 1958, A/C.4/ L.565, PP 3). For a summary of the proposed amendments and the voting, see Report of the Fourth Committee, 11 December 1958, A/4068, paras. 21–30.

[41] Summary record, Fourth Committee, 3 December 1958, A/C.4/SR.829, para. 19.
[42] Ibid., para. 7. See also Summary record, Fourth Committee, 28 November 1958, A/C.4/SR.820, para. 46.
[43] Summary record, Fourth Committee, 3 December 1958, A/C.4/SR.829, para. 24.
[44] Declaration on the granting of independence to colonial countries and peoples, 14 December 1960, A/RES/1514 (XV), PP 9.
[45] Report of the Committee on Information from Non-Self-Governing Territories, A/4371, para. 177.
[46] Ibid., para. 40.

That was another way of pointing to problems with the colonies of Australia, Portugal, and the United Kingdom.

The Fourth Committee adopted a resolution endorsing the conclusion of the Committee on Information that racial discrimination was not only a violation of human rights but also a deterrent to progress in all fields of development in the Non-Self-Governing Territories. Initially proposed by Afghanistan, Bolivia, Ethiopia, Ghana, India, Morocco, Nigeria, Sudan, Togo, and the United Arab Republic, these states were joined as co-sponsors by Guinea, Iraq, Liberia, Nepal, Panama, Senegal, and Somalia.[47] The operative paragraphs were more demanding than those of the two predecessors adopted in 1952 and 1958. The resolution recommended that Administering States 'immediately rescind or revoke all laws and regulations which tend to encourage or sanction, directly or indirectly, discriminatory policies and practices based on racial considerations, and that they do their utmost to discourage such practices by all other members possible'. They were also urged to extend to all inhabitants the full exercise of basic political rights, including the right to vote.[48]

Speakers complained that earlier resolutions had been ignored by colonial powers.[49] Guinea's representative said the resolution 'severely condemned' those who had ignored the declaration in article 73 of the Charter.[50] The United Kingdom's representative presented a lengthy defence of his country's conduct, claiming that great progress had been made in recent years. He proposed replacing the phrase 'immediately to rescind or revoke all laws' with 'to take steps as soon as possible to secure the revocation of all laws', and 'to give full and immediate effect' with 'to give full effect at the earliest possible time'.[51] The countries of the South were infuriated by Britain's unabashed refusal to accept the principle of immediate abolition of all distinctions based upon race.[52] The delegate from Ceylon described Africa as 'the scene of the most extreme racial discrimination ever known', focussing on discriminatory legislation 'in an acute form' in the British colonies of Northern and Southern Rhodesia, Kenya, and Uganda.[53] The Fourth Committee adopted the resolution by 74 to none, with two abstentions, Australia and the United Kingdom.[54] In the plenary General Assembly, the result was very similar, with 88 in favour and the same two abstentions.[55] In

[47] Draft resolution concerning racial discrimination in Non-Self-Governing Territories, 28 October 1960, A/C.4/L.643 and Add.1 and 2.

[48] Report of the Fourth Committee, 14 December 1960, A/4650, pp. 21–2.

[49] Summary record, Fourth Committee, 28 October 1960, A/C.4/SR.1027, paras. 22, 27; Summary record, Fourth Committee, 28 October 1960, A/C.4/SR.1028, para. 17.

[50] Summary record, Fourth Committee, 28 October 1960, A/C.4/SR.1027, para. 28.

[51] Ibid., para. 36; Report of the Fourth Committee, 14 December 1960, A/4650, para. 33.

[52] Summary record, Fourth Committee, 28 October 1960, A/C.4/SR.1027, para. 40; Summary record, Fourth Committee, 28 October 1960, A/C.4/SR.1028, paras. 3, 24, 39, 51–2, 60.

[53] Summary record, Fourth Committee, 28 October 1960, A/C.4/SR.1028, paras. 14–15.

[54] Ibid., para. 71.

[55] Verbatim record, plenary General Assembly, 15 December 1960, A/PV.948, para. 80.

208 COLONIALISM AND NEO-COLONIALISM AT THE UNITED NATIONS

explanation, the United Kingdom representative formulated two objections to the text. He said that removal of discriminatory legislation would jeopardize 'legislation of a differentiating character which is still required in some territories for the protection of the Interests of the indigenous people'. As for the demand of universal suffrage, he said this 'goes beyond the scope of removing racial discrimination'.[56]

In 1961, the racial discrimination issue in non-self-governing territories returned to the agenda of the General Assembly. The annual report of the Committee on Information from non-self-governing territories dealt with racial discrimination at some length. It cited verbatim the British submissions claiming that 'fundamental rights and freedoms which were part of the British tradition were established and protected by the laws of the Territories'. It then noted that delegates from Ghana, India, Iraq, and Liberia had pointed out that, contrary to the assertion made in the foregoing statement, in many United Kingdom Territories the right of suffrage was denied to indigenous inhabitants.[57] The United Kingdom representative in the Committee insisted that his government's policy 'was one of unequivocal rejection of racial discrimination in all forms and in all fields', but that 'there were limits to what Governments could do since a change in people's minds, attitudes and ways of life must take time'.[58] The Committee reported that 'the problem of race relations' was most acute in Kenya and Northern Rhodesia (Zambia), pointing to restriction of the movements and residence of Africans in European centres and of non-Africans in African centres.[59] According to the report of the Committee,

> The information laid before the Committee indicated that an African entering European towns and industrial areas in Northern Rhodesia to live and work there must obtain a permit to look for work; that if he decides to take advantage of housing accommodation provided to him by the employer, he must reside in a Native township or compound where he is registered by the superintendent; and that after he has found employment, he must register his contract with the superintendent. In this connexion, the representative of the United Kingdom stated that Africans were entitled to provide their own accommodation in any area if they so wished.[60]

The United Kingdom also came in for harsh criticism when racial discrimination in non-self-governing territories was discussed in the Fourth Committee.

---

[56] Ibid., para. 85.
[57] Report of the Committee on Information from self-governing territories, A/4785, para. 170.
[58] Ibid., para. 176.
[59] Ibid., para. 178.
[60] Ibid., para. 182.

RACISM IN NON-SELF-GOVERNING TERRITORIES 209

Iraq's representative said the difference between the racist policies in British East Africa and South Africa was 'simply one of degree'.[61] To Britain's insistence that it gave official positions to Africans, Burma's delegate said that in practice 'it would appear that the most responsible and highly paid posts were still held by overseas officers, while the indigenous personnel clung precariously to the lower rungs of the administrative ladder'. U Tin Maung said that in territories of east and central Africa, 'the proportion of expatriate officers in senior grades was still high. He feared that their number would remain high in view of the fact that the white settlers sought to protect their vested interests with the help of efficient civil administrators and technical personnel on whom they could rely for political or other reasons.'[62] The tone of the resolution was similar to the one adopted the previous year but with some new elements. It called for adoption of legislation making racial discrimination and segregation punishable by law. It made a clear link between racial discrimination and colonialism. Many speakers made eloquent condemnations of racial discrimination although there was little in the way of debate about the wording of the resolution. Of the colonial powers, only the United Kingdom and Australia participated actively. And in contrast with the previous years, the resolution was unanimous, without abstentions in both the Fourth Committee and the plenary General Assembly.[63]

In its 1962 report, the Committee on Information returned to the issue of racial discrimination in education, a matter it had been examining since the late 1940s.[64] During its session that year, Ecuador raised the issue, providing examples:

... in one African Territory, for instance, education was compulsory for the Europeans but not for the indigenous inhabitants. Sometimes, again, discrimination was not practised in the official schools but was to be found in independent and private schools. In one Territory African pupils were selected by means of a system of examinations which did not apply to the Europeans, with the result that the number of African children attending school declined from year to year. Elsewhere, again, Africans leaving primary school could not fill posts which were regarded as reserved for Europeans, whereas in theory employment opportunities were identical for the indigenous inhabitants and for the Europeans. In one African Territory discrimination was even sanctioned by legislation. Although in that Territory there were fifty-six African pupils for

---

[61] Summary record, Fourth Committee, 15 November 1961, A/C.4/SR.1211, para. 4.
[62] Summary record, Fourth Committee, 15 November 1961, A/C.4/SR.1210, para. 5.
[63] Racial discrimination in Non-Self-Governing Territories, 19 December 1961, A/RES/1698 (XVI); Summary record, Fourth Committee, 17 November 1961, A/C.4/SR.1215, para. 66; Verbatim record, plenary General Assembly, 19 December 1961, A/PV.1082, para. 182.
[64] See *supra*, p. 203.

each European pupil, the appropriations for African education amounted to £3 million and those for European education exceeded £1 million.[65]

In its report, the Committee said that in some non-self-governing territories, the school system was based on racial discrimination, particularly at the primary level. It noted that some efforts were being made to address this but that they were mainly confined to the secondary and higher levels. The Committee insisted 'that on no ground whatsoever could education on a racial basis be justified' and hoped efforts to abolish racial discrimination in education 'will be pursued with the greatest possible vigour'.[66]

The 1961 General Assembly resolution on racial discrimination in non-self-governing territories requested the Secretary-General to prepare a report on its implementation.[67] In accordance with the 1961 resolution, the Secretary-General submitted an extensive report on racial discrimination in non-self-governing territories. The General Assembly resolution also requested the Secretary-General to disseminate it in the non-self-governing territories using all appropriate media and using the languages of the indigenous peoples as well as those of the Administrating Power. The efforts seem generally to have been rather modest. The materials were distributed through UN offices in the regions. Radio talks were also prepared in the languages of the colonizers as well as in Bemba, Hindi, Kimbundu, Luganda, Malay, Maori, Mbundu, Niuean, Nyanja, Swahili, Thonga, and Zulu.[68] With the exception of Portugal, all of the 'Administrating Authorities' cooperated with the efforts of the Secretary-General.

Much of the Secretary-General's report was concerned with factual description of the racial or ethnic composition of non-self-governing territories. The Secretary-General used rather confused terminology, referring to 'negroid peoples', 'indigenous' and 'immigrant' groups, but also to 'European, Eurasian, Ceylonese and other races' and to the 'Melanesian race'. Sometimes he spoke of 'racial problems', 'the problem of race relations', and of 'the racial or colour problem' rather than of discrimination as such.[69] The report noted that several of the Administering Authorities, including Australia, the Netherlands, New Zealand, Spain, the United Kingdom, and the United States, claimed that there

---

[65] Summary record, Committee on Information, 27 April 1962, A/AC.35/SR.247, p. 7.
[66] Report of the Committee on Information from self-governing territories, A/5215, para. 64. See also the remarks of the chairman of the Committee: Summary record, Fourth Committee, 4 December 1962, A/C.4/SR.1409, para. 9.
[67] Racial discrimination in Non-Self-Governing Territories, 19 December 1961, A/RES/1698 (XVI), OP 4.
[68] Racial discrimination in Non-Self-Governing Territories, 2 October 1962, A/5249, Annexes I and II; Racial discrimination in Non-Self-Governing Territories, 18 September 1963, A/5524, para. 8.
[69] Racial discrimination in non-self-governing territories, 2 October 1962, A/5249, paras. 12–32.

was either no racial discrimination or that it was their policy to eliminate it.[70] Turning to actual evidence to confirm these claims by the colonial powers, the Secretary-General said the available information was 'not as up-to-date and comprehensive as might be desired' but that it indicated 'a trend towards the extension of basic political rights to local inhabitants' and the adoption of legal and administrative measures to eliminate racial discrimination.[71] The report focussed on various indicators illustrating the 'trend' that had been detected, relying on information provided by the colonizers. It was almost a rosy picture of the situation, although there were a few exceptional comments that were surely closer to the reality. On Northern Rhodesia, the report said that '[t]he problem of race relations . . . remains acute and in its conclusions on the conditions in the Territory the Special Committee of Seventeen noted that racial discrimination continued to be widespread'.[72] A British official was cited saying that 'some segregation has in fact existed, for historical reasons, but that it was no longer true that an African cannot live in a European area unless he has entered European domestic service'.[73] In any event, within two years Zambia was independent.

There was almost no discussion of the Secretary-General's report in the Fourth Committee, perhaps because it was so mediocre and uncritical. The delegate from Argentina referred to Spain's claim that the inhabitants of its African colonies and the Spanish metropolis 'enjoy the same privileges'. He asked Louis Joseph Maho of the Mouvement pour l'indépendance de la Guinée équatoriale, who was testifying before the Committee, for his comments on that statement.[74] Africans in the Spanish colonies were not allowed out of doors in the towns after 8 p.m., Maho replied. Furthermore, their access to the towns was restricted. Separate seats were set aside for them in the cinemas, cafés, and churches, and there were segregated cemeteries for whites and Blacks.[75] Spain offered a feeble reply that did not speak directly to Maho's charges.[76]

The Fourth Committee adopted a new resolution on racial discrimination in non-self-governing territories, as proposed by several States of the South together with Poland.[77] The resolution described racial discrimination as being 'utterly

---

[70] Ibid., paras. 33–41.

[71] Ibid., para. 43.

[72] Ibid., para. 71.

[73] Ibid., para. 73.

[74] Summary record, Fourth Committee, A/C.4/SR.1420, 12 December 1962, para. 86, citing Racial discrimination in non-self-governing territories, 2 October 1962, A/5249, paras. 40, 48.

[75] Summary record, Fourth Committee, A/C.4/SR.1420, 12 December 1962, para. 87.

[76] Summary record, Fourth Committee, A/C.4/SR.1423, 13 December 1962, paras. 29–34.

[77] Racial discrimination in the Non-Sell-Governing Territories: Bolivia, Brazil, Bulgaria, Burma, Ghana, Guinea, Mali, Mauritania, Mexico, Niger, Poland, and the United Arab Republic: joint draft resolution, 13 December 1962, A/C.4/L.769. Afghanistan, Cameroon, the Ivory Coast, Liberia, Syria, and Togo joined the list of sponsors (Summary record, Fourth Committee, 14 December 1962, A/C.4/SR.1424, para. 58).

212 COLONIALISM AND NEO-COLONIALISM AT THE UNITED NATIONS

repugnant to humanity'. It noted that racism had not been eradicated in non-self-governing territories. It reiterated the view that elimination of racial discrimination and segregation in non-self-governing territories was linked to 'faithful implementation of the Declaration on the granting of independence to colonial countries and peoples', in other words, independence and self-determination. The resolution was adopted without a vote in the Fourth Committee and in the plenary General Assembly.[78]

In 1963, the General Assembly decided to dissolve the Committee on Information from Non-Self-Governing Territories.[79] Its tasks were assigned to the Special Committee on the Situation with regard to the Implementation of the Declaration on the Granting of Independence to Colonial Countries and Peoples, known initially as the 'Special Committee of Seventeen', which had begun its work the previous year.[80] After the General Assembly expanded its membership, it was referred to as the 'Special Committee of Twenty-four' or the 'Decolonisation Committee'.[81] One-third of its Members were African States. The Western States were represented by Australia, the United Kingdom, and the United States. At the outset, the Committee decided that its work should emphasize territories in Africa, where the largest number of people continued to live under colonialism. In its first year of activities, the Committee held 117 meetings and provided the General Assembly with a report of nearly 200 pages.[82] The Committee considered the Secretary-General's Report on racial discrimination in non-self-governing territories. It informed the General Assembly that it would continue to give special attention to the eradication of racial discrimination in those territories where such discrimination was prevalent.[83]

The activities of the Committee concerned territories administered by Australia, France, New Zealand, Portugal, Spain, the United Kingdom, and the United States. Given the focus on Africa, the work very largely concerned Britain and its remaining colonies. With respect to racial discrimination, its focus

[78] Racial discrimination in Non-Self-Governing Territories, 19 December 1962, A/RES/1850 (XVII); Summary record, Fourth Committee, 14 December 1962, A/C.4/SR.1424, para. 60.

[79] Question of the continuation of the Committee on Information from Non-Self-Governing Territories, 16 December 1963, A/RES/1970 (XVIII).

[80] The situation with regard to the implementation of the Declaration on the granting of independence to colonial countries and peoples, 27 November 1961, A/RES/1654 (XVI).

[81] The situation with regard to the implementation of the Declaration on the granting of independence to colonial countries and peoples, 17 December 1962, A/RES/1810 (XVII). See Maurice Barbier, *Le Comité de Decolonisation des Nations Unies*, Paris: Librairie Générale de Droit et de Jurisprudence, 1974; Hollis W. Barber, 'Decolonization: The Committee of Twenty-four' (1975) 138 *World Affairs* 128.

[82] Report of the Special Committee on the Situation with regard to the Implementation of the Declaration on the Granting of Independence to Colonial Countries and Peoples, 8 October 1962, A/5238.

[83] Report of the Special Committee on the Situation with regard to the Implementation of the Declaration on the Granting of Independence to Colonial Countries and Peoples, 19 July 1963, A/5446/Rev.1, p. 287.

was on the white settler regime in Southern Rhodesia.[84] The Committee also assumed jurisdiction over South West Africa.[85] Along with the Portuguese colonies of Angola and Mozambique, these States formed a belt around South Africa. In effect, all of southern Africa was controlled by racist States that were ruled by white settler regimes or colonizers.

Trust Territories

The mandate system of the League of Nations was replaced by the international trusteeship system, governed by articles 75 to 91 of the Charter of the United Nations. The Charter specified that among the principles on which trusteeship was based was 'to encourage respect for human rights and for fundamental freedoms for all without distinction as to race, sex, language, or religion'.[86] In practice, of course, because the trusteeship system was little more than colonialism by another name, racial discrimination was endemic. The Trusteeship Council 'drew attention' to the importance of ensuring that there be no discrimination in wage rates.[87] In 1949, a General Assembly resolution on Trust Territories recommended 'the abolition of discriminatory laws and practices contrary to the principles of the Charter and the Trusteeship Agreements, in all Trust Territories in which such laws and practices still exist'.[88] Yet in a report on Tanganyika, the British explained that 'full application of the principle of non-discrimination . . . in wage and salary payments as between different races' raised 'particular difficulties'.[89]

Like the Permanent Mandates Commission of the League of Nations, the Trusteeship Council received petitions from those who lived in the territories. Some of these made charges of racial discrimination. For example, 22 indigenous residents of Shinyanga District, in Tanganyika, wrote that 'we should like to let the United Nations Mission and our local Government not to forget that there still exists a "COLOUR BAR" in this country, and that is a heart-breaking fact. Africans of not only Shinyanga Township but all over the Towns in Tanganyika would like to see that colour bar is put to an end at once'.[90] Francis Rukeba of

---

[84] Report of the Special Committee on the Situation with regard to the Implementation of the Declaration on the Granting of Independence to Colonial Countries and Peoples, Annex No. 8 (Part I), A/5800/Rev.1, pp. 30–107.

[85] Ibid., pp. 108–34.

[86] Charter of the United Nations, art. 76(c).

[87] Report of the Trusteeship Council covering its second and third sessions, 29 April 1947–5 August 1948, A/603, p. 32.

[88] Social advancement in Trust Territories, 15 November 1949, A/RES/323 (IV), OP 4.

[89] Report of the Trusteeship Council covering its second and third sessions, 29 April 1947–5 August 1948, A/603, p. 24.

[90] J. de la Roche to Trygve Lie, 22 August 1948, T/PET.2/51, p. 4.

Cyato Hill, Shangugu Territory, in Ruanda petitioned the Secretary-General with a range of grievances, several of which were clearly related to racial discrimination: 'Why are Europeans who want to buy land authorised to occupy such land, and thus to compel the occupants to leave their land and seek another? The natives cannot buy back lands sold to Europeans where there are deposits of gold, cassiterite, sand or clay for brick-making; if the Europeans, looking for land and mines increase in number and the natives have no right to refuse to give up their land to them, where shall we natives go?'[91] Another petition from Ruanda-Urundi spoke of injustice by the courts, explaining that any dispute between a European and an African would be heard by a European judge. 'The judge will never hear our complaints first without rebuking me and abuse me comparing me with monkey which they say in French Macaque', he wrote. 'They say that an African cannot tell the truth excepting European only.'[92] Another wrote from prison in Bujumbura claiming he had been waiting 17 months on his appeal of a conviction. 'Here in Usumbura, a native who has a case against a Belgian cannot even appeal. They condemn him with the statement that white men cannot tell a lie', he wrote.[93]

A Cameroonian postal worker residing in Paris, J.E. Alfred Togney, protested to the Council that 'a thousand promises were made to me that the clauses of the new Constitution would be observed and that racial discrimination against the black man in Africa would disappear'.[94] The petition of the *Évolution sociale camerounaise* formulated the desire 'that public places shall be open to everyone without discrimination of colour'.[95] In an early manifestation of intersectionality, the *Union démocratique des femmes camerounaise*s made the following submission:

> The social concept of colonialism lays strong stress on the inferiority of African to white women. We are being subjected daily to many forms of discrimination. For instance, African women (especially Cameroonians) give birth on the bare ground in the lying-in centres, and that gives rise to a high rate of infant mortality. Widows (sellers of foodstuffs) are often arrested in the markets for failure to pay the market fees. If you look at this from the point of view of morality, you yourself will see that these poor women, who have no other means of feeding their children, are thus wantonly penalised when they are forced to pay out all

---

[91] Francis Rukeba to Trygve Lie, 3 August 1948, T/PET.3/9.
[92] Petition from Mr. C.B. Muygutu concerning Ruanda-Urundi, 10 August 1951, T/PET.3/53.
[93] Petition from Mr. Jeean Sebukuavu concerning Ruanda-Urundi, 10 August 1951, T/PET.3/52.
[94] J.E. Alfred Togney to United Nations, 14 January 1950, T/PET.5/79.
[95] Petition of Évolution sociale camerounaise, 22 November 1949, T/PET.5/54, p. 6.

that they have earned during the day and remain empty-handed, thus leading a life as sad as it is onerous . . . [96]

The Council replied to the petition by informing the Cameroonian women that France had claimed '[n]o racial discrimination exists in the maternity wards of the country'.[97]

From Tanganyika, came the following, written in Swahili and signed by the African Association Mukindani:

> Why are Africans segregated from other races? For example, they are not given entry to European and Asian clubs or encouraged to mix with these races. Again, in times of food shortage relief to Africans is given only in the form of cassava, millet and maize in totally inadequate quantities. They are prohibited from obtaining rice, ghee, sugar etc., on the grounds that these do not form part of their customary diet, although these are obtainable in Africa.[98]

The Tanga Branch of the African Association sent a detailed description of grievances with the British regime in Tanganyika. It protested the tendency to 'Europeanise' the Senior Service, 'thus affording no chances to Africans to higher posts'. Even clerical and non-clerical posts 'are given to Europeans, non-Europeans, refugees, stateless and ex-enemies, and not to the African who suffered the horrors of World War II and contributed to the Allies' victory'. It protested the practice of only applying corporal punishment to Africans, saying this was incompatible with the principles of the United Nations Charter. The petition described the inadequacies of the educational system. Turning to health care, it said that

> hard beds in African wards are furnished with only one bedsheet and blanket. Mosquito-nets are not provided at all. The use of spray is not known. The food is of the worst kind known as 'whole meal'. In the non-native wards the patients enjoy all the comforts same as they get at home.

The petition also reported on medical research by which Africans suffering from malaria were denied quinine injections at the Tanga African Hospital. It said the rationale for this was to study the immunity of Africans from malaria. 'The

---

[96] Petition from the editorial board of the newspaper *'Femmes camerounaises'* concerning the Cameroons under French administration, 23 May 1955, T/PET.5/618.

[97] Petition from the Editorial Board of the newspaper *Femmes camerounaises* (T/PET.5/618), 23 April 1957, T/RES/1702 (XIX).

[98] Petition from the African Association, Mikindani concerning Tanganyika, 30 August 1951, T/PET.2/114.

216   COLONIALISM AND NEO-COLONIALISM AT THE UNITED NATIONS

consequences of this research may not be known, but the Africans detest to be used as guinea pigs.'[99]

The Trusteeship Council responded to the many petitions alleging racial discrimination with general resolutions on the subject. For Tanganyika, it noted that 'it is the policy of the Administering Authority to take every effective step practicable to end racial discrimination', urging the United Kingdom 'by appropriate legislation or other measures to further intensify its efforts to eliminate racial discrimination'.[100] For Cameroon, the Council noted France's claim that 'the complete eradication of the practice of racial discrimination is the policy of the Administration, that the principle of racial equality is taught in the schools of the Territory, that a number of European residents have been expelled from the Territory for their persistently discriminatory attitude . . . '[101]

A somewhat more exacting resolution was adopted with respect to the Belgian mandate over Ruanda-Urundi. The Council recommended that Belgium 're-view all legislation involving racial discrimination, particularly the laws on residence, land tenure, alcoholic beverages, firearms and the penitentiary system'.[102] Belgium's administration of Ruanda-Urundi featured particularly egregious examples of racial discrimination. For example, a curfew was imposed upon Africans, who were prohibited from circulating at night in urban areas. Corporal punishment was inflicted as a disciplinary measure in the prison system.[103] In its identification of the indigenous population, the Belgian administration distinguished between 'civilized' and 'uncivilized' persons. India was among the members of the Council who charged that this was discriminatory and that it 'relegated the indigenous people as a whole to an inferior status'.[104]

When the Council was examining the situation in individual Trust Territories, it would often make rather benign and friendly recommendations. This would be followed by the individual views of the various members. Typically, the colonial powers would come to the defence of one another. For example, commenting on the curfew imposed by the Belgians in Ruanda-Urundi, Australia thought

---

[99] Petition from the African Association, Tanga Branch, concerning Tanganyika, 8 September 1951, T/PET.2/130. See also Petition from the Tanganyika African Association, Dodoma concerning Tanganyika, 20 August 1951, T/PET.2/111; Petition from Mr M.D. Mdoe concerning Tanganyika, 5 September 1951, T/PET.2/149.

[100] Question of racial discrimination in Tanganyika, 23 March 1949, T/RES/50 (IV), T/295.

[101] Question of racial discrimination as raised in certain petitions concerning the Cameroons under French administration, 3 April 1950, T/RES/220 (VI), T/624.

[102] Question of racial discrimination in Ruanda-Urundi, 14 March 1949, T/RES/49 (IV), T/280.

[103] Report of the Trusteeship Council covering the period from 15 August 1956 to 12 July 1957, A/3595, paras. 167, 170–1, 197–8, 201–2; Report of the Trusteeship Council covering the period from 23 July 1955 to 14 August 1956, A/3170, p. 80; Report of the Trusteeship Council covering the period from 17 July 1954 to 22 July 1955, A/2933, pp. 94–5, 101–2; Report of the Trusteeship Council, 18 December 1951 to 25 July 1952, A/2150, pp. 94–5.

[104] Report of the Trusteeship Council covering the period from 23 July 1955 to 14 August 1956, A/3170, p. 73.

it to be rather insignificant, although it 'might sometimes seem to be superficially a little offensive to other ideas of human dignity'.[105] The Member States without colonies, some of them former colonies themselves, such as India, Burma, El Salvador, Guatemala, Haiti, Syria, and the Soviet Union, tended to be much harsher in their criticisms. When France insisted that there was no racial discrimination in the Cameroons, the Indian delegate politely 'accepted' this assurance, but then pointed out the existence of 'differential levels of amenities whether in hospitals or factories; differential levels of rewards, as in wages; difference, in treatment; differences in the franchise – all of which were based on racial differences. The fact was that race determined what emoluments, hospital conditions, educational facilities and political rights were extended to the people'.[106] Members of the Council questioned why if racial discrimination had been eliminated, as France contended, there were so many complaints from Africans about differential treatment.[107]

Schooling was an area where racial discrimination persisted. Belgium reported that in Ruanda-Urundi there were schools with a 'European syllabus' and schools with an 'African syllabus'. It told the Trusteeship Council that rules governing 'admission of non-European children to schools run on European lines have been made progressively more flexible'. According to the Belgians, 'these distinctions were prompted not by racial discrimination but by practical requirements arising from profound differences in customs, education and language, which made a single common system of education impossible'.[108]

The Trust Territory of Tanganyika, assigned to the United Kingdom, was frequently cited for racial discrimination by the Trusteeship Council. One report noted that in the country's hospital beds were labelled separately as 'European', 'Asian', and 'African'.[109] Britain's answer was that there was no 'legal discrimination' except to the extent that it was intended to protect Africans from exploitation. Admitting to differences in wages between Europeans and Africans, the British said this was not due to discrimination but to differences in experience and qualifications. As for discrimination in personal and social relations, it said this should be addressed by 'a process of normal evolution and education' rather

---

[105] Ibid., p. 83.

[106] Report of the Trusteeship Council covering the period from 22 July 1953 to 16 July 1954, A/2680, p. 174

[107] Report of the Trusteeship Council covering its First Special Session, its Second Special Session, and its Sixth and Seventh Sessions, 23 July 1949–21 July 1950, A/1306, pp. 57–8.

[108] Report of the Trusteeship Council, 7 August 1959–30 June 1960, A/4404, para. 230. Also Report of the Trusteeship Council, 2 August 1958–6 August 1959, A/4100, paras. 185–6; Report of the Trusteeship Council covering the work of its twenty-first and twenty-second sessions, A/3822, Vol. II, paras. 290–1.

[109] Report of the Trusteeship Council covering the period from 17 July 1954 to 22 July 1955, A/2933, p. 64; Report of the Trusteeship Council covering the period from 22 July 1953 to 16 July 1954, A/2680, p. 65.

218   COLONIALISM AND NEO-COLONIALISM AT THE UNITED NATIONS

than penal sanctions, as the Council had suggested. The Council expressed 'concern' that 'some vestiges of racial discrimination still persist in Tanganyika in fields outside the direct control of the Administering Authority'. It was 'encouraged' by the assurance that Britain was anxious to secure the eradication of the remaining vestiges of racial discrimination wherever they occur'.[110] The British representative in the Council referred to 'the few remaining traces of racial discrimination'.[111]

As Tanganyika was nearing full independence, the legislative assembly was restructured in a manner that reserved seats for 'non-Africans' of European or Asian descent. In the Trusteeship Council, Burma described this as a vestige of racial discrimination that should be immediately removed. The Soviet Union protested that this 'preserved the inadmissible racial discrimination against the African population'. It said that the Trusteeship Council 'should defend the interests of the indigenous population and recommend that the Administering Authority should abolish this system of racial representation, abolish the so-called reserved seats, and make all seats in the future Legislative Council open to representatives of any racial group so that the people of Tanganyika could elect to the legislative organ of the Territory those persons, irrespective of the colour of their skins, whom they considered to be worthy'.[112]

In 1957, a visiting mission of the Council to Ruanda-Urundi observed that 'the great majority of the non-Africans' were 'resolutely opposed to any form of racial discrimination'. It said that the indigenous inhabitants of the country, 'who wish to affirm increasingly their place in the community, are sometimes too much inclined to interpret or explain facts and situations in terms of racial discrimination. . . It appeared to the Mission, in fact, that many indigenous inhabitants retain the impression that racial discrimination in one form or another is still very common.'[113] The Council appeared to accept Belgium's preposterous claim that 'racial discrimination was rejected by everyone and that in all fields the Africans had broken the barriers, which were not based on colour, but on education, language and customs'.[114] The Soviet Union, which frequently took the lead

---

[110] Report of the Trusteeship Council covering the period from 15 August 1956 to 12 July 1957, A/3595, paras. 154–5. See also Report of the Trusteeship Council covering the period from 23 July 1955 to 14 August 1956, A/3170, pp. 56–7, 59; Report of the Trusteeship Council covering the period from 17 July 1954 to 22 July 1955, A/2933, pp. 63–5, 68–9; Report of the Trusteeship Council, 18 December 1951 to 25 July 1952, A/2150, pp. 56–7, 66; Report of the Trusteeship Council covering its Third Special Session and its Eighth and Ninth Sessions, 22 November 1950 to 30 July 1951, A/1866, pp. 44–5, 49.

[111] Report of the Trusteeship Council covering the period from 15 August 1956 to 12 July 1957, A/3595, para. 176.

[112] Report of the Trusteeship Council, 7 August 1959–30 June 1960, A/4404, paras. 67, 72.

[113] Report of the Trusteeship Council covering the work of its twenty-first and twenty-second sessions, A/3822, Vol. II, para. 221.

[114] Ibid., para. 222.

in condemning racial discrimination in the Trust Territories, was unconvinced, noting that the visiting mission had in fact observed many examples of racial discrimination in employment, education, health care, and criminal justice.[115]

By the early 1960s, all of the Trust Territories in Africa had achieved independence. Issues of racial discrimination were not, of course, confined to Africa. Australia was taken to task for its administration of Nauru, for example in the encouragement of 'uni-racial schools', by subsidizing white families who chose to send their children abroad.[116] Australian legislation applicable in Papua New Guinea prevented a young schoolteacher of Indian descent from being employed in the local schools because she was not eligible for Australian citizenship. The petitioner wrote: 'In other words, she could not be allowed to teach in New Guinea because of the colour of her skin, despite the fact that the people whom she would be teaching suffer a similar "disability".'[117]

Papua New Guinea became independent in 1975. That left the Trust Territory of the Pacific Islands as the only subject of the Trusteeship Council. Two parts of the Territory, the Marshall Islands and Micronesia, gained independence in 1986 and joined the United Nations. When Palau became independent, in 1994, the Trusteeship Council ceased to have any *raison d'être*.

At the time the International Convention on the Elimination of All Forms of Racial Discrimination was adopted, in 1965, there was a companion General Assembly resolution noting that cooperation between the Committee on the Elimination of Racial Discrimination and other United Nations bodies charged with receiving such petitions would further the purposes both of the Convention and of the Declaration on the Granting of Independence to Colonial Countries and Peoples. The General Assembly referred to the Special Committee of Twenty-four as well as to 'other bodies' although without specifying the Trusteeship Council.[118] Article 15(2)(a) of the International Convention on the Elimination of All Forms of Racial Discrimination declares that the Committee is to receive copies of relevant petitions submitted to United Nations bodies from inhabitants of Trust and Non-Self-Governing Territories. Moreover, the Committee is to 'submit expressions of opinion and recommendations' on such petitions.

Following the entry into force of the Convention on racial discrimination in 1969, the Secretary-General reminded the Trusteeship Council of the General Assembly resolution and article 15 of the Convention.[119] The Committee on

---

[115] Report of the Trusteeship Council covering the work of its twenty-first and twenty-second sessions, A/3822, Vol. II, para. 263.

[116] Report of the Trusteeship Council, 1 July 1960–19 July 1961, A/4818, para. 150.

[117] Petition from Mr. J.N. Peek concerning the Trust Territory of New Guinea, 2 December 1965, T/PET.8/20.

[118] International Convention on the Elimination of all Forms of Racial Discrimination, 21 December 1965, A/RES/2106 (XX) B.

[119] Note dated 18 February 1970 from the Secretary-General of the United Nations addressed to the President of the Trusteeship Council, T/1703.

220 COLONIALISM AND NEO-COLONIALISM AT THE UNITED NATIONS

the Elimination of Racial Discrimination took the initiative to address a series of requests for information to the Trusteeship Council.[120] The Committee's Decision was subsequently endorsed by the General Assembly.[121] At this point, the Council itself was concerned only with territories in the Asia Pacific region administered by Australia and the United States, neither of which had ratified the Convention.[122] Moreover, the Council's membership had shrunk to six, consisting of Australia and the five permanent members of the Security Council. The Trusteeship Council agreed that it would select appropriate petitions dealing with racial discrimination and forward them to the Committee. The Council decided to invite Australia and the United States to include the appropriate information in their reports to the Council.[123]

In 1971, the Trusteeship Council forwarded two petitions concerning Papua New Guinea to the Committee on the Elimination of Racial Discrimination.[124] The Council had already considered them summarily in the course of a meeting where the situation in the Territory was discussed more generally in light of the report of a recent mission there. The Soviet Union's delegate made a lengthy and very damning criticism of the Australian regime. 'Social inequality and discrimination against the indigenous people are everyday occurrences in the Territory', he said. 'A clear example of this fact is the enormous difference between the salaries paid to indigenous workers and those paid to white settlers, even in the cases where the indigenous persons perform the same work.'[125]

The first of the two petitions was from a young German who had moved to Papua New Guinea where he had married a Papuan. He warned of 'the danger of a rapidly increasing racism', writing of the racism of the European settlers but also of the growing anger of the indigenous people. 'Racism is inherent in the colonial political structure as well as in the economic and social ones, and it becomes more apparent with the increasing awareness of the indigenous people', he wrote.[126] The second petition, filed on the same date, reported an Australian police official describing how indigenous people had been intimidated by a fatal shooting of one of their number in 1958. He said that 'we had quiet for 11 years.

---

[120] Communication to be forwarded to the Trusteeship Council and the Special Committee on the Situation with regard to the Implementation of the Declaration on the Granting of Independence to Colonial Countries and Peoples, Decision 2 (III).

[121] Elimination of All Forms of Racial Discrimination, 6 December 1971, A/RES/2784 (XVI) III, OP 2.

[122] Australia and the United States both signed the Convention in 1966 (C.N.219.1966. TREATIES-5 and C.N.188.1966.TREATIES-4). Australia ratified the Convention on 30 September 1975 (C.N.272.1975.TREATIES-8). The United States ratified it on 21 October 1994 (C.N.356.l994. TREATIES-3).

[123] Verbatim record, Trusteeship Council, 8 June 1971, T/PV.1383, p. 17.

[124] Verbatim record, Trusteeship Council, 17 June 1971, T/PV.1386, pp. 16–7.

[125] Verbatim record, Trusteeship Council, 7 June 1971, T/PV.1382, p. 33.

[126] Petition from Mr. Uwe Lilye concerning the Trust Territory of New Guinea, 14 July 1970, T/ PET.8/33.

So let's shoot a couple more.'[127] Relying upon the materials submitted to the Trusteeship Council by Australia, the Committee on the Elimination of Racial Discrimination considered the situation in Papua New Guinea. The Committee confined its remarks to rather benign observations about the adoption of legislation and expressions of its hope to receive further information. It did not make any observations about the two petitions.[128] In its 1974 Report, the Committee discussed the petition mechanism at the Trusteeship Council but said 'no petition relating to racial discrimination has thus far been brought to the attention of the Committee'.[129]

Petitions were also forwarded to the Committee dealing with Namibia, Territories under Portuguese administration, and Southern Rhodesia.[130] It is striking that these areas, none of which fell under the jurisdiction of the Committee by virtue of ratification of the Convention, were the home to some of the worst racist abuse at the time and yet the Committee appears to have done nothing significant. Patrick Thornberry has written about 'the virtual non-functioning of the special procedure under Article 15'.[131]

Namibia's Struggle against Racism

The Republic of Namibia is a Member State of the United Nations with a population of about 2.5 million and a land area of approximately 825,000 square kilometres. It is the same size as Pakistan but with only about 1% of Pakistan's population. Namibia joined the United Nations in 1990 upon independence following a protracted armed conflict. When Europeans scrambled for Africa in the late nineteenth century, Namibia was formally recognized as the German colony of *Deutsch-Südwestafrika*, a status endorsed by other European colonial States assembled in Berlin in 1884. German rule over Namibia was characterized by extreme brutality. In May 2021, Germany's foreign minister, Heiko Mass, recognized the repression of the Herero and Nama peoples in 1904 as genocide.[132] South African troops drove Germany from South West Africa in 1915. The Paris Peace Conference agreed to confide the territories to South Africa as a category 'C' mandate in accordance with the Covenant of the League of Nations.

---

[127] Petition from Mataungan Association, Rabaul, concerning the Trust Territory of New Guinea, 14 July 1970, T/PET.8/34.

[128] Report of the Committee on the Elimination of Racial Discrimination, 1972, A/8718, pp. 49–50.

[129] Report of the Committee on the Elimination of Racial Discrimination, 1975, A/9618, p. 73.

[130] Report of the Committee on the Elimination of Racial Discrimination, 1970, A/8027, para. 55.

[131] Patrick Thornberry, *The International Convention on the Elimination of All Forms of Racial Discrimination*, Oxford: Oxford University Press, 2016, p. 63.

[132] Philip Olterman, 'Germany agrees to pay Namibia €1.1bn over historical Herero-Nama genocide', *The Guardian*, 28 May 2001.

222 COLONIALISM AND NEO-COLONIALISM AT THE UNITED NATIONS

South African rule, which proved to be no improvement for the Namibians, was regularly challenged before the Permanent Mandates Commission.[133]

At one of the first meetings of the United Nations General Assembly, in January 1946, South Africa announced its desire to annex South West Africa.[134] During the second part of the General Assembly's first session, South Africa returned to the issue, seeking authorization to annex the territory.[135] In the debate, Maharaj Singh of India remarked: 'It would be strange indeed if the South West African tribes wished to be incorporated in the Union of South Africa, where Africans, together with Asiatics and the members of the coloured communities, suffered under a system of discrimination.'[136] Singh said that annexation 'would place the South West African people in a worse position than during the term of the mandate.'[137] Chile made a formal statement alluding to the debate 'in which it was demonstrated that the democratic education of the natives consisted in teaching them to vote in favour of the whites since they were forbidden to elect men of their own race, and in passing discriminatory laws even after the adoption of the United Nations Charter.'[138] The General Assembly rejected annexation and requested South Africa to submit a trusteeship agreement for approval by the United Nations.[139] In the recorded vote, several Western States abstained, including the United Kingdom, France, Greece, Australia, the Netherlands, and New Zealand.[140] Because South African governance amounted to a system of white supremacy, the struggle against annexation and, subsequently, for full independence, was in very large part a fight against racial discrimination.

South West Africa was to remain on the agenda of the United Nations for the next 45 years. South Africa refused to negotiate a trusteeship agreement. Over time, the support South Africa received from countries in Europe and North America began to wither. Momentum for the cause of Namibian independence grew more or less in parallel with changes in the composition of the United Nations resulting from the end of colonialism. In 1968, the General Assembly proclaimed that henceforth, 'in accordance with the desires of its people', South West Africa would be known as 'Namibia'.[141] The following year, the Security Council decided that South Africa's occupation of Namibia

---

[133] See *supra*, pp. 72–80.

[134] See *supra*, p. 106.

[135] Statement by South Africa on Future Status of Mandated Territory, 14 October 1946, A/97.

[136] Summary record, Sub-Committee II of the Fourth Committee, 27 November 1946, A/C.4/Sub.2/33.

[137] Summary record, Sub-Committee II of the Fourth Committee, 29 November 1946, A/C.4/Sub.2/41.

[138] Trusteeship Agreements, Report of the Fourth Committee, 12 December 1946, A/258, pp. 20–1.

[139] Future Status of South-West Africa, 14 December 1946, A/RES/65 (I).

[140] Verbatim record, plenary General Assembly, 14 December 1946, A/PV.64, p. 1327.

[141] Question of South West Africa, 18 June 1968, 2372 (XXII), OP 1.

NAMIBIA'S STRUGGLE AGAINST RACISM   223

constituted 'an aggressive encroachment on the authority of the United Nations, a violation of the territorial integrity and a denial of the political sovereignty of the people of Namibia'.[142] There were four abstentions: Finland, France, the United Kingdom and the United States.[143] Although the United Nations General Assembly recognized the South West Africa People's Organisation as the legitimate representative of Namibia in 1973,[144] the country only became fully independent of South Africa in March 1990. The racist regime of occupation was regularly condemned by various bodies of the United Nations. The illegality of South Africa's rule was also confirmed in a series of advisory opinions of the International Court of Justice.[145]

In 1947, David Witbooi, the Chief of the Hottentot or Nama of South West Africa, together with 17 other community leaders, petitioned the United Nations in opposition to incorporation of the territory into South Africa. 'We support the petition of the Herero people for the return of their lands and of their Chief and people from exile, and we consider that the lands of other African people should be returned to them and the people protected from misrule', they said in a letter addressed to the Secretary-General. A similar petition was submitted by the people of Ovambo, who associated themselves with the Herero. These were presented together with other materials from indigenous peoples in South West Africa by Michael Scott and reproduced in the report of the Fourth Committee of the General Assembly.[146] An Anglican clergyman based in Johannesburg, Scott had earned much respect among Africans for his resistance to apartheid, which had landed him in jail in South Africa.[147] His communist affiliations were an obstacle to entry into the United States. However, his way was smoothed thanks to efforts from the Indian mission to the United Nations, the National Association for the Advancement of Colored People, and the International League for the Rights of Man. The dossier that Scott submitted to the Fourth Committee

---

[142] S/RES/269 (1969), OP 1.

[143] Verbatim record, Security Council, 12 August 1969, S/PV.1497, para. 22.

[144] Question of Namibia, 12 December 1973, A/RES/3111 (XXVII), OP 2.

[145] Marion Wallace and John Kinahan, *A History of Namibia, From the Beginning to 1990*, Oxford: Oxford University Press, 2011; John Dugard, *The South West Africa/Namibia Dispute: Documents and Scholarly Writings on the Controversy Between South Africa and the United Nations*, Berkeley: University of California Press, 1973.

[146] Question of South West Africa: communications received by the Secretary-General: letter from the Reverend Michael Scott transmitting petitions from inhabitants of South West Africa, A/C.4/96; Communications received by the Secretary-General relating to South West Africa, 9 December 1947, T/55/Add.l. See Roger Clark, 'The International League for Human Rights and South West Africa, 1947–1957: The Human Rights NGO as Catalyst in the International Legal Process' (1981) 3 *Human Rights Quarterly* 101, at pp, 109–10.

[147] Carol Anderson, 'International Conscience, the Cold War, and Apartheid: The NAACP's Alliance with the Reverend Michael Scott for South West Africa's Liberation, 1946–1951' (2008) 19 *Journal of World History* 297, at p. 303.

224 COLONIALISM AND NEO-COLONIALISM AT THE UNITED NATIONS

demonstrated the fraudulent nature of the referendum that the South African government had been claiming showed African support for annexation.[148]

Scott returned to the Fourth Committee in 1949 with several new petitions from the Nama, the Berg Damara, and the Herero peoples. A Sub-Committee ruled upon his credentials and authorized him as their representative.[149] In his statement to the Committee, Scott described being taken by the Herero to memorial sites of the attacks by the German colonizers at the beginning of the century. The petitions explained how Herero leaders had been refused permission from the South African regime to travel to Paris and present their case before the General Assembly at its Third Session, in 1948. Detailed information was provided about the denial of fundamental rights, including the right to democratic governance, the right to education, the right to food, and the right to property, and of inhuman conditions in the workplace and places of detention.[150] South Africa's representative boycotted Scott's presentation in the Fourth Committee but he attacked him furiously in the plenary General Assembly. Granting a hearing to Scott 'had been contrary to all precepts of law and procedure', he protested, explaining that the United Nations had no authority to allow the submission of petitions because South West Africa was not a Trust Territory.[151] South Africa took particular umbrage because Scott's submission to the Fourth Committee included 'no less than five pages of the most blatant propaganda on the alleged economic oppression of the indigenous inhabitants in the Union of South Africa'. It was 'not in keeping with the dignity' of the United Nations, said the South African, to allow a statement on the domestic affairs of a Member State to be part of an official document.[152]

The General Assembly decided to seek an advisory opinion of the International Court of Justice as to the obligations of South Africa under the League mandate and other relevant instruments.[153] The Advisory Opinion, issued in accordance with article 96 of the Charter of the United Nations, was the first of a series of judicial pronouncements by the International Court of Justice, described by one scholar as 'the most explosive and politically controversial cases' in the history of

---

[148] Anne Yates and Lewis Chester, *The Troublemaker, Michael Scott and His Lonely Struggle Against Injustice*, London: Aurum, 2006, pp. 97–9. Also Michael Scott, *A Time to Speak*, New York: Doubleday, 1958; Freda Troup, *In Face of Fear: Michael Scott's Challenge to South Africa*, London: Faber and Faber, 1950.

[149] Communications received by the Secretary General, 21 November 1949, A/C.4/L.57 and A/C.4/L.57/Corr.1; Report of Sub-Committee 7 to the Fourth Committee, 25 November 1949, A/C.4/L.62.

[150] Summary record, Fourth Committee, 26 November 1949, A/C.4/SR.138, pp. 258–65; Documents submitted by the Reverend Michael Scott, 29 November 1949, A/C.4/L.66.

[151] Verbatim record, plenary General Assembly, 6 December 1949, A/PV.269, para. 16.

[152] Ibid., para. 26

[153] Question of South West Africa: request for an advisory opinion of the International Court of Justice, 6 December 1949, A/RES/338 (IV).

the institution.[154] 'The central unspoken issue in all these cases was really apartheid', wrote Victor Kattan. The General Assembly was concerned that South Africa might alter the status of South West Africa without its consent, thereby extending the reach of its racially discriminatory laws, which indeed it did.[155]

At the time of the 1950 Advisory Opinion, the 15-member Court included only one judge from Africa, Abdel Hamid Badawi of Egypt. The first judge to be elected from Africa south of the Sahara was Isaac Forster of Senegal, in 1964. Besides South Africa, there were written submissions from Egypt, India, Poland, and the United States, and a statement by the Philippines made during the oral hearing in May 1950. The Court granted a request submitted by Robert Delson on behalf of the New York-based International League for Human Rights,[156] indicating that it was prepared to accept a written statement before 10 April 1950.[157] On 27 April 1950, the Registrar informed the Secretary-General of the United Nations that no submission had been received from the League.[158] Although Delson was apparently an experienced attorney, he had simply missed the filing date. Later, the League asked permission for Michael Scott to make oral representations at the Court hearing, but this was denied.[159]

In its Advisory Opinion, the Court confirmed that the obligations under the League of Nations mandate continued and that the supervisory function had passed to the United Nations. It also declared that the petition mechanism established under the League remained in force, as did the obligation to provide an annual report. Moreover, South Africa could not unilaterally change the status of South West Africa.[160] The Advisory Opinion changed the dynamics in the Fourth Committee. When it convened in November 1951, Cuba proposed that the traditional leaders of the Hereros, Namas, and Berg-Damaras, as well as their dynamic spokesman, Reverend Scott, be invited to appear before the Committee. The Cuban delegate cited a General Assembly resolution adopted after the Advisory Opinion[161] that referred to the submission of petitions from the inhabitants of South West Africa.[162] Several other Member States from the

---

[154] Victor Kattan, 'Decolonizing the International Court of Justice: The Experience of Judge Sir Muhammad Zafrulla Khan in the South West Africa Cases' (2015) 5 *Asian Journal of International Law* 310, at p. 310.

[155] Ibid., p. 327.

[156] 'Robert Delson, League for the Rights of Man, to the Registrar, 7 March 1950', in *International status of South-West Africa, Advisory Opinion, I.C.J. Reports 1950*, Pleadings, Oral Arguments, Documents, p. 324.

[157] 'The Registrar to Mr Robert Delson, League for the Rights of Man (telegram), 16 March 1950', ibid., p. 327.

[158] 'Le Greffier au Secrétaire-Général des Nations-Unies, 27 Avril 1950', ibid., p. 343.

[159] 'Mr Asher Lans, Counsel to the International League for the Rights of Man, to the Registrar, 9 May 1950', ibid., pp. 343–4; 'The Deputy Registrar to Mr Asher Lans, Counsel to the International League for the Rights of Man (telegram), 12 May 1950', ibid., p. 346.

[160] *International status of South-West Africa, Advisory Opinion, I.C.J. Reports 1950*, p. 128.

[161] Question of South West Africa, 13 December 1950, A/RES/449 (V), PP 3.

[162] Summary record, Fourth Committee, 14 November 1951, A/C.4/SR.201, para. 23.

226   COLONIALISM AND NEO-COLONIALISM AT THE UNITED NATIONS

Global South joined Cuba in a draft resolution whose purpose was to invite the indigenous representatives.[163] Aware of the danger that such a precedent could pose for them, the British, the French, the Belgians, and the Australians joined the South Africans in protesting.[164] The vote was very largely a north-south split, adopted by a strong majority with many predictable opponents: Australia, Belgium, France, the Netherlands, New Zealand, South Africa, and the United Kingdom. The United States, Canada, China, Denmark, Israel, Norway, and Peru abstained.[165] The British had counted on American support. They blamed the restraint of the United States delegation on its advisor, Channing Tobias, an African American who served as a trustee of the NAACP and was later elected its chairman.[166]

A few days after the vote, the Herero leader, Hosea Kutako, sent a telegram to the Fourth Committee explaining that he was still waiting for the South African government to reply to his request for authorization to travel to Paris.[167] On 8 December 1951, Michael Scott testified at length before the Fourth Committee. Scott spoke with characteristic humility, insisting that he was no substitute for the presence of the African representatives. Scott said it was important for the Committee to hear the 'life story of the old chiefs', Hosea Kutako and David Witbooi, before they died. He explained that 'it was right that they who had known such a long dark night of African history should live to see that dawn'. After the massacres of the Herero by Germany, they had been dispossessed of their traditional lands, which had never been restored to them, he said. He believed there were no hospitals on the Herero reservations, and they still lived under various forms of racial discrimination imposed by the South African legislation.[168]

Scott told the Committee of the attempts that had been made to facilitate travel to Paris by the Herero representatives and the apparent refusal of the South African government to allow this.[169] He explained that Hosea Kutako was over 80, yet despite mobility issues and poor eyesight, he had travelled hundreds of miles from his reserve by lorry over rough roads and by rail, in response to the invitation of the Fourth Committee.[170] Cuba's delegate, Guy Pérez-Cisneros,

[163] Requests for hearings on the question of South West Africa: Brazil, Cuba, Ecuador, Egypt, Guatemala, India, Indonesia, Pakistan, Philippines: draft resolution, 15 November 1951, A/C.4/L.136.

[164] Summary record, Fourth Committee, 16 November 1951, A/C.4/SR.203, paras. 2–5, 17–19, 42; Summary record, Fourth Committee, 16 November 1951, A/C.4/SR.204, paras. 6–9.

[165] Summary record, Fourth Committee, 16 November 1951, A/C.4/SR.204, para. 24.

[166] Carol Anderson, 'International Conscience, the Cold War, and Apartheid: The NAACP's Alliance with the Reverend Michael Scott for South West Africa's Liberation, 1946–1951' (2008) 19 Journal of World History 297, at p. 321.

[167] Summary record, Fourth Committee, 21 November 1951, A/C.4/SR.207, para. 1.

[168] Summary record, Fourth Committee, 8 November 1951, A/C.4/SR.222, para. 12.

[169] Ibid., paras. 16–17.

[170] Ibid., para. 19.

attacked South Africa's obstruction, describing it as a violation of the Charter and the Universal Declaration of Human Rights.[171] The Herero representatives never made it to Paris. On 15 December, Ralph Bunche read out a telegram sent by Kutako from Windhoek the previous day saying he was still waiting for permission.[172]

South Africa defied the requirement that it submit annual reports to the General Assembly, a consequence of the 1950 Advisory Opinion of the International Court of Justice. Its position was that it need only report to the three principal powers at the time the Covenant of the League of Nations was adopted in 1919, that is, France, the United Kingdom, and the United States. It was on good terms with all three and could comfortably expect a sympathetic reception. Furthermore, South Africa contended that decisions concerning the Mandate required unanimity. In other words, a resolution on the subject could only be adopted if South Africa voted in favour, which was improbable to say the least. A second Advisory Opinion of the International Court of Justice, issued in 1955, confirmed that the ordinary rule requiring a two-thirds majority for a General Assembly resolution remained in force.[173] Yet a third Advisory Opinion, issued in 1956, held that the Committee on South West Africa could hold oral hearings with petitioners from the Territory to the extent that this was required for international supervision.[174]

Setback at the International Court of Justice

In 1956 the General Assembly requested the Committee on South West Africa to examine the possibilities of legal action directed against South Africa either by organs of the United Nations or by its individual Member States.[175] One option that the Committee considered was a contentious case, rather than an advisory opinion, which would be taken by Member States of the League of Nations before the International Court of Justice.[176] The suggestion was pursued by the Second Conference of Independent African States, held in June 1960. Acting on the advice of Ernest A. Gross, a former State Department official practising law in New York, the Conference resolved to submit a contentious case on the question

---

[171] Ibid., para. 41.

[172] Summary record, Fourth Committee, 15 December 1951, A/C.4/SR.228, para. 85.

[173] *South-West Africa - Voting Procedure, Advisory Opinion, 7 June 1955, I.C.J. Reports 1955*, p. 67.

[174] *Admissibility of hearings of petitioners by the Committee on South West Africa, Advisory Opinion, 1 June 1956, I.C.J. Reports 1956*, p. 23.

[175] Special report of the Committee on South West Africa, Study of legal action to ensure the fulfilment of the obligations assumed by the Mandatory Power under the Mandate for South West Africa, 26 February 1957, A/RES/1060 (XI), para. 1.

[176] A study of legal action to ensure the fulfilment of the obligations assumed by the Mandatory Power under the Mandate for South West Africa, 1957, A/3625, para. 35.

228 COLONIALISM AND NEO-COLONIALISM AT THE UNITED NATIONS

of South West Africa to the International Court of Justice. The General Assembly Committee on South West Africa commended the decision, welcoming the willingness of Liberia and Ethiopia, both of them Member States of the League of Nations, to take the case.[177] The Committee said South Africa had continued to administer the Territory 'on the basis of a policy of apartheid and "White supremacy" which is contrary to the Mandate, the Charter of the United Nations, the Universal Declaration of Human Rights, the advisory opinions of the International Court of Justice and the resolutions of the General Assembly'.[178]

On 4 November 1960, Ethiopia and Liberia submitted essentially identical applications to the International Court of Justice stating that South Africa, 'by law and in practice, distinguishes as to race, colour, national and tribal origin in establishing the rights and duties of the peoples of South West Africa'. It has adopted legislation and decrees that are 'arbitrary, unreasonable, unjust, and detrimental to human dignity'.[179] The case was like nothing else that had ever come before the Court or its predecessor. It was being asked to decide that racial discrimination was a violation of international law. 'That the gravamen of the applicants' case before the Court was an attack on the segregation policies of the South African Government was beyond any doubt', wrote one commentator.[180] According to Rosalyn Higgins, 'the heart of the matter' was apartheid. 'The African states were presented with the chance of having behind them a judicial order to desist from the practice of apartheid.'[181] Ernest Gross, who argued the case before the Court as agent of the two African States, wrote that '[a]partheid, therefore, which as all of us here would agree is the reductio ad absurdum, the travesty of the policy of racial discrimination, is in this sense on trial before the World Court'.[182]

The application of Liberia and Ethiopia referred to racial segregation of residential areas, exclusion from trade union membership and exercise of various professions, restrictions on freedom of movement, and forcible deportations. It said that the right to vote was attributed only to persons of ' "European" descent'. Furthermore, South Africa 'has maintained racial discrimination in the

---

[177] Report of the Committee on South West Africa, 1960, A/4464, paras. 26–7.

[178] Ibid., para. 444.

[179] Application instituting proceedings by the government of Ethiopia, in *South West Africa Cases (Ethiopia v. Union of South Africa; Liberia v. South Africa)*, 1966, Pleadings, Oral Arguments, Documents, Vol. I, pp. 4–25, para. 4; Application instituting proceedings by the government of Liberia, ibid., pp. 26–7.

[180] Marinus Weichers, 'South West Africa: The Decision of 16 July 1966 and Its Aftermath' (1968) 1 *Comparative and International Law Journal of South Africa* 408, at p. 419.

[181] Rosalyn Higgins, 'The International Court and South West Africa: The Implications of the Judgment' (1966) 42 *International Affairs* 573, at p. 597. Also Rosalyn Higgins, *Themes and Theories: Selected Essays, Speeches, and Writings in International Law*, Vol. II, Oxford: Oxford University Press, 2009, p. 1071.

[182] Ernest A., Gross, 'The South West Africa Cases: On the Threshold of Decision' (1963) 3 *Columbia Journal of Transnational Law* 19, at p. 20.

educational system, has not permitted equal access by all children, according to merit, to all facilities for education, has denied to "native" children adequate educational facilities, . . . and, in general, has failed to make even a gradual endeavour to establish a common educational system open to all children according to merit rather than to colour'.[183] The Court was asked to declare that the Union of South Africa 'has practised apartheid, i.e. has distinguished as to race, colour, national or tribal origin in establishing the rights and duties of the inhabitants of the Territory; that such practice is in violation of Article 2 of the Mandate and Article 22 of the Covenant; and that the Union has the duty forthwith to cease the practice of apartheid in the Territory'.[184]

The racial discrimination practised by South Africa was set out much more fully in the Memorials of the two applicants. The Memorials relied very largely on official United Nations documents. The final submissions prayed the Court to adjudge and declare that South Africa 'has practised apartheid, i.e., has distinguished as to race, colour, national or tribal origin in establishing the rights and duties of the inhabitants of the Territory; that such practice is in violation of its obligations as stated in Article 2 of the Mandate and Article 22 of the Covenant of the League of Nations; and that the Union has the duty forthwith to cease the practice of apartheid in the Territory'.[185] South Africa had not really contest the argument that international law contained a norm prohibiting racial discrimination. Instead, it defended the view that such a norm was not part of the League of Nations mandate.[186] South Africa invoked the minorities treaties of the post-First World War period, explaining that they were designed to protect separate national groups and that therefore they 'necessarily involve a differentiation in the treatment of these respective groups'.[187]

In the Reply to the South African Counter-memorial, the applicants set out a detailed case for the prohibition of racial discrimination under international law. More specifically, they referred to 'a generally accepted international human rights norm' of 'non-discrimination' or 'non-separation' which, they explained,

[183] Application instituting proceedings by the government of Ethiopia, in *South West Africa Cases (Ethiopia v. Union of South Africa; Liberia v. South Africa)*, 1966, Pleadings, Oral Arguments, Documents, Vol. I, pp. 4–25, para. 4; Application instituting proceedings by the government of Liberia, ibid., pp. 26–7.

[184] Application instituting proceedings by the government of Ethiopia, in *South West Africa Cases (Ethiopia v. Union of South Africa; Liberia v. South Africa)*, 1966, Pleadings, Oral Arguments, Documents, Vol. I, pp. 4–25, at pp. 20–1; ibid., Application instituting proceedings by the government of Liberia, pp. 26–7.

[185] Memorial Submitted by the Government of Ethiopia, in *South West Africa Cases (Ethiopia v. Union of South Africa; Liberia v. South Africa)*, 1966, Memorials, Pleadings, Documents, Vol. I, pp. 32–199, at p. 197; Memorial Submitted by the Government of Liberia, ibid., p. 211.

[186] Rejoinder filed by the Government of the Republic of South Africa, in *South West Africa Cases (Ethiopia v. Union of South Africa; Liberia v. South Africa)*, 1966, Memorials, Pleadings, Documents, Vol. V, p.119.

[187] Ibid., p. 124.

230   COLONIALISM AND NEO-COLONIALISM AT THE UNITED NATIONS

refers to 'the absence of governmental policies or actions which allot status, rights, duties, privileges or burdens on the basis of membership in a group, class or race rather than on the basis of individual merit, capacity or potential: stated affirmatively, the terms refer to governmental policies and actions the objective of which is to protect equality of opportunity and equal protection of the laws to individual persons as such.[188] The Reply demonstrated that this norm had been applied by the Permanent Mandates Commission of the League of Nations. The Reply reviewed a large number of authorities, including the human rights clauses of the Charter of the United Nations, the Universal Declaration of Human Rights, the Trust Territories agreements, more than 30 resolutions of the United Nations General Assembly condemning racial discrimination or segregation, resolutions of the Security Council condemning racial discrimination and apartheid, the draft human rights covenants, the 1963 Declaration on the Elimination of All Forms of Racial Discrimination, the draft International Convention on the Elimination of All Forms of Racial Discrimination, conventions of the International Labour Organisation, and instruments of the Council of Europe and the Organisation of American States. 'Whether or not the norm of non-discrimination or separation on the basis of race has become a rule of customary international law, it is submitted that as a generally accepted legal norm, non-discrimination imparts a specific and objective content to Article 2, paragraph 2, of the Mandate', the Reply said.[189] In its conclusions during the oral hearing, Gross set out the position of Ethiopia and Liberia: 'Respondent, by laws and regulations, and official methods and measures, which are set out in the pleadings herein, has practised apartheid, i.e., has distinguished as to race, colour, national or tribal origin in establishing the rights and duties of the inhabitants of the Territory; that such practice is in violation of its obligations as stated in Article 2 of the Mandate and Article 22 of the Covenant of the League of Nations; and that Respondent has the duty forthwith to cease the practice of apartheid in the Territory.'[190]

They were good arguments, and a persuasive invitation to the judges to take a giant step in legal development. However, the Court never ruled on the merits of the claim. Although it had initially rejected South Africa's challenge to admissibility,[191] the Court effectively reversed that finding and, after 99 public sessions of oral hearings and six months of deliberations, concluded that Ethiopia

---

[188] Reply of the Governments of Ethiopia and Liberia, in *South West Africa Cases (Ethiopia v. Union of South Africa; Liberia v. South Africa)*, 1966, Memorials, Pleadings, Documents, Vol. IV, pp. 220–616, at p. 493.

[189] Ibid., pp. 510–11.

[190] Public hearing of 19 May 1965, in *South West Africa Cases (Ethiopia v. Union of South Africa; Liberia v. South Africa)*, 1966, Pleadings, Oral Arguments, Documents, Vol. IX, pp. 341–76, at p. 374.

[191] *South West Africa Cases (Ethiopia v. South Africa; Liberia v. South Africa), Preliminary Objections, Judgment of 21 December 1962, I.C.J. Reports 1962*, p. 319.

and Liberia lacked an adequate legal interest. Both parties assumed that the 1962 judgment on admissibility meant the judicial debate in the Court in 1965 was confined to the merits and the Court gave no indication to the contrary.[192] In its conclusions at the end of the hearings, South Africa did not even suggest that the Court reconsider questions of jurisdiction and admissibility, as Judge Jessup was to point out in his dissenting opinion.[193] The judges were actually tied, leaving the President of the Court with the casting vote which tipped the decision in favour of racist South Africa. One of the members of the Court, Muhammad Zafrulla Khan, did not participate in the judgment although he was apparently never formally recused. He had been misled by the President of the Court who had told him privately that his colleagues thought it inappropriate that he sit in the case because at an early stage, before he had been elected to the bench, his name had been proposed as an *ad hoc* judge for Ethiopia and Liberia.[194] Six years after the fateful judgment, by which point Khan had become President of the Court, he condemned apartheid, and it is generally assumed he would have ruled in favour of Ethiopia and Liberia in the 1966 judgment. The vote was also influenced by the absence of Judge Bustamente, who had ruled against South Africa in the 1962 judgment, but did not sit during the hearings on the merits because of illness. Another Judge who had previously voted against South Africa, Abdul Hamid Badawi, fell ill and died in the course of the proceedings. Beyond from this curious combination of serendipity and murky circumstances, the judgment revealed a divided Court where, in this case, conservative judges from the Global North prevailed.

The *ad hoc* South African judge, who of course voted with the 'majority', challenged the claim that 'non-separation' was actually recognized or applied under the League of Nations.[195] Dismissing the authorities invoked by Ethiopia and Liberia, he said 'the whole concept of "human rights and fundamental freedoms" is as yet an undefined and uncertain one with no clear content'.[196]

Several of the dissenting judges drafted opinions that spoke to the issue of racial discrimination. Judge Wellington Koo who, as a Chinese diplomat, had supported the Japanese amendment at the Paris Peace Conference and put forward an anti-racist provision for the Charter of the United Nations,[197] said 'the

---

[192] Richard Falk, 'The South West Africa Cases: An Appraisal' (1967) 21 *International Organization* 1, at p. 6.

[193] *South West Africa, Second Phase, Judgment, I.C.J. Reports 1966*, p. 6, Dissenting opinion of Judge Jessup, pp. 325–442, at p. 328.

[194] Victor Kattan, 'Decolonizing the International Court of Justice: The Experience of Judge Sir Muhammad Zafrulla Khan in the South West Africa Cases' (2015) 5 *Asian Journal of International Law* 310.

[195] *South West Africa, Second Phase, Judgment, I.C.J. Reports 1966*, p. 6, Separate opinion of Judge Van Wyk, pp. 67–215, para. 26.

[196] Ibid., para. 45.

[197] See *supra*, pp. 94–96.

232 COLONIALISM AND NEO-COLONIALISM AT THE UNITED NATIONS

policy of apartheid or separate development, as pursued in South West Africa, as far as the non-White groups are concerned, has not been and is not compatible with the basic principle of the "sacred trust of civilisation"' as set out in the Covenant of the League of Nations.[198] 'The assertion that "apartheid" is the only alternative to chaos, and that the peoples of South West Africa are incapable of constituting a political unity and be governed as a single State does not justify the official policy of discrimination based on race, colour or membership in a tribal group', wrote Judge Padilla Nervo.[199] 'Racial discrimination as a matter of official government policy is a violation of a norm or rule or standard of the international community', he said.[200] Judge Padilla Nervo considered that the United Nations General Assembly had the 'power to enact recommendations – regarding racial discrimination - which have evolved as principles or standards of general international acceptance'. He explained that '[t]he principle of non-discrimination on account of race or colour has a great impact in the maintenance of international peace'. For this reason, he considered that the United Nations had a 'duty' to ensure that all States, even non-Member States, act in according with the principles of the Charter, 'among them – to promote and encourage respect for human rights and fundamental freedoms for all, without racial discrimination'.[201]

Kōtarō Tanaka issued one of the most celebrated of the dissenting opinions. He acknowledged that the international law of human rights was in a process of development, and that there were 'legislative imperfections' in its definition as well as mechanisms for implementation. But that was not 'a reason for denying their existence and the need for their legal protection', he said. Moreover, he pointed to the Charter provisions that 'repeatedly emphasize the principle of equality before the law by saying, "without distinction as to race, sex, language or religion"'. Judge Tanaka said 'the equality principle, as an integral part of the Charter of the United Nations or as an independent source of general international law' applied to the case at bar.[202] He repeated the enumeration of legal instruments cited in the Reply of the Applicants in endorsing the view that these provided evidence of the emergence of a customary norm of 'non-discrimination or non-separation on the basis of race'.[203] John Dugard described

[198] *South West Africa, Second Phase, Judgment, I.C.J. Reports 1966*, p. 6, Dissenting opinion of Vice-president Wellington Koo, pp. 216–39, at p. 235.

[199] *South West Africa, Second Phase, Judgment, I.C.J. Reports 1966*, p. 6, Dissenting opinion of Judge Padilla Nervo, pp. 443–71, at p. 467.

[200] Ibid., p. 462.

[201] Ibid., p. 455

[202] *South West Africa, Second Phase, Judgment, I.C.J. Reports 1966*, p. 6, Dissenting opinion of Judge Tanaka, pp. 250–324, at p. 290.

[203] Ibid., p. 293. See the chapter on Judge Tanaka's dissenting opinion in Shiv R.S. Bedi, *The Development of Human Rights Law by the Judges of the International Court of Justice*. Oxford and Portland, OR: Hart, 2007, pp. 126–41.

the Tanaka dissent as 'exhilarating' but conceded that 'it remains an extreme statement'.[204]

The other major dissenting opinion, by Judge Jessup, was more cautious in its assessment of the law governing the prohibition of racial discrimination. Jessup made clear his rejection of the thesis that the prohibition of racial discrimination was a norm of customary international law. However, he said that the Mandate must be administered in light of 'the pertinent contemporary international community standard', which he indicated could be found in the numerous General Assembly resolutions condemning apartheid.[205]

The judgment 'stunned the world'.[206] Lester B. Pearson called it a blow to world law.[207] It was 'the most controversial judgment in its history', according to John Dugard.[208] While South Africa gloated about its success, States from the Global South expressed their fury in the General Assembly. 'The only interest deemed worthy of legal protection, according to the logic of the court – a logic that was not formulated, but logic just the same – is the interest of South Africa', said Senegal.[209] 'Here you have an organ based on the Charter, and this organ hands down a verdict contrary to the Charter!' protested the delegate of Cameroon.[210] Rosalyn Higgins, who decades later would serve as the Court's President, wrote that States from Africa and Asia 'feel bitter and hostile towards the Court, and their emotional reaction is to have no more part of it'. She added that 'the response of many Western persons to the surprising Judgment of the Court has been to denounce any suggestion of further recourse to the Court, and to insist that henceforth things proceed solely on the political level'.[211] In November 1966, a new slate of judges was elected, instilling some confidence of a better outcome should the matter return to the Court.[212] Leslie Green presciently observed that they came 'from a newer generation of legal scholars, which recognises the

---

[204] John Dugard, 'Namibia (South West Africa): The Court's Opinion, South Africa's Response, and Prospects for the Future' (1972) 11 *Colum Journal of Transnational Law* 14, at p. 16.

[205] *South West Africa, Second Phase, Judgment, I.C.J. Reports 1966*, p. 6, Dissenting opinion of Judge Jessup, pp. 325–442, at p. 441.

[206] Richard Falk, 'The South West Africa Cases: An Appraisal' (1967) 21 *International Organization* 1, at p. 5.

[207] 'Pearson Assails Ruling on Africa; South-West Africa Decision Called Blow to World Law', *New York Times*, 10 August 1966, p. 2.

[208] John Dugard, *The South West Africa/Namibia Dispute: Documents and Scholarly Writings on the Controversy Between South Africa and the United Nations*, Berkeley: University of California Press, 1973, p. 292.

[209] Verbatim record, plenary General Assembly, 23 September 1966, A/PV.1414, para. 210.

[210] Verbatim record, plenary General Assembly, 22 September 1966, A/PV.1412, para. 78.

[211] Rosalyn Higgins, 'The International Court and South West Africa: The Implications of the Judgment', in International Commission of Jurists, *South West Africa, The Court's Judgment*, Geneva: International Commission of Jurists, 1966.

[212] Victor Kattan, 'Decolonizing the International Court of Justice: The Experience of Judge Sir Muhammad Zafrulla Khan in the South West Africa Cases' (2015) 5 *Asian Journal of International Law* 310, at p. 350.

234   COLONIALISM AND NEO-COLONIALISM AT THE UNITED NATIONS

significance of functional and sociological approaches, and as such are determined to bring the Court and the law they are called upon to apply up-to-date and suitable for the mid-twentieth century world'.[213] The stage was set for another round.

In the aftermath of the World Court decision, the General Assembly voted to revoke South Africa's mandate over South West Africa. The preamble of the resolution cited the three advisory opinions issued in the 1950s, adding that the situation in the Territory 'has seriously deteriorated following the judgment of the International Court of Justice of 18 July 1966'. It said the administration had been conducted in a manner contrary to the Mandate, the Charter of the United Nations, and the Universal Declaration of Human Rights, making specific reference to the policies of apartheid and racial discrimination.[214] After hesitantly '[t]aking note of'[215] and '[t]aking into account'[216] the General Assembly's revocation of the mandate, the Security Council soon came to 'recognise' the termination of the Mandate by the General Assembly and declare South Africa's presence there to be 'illegal'.[217] France and the United Kingdom abstained in the vote.[218] In 1970, a similar Security Council resolution entitled 'The Situation in Namibia' was adopted.[219] The rationale for Security Council intervention was its primary responsibility under the Charter for the maintenance of international peace and security. But in effect it was adding its muscle to the General Assembly resolution of 1966 revoking the Mandate. The grounds for revocation were essentially the regime of apartheid and racial discrimination.

In 1971 the Security Council sought an advisory opinion from the International Court of Justice on the 'legal consequences for States of the continued presence of South Africa in Namibia, notwithstanding Security Council resolution 276 (1970)'.[220] The tables had turned since the 1966 judgment. The cohort of liberal judges had been considerably enhanced by new elections to the bench. Moreover, Muhammad Zafrulla Khan, who was excluded from sitting in the 1966 case because of alleged sympathies with the indigenous peoples of Namibia, was now president of the Court. The Court held that by declaring South Africa's presence in Namibia to be illegal, the Security Council not only placed an obligation on United Nations Member States to 'recognise the illegality and invalidity of South Africa's continued presence in Namibia' but also

---

[213] Leslie C. Green, 'South West Africa and the World Court' (1966–1967) 22 *International Journal* 39, at p. 67.
[214] Question of South West Africa, 27 October 1966, A/RES/2145 (XXI), PP 5, 6.
[215] The Question of South West Africa, 25 January 1968, S/RES/245 (1968), PP 1.
[216] The Question of South West Africa, 14 March 1968, S/RES/246 (1968), PP 2.
[217] The Situation in Namibia, 20 March 1969, S/RES/264 (1969), OP 1, 2.
[218] Verbatim record, Security Council, 20 March 1969, S/PV.1465, para. 165.
[219] The Situation in Namibia, 30 January 1970, S/RES/276 (1970).
[220] Namibia, 29 July 1970, S/RES/284 (1970), OP 1.

'to refrain from lending any support or any form of assistance to South Africa with reference to its occupation of Namibia'.[221] The Court described the people of Namibia as 'the injured entity', stating that it 'must look to the international community for assistance in its progress towards the goals for which the sacred trust was instituted'.[222]

South Africa had attempted to justify its policy of apartheid. To this, the Court said: 'Under the Charter of the United Nations, the former Mandatory had pledged itself to observe and respect, in a territory having an international status, human rights and fundamental freedoms for all without distinction as to race. To establish instead, and to enforce, distinctions, exclusions, restrictions and limitations exclusively based on grounds of race, colour, descent or national or ethnic origin which constitute a denial of fundamental human rights is a flagrant violation of the purposes and principles of the Charter'.[223] The Special rapporteur of the International Law Commission referred to this phrase as 'certainly an indication, though not definitive, that the International Court of Justice would include the prohibition of apartheid and racial discrimination as an example of *jus cogens*'.[224] Two judges, Fitzmaurice of the United Kingdom and Gros of France, dissented from the majority.

In his separate and concurring opinion, Judge Fouad Ammoun expounded on the bases of the General Assembly's revocation of the mandate, including the policy of apartheid and racial discrimination practiced by South Africa in Namibia. From his perspective, racial discrimination lay at the heart of the issues before the Court. Confronting France's objection to reference to the Universal Declaration of Human Rights on the ground that it was not a treaty, Judge Ammoun explained that the Declaration was also a source of customary law. 'One right which must certainly be considered a pre-existing binding customary

---

[221] *Legal Consequences for States of the Continued Presence of South Africa in Namibia (South West Africa) notwithstanding Security Council Resolution 276 (1970), Advisory Opinion, I.C.J. Reports 1971*, p. 16, para. 119. See Preston Brown, 'The I.C.J. 1971 Advisory Opinion on South West Africa (Namibia)' (1971) 5 *Vanderbilt Journal Transnational Law* 213; Brigitte Bollecker, 'L'avis consultatif en date du 21 juin 1971 de la Cour internationale de Justice dans l'affaire relative aux *conséquences juridiques pour les Etats membres de la présence continue de l'Afrique du Sud en Namibie (Sud-Ouest africain)*' (1971) 17 *Annuaire français de droit international* 281; John Dugard, 'Namibia (South West Africa): The Court's Opinion, South Africa's Response, and Prospects for the Future' (1972) 11 *Columbia Journal of Transnational Law* 14; John Dugard, *The South West Africa/Namibia Dispute: Documents and Scholarly Writings on the Controversy Between South Africa and the United Nations*, Berkeley: University of California Press, 1973; Victor Kattan, 'Decolonizing the International Court of Justice: The Experience of Judge Sir Muhammad Zafrulla Khan in the South West Africa Cases' (2015) 5 *Asian Journal of International Law* 310.

[222] *Legal Consequences for States of the Continued Presence of South Africa in Namibia (South West Africa) notwithstanding Security Council Resolution 276 (1970), Advisory Opinion, I.C.J. Reports 1971*, p. 16, para. 127.

[223] Ibid., para. 131.

[224] Fourth report on peremptory norms of general international law (*jus cogens*) by Dire Tladi, Special Rapporteur, 31 January 2019, A/CN.4/727, para. 93.

norm which the Universal Declaration of Human Rights codified is the right to equality, which by common consent has ever since the remotest times been deemed inherent in human nature.' He continued: 'The equality demanded by the Namibians and by other peoples of every colour, the right to which is the outcome of prolonged struggles to make it a reality, is something of vital interest to us here, on the one hand because it is the foundation of other human rights which are no more than its corollaries and, on the other, because it naturally rules out racial discrimination and apartheid, which are the gravest of the facts with which South Africa, as also other States, stands charged.'[225] Referring to the recognition of apartheid as a crime against humanity in the 1968 treaty on statutory limitation adopted by the General Assembly, Judge Ammoun said: 'Thus, in the eyes of the international community, violations of human rights by the practice of apartheid, itself a violation of equality and of the rights which are its corollaries, are no less punishable than the crimes against humanity and war crimes upon which the Charter of the Nuremberg Tribunal visited sanctions.'[226] Judge Padillo Nervo also dealt with racial discrimination in his separate opinion, although more briefly than Judge Ammoun, confirming his view that the General Assembly resolution revoking the mandate was premised on racial discrimination. He spoke of the competence and the power of the General Assembly to enact recommendations regarding racial discrimination which have evolved as principles or standards of general international acceptance.'[227] Later that year, in *Barcelona Traction*, the Court described protection against racial discrimination as one of the 'principles and rules concerning the basic rights of the human person.'[228]

Now condemned by all of the principal organs of the United Nations, including the International Court of Justice and the Security Council, the racist South African regime still had some important friends and supporters. Anthony Kershaw, the British Under-Secretary of State for Foreign and Commonwealth Affairs, told the House of Commons that the government considered the General Assembly had no authority to terminate the mandate. '[S]ince we have reached the conclusion that the mandate has not been validly terminated, we cannot accept the legal consequences deduced by the Court', he said.[229] Other powerful States, like France, were also aligned with Pretoria. This was related more to the important commercial interests of these countries in South Africa than any nostalgia for the glory days of colonialism. Nevertheless, the former

---

[225] *Legal Consequences for States of the Continued Presence of South Africa in Namibia (South West Africa) notwithstanding Security Council Resolution 276 (1970), Advisory Opinion, I.C.J. Reports 1971*, p. 16, Separate opinion of Vice-president Ammoun, para. 6.

[226] Ibid., para. 7.

[227] Ibid., Separate opinion of Judge Padillo Nervo, p. 111.

[228] *Barcelona Traction, Light and Power Company, Limited, Judgment, I.C.J. Reports 1970*, p. 3, para. 34.

[229] HC Deb, 19 October 1971, vol. 823, cols. 668 94 at cols. 678 83.

colonial powers were still imbued with the remnants of the white supremacism that had characterized their outlooks for centuries. They certainly did not share the fury of those who found it unthinkable that regimes based upon racial segregation could still survive.

'A Consortium of Racist States'

The tsunami of decolonization that swept over Africa in the late 1950s and early 1960s was not without resistance, especially in territories with a significant settler community. South Africa provided an anchor for this phenomenon, encouraging and supporting white supremacist movements and regimes elsewhere in the continent, particularly in the southern portion. By the middle of the 1960s, the General Assembly was speaking of the existence of an 'entente' in the southern part of Africa between South Africa, Portugal, and what was being called the 'illegal racist minority régime' of Southern Rhodesia.[230] The General Assembly said 'the increasing co-operation between the authorities of Southern Rhodesia, South Africa and Portugal is designed to perpetuate racist minority rule in southern Africa and constitutes a threat to freedom, peace and security in Africa'.[231] Speaking in the Security Council, the representative of Côte d'Ivoire described 'a general plan concocted by States that are well known to you, South Africa and Portugal, to create a consortium of racist States in the heart of Africa'.[232]

Portugal had evaded accountability before the Committee on Information, where it might have been challenged for its 'stubborn policy of racism and exploitation', to use the words of the representative of Senegal in the Fourth Committee.[233] After joining the United Nations in 1955, Portugal claimed its overseas territories were mere provinces rather than 'non-self-governing territories', and therefore they were outside the scope of article 73 of the Charter. In 1960, the General Assembly voted that Portugal's African colonies, consisting of the Cape Verde archipelago, Guinea, Sao Tome and Principe, Angola, and Mozambique, and a tiny enclave in Benin, were non-self-governing territories

---

[230] Implementation of the Declaration on the Granting of Independence to Colonial Countries and Peoples, 13 December 1966, A/RES/2189 (XXI), OP 10.

[231] Question of Southern Rhodesia, 5 November 1965, A/RES/2022 (XX), PP 4.

[232] Verbatim record, Security Council, 20 November 1965, S/PV.1265, para. 19.

[233] Summary record, Fourth Committee, 3 November 1961, A/C.4/SR.1196, para. 4. See Bruno Cardoso Reis, 'Portugal and the UN: A Rogue State Resisting the Norm of Decolonization (1956–1974)' (2013) 29 *Portuguese Studies* 251; Norrie MacQueen, 'Belated Decolonization and UN Politics against the Backdrop of the Cold War: Portugal, Britain, and Guinea-Bissau's Proclamation of Independence, 1973–1974' (2006) 8 *Journal of Cold War Studies* 29; Aurora Almada E Santos, 'The Role of the Decolonization Committee of the United Nations Organization in the Struggle Against Portuguese Colonialism in Africa: 1961–1974' (2012) 4 *Journal of Pan African Studies* 248.

238 COLONIALISM AND NEO-COLONIALISM AT THE UNITED NATIONS

within the meaning of the Charter, as well as Goa, Macau, and Timor in Asia.[234] There was a protracted debate in the Fourth Committee the following year. Over the objections of Portugal, which was supported by France and the United Kingdom, the Committee heard two representatives of the anti-colonial movement of Portuguese Guinea and the Cape Verde islands.

'Of all colonisations, Portuguese colonisation was the most totalitarian and the most tyrannical', Henry Labéry, speaking on behalf of the *Mouvement de libération de la Guinée et du Cap-Vert*, told the Fourth Committee.[235] He described racist legislation that formally distinguished between indigenous peoples and those from metropolitan Portugal, such as the 'Native Labour Code' which made this clear by its very title. 'An indigenous person was legally defined as a member of the Negro race or a descendant of a member of that race who was born or habitually resided in Guinea, Angola, or Mozambique, and did not as yet possess the level of education or the personal and social habits which were a condition for the unrestricted application of the public and private law pertaining to Portuguese citizens', he reported to the Fourth Committee.[236] Moreover, '[i]n the eyes of the Portuguese Administration, any white person must be "civilised", whereas any non-white person who had not adopted a European way of life and European habits was not "civilised". At the last census, the proportion of "civilised" Negroes in Portuguese Guinea had been 0.29 per cent, or 1,478 out of a population of 503,935.' Labéry observed that the 'civilized' Negroes knew how to read and write, whereas nearly a quarter of the 'civilized' white inhabitants of Guinea were illiterate.[237] At its next session, in 1962, the General Assembly created a 'Special Committee of Six' to take responsibility for Portuguese colonies.[238]

With respect to the Portuguese territories in Africa, the Security Council requested all States to refrain from offering assistance to Portugal 'which would enable it to continue its repression of the people of the Territories' and to impose an embargo on the sale and supply of arms and military equipment.[239] In 1965, the General Assembly recommended a package of measures aimed at Portugal with respect to the repression of the indigenous population of its African territories, although it did not employ the term 'racialism' or 'racism' and confined its characterization of the regime as a 'negative attitude'.[240] These included the

[234] Transmission of information under Article 73 e of the Charter, 15 December 1960, A/RES/1542 (XV).
[235] Summary record, Fourth Committee, 14 November 1961, A/C.4/SR.1209, para. 5.
[236] Ibid., para. 9.
[237] Ibid., para. 10.
[238] Non-compliance of the Government of Portugal with Chapter XI of the Charter of the United Nations and with General Assembly resolution 1542 (XV), 19 December 1961, A/RES/1699 (XVI).
[239] Question relating to territories under Portuguese administration, 23 November 1965, S/RES/218 (1965), OP 6.
[240] Question of Territories under Portuguese administration, 17 November 1967, A/RES/2270 (XXII), PP 6.

breaking off of diplomatic relations, closing of ports, refusal of landing rights, a trade boycott, and an embargo on arms and ammunition.[241] The General Assembly recommended that the Security Council make these measures obligatory.[242]

During the colonial period, Zimbabwe was known as Southern Rhodesia, named in honour of a British governor, Cecil Rhodes, whose posthumous honours and monuments are now slowly being undone.[243] In 1961, the hegemony of white settlers in the territory was ensured with a new constitution. The British took the position that Southern Rhodesia had been a self-governing colony since 1923 and was therefore beyond the reach of United Nations oversight. Of course, the so-called self-government was in reality that of the white settlers. The General Assembly determined that Southern Rhodesia remained a non-self-governing territory administered by the United Kingdom. It called for a new constitution to ensure the enfranchisement of the indigenous majority. The resolution was adopted by 73 votes with only one State opposed, South Africa. There were 27 abstentions, a mixture of European and South American States along with Australia, Canada, Japan, New Zealand, and the United States. Portugal and the United Kingdom were present but did not vote.[244]

In 1963, 32 African States called upon the Security Council to consider the situation in Southern Rhodesia. Their letter noted that the present government of the territory was elected by its European inhabitants, numbering less than 6 per cent of the overall population. 'All methods of constitutional protest or action have been denied to over 94 per cent of the population who are, on the grounds of their colour, subjected to most degrading and unjust laws', they said.[245] In the Security Council, Ghana, Morocco, and the Philippines proposed a resolution stating that 'the practice of racial discrimination is incompatible with the principles of the Charter of the United Nations' and calling for the United Kingdom

[241] Question of Territories under Portuguese administration, 21 December 1965, A/RES/2107 (XX), OP 7–8.
[242] Question of Territories under Portuguese administration, 12 December 1966, A/RES/2184 (XXI), OP 7.
[243] A. Kayum Ahmed, '#RhodesMustFall: How a Decolonial Student Movement in the Global South Inspired Epistemic Disobedience at the University of Oxford' (2020) 63 *African Studies Review* 271; Tebogo B. Sebeelo, 'Hashtag Activism, Politics and Resistance in Africa: Examining #ThisFlag and #RhodesMustFall online movements' (2021) 13 *Insight on Africa* 95.
[244] The Question of Southern Rhodesia, 28 June 1962, A/RES/1747 (XVI); Verbatim record, plenary General Assembly, 28 June 1962, A/PV.1121, para. 17.
[245] Letter dated 2 August 1963 from the representatives of Ghana, Guinea, Morocco and the United Arab Republic addressed to the president of the Security Council, 5 August 1963, S/5382, para. 4. They were subsequently joined by Algeria, Burundi, Cameroun, Central African Republic, Chad, Congo-Brazzaville, Congo-Leopoldville, Ivory Coast, Dahomey, Ethiopia, Gabon, Liberia, Libya, Madagascar, Mali, Mauritania, Niger, Nigeria, Rwanda, Senegal, Sierra Leone, Somalia, Sudan, Tanganyika, Togo, Tunisia, Uganda, Upper Volta (Letter dated 30 August 1963 from the chargé d'affaires of the permanent mission of the Congo (Brazzaville) addressed to the president of the Security Council, S/5409).

240 COLONIALISM AND NEO-COLONIALISM AT THE UNITED NATIONS

to implement the General Assembly resolutions.[246] Although eight Members of the Council voted in favour, the resolution was vetoed by the United Kingdom. France and the United States abstained.[247]

The authorities in Rhodesia threatened a unilateral declaration of independence. Britain said this was legally impossible and that the only path to independence was a vote of the House of Commons in London. In 1965 both the General Assembly and the Security Council adopted resolutions calling upon the United Kingdom not to allow the white settler regime to declare independence. The Security Council acted on the basis of a request from 35 African States.[248] The Council requested the United Kingdom not to accept a unilateral declaration of independence and not to transfer any attributes of sovereignty.[249] It was adopted by seven votes in favour, including China, with four abstentions, all of them permanent members of the Council.[250] The General Assembly resolution was largely addressed to the United Kingdom, calling for it to prevent a declaration of independence by various means including the use of force.[251]

The Rhodesian regime declared independence on 11 November 1965. The General Assembly reacted immediately with a new and very succinct resolution that condemned the unilateral declaration of independence made 'by the racialist minority in Southern Rhodesia.'[252] The vote was 107 in favour with two opposed, Portugal and South Africa. France abstained.[253] Then the Security Council adopted a resolution, on 20 November, by 10 votes with France abstaining.[254] It called upon the United Kingdom 'to quell this rebellion of the racist minority'.[255] It also told States not to recognize the illegal authority, not to entertain diplomatic or other relations, to refrain from any action which would assist and encourage the illegal regime and, in particular, to desist from providing it with arms, equipment, and military material, and to do their utmost in order to break all economic relations with Southern Rhodesia, including an embargo on oil and petroleum products.[256] As the African voice on the Security Council, Côte

---

[246] Ghana, Morocco and the Philippines: joint draft resolution, 11 September 1963, S/5425/Rev.1.
[247] Verbatim record, Security Council, 13 September 1963, S/PV.1069, para. 64.
[248] Letter dated 65/04/21 addressed to the President of the Security Council from the Representatives of Algeria, Burundi, Cameroon, Central African Republic, Chad, Congo (Brazzaville), Dahomey, Democratic Republic of the Congo, Ethiopia, Gabon, Ghana, Guinea, Ivory Coast, Kenya, Liberia, Libya, Madagascar, Malawi, Mali, Mauritania, Morocco, Niger, Nigeria, Rwanda, Senegal, Sierra Leone, Somalia, Sudan, Togo, Tunisia, Uganda, United Arab Republic, United Republic of Tanzania, Upper Volta and Zambia, 21 April 1965, S/6294/Add. 1.
[249] Question concerning the situation in Southern Rhodesia, 6 May 1965, S/RES/202 (1965).
[250] Verbatim record, Security Council, 6 May 1965, S/PV.1202, para. 87.
[251] The Question of Southern Rhodesia, 5 November 1965, A/RES/2022 (XX).
[252] The Question of Southern Rhodesia, 11 November 1965, A/RES/2024 (XX).
[253] Verbatim record, plenary General Assembly, 11 November 1965, A/PV.1375, para. 224.
[254] Verbatim record, Security Council, 20 November 1965, S/PV.1265, para. 4.
[255] Question concerning the situation in Southern Rhodesia, 20 November 1965, S/RES/217 (1965), OP 4.
[256] Ibid., OP 6, 8.

'A CONSORTIUM OF RACIST STATES' 241

d'Ivoire had proposed a much more militant resolution that noted the measures proposed by the United Kingdom would be ineffective without the use of force, and calling for 'a complete interruption of economic relations'.[257] It was clear that the African States were unimpressed by the measures adopted by the Security Council, which they thought insufficient to deal with the situation.[258]

The Security Council would soon impose mandatory measures. Resolutions adopted in 1966 described the situation in Southern Rhodesia as a 'threat to the peace',[259] implying the application of Chapter VII of the Charter, and then articles 39 and 41 were invoked more explicitly.[260] The Council first attempted to prohibit oil being pumped to Rhodesia by means of the pipeline from Beira, in Portuguese controlled Mozambique.[261] Subsequently, it adopted a package of sanctions aimed at blocking the export of important commodities from Rhodesia, including asbestos, iron ore, chrome, and tobacco, any trade in arms and ammunition, aircraft and motor vehicles, and oil and oil products. The Council resolution stated that any breach of the resolution would constitute a violation of article 25 of the Charter.[262]

In 1967, the General Assembly '[a]ffirme[ed] its conviction that the sanctions adopted so far will not put an end to the illegal racist minority regime and that sanctions, in order to achieve their objective, will have to be comprehensive and mandatory and backed by force'.[263] Subsequently, the General Assembly called upon all States 'to bring to an end the activities of financial, economic and other interests operated by their nationals in Southern Rhodesia'.[264] It also addressed the Security Council, indicating that it should further widen sanctions to include all measures in article 41 of the Charter, and impose sanctions on South Africa and Portugal, 'the Governments of which have blatantly refused to carry out the mandatory decisions of the Security Council'.[265]

The Security Council soon acknowledged the ineffectiveness of the measures it had taken two years earlier. A new resolution, adopted in 1968, that was aimed at choking the economy of Rhodesia required States to prevent entry into their countries by persons travelling with a Southern Rhodesian passport.

---

[257] Ivory Coast: Draft resolution, 15 November 1965, S/6929.
[258] Drew Middleton, 'Rhodesia Oil Embargo Demanded in U.N. Council', New York Times, 20 November 1965, p. 15.
[259] Question concerning the situation in Southern Rhodesia, 9 April 1966, S/RES/221 (1966), OP 1.
[260] Question concerning the situation in Southern Rhodesia, 16 December 1966, S/RES/232 (1966), PP 4.
[261] Question concerning the situation in Southern Rhodesia, 9 April 1966, S/RES/221 (1966), OP 1.
[262] Question concerning the situation in Southern Rhodesia, 16 December 1966, S/RES/232 (1966), PP 4.
[263] Question of Southern Rhodesia, 3 November 1967, A/RES/2262 (XXII), OP 5. See also Question of Southern Rhodesia, 7 November 1968, A/RES/2383 (XXIII), OP 4.
[264] Question of Southern Rhodesia, 7 November 1968, A/RES/2383 (XXIII), OP 8.
[265] Ibid., OP 9.

242 COLONIALISM AND NEO-COLONIALISM AT THE UNITED NATIONS

In the 1966 resolution, the Council had pointed to the obligation to comply with its decisions in accordance with article 25 of the Charter; this time it said more directly that any breach of its orders would be a violation of article 25. The Council established a Committee to monitor implementation of the resolution.[266] In 1970, the Council intervened once again, noting that the sanctions had not produced the desired effect, that some States were not complying, and imposing new measures.[267] The Security Council acknowledged the refusal of South Africa and Portugal to comply with its resolutions.[268] In 1979, a Council resolution condemned the efforts of Southern Rhodesia's 'illegal racist minority régime' to try to cling to power by holding sham elections, designed to perpetuate 'white racist minority rule'.[269] It was adopted by 12 votes with the typical three abstentions, France, the United Kingdom, and the United States.[270]

* * *

When the United Nations was established, large parts of the world and most of Africa were in a situation of colonization. This took various forms, including the prolongation of the mandate system of the League of Nations under the new guise of trusteeship. Two of the main colonizers, Britain and France, were permanent members of the Security Council. Over the two decades following the adoption of the Charter of the United Nations, most of the colonies became self-governing. During this period, United Nations oversight of the situation in the colonies became increasingly robust. The main prongs of United Nations monitoring was the requirement that the colonial powers present periodic reports on their conduct and the examination at the international level of petitions directed at abuses attributable to those powers. Inevitably, one of the main themes was racial discrimination.

The principal United Nations bodies in this process were the Fourth Committee of the General Assembly, the Trusteeship Council, and the Committee on Information from Non-Self-Governing Territories. The records that they left behind, although rarely consulted today, deserve to be revisited. They provide rich insight into the racial discrimination that was a *leitmotif* of

---

[266] Question concerning the situation in Southern Rhodesia, 29 May 1968, S/RES/253 (1968).

[267] Question concerning the situation in Southern Rhodesia, 18 March 1970, S/RES/277 (1970). Also Question concerning the situation in Southern Rhodesia, 17 November 1970, S/RES/288 (1970); Question concerning the situation in Southern Rhodesia, 28 February 1972, S/RES/314 (1972); Question concerning the situation in Southern Rhodesia, 28 July 1972, S/RES/318 (1972); Question concerning the situation in Southern Rhodesia, 22 May 1973, S/RES/333 (1973); Question concerning the situation in Southern Rhodesia, 6 April 1976, S/RES/388 (1976).

[268] Question concerning the situation in Southern Rhodesia, 29 September 1972, S/RES/320 (1972), PP 6.

[269] Question concerning the situation in Southern Rhodesia, 20 April 1979, S/RES/448 (1979), PP 5.

[270] Verbatim record, Security Council, 30 April 1979, S/PV.2143, para. 135.

colonialism. They also reveal the political forces that fought to bring an end to this intolerable situation. Colonialism did not die a natural death. Its demise was the result of struggles within the territories themselves. But constant political pressure at the international level was not insignificant. Bringing an end to colonialism was not set out in the Charter of the United Nations as a purpose of the organization. Nevertheless, the mechanisms that the Charter created, and some that were invented subsequently, made the struggle against colonialism a facet of its work and one of its great initial successes.

Independence largely brought an end to the colour line in the new States. Almost immediately, they were admitted as new Member States of the United Nations. When their delegates arrived in New York they brought with them creative approaches and inexorable energy to campaigns directed at combatting racial discrimination. The quota of people of colour in the delegations to the General Assembly, the Security Council, the Commission on Human Rights, and other United Nations bodies increased very dramatically.

Resistance to this process persisted within southern Africa. The situations were not identical although in white supremacy they found a common denominator. Portugal clung to its African colonies, principally Mozambique and Angola, but also Cape Verde, Guinea, and Sao Tome and Principe, until the 'Carnation revolution' of 1974 brought democracy to Portugal itself. After declaring independence from Britain, Rhodesia's white settlers clung to power and fought a civil war until the late 1970s. In 1980, democratic elections were held for the first time bringing white minority rule to an end. The country changed its name to Zimbabwe and joined the United Nations. South West Africa remained under South Africa's iron grip as long as apartheid prevailed. As Namibia, it only became independent in 1990.

South Africa, Portugal, and Rhodesia were all rogue or outlaw States. They were regularly condemned by United Nations bodies, especially the General Assembly. But the initiatives in the United Nations were constantly weakened, and in some cases completely undermined, by wealthy States in the Global North, many of them with sordid histories of colonialism. The fight for self-government, independence, and an end to racial discrimination, depended upon the determination and militancy of the countries of the Global South and especially of Africa for its momentum.

9

The International Convention on the Elimination of All Forms of Racial Discrimination

The Swastika Epidemic

The International Convention on the Elimination of All Forms of Racial Discrimination was adopted unanimously by the United Nations General Assembly on 21 December 1965. Speaking after the vote, Ghana's representative described it as the Assembly's 'finest hour'.[1] Haiti's representative spoke of 'a new landmark on the path to social progress'.[2] The Convention was the first component of what has over the years become a package of nine major human rights treaties that comprise the United Nations system. In a statement issued at the 1978 World Conference to Combat Racism and Racial Discrimination, the Committee on the Elimination of Racial Discrimination described the Convention as 'the international community's *only* tool for combating racial discrimination which is at one and the same time universal in reach, comprehensive in scope, legally binding in character, and equipped with built-in measures of implementation'.[3] Nearly six decades after adoption of the Convention, it remains the primary international legal instrument in the right against racism and racial discrimination.

That a web of human rights treaties would begin with an instrument on racial discrimination had not really been foreseen. Rather, until the early 1960s attention had been focussed on completing the 'international bill of rights' consisting of the Universal Declaration of Human Rights and the two Covenants. In 1948, when the General Assembly proceeded with adoption of the Universal Declaration, it was thought that completing the bill of rights would only take another year or two. However, negotiation of what soon became two general human rights treaties, reflecting the norms set out in the Universal

---

[1] Verbatim record, plenary General Assembly, 21 December 1965, A/PV.1406, para. 96.
[2] Ibid., para. 87.
[3] Report of the Committee on the Elimination of Racial Discrimination, 15 September 1978, A/33/18, Annex V, pp. 108–13, at p. 109.

The International Legal Order's Colour Line. William A. Schabas, Oxford University Press.
© Oxford University Press 2023. DOI: 10.1093/oso/9780197744475.003.0009

Declaration, would take nearly two decades. There was no sense of urgency. The International Covenant on Civil and Political Rights and the International Covenant on Economic, Social and Cultural Rights were only adopted by the General Assembly in 1966. It took another decade for them to obtain the requisite ratifications for entry into force.

While this process of codifying human rights proceeded at a most leisurely pace, an initiative emerged in the early 1960s for a universal treaty dealing only with racial discrimination. The newly independent African States that had only joined the United Nations were at the source of this development. They generated the moment for its speedy negotiation, adoption and entry into force. The International Court of Justice, in its 2021 judgment in the *Qatar v. United Arab Emirates* case, observed that the Convention was drafted 'against the backdrop of the 1960s decolonization movement.'[4]

The desecration of the Roonstrasse synagogue in Cologne, Germany on 25 December 1959 set off a wave of anti-Semitic vandalism in various parts of the world, including the United States.[5] Prompted by a request from the International League for the Rights of Man,[6] the Sub-Commission on the Prevention of Discrimination and the Protection of Minorities, which was meeting in Geneva in January 1960, took up the subject in the form of draft resolution entitled 'recent manifestations of anti-Semitism and other religious and so-called racial prejudices' proposed by several members.[7] The term 'so-called' had been inserted in light of the UNESCO declarations and to avoid any suggestion that Jews constituted a 'race'.[8] In proposing the resolution, the American delegate, Philip Halpern, referred to reports of anti-Semitic manifestations in 34 countries. Halpern was a cold warrior whose candidacy for the Sub-Commission had been put forward by the Eisenhower administration and whose focus had always been allegations of Soviet anti-Semitism.[9] He said the sponsors of the resolution

---

[4] *Application of the International Convention on the Elimination of All Forms of Racial Discrimination (Qatar v. United Arab Emirates), Preliminary Objections, Judgment, I.C.J. Reports 2021*, p. 71, para. 86.

[5] Sydney Gruson, 'Vandals Desecrate Synagogue Opened by Adenauer in Cologne: German Vandals Smear Synagogue', *New York Times*, 26 December 1959. See Howard J. Ehrlich, 'The Swastika Epidemic of 1959–1960: Anti-Semitism and Community Characteristics' (1962) 9 *Social Problems* 264; David Caplovitz and Candace Rogers, *Swastika 1960: The Epidemic of anti-Semitic Vandalism in America*, New York: Anti-Defamation League of B'nai B'rith, 1961; Nathan A. Kurz, *Jewish Internationalism and Human Rights after the Holocaust*, Cambridge: Cambridge University Press, 2021, pp. 114–15.

[6] Statement submitted by the International League for the Rights of Man, 7 January 1960, E/CN.4/Sub.2/NGO/12.

[7] Draft resolution on condemnation of manifestations of anti-Semitism and other religious and so-called racial prejudices and recommendations with respect to them, E/CN.4/Sub.2/L.159.

[8] Summary record, Sub-Commission on Prevention of Discrimination and Protection of Minorities, 27 January 1960, E/CN.4/Sub.2/SR.304, p. 14.

[9] James Loeffler, *Rooted Cosmopolitans, Jews and Human Rights in the Twentieth Century*, New Haven and London: Yale University Press, 2018, pp. 235–6.

246   ELIMINATION OF ALL FORMS OF RACIAL DISCRIMINATION

were 'particularly apprehensive because those events recalled, in a striking way, the odious acts committed by the Nazis before and during the Second World War'.[10]

The debates within the Sub-Commission do not indicate any suggestion that States were the actual perpetrators of racial discrimination. Indeed, governments were praised for their response to the anti-Semitic incidents and 'other forms of racial and national hatred and religious and racial prejudices of a similar nature, which have occurred in various countries, reminiscent of the crimes and outrages committed by the Nazis prior to and during the Second World War'. Rather, the resolution was entirely focussed on racist acts attributable to individuals. The purpose of the resolution was to affirm the need for States to take action to prevent racist conduct. It called for the Secretary-General to collect information on the subject, and for the Sub-Commission to review this at its 1961 session.[11] The plenary Commission on Human Rights, which met in February and early March of 1960, took up the Sub-Commission's resolution and, on 16 March 1960, it adopted a similar text.[12]

On 21 March 1960, five days after the adoption of the resolution by the Commission on Human Rights and three days after the conclusion of its annual session, South African police opened fire on anti-apartheid demonstrators in Sharpeville, killing 69 people and wounding nearly 200 more, including many children.[13] The world was in the throes of decolonization, with 17 Member States admitted to the United Nations in September and October 1960 after attaining independence, all but one of them in Africa. The General Assembly affirmed this profound change in the global order in its Declaration on the Granting of Independence to Colonial Countries and Peoples. The preamble of the Declaration underscores the relationship between racism and colonialism, stating that 'an end must be put to colonialism and all practices of segregation and discrimination associated therewith'.[14] In December 1961, the General

---

[10] Summary record, Sub-Commission on Prevention of Discrimination and Protection of Minorities, 27 January 1960, E/CN.4/Sub.2/SR.303, p. 9.

[11] Manifestations of anti-Semitism and Other Forms of Racial and National Hatred and Religious and Racial Prejudices of a Similar Nature, 26 January 1960, E/CN.4/Sub.2/RES/3 (XII); Report of the Twelfth Session of the Sub-Commission on Prevention of Discrimination and Protection of Minorities to the Commission on Human Rights, 8 February 1960, E/CN.4/800, para. 194.

[12] Manifestations of anti-Semitism and Other Forms of Racial Prejudice and Religious Intolerance of a Similar Nature, 16 March 1960, E/CN.4/RES/6 (XVI); Report of the 16th session, Commission on Human Rights, 29 February - 18 March 1960, E/CN.4/804, para. 200.

[13] Tom Lodge, *Sharpeville: An Apartheid Massacre and its Consequences*, Oxford: Oxford University Press, 2011; Philip H. Frankel, *An Ordinary Atrocity: Sharpeville and Its Massacre*, New Haven: Yale University Press, 2001.

[14] Declaration on the granting of independence to colonial countries and peoples, 14 December 1960, A/RES/1514 (XV), PP 9. See the references to the preamble of the Declaration by the International Court of Justice in *Legal Consequences of the Separation of the Chagos Archipelago from Mauritius in 1965, Advisory Opinion, I.C.J. Reports 2019*, p. 95, paras. 152–3.

THE SWASTIKA EPIDEMIC   247

Assembly unanimously adopted a resolution affirming that it shared the concern of the Sub-Commission about 'manifestations of racial and national hatred, religious intolerance and racial prejudice'.[15]

Patrice Lumumba was murdered on 17 January 1961 in what James Hicks, writing in the *New York Amsterdam News*, described as a 'lynching staged before the world under the auspices of the United Nations'.[16] Outraged by what they considered the complicity of the United Nations in the assassination, anti-racist demonstrators gathered on First Avenue before United Nations headquarters. Some infiltrated the building, erupting in cries of 'Vive Lumumba' and 'Hammarskjold murderer' when United States Ambassador Adlai Stevenson rose to make his first major address to the Security Council. The verbatim record of the Council meeting refers to a 'sustained interruption from the public gallery'.[17] When the meeting resumed, Stevenson told the Council 'that I deeply deplore this outrageous and obviously organised demonstration'. He added that '[t]o the extent that Americans may be involved, I apologise on behalf of my Government to the members of the Security Council.'[18]

The *New York Times* published a large photograph on the front page and described it as the most violent demonstration inside United Nations headquarters in the history of the organization.[19] Several United Nations security guards were reported injured in the melee, of which an official film exists.[20] Maya Angelou, who helped to organize the demonstration, wrote of how television cameras recorded 'black bodies hurtling out of the UN doors, and marchers chanting along 46th Street'.[21] 'It is obvious that something is seriously wrong', wrote *New York Times* journalist James Reston, recognizing 'a confluence of the world struggle for freedom in Black America and the struggle for equal rights in the Negro communities of America'.[22] James Baldwin discussed 'the spectacular disturbance in the gallery' in a piece in the *New York Times Magazine* published a month after the events. He referred to Stevenson's speech claiming that the United States was 'against' colonialism. 'God knows what the African nations,

---

[15] Manifestations of racial and national hatred, 12 December 1960, A/RES/1510 (XV); Verbatim record, plenary General Assembly, 12 December 1960, A/PV.943, para. 170–2; Report of the Third Committee, 6 December 1960, A/4615, paras. 54–71.

[16] James Hicks, 'Patrice Lumumba', *New York Amsterdam News*, 18 February 1961, p. 8.

[17] Verbatim record, Security Council, 15 February 1961, S/PV.934, para. 44.

[18] Ibid., para. 47.

[19] 'Riot in Gallery Halts UN Debate, American Negroes Ejected After Invading Session, Midtown March Balked', *New York Times*, 16 February 1961, p. 1.

[20] 934th meeting of the Security Council, https://www.unmultimedia.org/avlibrary/asset/2503/2503010/. The Pathé archive also contains film of the demonstration in the Security Council: https://www.youtube.com/watch?v=-yokrYoQfEo.

[21] Maya Angelou, *The Collected Autobiographies of Maya Angelou*, New York: Random House, 2012, p. 777.

[22] James Reston, 'Copper Sun, Scarlet Sea, What is Africa to Me?', *New York Times*, 17 February 1961, p. 26.

248   ELIMINATION OF ALL FORMS OF RACIAL DISCRIMINATION

who are 25 per cent of the voting stock in the United Nations, were thinking – they may, for example, have been thinking of the United States abstention when the vote on Algeria had been before the Assembly – but I think I have a fairly accurate notion of what the Negroes in the gallery were thinking', he wrote. 'I had intended to be there myself.'[23]

Like Baldwin, Martin Luther King Jr. was among those who were energized by the emergence of new African States and their increasingly important role within international politics and diplomacy. 'The nations of Africa and Asia are moving with jet-like speed toward gaining political independence', he wrote in his *Letter from Birmingham City Jail*, 'but we still creep at horse-and-buggy pace toward a cup of coffee at a lunch counter.'[24] In the final year of his life, before he was assassinated, Malcolm X took an internationalist turn. He began to speak of 'human rights' rather than 'civil rights', explaining that 'when you call it "human rights" it becomes international. And then you can take your troubles to the World Court. You can take them before the world. And anybody anywhere on this earth can become your ally.'[25]

African Initiatives in the General Assembly

The Sub-Commission returned to the issue of racial discrimination during its 1961 session. One of the ideas that emerged was an international convention, 'similar in scope to other conventions in the field of human rights, which would impose specific legal obligations on the signatory States to prohibit manifestations of racial and national hatred'. But there was no unanimity, and some members of the Sub-Commission pointed to the absence of any international authority capable of enforcement of such a treaty.[26] One member suggested convening an international conference where a treaty could be adopted, but he did not press the point.[27] The Sub-Commission adopted a mild resolution that called for the manifestations of racism to be subject to further study, recommending a role for UNESCO. It called upon States 'to take all the necessary steps to rescind discriminatory laws in those fields wherever they exist, to adopt legislation if necessary

---

[23] James Baldwin, 'A Negro Assays the Negro Mood', *New York Times Magazine*, 12 March 1961, p. 25.

[24] Martin Luther King Jr., *Letter from Birmingham City Jail*, Stamford, CT: Overbrook Press, 1968.

[25] Malcolm X, 'Not just an American problem, but a world problem', Address delivered in the Corn Hill Methodist Church, Rochester, New York, 16 February 1965.

[26] Report of the 13th session, Sub-Commission on Prevention of Discrimination and Protection of Minorities, 9 February 1961, E/CN.4/815, para. 176.

[27] Ibid., para. 185.

for prohibiting such discrimination, and to take such legislative or other appropriate measures to combat racial, national and religious hatred'.[28]

The modest initiative of the Sub-Commission in 1961 might well have been entirely neglected in the Commission and the General Assembly had it not been for proposals from countries of the Global South. Based upon a resolution that originated with India, the Commission on Human Rights endorsed the work of the Sub-Commission, changing the title somewhat by removing the focus on anti-Semitism.[29] The Commission's resolution was in turn approved by the Economic and Social Council.[30] In the Third Committee of the General Assembly, a resolution from Ethiopia, Ghana, and Guinea confirmed that the General Assembly would take up the question of racial prejudice and national and religious intolerance the following year, 'devot[ing] as many meetings as possible to its consideration'.[31]

As a general rule, initiatives and proposals in the Sub-Commission and the Commission tended to be softened and made more moderate by the time they reached the General Assembly. But with the issue of racial discrimination in the early 1960s, the opposite occurred. The Global South and especially Africa was underrepresented in the Sub-Commission and the Commission. In the General Assembly, by 1962, its influence was much greater and was only beginning to be felt throughout the entire system. That year, the General Assembly quickly agreed to a statement on racial prejudice and religious intolerance, similar in content to the earlier texts that can be traced back to the Sub-Commission in January 1960.[32] It also adopted a resolution calling for a declaration and a convention that was proposed by nine African States: Central African Republic, Chad, Dahomey (Benin), Guinea, Côte d'Ivoire, Mali, Mauritania, Niger, and Upper Volta (Burkina Faso).[33] All had been admitted to the United Nations in 1960 with the exceptions of Guinea (1958) and Niger (1961). None of the States could

---

[28] Manifestations of anti-Semitism and other forms of racial prejudice and religious intolerance of a similar nature, E/CN.4/Sub.2/RES/5 (XIII). The text appears included in Report of the 13th session, Sub-Commission on Prevention of Discrimination and Protection of Minorities to the Commission on Human Rights, 10 January to 3 February 1961, E/CN.4/Sub.2/211, para. 189.

[29] Manifestations of racial prejudice and national and religious intolerance, 10 March 1961, E/CN.4/RES/5 (XVII); Report of the 17th session, Commission on Human Rights, 20 February–17 March 1961, E/CN.4/817, paras. 99–124.

[30] Manifestations of racial prejudice and national and religious intolerance, 27 July 1961, E/RES/826 B (XXXII); Report of the 16th session, Economic and Social Council, 6 August 1960–4 August 1961, A/4820, para. 600.

[31] Manifestations of racial prejudice and national and religious intolerance, 18 December 1961, A/RES/1684 (XVI); Report of the Third Committee, 15 December 1961, A/5042.

[32] Manifestations of racial prejudice and national and religious intolerance, 7 December 1962, A/RES/1779 (XVII).

[33] Manifestations of racial prejudice and national and religious intolerance, preparation of an international convention on the elimination of racial discrimination, Central African Republic, Chad, Dahomey, Guinea, Ivory Coast, Mali, Mauritania, Niger and Upper Volta, draft resolution, 25 October 1962, A/C.3/L.1006.

250   ELIMINATION OF ALL FORMS OF RACIAL DISCRIMINATION

claim a delegate on the Sub-Commission on the Prevention of Discrimination and the Protection of Minorities, whose 12 members then counted only one African, from Sudan, and two Asians, from Lebanon and the Philippines.[34] Nor were any of them represented in the Commission on Human Rights, which then comprised 21 members including six from Asia (Afghanistan, China, India, Lebanon, Pakistan, and the Philippines) but none from Africa.[35] The sponsors of the General Assembly resolution calling for a convention and a declaration were subsequently joined by Ghana and Nigeria,[36] then by Brazil, Czechoslovakia, Madagascar, and Senegal,[37] and still later by Bulgaria, Cameroon, Liberia, and Mongolia.[38] Eventually, the proposal had 34 sponsors, virtually all from the Global South with a majority from Africa.

Debate on the resolution in the Third Committee of the General Assembly focussed on three issues; whether a declaration as well as a convention should be prepared; whether there should be a companion declaration and convention on religious intolerance; and designation of the proper organ of the United Nations to prepare the drafts. That a declaration should accompany the convention was not particularly controversial. After struggling with combining racial discrimination and religious intolerance in a single resolution, which was not favoured by several delegations, the Third Committee decided upon two separate resolutions, similar in form and content, one addressed to racial discrimination and the other to religious intolerance. According to Egon Schwelb, opposition to combining the two in a single resolution came from 'some of the Arab delegations' and reflected the Arab-Israeli conflict. He also said that many delegations, particularly those from Eastern Europe, did not consider the issue of religion to be as important as racial discrimination, and 'it was understood that the instruments relating to racial discrimination would receive priority'.[39] The two resolutions

[34] In 1953, members of the Sub-Commission from Haiti and Egypt were elected to three-year terms. In 1959, a member was elected from the United Arab Republic.

[35] Liberia was elected to the Commission in 1963 and Dahomey (Benin) the following year. Egypt had been elected to the Commission in 1950.

[36] Manifestations of racial prejudice and national and religious intolerance: Central African Republic, Chad, Dahomey, Guinea, Ivory Coast, Mali, Mauritania, Niger, and Upper Volta: revised draft resolution, 26 October 1962, A/C.3/L.1006/Rev.1.

[37] Manifestations of racial prejudice and national and religious intolerance: preparation of an international convention on the elimination of racial discrimination: Brazil, Central African Republic, Chad, Czechoslovakia, Dahomey, Ghana, Guinea, Ivory Coast, Madagascar, Mali, Mauritania, Niger, Senegal, and Upper Volta: revised draft resolution, 29 October 1962, A/C.3/L.1006/Rev.2.

[38] Manifestations of racial prejudice and national and religious intolerance: preparation of an international convention on the elimination of racial discrimination: Brazil, Bulgaria, Cameroon, Central African Republic, Chad, Czechoslovakia, Dahomey, Ghana, Guinea, Ivory Coast, Liberia, Madagascar, Mali, Mauritania, Mongolia, Niger, Nigeria, Senegal, and Upper Volta: revised draft resolution, 29 October 1962, A/C.3/L.1006/Rev.3.

[39] Egon Schwelb, 'The International Convention on the Elimination of All Forms of Racial Discrimination' (1966) 15 International and Comparative Law Quarterly 996, at p. 999.

were adopted without a vote and without any debate or explanations of vote in the plenary General Assembly.[40]

There was a new tension in the debates as the situation in the Middle East began to complicate United Nations activities addressed to racial discrimination. Israel was the first to take the floor in the Third Committee, focussing its remarks on anti-Semitism.[41] This provoked the Jordanian delegate to refer to the Deir Yassein massacre, when more than 100 Palestinians were murdered by right-wing Zionist extremists in 1948. She said she 'could not but view the statement of the representative of the so-called State of Israel in the light of the brutal actions of the Jews in the Middle East during and after the Palestine war'. She added that there were 'two classes of citizens in Israel', pointing to discrimination against Arabs.[42] Israel and its Arab neighbours skirmished repeatedly in the course of the debates.[43] The proceedings were very largely dominated by delegations from Africa and Asia, and many Western countries did not participate at all. Japan recalled its effort to condemn racial discrimination at the Paris Peace Conference.[44] There were mutual recriminations between the United States and the Soviet Union, with the former referring to persecution of Jews in Russia and the latter replying with comments about American treatment of persons of colour.[45]

Drafting the Declaration on Racial Discrimination

The General Assembly's expectation was that the initial study of the Convention would be undertaken by the Sub-Commission on the Prevention of Discrimination and the Protection of Minorities. The Sub-Commission did not attempt to do any work on the draft Convention at its 1963 session, postponing the matter to the following year and focussing its attention on the Declaration.[46] Three distinct proposals for a declaration on racial discrimination were considered at the January 1963 session of the Sub-Commission.[47] The drafts

[40] Preparation of a draft declaration and a draft convention on the elimination of all forms of racial discrimination, 7 December 1962, A/RES/1780 (XVII); Preparation of a draft declaration and a draft convention on the elimination of all forms of religious intolerance, 7 December 1962, A/RES/1781 (XVII); Verbatim record, plenary General Assembly, 7 December 1962, A/PV.1187, paras. 40–2.

[41] Summary record, Third Committee, 29 October 1962, A/C.3/SR.1165, paras. 8–17.

[42] Ibid., para. 32.

[43] For example, Summary record, Third Committee, 31 October 1962, A/C.3/SR.1168, paras. 9–14; Summary record, Third Committee, 31 October 1962, A/C.3/SR.1169, paras. 20, 50.

[44] Summary record, Third Committee, 31 October 1962, A/C.3/SR.1169, para. 53.

[45] Summary record, Third Committee, 1 November 1962, A/C.3/SR.1170, paras. 30–3; Summary record, Third Committee, 2 November 1962, A/C.3/SR.1171, paras. 34–7.

[46] Report of the 15th session, Sub-Commission on Prevention of Discrimination and Protection of Minorities, 14 January to 1 February 1963, E/CN.4/Sub.2/229, para. 187.

[47] E/CN.4/Sub.2/L.292 and Add.l, authored by Francesco Capotorti (Italy), Pierre Juvigny (France), Hernán Santa Cruz (Chile), and Wojciech Ketrzynski (Poland); E/CN.4/Sub.2/L.287, by

252 ELIMINATION OF ALL FORMS OF RACIAL DISCRIMINATION

defined racial discrimination in terms of distinctions based upon 'race, colour, or ethnic origin'. The Charter of the United Nations speaks only of distinction on grounds of 'race'. The term 'colour' was included by article 2 of the Universal Declaration of Human Rights. The addition of 'ethnic origin' was a contribution of the Sub-Commission. The Sub-Commission reached agreement on a text that was then submitted to the Commission on Human Rights, which met in March 1963.[48]

A Working Group of the Commission on Human Rights prepared a consolidated text. There was some controversy about whether racial discrimination should be associated with colonialism. Members of the Commission also disagreed about language in the Declaration condemning the propagation by individual or groups of notions of racial superiority, with some considering this might violate freedom of opinion and expression.[49] The final version adopted by the Commission referred to the 1960 General Assembly resolution on colonialism in a preambular paragraph and called for the condemnation of 'propaganda based on ideas or theories of the superiority of one race or group of persons of one colour or ethnic origin with a view to justifying or promoting racial discrimination in any form, and all incitement of hatred and violence against any race or group of persons of another colour or ethnic origin'.[50] After perfunctory treatment in the Economic and Social Council,[51] the Commission's text was forwarded to the General Assembly.

In the months between the conclusion of the 1963 session of the Commission on Human Rights and the opening of the General Assembly, 31 African States convened in Addis Ababa for a summit conference to found the Organization of African Unity, the forerunner of the African Union. In a resolution, the conference condemned racial discrimination 'in all its forms in Africa and all over the world, and '[e]xpresse[d] the deep concern aroused in all African peoples and

---

Morris Abram (United States); E/CN.4/Sub.2/L.291, by Wojciech Ketrzynski. The three texts are also included in Report of the 15th session, Sub-Commission on Prevention of Discrimination and Protection of Minorities to the Commission on Human Rights, 14 January to 1 February 1963, E/CN.4/Sub.2/229, paras. 184–6.

[48] Draft Declaration on the Elimination of All Forms of Racial Discrimination, E/CN.4/Sub.2/RES/7 (XV). The text appears included in Report of the 15th session, Sub-Commission on Prevention of Discrimination and Protection of Minorities to the Commission on Human Rights, 14 January to 1 February 1963, E/CN.4/Sub.2/229, para. 210.

[49] For the debates in the Commission, including the drafts that were submitted, see Report of the 19th session, Commission on Human Rights, 11 March–5 April 1963, E/CN.4/857, paras. 89–145. It provides a summary of E/CN.4/SR.740–4 and 757–67.

[50] Draft declaration on the elimination of all forms of racial discrimination, E/CN.4/857, pp. 93—5.

[51] Draft declaration on the elimination of all forms of racial discrimination, E/RES/958 E (XXXVI); Report of the 18th session, Economic and Social Council, 4 August 1962–2 August 1963, A/5503, paras. 485–6.

DRAFTING THE DECLARATION ON RACIAL DISCRIMINATION   253

governments by the measures of racial discrimination taken against communities of African origin living outside the continent and particularly in the United States of America'.[52] The Addis Ababa Summit was particularly concerned with the unfinished work of decolonization, the system of apartheid in force in South Africa, the white settler regime in Southern Rhodesia (Zimbabwe), and the remaining Portuguese colonies. In August 1963, Martin Luther King Jr delivered his legendary 'I have a dream' speech standing in front of the Lincoln Memorial, in Washington, before a crowd of 250,000 people. On 15 September 1963, four African American girls were killed by a bomb planted by members of the Ku Klux Klan in the 16th Street Baptist Church of Birmingham, Alabama. The next month, the Rivonia trial of Nelson Mandela began in Pretoria.

The General Assembly studied the draft Declaration on racial discrimination over the course of 30 meetings. Finally, the African States were actively involved in drafting the Declaration. To be entirely accurate, Liberia had been elected to the Commission on Human Rights the previous year. It was present during the debates within the Commission in March 1963 but does not appear to have played a prominent role. The negotiation of the Declaration in the General Assembly during September, October, and November was the first substantial participation by most African States in the development of international law within the United Nations. The debates provided an opportunity for an unprecedented condemnation of racial discrimination, unlike anything previously by the political bodies of the United Nations and the League of Nations. One after another, the African delegates took the floor to make eloquent statements. The Mauritanian representative, echoing the words of W.E.B. Du Bois, who had died in Accra only weeks earlier, described racial discrimination as 'the shame of the twentieth century'. She said that '[a]s long as it was not stamped out, mankind would not be entitled to pride itself on its scientific, technical and artistic progress; similarly, the young African countries could not devote themselves freely to the task of national development as long as the dignity of some of their brethren continued to be flouted'.[53] The delegate from Tanganyika said she would not even attempt to express her indignation at racial discrimination but 'wished to emphasise, on behalf of her delegation, the singular hypocrisy of States which, after signing the United Nations Charter, based on the principle of the dignity and equality of human beings, continued to practise racial discrimination, the very negation of that principle. Those States which loudly proclaimed their respect for the ideals of the Charter and at the same time flirted with a country like South Africa also displayed a form of hypocrisy which was an insult to the whole

---

[52] Apartheid and South Africa, Resolution B, SUMMIT CIAS/Plen.2/Rev.2, arts. 4–5.
[53] Summary record, Third Committee, 30 September 1963, A/C.3/SR.1215, para. 41.

254 ELIMINATION OF ALL FORMS OF RACIAL DISCRIMINATION

of mankind.[54] Liberia's representative said racial discrimination was 'one of the gravest social perils the world had ever known.[55]

In the General Assembly, several paragraphs were strengthened as a result of amendments proposed jointly by eight African states (Algeria, Cameroon, Chad, Guinea, Mauritania, Niger, Senegal, Togo) together with Iraq and Lebanon.[56] One striking feature in the participation of the African delegations is the number of women representing these newly independent countries. In the Third Committee debates, women spoke on behalf of Cameroon, Ghana, Guinea, Libya, Mali, Mauritania, Nigeria, Sierra Leone, Tanganyika, and Uganda.

Adlai Stevenson, the permanent representative of the United States to the United Nations, took the floor to present a rather frank and even contrite report on the situation in his country. Although emancipated from slavery, the American Negro 'had not been elevated to full citizenship', Stevenson explained. 'Scattered around an impoverished countryside, huddled in the slums of cities, he had become the forgotten man of American society.' Stevenson told the General Assembly that African Americans had been barred from the mainstream of national life, 'denied equal access to housing, to the polls and even to public facilities in some parts of the country'. He spoke of efforts to stamp out the practice of lynching, and told the Assembly of various measures taken at the federal level to address racial discrimination within the country. 'Unlike those Governments which, as the draft Declaration said, imposed racial discrimination by means of legislative, administrative and other measures, his own Government used such measures to destroy racial discrimination had been denied equal opportunities for education and hence for employment.[57] The *New York Times* described Stevenson's speech as particularly significant 'not because it contained any fresh ideas but because it offered foreign states an uncommonly candid recital of the racial struggle in the United States'.[58]

Concerns about anti-Semitism had launched the procedure in the Sub-Commission in 1960 that led to the Declaration. Until the proposal for a declaration and a convention had been made, the General Assembly and the subordinate bodies had dealt with the anti-Semitism issue under the heading 'Manifestations of racial prejudice and national and religious intolerance'. A resolution bearing this title continued to be adopted for a few years until the General

---

[54] Summary record, Third Committee, 27 September 1963, A/C.3/SR.1214, para. 28.
[55] Summary record, Third Committee, 1 October 1963, A/C.3/SR.1216, para. 57.
[56] Algeria, Cameroon, Chad, Guinea, Iraq, Lebanon, Mauritania, Niger, Senegal, and Togo: amendment to the draft declaration contained in document A/5459, A/C.3/L.1068/Rev.2/Add.1.
[57] Summary record, Third Committee, 1 October 1963, A/C.3/SR.1217, paras. 1–8.
[58] Kathleen Teltsch, 'Stevenson Gives Pledge on Rights, Tells U.N. the U.S. Intends to Destroy Discrimination', *New York Times*, 2 October 1963, p. 24.

DRAFTING THE DECLARATION ON RACIAL DISCRIMINATION   255

Assembly decided that it was no longer necessary.[59] Reports were submitted to the Secretary-General on compliance with the resolution.[60] By the time of the debates in the General Assembly on the draft declaration, in 1963, the focus on anti-Semitism had largely disappeared.

When the vote was taken in the Third Committee on the final text of the Declaration, 89 States were in favour with none against. But there were also 17 abstentions: Australia, Belgium, Canada, Denmark, Finland, France, Greece, Iceland, Ireland, Italy, Luxembourg, Netherlands, New Zealand, Norway, Sweden, the United Kingdom, and the United States of America.[61] After a rather trivial modification was made to one provision in the plenary General Assembly, these States agreed to join the consensus. The Declaration was then adopted without a vote by the plenary General Assembly on 20 November 1963.[62]

The Declaration on the Elimination of All Forms of Racial Discrimination consists of an 11-paragraph Preamble and 11 articles. When the Declaration was being debated by the General Assembly, great attention was given to its preamble. The United Kingdom presented an amendment to replace a general reference to equality with a specific phrase on 'equal rights of men and women', but the amendment was withdrawn when delegates suggested it would weaken the focus on racial discrimination. The word 'dignity' was added to 'equality' in the first preambular paragraph on a proposal from Nigeria, Paraguay, and Peru.[63] Six African States proposed adding a paragraph to the Preamble: 'Considering that any doctrine of racial differentiation or superiority is scientifically false, morally condemnable, socially unjust and dangerous, and that there is no justification for racial discrimination either in theory or in practice.'[64] The United States demanded a separate vote on the words 'differentiation or'. It was adopted, by 35 to 19, with 45 abstentions. Other than China and Jamaica, all of the negative votes were from Western States. Then the entire paragraph was adopted by the Third Committee on a roll-call vote, with 64 in favour, one against (the Netherlands) and 34 abstentions, almost all of them Western States.[65]

---

[59] Manifestations of racial prejudice and national and religious intolerance, 1 November 1965, A/RES/2019 (XX); Manifestations of racial prejudice and national and religious intolerance, 26 October 1966, A/RES/2143 (XXI).

[60] Manifestations of racial prejudice and national and religious intolerance, Report of the Secretary General, 9 August 1963, A/5473; Manifestations of racial prejudice and national and religious intolerance, Report of the Secretary General, 19 May 1964, A/5703; Manifestations of racial prejudice and national and religious intolerance, Report of the Secretary General, 8 August 1966, A/6347.

[61] Summary record, Third Committee, 28 October 1963, A/C.3/SR.1245, para. 2.

[62] Verbatim record, plenary General Assembly, 20 November 1963, A/PV.1261, para. 11.

[63] Nigeria, Paraguay and Peru: amendment to the draft declaration contained in document A/5459, 26 September 1963, A/C.3/L.1065; Summary record, Third Committee, 7 October 1963, A/C.3/SR.1222, para. 8.

[64] Algeria, Cuba, Guinea, Mali, Mauritania and Senegal: amendment to the draft declaration (A/5459), 4 October 1963, A/C.3/L.1092/Add.1.

[65] Summary record, Third Committee, 7 October 1963, A/C.3/SR.1222, para. 9.

256   ELIMINATION OF ALL FORMS OF RACIAL DISCRIMINATION

Article 1 of the Declaration states that '[d]iscrimination between human beings on the ground of race, colour or ethnic origin is an offence to human dignity and shall be condemned as a denial of the principles of the Charter of the United Nations, as a violation of the human rights and fundamental freedoms proclaimed in the Universal Declaration of Human Rights, as an obstacle to friendly and peaceful relations among nations and as a fact capable of disturbing peace and security among peoples'. Article 2 affirms that no State, institution, group or individual shall discriminate in matters of human rights and fundamental freedoms. It also recognizes the legitimacy of temporary 'special concrete measures' intended to 'secure adequate development or protection of individuals belonging to certain racial groups'.[66] This may well be the first recognition in international law of what has been sometimes described as 'affirmative action' or 'positive discrimination'.

The Declaration makes two references to apartheid. The Preamble expresses the 'alarm' about 'manifestations of racial discrimination still in evidence in some areas of the world, some of which are imposed by certain Governments by means of legislative, administrative or other measures, in the form, inter alia, of apartheid, segregation and separation, as well as by the promotion and dissemination of doctrines of racial superiority and expansionism in certain areas'. Article 5 states that '[a]n end shall be put without delay to governmental and other public policies of racial segregation and especially policies of apartheid, as well as all forms of racial discrimination and separation resulting from such policies'. Although many of the Western countries were quite tolerant of South Africa, there was no attempt to contest the condemnation of apartheid during the debates. South Africa itself took the floor on only one occasion in the General Assembly to object to the various negative comments that had been made. It said it would not participate in discussions about the text of the Declaration.[67]

The most controversial proposition in the Declaration concerned racist organizations, racist propaganda, and hate speech. Draft article 9 adopted by the Commission on Human Rights consisted of one paragraph: 'All propaganda based on ideas or theories of the superiority of one race or group of persons of one colour or ethnic origin with a view to justifying or promoting racial discrimination in any form, and all incitement of hatred and violence against any race or group of persons of another colour or ethnic origin, should be condemned.'[68] The provision was expanded considerably in the Third Committee with the addition of two new paragraphs. Paragraph 2 stated that incitement to violence against

---

[66] Commission on Human Rights, Report of the 19th session, 11 March–5 April 1963, E/3743, paras. 109–10.
[67] Summary record, Third Committee, 2 October 1963, A/C.3/SR.1218, paras. 21–2.
[68] Draft declaration on the elimination of all forms of racial discrimination, 2 April 1963, E/CN.4/RES/9 (XIX), art. 9.

DRAFTING THE DECLARATION ON RACIAL DISCRIMINATION   257

any race or group of another colour or ethnic origin was to be considered 'an of-fence against society and punishable under law'. The real stumbling block was the third paragraph. It required States to take 'immediate and positive measures, in-cluding legislative and other measures, to prosecute and/or outlaw organisations which incite racial discrimination or promote or use violence for purposes of discrimination based on race, colour or ethnic origin'.[69] The debates consumed the better part of three days. Several delegations argued that the provision unac-ceptably encroached upon freedom of expression and freedom of association.[70] Paragraph 3 was adopted on a roll call vote by 64 votes in favour to none against. There were 39 abstentions, essentially from the Western and Eastern blocs. All of the African States voted in favour.[71]

When they abstained in the final vote within the Third Committee on the Declaration as a whole, several Western States indicated their unhappiness with paragraph 3 of article 9.[72] Several weeks later, when the Declaration was debated by the plenary General Assembly, the 17 Western States that had abstained in the vote on the final text adopted by the Third Committee offered to join the consensus if the third paragraph of article 9 was amended.[73] Their request was quite petty, consisting of replacing the word 'promote' with 'incite' in the final phrase. A compromise whereby both terms would be used was proposed by Argentina and ultimately accepted.[74] The States of Africa and Asia, many of them United Nations members for only a few years, described by the Guinean delegate during the General Assembly debate as those 'who throughout history and in all continents have suffered the most from racial discrimination',[75] had prevailed. In effect, the Western States backed down. They were unable to defeat the basic premise of article 9 yet obviously felt it would be politically disastrous for them to abstain or oppose the Declaration.

In conjunction with the Declaration, the General Assembly adopted a res-olution requesting all States to 'undertake all necessary measures in order

---

[69] Bolivia, India, Libya, Nigeria, Peru, Spain, Sudan and United Arab Republic: amendment to the amendment submitted by Brazil, Burundi, Ceylon, Chile, Czechoslovakia, Mali, Tanganyika, USSR, and Yugoslavia (A/C.3/L.1090/Add.1), 14 October 1963, A/C.3/L.1127. See also Report of the Third Committee, 12 November 1963, A/5603, paras. 114–48.

[70] Summary record, Third Committee, 10 October 1963, A/C.3/SR.1227, paras. 3–31; Summary record, Third Committee, 10 October 1963, A/C.3/SR.1228, paras. 3–39; Summary record, Third Committee, 11 October 1963, A/C.3/SR.1229, paras. 1–5, 27–41; Summary record, Third Committee, 14 October 1963, A/C.3/SR.1230, paras. 1–19; Summary record, Third Committee, 15 October 1963, A/C.3/SR.1231, paras. 1–25; Summary record, Third Committee, 15 October 1963, A/C.3/SR.1232, paras. 21–59; Summary record, Third Committee, 16 October 1963, A/C.3/SR.1233, paras. 1–44.

[71] Summary record, Third Committee, 15 October 1963, A/C.3/SR.1232, paras. 58–9.

[72] Summary record, Third Committee, 28 October 1963, A/C.3/SR.1245, paras. 3 (Ireland), 7 (United Kingdom), 8 (Japan), 9 (Canada), 10 (United States), 14 (Austria), 21 (Belgium).

[73] Verbatim record, plenary General Assembly, 20 November 1963, A/PV.1260, paras. 6–8.

[74] Argentina, Amendment, A/L.435; Verbatim record, plenary General Assembly, 20 November 1963, A/PV.1261, paras. 9–10.

[75] Verbatim record, plenary General Assembly, 20 November 1963, A/PV.1260, para. 54.

258   ELIMINATION OF ALL FORMS OF RACIAL DISCRIMINATION

to implement fully, faithfully and without delay the principles contained' in the Declaration. They were also asked to publicize the text as widely as possible. The resolution invited States to report on their 'compliance' with the Declaration.[76] The following year, the Secretary-General produced a summary of the submissions received pursuant to the Resolution. Forty-three Member States provided reports, as well as several intergovernmental agencies and a host of non-governmental organizations. States provided information about national legislation, constitutional provisions and measures to publicize the Declaration. The Netherlands and Thailand both informed the United Nations that racial discrimination simply did not exist in their countries. Portugal, which at the time still had several colonies in Africa, presented itself as a pioneer in the prohibition of racial discrimination.[77] The report was only considered at the 1965 session of the General Assembly. A new resolution was adopted renewing the call for implementation of the Declaration, but also '[r]equest[ing] the States where organisations are promoting, or inciting to, racial discrimination to take all necessary measures to prosecute and/or outlaw such organisations'.[78] By 1967, the General Assembly was referring to the Declaration as one of several 'international instruments against racial discrimination'. It called upon the Secretary-General to continue reporting upon information from Member States on 'measures taken for the speedy implementation of the United Nations Declaration on the Elimination of All Forms of Racial Discrimination'.[79] In his separate opinion to the 1971 Advisory Opinion of the International Court of Justice, Judge Fouad Ammoun noted that the Declaration, adopted unanimously, condemned racial discrimination and apartheid.[80] Over time, the 1963 Declaration was eclipsed by subsequent instruments. The General Assembly continued to make reference to it in resolutions until about 1985.[81] The Declaration was not even mentioned in the 2001 Durban Declaration.

[76] Publicity to be given to the United Nations Declaration on the Elimination of All Forms of Racial Discrimination, 20 November 1963, A/RES/1905 (XVIII).

[77] Measures to Implement the United Nations Declaration on the Elimination of All Forms of Racial Discrimination, 8 June 1964, A/5698 and Corr.1, A/5698/Add.1 and Add.1/Corr.1, A/5698/Add.2-4.

[78] Measures to Implement the United Nations Declaration on the Elimination of All Forms of Racial Discrimination, 1 November 1965, A/RES/2017 (XX). See also Report of the Third Committee, 13 October 1965, A/6046.

[79] Measures for the speedy implementation of international instruments against racial discrimination, 18 December 1967, A/RES/2332 (XXII), para. 2.

[80] *Legal Consequences for States of the Continued Presence of South Africa in Namibia (South West Africa) notwithstanding Security Council Resolution 276 (1970), Advisory Opinion, I.C.J. Reports 1971*, p. 16, Separate opinion of Vice-president Ammoun, para. 8.

[81] Measures to be taken against Nazi, Fascist and neo-Fascist activities and all other forms of totalitarian ideologies and practices based on racial intolerance, hatred and terror, 13 December 1985, A/RES/40/148, PP 16.

The Declaration contains an important reference to 'peace and security'. Article 1 states that '[d]iscrimination between human beings on the ground of race, colour or ethnic origin ... shall be condemned ... as a fact capable of disturbing peace and security among peoples'. In the International Law Commission, Roberto Ago drew attention to the relationship between racial discrimination and the maintenance of peace and security, and the argument of some countries that collective action by the Security Council might be justified to the extent that a regime of apartheid constitutes a use of force that is 'inconsistent with the Purposes of the United Nations' in the sense of article 1 of the Charter. Accordingly, apartheid could amount to use of force prohibited by the final phrase of article 2(4) of the Charter.[82] Beginning in 1965, the General Assembly regularly drew the Security Council's attention to the threat to international peace and security posed by racist regimes in southern Africa.[83]

The Sub-Commission Meets Jim Crow in Atlanta

When genocide was first being discussed in the General Assembly, in 1946, the Soviet delegate thought the resolution might be amended to call for preparatory work on a draft international convention concerning the struggle against racial discrimination'.[84] He linked it to the Egyptian resolution on racial discrimination that had been voted a few days previously.[85] It was an isolated statement, however. In 1958, the Governing Body of the International Labour Organisation adopted a Convention on discrimination in employment which applies to distinctions based upon 'race, colour, sex, religion, political opinion, national extraction or social origin', an enumeration that is broadly similar to that of article 2 of the Universal Declaration of Human Rights.[86] Existing implementation mechanisms of the Organisation applied to the treaty. Earlier in the 1950s, the

---

[82] Fifth report on State responsibility, by Mr. Roberto Ago, Special Rapporteur, 22 March, 14 April and 4 May 1976, A/CN.4/291 and Add.l and 2, para. 108 and fn. 171.

[83] The policies of apartheid of the Government of the Republic of South Africa, 15 December 1965, A/RES/2054 A (XX). OP 6; The policies of apartheid of the Government of the Republic of South Africa, 16 December 1966, A/RES/2202 (XXI) A, OP 7; The policies of apartheid of the Government of the Republic of South Africa, 13 December 1967, A/RES/2307 (XXII) A, OP 4; The policies of apartheid of the Government of the Republic of South Africa, 2 December 1968, A/RES/2396 (XXIII), OP 4; The policies of apartheid of the Government of the Republic of South Africa, 8 December 1970, A/RES/2671 F (XXV), OP 6; etc.

[84] Summary record, Sixth Committee, 22 November 1946, A/C.6/SR.22, pp. 103–104.

[85] See *supra*, pp. 114–115.

[86] Convention (No. 111) concerning Discrimination in Respect of Employment and Occupation (1960) 362 UNTS 31. See Henrik Karl Nielsen, 'The Concept of Discrimination in ILO Convention no. 111' (1994) 43 *International and Comparative Law Quarterly* 827; Fergus Mackay, 'The ILO Convention No. 111: an alternative means of protecting indigenous peoples' rights?' (2020) 24 *International Journal of Human Rights* 144.

260 ELIMINATION OF ALL FORMS OF RACIAL DISCRIMINATION

International Labour Organisation had adopted a convention on equal remuneration, but this applied to discrimination on the basis of gender and not race or ethnicity.[87] Two years later, the General Conference of UNESCO adopted the Convention on Discrimination in Education. The UNESCO Convention resulted from an initiative of a Special rapporteur of the United Nations Sub-Commission on the Prevention of Discrimination and the Protection of Minorities.[88] The Convention calls for free and compulsory primary education as well as a range of other rights related to the subject. The Convention applies to distinctions based on race, colour, sex, language, religion, political or other opinion, national or social origin, economic condition or birth. It is striking for its explicit recognition of exceptions: separate systems or schools based upon gender, religion, and language and, in a general sense, private educational institutions provided that their object is not to secure exclusion, a rather vague notion. The UNESCO treaty requires States Parties to report on implementation on a periodic basis. It provides for disputes to be resolved by the International Court of Justice.[89] Implementation was also addressed by a Protocol to the Convention instituting a conciliation and good offices commission.[90]

Although the idea of a convention on racial discrimination had been mooted in the Sub-Commission, the first formal proposal came in the nine-power resolution of African States at the 1962 session of the General Assembly.[91] The 1962 resolution called upon the Sub-Commission to prepare a draft convention no later than the 1965 session of the General Assembly. Later that year, Czechoslovakia produced a 'working paper' that was, in effect, a draft convention.[92] Until that

[87] Convention (No. 100) concerning equal remuneration for men and women workers for work of equal value (1953) 165 UNTS 303.

[88] Study of discrimination in education by Charles D. Ammoun, Special Rapporteur of the Sub-Commission on Prevention of Discrimination and Protection of Minorities, 1957, E/CN.4/Sub.2/181, p. 238; Report of the Ninth Session of the Sub-Commission on the Prevention of Discrimination and the Protection of Minorities, 8 March 1957, E/CN.4/Sub. 2/186, para. 72–86. See also, in the Commission on Human Rights: Commission on Human Rights, Report of the Twelfth Session, 5–29 March 1956, E/CN.4/731, paras. 101–7.

[89] Convention against discrimination in education (1962) 429 UNTS 93, arts 7, 8. See Hanna Saba, 'La Convention et la Recommendation concernant la Lutte contre la Discrimination dans le Domaine de l'Enseignement' [1960] Annuaire français de droit international 646; Stephen Marks, 'UNESCO and Human Rights: The Implementation of Rights Relating to Education, Science, Culture, and Communication' (1977) 13 Texas International Law Journal 35; Natan Lerner, Group Rights and Discrimination in International Law, The Hague: Brill/Nijhoff, 2003, pp. 169–72; Kishore Singh, 'UNESCO's Convention against Discrimination in Education (1960): Key Pillar of the Education for All' (2008) 4 International Journal of Education Law and Policy 70.

[90] Protocol Instituting a Conciliation and Good Offices Commission to be Responsible for Seeking the settlement of any Disputes which may Arise between States Parties to the Convention against Discrimination in Education, 1962.

[91] Manifestations of racial prejudice and national and religious intolerance: preparation of an international convention on the elimination of racial discrimination: Central African Republic, Chad, Dahomey, Guinea, Ivory Coast, Mali, Mauritania, Niger, and Upper Volta: draft resolution, 25 October 1962, A/C.3/L.1006.

[92] Czechoslovakia: working paper concerning a draft International Convention on the Elimination of Racial Discrimination, 7 December 1962, E/CN.4/Sub.2/234, Annex IV, pp. 2–5.

point, the proposed treaty had been described as the 'convention on the elimination of racial discrimination'.

In 1963, the Sub-Commission focussed only on the draft declaration, which was due immediately, postponing work on the convention. As a polite reminder, several African States, joined with others from the Global South, included the proposal for a resolution calling for immediate work on the International Convention on the Elimination of All Forms of Racial Discrimination. It was sponsored by 22 States, all of them from Africa, Asia and South America, including Algeria, Ghana, Guinea, Liberia, Libya, Madagascar, Mali, Mauritania, and Nigeria.[93] The resolution accelerated the timetable, asking for materials to be prepared in time for the General Assembly session in 1964.[94]

The Sub-Commission convened in January 1964 only weeks after the adoption by the General Assembly of the Declaration on the Elimination of all Forms of Racial Discrimination. Western States were stung by their failure to weaken the text of article 9 of the Declaration, on hate speech and racist organizations, and hoped to reverse the current in the text of the Convention. For example, the American member of the Sub-Commission, Morris Abram, had been given a 'guidance paper' from the Department of State, that said 'coverage should be limited to basic rights and the approach should be along the lines of the 'equal protection' concept in our 14th Amendment' to the Constitution. It added: 'Provisions in line with the US Constitution and law should be supported on their merits. It can be pointed out that our Constitution is consistent with the Universal Declaration, which has been generally accepted as an international norm.'[95] Although theoretically the Sub-Commission was an expert body, where members served in their individual capacity and not as agents of their governments, in practice this distinction was blurred. The Sub-Commission allowed for an alternate member who was not elected but rather named by the government. When the Sub-Commission prepared its draft convention, the alternate member for the United States was an eminent African American lawyer,

---

[93] Brazil, Chile, Cyprus, Czechoslovakia, Ghana, Guinea, Lebanon, Liberia, Libya, Madagascar, Mali, Mauritania, Mongolia, Nigeria, Pakistan, Panama, Peru, Philippines, Uruguay, and Yugoslavia: draft resolution on the preparation of a draft international convention on the elimination of all forms of racial discrimination, 25 October 1963, A/C.3/L.1137/Add.1.

[94] Preparation of a draft international convention on the elimination of all forms of racial · discrimination, 20 November 1963, A/RES/1906 (XVII).

[95] 'Guidance Paper, Draft Convention on the Elimination of All Forms of Racial Discrimination', 7 January 1964, Abram Papers, Box 94, Folder 3, cited in H. Timothy Lovelace, Jr., 'Making the World in Atlanta's Image: The Student Nonviolent Coordinating Committee, Morris Abram, and the Legislative History of the United Nations Race Convention' (2014) 32 *Law and History Review* 385, at p. 401, fn. 52.

262 ELIMINATION OF ALL FORMS OF RACIAL DISCRIMINATION

Clyde Ferguson, then the Dean of the law school at Howard University. He stood in for Abram during a number of sessions of the Sub-Commission.[96]

At the outset of the discussions in 1964, Abram of the United States presented the Sub-Commission with a draft text,[97] as did the British member, Peter Calvocoressi.[98] The members from these two countries, with their long histories of racism and, in the case of Britain, colonialism, had set the bar as low as possible. Both of these initial drafts were extraordinarily short. They did not replicate many of the ideas that had been presented in the Declaration adopted only weeks earlier. They did not link the phenomenon of racial discrimination to colonialism, they overlooked General Assembly Resolution 1514, there was no reference to ideas of racial superiority, and they virtually ignored the issues of hate speech and racist organizations. Abram's text did not mention apartheid. Neither draft provided for any effective international mechanisms of implementation. After several sessions of discussion, the Polish and Soviet members of the Sub-Commission produced their own draft convention. This new version had a more exhaustive list of fundamental rights, a direct association of racism with colonialism, a rather elaborate definition of racial discrimination, and robust provisions on the suppression of hate speech and racist organizations.[99]

The debate about measures to deal with racial discrimination, including incitement and propaganda more generally, was the most controversial issue in the Sub-Commission. On this point, the drafts of Abram and Calvocoressi were at one end of the spectrum. Abram's text merely required States Parties to 'declare all incitement to racial hatred and discrimination resulting in or likely to cause acts of violence, whether by individuals or organizations, as an offence against society and punishable under law'.[100] Calvocoressi's was along the same lines: 'Within the territory of a Contracting State, it shall be an offence to commit, or to incite to commit, an act of violence against another person on the grounds of race, colour or ethnic origin.'[101] Imposition of such obligations was little more

---

[96] See Ferguson's account of some of the legal issues that arose during the drafting: Clarence Clyde Ferguson Jr, 'The United Nations Convention on Racial Discrimination: Civil Rights by Treaty' (1964) 1 *Law in Transition Quarterly* 61.

[97] Mr Abram: Suggested draft for United Nations Convention on the Elimination of All Forms of Racial Discrimination, 13 January 1964, E/CN.4/Sub.2/L.308. Abram later proposed some additions dealing with propaganda and incitement: Article IX, 13 January 1964k E/CN.4/Sub.2/L.308/Add.l; Article IX, 14 January 1964, E/CN.4/Sub.2/L.308/Add.l/Rev.1; Article IX, 14 January 1964, E/CN.4/Sub.2/L.308/Add.l/Rev.1/Corr.l.

[98] Mr Calvocoressi: Draft Convention on the Elimination of All Forms of Racial Discrimination, 13 January 1964, E/CN.4/Sub.2/L.309.

[99] Messrs Ivanov and Ketrzynski: Draft Convention on the Elimination of All Forms of Racial Discrimination, 15 January 1964, E/CN.4/Sub.2/L.314.

[100] Mr. Abram: Revised Suggested Draft for United Nations Convention on the Elimination of All Forms of Racial Discrimination, 13 January 1994, E/CN.4/Sub.2/L.308/Add.1, art. IX(1).

[101] Mr. Calvocoressi: Draft Convention on the Elimination of All Forms of Racial Discrimination, 13 January 1964, E/CN.4/Sub.2/L.309, art. II(3).

than empty rhetoric, given that most States, including the United States and the United Kingdom, already criminalized incitement of acts of violence regardless of the motive. Yet when Abram struggled to defend his proposal, he made the implausible claim that 'if his article had been incorporated in the substantive internal law of every state in the United States, racial discrimination would have been stamped out by now'.[102] Abram also told the Sub-Commission that in his opinion the State should not be given the power to prohibit or disband organizations practising racial discrimination.[103]

At the other end of the spectrum was the draft prepared by Ivanov and Ketrzynski, which imposed the following obligations on States Parties: 'to prohibit and disband racist, fascist and any other organisations practising or inciting to racial discrimination'; 'to admit no propaganda of any kind for the superiority of one race or national group over another, or any propaganda with a view to justifying or promoting racial discrimination in any form'; 'to consider all participation in the activity of such organisations . . . as well as incitement to or acts of violence against an individual or group of persons on the ground of their race, national or ethnic origin, a criminal offence . . . '[104] The ensuing debates in the Sub-Commission highlighted a profound dispute in international human rights law about the scope of permissible limitations on freedom of expression and freedom of association that has raged to the present day and on which there remains no consensus. The Sub-commission also consulted a draft convention prepared by Czechoslovakia in December 1962[105] and the generic non-discrimination treaties adopted by UNESCO and the International Labour Organisation.

In the course of the discussions within the Sub-Commission, some new ideas emerged that found their way into the final version of the Convention. There were early drafts of a text intended to exclude distinctions between citizens and non-citizens from the scope of racial discrimination.[106] The Sub-Commission also proposed, as a means of implementation, the establishment of a Fact-Finding and Conciliation Committee, a concept inspired by the Protocol to the UNESCO Convention on Discrimination in Education.[107]

[102] Summary record, Sub-Commission on the Prevention of Discrimination and the Protection of Minorities, 21 January 1964, E/CN.4/Sub.2/SR.417, p. 11.

[103] Summary record, Sub-Commission on the Prevention of Discrimination and the Protection of Minorities, 21 January 1964, E/CN.4/Sub.2/SR.418, p. 4.

[104] Messrs Ivanov and Ketrzynski: Draft Convention on the Elimination of All Forms of Racial Discrimination, 15 January 1964, E/CN.4/Sub.2/L.314, art. II.

[105] Czechoslovakia: working paper concerning a draft International Convention on the Elimination of Racial Discrimination, 7 December 1962, E/CN.4/Sub.2/234, Annex IV, pp. 2–5.

[106] Report of the 16th Session of the Sub-Commission on the Prevention of Discrimination and the Protection of Minorities, 11 February 1964, E/CN.4/Sub.2/241, paras. 103–11.

[107] Mr. Ingles: Proposed Measures of Implementation, E/CN.4/Sub.2/L.321; Report of the 16th session, Sub-Commission on the Prevention of Discrimination and the Protection of Minorities, E/CN.4/Sub.2/241, paras. 120–2.

264 ELIMINATION OF ALL FORMS OF RACIAL DISCRIMINATION

The Sub-Commission adopted a text consisting of a substantial preamble and 10 articles. With rare exceptions, the provisions were reached by consensus. Nevertheless, a vote was taken on the article dealing with incitement. A provision close to the position proposed by Abram and Calvocoressi was adopted by seven to two, presumably the votes of Ivanov and Ketrzynski, and two abstentions.[108] Assessing the work of the Sub-Commission on the draft convention, the Department of State praised Abram's 'good work' in restraining the provision on hate speech.[109] A second document, setting out detailed provisions for a Committee and entitled 'Additional measures of implementation', was also adopted. It was presented more tentatively, mainly because the Sub-Commission had given no more than summary attention to the text.[110]

The 1964 Sub-Commission session was punctuated by the most curious of incidents. Morris Abram organised a visit for its members to Atlanta on the final weekend of the January session. Although privately funded, it had the blessing of the Department of State. Abram hoped that the trip might strengthen his hand in the debates on the draft Convention, where he was fighting an uphill battle against proposals to require the criminalization of hate speech and racist organizations. In his memoirs, Abram made the preposterous claim that despite America's problems, 'we were without fault compared to the rest of the world'. He said he was 'keenly aware that I was representing the only great power that stands for human rights'.[111] The previous year he had cancelled a similar trip at the last minute because of a crisis provoked by racist measures of the municipal government. According to the principal academic study of the visit, '[f]rom the moment the Sub-Commission arrived in Atlanta on Friday evening, elite black Atlantans, handpicked from Abram's personal rolodex, used their world stage to offer crass endorsements of the city's race relations and the views Abram expressed during formal Sub-Commission meetings'.[112] But his best laid plans could not prevent demonstrators, organized by the Student Non-Violent Coordinating Committee. Placards reading 'Atlanta's image is a fraud' and 'Welcome to Atlanta, a Segregated City' greeted members of the Sub-Commission when they arrived at

---

[108] Summary record, Sub-Commission on the Prevention of Discrimination and the Protection of Minorities, 23 January 1964, E/CN.4/Sub.2/SR.422, p. 13. Ketrzynski declared he would vote against the text. The compromise was based upon Morris Abram's proposal: Mr. Abram: amendment to the Working Paper submitted by Mr. Cuevas Cancino and Mr. Ingles (E/CN.4/Sub.2/L.330), E/CN.4/Sub.2/L.332.

[109] Information Memorandum from the Assistant Secretary of State for International Organization Affairs (Cleveland) to Secretary of State Rusk, 20 March 1964, FRUS 1964–1968 XXXIV.

[110] Report of the 16th Session of the Sub-Commission on the Prevention of Discrimination and the Protection of Minorities, 11 February 1964, E/CN.4/Sub.2/241, para. 123.

[111] Morris Abram, *The Day is Short: An Autobiography*, New York: Harcourt Brace Jovanovich, 1982, pp. 150–1.

[112] H. Timothy Lovelace, Jr., 'Making the World in Atlanta's Image: The Student Nonviolent Coordinating Committee, Morris Abram, and the Legislative History of the United Nations Race Convention' (2014) 32 *Law and History Review* 385, at p. 412.

the airport.[113] Hooded Ku Klux Klansmen attacked the student demonstrators. At the insistence of members of the Sub-Commission, an impromptu meeting with the students took place.[114] 'You have a big problem', said one member of the Sub-Commission at the press conference that concluded the trip.[115] The events in Atlanta that weekend received wide international media coverage.[116]

The Commission on Human Rights debated the draft convention over the course of more than 40 sessions. The changes it made to the Sub-Commission text were relatively minor. The Commission's draft was shorter than that of the Sub-Commission. A provision requiring States to prohibit racial discrimination in their constitutions was dropped.[117] The Sub-Commission provision sheltering distinctions based upon 'national origin' was challenged.[118] The words were placed in square brackets, indicating that there was no agreement, along with a new sentence specifying that the term 'does not cover the status of any person as a citizen of a given State'.[119]

Paragraph 1 of the preamble was also modified in response to objections to the assertion in the Sub-Commission text that the Charter of the United Nations 'imposes on all Members of the United Nations the obligations to ensure, promote and encourage universal respect for, and observance of, human rights and fundamental freedoms for all'. This prompted a very striking exchange of views about whether the Charter imposed any obligations at all in the field of human rights.[120] Several States seized the occasion to insist that it did not. The British delegate, Samuel Hoare, said that if it was really correct to say the Charter imposed such obligations, then drafting a convention on racial discrimination was an entirely superfluous exercise.[121] Challenging a contention of the Ukrainian delegate that the Universal Declaration of Human Rights imposed obligations upon States, France's representative argued that it was actually addressed to ' "every individual and every organ of society", and not to States; and those individuals and organs were asked to "strive by teaching and education ... and by progressive measures" to secure universal observance of human rights, which was quite

---

[113] Ibid., p. 410.

[114] Ibid., p. 415.

[115] 'African Says U.S. Race Situation a Big Problem', *Los Angeles Times*, 27 January 1964, p. 16.

[116] See, for example, the British Pathé newsreel 'USA: Racial Demonstrators Arrested In Georgia', available at https://www.britishpathe.com/video/VLVAAN3AAQ2OZKSJ24WDXFPEOXDOB-USA-RACIAL-DEMONSTRATORS-ARRESTED-IN-GEORGIA/query/ARRESTED. For a survey of the international media on the visit, see H. Timothy Lovelace, Jr., 'Making the World in Atlanta's Image: The Student Nonviolent Coordinating Committee, Morris Abram, and the Legislative History of the United Nations Race Convention' (2014) 32 *Law and History Review* 385, at pp. 418–20.

[117] Commission on Human Rights, Report on the 20th Session, 17 February-18 March 1964, E/3873, paras. 257–70.

[118] Ibid., paras. 238–56.

[119] Ibid., paras. 71–101.

[120] Ibid., paras. 43–7.

[121] Summary record, Commission on Human Rights, 18 February 1964, E/CN. 4/SR.775, p. 11.

266 ELIMINATION OF ALL FORMS OF RACIAL DISCRIMINATION

different from being obliged to ensure immediate observance everywhere'.[122] Lebanon, the Philippines, and India came up with a viable compromise text, based upon the wording in articles 1(3) and 55 of the Charter. It declared that Members of the United Nations 'have pledged themselves to take joint and separate action in co-operation with the Organisation for the achievement of one of the purposes of the United Nations which is to promote and encourage universal respect for and observance of human rights and fundamental freedoms for all without distinction as to race, sex, language or religion'.[123] A reference elsewhere in the preamble to 'evil racial doctrines and practices of nazism in the past' was changed with the removal of a reference to 'nazism' after France requested a separate vote on use of the term.[124]

One of the core obligations involved a requirement that States prevent racial discrimination in the private sphere. The Sub-Commission provision read as follows: 'Each State Party shall prohibit racial discrimination by any person, group or organisation, and undertakes to adopt all necessary measures, including legislation, if appropriate.' In the Commission, the United Kingdom submitted a revised text that removed the word 'prohibit',[125] leading to considerable controversy. Defending the amendment, the British representative said that he thought the Sub-Commission's text would require adoption of legislation to make racial discrimination a criminal offence.[126] Turkey came up with an acceptable compromise text that retained the word 'prohibit'[127] and that corresponds to the text in the final version of the Convention.

As the Commission on Human Rights session was concluding, the United States proposed addition of a new article specifically addressed to anti-Semitism.[128] The Soviets reacted with an amendment replacing the reference to anti-Semitism with 'nazism, including all its new manifestations (neo-nazism), genocide, anti-Semitism'.[129] The American representative said the Soviet amendment 'tended to minimize the urgency of the question and to suggest that anti-Semitism was not a matter of immediate and basic concern'.[130] The argument of

[122] Summary record, Commission on Human Rights, 19 February 1964, E/CN. 4/SR.778, p. 5.
[123] India, Lebanon and Philippines: revised amendment to document E/CN.4/873, para. 119, resolution I (XVI), annex, E/CN.4/L.686/Rev.l; Summary record, Commission on Human Rights, 21 February 1964, E/CN. 4/SR.781, p. 9.
[124] Summary record, Commission on Human Rights, 21 February 1964, E/CN. 4/SR.782, pp. 4–6; Summary record, Commission on Human Rights, 25 February 1964, E/CN. 4/SR.784, pp. 4–7.
[125] United Kingdom: amendment to document E/CN.4/873, E/CN.4/L.689.
[126] Summary record, Commission on Human Rights, 27 February 1964, E/CN.4/SR.788, pp. 4–5.
[127] Ibid., pp. 4–10; Commission on Human Rights, Report on the 20th Session, 17 February-18 March 1964, E/3873, paras. 120–3.
[128] United States of America: revised amendment to document E/CN.4/873, para. 119, resolution I (XVI), annex, E/CN.4/L.701/Rev.2. See Commission on Human Rights, Report on the 20th Session, 17 February-18 March 1964, E/3873, paras. 271–80.
[129] Union of Soviet Socialist Republics: revised sub-amendment to the revised amendment of the United States of America (E/CN.4/L.701/Rev.1), E/CN.4/L.710/Rev.l.
[130] Summary record, Third Committee, 12 March 1964, E/CN.4/SR.807, p. 6.

urgency was not very convincing. The United States referred to the 1960 work of the Sub-Commission. But if the need was so imperative, why had this not occurred to the United States earlier, during drafting of the Declaration or in the more recent work of the Sub-Commission on the convention? Speaking in support of the Americans, the representative of Israel spoke of an anti-Semitic book published in the Soviet Union recently containing caricatures said to be reminiscent of Nazi publications.[131] After various views were expressed, the Commission welcomed India's observation that a hasty decision should not be taken and that it would be better to forward the matter to the Third Committee.[132]

Adopting the Convention

The General Assembly did not consider the Convention at its 1964 session. In 1965, between October and December, the Third Committee of the Assembly devoted 43 meetings to the Convention. The Third Committee decided not to have a general debate but rather to proceed article-by-article to discuss the draft adopted by the Commission along with the related amendments. Then it shifted gears, debating the issue of anti-Semitism that had been raised by the American delegation at the end of the Commission session earlier in the year. The issue was framed by a proposal, from Greece and Hungary, that the Committee decide not to include reference to 'specific forms of racial discrimination'.[133] The voting revealed the fault lines in the Assembly. The result was 82 in favour, 12 opposed, and 10 abstentions. All of the African and Asian countries voted for the resolution, with the exception of China and Côte d'Ivoire, which abstained, along with Haiti. Australia, Austria, Belgium, Bolivia, Brazil, Canada, Israel, Luxembourg, the Netherlands, the United Kingdom, the United States, and Uruguay voted against.[134] The Committee then returned to its article-by-article review of the text. The main addition to the text concerned the measures of implementation, an important issue that had been left unresolved by the Commission.

The text of the Convention was adopted by the General Assembly on 21 December 1995 in a roll call vote that was virtually unanimous.[135] Mexico abstained although it later said it wished to be included in the list of those who voted in favour. Ten Member States did not vote: Albania, Cambodia, Central

---

[131] Ibid., p. 12.
[132] Summary record, Third Committee, 12 March 1964, E/CN.4/SR.808, pp. 14–15; Commission on Human Rights, Report on the 20th Session, 17 February–18 March 1964, E/3873, para. 276.
[133] Greece and Hungary: draft resolution, 20 October 1965, A/C.3/L.1244.
[134] Ibid., para. 35. See also Report of the Third Committee, 18 December 1965, A/6181, paras. 7–11.
[135] Verbatim record, plenary General Assembly, 21 December 1965, A/PV.1406, para. 60; International Convention on the Elimination of All Forms of Racial Discrimination, 21 December 1965, A/RES/2106 (XX) A.

268 ELIMINATION OF ALL FORMS OF RACIAL DISCRIMINATION

African Republic, Ecuador, Gambia, Malawi, Malta, Nicaragua, Singapore, and South Africa. Ghana described the Convention as an 'infant step', saying it hoped that in a few years it would be subject to revision 'and a more effective instrument adopted'.[136] Haiti said the text was 'reasonably reassuring' but added that it still had 'some misgivings'.[137] Prior to the vote in the plenary General Assembly, an amendment adding an article authorizing reservations under limited circumstances was accepted by a very large majority.[138] A companion resolution provided General Assembly support to article 15 of the Convention by which the Committee on the Elimination of Racial Discrimination was empowered to examine petitions directed to the United Nations from colonial countries.[139] In effect, this gave the Committee jurisdiction over colonialist States even if they were not parties to the Convention.

The Convention was opened for signature and ratification or accession on 9 March 1966. Before the year was out, 47 States had signed the treaty. On 8 September 1966, Ghana became the first State to ratify the Convention. According to article 19, 27 ratifications or accessions were required for entry into force. That threshold was reached on 4 January 1969. As of 1 November 2022, the Convention had 182 States parties. Most of those who have yet to ratify the Convention are very small States with limited resources who indicate no issue of principle. Of the handful of larger States that are not parties, North Korea and Malaysia have manifested their intent to ratify or accede to the treaty.[140] Only Myanmar shows reluctance.[141]

The title of the International Convention on the Elimination of All Forms of Racial Discrimination can be traced to the 1962 General Assembly resolution proposed by nine African States.[142]

The preamble of the Convention went through a number of permutations from its origins in short drafts submitted to the Sub-Commission by several of

---

[136] Verbatim record, plenary General Assembly, 21 December 1946, A/PV.1406, para. 93.

[137] Ibid., para. 80.

[138] Verbatim record. plenary General Assembly, 21 December 1965, A/PV.1406, para. 57.

[139] International Convention on the Elimination of All Forms of Racial Discrimination, 21 December 1965, A/RES/2106 (XX) B.

[140] Democratic People's Republic of Korea, Views on conclusions and/or recommendations, voluntary commitments and replies presented by the State under review, 28 August 2019, A/HRC/42/10/Add.1, para. 9(a); Malaysia, Views on conclusions and/or recommendations, voluntary commitments and replies presented by the State under review, 18 February 2019, A/HRC/40/11/Add.1, para. 9.

[141] Myanmar has 'accepted in principle' recommendations that it ratify the Convention. See Myanmar, Views on conclusions and/or recommendations, voluntary commitments and replies presented by the State under review, 10 March 2016, A/HRC/31/13/Add.1, para. 7.

[142] Manifestations of racial prejudice and national and religious intolerance, preparation of an international convention on the elimination of racial discrimination, Central African Republic, Chad, Dahomey, Guinea, Ivory Coast, Mali, Mauritania, Niger, and Upper Volta, draft resolution, 25 October 1962, A/C.3/L.1006, OP 1; Preparation of a draft declaration and a draft convention on the elimination of all forms of racial discrimination, 7 December 1962, A/RES/1780 (XVII), OP 1.

its members.[143] The first two paragraphs are drawn from the Sub-Commission draft. They reference the Charter of the United Nations and the Universal Declaration of Human Rights. The third paragraph on equality before the law and equal protection of the law was added in the third Committee. It is derived from article 7 of the Universal Declaration. Preambular paragraph 4 links racial discrimination to colonialism, referring to General Assembly Resolution 1514 (XV). It too originated in the Sub-Commission. Paragraph 5 invokes the Declaration on the Elimination of All Forms of Racial Discrimination adopted by the General Assembly in 1963. Although the text can be traced to the Sub-Commission draft, the reference to human dignity was added by the Third Committee. Paragraph 6, drawn from the Sub-Commission draft, condemns doctrines of racial superiority. Paragraph 7 describes discrimination as an obstacle to friendly and peaceful relations among nations. A reference to Nazism in the Sub-Commission draft was removed by the Commission and never restored. Preambular paragraph 8 was added by the Third Committee: 'Convinced that the existence of racial barriers is repugnant to the ideals of any human society'. Paragraph 9 notes the persistence of racism 'in some areas of the world', referring specifically to apartheid. The drafts of the Sub-Commission and the Commission began with the word 'Concerned'. The Third Committee changed this to 'Alarmed'. In paragraph 10, the States parties resolve to adopt all necessary measures to prevent and combat racial discrimination. It originated in the Commission and was reinforced in the Third Committee with the idea of promotion of 'understanding between races'. The final paragraphs refer to the UNESCO and International Labour Organisation conventions and, once again, to the General Assembly Declaration of 1963.

In its 2021 judgment in the *Qatar v. United Arab Emirates* case, the International Court of Justice discussed the preamble of the Convention. It said that by underlining that 'any doctrine of superiority based on racial differentiation is scientifically false, morally condemnable, socially unjust and dangerous, and that there is no justification for racial discrimination, in theory or in practice, anywhere', the preamble clearly set out the object and purpose of the Convention. The Court said this was 'to bring to an end all practices that seek to establish a hierarchy among social groups as defined by their inherent characteristics or to impose a system of racial discrimination or segregation'. Basing itself on these provisions of the preamble, the Court concluded that the aim of the Convention was 'to eliminate all forms and manifestations of racial discrimination against

---

[143] For the debates in the Sub-Commission, see Report of the 16th Session of the Sub-Commission on the Prevention of Discrimination and the Protection of Minorities, 11 February 1964, E/CN.4/Sub.2/241, paras. 31–40. Also, Patrick Thornberry, *The International Convention on the Elimination of All Forms of Racial Discrimination, A Commentary*, Oxford: Oxford University Press, 2016, pp. 75–96.

human beings on the basis of real or perceived characteristics as of their origin, namely at birth'.[144] Dissenting judges also relied upon the preamble to support a broad and purposive interpretation of article 1.[145]

The Committee on the Elimination of All Forms of Racial Discrimination has made reference to the link between racial discrimination and the maintenance of friendly and peaceful relations among nations in its admissibility decision in the *Palestine v. Israel* case.[146] The Committee has also invoked the preambular reference to equality before the law and equal protection of the law in the context of racial profiling.[147]

Racial discrimination is defined in article 1 of the Convention. This central provision has provoked intense dispute as to its scope. In 2021, the International Court of Justice was quite dramatically split on the issue, with judges of the Global South generally favourable to a broad construction of the provision. However, they were in the minority. Paragraph 1 of article 1 states that 'racial discrimination' refers to 'any distinction, exclusion, restriction or preference based on race, colour, descent, or national or ethnic origin'. Inspired by article 2(1) of the Universal Declaration of Human Rights, it was somewhat challenged in the Commission on Human Rights where the term 'national' was placed in square brackets, indicating a lack of agreement on its inclusion. In an additional sentence, also in square brackets, the Commission provision stated that '[In this paragraph the expression 'national origin' does not cover the status of any person as a citizen of a given State.][148] The Third Committee opted to return to the original version of the Sub-Commission, thereby removing the square brackets, but added two new paragraphs in order to address the difficulty. Paragraph 2 of article 1 of the Convention states that it 'shall not apply to distinctions, exclusions, restrictions or preferences made by a State Party to this Convention between citizens and non-citizens'. Paragraph 3 says '[n]othing in this Convention may be interpreted as affecting in any way the legal provisions of States Parties concerning nationality, citizenship or naturalization, provided that such provisions do not discriminate against any particular nationality'.[149] The term 'descent' was added in the Third Committee on a proposal from India.[150]

---

[144] *Application of the International Convention on the Elimination of All Forms of Racial Discrimination (Qatar v. United Arab Emirates), Preliminary Objections, Judgment, I.C.J. Reports 2021*, p. 71, para. 86.

[145] Ibid., Separate opinion of Judge Iwasawa, 4 February 2021, paras. 32, 49; ibid., Dissenting opinion of Judge Bhandari, paras. 12–14.

[146] *Palestine v. Israel*, Jurisdiction decision, 12 December 2019, CERD/C/100/5, para. 3.35.

[147] General recommendation 36 on preventing and combating racial profiling by law enforcement officials, 17 December 2020, CERD/C/GC/36, para. 22.

[148] Commission on Human Rights, Report on the 20th Session, 17 February-18 March 1964, E/3873, paras. 71–86, 95, 99–101.

[149] Report of the Third Committee, 18 December 1965, A/6181, paras. 28–37.

[150] India: amendments to the provisions of the draft international convention on the elimination of all forms of racial discrimination adopted by the Commission on Human Rights, 11 October 1965,

According to Egon Schwelb, writing at the time the Convention was adopted, '[f]or the practical purposes of the interpretation of the Convention of 1965 the three terms "descent", "national origin" and "ethnic origin" among them cover distinctions both on the ground of present or previous "nationality" in the ethnographical sense and on the ground of previous nationality in the "politico-legal" sense of citizenship'.[151] In February 2021, in *Qatar v. United Arab Emirates*, a majority of the International Court of Justice concluded that the *travaux préparatoires* indicate an intent to exclude discrimination based on current nationality from the scope of the Convention.[152] Several of the judges from the Global South – India, Uganda, Jamaica, Somalia, Japan – issued individual dissenting opinions that argued for a more expansive understanding of 'racial discrimination'.[153] The majority ruling is at odds with the interpretation of the Convention adopted by the Committee on the Elimination of Racial Discrimination, as the majority judgment conceded.[154] In General Recommendation 30, the Committee concluded that 'differential treatment based on citizenship or immigration status will constitute discrimination if the criteria for such differentiation, judged in the light of the objectives and purposes of the Convention, are not applied pursuant to a legitimate aim, and are not proportional to the achievement of this aim'.[155] It applied the interpretation in ruling on admissibility in the interstate communications filed by Qatar against the United Arab Emirates and Saudi Arabia.[156]

The definition in article 1 makes no distinction between direct or intentional discrimination and what has sometimes been called indirect or 'effects'

A/C.3/L.1216, paras. 33. See David Keane, 'Descent-based Discrimination in International Law: A Legal History' (2005) 2 *International Journal on Minority and Group Rights* 93.

[151] Egon Schwelb, 'The International Convention on the Elimination of All Forms of Racial Discrimination' (1966) 15 *International and Comparative Law Quarterly* 996, at p. 1007.

[152] *Application of the International Convention on the Elimination of All Forms of Racial Discrimination (Qatar v. United Arab Emirates), Preliminary Objections, Judgment, I.C.J. Reports 2021*, p. 71, para. 97. See also *Application of the International Convention on the Elimination of All Forms of Racial Discrimination (Qatar v. United Arab Emirates), Provisional Measures, Order of 23 July 2018, I.C.J. Reports 2018*, p. 406, Separate opinion of Judges Tomka, Gaja and Gevorgian; ibid., Dissenting opinion of Judge Crawford, para. 1; ibid., Dissenting opinion of Judge Salam.

[153] *Application of the International Convention on the Elimination of All Forms of Racial Discrimination (Qatar v. United Arab Emirates), Preliminary Objections, Judgment, I.C.J. Reports 2021*, p. 71, Declaration of President Yusef; ibid., Dissenting opinion of Judge Sebutinde; ibid., Dissenting opinion of Judge Bhandari; ibid., Dissenting opinion of Judge Robinson; ibid., Dissenting opinion of Judge Iwasawa. Note the comment of Geir Ulfstein: 'It is striking that among the six dissenting judges, five come from former colonies (Yusuf, Cançado Trindade, Sebutinde, Bhandary [sic], and Robinson), whereas the sixth is Japanese (Iwasawa). Geir Ulfstein, 'Qatar v. United Arab Emirates' (2022) *American Journal of International Law* 397, at p. 401.

[154] Ibid., paras. 100–1.

[155] General recommendation 30 on discrimination against non-citizens, 5 August 2004, A/59/18, p. 93, para. 4.

[156] *Qatar v. United Arab Emirates*, Admissibility decision, 27 August 2019, CERD/C/99/4, paras. 53–63; *Qatar v. Saudi Arabia*, Admissibility decision, 27 August 2019, CERD/C/99/6, paras. 10–19.

discrimination. Judge Crawford of the International Court of Justice has explained that article 1 'does not require that the restriction in question be based expressly on racial or other grounds enumerated in the definition; it is enough that it directly implicates such a group on one or more of these grounds. Moreover, whatever the stated purpose of the restriction, it may constitute racial discrimination if it has the "effect" of impairing the enjoyment or exercise, on an equal footing, of the rights articulated in CERD.[157]

References to Apartheid and Anti-Semitism

By article 3, the shortest in the Convention, 'States Parties particularly condemn racial segregation and apartheid and undertake to prevent, prohibit and eradicate all practices of this nature in territories under their jurisdiction'. The source is the draft prepared by Morris Abram of the United States for the 1964 session of the Sub-Commission.[158] The final version corresponds to the text adopted by the Sub-Commission, but with the words 'in territories under their jurisdiction', which was added by the Commission along with a preambular reference to apartheid.[159] In his analysis of the Convention, Egon Schwelb said article 3 added nothing in terms of substantive obligations, and that even if it were not included States Parties would be under the obligation to prohibit, to bring to an end, and to eliminate racial segregation.[160] At a minimum, although it might have been legally superfluous the reference to apartheid was very important for many of the delegates. Patrick Thornberry has pointed out that [b]ecause of the centrality to the historical siting of the Convention as part of an anti-colonial project', many States have difficulty in the application of article 3 to their own internal situation.[161] Referring to implementation of article 3 in 2004, the Committee on the Elimination of Racial Discrimination said 'many States interpret the scope of the Article as directed exclusively to apartheid in South Africa and fail to examine whether forms of de facto racial segregation are occurring on their own territory.

---

[157] *Application of the International Convention for the Suppression of the Financing of Terrorism and of the International Convention on the Elimination of All Forms of Racial Discrimination (Ukraine v. Russian Federation), Provisional Measures, Order of 19 April 2017, I.C.J. Reports 2017*, p. 104, Declaration of Judge Crawford, para. 7.

[158] Mr Abram: Suggested draft for United Nations Convention on the Elimination of All Forms of Racial Discrimination, 13 January 1964, E/CN.4/Sub.2/L.308, art. III(2).

[159] Provisions of the Draft International Convention on the Elimination of All Forms of Racial Discrimination adopted by the Commission at its twentieth session, E/3873, Annex I, art. III.

[160] Egon Schwelb, 'The International Convention on the Elimination of All Forms of Racial Discrimination' (1966) 15 *International and Comparative Law Quarterly* 996, at p. 1021.

[161] Patrick Thornberry, *The International Convention on the Elimination of All Forms of Racial Discrimination, A Commentary*, Oxford: Oxford University Press, 2016, p. 261.

REFERENCES TO APARTHEID AND ANTI-SEMITISM   273

Segregation, as defined in Article 3 of the Convention, still occurs in various forms in a number of States, in particular in housing and education.'[162]

Abram's draft in the Sub-Commission made no reference to anti-Semitism. The only mention of the issue during the Sub-Commission's 1964 session arose when Israel's observer took the floor to make general comments in which he alluded to a statement by Bertrand Russell about Soviet newspapers that 'expressed that country's hostility towards the Jewish people'. Inevitably, this provoked an angry response from the Russian member, Boris Ivanov.[163] It was only in the Commission, which met later in 1964, that the United States decided to revive the issue, an initiative of its delegate, Marietta Tree. An internal report indicates that while the United States was 'not opposed' to the draft convention but it was hardly enthusiastic.[164] The United States and Brazil came up with the following: 'States Parties condemn anti-Semitism and shall take action as appropriate for its speedy eradication in the territories subject to their jurisdiction.'[165] Israel pointed to the adoption of article 3, which condemned apartheid, contending that anti-Semitism should be treated in the same way.[166] 'Implicitly', as Orla Friesel has written, the initiative 'embodied a censure of the Soviet Union'.[167] The United States was weaponizing the anti-Semitism issue in pursuit of its Cold War agenda directed against the Soviet Union.[168]

The Soviet Union responded with an amendment to the proposal of the United States and Brazil: 'States Parties condemn anti-Semitism, Zionism, Nazism, neo-Nazism and all other forms of the policy and ideology of colonialism, national and race hatred and exclusiveness and shall take action as appropriate for the speedy eradication of those inhuman ideas and practices in the territories subject to their jurisdiction.'[169] Speaking in the Third Committee, the Soviet

---

[162] Views of the Committee on the Elimination of Racial Discrimination on the Implementation of the International Convention on the Elimination of All Forms of Racial Discrimination and its Effectiveness, 17 September 2004, E/CN.4/WG.21/10.

[163] Summary record, Sub-Commission on Prevention of Discrimination and Protection of Minorities, 20 January 1964, E/CN.4/Sub.2/SR.416, pp. 9–10.

[164] Information Memorandum from the Assistant Secretary of State for International Organization Affairs (Cleveland) to Secretary of State Rusk, 20 March 1964, FRUS 1964–1968 XXXIV, doc. 315.

[165] Brazil and the United States: amendments to the provisions of the draft international convention on the elimination of all forms of racial discrimination adopted by the Commission on Human Rights (A/5921, annex), 8 October 1965, A/C.3/L.1211.

[166] Summary record, Third Committee, 20 October 1965, A/C.3/SR.1312, para. 5.

[167] Ofra Friesel, 'Equating Zionism with Racism: The 1965 Precedent' (2013) 97 *American Jewish History* 283, at p. 287.

[168] Nathan A. Kurz, *Jewish Internationalism and Human Rights after the Holocaust*, Cambridge: Cambridge University Press, 2021, pp. 128–32; Ofra Friesel, 'Race versus Religion in the Making of the International Convention against Racial Discrimination, 1965' (2014) 32 *Law and History Review* 351, at pp. 353–4; Ofra Friesel, 'Equating Zionism with Racism: The 1965 Precedent' (2013) 97 *American Jewish History* 283, at pp. 294–5.

[169] Draft international convention on the elimination of all forms of racial discrimination: USSR: amendment to the amendment of Brazil and the United States (A/C.3/L.1211), 13 October 1965, A/C.3/L.1231.

274 ELIMINATION OF ALL FORMS OF RACIAL DISCRIMINATION

representative said that the Convention must condemn and prohibit all forms of racial discrimination, 'all of which were equally dangerous; nazism and fascism were quite as dangerous as apartheid, and Zionism as anti-Semitism'.[170] Israel's representative promptly replied that mentioning Zionism in the same context as Nazism 'would be sacrilegious and tantamount to substituting the victims for the persecutors'.[171] This was the first skirmish in a controversy that would play a big role in United Nations action on racial discrimination for many years to come.[172] Egon Schwelb wrote of the 'provocative and politically loaded' position of the Soviet Union.[173] Yet the record suggests that if there was provocation, it came from Israel and the United States.

During the debate in the Third Committee, speakers favouring a reference to anti-Semitism tended to insist on the uniqueness of the problem, to the exclusion of all others. In its explanation of vote, the United States delegate described anti-Semitism as 'one of the gravest and most persistent problems facing Humanity'. He pointed to 'the explosion of anti-Semitism which the world had witnessed in 1959'.[174] But this needs to be put into perspective. The 'wave of anti-Semitism' that began in Germany and then spread to many countries consisted very largely of attacks on property rather than on persons. A report by the US-based Bnai Brith was entitled '*The Epidemic of anti-Semitic Vandalism in America*'.[175] A contemporary academic account referred to 'the relatively innocuous but highly visible and patently illegal character of the individual acts'.[176] The painting of swastikas on synagogues and desecration of cemeteries in 1959 and 1960 was appalling but governments moved promptly to address this. As for the Soviet Union, the persecution was part of a broader policy promoting secularism that applied to many other groups. An internal United States memorandum on the subject highlighted restrictions on the baking of matzoh bread, saying these had been relaxed since the fall of Khrushchev.[177] During the same period, there was a serious death toll in South Africa, of which the killing of 69 Black people at Sharpeville stands out. Several States in Africa remained subject to colonialism or, as in Southern Rhodesia, a white racist settler regime. There was also terrible racist violence in the United States itself in the years while the Convention

[170] Summary record, Third Committee, 12 October 1965, A/C.3/SR.1302, para. 3.
[171] Ibid., para. 7.
[172] See *infra*, pp. 356–359.
[173] Egon Schwelb, 'The International Convention on the Elimination of All Forms of Racial Discrimination' (1966) 15 *International and Comparative Law Quarterly* 996, at p. 1013.
[174] Summary record, Third Committee, 20 October 1965, A/C.3/SR.1312, para. 45.
[175] David Caplovitz and Candace Rogers, *Swastika 1960: The Epidemic of anti-Semitic Vandalism in America*, New York: Anti-Defamation League of B'nai B'rith, 1961.
[176] See Howard J. Ehrlich, 'The Swastika Epidemic of 1959–1960: Anti-Semitism and Community Characteristics' (1962) 9 *Social Problems* 264.
[177] Memorandum From Harold Saunders of the National Security Council Staff to the President's Special Assistant for National Security Affairs (Bundy), 5 October 1965, FRUS 1964–1968, XIV.

RACIST PROPAGANDA AND ORGANIZATIONS   275

was being negotiated, like the bomb attack that killed four girls in Birmingham, Alabama in 1963, and the murder of three civil rights workers, James Chaney, Michael Schwerner, and Andrew Goodman, in Mississippi in 1964. Although there were obvious historic cases of appalling anti-Semitism, its manifestations in the 1960s could not be reasonably compared with the violent atrocities to which people of African descent were subject.

The Afro-Asian group urged the United States and Brazil to drop their proposal on anti-Semitism. If this were done, the delegations with other proposals, notably the Soviets, had agreed that they would withdraw their amendments as well. However, the United States stubbornly insisted on a vote.[178] A brief debate followed, in which Greece, Hungary, France, and Ireland all expressed concerns about references to specific situations of racial discrimination.[179] Greece and Hungary proposed a resolution, rather than an amendment to the draft, by which 'any reference to specific forms of racial discrimination' would be excluded from the Convention.[180] Hungary made it clear that this did not affect the provision on apartheid, which had already been adopted by the Third Committee.[181] One of the States that opposed the resolution, the Netherlands, warned that support for the resolution 'might have been interpreted as a refusal to condemn anti-Semitism, or at least as a mark of indifference' and explained that it did not wish 'to minimise the magnitude of the scourge'.[182] After a relatively brief but very rancorous exchange about Zionism, Ghana called for a vote on the resolution of Greece and Hungary. It was adopted by 82 votes to 12, with 10 abstentions.[183]

Racist Propaganda and Organizations

The provision dealing with racist propaganda, incitement, and organizations, article 4 of the Convention, was the most controversial. A weak text in the Sub-Commission draft was further damaged in the Commission, only to be reinvigorated in the Third Committee of the General Assembly where the States of the Global South were strongest. Article 4 consists of an introductory paragraph stating a general principle followed by three paragraphs that contemplate specific aspects of the issue. The introductory paragraph requires States Parties to 'condemn all propaganda and all organisations which are based on ideas or theories of superiority of one race or group of persons of one colour or ethnic

---

[178] Summary record, Third Committee, 20 October 1965, A/C.3/SR.1311, paras. 1–5.
[179] Ibid., paras. 6–16.
[180] Ibid., para. 24. Proposed orally, it was later submitted as document: Greece and Hungary: draft resolution, 20 October 1965, A/C.3/L.1244.
[181] Summary record, Third Committee, 20 October 1965, A/C.3/SR.1311, para. 31.
[182] Summary record, Third Committee, 20 October 1965, A/C.3/SR.1312, para. 55.
[183] Ibid., para. 35.

276 ELIMINATION OF ALL FORMS OF RACIAL DISCRIMINATION

origin, or which attempt to justify or promote racial hatred and discrimination in any form'. Moreover, they are to 'undertake to adopt immediate and positive measures designed to eradicate all incitement to, or acts of, such discrimination'. The paragraphs that follow deal with punishment of hate speech including incitement, the outlawing of racist organizations, and the prohibition of racist incitement by public bodies.

On the issue of incitement, the Sub-Commission text required that States Parties make it an offence punishable by law to the extent that it resulted in or was likely to cause acts of violence. The Commission removed the words 'likely to cause' which further weakened the provision, adopting the following text: 'Shall declare an offence punishable by law all incitement to racial discrimination resulting in acts of violence, as well as all acts of violence or incitement to such acts against any race or group of persons of another colour or ethnic origin'.[184] A Soviet proposal to add the words 'and all other propaganda activities' following the word 'organised', so that the text required prohibition of racist propaganda that was not the work of organizations, was defeated.[185] The final compromise within the plenary General Assembly with respect to article 9 of the 1963 Declaration, one that had permitted the entire Declaration to be adopted unanimously, employed the phrase 'promote or incite to'. Western States had struggled, but without success, to change 'or' to 'and', which significantly narrowed the scope. The Sub-Commission text of the draft convention reverted to 'promote and incite'. In the Commission, the Soviet Union campaigned, unsuccessfully, for a text that was consistent with article 9 of the Declaration.[186] Nine of the 12 that voted for 'and' were from Europe and North America. The Philippines was the only State from Africa and Asia to vote for 'and' rather than 'or'.[187] India's delegate pointed out that the rejection of 'or' made the Commission's draft weaker than both the Declaration of the General Assembly and the draft of the Sub-Commission.[188]

In the Third Committee, Nigeria proposed a new text inspired by the earlier versions but with some significant additions.[189] The text resulted from protracted negotiations of which there is no official record.[190] The Nigerian text

---

[184] Commission on Human Rights, Report on the 20th Session, 17 February-18 March 1964, E/3873, paras. 161–2.

[185] Ibid., para. 178.

[186] Summary record, Commission on Human Rights, 28 February 1964, E/CN.4/SR.790, pp. 6–7; Summary record, Commission on Human Rights, 2 March 1964, E/CN.4/SR.792, p. 7; Commission on Human Rights, Report on the 20th Session, 17 February–18 March 1964, E/3873, paras. 169, 179.

[187] Summary record, Commission on Human Rights, 4 March 1964, E/CN.4/SR.795, p. 5.

[188] Summary record, Commission on Human Rights, 4 March 1964, E/CN.4/SR.796, p. 5.

[189] Nigeria: amendment to article IV of the draft international convention on the elimination of all forms of racial discrimination adopted by the Commission on Human Rights (A/5921, Annex), 22 October 1965, A/C.3/L/1250; Summary record, Third Committee, 22 October 1965, A/C.3/SR.1316, para. 1.

[190] Summary record, Third Committee, 25 October 1965, A/C.3/SR.1318, para. 9.

was adopted without any modification whatsoever. In the introductory paragraph, the Nigerian proposal added the following phrase: 'with due regard to the principles embodied in the Universal Declaration of Human Rights and the rights expressly set forth in article 5 of this Convention'. Article 5(2) of the Convention consisted of a list of civil and political rights including freedom of expression and freedom of association. This formulation addressed concerns of some States about conflicts with fundamental rights. Canada's delegate, Ronald St John Macdonald, described it as 'a reasonable accommodation between the requirement to create a new offence and the fundamental right to freedom of association'.[191] The views of Western States were also comforted by the phrase 'promote and incite' in paragraph (b), rather than the alternative, 'promote or incite', which was larger in extent. However, the Nigerian proposal also broadened the scope of the obligations relating to repression of racist propaganda in paragraph (a). The Commission draft required States Parties to declare incitement an offence punishable by law only when it resulted in acts of violence. Nigeria's proposal required States to make it an offence to disseminate ideas based on racial superiority or hatred as well as incitement to racial discrimination, with no requirement that any of these acts result in violence. It also required that States make punishable the provision of assistance to 'racist activities', including their financing. In paragraph (b), Nigeria removed the troublesome phrase 'as appropriate' in the Commission draft. But it also required that they recognize participation in racist organizations or activities as an offence punishable by law.

The Nigerian proposal was adopted by 88 votes to none, with five abstentions, which were not recorded.[192] The text appeared sufficiently ambiguous to satisfy delegations that were concerned about its encroachment upon freedom of expression and freedom of association. For example, the representative of the United States said the text 'did not impose on a State Party the obligation to take any action impairing the right to freedom of speech and freedom of association'.[193] But this was obviously not accurate. When it signed the Convention the following year, the United States felt compelled to make a declaration stating that 'nothing in the Convention shall be deemed to require or to authorise legislation or other action by the United States of America incompatible with the provisions of the constitution of the United States of America'.[194] Upon ratification of the Convention, in 1994, the United States made a formal reservation along the same lines that included a specific reference to article 4 of the Convention.[195] After the vote in the Sixth Committee, other delegations objected that paragraphs (a) and

[191] Ibid., para. 52.
[192] Ibid., para. 46.
[193] Ibid., para. 59.
[194] C.N.188.1966.TREATIES-4.
[195] C.N.356.1994.TREATIES-3.

278 ELIMINATION OF ALL FORMS OF RACIAL DISCRIMINATION

(b) contained obligations that 'taken by themselves would require States Parties to the Convention to legislate against racial discrimination without any regard to other fundamental freedoms'.[196] There were large numbers of abstentions when separate votes were taken on the two paragraphs.[197]

Explaining the apparent tension between the limitations imposed by the introductory paragraph of article 4 and the obligations set out in paragraph (a) and (b), the Committee on the Elimination of Racial Discrimination has said that 'it could not have been the intention of the drafters of the Convention to enable States parties to construe the phrase safeguarding the human rights in question as cancelling the obligations relating to the prohibition of the racist activities concerned. Otherwise, there would have been no purpose whatsoever for the inclusion in the Convention of the articles laying down those obligations.'[198]

Writing in the *American Journal of International Law* in 1985, Theodor Meron said that '[t]he overreach of Article 4 creates difficulties for democratic states that take their obligations seriously, and has prompted some of them to enter a relatively large number of reservations to that article'.[199] He returned to the same point in his dissenting opinion in the *Media case* at the International Criminal Tribunal for Rwanda, giving France as an example.[200] Actually, France only made an interpretative declaration with respect to article 4. Moreover, for additional clarity it subsequently informed the Secretary-General of the United Nations that its declaration 'did not purport to limit the obligations under the Convention in respect of the French Government, but only to record the latter's interpretation of article 4 of the Convention'.[201] French legislation regarding hate speech has been quite robust.[202]

When Meron published his article in the *American Journal* there had in fact been only one reservation to article 4, by Papua New Guinea.[203] Since then, there have been a handful of reservations,[204] of which the most significant is that of the United States: 'That the Constitution and laws of the United States contain extensive protections of individual freedom of speech, expression and association. Accordingly, the United States does not accept any obligation under this

---

[196] Summary record, Third Committee, 25 October 1965, A/C.3/SR.1318, para. 60 (New Zealand).

[197] Twenty-five for paragraph (a) and 16 for paragraph (b).

[198] Report of the Committee on the Elimination of Racial Discrimination, 15 September 1978, A/33/18, Annex V, p. 112.

[199] Theodor Meron, 'The Meaning and Reach of the International Convention on the Elimination of All Forms of Racial Discrimination' (1984) 79 *American Journal of International Law* 283, at p. 304.

[200] *Nahimana et al. v. Prosecutor* (ICTY-99-52-A), Partly dissenting opinion of Judge Meron, 15 March 2007, para. 5.

[201] C.N.151.1971.TREATIES-17.

[202] For example, *Faurisson v. France* (No. 550/1993), Views, 8 November 1996, CCPR/C/58/D/550/1993.

[203] C.N.32.1982.TREATIES-1.

[204] Ireland: C.N.1460.2000.TREATIES-10; Japan: C.N.469.1995.TREATIES-5; Monaco: C.N. 331.1995. TREATIES-3.

RACIST PROPAGANDA AND ORGANIZATIONS 279

Convention, in particular under Articles 4 and 7, to restrict those rights, through the adoption of legislation or any other measures, to the extent that they are protected by the Constitution and laws of the United States.'[205] Reservations have also been formulated by Ireland,[206] Japan,[207] Monaco,[208] and Switzerland.[209] A significant number of States have made statements labelled 'declaration',[210] 'interpretative statement',[211] 'explanatory statement'[212] or 'understanding'.[213] Although such labels may in some circumstances disguise what amount to reservations,[214] scrutiny of the actual texts confirms that this was not the case with the International Convention on the Elimination of All Forms of Racial Discrimination. Moreover, there is considerable evidence that those States formulating declarations asserting the importance of freedom of expression and freedom of association have in fact adopted adequate legislation implementing the obligations in article 4.

Views about the prohibition of racist organizations were sharply divided. The Sub-Commission text required the prohibition of associations. In the Commission, the American representative, Marietta Tree, explained that organizations as such could not be prohibited. She said she hoped the convention would not weaken the protection of freedom of association ensured by article 20 of the Universal Declaration of Human Rights.[215] The United States proposed an amendment to the text to add the words 'activities of' before 'associations'.[216] This was anathema to the Soviets, who countered that if American laws did not allow for prohibition of racist associations 'the United States would simply have to revise its legislation to bring it into line with the convention'.[217] The American position was supported by the British delegate, Samuel Hoare, who explained that '[h]is country, which had always preserved freedom, also had no laws under which it could prohibit organisations and, in any event, would not wish to do

---

[205] C.N.356.l994.TREATIES-3.

[206] C.N.1460.2000.TREATIES-10.

[207] Ibid.

[208] C.N. 331.1995. TREATIES-3.

[209] C.N.356.l994.TREATIES-3.

[210] Australia: C.N.272.1975.TREATIES-8; Austria: C.N.71.1972.TREATIES-4; France: C.N. 151.1971.TREATIES-17; Italy: C.N.3.1976.TREATIES-1, confirming its statement at the time of signature, C.N.50.1968.TREATIES-1; Tonga: C.N.35.1972.TREATIES-2.

[211] Barbados: C.N.213.1975.TREATIES-5; United Kingdom: C.N.40.1969.TREATIES-4, confirming a statement made at the time of signature, C.N.219.1966.TREATIES-5. Also Nepal: C.N.16.1971.TREATIES-3.

[212] Belgium: C.N.213.1975.TREATIES-5.

[213] Bahamas: C.N.220.1975.TREATIES-6; Malta: C.N.148.1968.TREATIES-5. The depository notification for Malta's ratification (C.N.90.1971.TREATIES-11) does not indicate that the declaration was renewed.

[214] *Belilos v. Switzerland*, Series A no. 132, p. 28, para. 60.

[215] Summary record, Commission on Human Rights, 28 February 1964, E/CN.4/SR.790, p. 8.

[216] United States of America: amendment to document E/CN.4/873, E/CN.4/L.688.

[217] Summary record, Commission on Human Rights, 28 February 1964, E/CN.4/SR.790, p. 8.

280   ELIMINATION OF ALL FORMS OF RACIAL DISCRIMINATION

so'.[218] His statement was not entirely accurate; the British had regularly prohibited organizations in its colonies. Birendra N. Chakravarty of India pointed to article 29(2) of the Universal Declaration of Human Rights which permits rights to be restricted under certain circumstances. He said '[h]e could not believe that the laws of the United States and the United Kingdom allowed unlimited liberty equalling licence'.[219] By a very strong majority, the Commission on Human Rights adopted a text requiring States Parties to 'declare illegal and prohibit organisations or the activities of organisations, as appropriate, and also organised propaganda activities, which promote and incite racial discrimination', based upon a proposal by Costa Rica that in effect complied with the American and the British position.[220]

In the Third Committee, the troublesome qualifier 'as appropriate' was removed and a phrase was added requiring States Parties to 'recognise participation in such organisations or activities as an offence punishable by law'. Egon Schwelb described the position of the United States and the United Kingdom as 'not fully convincing', giving as an example the post-Second World War peace treaties that they had made with Hungary, Bulgaria, Finland, Italy, Romania, and Austria requiring these States to prohibit fascist organizations.[221] During the debate in the Sixth Committee, Hungary pointed to its obligations not to permit fascist organizations on its territory, questioning whether 'the United States had the moral right to submit a sub-amendment which was in flagrant contradiction to an international treaty it had signed in the name of the United Nations'.[222] Reference might also be made to article 9 of the Charter of the International Military Tribunal, adopted by the United States, the United Kingdom, France, and the Soviet Union authorizing declarations that an organization is 'criminal'.[223]

---

[218] Ibid., p. 9.

[219] Ibid., p. 10.

[220] Costa Rica: sub-amendment to the amendment of the United States of America (E/CN.4/L.688), E/CN.4/L.702; Commission on Human Rights, Report on the 20th Session, 17 February–18 March 1964, E/3873, paras. 150–5.

[221] Egon Schwelb, 'The International Convention on the Elimination of All Forms of Racial Discrimination' (1966) 15 *International and Comparative Law Quarterly* 996, at p. 1022. See for example Treaty of Peace with Italy (1950) 49 UNTS 3, art. 17.

[222] Summary record, Third Committee, 22 October 1965, A/C.3/SR.1315, para. 11. See article 4 of the Treaty of Peace with Hungary (1949) 41 UNTS 135, to which the United States and the United Kingdom are parties: 'Hungary, which in accordance with the Armistice Agreement has taken measures for dissolving all organisations of a Fascist type on Hungarian territory, whether political, military or para-military, as well as other organisations conducting propaganda, including revisionist propaganda, hostile to the United Nations, shall not permit in future the existence and activities of organisations of that nature which have as their aim denial to the people of their democratic rights.'

[223] Agreement for the Prosecution and Punishment of Major War Criminals of the European Axis, and Establishing the Charter of the International Military Tribunal (IMT), annex (1951) 82 UNTS 279, art. 9.

Implementation of the Convention

A rather complex package of measures of implementation was also adopted in the Convention. The Philippines prepared a draft that was based upon the discussions and proposals in the Commission on Human Rights.[224] It was joined by two African States, Ghana and Mauritania, in preparing a revised version that also took into account various proposals that had been submitted to the Third Committee.[225] Measures of implementation of human rights obligations that had been debated at length during the still unfinished work of drafting the two Covenants were also an important influence.[226] John Humphrey later wrote that the implementation provisions of the Convention 'were largely the work of certain African delegations in the General Assembly'.[227] When the measures of implementation were being discussed, the rapporteur of the Third Committee, Ronald St John Macdonald of Canada, said it was unlikely that a petition mechanism would be acceptable universally: 'Many countries were not yet ready for it, and others did not share the traditional Western concept of human rights.'[228] The comment provoked an abrupt response from Venezuela's delegate, who said that 'Western countries had no reason to pride themselves on their advanced moral concepts, since it was in those countries that racial discrimination had originated and still existed, despite great efforts made by Governments to eliminate it'.[229] Waldo E. Waldron-Ramsay of Tanzania recalled that Canada had itself hesitated about voting in favour of the Universal Declaration of Human Rights.[230] 'The record of the Western countries in the matter of human rights gave those countries absolutely no right to take a patronising attitude towards others', he said. '[I]ndeed, it was the Western world that had given birth to colonialism and slavery, while the developing countries had suffered as a result.'[231]

---

[224] Philippines: articles relating to measures of implementation to be added to the provisions of the draft International Convention on the Elimination of All Forms of Racial Discrimination adopted by the Commission on Human Rights (A/5921, annex), 11 October 1965, A/C.3/L.1221.

[225] Ghana, Mauritania, and Philippines: articles relating to measures of implementation to be added to the provision of the draft International Convention on the Elimination of All Forms of Racial Discrimination adopted by the Commission on Human Rights (A/5921, annex), 18 November 1965, A/C.3/L.1291.

[226] Egon Schwelb, 'The International Convention on the Elimination of All Forms of Racial Discrimination' (1966) 15 *International and Comparative Law Quarterly* 996, at p. 1032.

[227] John P. Humphrey, 'The United Nations Sub-Commission on the Prevention of Discrimination and the Protection of Minorities' (1968) 62 *American Journal of International Law* 869, at p. 883.

[228] Summary record, Third Committee, 17 November 1965, A/C.3/SR.1345, para. 12.

[229] Ibid., para. 29.

[230] The reference appears to have been to Canada's abstention when the Third Committee adopted the draft Universal Declaration of Human Rights. See Summary record, Third Committee, 7 December 1948, A/C.3/SR.178, pp. 879–80; William A. Schabas, 'Canada and the Adoption of the *Universal Declaration of Human Rights*' (1998) 43 *McGill Law Journal* 403; A.J. Hobbins, 'Eleanor Roosevelt, John Humphrey and Canadian Opposition to the Universal Declaration of Human Rights: Looking Back on the 50th Anniversary of the UNDHR' (1998) 52 *International Journal* 325.

[231] Summary record, Third Committee, 17 November 1965, A/C.3/SR.1345, para. 39.

The Convention provides for the establishment of a 'treaty body' named the Committee on the Elimination of Racial Discrimination.[232] It is composed of 18 members 'of high moral standing and acknowledged impartiality',[233] elected by the States Parties from among their citizens to four-year terms. The first elections to the Committee were held in 1969 following the entry into force of the Convention. At its inaugural session in January 1970, the Committee elected its officers, adopted rules of procedure, and began consideration of reports from Argentina, Bulgaria, Costa, Rica, Czechoslovakia, India, Iran, Niger, Panama, Poland, and Spain. The submission of periodic reports to the Committee is one of the primary responsibilities of States Parties. The reports are examined in public sessions of the Committee which then issues concluding observations that contain comments and recommendations.

The Committee adjudicates individual petitions, known as 'communications', that are directed at those States Parties that have made a supplementary declaration in accordance with article 14. The first such petition was only filed in 1984. Directed at the Netherlands, it was submitted by a Turkish citizen resident in the Netherlands who complained of discriminatory statements made by her employer in the course of dismissal proceedings.[234] Since then, the Committee has received fewer than 60 communications, that is, not even two per year on average. Litigants would appear to have opted for human rights petition mechanisms before other treaty bodies, like the Human Rights Committee, and regional human rights courts like the European Court of Human Rights. The Committee also has jurisdiction over inter-State complaints, a mechanism that was first used in 2018. Two such petitions submitted by Qatar were subsequently discontinued. An inter-State communication submitted by Palestine against Israel was declared admissible in 2021.[235]

---

[232] Thomas Buergenthal, 'Implementing the UN Racial Convention' (1977) 12 *Texas International Law Journal* 187; Theodor Meron, 'The Meaning and Reach of the International Convention on the Elimination of All Forms of Racial Discrimination' (1985) 79 *American Journal of International Law* 283; Natan Lerner, *U.N. Convention on the Elimination of All Forms of Racial Discrimination*, Alphen aan den Rijn: Sijthoff and Noordhoff, 1980; Jose L. Gomez del Prado, 'United Nations Conventions on Human Rights: The Practice of the Human Rights Committee and the Committee on the Elimination of Racial Discrimination in Dealing with Reporting Obligations of States Parties' (1985) 7 *Human Rights Quarterly* 492; Michael Banton, 'Effective implementation of the UN Racial Convention' (1994) 20 *Journal of Ethnic and Migration Studies* 475; Patrick Thornberry, 'Confronting Racial Discrimination: A CERD Perspective' (2005) 5 *Human Rights Law Review* 239; Patrick Thornberry, *The International Convention on the Elimination of All Forms of Racial Discrimination, A Commentary*, Oxford: Oxford University Press, 2016.

[233] International Convention on the Elimination of All Forms of Racial Discrimination (1969) 660 UNTS 195, art. 8(1).

[234] *Yilmaz-Dogan v. the Netherlands* (no. 1/1984), Opinion, 10 August 1988, CERD/C/36/D/1/1988.

[235] Decision on the admissibility of the inter-State communication submitted by the State of Palestine against Israel, 30 April 2021, CERD/C/103/R.6.

The Convention also contains a compromissory clause by which the International Court of Justice is given jurisdiction in inter-State disputes, even with respect to States that have not made a general acceptance of the jurisdiction of the Court. In 2008, the Republic of Georgia filed an application against the Russian Federation alleging violations of the Convention during the armed conflict between the two countries. The Court issued a provisional measures order but subsequently granted Russia's preliminary challenge based upon jurisdiction on the grounds that Georgia had not attempted to resolve the dispute by negotiation prior to filing the application.[236] In 2017, Ukraine instituted proceedings against Russia based in part on the Convention. It alleged discrimination against Crimean Tatars and ethnic Ukrainians in the occupied Crimea involving measures directed at cultural and educational rights. The Court issued a provisional measures order protecting Crimean Tatar institutions and the right to education in Ukrainian.[237] Subsequently, Russia's challenge to the admissibility of the case was dismissed,[238] and the case has proceeded to the merits stage. The following year, Qatar filed an application against the United Arab Emirates concerning the treatment of its nationals. The Court issued a provisional measures order but then dismissed the case on the basis of a preliminary objection to jurisdiction. It held that Qatari nationals resident in the United Arab Emirates were not contemplated by article 1 of the International Convention.[239] Armed conflict in Azerbaijan prompted both Armenia and Azerbaijan to file applications based upon the Convention in 2021. The Court issued provisional measures with respect to both of the applications.[240]

---

[236] *Application of the International Convention on the Elimination of All Forms of Racial Discrimination (Georgia v. Russian Federation), Preliminary Objections, Judgment, I.C.J. Reports 2011*, p. 70. For the provisional measures order: *Application of the International Convention on the Elimination of all Forms of Racial Discrimination (Georgia v. Russian Federation), Provisional Measures, Order of 15 October 2008, I.C.J. Reports 2008*, p. 353.

[237] *Application of the International Convention for the Suppression of the Financing of Terrorism and of the International Convention on the Elimination of All Forms of Racial Discrimination (Ukraine v. Russian Federation), Provisional Measures, Order of 19 April 2017, I.C.J. Reports 2017*, p. 104. See Iryna Marchuk, 'Application of the International Convention for the Suppression of the Financing of Terrorism and of the International Convention on the Elimination of All Forms of Racial Discrimination (Ukraine v. Russia)' (2017) 18 *Melbourne Journal of International Law* 436.

[238] *Application of the International Convention for the Suppression of the Financing of Terrorism and of the International Convention on the Elimination of All Forms of Racial Discrimination (Ukraine v. Russian Federation), Preliminary Objections, Judgment, I.C.J. Reports 2019*, p. 558.

[239] *Application of the International Convention on the Elimination of All Forms of Racial Discrimination (Qatar v. United Arab Emirates), Preliminary Objections, Judgment, I.C.J. Reports 2021*, p. 71. For the provisional measures order: *Application of the International Convention on the Elimination of All Forms of Racial Discrimination (Qatar v. United Arab Emirates), Provisional Measures, Order of 14 June 2019, I.C.J. Reports 2019*, p. 361.

[240] *Application of the International Convention on the Elimination of All Forms of Racial Discrimination (Armenia v. Azerbaijan), Order (Provisional Measures)*, 7 December 2021; *Application of the International Convention on the Elimination of All Forms of Racial Discrimination (Azerbaijan v. Armenia), Order (Provisional Measures)*, 7 December 2021.

284 ELIMINATION OF ALL FORMS OF RACIAL DISCRIMINATION

Both the Declaration and the Convention were adopted with unprecedented speed, a sign of urgency but also of impatience. States of the Global South were not prepared for the Convention to be negotiated at the pace of the two international Covenants, which had taken nearly two decades. In 1962, when the General Assembly authorized the drafting of the declaration and the convention on racial discrimination, a second resolution using similar language did the same thing for religious intolerance. The Sub-Commission completed a draft declaration in 1964[241] and a draft convention in 1965.[242] The Commission reviewed these texts and forwarded them to the General Assembly where the negotiations stalled.[243] In 1973, the General Assembly decided to give priority to the declaration.[244] But it would take another eight years before the General Assembly adopted the Declaration on the Elimination of All Forms of Intolerance and of Discrimination Based on Religion or Belief in 1981.[245] As for the convention, nearly six decades have now passed since the initial General Assembly decision and its prospects of successful completion seem more remote than ever.[246]

The 1962 General Assembly resolution on religious intolerance began by recalling 'the principle of equality of all men and all peoples without distinction as to race, colour or religion, as stated in the Charter of the United Nations'.[247] This was not entirely accurate, as the reference to 'colour' was only added in

[241] Report of the 16th session of the Sub-Commission on Prevention of Discrimination and Protection of Minorities, 13 to 31 January 1964, E/CN.4/873, paras. 124–42.

[242] Report of the 17th session of the Sub-Commission on Prevention of Discrimination and Protection of Minorities, 11 to 29 January 1965, E/CN.4/882 and Corr.1, paras. 20–329.

[243] See Elimination of all forms of religious intolerance, 6 July 1971, A/8330 for details of the discussions in the Third Committee of the General Assembly. Also Roger S. Clark, 'The United Nations and Religious Freedom' (1978) 11 *New York University Journal of International Law and Policy* 197; John Claydon, 'The Treaty Protection of Religious Rights: U.N. Draft Convention on the Elimination of All Forms of Intolerance and of Discrimination Based on Religion or Belief' (1972) 12 *Santa Clara Lawyer* 403.

[244] Elimination of all forms of religious intolerance, 18 December 1972, A/RES/3027 (XXVII).

[245] Declaration on the Elimination of All Forms of Intolerance and of Discrimination Based on Religion or Belief, 25 November 1981, A/RES/36/55. See Donna J. Sullivan, 'Advancing the Freedom of Religion or Belief Through the UN Declaration on the Elimination of Religious Intolerance and Discrimination' (1988) 82 *American Journal of International Law* 487; Natan Lerner, 'Toward a Draft Declaration against Religious Intolerance and Discrimination' (1981) 11 *Israel Yearbook of Human Rights* 82; Natan Lerner, 'The Final Text of the U.N. Declaration Against Intolerance and Discrimination Based on Religion or Belief' (1982) 12 *Israel Yearbook of Human Rights* 185; Derek H. David, 'The Evolution of Religious Freedom as a Universal Human Right: Examining the Role of the 1981 United Nations Declaration on the Elimination of All Forms of Intolerance and of Discrimination Based on Religion or Belief' (2002) *BYU Law Review* 217; Peter Cumper, "The United Kingdom and the U.N. Declaration on the Elimination of Intolerance and Discrimination Based on Religious or Belief" (2007) 21:1 *Emory International Law Review* 13; Sidney Liskofsky, 'The UN Declaration on the Elimination of Religious Intolerance and Discrimination: Historical and Legal Perspectives', in James E. Wood, Jr. ed., *Religion and the State, Essays in Honor of Leo Pfeffer*, Waco, TX: Baylor University Press, 1985, pp. 441–76.

[246] Carolyn Evans, 'Time for a Treaty? The Legal Sufficiency of the Declaration on the Elimination of All Forms of Intolerance and Discrimination' (2007) 3 *Brigham Young University Law Review* 617.

[247] Preparation of a draft declaration and a draft convention on the elimination of all forms of religious intolerance, 7 December 1962, A/RES/1781 (XVII), PP 1.

article 2 of the Universal Declaration of Human Rights to the formulation in the Charter. But were 'intolerance' and 'discrimination' mere synonyms? The draft text of the religious intolerance convention adopted by the Commission on Human Rights in 1965 distinguished between the two notions although it did not define them. It was clear, nevertheless, that the prohibition of religious intolerance was focussed on issues of freedom of religion and the exercise of religion rather than on discrimination based upon religious belief.[248] There were clear commonalities but the issues were not at all identical. Western countries had insisted upon a focus on religion as well as race, and their treatment as parallel and equivalent phenomena, for political reasons related to the Cold War. A senior British official wrote in confidential instructions that government policy was 'to maintain a parity in order to prevent the UN from spending too much time on the racial item, where the West is on the defensive, and not enough on the religious item where the Soviet bloc is on the defensive. . . this policy was largely unsuccessful because of the enthusiasm of the Afro-Asians for eliminating racial discrimination.'[249]

* * *

The International Convention on the Elimination of All Forms of Racial Discrimination, adopted by the United Nations General Assembly in 1965, is the cornerstone of international law dealing with racial discrimination. The States of the Global South had played only a peripheral role in the preliminary stages of negotiation of the treaty, in the 1964 sessions of the Sub-Commission and the Commission of Human Rights. The reason was the inadequacy of their participation in these bodies. States from Africa, the Caribbean, and Asia were grossly underrepresented in the Sub-Commission and the Commission whereas they amounted to a majority of the General Assembly. It was only in the General Assembly that the importance of their place in the United Nations could be fully felt. There, these States struggled to transform a treaty whose initial drafts had been conceived by British and American diplomats in Whitehall and Foggy Bottom in an effort to produce a document that was as innocuous as possible.

It is often the case that in negotiations of a declaration or a treaty, the tone of the debate is strongly influenced by the initial drafts. These emerged in the Sub-Commission where they were initially the work of the United States and the United Kingdom, both of them States with sordid practices of racism and colonization. From the start, then, much of the negotiation involved 'damage control'

---

[248] Commission on Human Rights, Report on the 21st session, 22 March–15 April 1965, E/4024, p. 76.

[249] Samuel Falle, Consideration of the draft declaration on the elimination of all forms of racial intolerance at the 37th session of the Economic and Social Council in July, 2 July 1964, TNA FO 371/178331.

of the cautious and conservative proposals that launched the process. The story of the adoption of these two instruments, the Declaration and the Convention, is one of inadequate proposals developed within the Sub-Commission and the Commission, which were dominated by white men from Europe and North America, only to be made more intense and demanding in the General Assembly, where the influence of Africa and Asia was more effective.

10

Apartheid

Early Challenges to South African Racism

'It surely must be one of the great ironies of our age that this Assembly is being addressed for the first time in its 49 years' history by a South African head of State drawn from the African majority of what is an African country', said Nelson Mandela when he addressed the United Nations General Assembly on 3 October 1994. 'Future generations will find it strange in the extreme that it was only so late in the 20th century that it was possible for our delegation to take its seat in the Assembly, recognised both by our people and by the nations of the world as the legitimate representative of the people of our country.' Mandela noted how the organization had been confronted with the apartheid issue from its earliest days, 'undermin[ing] the credibility of the United Nations as an effective international instrument to end racism and secure the fundamental human rights of all peoples'. He said that the establishment and consolidation of apartheid constituted a brazen challenge to the very existence of the United Nations.[1]

In the late 1940s, South Africa began the adoption of a body of legislation that entrenched a system of racial discrimination known by the Afrikaans word apartheid, which is translated into English as 'separateness'. The Population Registration Act, 1950 classified South Africans into one of four racial groups, 'black', 'white', 'coloured', and 'Indian'. This designation affected such matters as place of residence and voting rights. Since 1946, South Africa had faced challenges within the General Assembly for its racist policies directed at persons of Indian descent as well as its administration of South-West Africa, the League of Nations mandate that it had been given over Germany's former colony.[2] Despite howls of protest from South Africa that article 2(7) of the Charter denied the United Nations any authority with respect to its internal policies,[3] the matter was soon an active item in the General Assembly.

The first explicit condemnation of apartheid by the General Assembly appeared in 1950, in a resolution dealing with treatment of persons of Indian

---

[1] Verbatim record, plenary General Assembly, 3 October 1994, A/49/PV.14, p. 6.
[2] See *supra*, pp. 106–113.
[3] See, for example, Verbatim record, plenary General Assembly, 17 October 1952, A/PV.381, paras. 9–66.

The International Legal Order's Colour Line. William A. Schabas, Oxford University Press.
© Oxford University Press 2023. DOI: 10.1093/oso/9780197744475.003.0010

288 APARTHEID

descent in South Africa. Referring to the Egyptian resolution at the 1946 session on racial persecution and discrimination,[4] as well as to the Universal Declaration of Human Rights, the resolution stated that 'a policy of "racial segregation" (Apartheid) is necessarily based on doctrines of racial discrimination.'[5] A roll-call vote was taken on this phrase. Twenty-nine States of the Global South voted in favour. Five States were opposed (Australia, Belgium, Greece, Luxembourg, South Africa) and 25 abstained, all from Europe and the Western hemisphere as well as Israel.[6] A similar resolution was adopted the following year,[7] this time with 39 votes to 3 and 12 abstentions in the vote on the preambular reference to apartheid.[8] Dantès Bellegarde of Haiti, who had collaborated decades earlier with W.E.B. Du Bois, and who had condemned South African racism in the Assembly of the League of Nations in the early 1920s, delivered an eloquent speech explaining that the issue of racism in South Africa went beyond an inter-State dispute with India:

We are of course well aware that in certain countries there are prejudices against coloured people and that, as a result of absurd customs, they are kept in an inadmissible and intolerable situation simply because they are of a different race. We maintain that such customs should be fought. They are indeed being fought, but the complete change that is necessary will still take much time. Even if this is so, it is none the less utterly inadmissible that a Member of the United Nations should today pass an act which flagrantly contravenes the principles of the Charter. This is a matter with which the United Nations as a whole must concern itself.

We know the misery, suffering and torture caused by racial prejudice. The experience of hitlerite racialism which led to the death of millions of human beings is still fresh in our memory. It has been recalled here repeatedly that six million human beings, because they were Jews, were murdered and burnt in the crematoria of Hitlerite Germany. The whole world was filled with the most profound indignation on learning of the horrors, tortures and cruelties suffered by the Jews. Hitlerite racialism was founded on a mistaken conception, that of the inequality of races. In defiance of all the teachings of anthropology and ethnology, there were men who actually believed in fundamental human differences and thought that, solely because they had yellow or black skins, certain human

---

[4] See *supra*, pp. 114–115.

[5] Treatment of people of Indian origin in the Union of South Africa, 2 December 1950, A/RES/395 (V), PP 4.

[6] Verbatim record, plenary General Assembly, 2 December 1950, A/PV.315, para. 45.

[7] Treatment of people of Indian origin in the Union of South Africa, 12 January 1952, A/RES/511 (VI).

[8] Verbatim record, plenary General Assembly, 12 January 1952, A/PV.360, para. 33.

beings should be condemned to occupy an inferior social position. This absurd and inhuman belief has caused untold unhappiness to mankind.[9]

On 12 September 1952, 13 Member States of the Global South asked that 'the question of race conflict in South Africa resulting from the policies of apartheid of the Government of the Union of South Africa' be placed on the agenda of the General Assembly. Their letter explained that the situation in South Africa was both a threat to international peace and a flagrant violation of fundamental human rights and freedoms enshrined in the Charter of the United Nations.[10] The request became a draft resolution that was then joined by Bolivia, Guatemala, Haiti, Honduras, and Liberia.[11] Speaking in support, India's representative, Vijaya Lakshmi Pandit, explained that the 13 States represented 600 million people, which at the time was not quite one-third of the world's population. 'They had felt that the deliberate attempt on the part of the South African Government to establish racial discrimination by a policy of apartheid, which implied permanent superiority of the white inhabitants over the non-white who comprised 80 per cent of the total population, had created a dangerous tension in South Africa with serious consequences for harmony among nations and peace in the world', she said. Furthermore, the objective was to force the non-European population into 'perpetual economic and social servitude by racial discrimination and segregation in violation of basic human rights and fundamental freedoms and of the principles of the Charter, to which all States, including South Africa, had pledged adherence'.[12] She invoked the Egyptian resolution adopted by the General Assembly in 1946, the preamble of the Universal Declaration of Human Rights, and the recent 'Uniting for Peace' resolution of the General Assembly,[13] which affirmed that 'genuine and lasting peace' depended 'especially upon respect for and observance of human rights'.[14]

South Africa warned of the precedent that was being set. It said that in the establishment of the proposed commission, the Assembly 'will be guilty of a specific act of intervention' in the domestic affairs of a Member State that would have serious consequences.[15] The United Kingdom supported South Africa in

[9] Verbatim record, plenary General Assembly, 12 January 1952, A/PV.360, paras. 24–5.

[10] Letter dated 12 September 1952 addressed to the Secretary-General by the permanent representatives of Afghanistan, Burma, Egypt, India, Indonesia, Iran, Iraq, Lebanon, Pakistan, Philippines, Saudi Arabia, Syrian Arab Republic, and Yemen, A/2183.

[11] A/AC.61/L.8/Rev.1. For a summary of the detailed negotiations of the draft resolutions, see the Report of the Ad Hoc Political Committee, 2 December 1952, A/2216.

[12] Summary record, Ad Hoc Political Committee, 12 November 1952, A/AC.61/SR.13, para. 16.

[13] Ibid., para. 20.

[14] Uniting for Peace, 3 November 1950, A/RES/377 E (V).

[15] Verbatim record, plenary General Assembly, 5 December 1952, A/PV.401, para. 86; Summary record, Ad Hoc Political Committee, 12 November 1952, A/AC.61/SR.13, paras. 5–13. See also Summary record, Ad Hoc Political Committee, 23 November 1953, A/AC.72/SR.32, paras. 2–14.

290 APARTHEID

attempts to obstruct the General Assembly from addressing apartheid, warning other States that they too might want to invoke article 2(7) in the future.[16] New Zealand also backed the South Africans with the strange argument that because apartheid was the development of 'certain trends of South Africa's internal policy' that were well-known at the time of the San Francisco Conference, the Member States of the United Nations had somehow accepted that it was consistent with the purposes and principles of the Charter.[17] South Africa's motion to reject the entire issue, premised upon article 2(7) of the Charter, was supported by Australia, Belgium, France, Luxembourg, and the United Kingdom. Abstentions were registered by Argentina, Dominican Republic, Greece, Netherlands, New Zealand, Peru, Turkey, and Venezuela. Forty-five States voted against the motion.[18]

Two resolutions on apartheid were adopted by the General Assembly in December 1952, in addition to one directed specifically at the situation of the Indian minority. The first established a Commission to examine 'the racial situation in the Union of South Africa in the light of the Purposes and Principles of the Charter'.[19] The resolution obtained 35 votes in favour to 1 against (South Africa), with 23 abstentions. The geographic division was stark, the resolution being supported by countries of the Global South together with the Soviet Union and its allies, and Israel.[20] China and a few Latin American States abstained, along with those of Western Europe and North America.[21] Britain and France made statements explaining their vote in which they insisted that the resolution went beyond the Charter by interfering in matters of domestic jurisdiction, in breach of article 2(7).[22]

The second resolution was hortatory in nature and more general in application, declaring 'that in a multi-racial society harmony and respect for human rights and freedoms and the peaceful development of a unified community are best assured when patterns of legislation and practice are directed towards ensuring equality before the law of all persons regardless of race, creed or colour, and when economic, social, cultural and political participation of all racial groups is on a basis of equality'. It affirmed that governmental policies not directed towards such goals, and that are designed to perpetuate or increase discrimination, are 'inconsistent with the pledges of the Members under Article 56

---

[16] Summary record, Ad Hoc Political Committee, 12 November 1952, A/AC.61/SR.14, para. 15. See also Australia: Summary record, Ad Hoc Political Committee, 14 November 1952, A/AC.61/SR.16, paras. 34–49; Belgium, ibid., paras. 72–6.

[17] Summary record, Ad Hoc Political Committee, 12 November 1952, A/AC.61/SR.14, para. 28.

[18] Summary record, Ad Hoc Political Committee, 20 November 1952, A/AC.61/SR.21, para. 34.

[19] The question of race conflict in South Africa resulting from the policies of *apartheid* of the Government of the Union of South Africa, 5 December 1952, A/RES/616 (VII) A, OP 1.

[20] On Israel's approach, see Rotem Giladi, 'Negotiating Identity: Israel, Apartheid, and the United Nations, 1949–1952' (2017) 132 *English Historical Review* 1440, at pp. 1460–3.

[21] Verbatim record, plenary General Assembly, 5 December 1952, A/PV.401, para. 98.

[22] Ibid., paras. 106–18.

of the Charter'.[23] The second resolution resulted from a Scandinavian proposal[24] although it was inspired by a draft prepared by the United States.[25] The roll-call vote indicated that this resolution was backed largely by Western States. The resolution was adopted by 24 to 1, and 34 abstentions.[26] India's Pandit explained that her country had abstained in the vote because the second resolution did not have a direct bearing on the race conflict in South Africa. 'It expressed general sentiments which are fine and with which we are in complete agreement, but it does not adequately provide a solution for the problem with which the world is faced today', she said.[27] There were several other resolutions adopted that year dealing with human rights. The resolutions spoke in generalities on such matters as freedom of information, refugees, and political rights of women. This was the only resolution addressed to a concrete situation where human rights were being violated.

The General Assembly debates in 1952 established the pre-eminent position of racial equality and the condemnation of discrimination based upon race and colour within the human rights law of the United Nations. They also confirmed the authority of the United Nations General Assembly to inquire into and investigate serious violations of human rights. Finally, they endorsed the view that the references to human rights in the Charter were not mere place-holders, awaiting formulation in subsequent treaties, but a source of substantive obligations imposing requirements on States like South Africa to address racial discrimination. This process was entirely driven by countries of the Global South, with India, Pakistan, and Haiti in the lead. Inevitably there were subtle differences in approach of the countries of the North. For example, the United States said '[i]t endorsed a national policy of attempting steady progress toward removal of discriminations which the Charter condemned and considered that no lasting solution of racial problems could be attained short of full participation of all races in the life of a nation'. The United States claimed it did not want to sit in judgment of South Africa although it questioned the wisdom of the apartheid policy because of its long-term repercussions within South Africa, adding that a policy of increased restriction was 'incompatible with the generally accepted interpretation of the obligations of the Charter'.[28] Canada said it doubted the competence

[23] The question of race conflict in South Africa resulting from the policies of apartheid of the Government of the Union of South Africa, 5 December 1952, A/RES/616 (VII) B.

[24] Report of the Ad Hoc Political Committee, 2 December 1952, A/2216, para. 10.

[25] Editorial note, FRUS 1952-54 IX, pp. 976–8. Also Department of State Position Paper, Question of race conflict in South Africa, 5 October 1952, FRUS 1952-54 IX, pp. 938–40; J.P. Brits, 'Tiptoeing Along the Apartheid Tightrope: The United States, South Africa, and the United Nations in 1952' (2005) 27 *International History Review* 754, at pp. 765, 771.

[26] Verbatim record, plenary General Assembly, 5 December 1952, A/PV.401, para. 105.

[27] Ibid., para. 121.

[28] Summary record, Ad Hoc Political Committee, 15 November 1952, A/AC.61/SR.17, paras. 9–14.

292   APARTHEID

of the General Assembly to establish a commission of inquiry.[29] European States with colonial empires tended to less subtlety. When Pakistan linked racial discrimination to colonialism in Africa generally,[30] France dismissed such a 'completely fantastic description' and 'revolting picture', claiming its colonial policy was driven 'by the greatest respect and by true and sincere love for the peoples concerned'.[31] The Belgian delegate, Count d'Aspremont Lynden, dismissed Pakistan's statement as a 'caricature'.[32] The delegate of the Netherlands said South Africa 'had done a good deal to improve the living conditions of the non-white population' and that 'racial segregation was not in itself a violation of human rights'.[33]

Commission of Inquiry into Apartheid

In accordance with the first of the resolutions, the General Assembly appointed a three-member Commission, composed of Hernán Santa Cruz of Chile, Ralph Bunche of the United States and Jaime Torres Bodet of Mexico.[34] A senior official in the Trusteeship Department, Bunche was the first person of African descent to be awarded the Nobel Prize. However, he could not be released from his United Nations functions. Bodet had just completed a term as Director-General of UNESCO. He too informed the Secretariat that he was unable to act. The two were replaced by Dantès Bellegarde of Haiti and Henri Laugier of France.[35] This was the first of many such commissions with human rights mandates to be established by organs of the United Nations. The United Nations Commission on the Racial Situation in the Union of South Africa began meeting in Geneva on 13 May 1953. Hernán Santa Cruz was elected chairman and rapporteur. The Commission heard a number of witnesses and received submissions from non-governmental organizations as well as the governments of Syria, India, and Pakistan. South Africa refused to co-operate with the Commission.

The 119-page report of the Commission was issued on 3 October 1953. It began with a lengthy analysis of the legal basis of the Commission and more generally of the role of the United Nations in the protection and promotion of human rights, including the scope to be given to article 2(7). The Commission discussed its own authority under the Charter, concluding that the General Assembly, and

---

[29] Summary record, Ad Hoc Political Committee, 19 November 1952, A/AC.61/SR.20, para. 15.
[30] Summary record, Ad Hoc Political Committee, 13 November 1952, A/AC.61/SR.15, paras. 12–18.
[31] Summary record, Ad Hoc Political Committee, 14 November 1952, A/AC.61/SR.16, paras. 52–5.
[32] Ibid., para. 70.
[33] Ibid., para. 29.
[34] Verbatim record, plenary General Assembly, 22 December 1952, A/PV.411, para. 518.
[35] Verbatim record, plenary General Assembly, 30 March 1953, A/PV.417, paras. 3–4.

any commission that it authorized, was competent to undertake studies and make recommendations in connection with implementation of the principles in the Charter. It stressed the importance of the activities of the General Assembly with respect to 'violations of the principle of non-discrimination, and more particularly when the discrimination is systematic and is based on a doctrine of racial inequality. It is precisely such situations that the authors of the Charter wished to prohibit when they included in the Charter the principle of non-discrimination based on grounds of race, thereby giving expression to mankind's deepest aspirations.'[36]

The report examined the demographic composition of South Africa. It turned to legislation affecting property rights, nationality, elections, access to services, social rights, education and the application of criminal law, and taxation, distinguishing between legislative measures adopted prior to the Charter and those adopted since its adoption. Proceeding to examine the applicable law, the Commission noted that South Africa's discriminatory policies were well-known to other Member States when it was admitted to the United Nations, who were not entitled to expect that 'this situation would be radically transformed overnight by the complete elimination of all discriminatory measures resulting either from statutory provisions or from administrative or private practices.'[37] On the other hand, however, they 'had the right to expect that the Union of South Africa would, as stated in Article 2, paragraph 2, of the Charter, fulfil in good faith the obligations assumed by it in accordance with that instrument: namely, the obligation to eliminate gradually all discriminatory measures based, inter alia, on race or colour in the sphere of human rights and fundamental freedoms; the obligation to cooperate with the Organisation for the achievement of universal respect for and observance of those rights and freedoms for all; and, most important of all, the obligation not to take any action calculated to aggravate or increase discrimination.'[38]

The report was tame by today's standards. But this was the first time that the United Nations or any international body—had produced such a damning assessment of a 'civilized nation'. It would not have happened had the initiative been left to the wealthy European States, who were anxious about their own vulnerabilities. Here was a United Nations expert body, one of whose members was a Black Haitian, calling to account a member of the British Commonwealth. It was a defining moment in the history of human rights within the United Nations, a turning point, and one whose success must be credited to countries

[36] Report of the United Nations Commission on the Racial Situation in South Africa, 1953, A/2505, p. 34.
[37] Ibid., para. 862.
[38] Ibid., para. 863.

294   APARTHEID

from the Global South. As one academic writer observed, decades later the report was still impressive for its objectivity, thoroughness, and detail.[39]

The chairman of the Commission, Hernán Santa Cruz, appeared before the Ad Hoc Political Committee of the General Assembly to present the report. He explained that the Commission had felt compelled to provide a thorough analysis of the legal issues given the 'injunction' of the United Kingdom, which had challenged the Commission's validity, refused all co-operation, and contended that it was improper to hear witnesses from non-governmental organizations.[40] Inevitably, South Africa, attacked the report's methodology, the lack of impartiality of its authors, and their 'anti-European bias'.[41] Santa Cruz took the floor again to answer the South African critique.[42] The South Africans attempted to revive the debate about article 2(7), with the support of Australia, Belgium, Colombia, France, Greece, New Zealand, and the United Kingdom.[43] Indeed, the debate in the Ad Hoc Political Committee, which lasted several days, focussed more on the interpretation of article 2(7) than it did on the substance of the Report. Nevertheless, as India's delegate pointed out, no delegation attempted to defend South Africa's racist policies.[44]

The General Assembly welcomed the report of the Commission, noting its conclusion that apartheid and its consequences were contrary to both the Charter of the United Nations and the Universal Declaration of Human Rights. It also decided that the Commission should continue its work.[45] The resolution followed the typical pattern, with African and Asian countries, and some of the Latin Americans, in favour, and those of the North (this includes Australia and New Zealand) abstaining or voting against. The draft resolution was adopted in the Political Committee by 37 to 10, with 9 abstentions. Canada and the Netherlands joined South Africa's supporters.[46] In the plenary General Assembly, the vote was the same.[47]

The Commission submitted a second report, of nearly 100 pages, in 1954. It consisted of two main sections, the first devoted to continued study of legislation in South Africa and the second to possibilities of a peaceful settlement.[48] The

[39] Newell M. Stultz, 'Evolution of the United Nations Anti-Apartheid Regime' (1991) 13 *Human Rights Quarterly* 1, at p. 9.

[40] Summary record, Ad Hoc Political Committee, 20 November 1953, A/AC.72/SR.31, paras. 7–8.

[41] Summary record, Ad Hoc Political Committee, 23 November 1953, A/AC.72/SR.32, paras. 1–26. Luxembourg joined the group for the vote in the plenary General Assembly: Verbatim record, plenary General Assembly, 8 December 1953, A/PV.469, para. 52.

[42] Summary record, Ad Hoc Political Committee, 24 November 1953, A/AC.72/SR.33, paras. 1–11.

[43] Summary record, Ad Hoc Political Committee, 5 December 1953, A/AC.72/SR.42, para. 60.

[44] Ibid., para. 1.

[45] The question of race conflict in South Africa resulting from the policies of apartheid of the Government of the Union of South Africa, 8 December 1953, A/RES/721 (VIII).

[46] Summary record, Ad Hoc Political Committee, 5 December 1953, A/AC.72/SR.42, para. 69.

[47] Verbatim record, plenary General Assembly, 8 December 1953, A/PV.469, para. 69.

[48] Second Report of the United Nations Commission on the Racial Situation in South Africa, A/2719.

COMMISSION OF INQUIRY INTO APARTHEID   295

ensuing debate in the Ad Hoc Political Committee rehearsed the same arguments as the previous year. South Africa did not persist with its resolution challenging the competence of the General Assembly on the basis of article 2(7). The General Assembly resolution noted 'the profound conviction of the Commission that the policy of apartheid constitutes a grave threat to the peaceful relations between ethnic groups in the world' and commended its 'constructive work'. The mandate of the Commission was renewed again. The vote was essentially identical to what it had been in 1953.[49]

The Commission's third and final report, of similar length to previous ones, was issued in 1955.[50] When discussion of the Report in the Ad Hoc Political Committee began, South Africa announced that it would not participate and that it was leaving the meeting.[51] The Committee adopted a resolution that was similar to that of previous years, renewing once again the mandate of the Commission. South Africa returned to vote against the motion, and the small group of its supporters, shrunk slightly with the departure of Colombia, which abstained.[52] After the vote in the Ad Hoc Political Committee, South Africa dramatically announced that its delegation to the United Nations was being withdrawn.[53] A few weeks later, the plenary General Assembly modified the draft and brought an end to the Commission. A majority of Member States supported continuing the mandate but the resolution required two-thirds of those voting to be in favour; the majority fell one vote short.[54] For the remainder of the decade, there were annual resolutions condemning South Africa adopted by large majorities.[55] In November 1959, only three Member States, the United Kingdom, France,

---

[49] The question of race conflict in South Africa resulting from the policies of apartheid of the Government of the Union of South Africa, 11 December 1954, A/RES/819 (IX); Summary record, Ad Hoc Political Committee, 8 December 1954, A/AC.76/SR.47, para. 69; Verbatim record, plenary General Assembly, 14 December 1954, A/PV.511, para. 129.

[50] Third Report of the United Nations Commission on the Racial Situation in South Africa, A/2953.

[51] Summary record, Ad Hoc Political Committee, 24 October 1955, A/AC.80/SR.3, para. 6.

[52] Summary record, Ad Hoc Political Committee, 9 November 1955, A/AC.80/SR.12, para. 44.

[53] Ibid.

[54] The question of race conflict in South Africa resulting from the policies of apartheid of the Government of the Union of South Africa, 6 December 1955, A/RES/917 (X); Verbatim record, plenary General Assembly, 6 December 1954, A/PV.551, para. 46.

[55] At the eleventh session: Question of race conflict in South Africa resulting from the policies of apartheid of the Government of the Union of South Africa, 30 January 1957, A/RES/1016 (XI); Verbatim record, plenary General Assembly, 30 January 1957, A/PV.648, para. 61, by 65 to 5 with 12 abstentions. At the twelfth session: Question of race conflict in South Africa resulting from the policies of apartheid of the Government of the Union of South Africa, 26 November 1957, A/RES/1178 (XII); Verbatim record, plenary General Assembly, 26 November 1957, A/PV.723, para. 104, by 59 to 6 with 14 abstentions. At the thirteenth session: Question of race conflict in South Africa resulting from the policies of apartheid of the Government of the Union of South Africa, 30 October 1958, A/RES/1248 (XIII); Verbatim record, plenary General Assembly, 30 October 1958, A/PV.723, para. 48, by 70 to 5 with 4 abstentions.

296 APARTHEID

and Portugal, voted against the resolution. Belgium, Canada, the Dominican Republic, Finland, Italy, Luxembourg, and the Netherlands abstained.[56]

Sharpeville and its Consequences

On 21 March 1960, armed South African police attacked peaceful demonstrators at Sharpeville, a Black township to the south of Johannesburg. Sixty-nine Black South Africans were killed, many of them shot in the back while fleeing. Another 186 were wounded. Four days after the Sharpeville massacre, 28 Member States from Africa and Asia, more than one-third of the total membership of the organization, petitioned the Security Council. Relying upon article 35(1) of the Charter of the United Nations, they called for an urgent meeting of the Security Council to consider 'the large-scale killings of unarmed and peaceful demonstrators against racial discrimination and segregation in the Union of South Africa'.[57] At the time, the Security Council consisted of 11 members.[58] Tunisia was the only African State on the Council. South Africa, as well as India, Ethiopia, Ghana, Guinea, Liberia, and Pakistan requested permission to speak during the debate, which continued over the course of three days. France and the United Kingdom opened the discussion by insisting that article 2(7) put such matters outside the authority of the United Nations, views they had already expressed on numerous occasions in the General Assembly.[59] When South Africa was given the floor, it too argued that this was a matter of purely domestic concern that was beyond the competence of the Security Council.[60] Its representative claimed that the annual discussion of South Africa's racial problems in the General Assembly had 'helped to inflame the situation', and that discussion by the Security Council could only embolden agitators and provoke further unrest. 'I am instructed to say that if this were to be the result the blame will rest squarely on the shoulders of the Security

[56] Question of race conflict in South Africa resulting from the policies of apartheid of the Government of the Union of South Africa, 17 November 1959, A/RES/1375 (XIV); Verbatim record, plenary General Assembly, 17 November 1958, A/PV.836, para. 24, by 62 to 3 with 7 abstentions.

[57] Letter dated 25 March 1960 from the Representatives of Afghanistan, Burma, Cambodia, Ceylon, Ethiopia, Federation of Malaya, Ghana, Guinea, India, Indonesia, Iran, Iraq, Japan, Jordan, Lebanon, Liberia, Libya, Morocco, Nepal, Pakistan, Philippines, Saudi Arabia, Sudan, Thailand, Tunisia, Turkey, United Arab Republic and Yemen addressed to the President of the Security Council, S/4279. Laos also joined the group (Letter dated 25 March 1960 from the Chargé d'Affaires a.i. of Laos to the United Nations addressed to the President of the Security Council, S/4279/Add.1).

[58] Initially, the Charter provided for six elected members of the Security Council. Egypt was elected to the Council in 1946 and again in 1949. From 1951 to 1959 there were no African members of the Council. Tunisia was elected in 1959, followed by Liberia (1961), Ghana (1962) and Morocco (1963). In 1965, the number of elected members was increased to 15, largely due to pressure from African and Asian Member States. Since 1966, there have always been three elected members of the Security Council from Africa, known as the 'A3'.

[59] Verbatim record, Security Council, 30 March 1960, S/PV.851, paras. 10–14.

[60] Ibid., paras. 46–58.

SHARPEVILLE AND ITS CONSEQUENCES   297

Council', he said.[61] Upon completing his remarks, the South African representative left the room.

Tunisia, which was the only African State sitting on the Council at the time, referred to the sessions of the General Assembly dealing with apartheid in South Africa that had been underway since 1952, and the resolutions adopted by majorities of over two-thirds. This confirmed that it was useless to invoke article 2(7) of the Charter, said the Tunisian representative.[62] During the debates, there were frequent references to the reports of the Santa Cruz Commission. Ecuador submitted a draft resolution[63] that was criticized by Tunisia for insufficiently addressing the gravity of the situation.[64] It disappointed many of the African and Asian States that had sought Security Council intervention.[65] The resolution was adopted by nine votes, with abstentions recorded for France and the United Kingdom.[66] It acknowledged the 'complaint' of the African and Asian States as well as the 'strong feelings and grave concern aroused among Governments and peoples of the world'. The operative paragraphs of the resolution 'called upon' South Africa to initiate measures aimed at bringing about racial harmony based on equality in order to ensure that the present situation does not continue or recur, and to abandon its policies of apartheid and racial discrimination'. The Secretary-General was requested to 'make such arrangements' to uphold the purposes and principles of the Charter and to report to the Council 'whenever necessary and appropriate'.[67]

A few weeks later the Secretary-General informed the Security Council that he had agreed to meet with the South African Prime Minister and the Minister of External Affairs in London in May, to be followed by a visit to the country.[68] Hammarskjöld's trip was delayed because of his responsibilities in the Congo.[69] In early January 1961, the Secretary-General travelled to South Africa. He met with the Prime Minister on several occasions and had informal contacts with various members of the community. He reported that talks with the South African leaders had been 'very useful' and that they had agreed to invite him back to Pretoria.[70] Hammarskjöld was criticized for failing to clarify what was

---

[61] Ibid., para. 80.

[62] Ibid., para. 116.

[63] Ecuador: Draft resolution, 31 March 1960, S/4299.

[64] Verbatim record, Security Council, 1 April 1960, S/PV.855, paras. 51–3.

[65] Verbatim record, Security Council, 1 April 1960, S/PV.856, para. 20.

[66] Ibid., para. 56.

[67] Resolution of 1 April 1960, S/RES/134 (1960).

[68] Interim report by the Secretary-General under Security Council Resolution S/4300, 19 April 1960, S/4305. Also Report of the Security Council to the General Assembly, 16 July 1959–15 July 1960, A/4494, paras. 118–21.

[69] Second interim report by the Secretary-General under Security Council Resolution S/4300, 11 October 1960, S/4551.

[70] Report by the Secretary-General under Security Council Resolution S/4300, 23 January 1961, S/4635. Also Report of the Security Council to the General Assembly, 16 July 1960–15 July 1961, A/4867, pp. 93–4.

298   APARTHEID

'useful' about the meetings.[71] According to Poland, 'nobody would have blamed the Secretary-General for failing in his efforts, but nobody could give his blessing to attempts to cover up a failure with cheerful phrases and hopeful assumptions, which in practice gave an excuse to those responsible for the present grave situation in South Africa.[72] Describing the visit as a 'whitewash', the Soviets said that during his visit he had made no effort to contact opposition parties and political organizations and had refused to receive their leaders. Hammarskjöld 'supported the position of the racists and colonialists', they charged.[73]

Only seven African States had actually participated in the initiative before the Security Council. However, later in the same year 16 newly independent African countries were admitted to the United Nations, and 12 more would join over the next five years. They wasted little time building on their success in the Security Council. In April 1961, 25 African Member States submitted a draft General Assembly resolution that was dramatically more demanding than those adopted during the 1950s. Besides harsh words of condemnation directed at the South African regime, it recommended that all States consider a range of sanctions.[74] A more moderate resolution proposed by India and several other Asian States was in line with previous resolutions adopted at earlier sessions of the General Assembly, describing South African racial policies as 'a flagrant violation of the Charter of the United Nations and the Universal Declaration of Human Rights and inconsistent with the obligations of a Member State'.[75]

During the debates in the Special Political Committee, many delegates warned of the danger of rebellion if South Africa did not alter its policies. One after another, they took the floor to condemn apartheid but also racial discrimination in general, sometimes making the link between colonialism and doctrines of white supremacy. Indonesia's representative pointed out that racism 'had been created by the expansion of European civilisation. The myth of the superiority of the white man, and of Western civilisation, had begun with the first contacts between Europeans and non-Europeans; and it was the survival of that myth, refuted by history, which was in 1961 plaguing the Union of South Africa.'[76] As a source of legal obligation, there were references to both the human rights clauses

---

[71] Summary record, Special Political Committee, 4 April 1961, A/SPC/SR.240, para. 4.

[72] Summary record, Special Political Committee, 3 April 1961, A/SPC/SR.238, para. 24.

[73] Summary record, Special Political Committee, 4 April 1961, A/SPC/SR.240, para. 14. Also Summary record, Special Political Committee, 4 April 1961, A/SPC/SR.241, paras. 5, 20.

[74] Draft resolution, Cameroon, Central African Republic, Chad, Congo (Brazzaville), Congo (Leopoldville), Dahomey, Ethiopia, Gabon, Ghana, Guinea, Ivory Coast, Liberia, Libya, Madagascar, Mali, Morocco, Niger, Nigeria, Senegal, Somalia, Sudan, Togo, Tunisia, Upper Volta, United Arab Republic, A/SPC/L.60.

[75] Draft resolution, Ceylon, Federation of Malaya, India, United Arab Republic, A/SPC/L.59. The United Arab Republic subsequently withdrew as a co-sponsor (A/SPC/L.59/Rev.1) and Afghanistan and Indonesia (A/SPC/L.59/Rev.1/Add.1) joined as co-sponsors.

[76] Summary record, Special Political Committee, 29 March 1961, A/SPC/SR.235, para. 19.

of the Charter and the provisions of the Universal Declaration of Human Rights. Ireland's representative said 'the policy of apartheid flagrantly violated both the letter and the spirit of the Charter and the Universal Declaration of Human Rights'. He 'feared that if the United Nations failed to uphold the purposes and principles of the Charter by not focussing the searchlight of a vigilant and aroused world public opinion upon that area of injustice its standing, prestige and authority would be seriously impaired'.[77] There was a perceptible shift in position of the United Kingdom with respect to article 2(7) of the Charter. It said it now considered apartheid to be 'exceptional'.[78]

The militant African resolution failed to obtain the required two-thirds majority in the plenary General Assembly. The paragraph containing the measures of implementation was adopted by the Special Political Committee, where only a simple majority was required,[79] but defeated in the plenary General Assembly, by 42 in favour to 34 against, with 21 abstentions.[80] The rejection of the operative paragraph 'effectively killed' the resolution, as the Ethiopian delegate put it, and the Assembly agreed not to proceed with a vote on the resolution as a whole.[81] The division could not have been more stark. Western countries were unanimous in opposing the resolution. The African countries were unanimous in supporting it, with the exception of Togo which abstained. The more moderate Asian resolution was adopted by 95 votes in favour with only Portugal, which by then was emulating South Africa, voting against.[82]

Six months later, the African States resumed their campaign for strict measures against South Africa. A draft resolution was submitted to the General Assembly, this time with more than 30 sponsors, including a number of Third World countries outside of Africa as well as Sierra Leone and Mauritania, who had been members of the United Nations for only a few weeks.[83] The resolution was adopted by the Special Political Committee with a majority of 55 in favour to 26 against, with 20 abstentions.[84] It was just shy of the two-thirds majority. In the plenary General Assembly, there was a separate vote on the paragraphs containing the measures and, as had been the case at the previous session, they

---

[77] Summary record, Special Political Committee, 30 March 1961, A/SPC/SR.237, para. 2.

[78] Summary record, Special Political Committee, 5 April 1961, A/SPC/SR.242, para. 13.

[79] Summary record, Special Political Committee, 10 April 1961, A/SPC/SR.245, para. 4; Report of the Special Political Committee, A/4728, para. 8.

[80] Verbatim record, plenary General Assembly, 13 April 1961, A/PV.981, para. 124.

[81] Ibid., para. 136.

[82] Ibid., para. 140.

[83] Draft resolution, Congo (Leopoldville), Ghana, Guinea, Iraq, Libya, Mali, Senegal, Sierra Leone, Somalia, Sudan, United Arab Republic, A/SPC/L.71 and Corr.1. Subsequently joined by Cameroun, Central African Republic, Chad, Congo (Brazzaville), Cuba, Dahomey, Ethiopia, Gabon, Indonesia, Ivory Coast, Liberia, Madagascar, Mauritania, Morocco, Niger, Nigeria, Saudi Arabia, Syria, Tunisia, and Upper Volta (A/SPC/L.71/Add.1-6).

[84] Summary record, Special Political Committee, 13 November 1961, A/SPC/SR, 287, para. 43; Report of the Special Political Committee, 14 November 1961, A4968, para. 11.

300   APARTHEID

were defeated by 48 votes to 31 with 22 abstentions because the special majority was not achieved.[85]

The sixteenth session of the General Assembly was also punctuated by a dramatic incident when the South African Foreign Minister, Eric Louw, was censured for a provocative speech he had made during the general debate. Louw questioned whether some newly independent African States were really ready for self-government.[86] At great length he praised the accomplishments of the apartheid system and its allege benefits. One after another, African delegates took the floor to condemn him for racism, misinformation, and dishonesty. Immediately following the speech, Liberia's representative moved that Louw's speech be deleted from the official records of the Assembly. 'It. is an insult to every African here, and not only to every African, but to every man of intelligence' he said. 'The whole speech is fictitious, and for him to come here and say that the Bantu tribe in Africa approves of everything the South African Government does is beyond human reason.'[87] Liberia moved the adoption of a 'motion of censure against the Government of South Africa, or its delegate, for a statement here today which was offensive, fictitious and erroneous, and of which the Assembly fully disapproves'.[88] The motion was adopted by 67 to 1 (South Africa) with 20 abstentions.[89] Upon his death in 1968, the *New York Times* wrote that if the effectiveness of his defences of apartheid was measured by the outrage it produced, his speech in the General Assembly on 11 October 1961 'was probably his most successful.'[90]

The following year, on 6 November 1962, the resolution succeeded, adopted by a vote of 67 to 16 with 23 abstentions.[91] Joining the original sponsors were two new African Member States, Algeria and Tanganyika.[92] The list of measures was expanded slightly by an explicit reference to boycott of 'arms and ammunition'. In addition to the list of recommended measures, the resolution called for establishment of a 'special committee' to monitor the situation and a request to

[85] Verbatim record, plenary General Assembly, 28 November 1961. A/PV.1067, para. 105.

[86] Verbatim record, plenary General Assembly, 11 October 1961, A/PV.1033, para. 82.

[87] Ibid., para. 151.

[88] Verbatim record, plenary General Assembly, 11 October 1961, A/PV.1034, para. 81.

[89] Ibid., para. 83. Belgium, Denmark, El Salvador, France, Iceland, Norway, Sweden, the United Kingdom the United States did not participate in the voting. The abstainers were Australia, Austria, Cambodia, Canada, China, Colombia, Costa Rica, Cyprus, Dominican Republic, Finland, Guatemala, Ireland, Italy, Japan, New Zealand, Nicaragua, Pakistan, Portugal, Spain, and Thailand.

[90] 'Eric Louw Dead: Diplomat was 77', *New York Times*, 24 June 1968, p. 37.

[91] The policies of apartheid of the Government of the Republic of South Africa, 6 November 1962, A/RES/1761 (XVII); Verbatim record, plenary General Assembly, 6 November 1962, A/PV.1165, para. 33.

[92] Draft resolution, Afghanistan, Algeria, Cameroun, Chad, Congo (Brazzaville), Congo (Leopoldville), Dahomey, Ethiopia, Gabon, Ghana, Guinea, India, Indonesia, Iraq, Ivory Coast, Liberia, Mali, Mauritania, Mongolia, Morocco, Nigeria, Pakistan, Saudi Arabia, Senegal, Sierra Leone, Somalia, Sudan, Syria, Tanganyika, Tunisia, United Arab Republic, A/SPC/L.83. Subsequently joined by Niger, Libya, and the Central African Republic (A/SPC/L.83/Add.1-3).

the Security Council 'to take appropriate measures, including sanctions, to se-cure South Africa's compliance with the resolutions of the Assembly and of the Council. . . and, if necessary, to consider action under Article 6 of the Charter'. Under article 6, a Member State may be expelled from the organization by the General Assembly following a recommendation of the Security Council. Among those voting against the resolution were South Africa's major trading partners: Australia, Belgium, Canada, France, Japan, the Netherlands, the United Kingdom, and the United States.[93] Besides South Africa itself, Ireland, Luxembourg, New Zealand, Portugal, Spain, and Turkey were also opposed. The result was facilitated when a procedural motion requiring only a simple majority prevented a vote on separate paragraphs, thereby forcing States that might have been uncomfortable with specific measures including a boycott to either op-pose the motion or abstain. Only the affirmative or negative votes and not the abstentions were counted in determining whether the special majority of two-thirds was attained.

Upon adoption of the resolution, the Secretary-General appointed the members of the Special Committee on *apartheid*: Algeria, Costa Rica, Ghana, Guinea, Haiti, Hungary, Malaya, Nepal, Nigeria, the Philippines, and Somalia.[94] States from Western Europe and North America refused to participate.[95] The Committee soon called for an expansion of its membership, highlighting the im-portance of 'full participation in the Committee' of permanent members of the Security Council as well as major trading partners of South Africa and broader geographic representation.[96] Its request prompted the General Assembly to increase the membership by six.[97] But when the President of the General Assembly requested Member States to join the Committee, few were willing. Argentina, Australia, Austria, Belgium, Brazil, Ceylon, France, Japan, Mexico, the Netherlands, Norway, Spain, Sweden, the United Kingdom, and the United States all declined. Denmark and Italy gave a conditional acceptance. Canada didn't even bother to reply. Only the Soviet Union provided a positive response.[98]

---

[93] Newell M. Stultz, 'The Apartheid Issue at the General Assembly: Stalemate or Gathering Storm' (1987) 86 *African Affairs* 25, at p. 33.

[94] The policies of apartheid of the Government of the Republic of South Africa, 18 February 1963, A/5400.

[95] Ram C. Malhotra, 'Apartheid and the United Nations' (1964) 354 *Annals of the American Academy of Political and Social Science* 135, at p. 143.

[96] Report of the Special Committee on the Policies of Apartheid of the Government of the Republic of South Africa, 8 December 1964, A/5825, para. 638. Also Report of the Special Committee on the Policies of Apartheid of the Government of the Republic of South Africa, 16 August 1965, A/5957, para. 183.

[97] The policies of apartheid of the Government of the Republic of South Africa, 15 December 1965, A/RES/2054 A (XX), OP 3.

[98] Report of the Special Committee on the Policies of Apartheid of the Government of the Republic of South Africa on the question of implementation of operative paragraph 3 of General Assembly res-olution 2054 A (XX) of 15 December 1965, 19 June 1966, S/7387.

302 APARTHEID

The General Assembly explicitly 'deplored' the attitude of South Africa's main trading partners, 'including three permanent members of the Security Council', for their failure to join the Special Committee.[99]

The Committee's goals, in practice, 'were overwhelmingly promotional in the broadest sense of the word'.[100] The Committee met an average of 25 times a year, assisting victims of apartheid as well as campaigning bodies, organizing conferences, seminars, hearings and similar activities. In 1966, the General Assembly established a special 'unit on apartheid' in order to assist the work of the Committee.[101] The following year, the General Assembly encouraged it to intensify co-operation with other special organs concerned with racial discrimination and colonialism in southern Africa.[102] Over the three decades of its existence, the Special Committee organized a huge number of activities. It set up subsidiary bodies, including a Task Force on Women and Children under Apartheid, a Task Force on Political Prisoners, and a Task force on Legal Aspects of Apartheid, and an Intergovernmental Group to Monitor the Supply and Shipping of Oil and Petroleum Products to South Africa. It organized conferences of trade unionists.[103] The Special Committee called upon writers, artists, and other personalities to boycott South Africa. It urged all academic and cultural institutions to terminate links with the country[104] and published a register of entertainers and artists who had performed in South Africa.[105] The basis was a General Assembly resolution specifying that States should 'cease any cultural and academic collaboration with South Africa, including the exchange of scientists, students and academic personalities, as well as co-operation research programmes'.[106] The Special Committee was also involved in an Art against Apartheid Collection, which was based in Paris. With the end of apartheid, the collection, of considerable value, was handed over to South Africa.[107] The Special Committee focussed on the role of transnational corporations in South Africa,

[99] The policies of apartheid of the Government of the Republic of South Africa, 16 December 1966, A/RES/2202 (XXI) A, OP 3.

[100] Newell M. Stultz, 'Evolution of the United Nations Anti-Apartheid Regime' (1991) 13 *Human Rights Quarterly* 1, at p. 11.

[101] Question of the violations of human rights and fundamental freedoms, including policies of racial discrimination and segregation and of apartheid, in all countries, with particular reference to colonial and other dependent countries and territories, 26 October 1966, A/RES/2144 (XXI), OP 13.

[102] The policies of apartheid of the Government of the Republic of South Africa, 13 December 1967, A/RES/2307 (XXII), OP 12–13.

[103] Second International Trade Union Conference for Action against Apartheid, 26 July 1977, S/12363/Add.1.

[104] Report of the Special Committee against Apartheid, A/35/33, para. 381. See Michael C. Beaubien, 'The Cultural Boycott of South Africa' (1982) 29(4) *Africa Today* 5.

[105] Report of the Special Committee against Apartheid, 31 October 1984, A/39/22, paras. 69–70.

[106] Cultural, Academic and other Boycotts of South Africa, 16 December 1980, A/RES/35/206 E, OP 2(b).

[107] Report of the Special Committee against Apartheid, 14 June 1994, A/48/22/Add.1, paras. 194–6.

holding a seminar on these subjects.[108] The seminar agreed upon a formal declaration that named names, among them: General Electric, IBM, Philips, Citicorp, Deutsche Bank, Credit Suisse, Barclay's Bank, Shell, BP Mobil, Total, General Motors, Volkswagen, Hoechst, Bayer, Hoffmann La-Roche, Ciba Geigy, and the British Steel Corporation.[109] This fit within a broader campaign for sanctions against South Africa including a boycott on the sale of oil.

In 1977, the General Assembly adopted the International Declaration against Apartheid in Sports. It called for a broad boycott of sporting activities involving South Africa.[110] This was followed, on 10 December 1985, by adoption of the International Convention Against Apartheid in Sports.[111] Pursuant to the Convention, a 15-member Commission on Apartheid in Sports was established. It issued annual reports for a few years until it stopped meeting in 1992.[112] For many years, the Special Committee against Apartheid compiled a register of athletes who had participated in sports events in South Africa. In 1989, shortly before the boycott was suspended, the Committee listed 3,404 athletes, of whom 650 participated in sports activities in South Africa, 'although most were not renowned'. The highest numbers were from the United States and the United Kingdom.[113]

Resistance to Mandatory Sanctions

During the 1940s and 1950s the United Nations confined its campaign against apartheid to 'naming and shaming'. But in 1960, the new Member States from Africa insisted that coercive measures were required. In the Special Political Committee of the General Assembly 26 African States, all but eight of them new Members, proposed a resolution calling for five concrete measures: breaking of diplomatic relations with the Government of South Africa; closing ports to South African vessels; prohibiting their own ships from entering South African ports; boycotting South African goods; refusing landing and passage facilities to South African aircraft.[114] The initiative was not successful. A similar resolution

---

[108] Report of the Special Committee against Apartheid, 24 October 1980, A/35/22, paras. 67–77.

[109] Declaration of the International Seminar on the Role of Transnational Corporations in South Africa, held in London from 2 to 4 November 1979, 6 November 1979, A/34/655, annex.

[110] Policies of apartheid of the Government of South Africa, 14 December 1977, A/RES/32/105 M.

[111] Policies of apartheid of the Government of South Africa, 10 December 1985, A/RES/40/64 G. The Convention entered into force three years later: (1988) 1500 UNTS 161.

[112] Report of the Commission on Apartheid in Sports, 27 October 1989, A/44/47; Report of the Commission on Apartheid in Sports, 14 September 1990, A/45/45; Report of the Commission on Apartheid in Sports, 10 November 1992, A/47/45.

[113] UN Yearbook 1989, p. 144.

[114] Cameroun, Central African Republic, Chad, Congo (Brazzaville), Congo (Leopoldville), Cuba, Dahomey, Ethiopia, Gabon, Ghana, Guinea, Indonesia, Ivory Coast, Liberia, Libya, Mali, Malagasy

304   APARTHEID

was submitted at the next session of the General Assembly.[115] It added a call for the Security Council to expel South Africa from the United Nations. The resolution was adopted by the Special Political Committee[116] and defeated in the General Assembly.[117] The separate vote on the operative paragraphs providing for coercive measures, which required a two-thirds majority for adoption, was 48 in favour to 31 against with 22 abstentions. Not enough, but a measurable improvement on the vote at the previous session, which had been 42 to 34 with 21 abstentions. When the operative paragraphs were rejected and the representative of the African group requested withdrawal of the draft, he added acerbically that his delegation 'would, however, like to say that the African countries hope the white peoples of Europe and America will admit that when that same doctrine was enforced against them by the Nazis, the black peoples were not deterred by economic considerations but gave their lives in order to save the world. Nazism has appeared in Africa under the name of apartheid.'[118]

In his remarks at the 1961 session following the defeat of the sanctions resolution, the spokesman for the African Group pledged that the same resolution would be submitted the following year. '[P]erhaps a majority of the Assembly will ultimately come to understand that it is more honourable to save the dignity of man than to cling to selfish material considerations. Our only regret is that in the meantime deaths will take place and men will be humiliated as human beings', he said.[119] And that is what happened. The African States made essentially the same proposal in 1962, adding a specific reference to an embargo on arms and ammunition.[120] On the third attempt, they met with success.[121] The vote in the General Assembly was 67 to 16 with 23 abstentions.[122] The Nordic States, Austria, and Italy changed their position and abstained rather than vote

Republic, Morocco, Niger, Nigeria, Senegal, Somalia, Sudan, Tunisia, United Arab Republic, Upper Volta: draft resolution, 3 April 1961, A/SPC/L.60 and Corr.1 and Add.1, 2.

[115] Cameroun, Central African Republic, Chad, Congo (Brazzaville), Congo (Leopoldville), Cuba, Dahomey, Ethiopia, Gabon, Ghana, Guinea, Indonesia, Iraq, Ivory Coast, Liberia, Libya, Madagascar, Mali, Mauritania, Morocco, Niger, Nigeria, Saudi Arabia, Senegal. Sierra Leone, Somalia, Sudan, Syria, Tunisia, United Arab Republic, Upper Volta: draft resolution, 30 October 1961, A/SPC/L.71 and Corr.1 and Add.1-6.

[116] Report of the Special Political Committee, 14 November 1961, A/4968, para. 11.

[117] Verbatim record, plenary General Assembly, 28 November 1961, A/PV.1067, paras. 105–10.

[118] Ibid., para. 111.

[119] Ibid.

[120] Afghanistan, Algeria, Cameroon, Central African Republic, Chad, Congo (Brazzaville), Congo (Leopoldville), Dahomey, Ethiopia, Gabon, Ghana, Guinea, India, Indonesia, Iraq, Ivory Coast, Liberia, Libya, Mali, Mauritania, Mongolia, Morocco, Niger, Nigeria, Pakistan, Saudi Arabia, Senegal, Sierra Leone, Somalia, Sudan, Syria, Tanganyika, Tunisia, United Arab Republic: draft resolution, 26 October 1962, A/SPC/L.83 and Add. 1–3.

[121] The policies of apartheid of the Government of the Republic of South Africa, 6 November 1962, A/RES/1761 (XVII).

[122] Verbatim record, plenary General Assembly, 6 November 1962, A/PV.1165, para. 33.

against the resolution. This was also the resolution that launched the Special Committee on Apartheid. In its first report, in September 1963, the Committee proposed a number of measures to be taken by the General Assembly and the Security Council aimed at dissuading South Africa from its racist policies including the prohibition or discouragement of foreign investments, loans, and emigration, denial of facilities for ships and planes to and from South Africa, and 'study of means to ensure an effective embargo on the supply of arms and ammunition, as well as petroleum, including a blockade, if necessary, under aegis of the United Nations'.[123] Weeks later, the General Assembly agreed to an embargo on arms and military equipment and on the supply of petroleum or petroleum products, but only with reference to Namibia.[124]

In December 1963, the Security Council adopted an embargo on sale and shipment of arms, ammunition of all types, and military vehicles to South Africa, by nine votes with France and the United Kingdom abstaining.[125] Nevertheless, the wording of the resolution was not mandatory, and in practice it was ignored, even by some of the permanent members of the Council who had adopted it. The Special Committee against Apartheid would later single out France for particular criticism, saying it 'had honoured the arms embargo more in the breach than in the observance and, by its actions, had encouraged other European States to break the embargo'. As for the United Kingdom and the United States, they 'had tried to honour their commitment' although they seemed to consider weapons to be destined for external defence when in fact they were being used extensively for internal security.[126]

Writing about the history of the anti-apartheid campaign within the United Nations, Boutros Boutros-Ghali explained that although there was 'virtual unanimity' in the organization in the condemnation of South Africa, there were nevertheless sharp differences of opinion about the measures that should be taken. A majority of Member States favoured total isolation of the South African regime, through diplomatic, economic, and other sanctions. Ideally, these would be ordered by the Security Council pursuant to Chapter VII of the Charter.

---

[123] Report of the Special Committee on the policies of apartheid of the Government of the Republic of South Africa, 16 September 1963, A/5497, para. 515.

[124] Question of South West Africa, 13 November 1963, A/RES/1899 (XVIII), OP 7. See also Question of South West Africa, 17 December 1965, A/RES/2074 (XX), OP 11.

[125] Question relating to the policies of apartheid of the Government of the Republic of South Africa, 7 August 1963, S/RES/181 (1963), OP 3. Also Question relating to the policies of apartheid of the Government of the Republic of South Africa, 4 December 1983, S/RES/182 (1963), OP 5; Question relating to the policies of apartheid of the Government of the Republic of South Africa, 18 June 1964, S/RES/191 (1964), OP 12; The Question of race conflict in South Africa resulting from the policies of apartheid of the Government of the Republic of South Africa, 23 July 1970, S/RES/282 (1970), OP 6.

[126] Report of the Special Committee on the policies of *apartheid* of the Government of the Republic of South Africa, 10 September 1970, A/8022/Rev.1, para. 37.

306   APARTHEID

But, as Boutros-Ghali noted, a large number of States, many of them newly independent and developing countries, 'ended their relations with South Africa,
often at considerable economic sacrifice, or refrained from establishing them'.[127]
This was not the case, however, with South Africa's major trading partners. In
1966, a resolution of the General Assembly 'deplored' the attitude of the main
trading partners of South Africa, 'including three permanent members of the
Security Council, which, by their refusal to join the Special Committee on the
Policies of Apartheid of the Government of South Africa and by their increasing
collaboration with the Government of South Africa, have encouraged the latter
to persist in its racial policies'.[128]

In 1968, the General Assembly called upon the Security Council to adopt 'comprehensive mandatory sanctions' against South Africa.[129] It also condemned collaboration with South Africa by 'the main trading partners of South Africa' and
'foreign financial and other interests' contrary to General Assembly and Security
Council resolutions.[130] Two new elements appeared: States were requested
to discourage the flow of immigrants to South Africa, particularly skilled and
technical personnel, and to suspend cultural, educational, sporting, and other
exchanges.[131] Subsequent resolutions reformulated the appeals for a range of
sanctions.[132] The General Assembly continued to call upon the Security Council
to adopt economic and other sanctions, pursuant to Chapter VII of the Charter,
as 'one of the essential means of achieving a peaceful solution of the grave situation in South Africa'.[133] The Programme of Action against Apartheid, adopted
by the General Assembly in 1976, devoted an entire page to precise measures
aimed at isolating South Africa in the following areas: diplomatic, consular, and
other official relations; military and nuclear collaboration; economic collaboration; airline and shipping lines; emigration; cultural, educational, sporting, and
other collaboration.[134]

---

[127] Boutros Boutros-Ghali, 'Introduction', in *The United Nations and Apartheid, 1948–1994*,
New York: United Nations, 1994, pp. 3–131, paras. 93–4.
[128] The policies of apartheid of the Government of South Africa, 16 December 1966, A/RES/2202
A (XXI), OP 3.
[129] The policies of apartheid of the Government of South Africa, 2 December 1968, A/RES/2396
(XXIII), OP 4.
[130] Ibid., OP 5.
[131] Ibid., OP 11, 12.
[132] For example, The policies of apartheid of the Government of South Africa, 21 November
1969, A/RES/2506 B (XXIV), OP 5–8; Arms embargo, 29 November 1971, A/RES/2775 A (XXVI);
Apartheid in sports, 29 November 1971, A/RES/2775 D (XXVI); Economic collaboration with South
Africa, 9 November 1976, A/RES/31/6 H; Situation in South Africa, 9 November 1976, A/RES/31/6
I, OP 7; Military and nuclear collaboration with South Africa, 14 December 1977, A/RES/32/105 F;
Investments in South Africa, 16 December 1977, A/RES/32/105 O.
[133] For example, Situation in South Africa resulting from the policies of apartheid, 15 November
1972, A/RES/2923 E (XVII), OP 7.
[134] Programme of Action against Apartheid, 9 November 1976, A/RES/31/6 J, Annex.

RESISTANCE TO MANDATORY SANCTIONS 307

The 1976 uprising in the Johannesburg suburb of Soweto, and the repressive response from the government in Pretoria, was a catalyst prompting the Security Council to transform the embargo on arms and ammunition from what had been only advisory into a binding obligation.[135] As usual, the initiative came from the African Group. A series of resolutions was proposed by the three African members of the Council, Benin, Libya, and Mauritius, directed at the imposition of embargos on arms and oil, and the end of foreign investment and economic co-operation.[136] They had initially been presented in March 1977 but, after a considerable debate, the Western countries asked for a postponement in order to pursue efforts of persuasion with the South African regime. After many months there had been no progress. In October, the African Group insisted that the debate be renewed. India held the rotating presidency of the Council. It was regularly reminded of, and congratulated for, its pioneering role in challenging racism in South Africa at the first session of the General Assembly, three decades previously. Initially, the Council heard from David Sibeko of the Pan Africanist Congress. 'While we have been impressed by the sharp criticisms pouring out from Bonn, London, Ottawa, Paris and Washington, and further impressed by tiny steps in the right direction like the recalling of ambassadors, it must be borne in mind that Vorster is no mere juvenile delinquent to be treated with mild rebukes', he warned.[137] For more than a week, speakers in the Council poured out their anger at the South African regime. The Western delegates all affirmed their support for a mandatory arms embargo. Only at the final session did Canada take the floor, apparently speaking for all of the Western members of the Council, to explain that it would only vote in favour of the first of the resolutions, describing it as 'a straight expression of opinion of the Council on the continuing oppressive actions of the Government of South Africa'.[138] Indeed, the first draft resolution was adopted by consensus.[139] The other three, including the draft resolution calling for an arms embargo, obtained 10 votes but were vetoed by France, the United Kingdom, and the United States.[140]

The President of the Council struggled to find an acceptable compromise, aware that his term was ending that evening and that a new President of the

[135] Special report of the Special Committee against Apartheid on 'The Soweto massacre and its aftermath', 3 August 1976, A/31/22/Add.1
[136] Benin, Libyan Arab Jamahiriya and Mauritius: revised draft resolution, 26 October 1977, S/12309/Rev.1; Benin, Libyan Arab Jamahiriya and Mauritius: draft resolution, 29 March 1977, S/12310; Benin, Libyan Arab Jamahiriya and Mauritius: revised draft resolution, 26 October 1977, S/12311/Rev.1; Benin, Libyan Arab Jamahiriya and Mauritius: draft resolution, 26 October 1977, S/12312/Rev.1.
[137] Verbatim record, Security Council, 24 October 1977, S/PV.2036, para. 36.
[138] Verbatim record, Security Council, 31 October 1977, S/PV.2045, paras. 30–5.
[139] South Africa, 31 October 1977, S/RES/417 (1977); Verbatim record, Security Council, 31 October 1977, S/PV.2045, para. 52.
[140] Verbatim record, Security Council, 31 October 1977, S/PV.2045, paras. 53–5.

308   APARTHEID

Council would take office the next day. Canada and West Germany presented a new draft resolution supporting a mandatory arms embargo,[141] but the meeting concluded without a decision and the draft was subsequently withdrawn. At the next meeting of the Council, a new text put forward by India achieved consensus.[142] It was adopted unanimously, without debate.[143] This was followed immediately by an intervention from the Secretary-General, Kurt Waldheim, who highlighted the unprecedented nature of the resolution. It was the result of a unanimous decision by the Council to impose sanctions on a Member State in accordance with Chapter VII of the Charter. 'It is abundantly clear that the policy of apartheid as well as the measures taken by the South African Government to implement this policy are such a gross violation of human rights and so fraught with danger to international peace and security that a response commensurate with the gravity of the situation was required', said Waldheim. 'Thus, we enter a new and significantly different phase of the long-standing efforts of the international community to obtain redress of these grievous wrongs.'[144]

The resolution began by 'strongly condemning the racist régime of South Africa for its resort to massive violence against and wanton killings of the African people, including schoolchildren and students and others opposing racial discrimination, and calling upon the South African racist régime urgently to end violence against the African people and to take urgent steps to eliminate apartheid and racial discrimination'. The preamble referred to the 'voluntary embargo' of previous resolutions. In operative paragraph 2, the Security Council '[d]ecide[d] that all States shall cease forthwith any provision to South Africa of arms and related *matériel* of all types, including the sale or transfer of weapons and ammunition, military vehicles and equipment, paramilitary police equipment, and spare parts for the aforementioned, and shall cease as well the provision of all types of equipment and supplies and grants of licensing arrangements for the manufacture or maintenance of the aforementioned'. Operative paragraph 3 targeted the termination of existing contracts and licences relating to the manufacture and maintenance of arms and ammunition. Operative paragraph 4 required all States to refrain from co-operation with South Africa in the manufacture and development of nuclear weapons. It was specified that all States, 'including States non-members of the United Nations', were 'to act strictly in accordance with the provisions of the present resolution'.[145]

---

[141]   Canada and Germany, Federal Republic of: draft resolution, 31 October 1977, S/12433.
[142]   Draft resolution, 4 November 1977, S/12436.
[143]   South Africa, 4 November 1977, S/RES/418 (1977); Verbatim record, Security Council, 31 October 1977, S/PV.2045, para. 4.
[144]   Verbatim record, Security Council, 31 October 1977, S/PV.2045, para. 6.
[145]   South Africa, 4 November 1977, S/RES/418 (1977).

RESISTANCE TO MANDATORY SANCTIONS   309

In May 1978, the Secretary-General reported that 106 Member States had said they would abide by the resolution.[146] The only Member State to decline such confirmation was Israel. It only indicated that it would be 'guided' by the resolution in formulating its policy.[147] On 1 April 1978, the *Economist* reported a cut of $147 million in the South African official budget for projected arms purchases, providing proof that the mandatory embargo was having an effect.[148] The Security Council never returned to the issue in order to adopt further sanctions.

From the very beginning of its activities, the Special Committee against Apartheid had promoted an oil embargo on South Africa. In its 1977 resolution on economic collaboration, the General Assembly had included a phrase calling for an embargo on the supply of petroleum and petroleum products to South Africa as well as on investment in the industry there.[149] In January 1979, the oil embargo on South Africa was the subject of an entire resolution of the Assembly.[150] It was adopted by 105 votes to 6 (Belgium, France, Germany, Luxembourg, United Kingdom, United States) with 16 abstentions.[151] A study prepared for the Special Committee against Apartheid concluded that oil sanctions would only be feasible and effective if imposed by a mandatory resolution of the Security Council.[152] On its recommendation, the General Assembly adopted a resolution recommending this course of action to the Council.[153] Although there was some progress in cutting oil shipments to South Africa, a decade later, in 1989, the General Assembly was still imploring the Security Council to impose a mandatory embargo.[154] The trend was clear. In 1979, the resolution was adopted by 124 to 7 with 13 abstentions,[155] whereas in 1989 the vote was 139 in favour to 2 with 14 abstentions.[156] The United States and the United Kingdom persisted in their opposition to the oil boycott until the *apartheid* regime collapsed.

---

[146] Report of the Secretary-General on the implementation of Resolution 418 (1977 on the question of South Africa, adopted by the Security Council at its 1046th meeting on 4 November 1977, 18 April 1978, S/12673.

[147] Note verbale dated 7 December 1977 from the permanent representative of Israel to the United Nations addressed to the Secretary-General, 7 December 1977, S/12475.

[148] *Economist*, 1 April 1978, p. 75.

[149] Economic collaboration with South Africa, 14 December 1977, A/RES/32/105 G, OP 3(d).

[150] Oil embargo against South Africa, 24 January 1979, A/RES/33/183 E.

[151] Verbatim record, plenary General Assembly, 24 January 1979, A/33/PV.93, para. 143.

[152] Special report of the Special Committee against Apartheid on oil sanctions against South Africa, 22 September 1978, A/33/22/Add.1, para. 8. For the report itself: Martin Bailey and Bernard Rivers, *Oil Sanctions Against South Africa*, New York: United Nations Centre Against Apartheid, 1978.

[153] Oil embargo against South Africa, 12 December 1979, A/RES/34/93 F, OP 3.

[154] Oil embargo against South Africa, 22 November 1989, A/RES/44/27 I, OP 4.

[155] Verbatim record, plenary General Assembly, 12 December 1979, A/34/PV.100, para. 256.

[156] Provisional verbatim record, plenary General Assembly, 22 November 1989, A/34/PV.63, p. 82.

310 APARTHEID

Dismantling Apartheid

In 1974, the General Assembly rejected the credentials of South Africa.[157] It called upon the Security Council to review South Africa's relationship with the United Nations 'in the light of the constant violation by South Africa of the principles of the Charter and the Universal Declaration of Human Rights'.[158] The Security Council considered the issue at 11 meetings in October 1974. On 30 October 1970, 10 members of the Council voted to expel South Africa from the United Nations but the resolution was not adopted because of the veto of three of the permanent members, France, the United Kingdom, and the United States.[159] Immediately after the vote, the president of the Council, from Cameroon, noted that South Africa only remained a member of the United Nations because of the veto power. '[P]ublic opinion in our various countries and world public opinion in general will surely understand who bears the overwhelming responsibility for the defeat of the draft resolution'.[160] In the corridors of the United Nations, and occasionally even in the recorded debates, delegates spoke of the 'triple veto' upon which the racist South African regime could rely.

Days later, the matter returned to the General Assembly. Tanzania, speaking on behalf of the African Group, observed that despite the refusal of the Security Council to expel South Africa, the record demonstrated the universal condemnation of apartheid. 'Indeed, even those who misused their responsibility under the Charter and cast their vetoes against the expulsion of that regime from our Organisation condemned that regime and its system of apartheid and racial segregation, which is based on the dangerous concept of racial supremacy', he said.[161] There was fierce denunciation of Britain, France, and the United States in the Assembly debate. 'Do we really need to be lectured on common law, international law or the Charter itself by the representative of a permanent member of the Security Council, when the permanent members and other Western European Powers in the Security Council have so often blatantly contravened mandatory resolutions of the Council which they themselves adopted', said the Nigerian delegate.[162] The President of the Assembly, Abdulaziz Bouteflika of Algeria, upheld the earlier decision on the credentials of South Africa and maintained its expulsion from the General Assembly,[163] reversing a precedent known as the 'Hambro

---

[157] Credentials of representatives to the 29th session of General Assembly, 30 September 2004, A/RES/3206 (XXIX); First report of the credentials committee, 28 September 1974, A/9779.

[158] Relationship between the United Nations and South Africa, 30 September 1974, A/RES/3207 (XXIX).

[159] Verbatim record, Security Council, 30 October 1974, S/PV.1808, para. 155.

[160] Ibid., paras. 158–9.

[161] Verbatim record, plenary General Assembly, 12 November 1974, A/PV.2281, para. 3.

[162] Ibid., para. 130.

[163] Ibid., para. 160.

ruling' and effectively neutralizing article 6 of the Charter.[164] Challenged by the United States, the President's ruling was upheld by 91 to 22 with 19 abstentions.[165]

The Soweto uprising that began in June 1976 marked the start of militant demonstrations and protests that were to continue in South Africa until the end of *apartheid*. At the international level, measures adopted by the United Nations including the arms embargo and the sports boycott, heightened pressure on the racist regime. Whereas in 1946, South Africa could count on a significant number of supporters in the General Assembly, by the 1980s that had withered as, inexorably, the camp of its opponents grew.[166] Nevertheless, wealthy States in Europe and North America continued to trade with South Africa and, to varying degrees, provide it with political support. Within these countries, pressure from civil society grew for governments to take a more resolute position against apartheid. In the United States, President Reagan vetoed anti-apartheid legislation only to be overruled by the Congress in 1986. The United Kingdom also applied limited sanctions, over the objections of Prime Minister Thatcher. In 1987, Israel's cabinet announced that it would not renew military contracts with South Africa. The following year, Israel told the United Nations that it was curtailing its relations with South Africa and that all cultural ties had been severed. The Special Committee against Apartheid acknowledged 'a step in the right direction' although it remained sceptical.[167] Multinational corporations chose to leave South Africa, damaging an already weakened economy. In 1988 South Africa agreed to withdraw from Namibia. The following year South Africa's leadership changed.

At a special session, held in December 1989, the General Assembly adopted without a vote the Declaration on Apartheid and its Destructive Consequences in Southern Africa. The Declaration spoke of a 'conjuncture of circumstances' that could enable apartheid to be brought to a speedy end through negotiation. It welcome 'the dawn of a new era of peace for all the peoples of Africa, in a continent finally free from racism, white minority rule and colonial domination'.[168] Early in the new year at the opening of the South African Parliament, President F.W. De Klerk announced that the ban on the African National Congress and other organizations was being repealed and that Nelson Mandela was being released from prison. On 22 June 1990, as part of his world tour, Mandela addressed the

---

[164] Verbatim record, plenary General Assembly, 11 November 1970, A/PV.1901, para. 286. For the legal opinion on which the President of the Assembly acted, see 'Scope of credentials in Rule 27 of the Rules of Procedure of the General Assembly', *UN Juridical Yearbook 1970*, pp. 169–71.

[165] Verbatim record, plenary General Assembly, 12 November 1974, A/PV.2281, para. 185.

[166] Newell M. Stultz, 'The Apartheid Issue at the General Assembly: Stalemate or Gathering Storm?' (1987) 86 *African Affairs* 25, at pp. 26–7.

[167] Report on recent developments concerning relations between South Africa and Israel, A/43/ 22, Annex.

[168] Declaration on Apartheid and its Destructive Consequences in Southern Africa, 14 December 1989, A/RES/S-16/1, PP 16, OP 1.

312 APARTHEID

Special Committee against Apartheid in the General Assembly hall at United Nations headquarters in New York City.[169]

* * *

The end of apartheid brought to a close the issue that had been at the heart of United Nations activity in the area of racial discrimination. In the early years, the battle had been waged by India and other States of the Global South. Civil society was also engaged, with particular credit due to African American organizations. By the early 1960s, the dramatic influx of African States that had only just won their independence transformed the United Nations and with it the campaign against apartheid. There was a consistent pattern over the four decades of resolutions and other initiatives being taken by countries of the Global South, and of rejection and obstruction by countries of the North, especially the three permanent members of the Security Council, Britain, France, and the United States.

Histories of international human rights often overlook the significance of the anti-apartheid struggle. They adopt a narrative that tends to exaggerate the progressive contribution of European and other Western States. In reality, the Western States held back human rights within the United Nations. Initially, the real logjam for the development of human rights activities in the United Nations was the domestic jurisdiction clause, article 2(7) of the Charter. It was the countries of the Global South that knocked it out, over the objections not only of South Africa but of its European supporters. The anti-apartheid campaign led to the first United Nations commission of inquiry into human rights violations. It confronted the General Assembly and the Security Council with the importance of mandatory sanctions, including measures affecting sports, culture, and academic activity. The struggle against apartheid was also responsible for the revival of international criminal prosecution, which had gone into a form of hibernation in the early 1950s. It is to this dimension of international law that the study now turns.

---

[169] Statement by Nelson Mandela to the Special Committee against Apartheid, 22 June 1990, A/44/1990, Annex VI.

11
Racial Discrimination as a Crime against Humanity

Nuremberg's Long Shadow

In the final years of the twentieth century, international criminal justice took on an important place in global efforts to address impunity for violations of fundamental human rights. Increasingly, in time of crisis and conflict, attention turned to the prospect of prosecution of individuals for their involvement in aggressive war and tyrannical regimes. Two specialized tribunals were established by the United Nations in the early 1990s, the International Criminal Tribunal for the former Yugoslavia and the International Criminal Tribunal for Rwanda. Both were addressed to situations involving racial discrimination, including its most extreme form, genocide. The institutions were temporary in nature.[1] However, with the negotiation and adoption of the Rome Statute of the International Criminal Court, in 1998, a permanent judicial body came into being.[2] Although all three tribunals are sometimes colloquially referred to as war crimes tribunals, two of the core crimes over which they may exercise jurisdiction, genocide and crimes against humanity, are profoundly linked to the issue of racial discrimination and may be prosecuted when perpetrated in peacetime.

The term 'crimes against humanity' can be traced to writers of the eighteenth century, including Voltaire and Beccaria.[3] Until the mid-twentieth century it remained undefined, in a legal sense, but the term seems to have been well understood as a way to describe atrocities on a grand scale. In 1915, as reports emerged of what we describe today as the genocide of the Armenians, the three Powers of the Entente, Britain, France, and Russia, condemned 'these new crimes of Turkey against humanity and civilisation' and pledged that those responsible would be

---

[1] On the *ad hoc* tribunals, see William A. Schabas, *The UN International Criminal Tribunals: the former Yugoslavia, Rwanda and Sierra Leone*, Cambridge: Cambridge University Press, 2006, and the authorities cited therein.

[2] On the International Criminal Court, see William A. Schabas, *Introduction to the International Criminal Court*, 6th ed., Cambridge: Cambridge University Press, 2020; William A. Schabas, *The International Criminal Court: A Commentary on the Rome Statute*, 2nd ed., Oxford: Oxford University Press, 2016, and the authorities cited therein.

[3] William A. Schabas, *Unimaginable Atrocities*, Oxford: Oxford University Press, 2011, pp. 51–2.

The International Legal Order's Colour Line. William A. Schabas, Oxford University Press.
© Oxford University Press 2023. DOI: 10.1093/oso/9780197744475.003.0011

314   RACIAL DISCRIMINATION AS A CRIME AGAINST HUMANITY

held to account when the War was over.[4] This was addressed in a provision of the Treaty of Sèvres proposing the trial of Ottoman leaders for 'massacres'.[5] However, the Treaty never entered into force and those responsible for the Armenian genocide escaped accountability.

As the Second World War was coming to a close, the four powers occupying Germany agreed to prosecute Nazi atrocities including those perpetrated within Germany itself as crimes against humanity. These were defined in the Charter of the International Military Tribunal as 'murder, extermination, enslavement, deportation, and other inhumane acts committed against any civilian population, before or during the war, or persecutions on political, racial or religious grounds in execution of or in connection with any crime within the jurisdiction of the Tribunal, whether or not in violation of the domestic law of the court where perpetrated'.[6] Nazi persecution and attempted destruction of Europe's Jewish population was prosecuted by the International Military Tribunal under the heading of crimes against humanity. First and foremost, crimes against humanity were about prosecuting the leaders of the paradigmatic racist state.

After an intense period of activity following the Second World War, marked by the trials at Nuremberg and Tokyo and the adoption of the Genocide Convention, in the mid-1950s international criminal law entered a period of virtual dormancy. Preparation of a draft code of crimes, mandated by General Assembly Resolution 95(I), fell off the agenda of the International Law Commission. The inactivity only lasted about a decade. It began to revive in the early 1960s under the impetus of States from the Global South who understood that individual accountability might prove to be a way forward in challenging racism's most egregious manifestation, apartheid, and other forms of racial discrimination practised by States of southern Africa. Their initiatives prompted many progressive developments in international criminal law including an expanded understanding of crimes against humanity and the promotion of the use of universal jurisdiction. These developments were generally opposed by States of the Global North, for whom another quarter century was necessary before their enthusiasm for international justice was to revive.

In 1965, the General Assembly began using the terminology 'crimes against humanity' to refer to racial discrimination, apartheid, and similar practices. The first of three resolutions adopted that year that referred to crimes against humanity emerged from the Fourth Committee of the General Assembly. The

---

[4] The Ambassador in France (Sharp) to the Secretary of State, Paris, 28 May 1915, FRUS 1915, Supplement, The World War, p. 981.

[5] Treaty of Sèvres, 10 August 1920, art. 230.

[6] Agreement for the Prosecution and Punishment of Major War Criminals of the European Axis, and Establishing the Charter of the International Military Tribunal (IMT), annex (1951) 82 UNTS 279, art. VI(c). A similar text, with minor differences, was included in the Charter of the International Military Tribunal for the Far East, also known as the Tokyo Tribunal.

resolution was intended to address the 'real substance' of the white supremacist regime that held power in Southern Rhodesia and that was threatening to declare independence in a perverse form of decolonization.[7] It '[c]ondemn[ed] the policies of racial discrimination and segregation practised in Southern Rhodesia, which constitute a crime against humanity'.[8] The text was proposed by 56 Member States, 35 of them from Africa. Yugoslavia and Cyprus were the only European sponsors of the resolution; Trinidad and Tobago was the only one from the western hemisphere.[9] There is no reported discussion of the crimes against humanity issue in the records of the Fourth Committee, where the debate focussed on whether the United Kingdom should be urged to use force to suppress the settler rebellion. The resolution was adopted in the Fourth Committee and then in the plenary General Assembly by large majorities, with Western States voting against or abstaining.[10]

Later in the 1965 session, the Fourth Committee adopted a resolution on South West Africa that condemned 'the policies of apartheid and racial discrimination practised by the Government of South Africa in South West Africa, which constitute crimes against humanity'.[11] The original draft resolution did not contain this paragraph.[12] It was proposed by Hungary, whose delegate explained that the reference to crimes against humanity in the earlier resolution on Southern Rhodesia 'was even more valid in the case of South West Africa'.[13] The only comment on the amendment came from the United States, which said it interpreted the term crime against humanity 'in the ordinary meaning of those words and not as a legal definition'.[14] The resolution was adopted in the Fourth Committee

---

[7] Summary record, Fourth Committee, 27 October 1965, A/C.4/SR.1540, para. 2.

[8] Question of Southern Rhodesia, 5 November 1965, A/RES/2022 (XX), OP 4. The same formulation is repeated in Question of Southern Rhodesia, 3 November 1967, A/RES/2262 (XXII), OP 2.

[9] Implementation of the Declaration on the Granting of Independence to Colonial Countries and Peoples: reports of the Special Committee: Southern Rhodesia: Afghanistan, Algeria, Burma, Burundi, Cameroun, Central African Republic, Ceylon, Chad, Congo (Brazzaville), Congo (Democratic Republic of), Cyprus, Dahomey, Ethiopia, Gabon, Ghana, Guinea, India, Iran, Iraq, Ivory Coast, Jordan, Kenya, Kuwait, Lebanon, Liberia, Libya, Madagascar, Malawi, Malaysia, Mali, Mauritania, Mongolia, Morocco, Nepal, Niger, Nigeria, Pakistan, Philippines, Rwanda, Saudi Arabia, Senegal, Sierra Leone, Somalia, Sudan, Syria, Thailand, Togo, Trinidad and Tobago, Tunisia, Uganda, United Arab Republic, United Republic of Tanzania, Upper Volta, Yemen, Yugoslavia, and Zambia, draft resolution, 27 October 1965, A/C.4/L.795 and Add.1-3; Report of the Fourth Committee, 3 November 1965, A/6041/Add.1, para. 4.

[10] Summary record, Fourth Committee, 1 November 1965, A/C.4/SR.1544, para. 76 (79 to 8 with 17 abstentions); Verbatim record, plenary General Assembly, 5 November 1965, A/PV.1368, para. 22 (82 to 9 with 18 abstentions).

[11] Question of South West Africa, 17 December 1965, A/RES/2074 (XX), OP 4.

[12] Question of South West Africa: Afghanistan, Algeria, Burma, Cameroon, Central African Republic, Chad, Congo (Brazzaville), Congo (Democratic Republic of), Cyprus, Dahomey, Ghana, Guinea, India, Iraq, Ivory Coast, Kenya, Libya, Madagascar, Mali, Mauritania, Morocco, Nepal, Niger, Nigeria, Pakistan, Rwanda, Saudi Arabia, Senegal, Sierra Leone, Somalia, Sudan, Syria, Togo, Uganda, United Arab Republic, United Republic of Tanzania, Yemen, Yugoslavia, and Zambia: joint draft resolution, 7 December 1965, A/C.4/L.812/Rev.1 and Add.1-3.

[13] Summary record, Fourth Committee, 9 December 1965, A/C.4/SR.1581, para. 11.

[14] Summary record, Fourth Committee, 9 December 1965, A/C.4/SR.1582, para. 67.

316   RACIAL DISCRIMINATION AS A CRIME AGAINST HUMANITY

and then in the plenary General Assembly by large majorities, with Western States voting against or abstaining.[15] Finally, on 20 December 1965 the General Assembly adopted a resolution on South Africa that had not been debated in committee. A preambular paragraph stated: 'Fully aware that the continuation of colonial rule and the practice of apartheid as well as all forms of racial discrimination threaten international peace and security and constitute a crime against humanity.'[16]

The following year, two resolutions of the General Assembly referred to crimes against humanity. The operative paragraphs of the main resolution on South Africa began with a condemnation of 'the policies of apartheid practised by the Government of South Africa as a crime against humanity'.[17] The resolution was proposed by a large group of non-aligned States, almost entirely from Africa and Asia.[18] When it was being debated in the Special Political Committee, the delegate from Guinea stated that '[e]veryone agreed that apartheid was a crime against humanity'.[19] This remark seemed to provoke the Italian representative to say that although it might be acceptable 'as an expression of moral condemnation, the Committee was not competent to use it in the full legal sense, as defined under existing international law'.[20] Guinea said Italy's objection was inappropriate given that moral and political condemnation should be obvious in a draft resolution for the General Assembly.[21] Italy could have called for a separate vote on the paragraph but it did not. The resolution was adopted in the Special Political Committee with only one negative vote, of Portugal, and 12 abstentions.[22] In the plenary General Assembly, South Africa joined Portugal in voting against the resolution.[23]

The other resolution adopted at the 1966 session condemned 'as a crime against humanity, the policy of the Government of Portugal, which violates the

---

[15] Ibid., para. 63 (83 to 2 with 15 abstentions); Verbatim record, plenary General Assembly, 17 December 1965, A/PV.1400, para. 26 (85 to 2 with 19 abstentions).

[16] Implementation of the Declaration on the Granting of Independence to Colonial Countries and Peoples, 20 December 1965, A/RES/2105 (XX), PP 9. Also Implementation of the Declaration on the Granting of Independence to Colonial Countries and Peoples, 13 December 1966, A/RES/2189 (XXI), OP 6.

[17] The policies of apartheid of the Government of the Republic of South Africa, 16 December 1966, A/RES/2202 (XXI) A, OP 1.

[18] Afghanistan, Algeria, Cameroon, Democratic Republic of the Congo, Cyprus, Dahomey, Ethiopia, Ghana, Guinea, Hungary, India, Indonesia, Iraq, Ivory Coast, Jordan, Kenya, Kuwait, Liberia, Libya, Madagascar, Malaysia, Mali, Mauritania, Morocco, Nepal, Niger, Nigeria, Pakistan, Philippines, Rwanda, Senegal, Sierra Leone, Singapore, Somalia, Sudan, Syria, Trinidad and Tobago, Tunisia, United Arab Republic, United Republic of Tanzania, Upper Volta, Yugoslavia, Zambia, 8 December 1966, A/SPC/L.135 and Add.1–2.

[19] Verbatim record, Special Political Committee, 8 December 1966, A/SPC/PV.537, para. 14.

[20] Verbatim record, Special Political Committee, 12 December 1966, A/SPC/PV.542, para. 27.

[21] Ibid., para. 30.

[22] Ibid., para. 34.

[23] Verbatim record, plenary General Assembly, 16 December 1966, A/PV.1496, para. 158,

economic and political rights of foreign immigrants in the Territories and by the exporting of African workers to South Africa'.[24] The text was similar to one in a resolution adopted the previous year with the exception of the qualification as a crime against humanity.[25] The resolution was proposed by 48 Member States, 31 of them from Africa and the others from Asia or Eastern Europe.[26] During the debate, Tanzania's delegate anticipated that some representatives might argue that the term 'crimes against humanity' was an exaggeration. He said that 'in Angola alone more than 300,000 people, including women and children, had been mercilessly killed by Portuguese soldiers. That was clearly a crime against humanity'.[27] But of course the allegation of crimes against humanity was about the rights of migrant workers rather than mass killing or extermination. Ireland, Jamaica, and South Africa all questioned use of the term.[28] After some discussion, a separate vote was taken and the paragraph adopted, by 71 votes to 13 with 20 abstentions.[29] The resolution as a whole was adopted by large majorities in the Fourth Committee and in the plenary General Assembly.[30]

On 4 March 1966 the Economic and Social Council adopted a resolution on implementation of the Convention on the Elimination of All Forms of Racial Discrimination that cited, in its second preambular paragraph, the General Assembly resolutions relating to crimes against humanity adopted at the previous session: 'Considering further that, in its resolutions 2022 (XX), of 5 November 1965, on the question of Southern Rhodesia, and 2074 (XX), of 17 December 1965, on the question of South West Africa, the General Assembly condemned such violations of human rights as policies of racial discrimination and segregation and the policies of apartheid and declared that they "constitute a crime against humanity"'.[31]

---

[24] Question of Territories under Portuguese administration, 12 December 1966, A/RES/2184 (XXI), OP 3.

[25] See Question of Territories under Portuguese administration, 21 December 1965, A/RES/2107 (XX), OP 5.

[26] Question of territories under Portuguese Administration: Afghanistan, Algeria, Bulgaria, Burundi, Cameroon, Ceylon, Chad, Congo (Democratic Republic of), Cyprus, Czechoslovakia, Dahomey, Ethiopia, Ghana, Guinea, Hungary, India, Indonesia, Iraq, Ivory Coast, Kenya, Kuwait, Liberia, Libya, Madagascar, Mali, Mauritania, Mongolia, Morocco, Nepal, Niger, Nigeria, Pakistan, Poland, Rwanda, Saudi Arabia, Senegal, Sierra Leone, Somalia, Sudan, Syria, Togo, Tunisia, Uganda, United Arab Republic, United Republic of Tanzania, Upper Volta, Yugoslavia, and Zambia: revised joint draft resolution, 5 December 1966, A/C.4/L.842/Rev.1.

[27] Summary record, Fourth Committee, 30 November 1966, A/C.4/SR.1648, para. 10.

[28] Summary record, Fourth Committee, 5 December 1966, A/C.4/SR.1654, paras. 36, 41, 43.

[29] Ibid., para. 70.

[30] Ibid., para. 74 (76 votes to 12, with 16 abstentions); Verbatim record, plenary General Assembly, 21 December 1965, A/PV.1407, para. 36.

[31] Measures for the speedy implementation of the United Nations Declaration on the Elimination of All Forms of Racial Discrimination, 4 March 1966, E/RES/1102 (XL), PP 2.

318   RACIAL DISCRIMINATION AS A CRIME AGAINST HUMANITY

The General Assembly returned to the issue of migrant workers in 1967, dropping the qualification of crimes against humanity.[32] In its place, it condemned, as a crime against humanity, 'the colonial war being waged by the Government of Portugal against the peaceful peoples of the Territories under its domination'.[33] As with previous resolutions, it was proposed by a large number of African and Asian countries.[34] Once again, Ireland expressed hesitation about the term,[35] but there was no separate vote on the paragraph, and the resolution as whole was adopted by a large majority.[36]

The suggestion that the General Assembly could not make declarations about the definition of international crimes was plainly incorrect. At its first session, in 1946, the General Assembly adopted a resolution endorsing the Nuremberg Principles, a notion that clearly encompassed the scope of crimes against humanity.[37] At the same session another resolution recognised genocide as an international crime and provided a definition. There had been no doubt since the 1940s that acts of persecution directed at a national, ethnic, or racial group could be punished as crimes against humanity under international law.[38] Nevertheless, the International Military Tribunal[39] as well as the International Law Commission, in the Nuremberg Principles it adopted in 1950,[40] had confined crimes against humanity to a situation of armed conflict. In condemning racial discrimination and apartheid perpetrated in time of peace, the General Assembly was contributing to an important advance in international law.

---

[32] Question of Territories under Portuguese administration, 17 November 1967, A/RES/2270 (XXII), OP 5.

[33] Ibid., OP 4.

[34] Implementation of the Declaration on the Granting of Independence to Colonial Countries and Peoples: question of territories under Portuguese administration: Afghanistan, Algeria, Botswana, Burma, Burundi, Cameroon, Ceylon, Central African Republic, Chad, Congo (Brazzaville), Congo (Democratic Republic of), Cyprus, Dahomey, Ethiopia, Gabon, Gambia, Ghana, Guinea, India, Indonesia, Iraq, Ivory Coast, Jordan, Kenya, Kuwait, Laos, Lebanon, Lesotho, Liberia, Libya, Madagascar, Malaysia, Mali, Mauritania, Mongolia, Morocco, Nepal, Niger, Nigeria, Pakistan, Rwanda, Saudi Arabia, Senegal, Sierra Leone, Somalia, Sudan, Syria, Togo, Tunisia, Uganda, United Arab Republic, United Republic of Tanzania, Upper Volta, Yemen, Yugoslavia, and Zambia: revised joint draft resolution, 10 November 1967, A/C.4/L.872/Rev.1.

[35] Summary record, Fourth Committee, 10 November 1967, A/C.4/SR.1717, para. 59.

[36] Ibid., para. 50 (80 votes to 8, with 15 abstentions). In the plenary General Assembly, Verbatim record, plenary General Assembly, 17 November 1967, A/PV.1599, para. 30 (82 votes to 7 with 21 abstentions).

[37] Affirmation of the principles of international law recognized by the Charter of the Nurnberg Tribunal, 11 December 1946, A/RES/95 (I).

[38] The crime of genocide, 11 December 1946, A/RES/96 (I). See the discussion at pp. 117–119.

[39] See p. 120.

[40] Report of the International Law Commission covering its 2nd session, 5 June–29 July 1950, A/1316, paras. 120–4.

Expanding the Scope of Crimes against Humanity

The Commission on Human Rights began studying crimes against humanity in 1965, giving priority to the issue of statutory limitation and the prosecution of Second World War crimes. There was no indication at the 1965 session that any substantive changes to the scope of crimes against humanity were being considered.[41] This is somewhat surprising in light of the definitional controversies in the International Law Commission when a United Nations body last considered crimes against humanity, in the early 1950s. It decided to request that the Secretary-General undertake a study of the issue.[42]

The following year, Austria, France, Israel, the Netherlands, New Zealand, and the United States proposed the preparation of a convention prohibiting statutory limitation for crimes against humanity.[43] The Commission based its discussions on the study prepared by the Secretary-General.[44] Once again, there was no consideration given to any progressive development of the definition of crimes against humanity.[45] At the same session, the Commission on Human Rights adopted a draft resolution on racial discrimination in which it recognised apartheid as a crime against humanity.[46]

The Secretary-General prepared a draft convention on statutory limitation for the Commission on Human Rights. The definition of crimes against humanity in article 1 of the Secretariat draft referred to 'the Charter of the International Tribunal of Nürnberg of 8 August 1945 and confirmed by resolutions 3 (I) of 11 February 1946 and 95 (I) of 11 December 1946 of the General Assembly of the United Nations'. Commenting on article 1, the Secretary-General referred to proposals that the definition of crimes against humanity take account of recent developments, with specific reference to General Assembly resolutions adopted that year referring to apartheid as a crime against humanity.[47]

The Secretariat draft was reviewed by an 11-member Working Group of the Commission on Human Rights that include three African States, Dahomey,

---

[41] Commission on Human Rights, Report on the 21st Session, 22 March–15 April 1965, E/4024, paras. 514–63.

[42] Question of Punishment of War Criminals and of Persons Who Have Committed Crimes Against Humanity, 9 April 1965, E/CN.4/RES/3 (XXI), OP 2. See also The Question of Punishment of War Criminals and of Persons Who Have Committed Crimes Against Humanity, 28 July 1965, E/RES/1074 D (XXXIX).

[43] Austria, France, Israel, the Netherlands, New Zealand and the United States, E/CN.4/L.830 and Add.1, para. 5.

[44] Study submitted by the Secretary-General, 15 February 1966, E/CN.4/906.

[45] Commission on Human Rights, Report on the 22nd Session, 8 March–5 April 1966, E/4184, paras. 223–89.

[46] Question of the violation of human rights and fundamental freedoms; including policies of racial discrimination and segregation and of apartheid in all countries, with particular reference to colonial and other dependent countries and territories, 25 March 1966, E/CN.4/RES/2 (XXII), PP 3.

[47] Draft convention, 25 January 1967, E/CN.4/928, art. 1, para. 6.

320 RACIAL DISCRIMINATION AS A CRIME AGAINST HUMANITY

Nigeria, and Senegal.[48] Never before had African countries been so engaged in the work of the Commission. There was no agreement in the Working Group on the definition of crimes against humanity. The version with the most support dropped the citations to the Charter of the International Military Tribunal and the early General Assembly resolutions and added a reference to 'inhuman acts resulting from apartheid'. It defined crimes against humanity as 'inhuman acts such as genocide, murder, extermination, enslavement, deportation or persecutions, including in the policy of apartheid'. A second version that received 'some' support stated that violations of the economic and political rights of indigenous populations as are the consequences of the policy of apartheid are crimes against humanity'. A third version that also received 'some' support made no mention of apartheid.[49] The Report of the Commission says that '[s]everal members were strongly in favour of including inhuman acts flowing from the policy of apartheid within the scope of the convention, even in a separate sentence'. It notes that '[a] few representatives' were opposed to mentioning apartheid in the definition because 'in their view, the proposed text was too broad to avoid misinterpretation, and that it might give the impression of defining a new crime in international law, a task which was outside the mandate of the Commission'.[50] For lack of time, the Commission was unable to prepare a final draft.[51]

The subject returned to the Third Committee of the General Assembly in late 1967.[52] Several States, principally those of eastern and central Europe, were concerned with offences perpetrated during the Second World War. They were reacting to developments in Germany where prosecution was to be time barred in 1969. For these States, the definition in the Secretary-General's draft referring to Nuremberg was satisfactory.[53] Other countries favoured developing the definition of crimes against humanity in order to address concerns of the present day, including apartheid.[54]

---

[48] Commission on Human Rights, Report on the 23rd session, 20 February–23 March 1967, E/4322, para. 153.

[49] Ibid., para. 155.

[50] Ibid., para. 178.

[51] Question of the punishment of war criminals and of persons who have committed crimes against humanity, 20 March 1967, E/CN.4/RES/4 (XXIII).

[52] For a summary of the general debate, see Report of the Third Committee, 15 December 1967, A/6989, para. 10.

[53] Summary record, Third Committee, 14 November 1967, A/C.3/SR.1514, paras. 19 (Poland), 34 (Yugoslavia), 38 (Czechoslovakia); Summary record, Third Committee, 15 November 1967, A/C.3/SR.1515, para. 8 (Belarus); Summary record, Third Committee, 15 November 1967, A/C.3/SR.1516, para. 11 (Soviet Union).

[54] Summary record, Third Committee, 15 November 1967, A/C.3/SR.1515, paras. 21–22 (Cuba), 24 (Saudi Arabia); Summary record, Third Committee, 15 November 1967, A/C.3/SR.1516, para. 16 (Cyprus); Summary record, Third Committee, 17 November 1967, A/C.3/SR.1518, para. 2 (Democratic Republic of the Congo); Summary record, Third Committee, 22 November 1967, A/C.3/SR.1523, paras. 10–11 (Syria), 20 (Mongolia), 28 (Tanzania), 32 (Poland).

EXPANDING THE SCOPE OF CRIMES AGAINST HUMANITY   321

Following the general debate, the Third Committee together with the Sixth Committee set up a Joint Working Group that prepared a draft convention, basing itself on the Secretary-General's text and the records of the Commission on Human Rights. The Joint Working Group adopted a draft convention by eight votes to none with seven abstentions. The first preambular paragraph of the draft referred to the Nuremberg principles but then went on to cite recent General Assembly resolutions 'which have expressly condemned as crimes against humanity the violation of the economic and political rights of the indigenous population on the one hand, and the policies of apartheid on the other'. Article 1 defined crimes against humanity as including 'inhuman acts resulting from the policy of apartheid, committed in time of war or in peacetime against the civil population or certain elements of that population on social, political, economic, racial, religious or cultural grounds by the authorities of the State or by private individuals acting at the instigation or with the toleration of such authorities'.[55] The draft was subsequently considered by the Third Committee, where '[a] great number of speakers' expressed general agreement with the preamble. There were '[a] few representatives' who objected to the reference to the recent General Assembly resolutions, arguing that such resolutions are without binding force and do not therefore amount to sources of international law, while '[s]everal members' maintained that the references should be retained 'in view of their relevance as regards contemporary forms of crimes against humanity'.[56] According to the Report of the Third Committee, '[m]any representatives strongly approved of the specific references, in article I (b), to "inhuman acts resulting from the policies of apartheid"', while 'one opinion was, however, that it was not appropriate to mention expressly specific policies such as apartheid in a legal text'.[57] It would appear that the United Kingdom was the one State to which the Report referred.[58] India was among those States speaking in support of the reference to apartheid. Its delegate noted that none of the countries opposing the mention of apartheid had been able to invoke valid arguments, 'which was the reason why the countries of the Afro-Asian group doubted the sincerity of the commitments undertaken by those countries to combat the policy of apartheid'.[59]

The General Assembly agreed to transmit the draft prepared by the Working Group to Member States for comments.[60] When the draft resolution was debated

[55] Report of the Third Committee, 15 December 1967, A/6989, para. 20; Draft Convention on the non-applicability of statutory limitations to war crimes and crimes against humanity, adopted by the Working Group on 30 November 1967, A/7174, Annex.

[56] Report of the Third Committee, 15 December 1967, A/6989, para. 23.

[57] Ibid., para. 25.

[58] Summary record, Third Committee, 12 December 1967, A/C.3/SR.1547, paras. 30–4; Summary record, Third Committee, 12 December 1967, A/C.3/SR.1548, paras. 20, 24–6.

[59] Summary record, Third Committee, 13 December 1967, A/C.3/SR.1549, para. 8.

[60] Question of the punishment of war criminals and of persons who have committed crimes against humanity, 18 December 1967, A/RES/2338 (XXII), PP 1. Adopted by 90 votes to 26 with 22 abstentions: Verbatim record, plenary General Assembly, 18 December 1967, A/PV.1638, para. 178.

322 RACIAL DISCRIMINATION AS A CRIME AGAINST HUMANITY

in the Third Committee, France proposed a separate vote on the reference in the preamble of the draft resolution to the two recent General Assembly resolutions including the mention of apartheid. The language was approved by 49 votes to 6, with 39 abstentions (including France). Canada, China, Honduras, Netherlands, South Africa, and the United States voted against.[61] There was also a similar vote in the plenary General Assembly on the first paragraph of the preamble, adopted by 67 to 46 with 41 abstentions.[62]

The Tehran Conference on Human Rights took place in April and May 1968. Resolution III of the Conference declared that 'the policy of apartheid or other similar evils are a crime against humanity punishable in accordance with the provisions of relevant international instruments dealing with such crimes'.[63] Another resolution recalled two General Assembly resolutions adopted in 1965 condemning apartheid and racial discrimination as crimes against humanity.[64] Introducing these resolutions to the plenary Conference, rapporteur Saadolah Ghaoucy of Afghanistan said that '[f]or the overwhelming majority of the delegations apartheid represented a crime against humanity'.[65] The Proclamation of Tehran, adopted at the conclusion of the Conference condemned the 'the repugnant policy of apartheid' was as a crime against humanity.[66]

Several countries referred to apartheid in their written comments on the draft convention on statutory limitation. Chile opposed the reference to apartheid.[67] Denmark, Greece, Italy, Madagascar, and the United States, without specifically mentioning apartheid, disagreed with widening the scope of crimes against humanity.[68] The United States was against making reference to recent General Assembly resolutions, claiming they were not intended to deal with crimes against humanity 'in a legal sense'.[69] Similarly, the United Kingdom described the General Assembly resolutions as 'vaguely worded propositions of questionable legal validity'.[70] It said the specific reference to apartheid in the definition of crimes against humanity was 'undesirable', explaining that 'either it adds nothing

[61] Summary record, Third Committee, 13 December 1967, A/C.3/SR.1550, para. 5.
[62] Verbatim record, plenary General Assembly, 18 December 1967, A/PV.1638, para. 177.
[63] Resolution III. Measures to achieve rapid and total elimination of all forms of racial discrimination in general and the policy of apartheid in particular, A/CONF.32/41, Part III, OP 4.
[64] Resolution VI. Measures to eliminate and all forms and manifestations of racial discrimination, A/CONF.32/41, Part III, PP 4.
[65] Statement by the Rapporteur of the First Committee, Mr. Saadollah Ghaoucy (Afghanistan), A/CONF.32/41, Annex IV.
[66] Proclamation of Tehran, A/CONF.32/41, Part II, para. 7.
[67] Question of punishment of war criminals and of persons who have committed crimes against humanity, 21 August 1968, A/7174, pp. 9–10.
[68] Ibid., pp. 16–21, 47; Question of punishment of war criminals and of persons who have committed crimes against humanity, 14 October 1968, A/7174/Add.2, p. 2.
[69] Question of punishment of war criminals and of persons who have committed crimes against humanity, 21 August 1968, A/7174, p. 46.
[70] Question of punishment of war criminals and of persons who have committed crimes against humanity, 18 September 1968, A/7174/Add.1, p. 2.

EXPANDING THE SCOPE OF CRIMES AGAINST HUMANITY   323

to the previous reference to inhuman acts, in which case it is unnecessary, or it adds something and implies that inhuman acts committed in consequence of a policy of apartheid are worse than identical acts committed elsewhere, in which case it is objectionable in principle'.[71] On the other hand, Dahomey insisted on the reference in the preamble as well as in article 1(b) because 'any omission of the policy of apartheid from the definition of crimes against humanity would mean encouraging the most backward type of racism'.[72] Cuba said it supported express mention of apartheid.[73] For Togo, apartheid was 'a perfect example of a crime against humanity'.[74]

During the debate in the Third Committee, many States of Africa, Asia, and the socialist countries in Europe spoke in favour of a reference to apartheid in the convention. The United States, France, Mexico, and the Netherlands proposed an amendment removing the reference to apartheid,[75] as did the United Kingdom.[76] Others opposing use of the term included Chile,[77] China,[78] Israel,[79] Italy,[80] and Norway.[81] At one point, the delegate from Congo (Brazzaville) said she was 'not surprised to note the zeal with which the United States, the United Kingdom, France and the other colonialist countries were attempting to exclude apartheid from the draft convention, for the African delegations had no illusions about the real motives behind the negative attitude of those countries'.[82] Article 1(b), with its reference to 'inhuman acts resulting from the policy of apartheid', was adopted by the Third Committee with 59 votes in favour to 12 against, with 27 abstentions. The following voted against the article: Australia, Belgium, Canada, France. Honduras, Luxembourg, the Netherlands, New Zealand, Portugal, South Africa, the United Kingdom, the United States.[83] There was a very similar result in the vote on the first paragraph of the preamble, with its reference to the 1966 General Assembly resolutions recognizing apartheid as a crime against humanity.[84]

---

[71] Ibid., p. 3.
[72] Question of punishment of war criminals and of persons who have committed crimes against humanity, 21 August 1968, A/7174, p. 15.
[73] Ibid., p. 14.
[74] Ibid., p. 41.
[75] France, Mexico, Netherlands, United States: amendment to the draft convention (A/7174, annex), 8 October 1968, A/C.3/L.1561
[76] United Kingdom: amendment to the draft convention (A/7174, annex), 9 October 1968, A/C.3/L.1564. Also Summary record, Third Committee, 8 October 1968, A/C.3/SR.1563, paras. 1–4; Summary record, Third Committee, 9 October 1968, A/C.3/SR.1566, paras. 1–2.
[77] Summary record, Third Committee, 8 October 1968, A/C.3/SR.1563, para. 36.
[78] Summary record, Third Committee, 10 October 1968, A/C.3/SR.1568, para. 5.
[79] Summary record, Third Committee, 10 October 1968, A/C.3/SR.1567, para. 11.
[80] Summary record, Third Committee, 9 October 1968, A/C.3/SR.1565, para. 35.
[81] Ibid., para. 22.
[82] Summary record, Third Committee, 10 October 1968, A/C.3/SR.1568, para. 8.
[83] Ibid., para. 41.
[84] Summary record, Third Committee, 15 October 1968, A/C.3/SR.1573, para. 5.

324 RACIAL DISCRIMINATION AS A CRIME AGAINST HUMANITY

The first preambular paragraph of the final text of the Convention cites resolutions 2184 (XXI) and 2202 (XXI) 'which expressly condemned as crimes against humanity the violation of the economic and political rights of the indigenous population on the one hand and the policies of apartheid on the other'. Article 1(b) affirms the application of the Convention to crimes against humanity, specifying that this includes 'inhuman acts resulting from the policy of apartheid'. The text as a whole was adopted in the plenary General Assembly by 58 to 7, with 36 abstentions.[85] Australia, El Salvador, Honduras, Portugal, South Africa, the United Kingdom, and the United States voted against. Other Western European States abstained.[86] Of those who had originally proposed the convention, only Israel voted in favour, while France, the Netherlands, and New Zealand abstained and the United States voted against. Belgium, which also abstained, said it 'regretted' the inclusion in the definition of crimes against humanity of 'certain acts of an essentially political nature which are not offences under the Belgian penal code'.[87] The United Kingdom put on record once again its objections to the inclusion of apartheid.[88] France criticized the reference, saying it was 'imprecise'.[89]

Writing nearly four decades later, Antonio Cassese said it was 'probably with the 1968 Convention on the Non-Applicability of it was Statutory Limitations that the process of a gradual crystallisation in international customary law of a rule proscribing crimes against humanity even in time of peace was set in motion'.[90] He did not refer to the earlier General Assembly resolutions or point to the fact that the 'process of crystallisation' originated from the Global South and was resisted by the Global North. A judgment of a Trial Chamber of the International Criminal Tribunal for the former Yugoslavia, presided over by Cassese, cited the 1968 Convention together with several other authorities, including the 1973 Apartheid Convention, as evidence of the 'gradual abandonment' of the link between crimes against humanity and armed conflict. But again, it made no

---

[85] Convention on the Non-Applicability of Statutory Limitations to War Crimes and Crimes Against Humanity, 25 November 1968, A/RES/2391 (XXIII). |For a thorough analysis of the provisions of the Convention, see Roger S. Clark, 'Apartheid', in M. Cherif Bassiouni, *International Criminal Law*, 3rd ed., Vol. I, New York: Transnational, 2008, 599–620). Also Ariel Bultz, 'Redefining Apartheid in International Criminal Law' (2013) 24 *Criminal Law Forum* 205; Max Du Plessis, 'International Criminal Law: The Crime of Apartheid Revisited' (2011) 24 *South African Journal of Criminal Justice* 423; Carola Lingaas, 'The Crime against Humanity of Apartheid in a Post-Apartheid World' (2015) 2 *Oslo Law Review* 86.

[86] Verbatim record, plenary General Assembly, 26 November 1968. A/PV.1727, para. 75.

[87] Ibid., para. 19.

[88] Ibid., para. 60.

[89] Ibid., para. 73.

[90] Antonio Cassese, 'Balancing the Prosecution of Crimes against Humanity and Non-Retroactivity of Criminal Law, The Kolk and Kislyiy v. Estonia Case before the ECHR' (2006) 4 *Journal of International Criminal Justice* 410.

reference to the General Assembly resolutions that began in 1965 and did not acknowledge the decisive role of the Global South in this process.[91]

The Convention on the non-applicability of statutory limitations to war crimes and crimes against humanity entered into force on 11 November 1970 after obtaining 10 ratifications.[92] As of 1 November 2022 it had 57 States Parties, of which the most recent are Palestine (2015) and Ecuador (2020). Although African States strongly supported the Convention during its adoption, only 10 of them have become States Parties. A similar treaty on statutory limitation was adopted by the Council of Europe in 1974 but only entered into force in 2003.[93] The European Convention on the Non-Applicability of Statutory Limitation to Crimes against Humanity and War Crimes does not refer to apartheid in its definition of crimes against humanity. The Convention has eight States Parties. France signed the Convention immediately following its adoption but has never ratified it.

Drafting the Apartheid Convention

The proposal to adopt a convention for the prevention and punishment of the crime against humanity of apartheid, consisting of a seven-paragraph pre-amble and six articles came from Guinea and the Soviet Union in October 1971.[94] Bulgaria, Syria, and Ukraine presented a draft General Assembly res-olution calling for the adoption of such a convention.[95] The Soviet represen-tative explained that its purpose was 'to affirm in juridical and concrete terms the rules of international law under which apartheid was denounced as a crime against humanity'.[96] The draft seemed influenced by the 1948 Convention on the Prevention and Punishment of the Crime of Genocide. Article 2 consisted of a definition of the crime, article 3 provided for modes of participation, article 4 required States to enact legislation, and article 5 comprised an obligation 'to participate in international measures adopted through the competent organs of the United Nations and aimed at the suppression and punishment of the crime of apartheid, including measures adopted under Chapter VII of the Charter

---

[91] *Prosecutor v. Kupreškić et al.* (IT-95-16-T), Judgment, 17 January 2000, para. 577.

[92] (1970) 754 UNTS 73.

[93] European Convention on the Non-Applicability of Statutory Limitation to Crimes against Humanity and War Crimes, CETS 82.

[94] Guinea and Union of Soviet Socialist Republics: draft of a Convention on the suppression and punishment of the crime of apartheid, 28 October 1971, A/C.3/L.1871.

[95] Bulgaria, Syrian Arab Republic, Ukrainian Soviet Socialist Republic, draft resolution, 3 November 1971, A/C.3/L.1875.

[96] Summary record, Third Committee, 5 November 1971, A/C.3/SR.1859, para. 13.

of the United Nations'. The draft resolution raised the idea of an 'international jurisdiction'.

Several delegates noted that the draft was weak on enforcement measures and required more work. Recognizing that conclusion of such a treaty 'would be an important contribution to the struggle against apartheid, racism, economic exploitation, colonial domination and foreign occupation', the General Assembly decided to transmit the text to the Commission on Human Rights with a view to preparing a draft convention the following year.[97] The resolution was adopted by 86 to 5 (Canada, the Netherlands, Portugal, the United Kingdom, the United States) with 23 abstentions. All African and Asian Member States, with the exception of the Central African Republic, Japan, and Madagascar, voted in favour.[98]

The Commission on Human Rights returned to the subject at its 1972 session. There was another proposal before it, from Nigeria, Pakistan, and Tanzania, for a protocol to the International Convention on the Elimination of All Forms of Racial Discrimination dealing with the crime of apartheid.[99] The protocol's purpose, it was explained, was the same as that of the draft convention on apartheid, but it was hoped that this might be facilitated by using the existing implementation machinery of the Convention on racial discrimination rather than creating something entirely new.[100] The draft protocol indicated an obligation to prosecute persons 'who are presently within their territorial jurisdiction', implying a form of universal jurisdiction over the crime of apartheid, something that had not been addressed in the draft convention proposed by Guinea and the Soviet Union. The Commission decided to transmit both draft instruments to Member States for their comments. It also called upon the General Assembly to 'give priority' to the adoption of an instrument.[101] An amendment by the United States to soften this so that the General Assembly was only being asked to 'consider' the question was defeated by 13 votes to 8, with 7 abstentions.[102]

In 1972, the Commission on Human Rights also examined a report it had requested the previous year from the Ad Hoc Working Group of Experts on the question of apartheid from the standpoint of international criminal law. By this time, General Assembly resolutions were referring simply to apartheid, rather

---

[97] Draft convention on the suppression and punishment of the Crime of apartheid, 6 December 1971, A/RES/2786 (XXVI).

[98] Verbatim record, plenary General Assembly. 6 December 1971, A/PV.2001, para. 36.

[99] Guinea and Union of Soviet Socialist Republics: draft of a Convention on the suppression and punishment of the crime of apartheid, 28 October 1971, E/CN.4/L.1871.

[100] Report of the 28th session of the Commission on Human Rights, 6 March–7 April 1972, E/5113, para. 44.

[101] Draft convention on the suppression and punishment of the crime of apartheid, 23 March 1972, E/CN.4/RES/4 (XXVIII).

[102] Report of the 28th session of the Commission on Human Rights, 6 March–7 April 1972, E/5113, para. 48.

DRAFTING THE APARTHEID CONVENTION 327

than to the policies of apartheid, as a crime against humanity.[103] The Working Group reviewed the history and development of international criminal law. Noting that the Convention on statutory limitations had identified apartheid as a crime against humanity, it said that this meant the punishable acts of crimes against humanity, namely, murder, extermination, enslavement, deportation, and persecution, as well as those of genocide, namely, killing, causing serious bodily or mental harm, imposing conditions of life calculated to destroy the group, imposing measures to prevent births, and forcibly transferring children, were all punishable acts with respect to apartheid.[104] On the other hand, the Working Group of Experts thought it doubtful that, 'morally condemnable as they may be, conspiracy, incitement and attempt to commit inhuman acts resulting from the policies of apartheid can be regarded as crimes punishable under general international law'.[105] The report discussed specific acts that might be punishable, including ill treatment of civilians, prisoners, detainees, and persons in police custody, murder through imposition of capital punishment and arbitrary execution, extermination and mass murder, servitude through slavery-like practices, and deportations. But the Working Group concluded that given the lack of effective national or international machinery to implement international criminal law, from the standpoint of international criminal law the apartheid issue was 'highly theoretical'.[106] The Working Group recommended that the Commission on Human Rights propose an amendment to the Genocide Convention so as to cover 'inhuman acts resulting from the policies of apartheid'. It also said that acts of 'cultural genocide' should be expressly declared to be crimes against humanity, and that the General Assembly should renew its work on both the code of crimes against the peace and security of mankind and the establishment of an international criminal jurisdiction.[107]

The General Assembly took up the question of the draft apartheid convention at its 1972 session. In the meantime, a number of comments had been submitted. There was no interest in a protocol to the Convention on racial discrimination. Support for the draft apartheid convention came from some African states as well as the Soviet Union and its allies. There was scepticism or downright opposition from the Nordic States.[108] Guinea, Nigeria, and the Soviet Union produced

---

[103] Elimination of all forms of racial discrimination, 6 December 1971, A/RES/2784 (XXVI), Section II, OP II.

[104] Study concerning the question of apartheid from the point of view of international penal law, 15 February 1972, E/CN.4/1075, para. 71(j).

[105] Ibid., para. 72(d).

[106] Ibid., para. 152.

[107] Ibid., paras. 161–7.

[108] Draft convention on suppression and punishment of crime of apartheid, 14 September 1972, A/8768; Draft convention on suppression and punishment of crime of apartheid, 29 September 1972, A/8768/Add.1.

328 RACIAL DISCRIMINATION AS A CRIME AGAINST HUMANITY

a revised draft convention.[109] An improvement on the version submitted the previous year was the requirement that persons charged with acts of apartheid 'shall be tried by a competent tribunal of the State in the territory of the State Party to this Convention'.[110] The clause bore a resemblance to article 6 of the 1948 Genocide Convention that said trial for genocide would be held before the courts of the State where the crime was committed. However, the clause in the 1972 draft apartheid convention contemplated something much broader, in effect, universal jurisdiction, by which any State can punish the crime regardless of where it has been committed. Clauses proposing universal jurisdiction had been rejected in 1948 when the Genocide Convention was being negotiated.[111]

In the Third Committee, the Afro-Asian Group made clear its support for the draft convention.[112] States that had proposed the alternative protocol indicated that they would support the convention.[113] The Committee briefly discussed the draft convention before voting to return the text to the Commission on Human Rights for more work.[114]

Debate in the Commission on Human Rights in 1973 focussed on the implementation machinery as well as the advisability of adopting the Convention. A working group of the Commission was set up to examine the draft. It proposed amendments together with comments by Member States. The Working Group was composed of Bulgaria, Chile, Ecuador, Egypt, India, the Philippines, Senegal, the Soviet Union, and Zaire (having changed its name from the Democratic Republic of the Congo in 1971), with Europe and North America virtually absent. Austria and the Netherlands attended its sessions as observers, taking care that their presence was 'without prejudice' to their position on the Convention.[115] The Commission endorsed a draft Convention complete with a preamble but without an article on implementation. It also asked for the report of the Ad Hoc Working Group of Experts to be sent to the International Law Commission for its comments.[116] On 13 July 1973, the International Law Commission produced a short and ultimately unhelpful reply indicating that it was aware of relationships between international criminal law and public

---

[109] Guinea, Nigeria, USSR: revised draft convention on suppression and punishment of crime of apartheid, 24 October 1972, A/C.3/L.1942/Rev.1; Report of the Third Committee, 13 November 1972, A/8880, para. 42.

[110] Ibid., art. IV(2).

[111] Summary record, Third Committee, 11 November 1948, A/C.6/SR.100, p. 406.

[112] Summary record, Third Committee, 23 October 1972, A/C.3/SR.1931, para. 1.

[113] Ibid., para. 3.

[114] Draft Convention on the Suppression and Punishment of the Crime of Apartheid, 15 November 1972, A/RES/2922 (XVII); Summary record, Third Committee, 25 October 1972, A/C.3/SR.1933, para. 16; Verbatim record, plenary General Assembly, 15 November 1972, para. 26.

[115] Report of the Working Group of the Commission on the Draft convention on the suppression and punishment of the crime of apartheid, 18 March 1973, E/CN.4/L 1252, para. 5.

[116] Draft convention on the suppression and punishment of the crime of apartheid, 2 April 1973, E/CN.4/RES/16 (XXIX).

ADOPTING THE APARTHEID CONVENTION   329

international law in general, and that it had previously addressed questions of relevance to international criminal law.[117]

Adopting the Apartheid Convention

The final negotiations took place during 1973 in the Third Committee of the General Assembly. The United States considered the convention to be unnecessary given that the International Convention on the Elimination of All Forms of Racial Discrimination dealt with apartheid. In the absence of an 'effective international penal jurisdiction', said the United States, the proposed convention added nothing. The United States also said it disagreed with describing apartheid as a crime against humanity, a term it said should be 'strictly construed' in accordance with the 1945 Charter of the International Military Tribunal.[118] The United States was critical of the 'vagueness' of the term 'mental harm' in article 2(a)(ii), which had been taken from article 2(b) of the Genocide Convention.[119] Concerns were expressed by Western delegations that the definition of apartheid was broad enough to apply to situations outside of southern Africa.[120]

The discussion of universal jurisdiction lacked real clarity. The United States said it would have 'considerable difficulty' accepting the recognition of universal jurisdiction in article 4.[121] Responding to a request for explanation from some delegates, the Director of Human Rights in the United Nations Secretariat said that the identification of apartheid as a crime against humanity under international law was sufficient to enable all States to punish offenders regardless of their nationality.[122] This was quite a misunderstanding. States have always had jurisdiction to prosecute nationals of other countries who commit crimes on their territory. The whole point of universal jurisdiction is to authorize prosecution of crimes committed on the territory of other States. A polite rectification followed from the Iraqi delegate, who explained that South African perpetrators of apartheid could be prosecuted anywhere.[123]

The debates on the draft convention in the Third Committee were quite brief and rather superficial, given that they concerned adoption of such an important

[117] Report of the International Law Commission on the work of its twenty-fifth session, 7 May–13 July 1973, A/9010/Rev.1 para. 11.
[118] Summary record, Third Committee, 22 October 1973, A/C.3/SR.2003, para. 12. Also Summary record, Third Committee, 26 October 1973, A/C.3/SR.2007, paras. 48–50.
[119] Summary record, Third Committee, 23 October 1973, A/C.3/SR.2003, para. 36. The United States delegate mistakenly referred to the term during the debate on article 1.
[120] Ibid., para. 36 (United States); Summary record, Third Committee, 23 October 1973, A/C.3/SR.2004, para. 4 (Australia).
[121] Summary record, Third Committee, 23 October 1973, A/C.3/SR.2003, para. 16.
[122] Ibid., para. 26.
[123] Ibid., para. 27. See also ibid., paras. 36, 49.

330 RACIAL DISCRIMINATION AS A CRIME AGAINST HUMANITY

text. Unusually, there were only a handful of amendments proposed by delegates. This did not escape comment from participants. The Soviets, who had initially proposed the convention, credited the smooth adoption process to conscientious preparation of the draft.[124] But it is evident from the summary records that many delegates were confused about the meaning of certain provisions. The haste to adoption of those who were campaigning for the convention was matched by a seeming indifference from many others. Beyond a few remarks from the United States and Australia, the Western countries boycotted the adoption process. Towards the end of the debates in the Third Committee, Finland took the floor on behalf of the Nordic States. After the usual perfunctory declaration of opposition to apartheid, the Finnish delegate expressed reservations about a legal instrument that would make apartheid subject to universal jurisdiction, adding that this would create an 'undesirable precedent'.[125] Belgium also took the floor to declare that the convention's provisions on 'the principle of extraterritoriality', that is, universal jurisdiction, were 'too broad'.[126] The Third Committee adopted the text by 93 votes to 1 (Portugal), with 24 abstentions.[127]

The International Convention on the Suppression and Punishment of the Crime of Apartheid was adopted by the General Assembly on an unrecorded vote, with 91 in favour to 4 against and 26 abstentions.[128] Only a few delegations made statements explaining their votes. The United States delegate spoke at length, repeating the arguments in the Third Committee. The principal sore point was universal jurisdiction, which the United States contended could only be exercised under limited circumstances with respect to piracy, air piracy, and war crimes. 'We do not, for example, accept that an American citizen vacationing in a foreign country could be extradited to another foreign country and tried in that third foreign country for something that he has said on the territory of the United States, a result which would flow quite clearly from the provisions of this convention', he said.[129] The United Kingdom delegate also spoke, but more briefly, indicating that his country had joined the United States in voting against the Convention. He too was preoccupied with universal jurisdiction. He said that '[t]he provisions in question purport to authorise contracting States to exercise criminal jurisdiction in respect of certain matters covered by the Convention over acts done outside their jurisdiction by persons who are not their nationals', something that was 'unacceptable'.[130]

[124] Summary record, Third Committee, 24 October 1973, A/C.3/SR.2005, paras. 36–37.
[125] Summary record, Third Committee, 26 October 1973, A/C.3/SR.2007, para. 34.
[126] Ibid., para. 44.
[127] Summary record, Third Committee, 26 October 1973, A/C.3/SR.2008, para. 6.
[128] International Convention on the Suppression and Punishment of the Crime of Apartheid, 30 November 1973, A/RES/3068 (XXVIII); Verbatim record, plenary General Assembly, 30 November 1973, A/PV.2185, para. 30.
[129] Verbatim record, plenary General Assembly, 30 November 1973, A/PV.2185, para. 25.
[130] Ibid., para. 45.

The Apartheid Convention entered into force on 18 July 1976 having obtained 20 ratifications. As of 1 November 2022, it had 110 States Parties. Since the end of the apartheid regime in South Africa, in the early 1990s, there have been a number of ratifications, by Azerbaijan (1996), Georgia (2005), Guatemala (2005), Honduras (2005), Montenegro (2006), Moldova (2005), Paraguay (2005), Serbia (2001), Palestine (2014), and Uruguay (2012). It has never been signed or ratified by any States of Western Europe or North America.[131] Rotem Giladi has described it as 'a largely forgotten and quite understudied instrument'.[132]

The Convention begins by affirming that apartheid is a crime against humanity. Article I also declares that 'inhuman acts resulting from the policies and practices of apartheid and similar policies and practices of racial segregation and discrimination' violate the principles of international law, in particular the purposes and principles of the Charter of the United Nations, and constituting a serious threat to international peace and security'. Article II states that the crime of apartheid 'shall include similar policies and practices of racial segregation and discrimination as practised in southern Africa'. It refers to 'inhuman acts committed for the purpose of establishing and maintaining domination by one racial group of persons over any other racial group of persons and systematically oppressing them'. A list of such acts follows, beginning with 'denial to a member or members of a racial group or groups of the right to life and liberty of person', 'murder of members of a racial group or groups' and 'infliction upon the members of a racial group or groups of serious bodily or mental harm by the infringement of their freedom or dignity, or by subjecting them to torture or to cruel, inhuman or degrading treatment or punishment', arbitrary arrest and illegal imprisonment, and imposition of living conditions calculated to destroy the group physically. Much of this language is clearly inspired by article 2 of the 1948 Genocide Convention. It goes on to list a range of legislative measures and other measures that deprive members of a racial group of 'basic human rights and freedoms', that are designed to divide a population along racial lines by creating separate reserves or ghettos, that prohibit mixed marriages, as well as the exploitation of labour including forced labour and persecution of opponents of apartheid.

The ad hoc Working Group interpreted the concept of 'inhuman acts resulting from the policy of apartheid' as acts 'perpetrated against blacks, Indians and coloured people on racial as well as political grounds, and against white people

---

[131] John Reynolds, 'Third World Approaches to International Law and the Ghosts of Apartheid', in David Keane and Yvonne McDermott, eds., *The Challenge of Human Rights*, Cheltenham: Elgar 2012, pp. 194–218, at p. 210.

[132] Rotem Giladi, 'Picking Battles: Race, Decolonization, and Apartheid', in Jochen von Bernstorff and Philipp Dann, eds., *The Battle for International Law, South-North Perspectives on the Decolonization Era*, Oxford: Oxford University Press, 2019, pp. 216–31, at p. 227.

332 RACIAL DISCRIMINATION AS A CRIME AGAINST HUMANITY

primarily on political grounds'.[133] In 1980, the Working Group analysed several cases of homicide and torture related to the apartheid policy. In addition to detailed description of the acts, it published a lengthy list of persons 'implicated',[134] although in the report it described them as 'persons guilty of the crime of apartheid within the meaning of the International Convention'.[135]

In 1984, the Security Council spoke of apartheid as 'a system characterised as a crime against humanity'.[136] Previously, it had described apartheid as 'a crime against the conscience and dignity of mankind [that] is incompatible with the rights and dignity of man, the Charter of the United Nations and the Universal Declaration of Human Rights, and seriously disturbs international peace and security'.[137]

Debate about the status of apartheid as a crime against humanity resumed in the International Law Commission as it studied the Code of Crimes Against the Peace and Security of Mankind. At its 1989 session, the Special Rapporteur, Doudou Thiam, declared that 'notwithstanding certain reservations of principle the Commission as a whole was in full agreement that it should be regarded as a crime against humanity'.[138] His statement was never challenged. There was a tendency to speak of 'genocide and apartheid' as the two paradigmatic examples of grave international crime. The Commission debated whether to simply list the crime of apartheid or to provide a detailed definition out of concern that some States had not ratified the Apartheid Convention. In 1991, the Commission adopted a revised draft Code of Crimes that did away with the label crimes against humanity altogether, replacing it with 'systematic or mass violations of human rights'. The Commission listed five categories of crimes against the peace and security of mankind: genocide, apartheid, systematic or mass violations of human rights, exceptionally serious war crimes, and wilful and severe damage to the environment.[139]

The 1991 draft Code of Crimes contained a detailed definition of the crime of apartheid that was based on Article II of the 1973 Convention but that was somewhat abbreviated. In its commentary on the text, the Commission said it thought it was 'more in the nature of a provision of criminal law' not to include examples. These had been removed from the Convention text 'simply for technical reasons'. The Commission included a major limitation on the

---

[133] Study concerning the question of apartheid from the point of view of international penal law, 15 February 1975, E/CN.4/1075, para. 50.

[134] Special report of the ad hoc Working Group of experts prepared in accordance with Resolution 12 (XXXV), paragraph 1, of the Commission on Human Rights, 31 January 1980, A/CN.4/1366, Annex III.

[135] Ibid., para. 385.

[136] South Africa, 23 October 1984, S/RES/556 (1984), OP 1.

[137] South Africa, 13 June 1980, S/RES/473 (1980), OP 3.

[138] Summary record, International Law Commission, 3 May 1989. A/CN.4/SR.2096, para. 13.

[139] Report of the International Law Commission, 43rd session, 1991, A/46/10, pp. 101–7.

crime by specifying that liability was confined to leaders or organisers', that is 'only those who are in a position to use the State apparatus for the planning, organisation or perpetration of the crime'.[140] The 1973 Convention had a much broader scope, imposing international criminal responsibility on 'individuals, members of organisations and institutions and representatives of the State'.[141] The International Law Commission also dropped the references to southern Africa. It said the definition of a crime as universally condemned as apartheid should be applicable without any restriction as to time or place.[142] In comments on the draft, Australia thought the definition should correspond more closely to that of the Apartheid Convention.[143] Some European countries expressed reservations about including the crime within the Code, arguing that the substance of the crime was covered by the general reference to 'systematic or mass violation of human rights'.[144] Austria proposed a more general formulation, such as 'institutionalised racial discrimination'.[145] The United Kingdom thought the whole matter should be reconsidered 'in the light of changed international circumstances'.[146]

The International Law Commission adopted the final version of the Code of Crimes in 1996. It removed apartheid altogether as an autonomous category of international crime, subsuming it, but only implicitly, within the definition of crimes against humanity. A new form of crime against humanity was added: 'institutionalised discrimination on racial, ethnic or religious grounds involving the violation of human rights and fundamental freedoms and resulting in seriously disadvantaging a part of the population'. The Commission said this amounted to 'the crime of apartheid under a more general denomination', noting in the commentary that such racial discrimination had been categorised as a crime against humanity in the 1973 Convention.[147]

The International Law Commission also considered apartheid within its work on State responsibility. In 1976, the Special Rapporteur on State responsibility of the International Law Commission, Roberto Ago, said that in his opinion an 'objective examination' led to the conclusion that 'maintenance by a State of a coercive policy of apartheid or absolute racial discrimination or of colonial domination over another people by force is henceforth considered within the United Nations system—and probably in general international law

---

[140] Ibid., pp. 102–3.
[141] International Convention on the Suppression and Punishment of the Crime of Apartheid (1976) 1015 UNTS 243, art. III.
[142] Report of the International Law Commission, 43rd session, 1991, A/46/10, p. 103.
[143] Comments and observations received from Governments, A/CN.4/448 and Add.l, Australia, paras. 28–30.
[144] Ibid., Nordic countries, para. 33, Netherlands, para. 58.
[145] Ibid., Austria, para. 24.
[146] Ibid., United Kingdom, para. 25.
[147] Report of the International Law Commission, 48th session, 1996, A/51/10, p. 49.

as well—as breaches of an established international obligation whereby countries should abstain from or put an end to such practices'. He said that given the seriousness of such breaches, they should entail consequences 'more severe than those attached to less serious internationally wrongful acts'.[148] Ago felt that the implications of this could not be clarified, given differing views of States. Nevertheless, he said that 'the international community as a whole now seems to recognize that acts such as the maintenance by force of apartheid and colonial domination constitute internationally wrongful acts and particularly serious wrongful acts'.[149]

The draft articles on State responsibility adopted in 2001 endorsed the notion of 'a serious breach by a State of an obligation arising under a peremptory norm of general international law'. The Commentary on the draft articles explains that it was not appropriate to provide examples in the text of the draft articles but that there was general agreement these would include the prohibitions of slavery and the slave trade, genocide, and 'racial discrimination and apartheid'. The obligations in question 'arise from those substantive rules of conduct that prohibit what has come to be seen as intolerable because of the threat it presents to the survival of States and their peoples and the most basic human values'.[150]

The International Law Commission retained the formulation 'racial discrimination and apartheid' in its study of *jus cogens*.[151] The Special rapporteur, Dire Tladi, pointed to the recognition of apartheid as a breach of *jus cogens* by the Study Group on fragmentation of international law.[152] The General Assembly appears to have described 'the elimination of racial discrimination' as a norm of *jus cogens*, referring to it as a 'pre-emptory obligation' in a companion resolution to the one adopting the International Convention on the Elimination of All Forms of Racial Discrimination. That it actually meant 'peremptory obligation' is confirmed in the French and Spanish versions of the resolution (*obligation primordiale, obligación imperativa*).[153]

---

[148] Fifth report on State responsibility, by Mr. Roberto Ago, Special Rapporteur, A/CN.4/291 and Add.1 and 2, para. 114.

[149] Ibid.

[150] Report of the International Law Commission, 53rd session, 2001, A/56/10 and Corr.1, p. 102.

[151] Report of the International Law Commission, 71st session, 2019, A/74/10, p. 203. Also Fourth report on peremptory norms of general international law (*jus cogens*) by Dire Tladi, Special Rapporteur, 31 January 2019, A/CN.4/727, paras. 91–101.

[152] Difficulties arising from the diversification and expansion of international law, Report of the Study Group of the International Law Commission finalized by Martti Koskenniemi, 13 April 2006, A/CN.4/L.682, para. 374.

[153] International Convention on the Elimination of All Forms of Racial Discrimination, 21 December 1965, A/RES/2106 (XX) B, PP 6.

Apartheid as Genocide

In addition to labelling apartheid a crime against humanity, attention was also given to its relationship with the crime of genocide. The Apartheid Convention itself pointed in this direction in a preambular reference to the Convention: 'Observing that, in the Convention on the Prevention and Punishment of the Crime of Genocide, certain acts which may also be qualified as acts of apartheid constitute a crime under international law . . . ' The discussion began in 1967 when the Commission on Human Rights set up an Ad Hoc Working Group of Experts to investigate charges of torture and ill-treatment of prisoners, detainees, or persons in police custody in South Africa. The Working Group was also empowered to receive petitions and to make recommendations.[154] This was an initiative of 10 states from the Global South, seven of them African: Democratic Republic of the Congo, Dahomey, Iraq, Iran, Jamaica, Morocco, Nigeria, the Philippines, Senegal, and the United Arab Republic. The Commission on Human Rights was a radically different body from what it had been a decade earlier when there was not a single member from Africa. The chairman of the Commission appointed five members: Ibrahima Baye of Senegal, who was elected chairman, Felix Ermacora of Austria, Branimir Jankovic of Yugoslavia, Luis Marchand Stens of Peru, and Waldo Emerson Waldron-Ramsey of Tanzania. Denied access to South Africa, whose government denounced the Working Group as a violation of sovereignty, it held a series of meetings in New York, London, Dar es Salaam, and Geneva, where it heard witnesses and received statements. The Working Group issued a report of some 435 pages, with detailed accounts of the testimony that was delivered about detention conditions, concluding that South Africa was becoming or had become a 'police state'. It made a number of recommendations, including a call for a study to ascertain whether elements of the crime of genocide were present in South Africa. 'The intention of the Government of South Africa to destroy a racial group, in whole or in part, not being established in law, the evidence nevertheless reveals certain elements which correspond to the acts described in article II (a), (b) and (c) of the United Nations Convention on the Prevention and Punishment of the Crime of Genocide and which may, as such, establish the existence of the crime of genocide', it said.[155]

The Commission on Human Rights studied the report of the ad hoc Working Group at its 1968 session. The genocide issue 'gave rise to a particular

---

[154] Communication dated 3 February 1967 from the Acting Chairman of the General Assembly's Special Committee on the Policies of Apartheid of the Government of the Republic of South Africa, 6 March 1967, E/CN.4/RES/2 (XXIII), OP 3.

[155] Report of the ad hoc Working Group of Experts set up under Resolution 2 (XXIII) of the Commission on Human Rights, 27 October 1967, E/CN.4/950, para. 1137.

336 RACIAL DISCRIMINATION AS A CRIME AGAINST HUMANITY

discussion.[156] By 22 votes to none, with 6 abstentions, the Commission adopted a resolution proposed by African and Asian States, as well as Yugoslavia[157] that endorsed the recommendations in the report and expanded the mandate of the Working Group to include a thorough investigation of the genocide issue and to expand its geographic scope so as to cover Namibia, Southern Rhodesia, and African territories under Portuguese domination.[158] In agreeing that the Working Group address the charge of genocide, the Commission had thereby greatly expanded its scope beyond the narrow question of prisoner abuse.

Genocide was declared to be an international crime in General Assembly Resolution 96(I), adopted in December 1946. A slightly different definition of the crime was employed by the General Assembly in the Convention on the Prevention and Punishment of the Crime of Genocide, adopted in December 1948. Prior to the study by the ad hoc Working Group, the scope of the Convention and of the crime of genocide had never been examined by a United Nations body although the International Law Commission has subsumed elements of the crime of genocide into its early drafts of the Code of Crimes.[159] That project had been in abeyance since 1954. The report of the Working Group devoted considerable attention to the views of those who had testified before it. This suggests an active discussion amongst participants in the anti-*apartheid* struggle about the application of the crime of genocide in that context.

At the time South Africa had neither signed nor ratified the Genocide Convention. It only acceded to the Convention in 1998. The ad hoc Working Group acknowledged that South Africa was not required to become a party to the Convention. 'This does not mean, however, that the obligation to prevent and punish genocide in itself is not binding on South Africa', said the Working Group, adding that the obligation was not 'newly created by the Convention. Its existence as a binding rule of general international law was rather presupposed by the Convention.'[160] Here, the Working Group was echoing the words of an Advisory Opinion of the International Court of Justice.[161] After a general theoretical discussion of the elements of the crime of genocide, the report concluded

[156] Report of the 24th session of the Commission on Human Rights, 5 February–12 March 1968, E/CN.4/972, para. 124.

[157] Dahomey, India, Lebanon, Madagascar, Morocco, Nigeria, Pakistan, Philippines, Senegal, United Arab Republic, United Republic of Tanzania, and Yugoslavia, Draft resolution, E/CN.4/L.990/Rev.1.

[158] Report of the ad hoc Working Group of Experts on the treatment of political prisoners in the Republic of South Africa, 16 February 1968, E/CN.4/RES/2 (XXIV); Report of the 24th session of the Commission on Human Rights, 5 February–12 March 1968, E/CN.4/972, para. 135.

[159] See art. 10(2) of the Draft code of crimes adopted in 1954, Report of the International Law Commission covering the work of its sixth session, 3 June-28 July 1954, A/2693, para. 54.

[160] Ad Hoc Working Group of Experts Established under Res. 2 (XXIII) of the Commission on Human Rights, Report, 28 February 1969, E/CN.4/984/Add.18, para. 19.

[161] *Reservations to the Convention on Genocide, Advisory Opinion, I.C.J. Reports 1951*, p. 15, at p. 23.

APARTHEID AS GENOCIDE 337

that 'in the present state of South African legislation, the Group cannot say that the South African Government has expressed an intention to commit genocide. However, the members of political groups who have testified consider that certain elements of genocide exist in the practice of apartheid.'[162] Noting that the drafters of the Genocide Convention did not explicitly contemplate the apartheid policies, which had not been fully developed at the time of its adoption, the Working Group said the Commission should request the General Assembly to revise the Convention so as to make the apartheid policies punishable.[163]

In 1969, the Commission on Human Rights extended the term of the Working Group for another two years. It also enlarged its mandate still further, requesting it to consider the issue of capital punishment in South Africa, with reference to a resolution of the General Assembly adopted the previous year.[164] The ad hoc Working Group was also charged with investigating the treatment of political prisoners and captured freedom-fighters in southern Africa, conditions in so-called 'Native reserves' and 'transit camps', and 'an investigation of all manifestations of colonialism and racial discrimination' in Namibia, Southern Rhodesia, and the Portuguese colonies in Africa, as well as South Africa itself.[165] At the same session, the Commission constituted a 'special Working Group of Experts' composed of the members of the ad hoc Working Group with a mandate to investigate violations of the fourth Geneva Convention by Israel in the occupied territories.[166]

The ad hoc Working Group returned to the genocide issue in its 1970 report. Witnesses at its hearings had denounced the 'Bantustan' policy involving forced displacement of African populations.[167] The Commission's resolution on the Working Group included a request that it 'study, from the point of view of international penal law, the question of apartheid, which has been declared a crime against humanity'.[168] There was no explicit reference to genocide, but during the debate speakers had said 'there were many indications that the policies and practices of the racist régimes in southern Africa might lead to genocide against

[162] Ibid., para. 36.

[163] Ibid., para. 39.

[164] Capital punishment in Southern Africa, 26 November 1968, A/RES/2394 (XXIII). See also Question relating to the policies of apartheid of the Government of the Republic of South Africa, 18 June 1964, S/RES/191 (1964), OP 4(a); Question concerning the situation in Southern Rhodesia, 29 May 1968, S/RES/253 (1968), PP 6,

[165] Report of the ad hoc working group of experts established under resolutions 2 (XXIII) and 2 (XXIV) of the Commission, 15 March 1969, E/CN.4/RES/21 (XXV).

[166] Question of human rights in the territories occupied as a result of hostilities in the Middle East, 4 March 1969, E/CN.4/RES/6 (XXV), OP 4.

[167] Report of the ad hoc Working Group of Experts on the investigation requested in Resolution 21 (XXV) of the Commission on Human Rights, 27 January 1970, E/CN.4/1020, paras. 60–5.

[168] Question of the violation of human rights and fundamental freedoms, including policies of racial discrimination and segregation and of apartheid, in all countries, with particular reference to colonial and other dependent countries and territories, 18 March 1970, E/CN.4/RES/8 (XXVI), OP 4.

338   RACIAL DISCRIMINATION AS A CRIME AGAINST HUMANITY

the African population.[169] The paragraph was controversial, adopted on a separate vote by 18 to none with 11 abstentions.

In 1983, the Ad Hoc Working Group of Experts issued a lengthy report on the impact of apartheid on women and children. In its conclusions, it noted that African women suffered from malnutrition, epidemics, and despair, with no medical care during pregnancy, and that new-born children grew up in 'wretched conditions which undermine their physical and mental health'. According to the Working Group, such criminal effects of apartheid amounted to a policy bordering on genocide'.[170] The Commission on Human Rights decided that in pursuing its activities the Working Group of Experts was to 'bear in mind' this conclusion about genocide.[171]

The Ad Hoc Working Group of Experts prepared a detailed study on the relationship between apartheid and genocide. The Experts confirmed their view 'that some aspects of apartheid, in view of their criminal effects on the non-white population, have certain features and amount to manifestations of the crime of genocide'.[172] They adopted a broad interpretation of the 1948 Convention, taking the view that genocide might involve acts falling short of physical extermination of the targeted group, and that it could even be the unintended consequence of certain acts. The Working Group explained that establishing the crime of genocide required a 'concurrence of two elements', the intent of the perpetrator and the results of the intended actions. With respect to the first, it wrote:

> The systematic repressive measures, including numerous death sentences, corporal punishment, all kinds of mistreatment and long. period detention, inflicted on recalcitrant individuals, who are in fact freedom fighters; underpayment for labour and maintenance of economic living conditions at a minimum level; numerous measures to suppress normal cultural and social development; and the atmosphere of terror and threat of the use of force through racist legislation - all this must definitely affect the physical and mental faculties of the group and must necessarily bring about consequences which will threaten its very survival. What could this be other than the international crime of genocide?[173]

---

[169] Report on the 26th session of the Commission on Human Rights (24 February–27 March 1970), E/4816, para. 162.

[170] Report of the ad hoc Working Group of Experts prepared in accordance with Commission on Human Rights Resolution 5 (XXXVIII) and Economic and Social Council Resolution 1981/41, 20 January 1983, E/CN.4/1983/38, para. 19.

[171] Violations of human rights in southern Africa: Report of the Ad Hoc Working Group of Experts, 18 February 1983, E/CN.4/RES/1983/9, OP 14.

[172] Violations of human rights in Southern Africa: Report of the Ad Hoc Working Group of Experts, 28 January 1985, E/CN.4/1985/14, para. 3.

[173] Ibid., para. 16(a).

APARTHEID AS GENOCIDE   339

Where the intent of the perpetrators is an inference drawn from their conduct, rather than a fact proven through direct evidence such as declarations and policy statements, it must be the only reasonable conclusion, to the exclusion of all others.[174] With its rhetorical question, the Working Group seemed to suggest that this was indeed the only possible conclusion. But the argument is not very persuasive.

The Ad Hoc Working Group turned to specific violations in support of the view it had taken, reviewing the five acts of genocide listed in article 2 of the 1948 Convention, of which the first is 'killing members of the group'. The report discussed the extensive use of capital punishment in South Africa. It said that in recent years, between 80 and 130 death sentences were pronounced annually, and that 'in all probability as many are carried out'. For the experts, '[t]he connection between skin-colour and capital punishment is obvious, and it is easy to explain the victims of discrimination will not reconcile themselves with their status; they oppose apartheid; they run foul of the laws that protect the system and are sentenced to death and liquidated'. They said this was 'undoubtedly an example of how criminal effects of the international crime of apartheid are closely related to that other international crime of genocide'.[175] The report then turned to the brutal suppression of strikes and demonstrations, sometimes with large numbers of lethal casualties. 'It is easy to appreciate how the life of non-whites in this country is threatened by a state of affairs that is in fact leading to a systematic annihilation of a group, in this case the destruction of a group on the grounds of race', said the Working Group.[176] According to the Working Group, these acts constituted the first act of genocide listed in article 2(a) of the Convention, 'killing members of the group'.

The Working Group turned to the other four punishable acts of genocide, misquoting article 2(b) of the Convention which it cited as 'serious violation of the physical or mental integrity of members of a group'. The Convention employs the phrase 'causing serious bodily or mental harm to members of the group'.[177] Whatever the formulation, there was no difficulty establishing that acts of torture and prisoner abuse fulfilled this element of the crime of genocide. The Working Group devoted several paragraphs to the situation of women and children, linking this to the third act of genocide which is imposing conditions of life calculated to destroy the group. But here it made an admission that undermined the case for genocidal intent: 'It might be an exaggeration to say that the living

---

[174] *Application of the Convention on the Prevention and Punishment of the Crime of Genocide (Croatia v. Serbia), Judgment, I.C.J. Reports 2015*, p. 3, paras. 145–8, 510.

[175] Violations of human rights in Southern Africa: Report of the Ad Hoc Working Group of Experts, 28 January 1985, E/CN.4/1985/14, para. 18.

[176] Ibid., para. 19.

[177] Ibid., para. 22.

340 RACIAL DISCRIMINATION AS A CRIME AGAINST HUMANITY

conditions imposed on the black population in South Africa are calculated to cause its or its members' physical destruction in whole or in part. But regardless of the legal question of the existence of intent, the living conditions give rise to consequences which could lead to the destruction of the black population or its members.'[178] The Working Group described various family planning measures, including the availability of birth control pills and abortion, explaining that such measures were aimed at reducing the growth in the Black African population. 'South African family planning is therefore mainly a population control programme which has elements of intent to destroy a group in whole or in part', the report concluded on this point.[179]

The Working Group appeared to concede that it was using the term 'genocide' in its 'etymological sense' and not necessarily in 'the technical or legal sense'. It acknowledged that it was interpreting the term 'broadly' so as to mean 'any act calculated to destroy the individual or prevent him from participating fully in national life'.[180] It spoke of 'social genocide', 'political genocide', and 'mental genocide'. It recommended that implementation of the policy of apartheid 'should henceforth be considered as a kind of genocide'.[181] The Working Group called for the General Assembly to request an advisory opinion from the International Court of Justice 'on the extent to which apartheid as a policy entails criminal effects bordering on genocide'. It also said the Commission on Human Rights should take steps to revise the 1948 Genocide Convention, concluding that '[t]hrough the practices described as "bordering on genocide", genocide has acquired new aspects, not only in, South Africa but also in other countries. The Working Group believes, therefore, that the Convention should be revised to establish what can still be regarded as genocide today, in the hope of arriving at a new and up-to-date definition of this international crime.'[182]

The final proposal seeking revision of the Genocide Convention was as close as the Working Group came to admitting that it was stretching the Convention's language in order to encompass various acts of apartheid. This can also be seen in its use of phrases like 'a kind of genocide' and 'bordering on genocide'. The report was only very sparsely supported with footnotes. The principal academic sources on the Convention available at the time were not referred to at all, nor was there any reference to the *travaux préparatoires* or to the limited case law, essentially the two judgments of the Israeli courts in the *Eichmann case*.

The Commission on Human Rights dealt with the Ad Hoc Working Group's genocide report with some equivocation, noting in a preambular paragraph that

[178] Ibid., para. 32.
[179] Ibid., para. 42.
[180] Ibid., paras. 56–7.
[181] Ibid., p. 23.
[182] Ibid., p. 24.

APARTHEID AS GENOCIDE   341

'the Ad Hoc Working Group has concluded that the effects of apartheid have resulted, in certain criminal consequences similar to those prohibited in the Convention on the Prevention and Punishment of the Crime of Genocide'.[183] An operative paragraph in the draft resolution used the word 'commends', and said affirmatively that 'acts of apartheid . . . constitute an element of genocide'.[184] The sponsors amended this, using the much more cautious words 'takes note of'. The Working Group was asked to. 'continue its investigation of the matter'.[185] In an operative paragraph, the resolution noted the studies and findings on the relationship between genocide and apartheid undertaken by the Ad Hoc Working Group and requested it to 'continue its investigation of the matter'.[186] The compromise worked, and the amended resolution was adopted by 41 votes to one (the United States) with one abstention (the United Kingdom).[187] The American representative said genocide had a 'clear meaning' and the term should only be used when it applies; '[w]rong as apartheid was it was not genocide'.[188] The Commission was less restrained in a resolution adopted a few minutes later where it said it was '[c]onvinced that the crime of apartheid, is a form of the crime of genocide'.[189] The resolution was adopted by 32 votes to 1 (the United States), but with 10 abstentions, essentially from States that were not positive about the Apartheid Convention.[190] At the same session, the Commission adopted a resolution condemning the massacre in the Palestinian refugee camps of Sabra and Shatilla, in Beirut, as 'an act of genocide'.[191]

---

[183] Situation of human rights in South Africa, 26 February 1985, E/CN.4/RES/1985/8, PP 5.

[184] Situation of human rights in South Africa – Afghanistan, Algeria, Angola, Bolivia, Cameroon, China, Congo, Cuba, Egypt, Ethiopia, Gambia, India, Kenya, Lesotho, Libyan Arab Jamahiriya, Mauritania, Mozambique, Nigeria, Pakistan, Senegal, Syrian Arab Republic, Uganda, and United Republic of Tanzania: draft resolution, 21 February 1985, E/CN.4/1985/L.23, OP 14.

[185] Situation of human rights in South Africa, 26 February 1985, E/CN.4/RES/1985/8, OP 14. See Summary record, Commission on Human Rights, 26 February 1985, E/CN.4/1985/SR.32/Add.1, para. 25.

[186] Situation of human rights in South Africa, 26 February 1985, E/CN.4/RES/1985/8, OP 14.

[187] Summary record, Commission on Human Rights, 26 February 1985, E/CN.4/1985/SR.32/Add.1, paras. 32–4.

[188] Ibid., para. 40.

[189] Implementation of the International Convention on the Suppression and Punishment of the Crime of Apartheid, 26 February 1985, E/CN.4/RES/1985/10, PP 6. Also Implementation of the International Convention on the Suppression and Punishment of the Crime of Apartheid, 28 February 1986, E/CN.4/RES/1986/7, PP 6; Implementation of the International Convention on the Suppression and Punishment of the Crime of Apartheid, 26 February 1987, E/CN.4/RES/1987/11, PP 6; Implementation of the International Convention on the Suppression and Punishment of the Crime of Apartheid, 29 February 1988, E/CN.4/RES/1988/14, PP 6; Implementation of the International Convention on the Suppression and Punishment of the Crime of Apartheid, 23 February 1989, E/CN.4/RES/1989/8, PP 6.

[190] Summary record, Commission on Human Rights, 26 February 1985, E/CN.4/1985/SR.32/Add.1, paras. 57–62.

[191] The right of peoples to self-determination and its application to peoples under colonial or alien domination or foreign occupation, 26 February 1985, E/CN.4/RES/1985/4, OP 3. Also Situation in occupied Palestine, 10 March 1986, E/CN.4/RES/1986/22, OP 5; Situation in occupied Palestine, 19 February 1987, E/CN.4/RES/1987/4, PP 8; Situation in occupied Palestine, 22 February 1988, E/

342 RACIAL DISCRIMINATION AS A CRIME AGAINST HUMANITY

The materials of the Ad Hoc Working Group were studied by the Special Rapporteur on genocide of the Sub-Commission on the Prevention of Discrimination and the Protection of Minorities. In his 1978 report, Nicodème Ruhashanyiko concluded that there was a clear tendency to view apartheid as a crime against humanity. He also felt that with the adoption of the Apartheid Convention, it was unnecessary to include apartheid in an amended definition of the international crime of genocide.[192] Ruhashanyiko's report was substantially reviewed in 1985 by Special rapporteur Benjamin Whitaker. He seemed to sit on the fence, reporting on the studies that had subsumed apartheid within the crime of genocide but also noting that the report of his predecessor had rejected the qualification. Although he discussed the findings of the Working Group, he took no firm position himself and made no mention of the position adopted by the Commission. 'It could seem pedantic to argue that some terrible mass-killings are legalistically not genocide, but on the other hand it could be counter-productive to devalue genocide through over-diluting its definition', he said.[193]

The Apartheid Convention called for the establishment of a 'Group of Three' charged with examining periodic reports of States Parties. The Group of Three observed that States Parties had not included information in their reports about the establishment of the tribunal that was contemplated by the Apartheid Convention. It considered convening a diplomatic conference of States Parties with a view to elaborating a statute for the tribunal. It also raised the possibility of preparing draft model penal legislation for domestic prosecutions of the crime of apartheid under the principle of universal jurisdiction.[194]

An International Court for Apartheid

Article 5 of the Apartheid Convention states that persons charged with the crime against humanity of apartheid could be tried by national courts or 'by an international penal tribunal having jurisdiction with respect to those States Parties which shall have accepted its jurisdiction'. This phrasing is almost identical to that of article 6 of the 1948 Genocide Convention. When the Genocide

CN.4/RES/1988/3, PP 8. This echoed a General Assembly resolution: The situation in the Middle East, 16 December 1982, A/RES/37/123 D, OP 2.

[192] Study of the question of the prevention and punishment of the crime of genocide, prepared by Nicodème Ruhashyankiko, Special Rapporteur, 4 July 1978, E/CN.4/Sub.2/416, paras. 404–5.
[193] Revised and updated report on the question of the prevention and punishment of the crime of genocide prepared by Mr. B. Whitaker, 2 July 1985, E/CN.4/Sub.2/1985/6, para. 24.
[194] Report of the Group of Three established under the Convention, 2 February 1979, E/CN.4/1328, para. 15. Also Report of the Group of Three established under the Convention, E/CN.4/1286, paras. 14, 18; Report of the Group of Three established under the Convention, 1 February 1980, E/CN.4/1558, para. 23.

AN INTERNATIONAL COURT FOR APARTHEID   343

Convention was adopted, a companion General Assembly resolution launched a process of preparing a statute for such an international penal tribunal.[195] After some initial work on the project, the General Assembly called a halt pending agreement on a definition of aggression.[196] But when that was accomplished, in 1974, the General Assembly did not then direct that preparation of a statute for an international criminal court should be resumed.

In 1979, in a General Assembly resolution sponsored by more than 25 African countries, the Ad Hoc Working Group of Experts was requested to study the 'establishment of the international jurisdiction envisaged by the Convention'.[197] The Group of Experts prepared a study on the history of efforts to establish a permanent international criminal jurisdiction.[198] In 1981, the Commission on Human Rights formally requested the Ad Hoc Working Group of Experts, in cooperation with the Special Committee against Apartheid, to undertake the task of drafting the statute of such a court.[199] The Working Group retained M. Cherif Bassiouni, a renowned Egyptian international lawyer and professor of law at DePaul University in Chicago, to undertake a study and to draft a statute. The report that he prepared discussed various features of the Apartheid Convention noting that in many respects it duplicated earlier instruments dealing with racial discrimination. 'It is as a declaration of international criminal law that the Apartheid Convention merits special attention', wrote Bassiouni.[200]

The actual draft statute that Bassiouni prepared contemplated an international criminal tribunal with jurisdiction over the crime of humanity but also over certain other international crimes, provided that these were recognized by States Parties by means of an additional protocol. The core crime was identified as 'grave breaches' of the Apartheid Convention, namely murder, torture, cruel, inhuman or degrading treatment, or punishment and arbitrary arrest and detention. It did not define apartheid as a crime against humanity.[201]

---

[195] Study by the International Law Commission of the question of an international criminal jurisdiction, 9 December 1948, A/RES/260 B (III).

[196] International criminal jurisdiction, 14 December 1954, A/RES/898 (IX), OP 2.

[197] Programme of activities to be undertaken during the second half of the Decade for Action to Combat Racism and Racial Discrimination, 15 November 1979, A/RES/34/24, Annex, para. 20. See also Report of the Third Committee, 29 October 1979, A/34/618, para. 8.

[198] Étude sur les moyens à mettre en œuvre pour appliquer les instruments internationaux pertinents, tels que la Convention internationale sur l'élimination et la répression du crime d'apartheid, y compris la création de la juridiction internationale envisagée par ladite convention, 25 July 1980, E/CN.4/AC.22/1980/WP.2.

[199] Implementation of the International Convention on the Prevention and Suppression of the Crime of Apartheid, 26 February 1980, E/CN.4/RES/12 (XXXVI); Report on the 37th session of the Commission on Human Rights, 2 February–13 March 1981, E/1981/25, para. 73.

[200] Study on the ways and means of the implementation of international instruments such as the International Convention on the Suppression and Punishment of the Crime of Apartheid, including the establishment of the international jurisdiction envisaged by the Convention, 19 January 1980, E/CN.4/1426, para. 30.

[201] Ibid., p. 21.

344 RACIAL DISCRIMINATION AS A CRIME AGAINST HUMANITY

The chairman of the Ad Hoc Working Group, Branimír Janković, presented the report to the 1981 session of the Commission on Human Rights, appealing to the international community to suppress apartheid by establishing an international criminal tribunal.[202] According to the Report of the Commission, '[a] large number of delegations unreservedly supported the recommendations made by the Ad Hoc Working Group of Experts in the reports submitted to the Commission'.[203] Moreover, '[s]everal representatives favoured the elaboration of legal rules and the establishment of a procedure for the creation of an international penal tribunal to try crimes of apartheid'.[204] The Commission adopted a resolution inviting Member States to make observations on the draft statutes of the proposed international criminal court.[205] Later in the year, an expert meeting on the proposed tribunal was convened at the International Institute for Higher Studies in Criminal Sciences, in Siracusa, Italy, of which Bassiouni was the director.[206]

The Commission renewed its request to Member States in 1982.[207] By December 1982 it had received replies from nine States Parties to the Convention and from 12 non-party States. The Ad Hoc Working Group of Experts considered that this was insufficient for it to prepare a study and asked the Commission to try once again to encourage submissions.[208] The resolution was duly adopted by the Commission.[209] In 1984, the Ad Hoc Working Group reported on submissions from the Soviet Union, Bulgaria, Hungary, and East Germany, who said that they saw no need for an international tribunal.[210] Yugoslavia, on the other hand, expressed its support for the initiative.[211] Australia was the only Western State to make substantive comments. It said consideration should be given to a

---

[202] Summary record, Commission on Human Rights, 16 February 1981, E/CN.4/SR.1596, para. 50; Report on the 37th session of the Commission on Human Rights (2 February–13 March 1981), E/1981/25, para. 74.

[203] Report on the 37th session of the Commission on Human Rights (2 February–13 March 1981), E/1981/25, para. 76.

[204] Ibid., para. 82.

[205] Violations of human rights in southern Africa: report of the Ad Hoc Working Group of Experts, 23 February 1981, E/CN.4/RES/5 (XXXVII), OP 11.

[206] Report on the Seminar on 'The draft international criminal code and the draft statute for the creation of an international criminal court' held from 17 to 23 May 1981 in Siracusa (Italy), 8 June 1982, E/CN.4/1485, Annex I.

[207] Violations of human rights in southern Africa; report of the Ad Hoc Working Group of Experts, 25 February 1982, E/CN.4/RES/1982/8, OP 8.

[208] Report of the Ad Hoc Working Group of Experts prepared in accordance with Commission on Human Rights Resolution 5 (XXXVII) and Economic and Social Council Resolution 1982/40, 21 January 1983, E/CN.4/1983/10, para. 9.

[209] Violations of human rights in southern Africa: Report of the Ad Hoc Working Group of Experts, 18 February 1983, E/CN.4/RES/1983/9, OP 5.

[210] Progress report of the Ad Hoc Working Group of Experts prepared in accordance with Commission on Human Rights Resolutions 1983/9 and 1983/10 and Economic and Social Council Decision 1983/135, 24 January 1984, E/CN.4/1984/8, paras. 509–10.

[211] Ibid., para. 517.

tribunal with a broader subject-matter jurisdiction than apartheid.[212] Algeria, the only African State to reply, made a number of detailed suggestions aimed at improving the proposal.[213] The Ad Hoc Working Group drew no conclusions. The Commission on Human Rights put out further calls for submissions in 1984 and again in 1985.[214] Then the effort seemed to run out of momentum, at least as far as the Commission on Human Rights was concerned. Writing on the subject three decades later, Cherif Bassiouni offered a straightforward explanation: 'The "Western bloc" was not ready to establish an international criminal court only for the prosecution of the crime of apartheid. Thus, no further United Nations action ensued.'[215] However, the work of the Commission on Human Rights undoubtedly contributed to a growing momentum for the international criminal court project.

The International Law Commission began raising the issue of an international criminal court in its reports to the General Assembly in 1983, and again in 1986 and 1987.[216] Its persistence resulted in a request to the Commission from the General Assembly in 1989 'to address the question of establishing and international criminal court or other international criminal trial mechanism' with jurisdiction over crimes in the Draft Code of Crimes against the Peace and Security of Mankind.[217] In 1992, a Special rapporteur of the International Law Commission made initial proposals for the statute of the international criminal court. Under subject-matter jurisdiction were listed five categories of international crime, one of them apartheid.[218] The same year, a Working Group of the Commission concluded that the proposed court's jurisdiction should 'certainly include' crimes set out in international conventions, giving those governing genocide and

---

[212] Ibid., para. 520.

[213] Ibid., para. 518. The Working Group subsequently received a report from Madagascar that was relatively positive about the proposed tribunal: Note from the Government of Madagascar concerning the draft Convention on the Establishment of an International Penal Tribunal for the Suppression and Punishment of the Crime of Apartheid and Other International Crimes, 23 January 1985, E/CN.4/1985/8, Annex I.

[214] Violations of human rights in southern Africa: Report of the Ad Hoc Working Group of Experts, 28 February 1984, E/CN.4/RES/1984/5, OP 11; Situation of human rights in South Africa, 26 February 1985, E/CN.4/RES/1985/8, OP 20.

[215] M. Cherif Bassiouni, 'Chronology of Efforts to Establish an International Criminal Tribunal' (2015) 86 *Revue internationale de droit pénal* 1183, at p. 1169.

[216] Report of the International Law Commission, 35th session, 1983, A/38/10, para. 69(c)(i); Report of the International Law Commission, 38th session, 1986, A/41/10, para. 185; Report of the International Law Commission, 39th session, 1987, A/42/10, para. 67(c).

[217] International criminal responsibility of individuals and entities engaged in illicit trafficking in narcotic drugs across national frontiers and other transnational criminal activities: establishment of an international criminal court with jurisdiction over such crimes, 4 December 1989, A/RES/44/39, OP 2.

[218] Tenth report on the draft Code of Crimes against the Peace and Security of Mankind, by Mr. Doudou Thiam, Special Rapporteur, 20 March 1992, A/CN.4/442, para. 36.

346   RACIAL DISCRIMINATION AS A CRIME AGAINST HUMANITY

apartheid as examples.[219] The final draft adopted by the Commission in 1994 recognised jurisdiction over genocide, aggression, violations of the laws and customs of war, crimes against humanity, and 'Crimes, established under or pursuant to the treaty provisions listed in the Annex, which, having regard to the conduct alleged, constitute exceptionally serious crimes of international concern'.[220] Apartheid was listed in the annex.[221]

The temporary tribunals established by the United Nations Security Council for the former Yugoslavia and Rwanda, in 1993 and 1994 respectively, did not recognize apartheid as a crime against humanity. The logical explanation is that the drafters did not see the relevance of the crime in the circumstances being addressed by those institutions.[222] In one of the early judgments of the International Criminal Tribunal for the former Yugoslavia, a Trial Chamber spoke of the 'customary law status of the prohibition of crimes against humanity, as well as two of its most egregious manifestations, genocide and apartheid'.[223]

In 1994, the General Assembly designated an *ad hoc* Committee to examine the draft statute prepared by the International Law Commission. During its sessions, the United States objected to the inclusion of the Apartheid Convention in the list of treaty-based crimes.[224] One of the reports of the Committee said there were doubts about the clarity of the definition of apartheid and whether it should be considered in the definition of crimes against humanity or treated as a separate crime.[225] In a position paper, Canada said that international custom was a source of substantive law, giving as examples 'the crime of piracy and, arguably, apartheid (which may be considered a crime against the peace and security of mankind, even by states that have not ratified the International Convention on the Suppression and Punishment of the Crime of Apartheid)', which was indeed the case for Canada.[226] However, at the time Canada was a State Party to the Additional Protocol to the Geneva Conventions applicable to international armed conflict, where apartheid was listed as a grave breach ('when committed wilfully and in violation of international humanitarian law. . . Practices of

---

[219] Report of the Working Group on the Question of an International Criminal Jurisdiction, A/47/40, Annex, para. 57. Also Revised Report of the Working Group on the Draft Statute for an International Criminal Court, 19 July 1993, A/CN.4/L.490, p. 21

[220] Draft Statute for an International Criminal Court, including Annex and Appendices I to III, A/CN.4/SER.A/1994/Add.1 (Part 2), p. 38, art. 20

[221] Ibid., Annex (Crimes pursuant to treaties (see art. 20, sub-para. (e)), pp. 67–8.

[222] Guénaël Mettraux, *Crimes against Humanity*, Oxford: Oxford University Press, 2020, p. 737.

[223] *Prosecutor v. Tadić* (IT-94-1-T), Opinion and judgment, 7 May 1997, para. 622.

[224] Comments received pursuant to paragraph 4 of General Assembly resolution 49/53 on the establishment of an international criminal court, 20 March 1995. A/AC.244/1/Add.2, para. 104 (United States).

[225] Summary of the proceedings of the ad hoc Committee during the period 3–13 April 1995, 21 April 1995, A/AC.244/2, para. 36.

[226] Options paper on 'applicable law' by Canada, 14–25 August 1995, p. 2.

AN INTERNATIONAL COURT FOR APARTHEID   347

apartheid and other inhuman and degrading practices involving outrages upon personal dignity, based on racial discrimination').[227]

From 1996 to 1998, the Preparatory Committee established by the General Assembly in 1995 was the forum for negotiations of permanent court's statute. The 1996 report of the Preparatory Committee noted laconically that '[s]ome delegations favoured including apartheid and other forms of racial discrimination as defined in the relevant conventions'.[228] Its final report, issued immediately prior to the Rome Conference, listed apartheid under the heading 'war crimes' as a form of 'outrages upon personal dignity', presumably because of the reference in the Additional Protocol rather than to the Apartheid Convention, where it would properly be described as a crime against humanity.[229] There was only a hint that it belonged within crimes against humanity, buried in a footnote stating: 'It was also suggested that the list of acts should include institutionalised discrimination.'[230]

At the Rome Conference in June-July 1998, the first call to include apartheid in the list of crimes against humanity in the recorded debates was from the Mexican representative, Socorro Flores, who was elected as a judge of the Court in 2020.[231] There was broad support for listing apartheid,[232] but also substantial opposition.[233] Several States of the Global South proposed including the following: 'Institutionalised racial discrimination, including the practices of apartheid.'[234] The proposal was then picked up as 'The crime of apartheid' by the

---

[227] Additional Protocol to the 1949 Geneva Conventions and Relating to the Protection of Victims of International Armed Conflicts (1979) 1125 UNTS 3, art. 85(4)(c). According to the *Commentary* of the International Committee of the Red Cross on the provision, 'the practices concerned were already grave breaches of the Conventions, whatever their motive; this is simply a special mention of reprehensible conduct for which the motive is particularly shocking' (Bruno Zimmermann, 'Article 85 – Repression of breaches of this Protocol', in Yves Sandoz, Christophe Swinarski, and Bruno Zimmermann, eds., *Commentary on the Additional Protocols of 8 June 1977 to the Geneva Conventions of 12 August 1949*, Geneva: Martinus Nijhoff, 1987, pp. 989–1004, at p. 1002).

[228] Preparatory Committee 1996 Report, A/51/22, Vol. I, para. 108. Also: Preparatory Committee 1996 Report, A/51/22, Vol. II, p. 60.

[229] Report of the Preparatory Committee on the Establishment of an International Criminal Court, A/CONF.183/13 (Vol. III), p. 18.

[230] Ibid., p. 26.

[231] Summary record, Committee of the Whole, 17 June 1998, A/CONF.183/C.1/SR.3, para. 125.

[232] Summary record, Committee of the Whole, 17 June 1998, A/CONF.183/C.1/SR.4, paras. 44 (Syria), 48 (Lebanon), 63 (Libya), 65 (China), 66 (United Arab Emirates), 67 (Greece), 69 (Viet Nam), 70 (Bahrain); Summary record, Committee of the Whole, 18 June 1998, A/CONF.183/C1/SR.5, paras. 9 (Kuwait), 19 (Republic of Korea), 23 (Tunisia), 26 (Thailand), 33 (Egypt), 46 (Brazil), 48 (Algeria), 56 (Japan), 62 (Morocco), 69 (Cuba), 70 (Turkey), 72 (Iran), 83 (Senegal), 97 (South Africa).

[233] Summary record, Committee of the Whole, 17 June 1998, A/CONF.183/C.1/SR.4, paras. 62 (Costa Rica), 75 (Sweden); Summary record, Committee of the Whole, 18 June 1998, A/CONF.183/C1/SR.5, paras. 7 (Belgium), 36 (Russia), 40 (United Kingdom), 58 (Switzerland), 60 (Macedonia), 66 (Italy), 92 (Chile).

[234] Bangladesh, India, Lesotho, Malawi, Mexico, Namibia, South Africa, Swaziland, Trinidad and Tobago, and United Republic of Tanzania: proposal regarding article 5, 22 June 1998, A/CONF.183/C.1/L.12.

Bureau of the Conference in a 'discussion paper' as it sought to find texts that would be generally acceptable.[235] The Bureau proposal also included a number of detailed definitions of some of the categories of crimes against humanity that do not seem to have been proposed by any State and that emerged in the course of the Rome Conference. One of them described apartheid as 'inhumane acts of a character similar to those referred to in paragraph 1, committed in the context of an institutionalised regime of systematic oppression and domination by one racial group over any other racial group or groups and committed with the intention of maintaining that regime'. Timothy McCormack has suggested that many States showed a lot of deference to South Africa, 'understandably reticent to be seen to be prolonging South Africa's apartheid induced suffering by arguing against the explicit inclusion of apartheid'. He wrote that the United States was one of the few delegations that was concerned about the breadth of the definition, 'to ensure that the practices of white supremacy organisations operating within the US were not covered'. This seems to have been achieved by the requirement of an institutionalized regime of systematic oppression and domination. McCormack said the South African delegation and the other African States supporting inclusion of apartheid had no objection to this additional element, given its obvious application to the racist regimes in southern Africa in previous decades.[236] The Rome Statute definition is therefore somewhat narrower than that of the Convention although this does not have consequences with respect to customary law, where the Convention definition is authoritative.[237]

There have been no prosecutions at the International Criminal Court for the crime against humanity of apartheid. It does not appear that it was ever charged within South Africa itself. South Africa took a political decision by which the crimes of the apartheid regime were, as a general rule, left unpunished. In itself, that is not an obstacle to national courts in other countries from prosecuting the crime under the principle of universal jurisdiction. Given the growing enthusiasm for the use of universal jurisdiction, attention to the unpunished crimes of apartheid in South Africa prior to 1990 might be expected. The absence of such prosecutions outside South Africa provides confirmation of broad international approval of the path it chose, one of reconciliation, to deal with the crimes of the

---

[235] Bureau: discussion paper regarding part 2, 6 July 1998, A/CONF.183/C.1/L.53. Also Bureau: proposal regarding part 2, 10 July 1998, A/CONF.183/C.1/L.59.

[236] Timothy L.H. McCormack, 'Crimes Against Humanity', in Dominic McGoldrick, Peter Rowe, and Eric Donnelly, eds., *The Permanent International Criminal Court: Legal and Policy Issues*, Oxford: Hart 2004, pp. 179–202, at p. 199.

[237] Miles Jackson, 'The Definition of Apartheid in Customary International Law and the International Convention on the Elimination of All Forms of Racial Discrimination' (2022) 71 *International and Comparative Law Quarterly* 831, at p. 844

white supremacists. Nevertheless, calls continue for the application of international criminal justice to those responsible for the apartheid regime.[238]

Israel has frequently been accused of apartheid with respect to its treatment of Palestinians. The Special rapporteur on the occupied Palestinian territories, John Dugard, said Israel's intent 'to establish and maintain domination by one racial group (Jews) over another racial group (Palestinians) and systematically oppressing them', in violation of the Apartheid Convention, could be inferred from various acts.[239] 'Israel's laws and practices in the OPT certainly resemble aspects of apartheid', wrote Dugard.[240] His successor, Richard Falk, endorsed Dugard's findings and said that the evidence was even stronger than it had been in 2007.[241] In 2017 Falk and his co-author, Virginia Tilley, produced a report for the United Nations Economic and Social Commission for Eastern Asia entitled 'Israeli Practices towards the Palestinian People and the Question of Apartheid'. The report concluded, 'on the basis of scholarly inquiry and overwhelming evidence, that Israel is guilty of the crime of apartheid'.[242] In Concluding Observations on Israel's periodic reports, the Committee on the Elimination of Racial Discrimination has 'drawn the attention' of the State Party to article 3 of the Convention, which refers to apartheid, and has urged it 'to give full effect to article 3 of the Convention to eradicate all forms of segregation between Jewish and non-Jewish communities and any such policies or practices that severely and disproportionately affect the Palestinian population in Israel proper and in the Occupied Palestinian Territory'.[243] Human Rights Watch and Amnesty International have called for the International Criminal Court to consider the crime of apartheid in the context of its investigation into the Situation in Palestine.[244] However, in reports on the preliminary examination and investigation of the *Situation in the State of Palestine*, the Prosecutor of the International Criminal Court has not referred to the crime against humanity of apartheid.

* * *

[238] Yasmin Sooka and Christopher Gevers, 'FW De Klerk Has a Case to Answer', *Independent Online*, 4 July 2020.

[239] Report of the Special Rapporteur on the situation of human rights in the Palestinian territories occupied since 1967, John Dugard, 29 January 2007, A/HRC/4/17, para. 50.

[240] Ibid., para. 61.

[241] Report of the Special Rapporteur on the situation of human rights in the Palestinian territories occupied since 1967, 30 August 2010, A/65/331, para. 3. Also Report of the Special Rapporteur on the situation of human rights in the Palestinian territories occupied since 1967, Richard Falk, 13 January 2014, A/HRC/25/67, paras. 51–77.

[242] Richard Falk and Virginia Tilley, *Israeli Practices towards the Palestinian People and the Question of Apartheid*, Beirut: Economic and Social Commission for Eastern Asia, 2017.

[243] Concluding observations on the combined seventeenth to nineteenth reports of Israel, 27 January 2020, CERD/C/ISR/CO/17-19, para. 20. Also Concluding observations of the Committee on the Elimination of Racial Discrimination, Israel, 3 April 2012, CERD/C/ISR/CO/14-16, para. 11.

[244] Human Rights Watch, *A Threshold Crossed, Israeli Authorities and the, Crimes of Apartheid and Persecution* April 2021, pp. 20, 207; Amnesty International, Israel's *Apartheid against Palestinians, Cruel System of Domination and Crime against Humanity*, MDE 15/5141/2022, January 2022, p. 32.

The changing position of Western States on the crime against humanity of apartheid is remarkable. They attempted to fight off the initiatives from African and Asian States during the 1960s and 1980s but gradually gave way. There was no serious resistance to including the crime in the subject-matter jurisdiction of the International Criminal Court. Several States Parties have now incorporated it within their domestic legislation in fulfilment of their obligations under the Rome Statute.

There has been criticism of the inclusion of apartheid within the definition of crimes against humanity in the academic literature.[245] Generally, it rests on the charge that the notion is either superfluous or that it is vague. The same objections were made when the Apartheid Convention was being drafted. Nevertheless, including apartheid within the enumerated acts of crimes against humanity effected a sea change in the concept because it confirmed the application of crimes against humanity with respect to violations committed in peacetime and without the requirement of any armed conflict. As for the superfluous nature, this complaint can be made about many of the crimes against humanity on the list. For example, a crime of 'extermination' is surely unnecessary given that 'murder' is the first of the crimes on the list. Similarly, various acts of sexual violence add detail, and emphasis, to certain criminal conducts but they are hardly essential. The explicit inclusion of apartheid helps emphasize the importance of racial discrimination within crimes against humanity generally. After all, the category of crimes against humanity was first codified at Nuremberg so that racist Nazi crimes of persecution against minorities would not go unpunished.

---

[245] Adam Sitze, 'The crime of apartheid: genealogy of a successful failure' (2019) 7 *London Review of International Law* 181, at p. 195; Alexander Zahar, 'Apartheid as an international crime', in Antonio Cassese, ed., *The Oxford Companion to International Criminal Law*, Oxford: Oxford University Press, 2009, pp. 245–6.

12

Days, Years, Decades, and Conferences on Racial Discrimination

An International Year to Combat Racism

The fashion of General Assembly resolutions designating 'international years' began in 1958 when two such years were announced to highlight health and medical research[1] and the 'refugee problem'.[2] In 1963, the United Nations General Assembly decided that 1968, the twentieth anniversary of its adoption of the Universal Declaration of Human Rights, would be the 'International Year for Human Rights'.[3] Racial discrimination emerged as one of the central themes to be addressed by the Conference held in Tehran.[4] A resolution adopted by the Conference invoked the Charter of the United Nations, the Universal Declaration of Human Rights, and the International Convention on the Elimination of All Forms of Racial Discrimination. It urged the General Assembly to consider declaring 1969 'or the following year' as the International Year for Action to Combat Racism and Racial Discrimination.[5] Adopted unanimously, only the United States expressed reservations on the very unconvincing ground that 'every year should be a year for action to combat racism and racial discrimination and that too many International Years would render the idea meaningless'.[6] The General Assembly endorsed the proposal and asked the Secretary-General to prepare a programme for the year.[7] After seeking the views of Member States,

[1] International Health and Medical Research Year, 5 December 1958, A/RES/1283 (XIII).

[2] World Refugee Year, 5 December 1958, A/RES/1285 (XIII).

[3] Designation of 1968 as International Year for Human Rights, 12 December 1963, A/RES/1961 (XVIII).

[4] Steven L.B. Jensen, *The Making of International Human Rights, The 1960s, Decolonisation, and the Reconstruction of Global Values*, Cambridge: Cambridge University Press, 2016, pp. 97–9. On the Tehran Conference, see generally Roland Burke, 'From Individual Rights to National Development: The First UN International Conference on Human Rights, Tehran, 1968' (2008) 19 *Journal of World History* 275; Andrew S. Thompson, 'Tehran 1968 and Reform of the UN Human Rights System' (2015) 14 *Journal of Human Rights* 84.

[5] International Year for Action to Combat Racism and Racial Discrimination, A/CONF.32/RES/24.

[6] Summary record, Committee II, Tehran Conference, 9 May 1968, A/CONF.32/C.2/SR.13, p. 158.

[7] Measures to achieve the rapid and total elimination of all forms of racial discrimination in general and of the policy of apartheid in particular, 19 December 1968, A/RES/2446 (XXIII), OP 9.

The International Legal Order's Colour Line. William A. Schabas, Oxford University Press.
© Oxford University Press 2023. DOI: 10.1093/oso/9780197744475.003.0012

352 INITIATIVES ON RACIAL DISCRIMINATION

the Secretary-General prepared a draft programme of an International Year for action to combat racism and racial discrimination for consideration by the General Assembly.[8]

There was only perfunctory discussion in the Third Committee of the proposed programme for the International Year for Action to Combat Racism and Racial Discrimination. The general debate manifested the global tensions that swirled around the debates about apartheid, racism, and racial discrimination. The United States argued that too much attention was being given to apartheid and racial discrimination. It thought that there should be a greater focus on other issues such as prisoners of conscience. The United States also suggested that the Third Committee might take up the question of the fundamental rights of American prisoners of war captured by the Vietnamese.[9] This provoked a spirited reply from the Soviet Union, which said the issue was 'nothing but a trick to divert the Committee's attention from other matters, such as the violation of human rights by Israel in the Middle East'.[10] Citing both Raphaël Lemkin and Jean-Paul Sartre, Cuba implied that the Vietnam war was genocidal in nature.[11]

When the resolution on the International Year came to a vote, the United Kingdom abruptly proposed that the name be changed from 'International Year for Action to Combat Racism and Racial Discrimination' to 'International Year for Social Justice'.[12] The United Kingdom had not previously spoken to such a radical proposal,[13] although it had obviously been manoeuvring behind the scenes to build support. There were 26 votes in favour of the British proposal, including those of Australia, Canada, New Zealand, and the United States, as well as other Western European states and three African states, Gabon, Lesotho, and Malawi. The explanations of vote suggest that there may have been a degree of misunderstanding, with some delegates thinking that Britain's oral amendment referred to 'racial justice'.[14] The 59 negative votes on the amendment came almost entirely from States in Africa and Asia, as well as the Soviet bloc.[15] At the domestic level, the United Kingdom eventually chose to refer to the 'International Year for Racial Harmony'.[16]

---

[8] Programme for the celebration in 1971 of the International Year for action to combat racism and racial discrimination, 17 September 1969, A/7649.

[9] Summary record, Third Committee, 10 November 1969, A/C.3/SR.1698, paras. 23–30.

[10] Ibid., para. 31.

[11] Summary record, Third Committee, 12 November 1969, A/C.3/SR.1700, para. 58

[12] Summary record, Third Committee, 21 November 1969, A/C.3/SR.1711, para. 58.

[13] See, nevertheless, its indifferent comment about the International Year in its communication to the Secretary-General dated 18 October 1968, Programme for the celebration in 1971 of the International Year for action to combat racism and racial discrimination, Addendum, 21 October 1961, A/7649/Add.1, p. 22.

[14] Summary record, Third Committee, 21 November 1969, A/C.3/SR.1711, paras. 59–60.

[15] Ibid., para. 58.

[16] Elimination of all forms of racial discrimination: International Year for Action to Combat Racism and Racial Discrimination, 24 September 1971, A/8367, p. 79.

On 11 December 1969, the General Assembly voted unanimously to recognize 1971 as the International Year for Action to Combat Racism and Racial Discrimination. The resolution reaffirmed the resolve of the General Assembly 'to achieve the total and unconditional elimination of racial discrimination and racism', recalling its decisions and those of other United Nations organs condemning apartheid as being incompatible with the Charter of the United Nations and as a crime against humanity.[17] Michael Banton noted an innovation in the use of the term 'racism', concluding that the General Assembly 'meant to extend the scope of the action proposed', although he did not point to any evidence in the debates that might confirm such a suggestion.[18] During 1970, various United Nations bodies addressed possible activities during the upcoming International Year. The Commission on Human Rights considered the matter in some detail although its recommendations were rather unimaginative, consisting essentially of campaigns for ratification of the International Convention on the Elimination of All Forms of Racial Discrimination and the dissemination of information.[19]

The Sub-Commission on the Prevention and Discrimination and the Protection of Minorities proposed that the United Nations convene a meeting 'to be held in an African capital situated not far from South Africa, such as that of Namibia, Territory under the direct responsibility of the United Nations ... ' Given effective control of Namibia by South Africa, that was an impossibility. The Sub-Commission thought this 'would be an important occasion for bringing to the people of South Africa in particular and to other oppressed peoples and victims of discrimination in general the support of the international community in their struggle to regain their dignity and freedom and to enjoy with the other peoples of the world all the rights embodied in the Universal Declaration of Human Rights'.[20]

The International Year focussed global attention on the issues of racism and racial discrimination. Various United Nations organs took special initiatives. The Commission on Human Rights appealed to international public opinion to protest any attempt to violate the relevant provisions of the Security Council resolutions imposing an embargo on the sale of arms to South Africa.[21] Similar

---

[17] Programme for the observance in 1971 of the International Year for Action to Combat Racism and Racial Discrimination, 11 December 1969, A/RES/2544 (XXIV), PPs 1, 2.

[18] Michael Banton, *International Action against Racial Discrimination*, Oxford: Clarendon Press, 1996, p. 71.

[19] For example, Commission on Human Rights, Report on the 26th session (24 February–27 March 1970), E/4816, paras. 15–21; International action against racial discrimination: programme for the observance in 1971 of the International Year for Action to Combat Racism and Racial Discrimination, 26 February 1970, E/CN.4/RES/3 (XXVI).

[20] Elimination of racial discrimination; International Year for Action to Combat Racism and Racial Discrimination, 26 August 1970, E/CN.4/Sub.2/RES/5 (XXIII), OP 3.

[21] Observance in 1971 of the International Year for Action to Combat Racism and Racial Discrimination, 1 March 1971, E/CN.4/RES/1 (XXVII).

354   INITIATIVES ON RACIAL DISCRIMINATION

resolutions were adopted by the Economic and Social Council[22] and the Sub-Commission on Prevention of Discrimination and Protection of Minorities,[23] as well as by the International Labour Organisation[24] and UNESCO. Regional organizations like the Council of Europe also marked the International Year.[25] The Secretary-General's report on the activities of the International Year runs to nearly 150 pages. It describes a range of initiatives by various Member States involving meetings, conferences, publication, treaty ratifications, legislative changes, decrees, media coverage, rallies, art exhibitions, changes to school curricula, official statements, and speeches.[26] Many countries issued commemorative stamps or adopted special cancellations to mark the International Year, including Afghanistan, Algeria, Brazil, Cambodia, Cameroon, Canada, Central African Republic, Chad, Congo (Brazzaville), Côte d'Ivoire, Dahomey, Ethiopia, Gabon, German Democratic Republic, Guinea, Hungary, Iraq, Ireland, Kuwait, Laos, Libya, Mongolia, Niger, Qatar, Romania, Rwanda, Senegal, Syria, Tunisia, Turkey, Upper Volta, Uruguay, and Vatican City, as well as the United Nations postal service itself.[27]

The United Nations General Assembly has from time to time proclaimed a 'decade' on specific subjects. The first initiative seems to have come from United States President John Kennedy in 1961. In the General Assembly's general debate, he proposed that the 1960s be officially designated as the 'United Nations Development Decade'.[28] The proposal for a decade on racial discrimination can be traced to the stocktaking as the International Year drew to a close. In December 1971, the General Assembly adopted a resolution that spoke of the opening year of an ever-growing struggle against racial discrimination in all its forms and manifestations and for the purpose of promoting international solidarity with all those struggling against racism. The Assembly considered that by arousing world public opinion and promoting action against racism, the International Year would contribute to the expansion of national and international efforts towards ensuring the rapid and total eradication of racial

---

[22] Racial Discrimination in the political, economic, social and cultural spheres, 21 May 1971, E/RES/1588 (L).

[23] International Year for Action to Combat Racism and Racial Discrimination, 18 August 1971, E/CN.4/Sub.2/RES/5 (XXIV).

[24] Resolution concerning apartheid and the contribution of the International Labour Organisation to the International Year for Action to Combat Racism and Racial Discrimination, June 1971.

[25] International Year for Action to Combat Racism and Racial Discrimination, Resolution 468, Consultative Assembly, Minutes of Proceedings, 21 January 1971, p. 21.

[26] International Year for Action to Combat Racism and Racial Discrimination, 24 September 1971, A/8367.

[27] On the issuance of stamps to commemorate human rights, see Roland Burke, 'Premature Memorials to the United Nations Human Rights Program: International Postage Stamps and the Commemoration of the 1948 Universal Declaration of Human Rights' (2016) 28 *History and Memory* 15.

[28] Verbatim record, plenary General Assembly, 25 September 1961, A/PV.1013, para. 73.

AN INTERNATIONAL YEAR TO COMBAT RACISM   355

discrimination in all its forms. Then the Assembly, amongst other things, invited the Economic and Social Council to request the Commission on Human Rights to submit suggestions with a view to launching a 'Decade for vigorous and continued mobilisation against racism and racial discrimination in all its forms'.[29] The initial proposal for such a Decade was made by 24 African States in addition to Yugoslavia and several from Asia.[30]

At its 1972 session, responding to a request from the Commission on Human Rights,[31] the Sub-Commission on Prevention of Discrimination and Protection of Minorities drew up a draft programme for the Decade. A range of international and national actions were proposed, including a 'world conference on combating racism and racial discrimination' to be a 'major feature of the Decade', regional seminars, preparation of support for oppressed peoples, the denial of support to racist regimes, the imperative implementation of United Nations resolutions and adoption of new international instruments. Deadlines were proposed for the achievement of various objectives.[32] After discussion of the Sub-Commission's proposals in the Third Committee,[33] the General Assembly agreed that the Decade for Action to Combat Racism and Racial Discrimination should begin on 10 December 1973, the twenty-fifth anniversary of the adoption of the Universal Declaration of Human Rights.[34] The following year, the General Assembly formally endorsed the detailed programme for the Decade. This included adoption of national legislation to provide recourse against racial discrimination, measures related to education, support for liberation movements, and studies on a range of issues including the crime of apartheid under international criminal law. As a 'major feature' of the Decade, a world conference on combating racial discrimination was to be convened 'as soon as possible, but preferably not later than 1978'. The conference was to focus on effective ways and means 'for securing the full and universal implementation of United Nations decisions and resolutions on racism, racial discrimination, apartheid,

---

[29] Elimination of All Forms of Racial Discrimination, 6 December 1971, A/RES/2784 (XXVI).

[30] Elimination of all forms of racial discrimination: Afghanistan, Algeria, Cameroon, Dahomey, Egypt, Ethiopia, Ghana, Guinea, India, Kenya, Liberia, Libyan Arab Republic, Mali, Mauritania, Morocco, Niger, Nigeria, Pakistan, People's Republic of the Congo, Senegal, Sierra Leone, Somalia, Sudan, Syrian Arab Republic, Uganda, United Republic of Tanzania, Upper Volta, Yemen, Yugoslavia, and Zambia: revised draft resolution, 8 November 1971, A/C.3/L.1874/Rev.1. Togo subsequently joined the co-sponsors.

[31] Continued international action to combat racism and racial discrimination, 9 March 1973, E/CN.4/RES/1 (XXVIII), OP 1.

[32] Draft programme for a 'Decade for action to combat racism and racial discrimination', 29 August 1972, E/CN.4/Sub.2/RES/3 (XXV), Annex; Report of the Sub-Commission on Prevention of Discrimination and Protection of Minorities, 14 August-1 September 1972, E/CN.4/Sub.2/332, paras. 16–68.

[33] Report of the Third Committee, 13 November 1972, A/8880, paras. 13–18.

[34] Decade for Action to Combat Racism and Racial Discrimination, 15 November 1972, A/RES/2919 (XXVII).

356 INITIATIVES ON RACIAL DISCRIMINATION

decolonisation and self-determination'.[35] When the programme for the Decade was first discussed by the Third Committee, in 1973, the United Kingdom contested the proposed world conference, arguing that it 'was likely to require a large financial outlay by an organisation which could not afford it and to produce few, if any, positive results'.[36] Several other delegations were also lukewarm about holding a conference.[37]

'Zionism is Racism'

During the debate in the Third Committee in 1973, some Western States warned that a focus on racism and racial discrimination might lead to neglect of other issues. For example, Canada's delegate pointed to the possibility 'that other forms of discrimination, especially on the grounds of sex, religion and social origin, would not be accorded due attention during the following 10 years'.[38] Belgium's representative said 'the non-white nations must recognise that decolonisation and the eradication of apartheid in Africa were not the only human rights issues meriting world attention'.[39] Arab States of the Middle East used the debate to denounce Zionism, which they said was a racist ideology.[40] The issue had been simmering since the late 1960s following the war and subsequent occupation of the West Bank and Gaza. The spark, according to some writers, was a Soviet suggestion during the final negotiations of the International Convention on the Elimination of All Forms of Racial Discrimination as Moscow fought off American attempts to condemn anti-Semitism.[41] Although many of the African countries generally kept their distance from the issue, Israel's growing relationship with South Africa did nothing to calm the waters. They were understandably infuriated that at a time when they were trying to build momentum for campaigns to isolate South Africa, Israel was pushing in the other direction.

---

[35] Decade for Action to Combat Racism and Racial Discrimination, 2 November 1973, A/RES/3057 (XXVIII), para. 13(a).

[36] Summary record, Third Committee, 1 October 1973, A/C.3/SR.1982, para. 57.

[37] Summary record, Third Committee, 27 September 1973, A/C.3/SR.1980 (Poland, para. 3); Summary record, Third Committee, 28 September 1973 (Iran, para. 48; France, para. 54); Summary record, Third Committee, 1 October 1973, A/C.3/SR.1983 (Australia, para. 19; Hungary, para. 26); Summary record, Third Committee, 3 October 1973, A/C.3/SR.1986 (Israel, para. 9).

[38] Summary record, Third Committee, 2 October 1973, A/C.3/SR.1984, para. 18.

[39] Ibid., para. 24.

[40] Summary record, Third Committee, 1 October 1973, A/C.3/SR.1983, para. 32 (Algeria); Summary record, Third Committee, 3 October 1973, A/C.3/SR.1986, paras. 30 (Egypt), 42–6 (Syria), 56 (Saudi Arabia).

[41] Nathan A. Kurz, *Jewish Internationalism and Human Rights after the Holocaust*, Cambridge: Cambridge University Press, 2021, pp. 128–32; Ofra Friesel, 'Equating Zionism with Racism: The 1965 Precedent' (2013) 97 *American Jewish History* 283.

In its early years, Israel was generally aligned with the States of the Global South on the subject of apartheid. In 1952, Israel voted in favour of the General Assembly resolution establishing a Commission to examine racism in South Africa while the Western States all abstained.[42] A decade later, Israel voted for a resolution setting up the Special Committee on Apartheid, an initiative that was opposed by 16 Western States, including France, the United Kingdom, and the United States.[43] Days later, Foreign Minister Golda Meir felt compelled to explain this to the Knesset: '[I]t would have been contrary to Jewish morality for Israel to have failed to raise its voice against the "shameful iniquity" of South Africa's apartheid policy'. She added that racism in South Africa 'touched "the very souls" of the African members of the United Nations'.[44] Addressing the General Assembly in 1963, Golda Meir spoke of the 'universal condemnation' of apartheid, invoking Israel's 'deep abhorrence for all forms of discrimination on the grounds of race, colour or religion. This stems from our age-old spiritual values, and from our long and tragic historical experience as a victim of man's inhumanity to man'.[45] In 1963 Israel lowered its representation within South Africa to the consular level. Israel joined efforts within the United Nations in 1966 to relieve South Africa of its mandate over Namibia. By 1967, 'real contacts had dwindled to a mere trickle'.[46]

Israel's occupation of much of Palestine following the 1967 war was followed by a thaw in its relations with South Africa. The policy shifted quite visibly in 1973, a result of the Yom Kippur War, the Arab oil boycott, and the fact that many African States had severed diplomatic relations with Israel in solidarity with the Palestinians. Israel's growing affinities with South Africa were first criticized by the General Assembly in 1973.[47] A General Assembly resolution referred to 'the collusion between Portuguese colonialism, the apartheid regime and zionism, as exemplified by the political military and financial aid supplied to each other by Portugal, South Africa and Israel'. It 'condemn[ed], in particular, the unholy alliance between Portuguese colonialism, South African racism, zionism and Israeli imperialism'.[48] These paragraphs were proposed by Burundi in the plenary General Assembly as it prepared to vote on a series of resolutions related to South

---

[42] On Israel's approach, see Rotem Giladi, 'Negotiating Identity: Israel, Apartheid, and the United Nations, 1949–1952' (2017) 132 *English Historical Review* 1440, at pp. 1460–3.

[43] Verbatim record, plenary General Assembly, 6 November 1962, A/PV.1165, para. 33.

[44] 'Golda Meir defends Israel's condemnation of South Africa at U.N', *Jewish Telegraphic Agency*, 14 November 1962. Also Sasha Polakow-Suransky, *The Unspoken Alliance: Israel's Secret Relationship with Apartheid South Africa*, New York: Vintage Books, 2013, p. 5.

[45] Verbatim record, plenary General Assembly, 2 October 1963, A/PV.1224, paras. 101–2.

[46] Naomi Chazan, 'The Fallacies of Pragmatism: Israeli Foreign Policy towards South Africa' (1983) 82 *African Affairs* 169, at p. 172.

[47] Situation in South Africa resulting from the policies of apartheid, 14 December 1973, A/RES/3151 G (XXVIII), OP 5.

[48] Ibid.

358 INITIATIVES ON RACIAL DISCRIMINATION

Africa.[49] Referring to the recent armed conflict in the region, the representative of Burundi said the attitude of Portugal and South Africa 'proved that the Tel Aviv-Pretoria-Lisbon axis is a reality'.[50] Israel denounced the amendment as the work of 'the Arab propaganda machine'. Its representative read out a statement explaining the nature of Zionism that had been delivered several weeks earlier in the Security Council, describing it as 'the Jewish people's liberation movement'.[51]

General Assembly resolutions in 1974 and 1975 condemned 'the strengthening of political, economic, military and other relations between Israel and South Africa'.[52] In 1975, the World Conference of the International Women's Year condemned Zionism in the Declaration of Mexico on the Equality of Women and their Contribution to Development and Peace. Two preambular paragraphs and two operative paragraphs in the Declaration place the reference in an enumeration that includes imperialism, colonialism, neo-colonialism, foreign occupation, racial discrimination, and apartheid.[53]

Later in 1975, an amendment was proposed to a draft resolution on the Decade[54] by Cuba, Libya, Syria, Somalia, and Yemen to add several references to Zionism.[55] Several days later, Somalia asked permission of the Committee to present a revised version of the amendments. The Third Committee determined that the revised amendment was admissible, by a vote of 75 to 22 with 26 abstentions. Ten African States were among the abstainers.[56] But on the following day, rather than a reformulation of the amendments to the resolution on the Programme for the Decade, Somalia produced an entirely new resolution consisting of several preambular paragraphs and a single operative paragraph declaring Zionism to be a form of racism and of racial discrimination. Of the many sponsors, Dahomey was the only one from Africa south of the Sahara.[57]

---

[49] Verbatim record, plenary General Assembly, 14 December 1973, A/PV.2201, para. 104.

[50] Ibid., para. 105.

[51] Ibid., paras. 175–6. For the statement by Ambassador Yosef Tekoah, see Verbatim record, Security Council, 21 October 1973, S/PV.1747, paras. 76–80.

[52] Situation in South Africa, 16 December 1974, A/RES/3324 E (XXIX), OP 5; Situation in South Africa, 28 November 1975, A/RES/3411 G (XXX), OP 4.

[53] Declaration of Mexico on the Equality of Women and their Contribution to Development and Peace, 1975, in Report of the World Conference of the International Women's Year, Mexico City, 19 June-2 July 1975, E/CONF.66/34, pp. 2–7. For the voting on the references, see ibid., pp. 149–50. See also Palestinian and Arab women, Resolution 32, ibid., pp. 110–11.

[54] Programme for the Decade for Action to Combat Racism and Racial Discrimination, 6 May 1975, E/RES/1938 (LVIII).

[55] Cuba, Libyan Arab Republic, Syrian Arab Republic, Somalia and Democratic Yemen: amendment to draft resolution recommended by the Economic and Social Council (A/10145, annex), 1 October 1975, A/C.3/L.2157. Afghanistan, Algeria, Guinea, Iraq, Jordan, Morocco, Sudan, the United Arab Emirates and Yemen subsequently became co-sponsors.

[56] Summary record, Third Committee, 16 October 1975, A/C.3/SR.2131, para. 19.

[57] Afghanistan, Algeria, Saudi Arabia, Bahrein, Cuba, Dahomey, Democratic Yemen, Egypt, Guinea, Iraq, Jordan, Kuwait, Lebanon, Morocco, Mauritania, Oman, Qatar, Libya, Somalia, Soudan, Syria, Tunisia, United Arab Emirates, Yemen: draft resolution, 15 October 1975, A/C.3/L.2159. Mali and Ukraine subsequently became sponsors.

'ZIONISM IS RACISM' 359

The decision to propose a separate resolution may have been a response aimed at those, including African States, who were concerned that linking the Zionism question directly to other initiatives directed at apartheid and racial discrimination might undermine the latter and reduce the important consensus that had been built over the years. One delegate described the new resolution as a reaction to the refusal of many States within the African group to support the amendments that had initially been proposed.[58] Sierra Leone and Zambia tried, but without success, to postpone the issue to the following year. Their resolution was supported by 12 African States, with another 3 abstaining, demonstrating the unease.[59] The 'Zionism is racism' resolution was adopted by 72 votes to 35, with 32 abstentions.[60] Seventeen African States voted against the resolution or abstained, concerned that introducing the Zionism issue would compromise the objectives of the Decade and its Programme.[61]

In the plenary General Assembly, the resolution on the Decade was adopted by 117 to 19, with 5 abstentions.[62] The resolution on the Conference, which did little more than acknowledge Ghana's invitation to host the event, had a very similar result.[63] Several of those who did not vote in favour explained that this was a consequence of the inevitable association of the Zionism issue with the campaigns against racial discrimination. The only African and Asian States to vote against or abstain were the Central African Republic and Malawi.

In 1991, the General Assembly resolution describing Zionism as racism was revoked. Speaking in support, the US delegate explained that the 1975 determination had been a product of cold war tensions that were no longer present.[64] A simple one-paragraph resolution was put forward: 'The General Assembly, Decides to revoke the determination contained in its resolution 3379 (XXX) of 10 November 1975.' The Arab States attempted to block the American resolution by imposing a requirement of a special majority.[65] Even if it had succeeded, the outcome would have been no different because the revocation resolution passed by 111 votes to 25, with 13 abstentions. Other than States with a large Arab or

---

[58] Summary record, Third Committee, 17 October 1975, A/C.3/SR.2133, para. 6.

[59] Ibid., para. 13.

[60] Elimination of all forms of racial discrimination, 10 November 1975, A/RES/3379 (XXX).

[61] See, for example, Verbatim record, plenary General Assembly, 10 November 1975, A/PV.2400, para.193.

[62] Verbatim record, plenary General Assembly, 10 November 1975, A/PV.2400, para. 295; Implementation of the Programme for the Decade for Action to Combat Racism and Racial Discrimination, 10 November 1975, A/RES/3377 (XXX).

[63] Verbatim record, plenary General Assembly, 10 November 1975, A/PV.2400, para. 296; World conference to combat racism and racial discrimination, 10 November 1975, A/RES/3378 (XXX).

[64] Verbatim record, plenary General Assembly, 16 December 1991, A/46/PV.74, pp. 11–15.

[65] Ibid., p. 37.

360 INITIATIVES ON RACIAL DISCRIMINATION

Islamic population, only Cuba, North Korea, and Vietnam voted against the resolution.[66]

The World Conference of 1978

The World Conference to Combat Racism and Racial Discrimination was held in Geneva from 14 to 25 August 1978. Initially, Ghana had volunteered to host the gathering, asking only that the United Nations defray half the costs of the event.[67] However it subsequently withdrew citing the expense.[68] One hundred and twenty-five Member States participated in the Conference. Israel and the United States were absent, the former citing the 1975 resolution on Zionism and racism, saying this would contaminate the Conference, and the latter because it had chosen not to participate in any activities related to the Decade.[69]

The Declaration adopted by the Conference stated that any doctrine of racial superiority was scientifically false, morally condemnable and socially unjust. It labelled apartheid as a crime against humanity and a threat to peace and security. It called for racist regimes to be isolated in accordance with United Nations sanctions. The Declaration said governments had an obligation to ensure that transnational corporations ceased assisting the racist regimes of South Africa and Rhodesia (Zimbabwe). According to the Declaration, those who 'profit from racist domination and exploitation in South Africa, or assist the apartheid regime, or facilitate the propaganda in favour of apartheid, are accomplices in the perpetuation of this crime against humanity.[70]

Much of the Declaration was focussed on the racist governments in South Africa and Rhodesia. The Declaration condemned cooperation with the apartheid regime in the military and nuclear fields, stating that provision of training, supply of equipment and fissionable material, the construction of nuclear facilities, and the transfer of any form of nuclear technology to South Africa was a threat to international peace and security. This was consistent with a Security Council resolution adopted in 1977 expressing grave concern that South Africa was 'at the threshold of producing nuclear weapons' and imposing a mandatory

---

[66] Elimination of racism and racial discrimination, 16 December 1991, A/RES/46/86; Verbatim record, plenary General Assembly, 16 December 1991, A/46/PV.74, p. 39–40. See Gil Troy, *Moynihan's Moment, America's Fight against Zionism as Racism*, Oxford: Oxford University Press, 2012.

[67] World conference to combat racism and racial discrimination, 13 December 1976, A/RES/31/78.

[68] Letter of 4 February 1977 from Ghana, E/5911.

[69] Telegram from the Department of State to All Diplomatic and Consular Posts, 12 August 1978, FRUS 1977–1980 II.

[70] Report of the World conference to combat racism and racial discrimination, Geneva, 14–25 August 1978, A/CONF.92/40, p. 11.

arms embargo on arms and related *matériel*.[71] Although it has consistently denied this, Israel almost certainly assisted South Africa in its attempts to develop nuclear weapons.[72]

The sticking point for the Western delegations was references to Israel in two lengthy paragraphs of the Declaration. The first paragraph condemned the relationship between Israel and South Africa in both economic and military fields, warning of cooperation in the nuclear field. It described the cooperation as 'a hostile act against the oppressed people of South Africa', noting that it was in defiance of United Nations resolutions. The second paragraph spoke of the 'cruel tragedy which befell the Palestinian people', calling for 'the cessation of all practices of racial discrimination to which Palestinians, as well as other inhabitants of the Arab territories occupied by Israel, are being subjected'.[73] But the Declaration did not repeat the 'Zionism is racism' allegation.

In the version finalized by the First Committee of the Conference, which had been given responsibility for drafting the Declaration, the paragraphs concerning Israel appeared in square brackets, indicating a lack of consensus.[74] The paragraphs were adopted by strong majorities in recorded votes, 67 for one and 65 for the other, with about 18 against and 18 abstentions. The negative votes were from Western States, the abstentions were almost entirely from Latin America.[75] Immediately following the vote on the two paragraphs, the nine members of the European Economic Community as well as Australia, Canada, and New Zealand announced that they could not associate themselves with the results and that they would no longer participate in the Conference proceedings.[76]

The Declaration was linked with a Programme of Action consisting of a range of measures to be adopted at the national and international level.[77] It was drafted in Committee II of the Conference. The Programme referred to the special responsibility of the United Nations and the international community 'to the oppressed peoples of South Africa, Namibia, Zimbabwe, Palestine and their liberation movements', which the Western States also found to be objectionable. But their difficulties with the Programme also could be attributed to its call for 'prohibition of all loans to and investments in South Africa and the termination of all promotion of trade with South Africa'. At the time, many Western States

---

[71] South Africa, 4 November 1977, S/RES/418 (1977).

[72] Sasha Polakow-Suransky, *The Unspoken Alliance: Israel's Secret Relationship with Apartheid South Africa*, New York: Pantheon, 2010; Peter Liberman, 'Israel and the South African bomb' (2004) 11 *Non-proliferation Review* 46.

[73] Report of the World conference to combat racism and racial discrimination, Geneva, 14–25 August 1978, A/CONF.92/40, p. 13.

[74] Ibid., pp. 62–3.

[75] Ibid., pp. 66–7.

[76] Ibid., p. 69. For the text of the various statements made by Germany on behalf of the nine European Economic Community Member States, see ibid., pp. 115–18.

[77] Ibid., pp. 15–16

362 INITIATIVES ON RACIAL DISCRIMINATION

continued to have important commercial relationships with the apartheid State. Only in the mid-1980s did the European Community and the Commonwealth impose trade and financial sanctions on South Africa, and even these were limited in scope. There was also a call for 'research studies and educational material on the situation of women living under racist regimes in southern Africa, especially under apartheid',[78] and a similar reference dealing with children.[79] The word 'Palestine' received 63 votes in favour to 21 with 5 abstentions.[80] The Committee agreed that the result should be the same for the references to the 'occupied Arab and other territories'.[81]

A very large number of reservations were formulated by many of the States that participated in the Conference.[82] Several of the Western States that chose not to participate in the final votes provided explanations, often reserving their right to object to specific aspects of the Programme of Action. Some delegations that voted in favour of the Declaration and Programme of Action also expressed their concerns about the language on Israel. When the Third Committee assessed the Conference later that year, there were mixed reactions to the attention given to the reservations. That no summary records were prepared of the Conference sessions strengthened the need to allow some way to express disagreement. At the same time, there was a danger that publication of the reservations might only exaggerate the significance of isolated objections and detract from the fact that the vast majority of States participating in the Conference accepted the results unconditionally.

Introducing the subject in the Third Committee, the President of the Conference noted that the Secretary-General's report contained a 'Final Act' that, while not intended to replace the Programme of Action, spelled out certain details. He said the Final Act 'contained a declaration condemning the evils of racism, apartheid, colonialism, and foreign domination and specific proposals for action to fight those evils. It contained many examples of practical action to be taken to promote and protect human rights.'[83] Nevertheless, there is no record of any 'Final Act' in the Report of the Conference nor does one appear in the Report of the Secretary-General despite the puzzling statement of the President. The Secretary-General of the Conference was almost apologetic, explaining that the number of days available was insufficient given the 'highly political' nature of the issues being discussed. Moreover, the facilities had been 'inadequate'.

---

[78] Ibid., p. 84.

[79] Ibid., p. 85.

[80] Ibid., pp. 91–2.

[81] Ibid., p. 92.

[82] Ibid., pp. 107–30; World Conference to Combat Racism and Racial Discrimination, 9 October 1978, A/33/262, Annex. For a summary of the reservations and declarations, see *UN Yearbook*, 1978, pp. 666–7.

[83] Summary record, Third Committee, 17 October 1978, A/C.3/33/SR.20, para. 4.

Accordingly, 'participants had been unable to establish genuine dialogue and it had proved impossible to reconcile the differences which had emerged towards the end', especially the two paragraphs on Israel.[84]

Disappointment with the First Conference

When the Conference was assessed in the Third Committee of the General Assembly, Nigeria spoke of 'disappointment'.[85] Burundi said it had 'not been as successful as had been hoped'.[86] Ghana, on the other hand, was 'generally satisfied' although it 'could have achieved more than it had'.[87] Speaking on behalf of the nine European Community Member States, Germany said there were 'great difficulties' as a consequence of references to 'the question of the Middle East' in the texts that were adopted. 'The Nine believed that the nature of that question differed fundamentally from that of the situation in southern Africa, and they could not accept that a racist character that it did not possess should be attributed to it; they had consequently been forced to dissociate themselves from the final document of the Conference.'[88] He was followed immediately by Benin, whose delegate condemned 'the collaboration of the Western Powers, in particular France and Great Britain', who had helped to arm South Africa and whose transnational corporations had strengthened the racism regimes in the region.[89] Many States of the Global South considered that the Western States only used the Israel/Palestine issue as an excuse for their refusal to support robust measures against Pretoria.

There may have been some hope that the Third Committee might be able to heal the rift that had afflicted the Conference. Ghana prepared a draft resolution that enjoyed support from several Western countries. It praised the Conference but without formally endorsing the Declaration and Programme of Action and instead referred positively to the Secretary-General's report on the Conference. It also contained a lengthy section of proposed measures that was, in reality, a lean version of the Programme of Action adopted at the Conference. There were no references to Israel.[90] An amendment proposed by 15 African States added an explicit endorsement of the Declaration and Programme of Action adopted by the Conference.[91] The same States also put forward a new draft resolution

---

[84] Ibid., paras. 12–13.

[85] Summary record, Third Committee, 18 October 1978, A/C.3/33/SR.22, para. 17.

[86] Summary record, Third Committee, 26 October 1978, A/C.3/33/SR.30, para. 30.

[87] Summary record, Third Committee, 23 October 1978, A/C.3/33/SR.26, para. 17.

[88] Summary record, Third Committee, 23 October 1978, A/C.3/33/SR.25, para. 42.

[89] Ibid., paras. 43–4.

[90] Ghana: Draft resolution, 17 October 1978, A/C.3/33/L.17. Liberia later became a co-sponsor.

[91] Algeria, Angola, Benin, Burundi, Congo, Djibouti, Libya, Madagascar, Mali, Mauritania, Mozambique, Sao Tomé and Principe, Senegal, Tunisia, Zambia: draft amendment to draft resolution

364 INITIATIVES ON RACIAL DISCRIMINATION

along similar lines.[92] Some of the Western States indicated they would vote for Ghana's resolution but only if the amendments were rejected; otherwise, they would oppose it.[93] The delegate of the Netherlands put the matter rather bluntly: 'The Committee was therefore facing a choice and would have to decide whether to try to adopt a common line of action with regard to apartheid or whether to endorse the final documents of the World Conference and thereby exclude from that common action - and possibly from the Decade as a whole – a large number of Western countries, the very countries to which the African delegations addressed themselves when they were speaking of the struggle against apartheid.'[94]

The African States were called to task for refusing to bend, including by a few of their own.[95] The separate resolution they had proposed would pass in any event, although with negative votes and abstentions. On the other hand, if they had withdrawn their amendments to Ghana's resolution it would then have been sure of adoption by consensus. But consensus for what? It would be a unanimous resolution giving a General Assembly blessing to a Conference whose vital organs had been removed, in particular the requirement that sanctions against South Africa be mandatory. Their intransigence is understandable.

The amendments to Ghana's resolution were adopted by strong majorities, but with very significant negative votes and abstentions, several of them from African States.[96] The resolution as a whole, with the amendments endorsing the Declaration and Programme of Action, received 101 votes to 18, with 13 abstentions. The negative votes were cast by Western States, including Israel. The following abstained: Bahamas, Central African Empire, Costa Rica, Gabon, Ghana, Guatemala, Ivory Coast, Malawi, Nicaragua, Papua New Guinea, Swaziland, Upper Volta, and Zaire.[97] The separate resolution endorsing the Conference that had also been proposed by the African States was adopted by 87 votes to 19, with 14 abstentions.[98] In the plenary General Assembly, the first

published as A/C.3/33/L.17, 16 November 1978, A/C.3/33/L.34. Cuba, East Germany, Guinea, Guinea-Bissau, Mongolia, Pakistan, Syria, and Viet Nam joined as co-sponsors.

[92] Algeria, Angola, Benin, Burundi, Congo, Libya, Madagascar, Mali, Mauritania, Mozambique, Niger, Sao Tomé and Principe, Senegal, Tunisia, Zambia: draft resolution, 16 November 1978, A/C.3/33/L.35. Subsequently, several States joined as co-sponsors: Afghanistan, Bulgaria, Cuba, Czechoslovakia, Djibouti, Egypt, Ethiopia, East Germany, Iraq, Jordan, Mongolia, Pakistan, Sudan, Syria, Ukraine, Tanzania, and Viet Nam. Senegal withdrew as a co-sponsor.
[93] Summary record, Third Committee, 4 December 1978, A/C.3/33/SR.65, paras. 26 (Australia), 31 (the Netherlands), 37 (Ireland), 40 (Canada), 57 (Germany, on behalf of the European Economic Community), 78 (Norway), 82 (Finland).
[94] Summary record, Third Committee, 4 December 1978, A/C.3/33/SR.65, para. 29.
[95] Ibid., paras. 66–7 (Lesotho), 74–6 (Ghana), 84–5 (Nigeria).
[96] Ibid., paras. 94–5, 101–2.
[97] Ibid., paras. 104–5.
[98] Summary record, Third Committee, 4 December 1978, A/C.3/33/SR.66, paras. 17–18.

resolution, that had initially been drafted as a compromise with a view to adoption by consensus, was adopted by 107 votes to 18, with 11 abstentions.[99] The second resolution obtained a similar result.[100] Israel charged that the resolutions had 'introduced by a semantic device the infamous formula, "Zionism equals racism"'.[101] However, condemning either Israel's collaboration with South Africa or racial discrimination against Palestinians was not the same as a blanket denunciation of Zionism and of the ideology underpinning Israel's existence.

The Declaration and Programme of Action might have served as an important landmark in the international struggle against racial discrimination. Alas, its potential impact was surely diminished because of the controversies and the failure to obtain anything resembling a consensus. But sometimes, when positions are far apart, consensus is impossible, however desirable it may seem in principle. Could the African States really be expected to abandon their insistence on mandatory sanctions in order to hasten the end of the apartheid regime? Israel's growing assistance to Pretoria, up to and including suspicion that it was supplying weapons of mass destruction, could hardly be ignored, even if there was room for reasonable disagreement about how to characterize the Jewish State's prevailing ideology. References to the Apartheid Convention, and to apartheid as a crime against humanity, were also troublesome. Some States expressed concern that the Apartheid Convention appeared to approve of the exercise of universal jurisdiction. For example, Uruguay said it did not agree with exercise of jurisdiction over the crime of apartheid by States Parties to the Convention 'with respect to acts committed outside their territory by persons who were not their nationals'.[102] In reality, the paragraphs in the Declaration and Programme of Action about Israel and Palestine had probably been toned down in the hopes of reaching agreement.

In 1979, the General Assembly endorsed a recommendation in the Programme of Action to hold a second World Conference, 'preferably at the end of the Decade'.[103] A formal decision to hold the Second World Conference was taken in 1980.[104] Held in Geneva during the first two weeks of August in 1983, the Conference was attended by 128 States. The pattern in 1983 followed the script that had been set in 1978 at the first World Conference. A Declaration

[99] World Conference to Combat Racism and Racial Discrimination, 16 December 1978, A/RES/33/99; Verbatim record, plenary General Assembly, 16 December 1978, A/33/PV.86, para. 92.

[100] Results of the World Conference to Combat Racism and Racial Discrimination, 16 December 1978, A/RES/33/100; Verbatim record, plenary General Assembly, 16 December 1978, A/33/PV.86, para. 93.

[101] Verbatim record, plenary General Assembly, 16 December 1978, A/33/PV.86, para. 81.

[102] Summary record, Third Committee, 24 October 1978, A/C.3/33/SR.28, para. 95.

[103] Programme of activities to be undertaken during the Second half of the Decade for Action to Combat Racism and racial Discrimination, 15 November 1979, A/RES/34/24, Annex, para. 26.

[104] Decade for Action to Combat Racism and Racial Discrimination, 14 November 1980, A/RES/35/33, OP 18.

366 INITIATIVES ON RACIAL DISCRIMINATION

was adopted with a prominent condemnation of Israel's 'existing and increasing relations' with South Africa, 'in particular those in the economic and military fields' with a specific warning against cooperation in the nuclear fields. It also recalled 'practices of racial discrimination against the Palestinians as well as other inhabitants of the Arab occupied territories'.[105] The two paragraphs were adopted by the plenary Conference on recorded votes. The condemnation of Israel's relations with South Africa received 84 votes to 15 with 16 abstentions, indicating a softening of sympathy for Israel. Among the abstainers were a number of European States, namely Austria, Finland, Greece, Portugal, Spain, and Sweden, some of whom had voted against a similar condemnation at the 1978 Conference.[106] The paragraph on racial discrimination against Palestinians in the occupied territories was adopted by 87 to 17 with 11 abstentions.[107]

The Declaration as a whole was adopted by 101 votes to 12, with 3 abstentions.[108] The Programme of Action was adopted by 104 votes with no negative votes and 10 abstentions.[109] The successful adoption of the Programme is confirmed by its endorsement in a resolution of the General Assembly, adopted without a vote, to which it is annexed.[110] In that resolution the General Assembly recognized the Conference as 'a positive contribution'.[111] As had been the case at the First Conference, there were many reservations to various provisions of the Declaration and the Programme of Action.[112] Major differences remained and this made full agreement on the text impossible but there was very perceptible movement in the right direction. Austria and Finland indicated they had voted in favour of the Declaration, whereas they had voted against it in 1978. Speaking on behalf of the Nordic countries as a whole, Norway said they had voted in favour, whereas Norway and Sweden had walked out in 1978. New Zealand, which had also walked out in 1978, said it had abstained. Canada, Denmark, France, Germany, and the Netherlands, all of whom had walked out in 1978, stated they had cast negative votes on the Declaration but couched this in language indicating support for much of the document as a whole. As the chairman of the Conference explained in his report to the Third Committee, 'an ethical consensus on condemning all forms of racism had been forged' and 'an operational consensus had developed in favour of strengthening that condemnation

---

[105] Declaration, A/CONF.119/26, pp. 11–17, paras. 19–20.

[106] Report of the Second World Conference to Combat Racism and Racial Discrimination, Geneva (1–12 August 1983), A/CONF.119/26, p. 73.

[107] Ibid., pp. 73–4.

[108] Ibid., p. 74.

[109] Ibid., p. 94.

[110] Second Decade to Combat Racism and Racial Discrimination, 22 November 1983, A/RES/38/14, OP 3.

[111] Ibid., PP 8.

[112] Report of the Second World Conference to Combat Racism and Racial Discrimination, Geneva (1–12 August 1983), A/CONF.119/26, pp. 95–116.

CONTEMPORARY FORMS OF RACISM   367

and of finding a solid basis for the work of the Second Decade'.[113] During the debate in the Third Committee, several Western delegations ventured positive assessments of the Conference.[114] Even Israel conceded that 'some constructive work had been undertaken by the Second World Conference' although it protested that it had been 'undermined for the sake of another unfounded attack upon Israel'.[115] A degree of consensus had been re-established, thanks in large part to efforts of the African States. The General Assembly linked the Conference results to the proposal for a Second Decade.[116] In 1993, the Commission on Human Rights described the Second World Conference as 'a positive contribution by the international community towards attaining the objectives of the Decade, through its adoption of a Declaration and an operational Programme of Action for the Second Decade to Combat Racism and Racial Discrimination'.[117]

Contemporary Forms of Racism

International action against racial discrimination had been focussed on Africa since the first days of the United Nations. After the collapse of colonialism and the virtual end of the Trust Territory scheme in the 1960s there remained a hard core of racist regimes in southern Africa. Over the decades, its components became detached. Portugal was the first, giving up its territories in Africa in 1974. Immediately, Mozambique and Angola became front line States in the battle against apartheid and its allies. Southern Rhodesia was next. After a protracted armed struggle, a negotiated peace brought majority rule to a territory that had been ruled by a small white minority for decades. Then Namibia, a territory that had suffered the worst abuses including the scourge of genocide, dating from the first years of the twentieth century when it was still under German administration, achieved independence. And finally, the linchpin of this racist axis, apartheid, came to an abrupt end.

The campaign against racial discrimination began to refocus its attention. In 1989, Asbjørn Eide, one of Norway's great international human rights experts,

---

[113] Summary record, Third Committee, 7 October 1983, A/C.3/38/SR.5, para. 3.

[114] For example, Summary record, Third Committee, 12 October 1983, A/C.3/38/SR.7, para. 8 (United Kingdom); Summary record, Third Committee, 12 October 1983, A/C.3/38/SR.8, paras. 10–15 (France), 28–33 (Canada); Summary record, Third Committee, 14 October 1983, A/C.3/38/SR.10, para. 47 (Spain); Summary record, Third Committee, 17 October 1983, A/C.3/38/SR11, para. 41 (New Zealand).

[115] Summary record, Third Committee, 26 October 1983, A/C.3/38/SR.21, para. 11.

[116] Second World Conference to Combat Racism and Racial Discrimination, 22 November 1983, A/RES/38/15, PP 3.

[117] Implementation of the Programme of Action for the Second Decade to Combat Racism and Racial Discrimination and launching of a third decade to combat racism and racial discrimination, 26 February 1993, E/CN.4/RES/1993/11, PP 9.

368 INITIATIVES ON RACIAL DISCRIMINATION

produced an assessment of the results and achievements of the first Decade and of the first five years of the second Decade at the request of the Sub-Commission on the Prevention of Discrimination and the Protection of Minorities. Eide explained that United Nations activity with respect to racial discrimination had confronted two quite different situations. The first was the 'stubborn and defiant' system of apartheid in South Africa which needed to be defeated. But with regard to most other States, who did not condone racial discrimination as official policy, he said the task was one of patient persuasion.[118] Although Eide did not take an overtly critical tone, the message he delivered was that the United Nations had largely focussed its attention on racist regimes in southern Africa while neglecting other important aspects of racial discrimination, in particular national minorities, indigenous peoples, and migrant workers.[119] Eide also acknowledged the issue of people of African descent, although he described it under the heading 'Situations originating in slavery', discussing exclusively the condition of African Americans.[120] Eide reviewed the contributions made by different United Nations agencies to the anti-apartheid struggle, including UNESCO, the International Labour Organisation, the World Health Organisation, the Food and Agriculture Organisation, and the International Civil Aviation Organisation.[121]

The Decade that began in 1983 was labelled as one to 'combat racism and racial discrimination'. In the early 1990s, new formulations began to be employed, adding the terms 'xenophobia' and 'related intolerance'. The nomenclature had evolved considerably over the decades. In the early years of the United Nations, there were only very rare references to 'racism', 'racialism', and 'racists'.[122] In 1952, at the request of several States of the Global South, '[t]he question of race conflict in South Africa' was added to the agenda of the General Assembly. Lest this imply that both sides were in the wrong, the words 'resulting from the policies of apartheid' were included.[123] Within a decade, the expression 'race conflict' disappeared from United Nations materials.

The word 'xenophobia' first appeared in United Nations documents in a 1990 resolution of the Sub-Commission on the Prevention of Discrimination

---

[118] Study on the achievements made and obstacles encountered during the Decades to Combat Racism and Racial Discrimination, 7 November 1989, E/CN.4/Sub.2/1989/8 and Add.1, paras. 15–16. At the request of the General Assembly, it was later circulated as A/45/525.

[119] Ibid., paras. 41–9.

[120] Ibid., paras. 361–9.

[121] Ibid., paras. 119–38.

[122] The earliest is probably from the Soviet delegate, Alexey P. Pavlov, in the plenary Economic and Social Council, in 1948: Summary record, Economic and Social Council, 23 August 1948, E/SR.210, p. 582. But it was really the Russian interpreter who used the word 'racism'. Pavlov's amendment used the term 'racism': E/AC.27/W.18.

[123] Letter dated 12 September 1952 addressed to the Secretary-General by the permanent representatives of Afghanistan, Burma, Egypt, India, Indonesia, Iraq, Iran, Lebanon, Pakistan, the Philippines, Saudi Arabia, Syria, and Yemen, 12 September 1952, A/2183.

and the Protection of Minorities that referred to 'an upsurge of racism, with accompanying manifestations of prejudice, discrimination, intolerance and xenophobia in many parts of the world'.[124] When the Economic and Social Council reviewed the Second Decade, delegations expressed their concern about 'racism, racial discrimination, intolerance and xenophobia in various parts of the world'.[125] In 1993, the Commission on Human Rights adopted a resolution to establish a new special procedure, the Special rapporteur on contemporary forms of racism, racial discrimination, xenophobia, and related intolerance.[126] A General Assembly resolution of 1994 was entitled 'contemporary forms of racism, racial discrimination, xenophobia and related intolerance'.[127] Use of the term seems to have been inspired by European sources. As early as 1986, the European Parliament and related ancestors of the European Union adopted a succinct declaration against 'racism and xenophobia'.[128] Reports of the French Commission nationale consultative des droits de l'homme had been referring to 'le racisme et la xénophobie' since the late 1980s.[129]

References to 'intolerance' appear in General Assembly resolutions as early as 1960, for example in the phrases 'racial and national hatred, religious intolerance and racial prejudice',[130] 'racial prejudice and national and religious intolerance',[131] 'nazism and racial intolerance',[132] and 'racial or ethnic exclusiveness or intolerance'.[133] The 1981 Declaration on the Elimination of All Forms of Intolerance and of Discrimination Based on Religion or Belief offers a definition: 'For the purposes of the present Declaration, the expression "intolerance and discrimination based on religion or belief" means any distinction, exclusion, restriction or preference based on religion or belief and having as its purpose or as its effect

---

[124] Measures to combat racism and racial discrimination and the role of the Sub-Commission, 20 August 1990, E/CN.4/Sub.2/RES/1990/2, PP 5.

[125] Implementation of the Programme of Action for the Second Decade to Combat Racism and Racial Discrimination and launching of a third decade to combat racism and racial discrimination Report of the Secretary-General, 23 September 1992, A/47/432, para. 27.

[126] Measures to combat contemporary forms of racism, racial discrimination, xenophobia and related intolerance, 2 March 1993, E/CN.4/RES/1993/20, OP 10.

[127] Measures to combat contemporary forms of racism, racial discrimination, xenophobia and related intolerance, 23 December 1994, A/RES/49/147.

[128] Joint Declaration by the European Parliament, the Council and the Commission against racism and xenophobia, 11 June 1986 (OJ C 158, 25.6.1986).

[129] La lutte contre le racisme et la xénophobie, Paris: La Documentation française, 1990.

[130] Manifestations of racial and national hatred, 12 December 1960, A/RES/1510 (XV), PP 2.

[131] Manifestations of racial prejudice and national and religious intolerance, 7 December 1962, A/RES/1779 (XVII).

[132] Measures to be taken against nazism and racial intolerance, 15 December 1970, A/RES/2713 (XXV).

[133] Measures to be taken against Nazi, Fascist and neo-Fascist activities and all other forms of totalitarian ideologies and practices based on racial intolerance, hatred and terror, 16 December 1981, A/RES/36/162, OP 1.

370 INITIATIVES ON RACIAL DISCRIMINATION

nullification or impairment of the recognition, enjoyment or exercise of human rights and fundamental freedoms on an equal basis.'[134]

Giving autonomous meanings to 'xenophobia' and 'related intolerance' is not straightforward. If a narrow approach to 'racism' is adopted, then 'xenophobia' broadens the concept by including policies and measures focussed not only upon race or colour but on ethnicity and national origin more generally. However, it cannot have been the intent of the United Nations bodies to restrict the existing understanding of racism by adding a new category to the enumeration. As for 'related intolerance', it seems associated with a distinction between racial discrimination as a matter of government or public policy and circumstances where individuals or groups are responsible for acts of prejudice and hatred. For the former the obligation upon the State is one of result whereas for the latter it is one of means. A resolution of the Commission on Human Rights made this distinction: 'Conscious of the fundamental difference between, on the one hand, racism and racial discrimination as an institutionalized governmental policy, such as apartheid, or resulting from official doctrines of racial superiority or exclusivity, and on the other hand, other manifestations of racism, racial discrimination, xenophobia and related intolerance taking place in segments of many societies and perpetrated by individuals or groups'.[135] The same resolution implied a hierarchy whereby 'forms of racism and racial discrimination, particularly in their institutionalised form, such as apartheid, or resulting from official doctrines of racial superiority or exclusivity, were among the most serious violations of human rights'.[136] The language was taken from a 1990 General Assembly resolution.[137]

In his first report to the United Nations Commission on Human Rights, the Special rapporteur on contemporary forms of racism said the emphasis of the mandate was placed on 'recent manifestation of racism and xenophobia in the developed countries, and in particular on the situation of migrant workers and other vulnerable groups'.[138] This was consistent with the 1992 report to the Sub-Commission prepared by the Secretary-General which was almost entirely devoted to racism and measures to address it in European States. Asia and Africa

---

[134] Declaration on the Elimination of All Forms of Intolerance and of Discrimination Based on Religion or Belief, 25 November 1981, A/RES/36/55, art. 2(2).

[135] Measures to combat contemporary forms of racism, racial discrimination, xenophobia and related intolerance, 2 March 1993, E/CN.4/RES/1993/20, PP 6.

[136] Ibid., PP 4.

[137] Second decade to combat racism and racial discrimination, 14 December 1990, A/RES/45/105, OP 1.

[138] Report by Mr. Maurice Glélé-Ahanhanzo, Special Rapporteur on contemporary forms of racism, racial discrimination, xenophobia and related intolerance, submitted pursuant to Commission on Human Rights resolution 1993/20, E/CN.4/1994/66, para. 13.

were entirely absent from the study.[139] The Special rapporteur also noted the importance of the situation of indigenous peoples.[140]

European Initiatives

Associated with the new focus on racial discrimination in the developed countries were unprecedented initiatives within the regional organizations to which those States belonged. The focus was on ethnic violence within Europe and on anti-Semitism and persecution of Roma rather than on the colour line. It was 'colour blind'. For example, in 1994 the European Parliament adopted a detailed resolution noting that 'racism, xenophobia, anti-semitism and ethnic cleansing strategies and expulsions, which have caused great conflicts and suffering to various regions and nations of Europe throughout history, have left deep and lasting wounds and yet are still rampant as the twentieth century draws to a close'.[141] Undoubtedly racism had done much harm to Europe over the centuries, but shouldn't the European Parliament have at least acknowledged the consequences of European racism for the rest of the world? After all, as Asbjørn Eide noted in his 1989 report, if there is any truth in the claim that human rights originated in Europe, it must also be said that racism too originated there, and at about the same time.[142]

In 1993, the Council of Europe set up the European Commission against Racism and Intolerance. Its mandate was to combat 'racism, xenophobia, antisemitism and intolerance at the level of greater Europe and from the perspective of the protection of human rights'.[143] Composed of one delegate from each Member State, the Commission undertakes a number of functions, including

[139] Elimination of racial discrimination: measures to combat racism and racial discrimination and the role of the Sub-Commission on Prevention of Discrimination and Protection of Minorities, 14 July 1992, E/CN.4/Sub.2/1992/11, paras. 35–43.

[140] Report by Mr. Maurice Glélé-Ahanhanzo, Special Rapporteur on contemporary forms of racism, racial discrimination, xenophobia, and related intolerance, submitted pursuant to Commission on Human Rights resolution 1993/20, E/CN.4/1994/66, para. 13.

[141] Resolution of the European Parliament on racism, xenophobia, and anti-semitism, 27 October 1994 (OJ C 323/154, 20.11.1994). Also Resolution of the European Parliament on racism, xenophobia, and anti-semitism, 26 October 1995 (OJ C 308/140, 20.11.1995).

[142] Study on the achievements made and obstacles encountered during the Decades to Combat Racism and Racial Discrimination, 7 November 1989, E/CN.4/Sub.2/1989/8 and Add.1, para. 5.

[143] Lanna Yael Hollo, 'The European Commission against Racism and Intolerance', in Gauthier de Beco, ed., *Human Rights Monitoring Mechanisms of the Council of Europe*, London: Routledge, 2012, pp. 127–49; Lanna Yael Hollo, *The European Commission against Racism and Intolerance (ECRI) – Its first 15 years*, Strasbourg: Council of Europe, 2009; Mark Kelly, *ECRI 10 years of combating racism: A review of the work of the European Commission against Racism and Intolerance*, Strasbourg: Council of Europe, 2004; Lauri Hannikainen, 'Dialogue Between States and International Human Rights Monitoring Organs – Especially the European Commission Against Racism and Intolerance', in Asbjørn Eide, Jakob Th. Moller, and Inete Ziemele, eds., *Making Peoples Heard: Essays on Human Rights in Honour of Gudmundur Alfredsson*, The Hague: Brill, 2011, pp. 323–40.

372 INITIATIVES ON RACIAL DISCRIMINATION

evaluating periodic reports, visits to States to assess the situation, and issuance of thematic recommendations.

At the heart of the Council of Europe are the bodies established under the European Convention on Human Rights, both the European Court of Human Rights as well as the European Commission on Human Rights, an organ that began activities in the early 1950s and whose functions ceased in 1998. Although the European Convention only addresses racism generally, in a provision dealing with equality in a broad sense, the European Commission on Human Rights held, in 1973, that 'as generally recognised, a special importance should be attached to discrimination based on race; that publicly to single out a group of persons for differential treatment on the basis of race might, in certain circumstances, constitute a special form of affront to human dignity; that differential treatment of a group of persons on the basis of race might therefore be capable of constituting degrading treatment when differential treatment on some other ground would raise no such question'.[144] In this way, the prohibition on discrimination was linked to another provision of the European Convention, article 3, on inhuman or degrading treatment or punishment. Decades later, the Grand Chamber of the European Court of Human Rights invoked this statement of the Commission.[145] Along similar lines, the European Court referred to 'the need to reassert continuously society's condemnation of racism and ethnic hatred and to maintain the confidence of minorities in the ability of the authorities to protect them from the threat of racist violence'.[146] The Court has said that 'racial discrimination is a particularly egregious kind of discrimination and, in view of its perilous consequences, requires from the authorities special vigilance and a vigorous reaction'.[147] In 2021, for the first time, judges of the Court spoke of a 'duty to combat racial discrimination' that they said was implied by the European Convention's rather modest equality rights provision.[148]

The Conference on Security and Cooperation in Europe dates to the early 1970s. In 1995, it was transformed into the Organisation for Security and Cooperation in Europe. Its name indicates the region to which it applies. But its

---

[144] *East African Asians v. the United Kingdom,* nos. 4403/70-4419/70, 4422/70, 4423/70, 4434/70, 4443/70, 4476/70-4478/70, 4486/70, 4501/70, and 4526/70-4530/70, Commission report of 14 December 1973, § 207, DR 78-A, p. 5.

[145] *Cyprus v. Turkey* [GC], no. 25781/94, § 306, ECHR 2001-IV.

[146] *Nachova and Others v. Bulgaria,* nos. 43577/98 and 43579/98, §§ 156–9, 26 February 2004; *Nachova and Others v. Bulgaria* [GC], nos. 43577/98 and 43579/98, §§ 160–1, ECHR 2005-VII; *Šečić v. Croatia,* no. 40116/02, §§ 66–70, 31 May 2007.

[147] *Muhammad v. Spain,* no. 34085, § 65, 18 October 2022. Also *Basu v. Germany,* no. 215/19, §§ 24, 34, 18 October 2022; *Paketova et al. v. Bulgaria,* nos. 17806/19 and 36972/19, § 152, 4 October 2022; *L.F. v. Hungary,* no. 621/14, § 86, 19 May 2022; *Timishev v. Russia,* nos. 55762/00 and 55974/00, § 56, ECHR 2005-XII.

[148] *Budinova et al. v. Bulgaria,* no. 12567/13, § 91, 16 February 2021; *Behar et al. v. Bulgaria,* no 29335/13, § 102, 16 February 2021.

membership goes beyond Europe to include the United States and Canada. In the 1992 Helsinki Declaration the participating States '[e]xpress[ed] their concern over recent and flagrant manifestations of intolerance, discrimination, aggressive nationalism, xenophobia, anti-semitism and racism and stress the vital role of tolerance'.[149] Two years later, in the Budapest Summit Document, they condemned 'manifestations of intolerance, and especially of aggressive nationalism, racism, chauvinism, xenophobia and anti-semitism'.[150]

The European Communities, the ancestor of the European Union, was compelled to confront the issue of apartheid in the 1970s. A Code of Conduct for European firms operating in South Africa required them to observe certain minimum standards of non-discrimination in terms of employment.[151] It was a pretty feeble gesture at a time when African countries were calling for proper sanctions. In 1996, the European Union declared that 1997 would be the European Year Against Racism.[152] The following year, the Council of Ministers also decided to set up the European Monitoring Centre on Racism and Xenophobia. As its name suggests, it was essentially concerned with study and analysis. Later, it was folded into a new institution with a much broader remit, the European Fundamental Rights Agency.

Durban 2001

The resolutions adopted at the 1983 World Conference did not propose that there be a third conference. Nor was a conference called for in the Secretary-General's list of proposed elements for the Third Decade, issued in September 1992.[153] The initiative seems to have originated in 1994 in the Sub-Commission on the Prevention of Discrimination and the Protection of Minorities.[154] Its

[149] Conference for Security and Co-operation in Europe, Helsinki Summit Declaration, 1992, para. 30.

[150] Conference for Security and Co-operation in Europe, Budapest Summit Document, 1994, para. 25.

[151] See Specific measures to be taken with a view to ending all forms of commercial, financial and technological assistance to the economy of South Africa: study prepared in accordance with paragraph 18 of General Assembly resolution 34/24, A/CONF.119/13; Transnational corporations in southern Africa: update on financial activities and employment practices, E/C.10/83.

[152] Proposal by the Commission for a Council Decision designating 1997 as European Year against Racism, COM (95) 653 final, 26 March 1996, [1996] O.J. C 89/7. See Pieter Batelaan and Carla Van Hoof, 'The European Year against Racism and other Issues' (1998) 9 *European Journal of Intercultural Studies* 179; Jorg Monar, 'The EU's Role in the Fight Against Racism and Xenophobia: Evaluation and Prospects After Amsterdam and Tampere' (2000) 22 *Liverpool Law Review* 7.

[153] Implementation of the Programme of Action for the Second Decade to Combat Racism and Racial Discrimination and launching of a third decade to combat racism and racial discrimination, 23 September 1992, A/47/432.

[154] A world conference against racism, racial and ethnic discrimination, xenophobia and other related contemporary forms of intolerance, 12 August 1994, E/CN.4/Sub.2/RES/1994/2; Summary record, Sub-Commission on the Prevention of Discrimination and the Protection of Minorities, 12

374   INITIATIVES ON RACIAL DISCRIMINATION

recommendation for a conference to be held in 1997 was endorsed by the newly-appointed High Commissioner for Human Rights, José Ayala Lasso, who spoke at the conclusion of the session.[155] Later that year, the General Assembly took note of the recommendation of the Sub-Commission.[156] In 1995, the General Assembly requested the Secretary-General to consult Member States, intergovernmental, and non-governmental organizations on the possibility of holding a third world conference 'to combat racism, racial discrimination, xenophobia and other related contemporary forms of intolerance'.[157] The General Assembly requested the Commission on Human Rights to take up the matter.[158] In 1997, the Commission on Human Rights proposed a world conference on racism, xenophobia, and intolerance in a resolution adopted without a vote[159] on the basis of a draft resolution from China, Cuba, the African Group, India, and Nicaragua.[160] The summary records only indicate a very limited consideration of the subject. Canada, speaking on behalf of Japan, Liechtenstein, Norway, and Switzerland, said it was very much in favour of the organization of a high-level conference on racism 'which should focus on specific action to combat racism rather than at the elaboration of new standards'.[161] Later in the year, the Sub-Commission endorsed the Commission's proposal.[162] In January 1998, the General Assembly voted to convene the World Conference against Racism, Racial Discrimination, Xenophobia and Related Intolerance, to be held no later than 2001. It did not label it the 'Third' Conference, although the preamble of the resolution 'recalled'

August 1994, E/CN.4/Sub.2/1994/SR.17, para. 123; A world conference against racism, racial and ethnic discrimination, xenophobia and other related contemporary forms of intolerance: draft resolution, Mr. Alfonso Martínez, Mr. Bengoa, Mr. Bossuyt, Mr. Boutkevitch, Ms. Chavez, Mr. Chernichenko, Mr. Eide, Mr. El-Hajje, Mrs. Forero Ucros, Mr. Guissé, Mrs. Gwanmesia, Mr. Hakim, Mr. Hatano, Mr. Joinet, Mr. Khan, Mrs. Koufa, Mr. Limón Rojas, Mr. Lindgren Alves, Mr. Maxim, Mrs. Mbonu, Ms. Palley, Mr. Ramadhane, and Ms. Warzazi, 9 August 1994, E/CN.4/Sub.2/1994/L.3.

[155] Summary record, Sub-Commission on the Prevention of Discrimination and the Protection of Minorities, 26 August 1994, E/CN.4/Sub.2/1994/SR.37/Add.1, para. 37.
[156] Third Decade to Combat Racism and Racial Discrimination, 23 December 1994, A/RES/49/146, PP 6.
[157] Third Decade to Combat Racism and Racial Discrimination, 21 December 1995, A/RES/50/136, OP 12.
[158] Third Decade to Combat Racism and Racial Discrimination, 12 December 1996, A/RES/51/81, OP 22.
[159] Summary record, Commission on Human Rights, 18 April 1997, E/CN.4/1997/SR.68, para. 40; Racism, racial discrimination, xenophobia and related intolerance, 18 April 1997, E/CN.4/RES/1997/74, OPs 44–9.
[160] Racism, racial discrimination, xenophobia and related intolerance: [draft resolution]/China, Cuba, Egypt (on behalf of the African Group), India and Nicaragua, 15 April 1997, E/CN.4/1997/L.12/Rev.1, paras. 44–8.
[161] Summary record, Commission on Human Rights, 18 April 1997, E/CN.4/1997/SR.68, para. 26.
[162] Racism and racial discrimination, 21 August 1997, E/CN.4/Sub.2/RES/1997/5, OP 5.

DURBAN 2001   375

the outcome of the 1978 and 1983 events,[163] and informally it was often referred to as the 'Third World Conference' although, of course, this title might suggest something entirely different.

Holding the World Conference in South Africa's second largest city, Durban, was rich in symbolism. South Africa had been a racist pariah since the beginnings of the United Nations. For many years it was hardly alone, with allies elsewhere in southern Africa and wealthy trading partners in the North. But over the decades, South Africa became increasingly isolated. The two previous World Conferences had been held in the rather sterile environment of Geneva. The Durban Conference dwarfed its predecessors in terms of participation. Some 163 States were represented by 2,300 delegates, including 16 heads of State and 58 foreign ministers.[164]

The Conference was preceded by a series of preliminary regional meetings, convened in Strasbourg, Santiago, Dakar, and Tehran, in the latter part of 2000 and early 2001. Each of the four regional meetings was tasked with preparing a draft declaration and plan of action.[165] The products of these regional meetings reflected different priorities. The declaration from the Dakar meeting included the requirement of an apology by the former colonial powers to victims and descendants of the slave trade and colonialism, and a commitment that reparations be furnished.[166] The Santiago statement contained a very strong paragraph about reparations for 'Africans and their descendants and of the indigenous peoples of the Americas'.[167] Canada and the United States registered their reservations about the reparations issue.[168] The Tehran declaration included references to 'racial discrimination against the Palestinians as well as other inhabitants of the Arab occupied territories'.[169] Europe's declaration focussed on regional issues such as the treatment of Roma and anti-Semitism, and made no mention of discrimination based upon colour. There was a perfunctory recognition that 'all States must acknowledge the suffering caused by slavery and

---

[163] Third Decade to Combat Racism and Racial Discrimination and the convening of a world conference against racism, racial discrimination, xenophobia, and related intolerance, 12 November 1997, A/RES/52/111.

[164] Michael Banton, 'Lessons from the 2001 World Conference Against Racism' (2002) 28 *Journal of Ethnic and Migration Studies* 355, at p. 359.

[165] For a summary of regional meetings prepared by an American diplomat, see Christopher N. Camponovo, 'Disaster in Durban: The United Nations World Conference against Racism, Racial Discrimination, Xenophobia, and Related Intolerance' (2003) 34 *George Washington International Law Review* 659, at pp. 678–87.

[166] Report of the Regional Conference for Africa (Dakar, 22–24 January 2001), A/CONF.189/PC.2/8, p. 6.

[167] Report of the Regional Conference of the Americas, Santiago, Chile, 5–7 December 2000, p. 14.

[168] Ibid., p. 52.

[169] Report of the Asian Preparatory Meeting (Tehran, 19–21 February 2001), A/CONF.189/PC.2/9, p. 21.

376 INITIATIVES ON RACIAL DISCRIMINATION

colonialism'.[170] These versions from the regional meetings, together with other materials, were then compiled by the High Commissioner for Human Rights, Mary Robinson, who acted as Secretary-General of the Conference.[171]

The Durban Declaration and Programme of Action was adopted by consensus. The United States and Israel announced their withdrawal once it was clear that the Conference documents would contain references to racist treatment of Palestinians. In fact, they never formally rescinded their credentials although they chose not to participate in the adoption of the final documents.[172] This was nothing more than *déjà vu*, both of them having boycotted the two earlier World Conferences along with racist South Africa.[173] Moreover, the United States had exuded negativity from the earliest discussions about the Third Conference.[174] In this way, one of the great beneficiaries of slavery and the slave trade found a pretext to avoid participation in a Conference that was to have a strong focus on the past.[175] The reservations that the United States formulated at the Santiago preparatory meeting confirm that Israel was far from being its only concern. The question of reparations for slavery was a major difficulty. One of the American delegates, a Congressman, described the Conference as 'a disaster for the United States'.[176] But diplomatic 'disasters' for the United States are frequently good news for the rest of the world, and this was no exception. America's isolation only underscores the significance of the achievement at Durban. The Declaration and Programme of Action contained several new elements that constituted progressive development of law and practice concerning racial discrimination.

The Conference confronted the issue of historic injustices associated with slavery, the slave trade, and colonialism, as well as demands for both apology and reparation. Inevitably, securing a consensus in this area required compromise on all sides. The Declaration recognizes that 'colonialism has led to racism, racial discrimination, xenophobia and related intolerance'.[177] Speaking on behalf of the

---

[170] Final documents of the European Conference against Racism (Strasbourg, France, 11–13 October 2000), A/CONF.189/PC.2/6, p. 8; also, ibid., p. 3.

[171] Elements for a draft declaration and programme of action for the World Conference, 22 February 2001, A/CONF.189/WG.1/3.

[172] Ulrike Sundberg, 'Durban: The Third World Conference against Racism, Racial Discrimination, Xenophobia and Related Intolerance' (2002) 73 *International Review of Penal Law* 301, at p. 303.

[173] Jerry V. Leaphart, 'The World Conference against Racism: What Was Really Achieved' (2002) 26 *Fletcher Forum of World Affairs* 153, at p. 153. See also Christopher N. Camponovo, 'Disaster in Durban: The United Nations World Conference against Racism, Racial Discrimination, Xenophobia, and Related Intolerance' (2003) 34 *George Washington International Law Review* 659, at p 708.

[174] Summary record, Third Committee, 2 November 1995, A/C.3/50/SR.18, paras. 18–19; Summary record, Commission on Human Rights, 18 April 1997, E/CN.4/1997/SR.68, para. 37.

[175] Lorenzo Morris, 'Symptoms of Withdrawal - The U.N., The U.S., Racism and Reparations' (2003) 6 *Howard Scroll: The Social Justice Law Review* 49.

[176] Tom Lantos, 'The Durban Debacle: An Insider's View of the UN World Conference against Racism' (2002) 26 *Fletcher Forum of World Affairs* 31, at p. 31.

[177] Declaration, A/CONF.189/12, pp. 5–26, para. 14.

African States at the conclusion of the Conference, Kenya declared: 'Africa had a rendezvous with history and I dare say that rendezvous was productive, constructive and unforgettable. We believe we made history in Durban and rightfully so.'[178]

The Declaration recognizes that slavery and the slave trade 'were appalling tragedies in the history of humanity not only because of their abhorrent barbarism but also in terms of their magnitude, organized nature and especially their negation of the essence of the victims' and then acknowledges that 'slavery and the slave trade are a crime against humanity and should always have been so'.[179] The 'should always have been so' phrase was a concession to some Western States who 'feared the implications that admission might have in litigation for reparations in national courts'.[180] Barbados, speaking on behalf of Belize, Cuba, Guyana, Haiti, Honduras, Jamaica, Saint Vincent and the Grenadines, and Trinidad and Tobago, made the following reservation to the Declaration: 'We declare that the transatlantic slave trade and the related system of racialized chattel slavery of Africans and people of African descent constitute crimes against humanity.'[181] Speaking on behalf of the African Group, Kenya said that 'slavery and the slave trade, especially the transatlantic slave trade [are] a crime against humanity; not today, not tomorrow, but always and for all time'.[182]

On the other hand, Canada issued a statement setting out its understanding that 'widespread and systematic enslavement directed against a civilian population today constitutes a crime against humanity' but that 'under international law there is no right to a remedy for historical acts that were not illegal at the time at which they occurred'.[183] Canada's involvement in slavery and the slave trade was perhaps not as significant as in other countries of the hemisphere, but it has a huge and terrible legacy in its treatment of indigenous peoples. The European Union said it had joined consensus on a reference in the Declaration 'to measures to halt and reverse the lasting consequences of certain practices of the past. This

---

[178] Report of the World Conference against Racism, Racial Discrimination, Xenophobia and Related Intolerance, A/CONF.189/12, p. 141.

[179] Declaration, A/CONF.189/12, pp. 5–26, para. 13. See also Ulrike Sundberg, 'Durban: The Third World Conference against Racism, Racial Discrimination, Xenophobia and Related Intolerance' (2002) 73 International Review of Penal Law 301, at p. 304.

[180] Gay McDougall, 'The World Conference against Racism: Through a Wider Lens' (2002) 26 Fletcher Forum of World Affairs 135, at p. 138. Also Antony Anghie, 'Slavery and International Law: The Jurisprudence of Henry Richardson' (2017) 31 Temple International and Comparative Law Journal 11, at p. 18; Christopher N. Camponovo, 'Disaster in Durban: The United Nations World Conference against Racism, Racial Discrimination, Xenophobia, and Related Intolerance' (2003) 34 George Washington International Law Review 659, at pp. 677.

[181] Report of the World Conference against Racism, Racial Discrimination, Xenophobia and Related Intolerance, A/CONF.189/12, p. 128. See also the statement of Trinidad and Tobago, ibid., pp. 130–1.

[182] Ibid., p. 141.

[183] Ibid., pp. 120–1.

378 INITIATIVES ON RACIAL DISCRIMINATION

should not be understood as the acceptance of any liability for these practices.' The European Union added that 'nothing in the Declaration or the Programme of Action can affect the general legal principle which precludes the retrospective application of international law in matters of State responsibility'.[184]

In her closing speech, Dlamini Zuma, President of the World Conference and South Africa's minister of foreign affairs, said: 'We agreed that slavery is a crime against humanity and that an apology is necessary, not for monetary gain, but to restore the dignity and humanity of those who suffered'.[185] Instead of a full apology, as the African States had sought, the Declaration 'note[s] that some States have taken the initiative to apologise and have paid reparation, where appropriate, for grave and massive violations committed'.[186] It speaks of 'the moral obligation on the part of all concerned States' and it 'call[s] upon these States to take appropriate and effective measures to halt and reverse the lasting consequences of those practices'.[187] Although the Durban Declaration acknowledged that some States had provided reparation for past injustices related to 'slavery, the slave trade, the transatlantic slave trade, apartheid, colonialism and genocide', its support for any sense of legal obligation was modest.[188]

The Durban Declaration confirms that apartheid is a crime against humanity.[189] Although the Declaration of the 1983 Conference contained the same statement, it was accompanied by reservations from Western States who challenged this characterization of apartheid. There were no similar reservations in 2001, perhaps because the opposition lost its *raison d'être* with the recognition of apartheid as a crime against humanity in article 7 of the Rome Statute of the International Criminal Court in July 1998. States like Germany, Canada, and the United Kingdom that had previously objected were now introducing the crime against humanity of apartheid into their domestic legislation so as to comply with their obligations under the Rome Statute.[190] Use of the term 'crime against humanity' in the singular was apparently intended to indicate that historic wrongs do not constitute individual crimes,[191] although this seems quite theoretical because criminal prosecution only applies to persons who are alive.

---

[184] Ibid., p. 144.

[185] Gay McDougall, 'The World Conference against Racism: Through a Wider Lens' (2002) 26 *Fletcher Forum of World Affairs* 135, at p. 139.

[186] Declaration, A/CONF.189/12, pp. 5–26, para. 100.

[187] Ibid., para. 102.

[188] Ibid., paras. 99–100.

[189] Ibid., para. 12.

[190] United Kingdom: International Criminal Court Act 2001, s. 50(1); Canada: Crimes Against Humanity and War Crimes Act (S.C. 2000, c. 24), s. 4(4).

[191] Ulrike Sundberg, 'Durban: The Third World Conference against Racism, Racial Discrimination, Xenophobia and Related Intolerance' (2002) 73 *International Review of Penal Law* 301, at pp. 303–4.

It has been suggested that Israel was singled out for attack at Durban, and that this was a manifestation of anti-Semitism.[192] The paragraphs in the Declaration dealing with racial discrimination against Palestinians are diplomatic reflections of compromise.[193] They are hardly the 'show trial of Israel' described by one impassioned critic.[194] The Durban Declaration explicitly recognizes 'the increase in anti-Semitism and Islamophobia in various parts of the world, as well as the emergence of racial and violent movements based on racism and discriminatory ideas against Jewish, Muslim and Arab communities'.[195] Paragraph 58 declares: 'We recall that the Holocaust must never be forgotten'. The High Commissioner for Human Rights, Mary Robinson, adroitly navigated this difficult terrain in efforts to find formulations that might be acceptable to all,[196] but the challenge was daunting. Syria put forward a 'killer amendment' in the final negotiations that referred to the suffering of the Palestinian people and foreign occupation as a source of racism. It was blocked by a procedural gambit known as a no-action motion.[197]

In marked contrast with the first two Conferences on racial discrimination, at Durban there was a very active and visible engagement of non-governmental organizations. It is estimated that more than 3,000 of them attended, informally grouped into more than 30 caucuses.[198] An 'NGO Forum' that convened prior to the main Conference adopted its own declaration and programme of action. The tone was militant on a range of issues including the Middle East. It condemned Israel as a 'racist apartheid state' and charged it with 'genocide' against the Palestinians.[199] According to Swedish diplomat Ulrike Sundberg, the language of the NGO Declaration was 'highly inflammatory, which prevented its formal annexation to the report from the Conference'.[200] Mary Robinson declined recommending the documents from the NGO Forum to the World Conference.[201]

---

[192] Anne Bayefsky, 'The UN World Conference Against Racism: A Racist Anti-racism Conference' [2002] *Proceedings of the American Society of International Law Annual Meeting* 65.

[193] Corinne Lennox, 'Reviewing Durban: Examining the Outputs and Review of the 2001 World Conference against Racism' (2009) 27 *Netherlands Quarterly of Human Rights* 191, at pp. 203–5.

[194] Ruth Wedgewood, 'Zionism and Racism Again, Durban II' (2009) 171 *World Affairs* 84, at p. 84.

[195] Declaration, A/CONF.189/12, pp. 5–26, para. 61.

[196] Gay McDougall, 'The World Conference against Racism: Through a Wider Lens' (2002) 26 *Fletcher Forum of World Affairs* 135, at p. 147.

[197] Chapter IV. Report of the Main Committee, A/CONF.189/12, pp. 103–11, paras. 17–20. See Ulrike Sundberg, 'Durban: The Third World Conference against Racism, Racial Discrimination, Xenophobia and Related Intolerance' (2002) 73 *International Review of Penal Law* 301, at pp. 301–2.

[198] Maria Miguel Sierra, 'The World Conference against Racism and the Role of the European NGOs' (2002) 4 *European Journal of Migration and Law* 249, at p. 255.

[199] Ibid.

[200] Ulrike Sundberg, 'Durban: The Third World Conference against Racism, Racial Discrimination, Xenophobia and Related Intolerance' (2002) 73 *International Review of Penal Law* 301, at p. 302.

[201] Maria Miguel Sierra, 'The World Conference against Racism and the Role of the European NGOs' (2002) 4 *European Journal of Migration and Law* 249, at p. 258.

380 INITIATIVES ON RACIAL DISCRIMINATION

There were some very ugly manifestations of anti-Semitism at the NGO Forum that had no place at any event associated with the United Nations. For example, there were reports of placards stating 'Hitler should have finished the job' and distribution by one delegation of the notorious 'Protocols of the elders of Zion'. Mary Robinson denounced the anti-Semitism that was roiling the NGO Forum.[202] But some reports exaggerated the extent of the problem or confounded criticism of Israel with anti-Jewish racism. One academic writer alleged it was 'the worst manifestation of anti-Semitism since World War II',[203] attributing this hyperbole to Tom Lantos in an article where he said no such thing. After the Conference, a representative of the United States greatly overstated the situation when he claimed the Conference 'was accompanied in the streets of Durban by some of the worst examples of hate and intolerance witnessed in many decades'.[204] In the United States alone, there had been many examples of hate and intolerance in previous decades that were far more grievous than anything witnessed in Durban in 2001. In a personal memoir of the conference, a senior UN official provided the sale of t-shirts with messages like 'End Israeli apartheid' and 'Zionism = racism' as examples of anti-Semitism.[205] These are perfectly legitimate criticisms of Israel that are quite distinguishable from glorification of Nazi atrocities. Of course, some of those who attacked Israel may have been driven by anti-Semitism but it is just as true to contend that some of those who have supported it have been animated by Islamophobia.

Whereas the first two World Conferences had focussed on apartheid and the racist regimes in southern Africa, the third World Conference dealt with Africa more generally. The Durban Declaration and Programme of Action identifies the principal victims of racial discrimination as 'Africans and people of African descent, Asians and people of Asian descent and indigenous peoples'.[206] Several paragraphs of the Declaration deal with these groups individually, beginning with Africans and people of African descent[207] and followed by 'Asians and people of Asian descent'[208] and indigenous peoples.[209] Some have suggested there was an intent to recognize a hierarchy.[210] Other groups entitled to special

---

[202] Laurie Weisberg, NGOs and the World Conference Against Racism: Nearly Twenty Years On, A Very Personal Experience (August 2021), p. 90 (on file with the author).

[203] Dimitrina Petrova, ' "Smoke and Mirrors": The Durban Review Conference and Human Rights Politics at the United Nations' (2010) 10 *Human Rights Law Review* 129, at p. 130.

[204] Verbatim record, plenary General Assembly, 27 March 2002, p. 3.

[205] Laurie Weisberg, NGOs and the World Conference Against Racism: Nearly Twenty Years On, A Very Personal Experience (August 2021), p. 89 (on file with the author).

[206] Declaration, A/CONF.189/12, pp. 5–26, paras. 13, 14,

[207] Ibid., paras. 33–5.

[208] Ibid., paras. 36–8.

[209] Ibid., paras. 39–45.

[210] Ulrike Sundberg, 'Durban: The Third World Conference against Racism, Racial Discrimination, Xenophobia and Related Intolerance' (2002) 73 *International Review of Penal Law* 301, at pp 307–8.

DURBAN 2001   381

recognition are migrants,[211] refugees, asylum-seekers, and internally displaced persons.[212] Unfortunately, the Declaration does not recognize discrimination based on descent, despite vigorous efforts by Indian Dalits.[213] The Declaration also provides significant recognition of intersectionality, notably in the attention it gives to gender.

***

The very central role that the issues of racism and racial discrimination have played within the general framework of human rights, both within the United Nations and to a somewhat lesser extent in regional human rights bodies, was highlighted by the years, decades, and conferences. The International Day against Racial Discrimination was proclaimed by the General Assembly in 1966 and observed the following year on 21 March.[214] It commemorates the Sharpeville massacre that took place on that date in 1960. In 2007, the General Assembly designated 25 March as the annual International Day of Remembrance of the Victims of Slavery and the Transatlantic Slave Trade.[215] Already, UNESCO had recognized 23 August as the International Day for the Remembrance of the Slave Trade and its Abolition.[216] It commemorates the uprising of slaves in Saint-Domingue in 1791. In 2020, the General Assembly established 31 August as the International Day for People of African Descent.[217]

The Durban Conference continues to emit a mixed message. Its impact has been clouded by the allegations of anti-Semitism. This would not be an issue if there was greater awareness of how limited the phenomenon actually was, that it was confined to an NGO conference, and that many of the charges in reality deal with perfectly legitimate criticism of Israeli policies. States that have harped on the issue, notably Canada and the United States, are in reality concerned more with the reparations issue than they are with criticism of Israel's conduct. Since the United Nations was founded in 1945, the United States has been making periodic statements of contrition, explaining that it is doing its best to deal with

[211] Declaration, A/CONF.189/12, pp. 5–26, paras. 46–51.

[212] Ibid., paras. 52–4.

[213] Peter Prove, 'Caste at the World Conference Against Racism', in Sukhadeo Thorat, ed., *Caste, Race and Discrimination: Discourses in International Context*, New Delhi: Rawat Publications, 2004, pp. 322–5; Corinne Lennox, 'Reviewing Durban: Examining the Outputs and Review of the 2001 World Conference against Racism' (2009) 27 *Netherlands Quarterly of Human Rights* 191, at pp. 213–16. See also Summary record, Committee on the Elimination of Racial Discrimination, 16 August 2002, CERD/C/SR.1531.

[214] Elimination of all forms of racial discrimination, 26 October 1966, A/RES/2142 (XXI), OP 8.

[215] Permanent memorial to and remembrance of the victims of slavery and the transatlantic slave trade, 17 December 2007, A/RES/62/122, OP 3.

[216] International Day for the Remembrance of the Slave Trade and its Abolition, UNESCO, General Conference, 29th session, 1997, General Conference, Res. 40, OP 2.

[217] International Day for People of African Descent, 28 December 2020, A/RES/75/170, OP 1. See *infra*, p. 390.

racial discrimination. It has managed to put a man on the moon, amongst other accomplishments, yet somehow it cannot wrestle the monster of racism to the ground. Moreover, in the campaigns against racism and apartheid within the United Nations, its engagement is a long saga of negative votes, abstentions, vetos, and walkouts. This pattern that can be traced back to the 1940s. If the views of the United States had prevailed, the United Nations would never have done anything to confront racial discrimination.

The Declaration and Programme of Action may be seen as a kind of capstone on the work of the United Nations on racism and racial discrimination. It provided an important correction in the post-apartheid era by restoring the focus on discrimination against people of colour. It also represents an important marker with regard to reparations for slavery, the slave trade, and racial discrimination. It should have been a celebration declaring the end of W.E.B. Du Bois's century of the colour line. Instead, it set an agenda for further initiatives directed at the persistence of racism and racial discrimination.

13

The Colour Line's Long Twentieth Century

Durban's Aftermath

The tensions of the Durban Conference did not dissipate for many years as States wrestled with the implementation of the Declaration and Programme of Action. At a special meeting of the General Assembly held to mark the tenth anniversary of the Conference, the Secretary-General noted that Durban had caused 'immense controversy'. He said that '[w]e should condemn anyone who uses this platform to subvert that effort with inflammatory rhetoric, baseless assertions and hateful speech. Our common commitment must be to focus on the real problems of racism and intolerance.'[1]

The General Assembly took several months to finalize its resolution on the Durban Conference due to ongoing negotiations involving the High Commissioner for Human Rights, the African Group, and the European Union.[2] Only in March 2002 was the resolution adopted, by 134 votes in favour, with the United States and Israel voting against and Canada and Australia abstaining.[3] The Assembly said it was '[c]onvinced that the Conference made an important contribution to the cause of the eradication of racism, racial discrimination, xenophobia and related intolerance'.[4] It endorsed the Declaration and Programme of Action.[5] The Assembly decided that 'independent eminent experts', one from each of the five regions, were to be appointed by the Secretary-General, from a list proposed by the Chairperson of the Commission on Human Rights, with the mandate to follow the implementation of the provisions of the Declaration and Programme of Action'.[6] The appointment of the experts took more than a year, and their first report was only issued in early 2004.[7]

---

[1] Verbatim record, plenary General Assembly, 22 September 2011, A/66/PV.14, p. 3.

[2] Ulrike Sundberg, 'Durban: The Third World Conference against Racism, Racial Discrimination, Xenophobia and Related Intolerance' (2002) 73 *International Review of Penal Law* 301, at p. 315.

[3] Verbatim record, plenary General Assembly, 27 March 2002, A/56/PV.97, p. 5.

[4] Comprehensive implementation of and follow-up to the World Conference against Racism, Racial Discrimination, Xenophobia and Related Intolerance, 27 March 2002, A/RES/56/266, PP 4.

[5] Ibid., OP 2.

[6] Ibid., OP 13.

[7] Views of the independent eminent experts on the implementation of the Durban Declaration and Programme of Action, 10 February 2004, E/CN.4/2004/112.

The International Legal Order's Colour Line. William A. Schabas, Oxford University Press.
© Oxford University Press 2023. DOI: 10.1093/oso/9780197744475.003.0013

384 THE COLOUR LINE'S LONG TWENTIETH CENTURY

The Durban Declaration and Programme of Action recommended that the Commission on Human Rights 'prepare complementary international standards to strengthen and update international instruments against racism, racial discrimination, xenophobia and related intolerance in all their aspects'.[8] The Commission entrusted this task to the Intergovernmental Working Group that it set up to implement the Durban Declaration and Programme of Action.[9] The Working Group held a 'high-level seminar' on the subject in 2006. There were a number of interesting suggestions but little in the way of common ground or consensus about gaps that required filling.[10]

Later in 2006, the newly-formed Human Rights Council asked the High Commissioner for Human Rights to designate five experts for a study of 'substantive gaps in the existing international instruments to combat racism, racial discrimination, xenophobia and related intolerance'.[11] At its December 2006 session, the Council decided, with reference to the Durban Declaration and Programme of Action, to establish an Ad Hoc Committee of the Human Rights Council on the Elaboration of Complementary Standards. Its mandate was to elaborate 'complementary standards in the form of either a convention or additional protocol(s) to the International Convention on the Elimination of All Forms of Racial Discrimination, filling the existing gaps in the Convention and also providing new normative standards aimed at combating all forms of contemporary racism, including incitement to racial and religious hatred'.[12] Several States were opposed or abstained in the vote, voicing concern about the final phrase that seemed to direct the outcome.[13] The reference was understood to signal the new and controversial notion of 'defamation of religions' being promoted by some States in the Middle East and Asia.[14]

---

[8] Programme of Action, A/CONF.189/12, pp. 28–66, para. 199.

[9] Racism, racial discrimination, xenophobia, and related intolerance, 25 April 2002, E/CN.4/RES/2002/68, OP 7(b).

[10] Report of the Intergovernmental Working Group on the effective implementation of the Durban Declaration and Programme of Action on its fourth session, 20 March 2006, E/CN.4/2006/18, paras. 49–85; Information on the elaboration of complementary international standards as part of the follow-up to the Durban Declaration and Programme of Action, 7 February 2008, A/HRC/AC.1/1/2, paras. 1–20.

[11] Intergovernmental Working Group on the effective implementation of the Durban Declaration and Programme of Action, 29 June 2006, A/HRC/RES/1/5, OP 2.

[12] Global efforts for the total elimination of racism, racial discrimination, xenophobia and related intolerance and the comprehensive follow-up to the World Conference against Racism, Racial Discrimination, Xenophobia and Related Intolerance and the effective implementation of the Durban Declaration and Programme of Action, 8 December 2006, A/HRC/DEC/3/103, para. (a).

[13] Summary record, Human Rights Council, 8 December 2006, A/HRC/3/SR.14, paras. 4, 9, 10.

[14] Dimitrina Petrova, ' "Smoke and Mirrors": The Durban Review Conference and Human Rights Politics at the United Nations' (2010) 10 *Human Rights Law Review* 129, at p. 135. On this subject, see Report of the Special Rapporteur on contemporary forms of racism, racial discrimination, xenophobia, and related intolerance, Doudou Diène, on the manifestations of defamation of religions and in particular on the serious implications of Islamophobia on the enjoyment of all rights, 2 September 2008, A/HRC/9/12.

In the meantime, the experts designated by the High Commissioner produced a report that assessed the development of complementary standards with respect to specific groups: religious groups; refugees, asylum-seekers, migrant workers, and stateless persons; internally displaced persons; descent-based communities; indigenous peoples; minorities; people under foreign occupation. It also considered whether there should be new norms to deal with multiple discrimination or aggravated forms of racial discrimination, ethnic cleansing, genocide, religious intolerance and defamation of religious symbols, racial discrimination in the private sphere, and incitement to racial hatred and dissemination of hate speech and xenophobic and caricatural pictures, through traditional mass media and information technology, including the Internet. There were a number of recommendations, some involving interpretative developments by United Nations treaty bodies. In certain cases, such as the crime of genocide, the experts considered that there was no gap and no need for complementary standards. The experts concluded that the existing law applicable to racist speech directed at religions or religious groups was satisfactory.[15]

The Human Rights Council reacted negatively, declaring that the expert report 'was not accomplished in accordance with the requirements set out in its decision 3/103'.[16] At the same session, the Council decided to 'realign' the work and name of the Anti-Discrimination Unit in the Office of the United Nations High Commissioner for Human Rights. It said that henceforth it was to be known as 'The Anti-Racial Discrimination Unit' and that its operational activities 'shall focus exclusively on racism, racial discrimination, xenophobia and related intolerance, as defined in paragraphs 1 and 2 of the Durban Declaration'.[17] When after six years the change had still not taken place, the General Assembly called upon the High Commissioner for Human Rights to implement the 'realignment'.[18] In the same resolution, the General Assembly said it '[r]egrets that the High Commissioner omitted to include the historic and landmark World Conference against Racism, Racial Discrimination, Xenophobia and Related Intolerance of 2001 among the twenty major achievements of her Office since the adoption of the 1993 Vienna Declaration and Programme of Action'.[19] The dispute involved the independence of the High Commissioner but it also reflected resistance

---

[15] Report on the study by the five experts on the content and scope of substantive gaps in the existing international instruments to combat racism, racial discrimination, xenophobia, and related intolerance, 27 August 2007, A/HRC/4/WG.3/6.

[16] Elaboration of international complementary standards to the International Convention on the Elimination of All Forms of Racial Discrimination, 28 September 2007, A/HRC/RES/6/21, PP 10.

[17] From rhetoric to reality: a global call for concrete action against racism, racial discrimination, xenophobia and related intolerance, 28 September 2007, A/HRC/RES/6/22, OP 1.

[18] Global efforts for the total elimination of racism, racial discrimination, xenophobia and related intolerance and the comprehensive implementation of and follow-up to the Durban Declaration and Programme of Action, 18 December 2013, A/RES/68/151, para. 10.

[19] Ibid., para. 11.

386   THE COLOUR LINE'S LONG TWENTIETH CENTURY

from European Union Member States who took the view that 'the Office's Anti-Discrimination Section should not focus solely on racial discrimination to the exclusion of other forms of discrimination'.[20] After the General Assembly resolution was adopted, the Office of the High Commissioner reported that the name had been changed to the 'Anti-Racial Discrimination Section'.[21]

In December 2006, the General Assembly voted to convene a review conference in 2009 on the implementation of the Durban Declaration and Programme of Action. It assigned the Human Rights Council to take responsibility for the preparations.[22] The United States and Israel opposed the resolution, and Canada and Australia, as well as Palau and the Marshall Islands, abstained. The European Union insisted that the Durban Declaration and Programme of Action was not to be reopened.[23] As had been the case with the three World Conferences, in 1978, 1983, and 2001, States from Africa and Asia were the most enthusiastic. States of the Global North had no appetite for activities that would inexorably dwell on historic injustices, persistent global inequalities that were linked to colonialism, and failure to achieve peace in the Middle East. Moreover, they were vehemently opposed to any discussion of new standards that might strengthen international law in the area of racial discrimination.

The Durban Review Conference took place over five days in April 2009, at the United Nations Office in Geneva, and was relatively modest in scale by comparison with the 2001 event.[24] Well before the start of the Conference, Canada announced it would not participate. The United States initially sent conflicting signals but also decided not to attend, as did Australia, Germany, Israel, Italy, and the Netherlands. Only one head of State participated at the opening high-level session. Iran's President, Mahmoud Ahmadinejad, provoked a temporary walk-out of several delegations when he referred to Israel as a racist State. Such a disturbance was nothing new for United Nations Conferences on racism. The 'Outcome Document' adopted by the Review Conference reaffirmed the conclusions reached at Durban in 2001 but there was little in the way of significant new developments.[25] To the condemnation of anti-Semitism and Islamophobia were added two new categories of intolerance, Christianophobia and anti-Arabism.[26] The issue of racism against Palestinians was avoided entirely.

[20] Summary record, Third Committee, 27 November 2013, A/C.3/68/SR.54, para. 7.
[21] Progress report of the High Commissioner for Human Rights on the realignment of work and name of the Anti-Discrimination Unit, 25 July 2014, A/69/186, para. 6.
[22] Global efforts for the total elimination of racism, racial discrimination, xenophobia and related intolerance and the comprehensive implementation of and follow-up to the Durban Declaration and Programme of Action, 19 December 2006, A/RES/61/149, OP 33.
[23] Verbatim record, plenary General Assembly, 19 December 2006, A/61/PV.81, pp. 8–10.
[24] Corinne Lennox, 'Reviewing Durban: Examining the Outputs and Review of the 2001 World Conference against Racism' (2009) 27 Netherlands Quarterly of Human Rights 191, at pp. 223–35.
[25] Report of the Durban Review Conference Geneva, 20–24 April 2009, A/CONF.211/8.
[26] Outcome Document of the Durban Review Conference, A/CONF.211/8, pp. 1–16, para. 12. It seems that the term 'Christianophobia' may have first appeared in a 2003 General Assembly

The Ad Hoc Committee of the Human Rights Council on the Elaboration of Complementary Standards, whose establishment had been decided in late 2006, only became operational in 2009, after the Durban Review Conference. That year the Chairperson of the Committee prepared a summary of submissions from Member States that revealed a broad diversity of views on the subject of complementary standards.[27] The Ad Hoc Committee met annually although with little to show for its work. In December 2016, the General Assembly 'expressed its concern at the lack of progress' in elaborating complementary standards, calling upon the Chairperson-Rapporteur of the Ad Hoc Committee 'to ensure the commencement of the negotiations on the draft additional protocol to the Convention criminalising acts of a racist and xenophobic nature'.[28] The European Union and other Western States opposed the initiative, taking the view that the International Convention on the Elimination of All Forms of Racial Discrimination does not have 'gaps' and that there is no need for an additional protocol.[29]

On the occasion of the tenth anniversary of the adoption of the Durban Declaration and Programme of Action the General Assembly held a one-day 'High-level meeting' in New York. A political declaration entitled 'United against racism, racial discrimination, xenophobia and related intolerance' was adopted '[r]eaffirm[ing] that the Durban Declaration and Programme of Action, adopted in 2001, and the outcome document of the Durban Review Conference, adopted in 2009, provide a comprehensive United Nations framework and solid foundation for combating racism, racial discrimination, xenophobia and related intolerance'.[30]

In 2013, the Secretary-General of the United Nations issued a 'Guidance Note on Racial Discrimination and Protection of Minorities'. The Secretary-General explained the rationale behind linking the two concepts. He said standards and

---

resolution: Global efforts for the total elimination of racism, racial discrimination, xenophobia and related intolerance and the comprehensive implementation of and follow-up to the Durban Declaration and Programme of Action, 22 December 2003, A/RES/58/160. para. 46. See the discussion of Christianophobia in Report submitted by Mr. Doudou Diène, Special Rapporteur on contemporary forms of racism, racial discrimination, xenophobia, and related intolerance, 13 December 2004, E/CN.4/2005/18/Add.4, paras. 52–62.

[27] Outcome referred to in paragraph 2(d) of the Road Map on the elaboration of complementary standards, Prepared by the Chairperson-Rapporteur of the Ad Hoc Committee on the Elaboration of Complementary Standards, 26 August 2009, A/HRC/AC.1/2/2.

[28] A global call for concrete action for the total elimination of racism, racial discrimination, xenophobia and related intolerance and the comprehensive implementation of and follow-up to the Durban Declaration and Programme of Action, 19 December 2016, A/RES/71/181, OP 5.

[29] Report of the Ad Hoc Committee on the Elaboration of Complementary Standards on its tenth session, 20 August 2019, A/HRC/42/58, paras. 27–30.

[30] United against racism, racial discrimination, xenophobia and related intolerance, 22 September 2011, A/RES/66/3, OP 1.

388 THE COLOUR LINE'S LONG TWENTIETH CENTURY

mechanisms devoted to combatting racial discrimination benefit minorities, who are often targets of racial discrimination, and that 'minority rights contribute to the efforts to combat racial discrimination'.[31] The Guidance Note drew attention to 'institutional racism' in such areas as education and criminal justice. Writing in 2022, the Special rapporteur on minorities issues appeared to credit the Guidance Note's contribution to 'significant progress for the mainstreaming of racial anti-discrimination' but he lamented 'a near complete failure to mainstream and integrate the rights of minorities at the United Nations, despite the call to do so by the Secretary-General in his 2013 Guidance Note'.[32]

People of African Descent

The Durban Declaration brought the notion of 'people of African descent' into the mainstream of United Nations human rights activity. The Durban Conference gave 'greater recognition and visibility' to people of African descent, observed the Committee on the Elimination of Racial Discrimination.[33] Referring to 'countries in the region of the Americas and all other areas of the African Diaspora', the Declaration called for recognition of cultural, economic, political, and scientific contributions of the population of African descent as well as the persistence of racism, racial discrimination, xenophobia, and related intolerance that specifically affect them, including long-standing inequality in access to education, health care, and housing.[34] The identification of racism and racial discrimination directed at 'people of African descent' refocussed the attention of international organizations and international law. It is a new concept that in reality largely corresponds to that of the 'colour line' identified by Frederick Douglass and W.E.B. Du Bois more than 100 years earlier.

In 2002, African States successfully pushed the Commission on Human Rights to establish an expert panel to study the problems of racial discrimination faced by people of African descent living in the diaspora.[35] The mandate of the five-member Working Group of Experts on People of African Descent has been regularly renewed. In 2017, the Human Rights Council requested the Working Group to focus on 'the rising tide of racism and racial hatred, as evidenced by the

---

[31] Guidance Note of the Secretary-General on Racial Discrimination and the Protection of Minorities, March 2013, para. 7.

[32] Report of the Special Rapporteur on minority issues, Fernand de Varennes, Protection of the rights of minorities in the institutions, structures and initiatives of the United Nations, 29 July 2022, A/77/246, para. 70.

[33] Racial discrimination against people of African descent, General recommendation 34, 3 October 2011, CERD/C/GC/34, PP 2.

[34] Declaration, A/CONF.189/12, pp. 5–26, para. 33.

[35] Racism, racial discrimination, xenophobia, and related intolerance, 25 April 2002, E/CN.4/RES/2002/68, OP 8.

PEOPLE OF AFRICAN DESCENT 389

resurgence of white supremacist ideologies, and extremist nationalist and populist ideologies, and to make specific recommendations in this regard.[36] In the course of its activities, the Working Group has prepared thematic reports on such issues as environmental justice and climate change,[37] COVID-19,[38] and negative racial stereotypes.[39] The Working Group has conducted field missions to more than 15 countries, visiting the United States, Belgium, and Ecuador twice. Reporting on a mission to Belgium in 2019, the Working Group referred to racist stereotypes of people of African descent, giving as an example the book *Tintin in the Congo* and suggesting it should be either withdrawn or contextualized with an addendum reflecting current commitments to anti-racism.[40] The Netherlands was called to task for manifestations of racism in its traditional Christmas celebrations, which involve a personality known as 'Zwarte Piet' or Black Pete who serves as helper of 'Sinterklaas', although the Working Group stopped short of calling for a ban.[41] A 2020 mission to Peru observed a 'comprehensive lack of access to basic services and the denial of core human rights for many Afro-Peruvians'.[42] The Working Group's mission to Canada found 'clear evidence that racial profiling is endemic in the strategies and practices used by law enforcement. Furthermore, arbitrary use of "carding", or street checks – the police practice of stopping, questioning and documenting people suspected of a crime – disproportionately affects people of African descent'.[43]

Reassessing history requires scrutiny of some of the hitherto distinguished personalities, whose involvement in slavery, the slave trade, racial discrimination, and colonialism has been downplayed or simply left unmentioned. Most of these individuals belong to 'civilized' Europe and the European diaspora. When the Working Group of Experts on People of African Descent conducted its mission to Belgium, it 'noted with concern' the public monuments to Leopold II.[44] Perhaps the Working Group will turn its attention to the Palais Wilson in

[36] Mandate of the Working Group of Experts on People of African Descent, 29 September 2017, A/HRC/RES/36/23, OP 5.
[37] Environmental justice, the climate crisis and people of African descent, 21 September 2021, A/HRC/48/78.
[38] COVID-19, systemic racism and global protests, 21 August 2020, A/HRC/45/44, paras. 15–29.
[39] Report of the Working Group of Experts on People of African Descent, 2 August 2019, A/74/274.
[40] Visit to Belgium, Report of the Working Group of Experts on People of African Descent, 14 August 2019, A/HRC/42/59/Add.1, para. 47.
[41] Mission to the Netherlands, 20 July 2015, A/HRC/30/56/Add.1, paras. 104–9. See also Mission to the Netherlands and Curaçao: comments by the State on the report of the Working Group, 2 September 2015, A/HRC/30/56/Add.3, paras. 56–60.
[42] Visit to Peru, Report of the Working Group of Experts on People of African Descent, 21 August 2020, A/HRC/45/44/Add.2, para. 21.
[43] Visit to Canada, Report of the Working Group of Experts on People of African Descent, A/HRC/36/60/Add.1, 16 August 2017, para. 35.
[44] Visit to Belgium Report of the Working Group of Experts on People of African Descent, 14 August 2019, A/HRC/42/59/Add.1, para. 32.

390 THE COLOUR LINE'S LONG TWENTIETH CENTURY

Geneva, the home of the High Commissioner for Human Rights and the venue for its meetings. The Palais Wilson was named to honour the man who praised racist films glorifying the Ku Klux Klan and who effectively vetoed the text on racial equality proposed by Japan for the Covenant of the League of Nations.

The General Assembly declared 2011 to be the International Year of People of African Descent.[45] Then, it proclaimed 2014–2024 as the International Decade of People of African Descent.[46] In its 2020 resolution recognizing 31 August as the International Day for People of African Descent, the General Assembly said this was 'to promote greater recognition and respect for the diverse heritage, culture and contribution of people of African descent to the development of societies, and to promote respect for human rights and fundamental freedoms of people of African descent'.[47] The date of 31 August is intended to commemorate the Declaration of Rights of the Negro Peoples of the World, adopted in 1920 in New York at the first International Convention of the Negro Peoples of the World 'as a result of the discussions led by Marcus Garvey'.[48] The 1920 Declaration proclaimed 31 August as 'an international holiday to be observed by all Negroes'.[49]

Within Europe, the continent that was at the epicentre of the slave trade and colonialism, the main international organizations to some extent neglected the colour line in their activities in the field of racism and racial discrimination, diluting the issue within the broader rubric of 'xenophobia and related intolerance'. Yet as migration from Africa to Europe continues, its population of people of colour becomes increasingly significant. Europe has been compelled to confront the very specific issues of 'people of African descent'. Thus, in 2018 the European Union's Fundamental Rights Agency issued a report entitled 'Being Black in the EU'. 'It is a reality both shameful and infuriating: racism based on the colour of a person's skin remains a pervasive scourge throughout the European Union', wrote the Agency's director, Michael O'Flaherty, in the preface to this study.[50] The report highlights police violence and harassment directed against people of colour, including racial profiling, and inequalities in such areas as

[45] International Year for People of African Descent, 18 December 2009, A/RES/64/169. See Gina Thésée and Paul R. Carr, 'The 2011 International Year for People of African Descent: The paradox of colonized invisibility within the promise of mainstream visibility' (2012) 1 *Decolonization: Indigeneity, Education and Society* 158.

[46] Proclamation of the International Decade for People of African Descent, 23 December 2013, A/RES/68/237.

[47] International Day for People of African Descent, 28 December 2020, A/RES/75/170, OP 1.

[48] Ibid., PP 16. See also Summary record, Third Committee, 17 February 2021, A/C.3/75/SR.14, para. 61.

[49] 'Declaration of Rights of the Negro Peoples of the World', in Robert Hill, ed., *The Marcus Garvey and Universal Negro Improvement Papers*, Vol. 2, Berkeley: University of California Press, 1983, pp. 571–80; Marcus Garvey, Declaration of Rights of the Negro Peoples of the World' (2021) 13 *Black Camera* 335.

[50] Agency for Fundamental Rights, *Being Black in the EU*, Vienna, 2018, p. 3.

housing and education. A European Parliament resolution adopted in 2019 called for the European Commission 'to include a focus on people of African descent in its current funding programmes' and 'to set up a dedicated team within the relevant services, with a specific focus on Afrophobia issues'.[51] The Organisation for Security and Cooperation in Europe has also focused attention on people of African descent.[52]

The Council of Europe institutions have shown a preference for the terms 'Afrophobia' and 'anti-Black racism', which seem to be considered as synonymous with discrimination directed at people of African descent. The Commissioner for Human Rights of the Council of Europe has spoken of 'Afrophobia', pointing to the campaigns of certain politicians directed at migrants from the South.[53] The European Parliament cited the terminology of the Commissioner for Human Rights in its own resolution on the right of people of African descent in Europe: 'whereas the terms "Afrophobia", "Afri-phobia" and "anti-black racism" refer to a specific form of racism, including any act of violence or discrimination, fueled by historical abuses and negative stereotyping, and leading to the exclusion and dehumanisation of people of African descent; whereas this correlates to historically repressive structures of colonialism and the transatlantic slave trade, as recognised by the Council of Europe's High [sic] Commissioner for Human Rights'.[54] In 2020, the Commissioner for Human Rights hosted a round table on racism and racial discrimination against people of African descent in Europe. Her report reached the unsurprising conclusion that people of African descent in Europe experience worse economic, social, and health outcomes than other groups.[55] A report from the Parliamentary Assembly of the Council of Europe pointed to the origins of anti-Black racism in colonial history, enslavement, and the transatlantic slave trade. It said that Council of Europe Member States should acknowledge this link and recognize Afrophobia as a specific form of racism.[56]

---

[51] European Parliament resolution of 26 March 2019 on fundamental rights of people of African descent in Europe (2018/2899(RSP), OP 13, 14.

[52] Roundtable on the contemporary forms of racism and xenophobia affecting people of African Descent in the OSCE region, Summary meeting report, 12 February 2012, ODIHR.GAL/81/11/Corr.1.

[53] Commissioner for Human Rights, 'Afrophobia: Europe should confront this legacy of colonialism and the slave trade', Human Rights Comment, 25 June 2017. Note also the reference to 'Afrophobia' by the United Nations Human Rights Council: From rhetoric to reality: a global call for concrete action against racism, racial discrimination, xenophobia, and related intolerance, 25 October 2012, A/RES/21/33, OP 13.

[54] European Parliament resolution of 26 March 2019 on fundamental rights of people of African descent in Europe (2018/2899(RSP), PP B.

[55] Combatting racism and racial discrimination against people of African descent in Europe, Report, 19 March 2021, CommDH(2021)2.

[56] Combating Afrophobia, or anti-Black racism, in Europe, 16 March 2021, AS/ega (2021) 09. See also Committee on Equality and Non-Discrimination, Taking a stand against systemic discrimination and institutional racism in Europe: parliamentary response, Information document prepared by the Secretariat, 3 July 2020, AS/Ega/Inf (2020) 19.

392 THE COLOUR LINE'S LONG TWENTIETH CENTURY

About 30% of the population of the western hemisphere, said to be slightly more than 1 billion, consists of people of African descent.[57] The United States was not alone in being the destination of the Middle Passage. Africans were also taken in huge numbers to South and Central America, and to the islands of the Caribbean. Although racial discrimination was condemned in some early declarations of inter-American institutions,[58] for most of the twentieth century the organs of the Organization of American States gave the issue only perfunctory attention. For example, in 1954, when a resolution on communist intervention in the Americas was being debated at the Tenth Inter-American Conference, Panama urged the adoption of a resolution condemning racial discrimination saying it would assist in fighting communism in the United States-controlled Canal Zone, where there were said to be many abuses.[59]

The preliminary activities associated with the 2001 Durban Conference of the United Nations appear to have stimulated activity within the institutions of the western hemisphere. The Regional Conference of the Americas, held in Santiago, Chile in December 2000, adopted a statement that the Inter-American Commission on Human Rights refers to as the 'Santiago Declaration'.[60] The Declaration '[r]eaffirm[ed] . . . that the history of the Americas has often been characterised by racism, racial discrimination, xenophobia and related intolerance, and that telling the truth about the history of and ongoing manifestations of racism in the Americas is essential for reconciliation and to build societies based on justice, equality and solidarity'.[61] Detailed provisions were devoted to the rights of 'people of African descent', including their rights to culture and their own identity, to their own forms of organization and mode of life, to maintain and use their own languages and to the protection of their traditional knowledge.[62]

The first Summits of the Americas, during the 1990s, had addressed discrimination in general but with no special emphasis on race. Only in 2001, when the Summit of the Americas was held in Quebec City, did the Declaration specifically deal with 'the eradication of all forms of discrimination, including racism, racial discrimination, xenophobia and other related intolerance in our societies'.[63] The Plan of Action adopted at the 2001 Summit stated that 'political platforms based

[57] Inter-American Commission on Human Rights, The Situation of People of African Descent in the Americas, 5 December 2011, OEA/Ser.L/V/II., Doc. 62, para. 9.

[58] 'Persecution for racial or religious motives, Resolution XXXVI' (1940) 34 American Journal of International Law Supplement 198; Acta Final de la Conferencia Interamerican sobre Problemas de la Guerra y de la Paz, Ciudad de Mexico, 21 February to 8 May 1945, Washington: Pan American Union, pp. 96–7.

[59] 'Tenth Inter-American Conference', pp. 604–10, at p. 605.

[60] Proyecto de Declaración y Plan de acción, 20 December 2000, WCR/RCONF/SANT/2000/L.1/Rev.4.

[61] Draft Declaration and Plan of Action, A/CONF.189/PC.2/7, PP 12.

[62] Ibid., paras. 27–32.

[63] Declaration of Quebec City, Summit of the Americas, 20–2 April 2001.

PEOPLE OF AFRICAN DESCENT 393

on racism, xenophobia or doctrines of racial superiority must be condemned as incompatible with democracy and transparent and accountable governance'.[64]

The Plan of Action of the Quebec City Summit also supported efforts underway within the Organization of American States directed at developing an inter-American convention against racism and related forms of discrimination and intolerance. In 2005, the General Assembly of the Organization of American States adopted a resolution calling for preparation of a new convention on 'the prevention of racism and all forms of discrimination and intolerance'. Attached to the resolution was a declaration from the United States: 'As there is already a robust global treaty regime on this topic, most notably the International Convention on the Elimination of All Forms of Racial Discrimination to which some 170 countries are States Parties, a regional instrument is not necessary and runs the risk of creating inconsistencies with this global regime'.[65] In the course of negotiations a very detailed and controversial list of prohibited grounds emerged that included sexual orientation, gender identity and expression, educational level, and debilitating psychological condition amongst others.[66] The solution was to split the draft into two instruments, a convention dealing with discrimination on grounds of race, colour, lineage, and national or ethnic origin, and a second convention covering all of the other grounds. The General Assembly of the Organization of American States adopted the Inter-American Convention against Racism, Racial Discrimination and Related Forms of Intolerance in 2013.[67] The Convention gives special attention to people of African descent as victims of racism, racial discrimination, and other related forms of intolerance in the Americas.[68] Again, the United States made a declaration of objection. This time, it was joined by Canada, which stated that it 'has consistently raised concerns about the negotiation of an inter-American convention against all forms of discrimination and intolerance, and is not endorsing the resulting text'.[69] Upon the second ratification, in 2017, it entered into force. As of 1 November 2022, nine years after its adoption, the Convention had only six States Parties. The Inter-American Convention on the Elimination of All Forms of Discrimination and Intolerance, also adopted in 2013, contains a lengthy enumeration of prohibited grounds but no mention whatsoever of either race or colour.[70] Readers who are unaware of the history

---

[64] Plan of Action, Summit of the Americas, 20–2 April 2001.

[65] Prevention of Racism and All Forms of Discrimination and Intolerance and Consideration of the Preparation of a Draft Inter-American Convention, 7 June 2005.

[66] Draft Inter-American Convention against Racism and All Forms of Discrimination and Intolerance, 13 October 2010, OEA/Ser.G CAJP/GT/RDI-148/10, art. 1(1).

[67] Inter-American Convention against Racism, Racial Discrimination and Related Forms of Intolerance, 6 June 2013, OEA/Ser.P AG/RES. 2804 (XLIII-O/13).

[68] Inter-American Convention against Racism, Racial Discrimination and Related Forms of Intolerance, OASTS 68, preamble, para. 6.

[69] Ibid., footnotes 1 and 2.

[70] Inter-American Convention against All Forms of Discrimination and Intolerance, OASTS 69.

of the two instruments will find this to be a bizarre result. The Convention on 'other grounds' entered into force on 20 February 2020 and has only two States Parties. The two Conventions contain identical clauses providing for the creation of the Inter-American Committee for the Prevention and Elimination of Racism, Racial Discrimination, and All Forms of Discrimination and Intolerance. The Committee is only activated when 10 States have ratified one or other of the Conventions.

The human rights institutions of the Organization of American States have devoted attention to discrimination directed at what they refer to as 'Afro-descendant' peoples. In 2005, the Inter-American Commission on Human Rights established the position of Special Rapporteur on the Rights of Persons of African Descent and against Racial Discrimination.[71] The Inter-American Commission on Human Rights issued a substantial report on the situation of people of African descent in the Americas.[72] The General Assembly of the Organization of American States adopted resolutions recognizing the international year and the international decade for people of African Descent.[73] Citing an amicus curiae brief from the Human Rights Clinic of the Universidade da Bahia, the Inter-American Court of Human Rights recognized that following the abolition of slavery, 'the Afro-descendant population of Brazil were denied a series of rights by the State, because the exercise of citizenship was extremely restricted and the rights to housing and property, and entry into the labour market were obstructed'.[74]

Reparations for Slavery, Colonialism

That there should be reparations for serious violations of human rights and for international crimes is uncontroversial. The Basic Principles and Guidelines on the Right to a Remedy and Reparation for Victims of Gross Violations of International Human Rights Law and Serious Violations of International Humanitarian Law, proclaimed by the United Nations General Assembly in 2005, explain that '[a]dequate, effective and prompt reparation is intended to promote justice by redressing gross violations of international human rights law

---

[71] 'IACHR creates Special Rapporteurship on the Rights of Afro-descendants and on Racial Discrimination', Inter-American Commission on Human Rights, Press Release 3/05, 25 February 2005.

[72] The situation of people of African descent in the Americas, 5 December 2011, OEA Ser.L/V/II. Doc.62.

[73] Recognition of the International Year for People of African Descent, 8 June 2010, AG/RES. 2550 (XL-O/10); Recognition of the International Decade for People of African Descent, 4 June 2014, AG/ RES. 2824 (XLIV-O/14).

[74] *Workers of the Fireworks Factory in Santo Antônio de Jesus and their families v. Brazil*, Preliminary objections, merits, reparations and costs, 15 July 2020, para. 57.

REPARATIONS FOR SLAVERY, COLONIALISM   395

or serious violations of international humanitarian law'.[75] The burning question is the temporal scope of this obligation. At what point in history does it begin?

Issues relating to reparation for slavery and colonialism were among the most contentious at the 2001 Durban Conference. The draft Declaration adopted at the regional preparatory meeting for the Americas, held in Santiago, Chile, stated that 'the enslavement and other forms of servitude of Africans and their descendants and of the indigenous peoples of the Americas, as well as the slave trade, were morally reprehensible, in some cases constituted crimes under domestic law and, if they occurred today, would constitute crimes under international law'. Moreover, the Declaration '[a]cknowledge[d] that these practices have resulted in substantial and lasting economic, political and cultural damage to these peoples and that justice now requires that substantial national and international efforts be made to repair such damage. Such reparation should be in the form of policies, programmes and measures to be adopted by the States which benefited materially from these practices, and designed to rectify the economic, cultural and political damage which has been inflicted on the affected communities and peoples'.[76] Canada and the United States of America did not agree to the inclusion of this paragraph.[77]

The African regional preparatory meeting for the Durban Conference, held in Dakar, decided upon an 'International Compensation Scheme' for 'victims of the slave trade, as well as victims of any other transnational racist policies and acts'. It also called for a 'Development Reparation Fund' to provide resources for the development process in countries affected by colonialism. Echoing the formulation at the Santiago meeting, the Dakar declaration concluded that '[o]n a collective basis, such reparation should be in the form of enhanced policies, programmes and measures to be adopted by States which benefit materially from these practices in order to rectify, through affirmative action, the economic, cultural and political damage which has been inflicted on the affected communities and peoples in the full implementation of their right to development'. The meeting included the requirement of an apology by the former colonial powers to victims and descendants of the slave trade and colonialism, and a commitment that reparations be furnished.[78]

The result at the Durban Conference itself on the issue of reparations, according to Marc Bossuyt and Stef Vandeginste, was an 'honourable compromise'

[75] Basic Principles and Guidelines on the Right to a Remedy and Reparation for Victims of Gross Violations of International Human Rights Law and Serious Violations of International Humanitarian Law, 21 March 2006, A/RES/60/147, Annex, paras. 15–23.
[76] Report of the Regional Conference of the Americas (Santiago, Chile, 5–7 December 2000), A/CONF.189/PC.2/8, p. 14, para. 70.
[77] Ibid., Annex IV, p. 52.
[78] Report of the Regional Conference for Africa (Dakar, 22–24 January 2001), A/CONF.189/PC.2/8, p. 8.

based upon common ground for positions that initially seemed irreconcilable.[79] The Durban Declaration recognized that 'some States have taken the initiative to apologise and have paid reparation, where appropriate, for grave and massive violations committed'.[80] In 2019, the Secretary-General referred to this passage in the Durban Declaration and said '[f]ull recognition of past injustices is a constructive foundation for fulfilling the right to development for people of African descent'.[81] But the Durban Declaration stopped short of a clear message setting out an obligation upon States to make reparation for slavery, the slave trade, colonialism, and other wrongs related to racial discrimination perpetrated in the somewhat distant past. The modest and equivocal formulations on reparations in the Durban Declaration nevertheless gave impetus to both legal and political campaigns.[82]

General Assembly resolutions on racial discrimination adopted in 2021 and 2022 '[w]elcom[e] the call upon all the former colonial Powers for reparations, consistent with paragraphs 157 and 158 of the Durban Programme of Action, to redress the historical injustices of slavery and the slave trade, including the transatlantic slave trade'.[83] The paragraphs in question do not refer explicitly to reparations, but they speak of 'historical injustices' that 'have undeniably contributed to the poverty, underdevelopment, marginalization, social exclusion, economic disparities, instability and insecurity that affect many people in different parts of the world, in particular in developing countries'.[84] The reference to 'former colonial powers' rankled. Several voted against the resolution, including Australia, France, Germany, the Netherlands, Spain, the United Kingdom, and the United States of America, as well as some of their close allies such as Canada and Israel.[85]

[79] Marc Bossuyt and Stef Vandeginste, 'The Issue of Reparation for Slavery and Colonialism and the Durban World Conference Against Racism' (2001) 22 *Human Rights Law Journal* 341, at p. 350.

[80] Declaration, A/CONF.189/12, pp. 5–26, paras. 99–100.

[81] Implementation of the activities of the International Decade for People of African Descent, Report of the Secretary-General, 19 August 2019, A/74/308, para. 54.

[82] Michelle E. Lyons, 'World Conference Against Racism: New Avenues for Slavery Reparations?' (2002) 35 *Vanderbilt Journal of Transnational Law* 1235; Penelope E. Andrews, 'Reparations for Apartheid's Victims: The Path to Reconciliation' (2004) 53 *DePaul Law Review* 1155; Martha Biondi, 'The Rise of the Reparations Movement' (2003) 87 *Radical History Review* 5; Eric A. Posner and Adrian Vermeule, 'Reparations for Slavery and Other Historical Injustices' (2003) 103 *Columbia Law Review* 689; Lorenzo Morris, 'Symptoms of Withdrawal – The U.N., The U.S., Racism and Reparations' (2003) 6 *Howard Scroll: The Social Justice Law Review* 49.

[83] A global call for concrete action for the elimination of racism, racial discrimination, xenophobia and related intolerance and the comprehensive implementation of and follow-up to the Durban Declaration and Programme of Action, A/RES/76/226, 24 December 2021, PP 25; A global call for concrete action for the elimination of racism, racial discrimination, xenophobia, and related intolerance and the comprehensive implementation of and follow-up to the Durban Declaration and Programme of Action, A/RES/77/205, 15 December 2022, PP 29.

[84] Declaration, A/CONF.189/12, pp. 5–26, para. 158.

[85] Summary record, Third Committee, 15 November 2021, A/C.3/76/SR.11, para. 132–133.

In its final statement at the Durban Conference, Trinidad and Tobago argued that the World Conference on Racism and Racial Discrimination 'should recognise that these crimes and injustices have undeniably contributed to poverty, underdevelopment, marginalisation, social exclusion, economic disparities, instability and insecurity, which affect many people in different parts of the world, in particular in developing countries. It should therefore call upon those States that practised, benefited or enriched themselves from slavery, the transatlantic slave trade and indentureship to provide reparations to countries and peoples affected, and to adopt appropriate remedial and other measures in order to repair these consequences.'[86] On the other hand, Canada stated, for the record, that 'under international law there is no right to a remedy for historical acts that were not illegal at the time at which they occurred'.[87]

The position put forward by Canada about crimes against humanity, which finds an echo in the Durban Declaration in the strange 'should always have been so' formulation, presents itself as one of strict legality. But it is a flawed proposition. The most extreme form of crime against humanity, genocide, is codified in a Convention adopted in 1948 that recognizes 'that at all periods of history genocide has inflicted great losses on humanity'. The General Assembly resolution that preceded the Convention, adopted unanimously in 1946, says that genocide is 'contrary to moral law'. Did Canada also mean to say that genocide was 'not illegal' when committed prior to 1946? Indeed, this was the very argument advanced by the Nazi defendants at Nuremberg and dismissed by the International Military Tribunal.

Some of the statements at Durban about the temporal application of crimes against humanity were inapposite because the issue is not one of criminal prosecution of individuals for acts perpetrated in the eighteenth and nineteenth centuries. Criminal prosecution does not concern itself with suspects who are already known to be dead and who cannot therefore be punished.[88] The issue of retroactive application of criminal law simply does not arise. Moreover, determining whether slavery and the slave trade were crimes against humanity in past centuries does not resolve whether these practices were illegal, however. The real question is whether the slave trade, slavery, colonialism, and racial discrimination may be considered 'internationally wrongful acts' for which reparation, in various forms, may be required. There can be no principled objection to

---

[86] Report of the World Conference against racism, racial discrimination, xenophobia, and related intolerance, Durban, 31 August–8 September 2001, A/CONF.189/12, p. 131.

[87] Ibid., p. 121.

[88] Wolfgang Kaleck, 'On Double Standards and Emerging European Custom on Accountability for Colonial Crimes', in Morten Bergsmo, Wolfgang Kaleck, and Kyaw Yin Hlaing, eds., *Colonial Wrongs and Access to International Law*, Brussels: Torkel Opsahl Academic EPublisher, 2020, pp. 1–40, at p. 38; Transitional justice measures and addressing the legacy of gross violations of human rights and international humanitarian law committed in colonial contexts, 19 July 2021, A/76/180, para 32.

international law recalibrating its assessment of the past and declaring that certain acts perpetrated in the past are, in light of evolving values, now deemed to be wrongful and therefore deserving of compensation or reparation. The technical arguments mounted by Canada and others seemingly suggest that the whole notion of reparation is inadmissible whereas in fact the real rationale is simply the refusal to recognize an obligation arising from wrongful acts in the past.[89]

The intertemporality objection also disregards the fact that the alleged legality of colonialism and the slave trade in the past is premised on legal norms that were not at all universal. It was the colonialists, not the colonized, who declared that their practises were legal under international law. It was those who traded in slaves who made the rule permitting this barbaric and inhumane practise in previous centuries. The prohibition of slavery and the slave trade is recognized as a norm of *jus cogens*.[90] Such fundamental principles are often confounded with norms of customary law but in fact they are a quite distinct source of international law. They constitute a body of human values, universal in nature. To contend that practices rooted in racism were actually lawful only a few hundred years ago merely because they were then carried out with impunity by a small number of powerful states is a preposterous suggestion.

The struggle to recognize an obligation of reparation as a matter of international law continues. As the Special rapporteur on contemporary forms of racism, racial discrimination, xenophobia, and related intolerance, Tendayi Achiume, has explained, 'the pursuit and achievement of reparations for slavery and colonialism require a genuine "decolonisation" of the doctrines of international law that remain barriers to reparations'.[91] The Special rapporteur issued a thematic report on reparations in 2019. She explained that reparations for slavery and colonialism go beyond justice and accountability for historic wrongs. They also involve 'eradication of persisting structures of racial inequality, subordination and discrimination that were built under slavery and colonialism to deprive non-whites of their fundamental human rights'. According to the Special rapporteur, a persisting legacy of slavery and colonialism contributes to the unequal application of the law to descendants of historically enslaved and colonized people.[92] She said that 'the urgent project of providing reparations for slavery and colonialism requires States not only to fulfil remedial obligations resulting from specific historical wrongful acts, but also to transform contemporary

[89] On the subject of 'intertemporality', see Andreas von Arnauld, 'How to Illegalize Past Injustice: Reinterpreting the Rules of Intertemporality' (2021) 32 *European Journal of International Law* 401.

[90] Fourth report on peremptory norms of general international law (*jus cogens*) by Dire Tladi, Special Rapporteur, A/CN.4/727, paras. 102–7.

[91] Contemporary forms of racism, racial discrimination, xenophobia and racial intolerance, 21 August 2019, A/74/321, para. 10.

[92] Ibid., para. 7.

structures of racial injustice, inequality, discrimination and subordination that are the product of the centuries of racial machinery built through slavery and colonialism'.[93] The Special rapporteur has set out a detailed demonstration of the basis in contemporary international law of the obligation upon those States that bear some responsibility for slavery, the slave trade, and colonialism, and those who profited from these abuses, to provide reparations. 'The intention of the Special Rapporteur is not to trivialize the practical hurdles to the legal determination of reparations; her intention is instead to insist that, with the requisite political will and moral courage, much more could be done through legal and political channels to pursue meaningful reparations for colonialism and slavery', she explained.[94]

'People of African descent have a right to reparations, which should be proportional to the gravity of the violations and the harm suffered', the Working Group of Experts on People of African Descent has stated. In addition to financial inequalities associated with the consequences of the trade in enslaved Africans, the Working Group has pointed to other injustices, 'such as intergenerational health issues, disproportionately high illiteracy rates and the erasure of collective culture, history and identity. Reparations include the right to restitution, rehabilitation, compensation, and safeguarding and protection from future violations.'[95] In a report on the United Kingdom, the Working Group contemplated an acknowledgement of 'the historic reasons for the current situation of people of African descent' and urged that they be addressed through an apology for colonial wrongs and reparation.[96] It has encouraged the initiatives within the Congress of the United States to address reparations for slavery and racial discrimination.[97] The Working Group recommended that Canada issue an apology and consider providing reparations to African Canadians 'for enslavement and historical injustices'.[98]

The Office of the High Commissioner for Human Rights, in its 2021 report to the Human Rights Council, referred to a number of measures that have been taken in the spirit of addressing responsibility for historic injustices. 'Yet, no State has comprehensively accounted for the past or for the current impact of systemic racism', said the report. 'Some have argued against accountability and redress for

---

[93] Ibid., para. 8.

[94] Ibid., para. 51.

[95] Report of the Working Group of Experts on People of African Descent on its 21st and 22nd sessions, 15 August 2018, A/HRC/39/69, para. 61.

[96] Report of the Working Group of Experts on People of African Descent on its 12th session, Addendum, Mission to the United Kingdom of Great Britain and Northern Ireland, 5 August 2013, A/HRC/24/52/Add.1, para. 109.

[97] Report of the Working Group of Experts on People of African Descent on its mission to the United States of America, 18 August 2016, A/HRC/33/61/Add.2, para. 94.

[98] Report of the Working Group of Experts on People of African Descent on its mission to Canada, 16 August 2017, A/HRC/36/60/Add.1.

historical legacies, citing the complexity of considering centuries-old serious human rights violations and abuses involving now-deceased perpetrators and victims and the presumption that the harms of systemic racism ended with the abolition of chattel slavery. Additionally, delineations of State responsibility and the design and financing of effective reparations programmes that address the temporal and material scope and possible beneficiaries require further definition and negotiation – including but not limited to specific concerns about financial compensation claims.' According to the Office of the High Commissioner, overcoming these hurdles is simply a matter of 'political leadership, creative responses, empowerment measures and honest dialogue about the impact of these legacies on contemporary forms of racism'.[99]

The Caribbean Community (CARICOM) has undertaken an ambitious campaign for reparations. In 2013, the Caricom Reparations Commission was established to prepare the case. The Commission has highlighted the special role and status of European governments as the bodies that instituted the framework and sustained the historic crimes against humanity. Moreover, they were the primary agencies for the wealth that the slave-based economies generated. The Commission developed a Ten-Point Action Plan for reparations.[100] Reparations are understood in a broad sense, 'a creative way of weaving together different elements of reparatory justice. Apology, repatriation, indigenous people's development, cultural institutions such as museums and research centres, public health initiatives, literacy, African knowledge programmes, technology transfer and debt cancellation, are among the points raised in this action plan.'[101]

Intersectionality

The preamble to the Convention on the Elimination of All Forms of Discrimination Against Women, adopted by the General Assembly in 1979 and in force since 1981, '[e]mphasi[ses] that the eradication of apartheid, of all

---

[99] Promotion and protection of the human rights and fundamental freedoms of Africans and of people of African descent against excessive use of force and other human rights violations by law enforcement officers, 1 June 2021, A/HRC/47/53, para. 60.

[100] Jose Atiles-Osoria, 'Colonial State Crimes and the CARICOM Mobilization for Reparation and Justice' (2018) 7 *State Crime Journal* 349, at pp. 361–3. See also V.P. Franklin, 'Commentary – Reparation as Development Strategy: The CARICOM Reparations Commission' (2013) 98 *Journal of African American History* 363; Jada Benn Torres, '"Reparational" Genetics: Genomic Data and the Case for Reparations in the Caribbean' (2018) 2 *Genealogy* 7; James B. Stewart, 'V.P. Franklin and the Case for Reparations' (2017) 102 *Journal of African American History* 341; David Jobbins, 'Has the Commonwealth a Role to Play in the Row over Reparations for the Slave Trade?' (2014) 103 *The Round Table* 343.

[101] Report of the Working Group of Experts on People of African Descent on its 17th and 18th sessions, 19 July 2016, A/HRC/33/61, para. 54.

forms of racism, racial discrimination, colonialism, neo-colonialism, aggression, foreign occupation and domination and interference in the internal affairs of States is essential to the full enjoyment of the rights of men and women'.[102] Kimberlé Crenshaw's seminal essay, published in 1989, introduced the term 'intersectionality' to highlight the relationship between racial discrimination and discrimination against women.[103] She described it in this way:

> Consider an analogy to traffic in an intersection, coming and going in all four directions. Discrimination, like traffic through an intersection, may flow in one direction, and it may flow in another. If an accident happens in an intersection, it can be caused by cars traveling from any number of directions and, sometimes, from all of them. Similarly, if a Black woman is harmed because she is in an intersection, her injury could result from sex discrimination or race discrimination. . . But it is not always easy to reconstruct an accident: Sometimes the skid marks and the injuries simply indicate that they occurred simultaneously, frustrating efforts to determine which driver caused the harm.[104]

The metaphor suggests an inability to identify a specific cause whereas intersectionality has probably come to be understood as a cumulative phenomenon.

Crenshaw brought the issue to a preparatory session for the Durban Conference, for which she was the Rapporteur, in a background paper entitled 'Gender-related aspects of race discrimination'.[105] It was subsequently endorsed in a submission to the Conference by Radhika Coomaraswamy, Special Rapporteur on violence against women, on the subject of race, gender and violence against women. 'Gender-based discrimination intersects with discriminations based on other forms of "otherness", such as race, ethnicity, religion and economic status, thus forcing the majority of the world's women into situations of double or triple marginalization', wrote Coomaraswamy. 'The combined effects of racism and gender discrimination on migrant, immigrant, indigenous, minority and marginalized women, in particular, around the world has had devastating consequences for their full enjoyment of equality and fundamental human rights in both the public and private spheres.'[106]

---

[102] Convention on the Elimination of All Forms of Discrimination Against Women (1981) 1249 UNTS 13, PP 10.

[103] Kimberlé Crenshaw, 'Demarginalizing the Intersection of Race and Sex: A Black Feminist Critique of Antidiscrimination Doctrine, Feminist Theory and Antiracist Politics' [1989] *University of Chicago Legal Forum* 139.

[104] Ibid., p. 149.

[105] Kimberlé Crenshaw, 'Gender-related aspects of race discrimination, background paper for Expert Meeting on Gender and Racial Discrimination, 21–24 November 2000, Zagreb, Croatia', EM/GRD/ 2000/WP.1.

[106] Review of reports, studies and other documentation for the Preparatory Committee and the World Conference, 27 July 2001, A/CONF.189/PC.3/5, para. 2.

The notion was reflected, but only modestly, in the Durban Declaration, where there is a reference to 'the multiple forms of discrimination which women can face' and the assertion that 'that racism, racial discrimination, xenophobia and related intolerance reveal themselves in a differentiated manner for women and girls'. It also referred to multiple forms of discrimination that afflict indigenous and migrant women. Over time, the concept of intersectionality has been extended to a broad range of inequalities, in some cases departing entirely from any focus on racial discrimination. According to the Committee for the Elimination of Discrimination Against Women, intersectionality means that 'discrimination of women based on sex and gender is inextricably linked with other factors that affect women, such as race, ethnicity, religion or belief, health, status, age, class, caste and sexual orientation and gender identity'.[107]

Intersectionality has been embraced within the Inter-American regional system for the protection of human rights. The Inter-American Commission on Human Rights has said it considers it 'essential that States recognize the multiple discrimination endured by Afro-descendant women because of their gender and race, and that they compile disaggregated data on the situation and living conditions of Afro-descendant women'.[108] In a 2020 judgment, the Inter-American Court of Human Rights condemned the 'intersection of factors of discrimination' where victims 'suffered a specific form of discrimination owing to the confluence' of poverty, gender, and Afrodescendance.[109]

Tendayi Achiume has warned against reducing intersectionality to the inclusion of references to gender in policy documents. 'Intersectionality is vital to achieving substantive equality but it requires attention to all the operational social categories that shape the experience of discrimination and intolerance: race, gender, ethnicity, national origin, class, religion, disability status, sex, sexual orientation and others', she has written. 'True racial equality requires taking seriously the experiences and expertise of cis and transwomen, LGBTQ persons, persons with disabilities, the poor, the undocumented and other marginalized groups.'[110]

---

[107] General Recommendation No. 28 on the Core Obligations of States Parties under Article 2 of the Convention on the Elimination of All Forms of Discrimination against Women, 18 December 2010, CEDAW/C/GC/28, para. 18.

[108] The situation of people of African descent in the Americas, 5 December 2011, OEA Ser.L/V/II. Doc.62, pp. 23–9.

[109] *Workers of the Fireworks Factory in Santo Antônio de Jesus and their families v. Brazil*, Preliminary objections, merits, reparations and costs, 15 July 2020, Series C, No. 407, para. 191. Also para. 197.

[110] E. Tendayi Achiume, 'Putting Racial Equality onto the Global Human Rights Agenda' (2018) 28 *SUR – International Journal on Human Rights* 141, at p. 146.

The Murder of George Floyd

On 25 May 2020, an African American man of 46 years of age, George Floyd, was killed when a white American policeman, Derek Chauvin, knelt on his neck for several minutes. Floyd was being apprehended by the Minneapolis police on suspicion of using a counterfeit $20 bill. At the time Floyd was handcuffed and lying face down on the street. This was all filmed by several bystanders, some of whom pleaded with the police to release Floyd. Before he lost consciousness, Floyd had said 'I can't breathe'. Chauvin was later convicted of his murder.

The crime provoked global protests centred on the slogan 'Black Lives Matter'. Within days, nearly 70 of the Human Rights Council's independent experts issued a joint statement on systemic racism in the United States. 'The protests the world is witnessing, are a rejection of the fundamental racial inequality and discrimination that characterise life in the United States for black people, and other people of colour', they said. The human rights experts said that '[r]eparative intervention for historical and contemporary racial injustice is urgent' and that it was required by international human rights law. They also condemned the President of the United States, Donald Trump, for a response that threatened more state violence and that used 'language directly associated with racial segregationists from the nation's past, who worked hard to deny black people fundamental human rights'.[111] Previously, the Committee on the Elimination of Racial Discrimination had denounced 'the failure at the highest political level of the United States of America' following the violent demonstrations in Charlottesville in 2017,[112] but actually naming the American President was unprecedented.

Shortly thereafter, the Committee on the Elimination of Racial Discrimination issued a statement in accordance with its Early Warning and Urgent Action Procedures that expressed alarm at the 'horrific killing' of George Floyd but also at 'the recurrence of killings of unarmed African Americans by police officers and individuals over the years'. The Committee said it was '[c]onvinced that systemic and structural discrimination permeates State institutions and disproportionately promotes racial disparities against African Americans, notably in the enjoyment of the rights to equal treatment before the tribunals, security of person and protection by the State against violence or bodily harm, and other civil, economic, social and cultural rights'. The Committee urged the United States Government to recognize 'the existence of structural racial discrimination in the society, as well as to unequivocally and unconditionally reject and condemn racially motivated killings of African Americans and other minorities'.[113]

---

[111] Statement on the Protests against Systemic Racism in the United States, 5 June 2020.

[112] Decision 1 (93) on the United States of America, 18 August 2017, A/73/186, p. 6.

[113] Committee on the Elimination of All Forms of Racial Discrimination, Statement 1 (2020), United States of America, 12 June 2020.

404   THE COLOUR LINE'S LONG TWENTIETH CENTURY

On 17 June 2020, Philonese Floyd, George's brother, addressed the Human Rights Council during an Urgent Debate called for by the African Group. He emphasized the fact that his brother was unarmed, describing how he and his family had witnessed the murder which had been captured on camera. After the killing, the Minneapolis police used tear gas and rubber bullets in attacking those who demonstrated peacefully. The sad truth was that George Floyd's case was not unique; it represented the way Black people were treated in the United States, his brother told the Human Rights Council. Philonese Floyd specifically called for the Council to establish an independent commission of inquiry to investigate police killings of Black people in the United States and the violence used against peaceful protesters.[114]

The Council subsequently adopted a resolution that '[s]trongly condemns the continuing racially discriminatory and violent practices perpetrated by law enforcement agencies against Africans and people of African descent, in particular which led to the death of George Floyd on 25 May 2020 in Minnesota . . . and the deaths of other people of African descent, and also condemns the structural racism in the criminal justice system'.[115] A fierce text prepared by the African Group[116] was much diluted, a consequence of 'geopolitical bullying' by the United States, the European Union and other members of the Western European and Other Group.[117] In its resolution, the Council recalled the Durban Declaration and Programme of Action. The resolution made an extraordinary historical reference, taking note of a resolution on racial discrimination in the United States of America adopted at the first ordinary session of the Assembly of African Heads of State and Government of the Organization of African Unity, in July 1964. That Declaration had welcomed the enactment of the Civil Rights Act but also said the Assembly was '[d]eeply disturbed, however, by continuing manifestations of racial bigotry and racial oppression against Negro citizens of the United States of

[114] Press release, 'Human Rights Council Holds an Urgent Debate on Current Racially Inspired Human Rights Violations, Systemic Racism, Police Brutality, and Violence against Peaceful Protests', 17 June 2020.

[115] Promotion and protection of the human rights and fundamental freedoms of Africans and of people of African descent against excessive use of force and other human rights violations by law enforcement officers, 19 June 2020, A/HRC/RES/43/1, OP 1.

[116] Burkina Faso, Iran (Islamic Republic of) and State of Palestine: draft resolution, A/HRC/43/L.50, 17 June 2020.

[117] E. Tendayi Achiume, 'Transnational Racial (In)Justice in Liberal Democratic Empire' (2021) 134 *Harvard Law Review Forum* 378, at pp. 387–8. Also Sejal Parmar, 'The Internationalisation of Black Lives Matter at the Human Rights Council', *EJIL Talk!*, 26 June 2020; Lawrence Hill-Cawthorne, 'Racism will not Pass', *EJIL Talk!*, 20 July 2020; Thiago Amparo and Andressa Vieira e Silva, 'George Floyd at the UN: Whiteness, International Law' (2022) 7 *UC Irvine Journal of International, Transnational and Comparative Law* 91; Balthazar I. Beckett and Salimah K. Hankins, ' "Until We Are First Recognized as Humans": The Killing of George Floyd and the Case for Black Life at the United Nations' (2021) *International Journal of Human Rights Education* 1.

America'.[118] The reference to the OAU resolution had originated in the African Group draft. But the final resolution treads softly on the United States. An NGO statement charged that '[s]hifting the resolution from being specific to the U.S. to being generic has served to subvert the debate into an "all lives matter" discussion which has rendered invisible those who needed to be at the very centre of the Council's action'.[119]

The African Group draft had called for creation of a commission of inquiry, a radical proposal that did not succeed. Instead, the Human Rights Council mandated the High Commissioner for Human Rights to prepare a report on systemic racism, violations of international human rights law against Africans and people of African descent by law enforcement agencies, especially those incidents that resulted in the death of George Floyd and other Africans and people of African descent.[120] When the report was issued in June 2021 the High Commissioner praised the Black Lives Matter movement, saying that 'the worldwide mobilisation of people calling for racial justice has forced a long-delayed reckoning with racism and shifted debates towards a focus on the systemic nature of racism and the institutions that perpetrate it'.[121] The High Commissioner's report charged that 'some States – especially those with links to enslavement, the transatlantic trade in enslaved Africans and colonialism – continue to deny or have failed to acknowledge the existence and impact of systemic racism, especially institutional racism, against Africans and people of African descent; or its linkages with enslavement and colonialism'.[122]

'The murder of George Floyd on 25 May 2020 and the ensuing mass protests worldwide have marked a watershed in the fight against racism', said the High Commissioner's report. It noted that '[t]he dehumanisation of people of African descent . . . has sustained and cultivated a tolerance for racial discrimination, inequality and violence'. According to the report, available data produces 'an alarming picture of system-wide, disproportionate and discriminatory impacts

---

[118] Promotion and protection of the human rights and fundamental freedoms of Africans and of people of African descent against excessive use of force and other human rights violations by law enforcement officers, 19 June 2020, A/HRC/RES/43/1, PP 9. See Racial Discrimination in the United States of America: Resolution Adopted by the Assembly of Heads of State and Government of the OAU, Cairo, 21 July 1964, in *American Foreign Policy, Current Documents, 1964*, Washington: Department of State, 1967, p. 739.

[119] Joint NGO statement following the adoption of HRC resolution on systemic racism and police violence following the Urgent Debate, 23 June 2020.

[120] Promotion and protection of the human rights and fundamental freedoms of Africans and of people of African descent against excessive use of force and other human rights violations by law enforcement officers, A/HRC/RES/43/1, OP 3.

[121] UN Human Rights Chief urges immediate, transformative action to uproot systemic racism, 28 June 2021.

[122] Promotion and protection of the human rights and fundamental freedoms of Africans and of people of African descent against excessive use of force and other human rights violations by law enforcement officers, 28 June 2021, A/HRC/47/CRP.1, para. 41.

on people of African descent in their encounters with law enforcement and the criminal justice system in some States'. Seven illustrative cases, four of them drawn from permanent members of the Security Council, were examined in some detail: Luana Barbosa dos Reis Santos and João Pedro Matos Pinto (Brazil); George Floyd and Breonna Taylor (United States); Kevin Clarke (United Kingdom); Janner (Hanner) García Palomino (Colombia), and Adama Traoré (France). The Report addressed the repression of anti-racism demonstrations in the wake of the murder of George Floyd. It also identified a 'long-overdue need to confront the legacies of enslavement, the transatlantic trade in enslaved Africans and colonialism, and to seek reparatory justice'.[123]

The High Commissioner's report also spoke to the issue of health care for people of African descent. Citing higher mortality rates at all ages as well as higher incidences of poor health compared with other groups. The report described incidents of racial prejudice and stereotypes from health care providers. It said that in the United Kingdom, although maternal mortality is now at very low levels the disparity between Black and white women has actually widened, with Black British mothers five times more likely than white women to die during pregnancy or in the weeks following.[124] Obstacles in gaining equal access to quality education are also encountered, with reports of children of African descent being awarded lower grades and being diverted to vocational or manual training.[125]

Prompted by the High Commissioner's report, and with an explicit reference to the murder of George Floyd, in July 2021 the Human Rights Council voted to establish the International Independent Expert Mechanism to Advance Racial Justice and Equality in the context of Law Enforcement, in order to further transformative change for racial justice and equality in the context of law enforcement globally, especially where relating to the legacies of colonialism and the Transatlantic slave trade in enslaved Africans, to investigate Governments' responses to peaceful anti-racism protests and all violations of international

---

[123] Promotion and protection of the human rights and fundamental freedoms of Africans and of people of African descent against excessive use of force and other human rights violations by law enforcement officers, Report of the United Nations High Commissioner for Human Rights, 1 June 2021, A/HRC/47/53. The 23-page Report is accompanied by a much longer version, known as a 'Conference Room Paper': Promotion and protection of the human rights and fundamental freedoms of Africans and of people of African descent against excessive use of force and other human rights violations by law enforcement officers: Promotion and protection of the human rights and fundamental freedoms of Africans and of people of African descent against excessive use of force and other human rights violations by law enforcement officers, 28 June 2021, A/HRC/47/CRP.1. Conference room papers are a technique to bypass General Assembly regulations on the length of reports. They are not normally translated into the official languages of the United Nations.

[124] Promotion and protection of the human rights and fundamental freedoms of Africans and of people of African descent against excessive use of force and other human rights violations by law enforcement officers, 28 June 2021, A/HRC/47/CRP.1, para. 28.

[125] Ibid., para. 26.

human rights law and to contribute to accountability and redress for victims'.[126] The Mechanism is chaired by Yvonne Mokgoro, a former justice of the South African Constitutional Court, who is joined by two other experts, Tracie Keesee and Juan Méndez. Its initial focus has been on the collection of data on criminal justice and policing that is disaggregated by race and ethnic origin.[127]

The legacy of Durban has remained controversial. In 2020, the Human Rights Council was able to adopt a resolution marking the twentieth commemoration of the great conference without a vote.[128] However, in the Third Committee of the General Assembly there were objections from the usual sources. Israel called for a vote.[129] It opposed the resolution, along with Australia, Canada, Czechia, France, Germany, Hungary, Marshall Islands, Nauru, Slovenia, the United Kingdom, and the United States.[130] The European Union, on the other hand, insisted that it 'remained firmly committed to the primary objectives and commitments undertaken' at Durban, while expressing disappointment that none of its suggestions had been incorporated into the text.[131] Its Member States abstained in the vote. A resolution setting out the modalities of the commemoration was adopted without a vote.[132]

On 22 September 2021, a high-level session of the General Assembly commemorated the Durban Declaration and Programme of Action. South Africa's President, Matamela Cyril Ramaphosa, called upon the United Nations to place the issue of reparations for victims of the slave trade on its agenda, expressing support for such special measures as affirmative action programmes and targeted financial assistance. The High Commissioner for Human Rights, Michelle Bachelet, cautioned that the legacy of colonialism and enslavement continued to have real and lasting consequences. She said they must be addressed by the provision of broad-based reparations, formal acknowledgement of, and apologies for, past harms, and by implementation of educational reforms and other systemic measures.[133]

---

[126] Promotion and protection of the human rights and fundamental freedoms of Africans and of people of African descent against excessive use of force and other human rights violations by law enforcement officers through transformative change for racial justice and equality, A/HCR/RES/47/21, 13 July 2021, para. 10.

[127] Report of the International Independent Expert Mechanism to Advance Racial Justice and Equality in Law Enforcement, 4 August 2022, A/HRC/51/55.

[128] Commemoration of the twentieth anniversary of the adoption of the Durban Declaration and Programme of Action, 6 October 2020, A/HRC/RES/45/23.

[129] Summary record, Third Committee, 19 November 2020, A/C.3/75/SR.15, para. 14.

[130] Ibid., paras. 23–4.

[131] Ibid., para. 10.

[132] Commemoration of the twentieth anniversary of the adoption of the Durban Declaration and Programme of Action, 6 October 2020, A/HRC/RES/45/23; Scope, modalities, format and organization of the high-level meeting of the General Assembly to commemorate the twentieth anniversary of the adoption of the Durban Declaration and Programme of Action, 2 September 2021, A/RES/75/320; Verbatim record, plenary General Assembly, 2 September 2021, A/75/PV.100, pp. 1–4.

[133] World Leaders Vow Accelerated Fight against Racism, as General Assembly Adopts Text Marking Adoption of Durban Declaration, Action Programme, 22 September 2021, GA/12365.

The political declaration adopted on 22 September 2021 '[r]eaffirm[ed] that the Durban Declaration and Programme of Action, adopted in 2001, and the outcome document of the Durban Review Conference, adopted in 2009, as well as the political declaration on the occasion of the tenth anniversary of the adoption of the Durban Declaration and Programme of Action, provide a comprehensive United Nations framework and solid foundation for combating racism, racial discrimination, xenophobia and related intolerance, and reaffirm[ed] our commitment to their full and effective implementation'.[134] The political declaration was significantly longer and more robust than the one adopted a decade earlier.

Coda: Some Conclusions

This book began with a project focussed on the issue of racial discrimination and its place within the development of international human rights law more generally. Racial discrimination is one of many issues within the broader rubric of human rights. That it is particularly prominent seems self-evident given that one of the nine core human rights treaties, of the United Nations system, and indeed the first of the nine to be adopted and to enter into force, is devoted to the subject. Furthermore, it has been the subject of a series of important international conferences convened by the United Nations. Yet it has had to struggle, constantly, for its rightful place at the epicentre of human rights activities. The Special rapporteur, Tendayi Achiume, has spoken of the 'general marginality of racial equality within the global human rights agenda, and among those who wield power in the formation and execution of this agenda'.[135] She has observed that since the International Convention on the Elimination of All Forms of Racial Discrimination was adopted, in 1965, 'racial equality has seemingly drifted to the margins of the global human rights agenda'.[136] The human rights movement owes a great debt to the campaign against racism and racial discrimination because its contribution went well beyond the issues with which it was directly concerned. The campaign against racial discrimination has served as the beating heart of international human rights. This is one of the themes that emerged in the course of this research.

'People of African descent continue to suffer from a lack of knowledge and recognition of their history, including the wrongs and racial injustices they suffer,

---

[134] United against racism, racial discrimination, xenophobia and related intolerance, 22 September 2021, A/RES/76/1, OP 1.

[135] E. Tendayi Achiume, 'Putting Racial Equality onto the Global Human Rights Agenda' (2018) 28 *SUR – International Journal on Human Rights* 141, at p. 142.

[136] Ibid., p. 144.

culture, heritage and contributions', explains the 2021 report of the Office of the High Commissioner for Human Rights. 'Their history remains insufficiently or inaccurately addressed in educational curricula, particularly in relation to enslavement, the transatlantic trade in enslaved Africans and colonialism.'[137] The Programme of Action adopted at the Durban Conference urged that 'the marginalisation of Africa's contribution to world history and civilisation' be redressed.[138] One of the objectives of this study has been to record the contribution made by people of colour, especially by people of African descent, to the progressive development of international law. International human rights law is no exception to a pattern whereby their role has been neglected, overlooked, and even deliberately ignored. In particular, histories of the development of international human rights law and the international human rights movement emphasize the role of intellectuals from Europe and North America. Little if anything is said of the pivotal contribution that States of the Global South, their leaders, diplomats, and activists, have played in promoting the global human rights agenda. Henry Richardson cited the great Howard Law School Dean Charles Hamilton Houston, who often observed that 'nobody needs to explain to African Americans the difference between law in the books and law in action. In international law the racial battle lines are not yet quite as clear as in American law, but the discrimination and marginalisation of peoples of colour are no less real.'[139]

The narrative of the engagement of people of African descent in international law can be traced to the efforts of W.E.B. Du Bois, Marcus Garvey, Dantès Bellegarde, and Blaise Diagne, who campaigned at the Paris Peace Conference and in the early years of the League of Nations. Nor should the contributions of diplomats and activists from Asia be gainsaid, including the Japanese and Chinese delegates to the Peace Conference. The voices of these pioneers were loud and determined, but also polite, and the impact was modest. At the next great moment in international law-making, following the Second World War, there was a somewhat more developed participation from the Global South. Although grossly under-represented in the United Nations General Assembly, the delegates from India, Egypt, Haiti, Liberia, amongst others, nevertheless took the lead in promoting fundamental human rights, where their attention was focussed on racial equality and related issues.

---

[137] Promotion and protection of the human rights and fundamental freedoms of Africans and of people of African descent against excessive use of force and other human rights violations by law enforcement officers, 28 June 2021, A/HRC/47/CRP.1, para. 38.

[138] Programme of Action, A/CONF.189/12, pp. 28–66, para. 118.

[139] Henry J. Richardson III, 'Excluding Race Strategies from International Legal History: The Self-Executing Treaty Doctrine and the Southern Africa Tripartite Agreement' (2000) 45 *Villanova Law Review* 1091, at p. 1093.

The purpose is not to dispute the validity of well-known elements of the Eurocentric vision but rather to demonstrate that it provides an incomplete picture of the origins of human rights within international law. The Global South contributed not by means of precedents drawn from constitutional documents that had emerged in rebellions against feudalism but through inexorable pressure to promote equality, and especially racial equality, to the top of the agenda. These efforts were all the more essential because they were constantly resisted by the very States of the Global North who claimed authorship of the great statements of human rights. The political and legal culture of Britain, France, and the United States was the source of noble declarations recognizing freedom and equality. Yet that same culture had been infected for centuries with racism and notions of white supremacy which were the inseparable accompaniments of colonialism, the slave trade, and segregation. The Western States vaunted the entrenchment of fundamental rights within their domestic legal orders, offering it as a contribution to universality. Yet they could never rid themselves of the pervasive racism that seemed inseparable from their sense of moral entitlement. Too often, historians ask us to overlook this dimension as if it were nothing more than an inconvenient detail.

Students of international human rights law are often intrigued about the pattern of development of specific treaties and other instruments. Why is it that the General Assembly adopted a specialized convention on racial discrimination, in 1965, even before it could agree on general overarching treaties on human rights? The answer, of course, is hiding in plain sight. In 1945, when the Charter of the United Nations was adopted, there was no master plan for the development of human rights law whereby racial discrimination would be given priority, taking precedence over all other issues. Indeed, as Chapter 2 of this study explains, racial discrimination did not receive appropriate attention in the Charter, something largely explained by the profile of the delegates in San Francisco. Yet almost immediately racial discrimination jumped to the top of the agenda as the theme of the major human rights resolutions adopted by the General Assembly at its first session, in 1946. The first human rights treaty adopted within the United Nations system, the Convention on the Prevention and Punishment of the Crime of Genocide, dealing with the ultimate form of racial discrimination, followed in 1948. It was proposed by countries of the South who were dissatisfied with the shortcomings of the Nuremberg judgment. The first United Nations fact-finding commission into human rights abuses, in the early 1950s, focussed on another manifestation of racial discrimination, apartheid. It was a pioneering initiative in an organization where many States thought such inquiries to be beyond the organization's authority under the Charter.

But until the 1960s, the work of the human rights organs of the United Nations was modest indeed. The Commission on Human Rights and the Sub-Commission on the Prevention of Discrimination and the Protection of Minorities remained dominated by representatives of Western States. That began to change in 1960, as newly independent African States joined the United Nations and quickly put pressure to reshape the agenda. Their passion, first and foremost, was the elimination of racial discrimination. Had they not insisted, it is impossible that the International Convention on the Elimination of All Forms of Racial Discrimination would have been adopted so quickly. Indeed, it might never have been adopted at all. Arguably, the momentum that they generated also helped get the two Covenants, which had lingered in the doldrums for many years, over the finish line. From that great success of the Convention on racial discrimination, the Global South turned its attention to the Apartheid Convention, which was adopted in 1973. An independent observer in the mid-1970s, assessing the development of human rights law, might well have concluded that racial discrimination was the overarching theme. As this book has attempted to show, such development took place in the face of resistance by Western States, the very countries who in previous centuries had developed a world order premised on the colour line. Without the inexorable pressure from countries of the South, especially Africa, the United Nations human rights regime more generally would have been weaker and less effective.

During this period, Western States that would later present themselves as the vanguard of global human rights were either silent or quite deliberately obstructive. When the African States put forward progressive resolutions in the General Assembly on issues like racial discrimination and accountability for international crimes, the Western States cast negative votes or abstained. They also opposed initiatives from African States and their allies aimed at creation of a permanent international criminal court and recognition of the principle of universal jurisdiction. By the 1990s, governments in European and North America were vocal advocates of international justice, conveniently forgetting how they had stymied its development only a decade or two earlier. Some of them had a vision of an international criminal court that would be directed from the North but that would target the South. Indeed, to some extent it seems that this is what they got. After nearly two decades of activity, the International Criminal Court has yet to try anyone who is not African. The photos of the accused persons on the website of the Court are reminiscent of those on the 'most wanted men' posters of apartheid South Africa and in the United States of Jim Crow. The 2021 report of the Office of the High Commissioner for Human Rights pointed to distortions in the national criminal justice systems of many countries, where the presence of persons of African descent is disproportionate to their place in the overall population. The report might well have added the International Criminal Court.

Historian Eric Hobsbawm wrote of a 'long nineteenth century' that began with the French revolution and ended with the First World War. It was followed by the 'short twentieth century', barely 80 years long, concluding with the end of the Cold War around 1990. Conceptualizing history in terms of 'ages' or 'eras' is nothing new, of course. When W.E.B. Du Bois described the twentieth century as that of the colour line he surely did not contemplate a period of exactly 100 years with a precise beginning and an end. Rather, his was an inspired attempt to understand one of the great themes of the modern era. It is tempting to merge the Du Bois thesis with Hobsbawm's 'short twentieth century', starting with the frustrated Japanese initiative at the Paris Peace Conference in 1919 and concluding with the end of apartheid, which conveniently coincides with the fall of the Berlin wall and the collapse of the Soviet Union. Another approach might be to end the twentieth century of W.E.B. Du Bois with the Durban Conference of 2001.

The colour line did not come to an end in either 1990 or in 2001. The global colour line continues to mark our planet. It manifests itself in many ways. The reparations debate that took on so much importance at the Durban Conference was left unresolved. It is underpinned by a recognition that contemporary inequalities that can be explained by race or colour are the consequence of historic crimes associated with slavery, the slave trade, and colonialism. Mere acknowledgement of this is not enough. The colour line also appears in patterns of State violence. Here the murder of George Floyd in 2020 is the paradigm. The COVID-19 pandemic highlighted the unequal treatment, where persons living on one side of the colour line did not have the same access to vaccines and other medical treatment as those who lived on the other. It was painfully visible during the Russian invasion of Ukraine in 2022, with the generous welcome provided to war refugees by countries that had closed their borders to those fleeing persecution from the other side of the colour line.[140] The Committee on the Elimination of Racial Discrimination expressed alarm about 'reports of discriminatory treatment of people attempting to flee Ukraine into neighbouring countries, in particular people of African, Asian, Middle Eastern and Latin American descent'.[141]

---

[140] See 'Ukraine: UN experts concerned by reports of discrimination against people of African descent at border' of 3 March 2022, issued by the Working Group of Experts on People of African Descent, the Special Rapporteur on contemporary forms of racism, racial discrimination, xenophobia, and related intolerance, and the Special Rapporteur on the human rights of migrants.

[141] Racial Discrimination against persons fleeing from the armed conflict in Ukraine, Statement 1 (2022), 17 March 2022.

As Marisa Jackson Sow noted, writing in the *American Journal of International Law*, '[t]he Ukrainian crisis has exposed, for scholars and the public alike, the impact of widely held beliefs concerning white supremacy and humanity upon the provision of humanitarian protection'.[142] The responsibility of the United Nations to lead the struggle against racism and racial discrimination is as acute as it was three quarters of a century ago, when the organization rose from the ashes of the Second World War.

---

[142] Marisa Jackson Sow, 'Ukrainian Refugees, Race and International Law's Choice Between Order and Justice' (2022) 116 *American Journal of International Law* 698, at p. 707. Also Cathryn Costello and Michelle Foster, '(Some) Refugees Welcome: When is Differentiating between Refugees Unlawful Discrimination? (2022) 22 *International Journal of Discrimination and the Law* 244.

Bibliography

Abi-Saab, Georges, 'International Law and the International Community: The Long Road to Universality', in Ronald St. John Macdonald, ed., *Essays in Honour of Wang Tieya*, Dordrecht: Martinus Nijhoff, 1994, pp. 31–41

Abi-Saab, Georges, 'The Development of International Law by the United Nations', in Frederick Snyder and Surakiart Sathirathai, eds., *Third World Attitudes to International Law: An Introduction*, Dordrecht: Martinus Nijhoff, 1987, pp. 221–30

Abi-Saab, Georges, 'The Newly Independent States and the Rules of International Law: An Outline' (1962) 8 *Howard Law Journal* 95

Abram, Morris, *The Day is Short: An Autobiography*, New York: Harcourt Brace Jovanovich, 1982

Aceves, William J., 'Two Stories about Skin Color and International Human Rights Advocacy' (2015) 14 *Washington University Global Studies Law Review* 563

Achiume, E. Tendayi and Devon W. Carbado, 'Critical Race Theory Meets Third World Approaches to International Law' (2021) 67 *UCLA Law Review* 1462

Achiume, E. Tendayi, 'Beyond Prejudice: Structural Xenophobic Discrimination against Refugees' (2014) 45 *Georgetown Journal of International Law* 323

Achiume, E. Tendayi, 'Putting Racial Equality onto the Global Human Rights Agenda' (2018) 28 *SUR – International Journal on Human Rights* 141

Achiume, E. Tendayi, 'Race, Refugees, and International Law', in Cathryn Costello, Michelle Foster and Jane McAdam, eds., *The Oxford Handbook of International Refugee Law*, Oxford: Oxford University Press, 2021, pp. 42–59

Achiume, E. Tendayi, 'Transnational Racial (In)Justice in Liberal Democratic Empire' (2021) 134 *Harvard Law Review Forum* 378

Aderinto, Saheed, ' "The problem of Nigeria is slavery, not white slave traffic": Globalization and the Politicization of Prostitution in Southern Nigeria, 1921–1955' (2012) 46 *Canadian Journal of African Studies / La Revue canadienne des études africaines* 1

Ahmed, A. Kayum, '#RhodesMustFall: How a Decolonial Student Movement in the Global South Inspired Epistemic Disobedience at the University of Oxford' (2020) 63 *African Studies Review* 271

Aiyetoro, Adjoa A. and Adrienne D. Davis, 'Historic and Modern Social Movements for Reparations: The National Coalition of Blacks for Reparations in America (N'Cobra) and Its Antecedents' (2010) 16 *Texas Wesleyan Law Review* 687

Aiyetoro, Adjoa A., 'Achieving Reparations While Respecting Our Differences: A Model for Black Reparations' (2020) 63 *Howard Law Journal* 329

Aiyetoro, Adjoa A., 'The Development of the Movement for Reparations for African Descendants' (2002) 3 *Journal of Law in Society* 133

Aiyetoro, Adjoa A., 'Why Reparations to African Descendants in the United States are Essential to Democracy' (2011) 14 *Journal of Gender, Race and Justice* 633

Al Attar, Mohsen and Rosalie Miller, 'Towards an Emancipatory International Law: the Bolivarian reconstruction' (2010) 31 *Third World Quarterly* 347

416 BIBLIOGRAPHY

Alkhazragi, Hussein D., 'Un Petit Prince à la SDN: La lutte du Roi Hussein du Hedjaz pour l'indépendance des provinces arabes de l'empire Ottoman' (2011–2012) 146 *Rélations internationales* 7

Allain, Jean, 'Decolonisation as the Source of the Concepts of *Jus Cogens* and Obligations *Erga Omnes*', in Zeray Yihdego, Melaku Geboye Desta, and Fikremarkos Merso, eds., *Ethiopian Yearbook of International Law 2016*, Cham: Springer, 2017, pp. 35–59

Allain, Jean, 'Slavery and the League of Nations: Ethiopia as a Civilised Nation' (2006) 8 *Journal of the History of International Law* 213

Allain, Jean, 'White Slave Traffic in International Law' (2017) 1 *Journal of Trafficking and Human Exploitation* 1

Allain, Jean, *The Legal Understanding of Slavery: From the Historical to the Contemporary*, Oxford: Oxford University Press, 2012

Allerfeldt, Kristofer, 'Wilsonian Pragmatism? Woodrow Wilson, Japanese Immigration, and the Paris Peace Conference' (2004) 15 *Diplomacy and Statecraft* 545

Amparo, Thiago and Andressa Vieira e Silva, 'George Floyd at the UN: Whiteness, International Law' (2022) 7 *UC Irvine Journal of International, Transnational and Comparative Law* 91

Alston, Philip, 'Does the Past Matter? On the Origins of Human Rights, An Analysis of Competing Histories of the Origins of International Human Rights Law' (2013) 126 *Harvard Law Review* 2043

Alvarez Molinero, Natalia, 'La Convención para la Eliminación de Todas las Formas de Discriminación Racial', in Felipe Gómez Isa and José Manuel Pureza, eds., *La protección internacional de los derechos humanos en los albores del siglo XXI*, Bilbao: Universidad de Deusto, 2004, pp. 215–41

Ambrosius, Lloyd E., 'Woodrow Wilson and the Birth of a Nation: American Democracy and International Relations' (2007) 18 *Diplomacy and Statecraft* 689

Anand, R.P., 'Attitude of the Asian-African States toward Certain Problems of International Law' (1966) 15 *International and Comparative Law Quarterly* 55

Anand, R.P., 'Role of the "New" Asian-African States in the Present International Legal Order' (1962) 66 *American Journal of International Law* 895

Anand, R.P., 'The Formation of International Organizations and India: A Historical Study' (2010) 23 *Leiden Journal of International Law* 5

Anderson, Carol, 'African Americans, the United Nations, and the Struggle for Human Rights, 1944–1947' (1996) 29 *Diplomatic History* 531

Anderson, Carol, 'Bleached Souls and Red Negroes, The NAACP and Black Communists in the Early Cold War, 1948–1952', in Brenda Gayle Plummer, ed., *Window on Freedom: Race, Civil Rights, and Foreign Affairs, 1945–1988*, Chapel Hill and London: University of North Carolina Press, 2003, pp. 93–113

Anderson, Carol, 'From Hope to Disillusion: African Americans, the United Nations, and the Struggle for Human Rights, 1944–1947' (1996) 29 *Diplomatic History* 531

Anderson, Carol, 'International Conscience, the Cold War, and Apartheid: The NAACP's Alliance with the Reverend Michael Scott for South West Africa's Liberation, 1946–1951' (2008) 19 *Journal of World History* 297

Anderson, Carol, *Bourgeois Radicals, The NAACP and the Struggle for Colonial Liberation, 1941–1960*, Cambridge: Cambridge University Press, 2014

Anderson, Carol, *Eyes Off the Prize, African-Americans, the United Nations and the Struggle for Human Rights, 1944–1955*, New York: Cambridge, 2002

BIBLIOGRAPHY 417

Anderson, Karen, *Little Rock: Race and Resistance at Central High School*, Princeton: Princeton University Press, 2010

Andrews, Penelope E., 'Making Room for Critical Race Theory in International Law: Some Practical Pointers' (2000) 45 *Villanova Law Review* 855

Andrews, Penelope E., 'Reparations for Apartheid's Victims: The Path to Reconciliation' (2004) 53 *DePaul Law Review* 1155

Angelou, Maya, *The Collected Autobiographies of Maya Angelou*, New York: Random House, 2012

Anghie, Antony and Bhupinder S. Chimni, 'Third World Approaches to International Law and Individual Responsibility in Internal Conflicts' (2003) 2 *Chinese Journal of International Law* 77

Anghie, Antony, '"The Heart of My Home": Colonialism, Environmental Damage, and the Nauru Case' (1993) 34 *Harvard International Law Journal* 445

Anghie, Antony, 'Colonialism and the Birth of International Institutions: Sovereignty, Economy, and the Mandate System of the League of Nations' (2002) 34 *New York University Journal if International Law and Policy* 513

Anghie, Antony, 'Finding the Peripheries: Sovereignty and Colonialism in Nineteenth-Century International Law' (1999) 40 *Harvard International Law Journal* 1

Anghie, Antony, 'Francisco de Vitoria and the Colonial Origins of International Law' (1996) 5 *Social and Legal Studies* 321

Anghie, Antony, 'Slavery and International Law: The Jurisprudence of Henry Richardson' (2017) 31 *Temple International and Comparative Law Journal* 11

Anghie, Antony, 'Whose Utopia? Human Rights, Development, and the Third World' (2013) 22 *Qui Parle* 63

Anghie, Antony, *Imperialism, Sovereignty and International Law*, Cambridge: Cambridge University Press, 2007

Anievas, Alexander, Nivi Manchanda, Robbie Shilliam, eds., *Race and Racism in International Relations: Confronting the Global Colour Line*, London: Routledge, 2014

Apor, Péter, Tamás Kende, Michala Lônčíková, and Valentin Săndulescu, 'Post-World War II Anti-Semitic Pogroms in East and East Central Europe: Collective Violence and Popular Culture' (2019) 26 *European Review of History / Revue européenne d'histoire* 913

Appiah, Anthony, 'Race in the Modern World: The Problem of the Color Line' (2015) 94 *Foreign Affairs* 1

Appiah, Anthony, 'The Uncompleted Argument: Du Bois and the Illusion of Race' (1985) 12 *Critical Inquiry* 21

Araujo, Ana Lucia, *Reparations for Slavery and the Slave Trade: A Transnational and Comparative History*, London and New York: Bloomsbury Publishing, 2017

Asamoah, Obed Y., *The Legal Significance of the Declarations of the General Assembly of the United Nations*, Dordrecht: Springer, 1966

Asamoah, Obed Y., 'The Declaration on the Elimination of All Forms of Racial Discrimination', in Obed Y. Asamoah, *The Legal Significance of the Declarations of the General Assembly of the United Nations*, Dordrecht: Springer, 1966, pp. 192–213

Atiles-Osoria, José, 'Colonial State Crimes and the CARICOM Mobilization for Reparation and Justice' (2018) 7 *State Crime Journal* 349

Atkinson, Nolan N. Jr. and Alan Ira Neuman, 'International Law and the South West Africa Cases' (1967) 13 *Howard Law Journal* 120

418   BIBLIOGRAPHY

Axtmayer, Jose Alberto, 'Non-Self-Governing Territories and the Constitutive Process of the United Nations: A General Analysis and the Case Study of Puerto Rico' (1976) 45 *Revista Juridica de la Universidad de Puerto Rico* 211

Bakan, Abigail B. and Yasmeen Abu-Laban, 'The Israel/Palestine Racial Contract and the challenge of anti-Racism: a case study of the United Nations World Conference Against Racism' (2021) 44 *Ethnic and Racial Studies* 2167

Baker, Ray Stannard, *Woodrow Wilson and World Settlement*, Vol. II, Garden City and New York: Doubleday, Page, 1922

Baldwin, James, 'A Negro Assays the Negro Mood', *New York Times Magazine*, 12 March 1961, p. 25

Balibar, Étienne, 'Racism Revisited: Sources, Relevance, and Aporias of a Modern Concept' (2008) 123 *Publications of the Modern Language Association of America* 1633

Ballinger, Ronald B., 'The International Court of Justice and the South West Africa Cases: Judgment of 21st December, 1962' (1964) 81 *South Africa Law Journal* 35

Bangham, Jenny, 'What Is Race? UNESCO, Mass Communication and Human Genetics in the Early 1950s' (2015) 28 *History of the Human Sciences* 80

Bankier, David, *The Jews Are Coming Back: The Return of the Jews to Their Countries of Origin after WWII*, Jerusalem: Yad Vashem and Berghahn Books, 2005

Banton, Michael, 'Colour as a Ground of Discrimination', in Nazila Ghanea and Alexandra Xanthaki, eds., *Minorities, Peoples and Self-Determination*, Leiden/Boston: Martinus Nijhoff Publishers, 2005, pp. 237–47

Banton, Michael, 'Decision-Taking in the Committee on the Elimination of Racial Discrimination', in Philip Alston and James Crawford, eds., *The Future of UN Human Rights Treaty Monitoring*, Cambridge: Cambridge University Press, 2000, pp. 55–78

Banton, Michael, 'Effective Implementation of the UN Racial Convention' (1994) 20 *Journal of Ethnic and Migration Studies* 475

Banton, Michael, 'Lessons from the 2001 World Conference Against Racism' (2002) 28 *Journal of Ethnic and Migration Studies* 355

Banton, Michael, 'Racial Rhetoric at the United Nations' (1991) 5 *International Journal of Politics, Culture and Society* 5

Banton, Michael, 'The International Defence of Racial Equality' (1990) 13 *Ethnic and Racial Studies* 568

Banton, Michael, 'The Vertical and Horizontal Dimensions of the Word Race' (2010) 10 *Ethnicities* 127

Banton, Michael, *International Action against Racial Discrimination*, Oxford: Oxford University Press, 1996

Banton, Michael, *The International Politics of Race*, Cambridge: Polity Press, 2002

Barber, Hollis W., 'Decolonization: The Committee of Twenty-four' (1975) 138 *World Affairs* 128

Barbier, Maurice, *Le Comité de Decolonisation des Nations Unies*, Paris: Librairie Générale de Droit et de Jurisprudence, 1974

Barkan, Elazar, 'Introduction: Reparation: A Moral and Political Dilemma', in Jon Miller and Rahul Kumar, eds., *Reparations: Interdisciplinary Inquiries*, Oxford: Oxford University Press, 2013, pp. 1–19

Barkan, Elazar, 'The Politics of the Science of Race: Ashley Montagu and UNESCO's Anti-Racist Declarations', in Larry T. Reynolds and Leonard Lieberman, eds., *Race and Other Misadventures: Essays in Honor of Ashley Montagu in His Ninetieth Year*, Dix Hall, NY: Altamira Press, 1996, pp. 96–105

BIBLIOGRAPHY 419

Barkan, Elazar, *The Retreat of Scientific Racism: Changing Concepts of Race in Britain and the United States Between the World Wars*, Cambridge: Cambridge University Press, 1992

Barnes, Teresa, '"The best defence is to attack": African Agency in the South West Africa Case at the International Court of Justice, 1960–1966' (2017) 69 *South African Historical Journal* 162

Barrett, Michèle, 'Dehumanization and the War in East Africa' (2017) 10 *Journal of War & Culture Studies* 238

Barrett, Michèle, 'Subalterns at War' (2007) 9 *Interventions* 451

Barrett, Michèle, 'White Graves and Natives: The Imperial War Graves Commission in East and West Africa, 1918–1939', in Paul Cornish and Nicholas J. Saunders, eds., *Bodies in Conflict: Corporeality, Materiality, and Transformation*, London: Routledge, 2013, pp. 80–90

Barrington, J.M., 'The Permanent Mandates Commission and Educational Policy in Trust Territories' (1976) 22 *International Review of Education* 88

Barsalou, Olivier, 'The United States and Human Rights Marginalization at the International Court of Justice, 1945–1950' (2021) 24 *Journal of the History of International Law* 102

Barsalou, Olivier, *La Diplomatie de l'universel: La guerre froide, les Etats-Unis et la genèse de la Déclaration universelle des droits de l'homme*, Brussels: Bruylant, 2012

Bassiouni, M. Cherif and Daniel H. Derby, 'Final Report on the Establishment of an International Criminal Court for the Implementation of the Apartheid Convention and Other Relevant International Instruments' (1981) 9 *Hofstra Law Review* 523

Bassiouni, M. Cherif, 'Chronology of Efforts to Establish an International Criminal Tribunal' (2015) 86 *Revue internationale de droit pénal* 1183

Batelaan, Pieter and Carla Van Hoof, 'The European Year against Racism and other Issues' (1998) 9 *European Journal of Intercultural Studies* 179

Bayefsky, Anne, 'The UN World Conference Against Racism: A Racist Anti-racism Conference' [2002] *Proceedings of the American Society of International Law Annual Meeting* 65

Beaubien, Michael C., 'The Cultural Boycott of South Africa' (1982) 29(4) *Africa Today* 5

Beckett, Balthazar I. and Salimah K. Hankins, '"Until We Are First Recognized as Humans": The Killing of George Floyd and the Case for Black Life at the United Nations' (2021) *International Journal of Human Rights Education* 1

Beckles, Hilary McD., *Britain's Black Debt: Reparations for Caribbean Slavery and Native Genocide*, Kingston: University of the West Indies, 2012

Bedau, Hugo Adam, 'Compensatory Justice and the Black Manifesto' (1972) 56 *Philosophy and Public Policy* 20

Bedi, Shiv R.S., *The Development of Human Rights Law by the Judges of the International Court of Justice*, Oxford and Portland, OR: Hart, 2007

Belanger, Yale D., 'The Six Nations of Grand River Territory's Attempts at Renewing International Political Relationships, 1921–1924' (2007) 13 *Canadian Foreign Policy Journal* 29

Bell, Mark, *Racism and Equality in the European Union*, New York: Oxford University Press, 2008

Bellegarde-Smith, Patrick, 'International Relations/Social Theory in a Small State: An Analysis of the Thought of Dantès Bellegarde' (1982) 39 *The Americas* 167

Bellegarde-Smith, Patrick, *In the Shadow of Powers: Dantes Bellegarde in Haitian Social Thought*, Atlantic Highlands, N.J.: Humanities Press International, 1985

420   BIBLIOGRAPHY

Bellegarde, Dantès and Mercer Cook, 'Haiti and the Rights of Man' (1950) 14 *Negro History Bulletin* 41

Bellegarde, Dantès, 'Haiti and the Rights of Man' (1950) 14 *Negro History Bulletin* 41

Beresford, Quentin and Gary Partington, eds., *Reform and Resistance in Aboriginal Education*, Crawley: University of West Australia Press, 2003

Berghe, Pierre L. van den, 'Miscegenation in South Africa' (1960) 1 *Cahiers d'Études Africaines* 68

Berman, Edward H., 'American Influence on African Education: The Role of the Phelps-Stokes Fund's Education Commissions' (1970) 15 *Comparative Education Review* 132

Bernstorff, Jochen von and Philipp Dann, eds., *The Battle for International Law, South-North Perspectives on the Decolonization Era*, Oxford: Oxford University Press, 2019

Bhatia, Amar, 'The South of the North: Building on Critical Approaches 137 to International Law with Lessons from the Fourth World' (2012) 14 *Oregon Review of International Law* 131

Biddiss, Michael D., 'The Universal Races Congress of 1911' (1971) 13 *Race* 37

Biddiss, Michael D., *Father of Racist Ideology: The Social and Political Thought of Count Gobineau*, London: Weidenfeld and Nicolson, 1970

Bielefeldt, Heiner, *The Durban Review Conference – why EU governments should participate*, Berlin: Deutsches Institut für Menschenrechte, 2009

Biondi, Martha, 'The Rise of the Reparations Movement' (2003) 87 *Radical History Review* 5

Black, Allida, ed., *The Eleanor Roosevelt Papers, Vol. I, The Human Rights Years, 1945–1948*, Charlottesville and London: University of Virginia Press, 2007

Bollecker, Brigitte, 'L'avis consultatif en date du 21 juin 1971 de la Cour internationale de Justice dans l'affaire relative aux conséquences juridiques pour les États membres de la présence continue de l'Afrique du Sud en Namibie (Sud-Ouest africain)' (1971) 17 *Annuaire français de droit international* 281

Booysen, Hercules, 'Convention on the Crime of Apartheid' (1976) 2 *South African Yearbook of International Law* 56

Borgwardt, Elizabeth, 'Race, Rights and Nongovernmental Organisations at the UN San Francisco Conference', in Kevin M. Kruse and Stephen Tuck, eds., *The Fog of War: The Second World War and the Civil Rights Movement*, Oxford: Oxford University Press, 2012, pp. 188–207

Borgwardt, Elizabeth, 'When You State a Moral Principle, You Are Stuck with It: The 1941 Atlantic Charter as a Human Rights Instrument' (2006) 46 *Virginia Journal of International Law* 501

Borgwardt, Elizabeth, *A New Deal for the World, America's Vision for Human Rights*, Cambridge, MA and London: Harvard University Press, 2005

Borstelmann, Thomas, 'Jim Crow's Coming Out: Race Relations and American Foreign Policy in the Truman Years' (1999) 29 *Presidential Studies Quarterly* 549

Borstelmann, Thomas, *Apartheid's Reluctant Uncle: The United States and Southern Africa in the Early Cold War*, New York: Oxford University Press, 1993

Borstelmann, Thomas, *The Cold War and the Color Line: American Race Relations in the Global Arena*, Cambridge, MA: Harvard University Press, 2001

Bossuyt, Marc and Stef Vandeginste, 'The Issue of Reparation for Slavery and Colonialism and the Durban World Conference Against Racism' (2001) 22 *Human Rights Law Journal* 341

Bossuyt, Marc, *L'interdiction de la discrimination dans le droit international des droits de l'homme*, Brussels: Bruylant, 1976

Boutros-Ghali, Boutros, 'Introduction', in *The United Nations and Apartheid, 1948–1994*, New York: United Nations, 1994, pp. 3–131

Boven, Theo van, 'Racial and Religious Discrimination', in Rüdiger Wolfrum, ed., *The Max Planck Encyclopaedia of Public International Law*, Vol. VIII, Oxford: Oxford University Press, 2012, pp. 608–17

Boven, Theo van, 'United Nations Strategies to Combat Racism and Racial Discrimination', in M. Castermans-Holleman, F. van Hoof, and J. Smith, eds., *The Role of the Nation-State in the 212st Century: Human Rights, International Organisations and Foreign Policy; Essays in Honour of Peter Baehr*, The Hague: Kluwer, 1998, pp. 251–64

Boven, Theo van, 'World Conference Against Racism: An Historic Event?' (2001) 19 *Netherlands Quarterly of Human Rights* 379

Boven, Theo van, *World Conference to Combat Racism and Racial Discrimination: A New Step Forward*, New York: United Nations, 1978

Bowden, Brett, 'The Colonial Origins of International Law – European Expansion and the Classical Standard of Civilization' (2005) 7 *Journal of the History of International Law* 1

Bowden, Brett, *The Empire of Civilization: The Evolution of an Imperial Idea*, Chicago: University of Chicago Press, 2009

Boyle, Kevin and Anneliese Baldaccini, 'A Critical Evaluation of International Human Rights Approaches to Racism', in Sandra Fredman, ed., *Discrimination and Human Rights: The Case of Racism*, Oxford University Press, Oxford, 2001, pp. 135–92

Brackman, Harald, ' "A Calamity Almost Beyond Comprehension": Nazi Anti-Semitism and the Holocaust in the Thought of W.E.B. Du Bois' (2000) 88 *American Jewish History* 53

Bradley, Anna Spain, 'Human Rights Racism' (2019) 32 *Harvard Human Rights Journal* 1

Brattain, Michelle, 'Race, Racism, and Antiracism: UNESCO and the Politics of Presenting Science to the Postwar Public' (2007) 112 *American Historical Review* 1387

Breitman, George, ed., *Malcolm X Speaks: Selected Speeches and Statements*, New York: Grove Press, 1965

Brits, J.P., 'Tiptoeing Along the Apartheid Tightrope: The United States, South Africa, and the United Nations in 1952' (2005) 27 *International History Review* 754

Brooks, Roy L., 'Getting Reparations for Slavery Right-Response to Posner and Vermeule' (2004) 80 *Notre Dame Law Review* 251

Brophy, Alfred L., 'The Cultural War over Reparations for Slavery' (2004) 53 *DePaul Law Review* 1181

Brown, Preston, 'The I.C.J. 1971 Advisory Opinion on South West Africa (Namibia)' (1971) 5 *Vanderbilt Journal Transnational Law* 213

Browning, James R., 'Anti-Miscegenation Laws in the United States' (1951) 1 *Duke Bar Journal* 26

Brugel, J.W., 'The Bernheim Petition: A Challenge to Nazi Germany in 1933' (1983) 17(3) *Patterns of Prejudice* 17

Buell, Raymond Leslie, 'The Development of Anti-Japanese Agitation in the United States' (1923) 38 *Political Science Quarterly* 57

Buelli, Arlena, 'The Hands Off Ethiopia Campaign, Racial Solidarities and Intercolonial Antifascism in South Asia (1935–36) – CORRIGENDUM' (2022) 21 *Journal of Global History* 1

422 BIBLIOGRAPHY

Buergenthal, Thomas, 'Implementing the UN Racial Convention' (1977) 12 *Texas International Law Journal* 187

Bultz, Ariel, 'Redefining Apartheid in International Criminal Law' (2013) 24 *Criminal Law Forum* 205

Burke, Roland, '"The Compelling Dialogue of Freedom": Human Rights at the 1955 Bandung Conference' (2006) 28 *Human Rights Quarterly* 947

Burke, Roland, 'Decolonization, Development, and Identity: The Evolution of the Anticolonial Human Rights Critique, 1948–78' in Jean H. Quaetart and Lora Wildenthal, eds., *The Routledge History of Human Rights*, London and New York: Routledge, 2021, pp. 222–40

Burke, Roland, 'Despairing at "A World Made New"? South Africa Encounters the Postwar Human Rights Idea' (2020) 48 *Journal of Imperial and Commonwealth History* 351

Burke, Roland, 'From Individual Rights to National Development: The First UN International Conference on Human Rights, Tehran, 1968' (2008) 19 *Journal of World History* 275

Burke, Roland, 'Premature Memorials to the United Nations Human Rights Program: International Postage Stamps and the Commemoration of the 1948 Universal Declaration of Human Rights' (2016) 28 *History and Memory* 15

Burke, Roland, *Decolonization and the Evolution of International Human Rights*, Philadelphia: University of Pennsylvania Press, 2013

Burleigh, Michael and Wolfgang Wippermann, *The Racial State, Germany 1933–1945*, Cambridge: Cambridge University Press, 1991

Butcher, Goler Teal, 'Legal Consequences for States of the Illegality of Apartheid' (1986) 8 *Human Rights Quarterly* 404

Buys, Cindy Galway, 'International Decisions: Application of the International Convention on the Elimination of All Forms of Racial Discrimination: International Court of Justice Order on Provisional Measures and Application of CERD as Basis of Jurisdiction' (2009) 103 *American Journal of International Law* 294

Búzás, Zoltán I., *Evading International Norms: Race and Rights in the Shadow of Legality*, Philadelphia: University of Pennsylvania Press, 2021

Caballero, Chamion and Peter J. Aspinall, 'Redefining Race: UNESCO, the Biology of Race Crossing, and the Wane of the Eugenics Movement', in Chamion Caballero and Peter J. Aspinall, eds., *Mixed Race Britain in The Twentieth Century*, London: Palgrave Macmillan, 2018, pp. 293–312

Cahn, Claude, 'Court of Justice of the EU Rules Collective and Inaccessible Electrical Metres Discriminate against Roma: CHEZ Razpredelenie Bulgaria AD v. Komisia za zashtita ot diskriminatsia (C-83/14)' (2016) 18 *European Journal of Migration* 112

Callahan, Michael D., *A Sacred Trust: The League of Nations and Africa, 1929–1946*, Brighton: Sussex Academic Press, 2004

Callahan, Michael D., *Mandates and Empire: The League of Nations and Africa, 1914–1931*, Brighton: Sussex Academic Press, 1999

Campbell, Peter, 'The "Black Horror on the Rhine": Idealism, Pacifism, and Racism in Feminism and the Left in the Aftermath of the First World War' (2014) 49 *Histoire sociale / Social History* 471

Camponovo, Christopher N., 'Disaster in Durban: The United Nations World Conference against Racism, Racial Discrimination, Xenophobia, and Related Intolerance' (2003) 34 *George Washington International Law Review* 659

Cançado Trindade, Antonio, 'The Domestic Jurisdiction of States in the Practice of the United Nations and Regional Organisations' (1976) 25 *International and Comparative Law Quarterly* 715

Canyes, Manuel S., 'The Inter-American System and the Conference of Chapultepec' (1945) 39 *American Journal of International Law* 504

Caplovitz, David and Candace Rogers, *Swastika 1960: The Epidemic of anti-Semitic Vandalism in America*, New York: Anti-Defamation League of B'nai B'rith, 1961

Cassese, Antonio, 'Il sistema de garanzia della Convenzione dell' onu sull'eliminazione di ogni forma di discriminazione razziale' [1967] *Rivista di Diritto Internazionale* 270

Castillo Jiménez, Elina, 'Racial Justice to the Forefront: Do Black Lives Matter in International Law?', in Morten Kjaerum, Martha F. Davis, & Amanda Lyons, eds., *COVID-19 and Human Rights*, London: Routledge, 2021, pp. 82–99

Chakma, Suhas, 'The Issue of Compensation for Colonialism and Slavery at the World Conference against Racism: A Fine Balance Between Rhetoric and Legality', in George Ulrich and Louise Krabbe-Boserup, eds., *Human Rights in Development Yearbook 2001*, Frederick, MD: Kluwer Law International, 2003, pp. 57–71

Chalk, Frank, 'Du Bois and Garvey Confront Liberia: Two Incidents of the Coolidge Years' (1967) 1 *Canadian Journal of African Studies / Revue Canadienne des Études Africaines* 135

Chase, Garrett, 'The Early History of the Black Lives Matter Movement, and the Implications Thereof' (2018) 18 *Nevada Law Journal* 1091

Chazan, Naomi, 'The Fallacies of Pragmatism: Israeli Foreign Policy towards South Africa' (1983) 82 *African Affairs* 169

Cheng, Bin, 'The 1966 South West Africa Judgment of the World Court' (1967) 20 *Current Legal Problems* 181

Chimni, Bhupinder S., 'Third World Approaches to International Law: A Manifesto' (2006) 8 *International Community Law Review* 3

Cimiotta, Emanuele, 'Parallel Proceedings before the International Court of Justice and the Committee on the Elimination of Racial Discrimination' (2020) 19 *The Law and Practice of International Courts and Tribunals* 388

Clark, Roger S., 'Apartheid', in M. Cherif Bassiouni, ed., *International Criminal Law*, 3rd ed., Vol. I, New York: Transnational, 2008, pp. 599–620

Clark, Roger S., 'The International League for Human Rights and South West Africa, 1947–1957: The Human Rights NGO as Catalyst in the International Legal Process' (1981) 3 *Human Rights Quarterly* 101

Clark, Roger S., 'The United Nations and Religious Freedom' (1978) 11 *New York University Journal of International Law and Policy* 197

Claydon, John, 'The Treaty Protection of Religious Rights: U.N. Draft Convention on the Elimination of All Forms of Intolerance and of Discrimination Based on Religion or Belief' (1972) 12 *Santa Clara Lawyer* 403

Cohen, Benjamin V., 'Human Rights under the United Nations Charter' (1949) 14 *Law and Contemporary Problems* 430

Cohen-Jonathan, Gérard, 'Le droit de l'homme à la non-discrimination raciale' [2001] *Revue trimestrielle des droits de l'homme* 665

Coleman, Howard D., 'The Problem of Anti-semitism under the International Convention on the Elimination of All Forms of Racial Discrimination' (1969) 2 *Revue des Droits de l'Homme/Human Rights Journa l*609

424 BIBLIOGRAPHY

Comas, Juan, ' "Scientific" Racism Again?' (1961) 2 *Current Anthropology* 303

Contee, Clarence G., 'Du Bois, the NAACP, and the Pan-African Congress of 1919' (1972) 57 *Journal of Negro History* 13

Cook, Mercer, 'Dantès Bellegarde' (1940) 1 *Phylon* 125

Cooper, John, *Raphael Lemkin and the Struggle for the Genocide Convention*, Basingstoke: Palgrave Macmillan, 2008

Costello, Cathryn and Michelle Foster, '(Some) Refugees Welcome: When is Differentiating Between Refugees Unlawful Discrimination?' (2022) 22 *International Journal of Discrimination and the Law* 244

Costello, Cathryn and Michelle Foster, 'Race Discrimination Effaced at the International Court of Justice' (2021) 115 *AJIL Unbound* 339

Cox, Graham B., *Seeking Justice for the Holocaust, Herbert C. Pell, Franklin D. Roosevelt and the Limits of International Law*, Norman: University of Oklahoma Press, 2019

Craven, Matthew, 'Colonialism and Domination', in Bardo Fassbender and Ann Peters, eds., *The Oxford Handbook of the History of International Law*, Oxford: Oxford University Press, 2012, pp. 862–89

Crenshaw, Kimberlé, 'Mapping the Margins: Intersectionality, Identity Politics, and Violence Against Women of Color' (1991) 43 *Stanford Law Review* 1241

Crook, John R., 'United States Boycotts Durban Review Conference, Will Seek Election to Human Rights Council' (2009) 103 *American Journal of International Law* 359

Crooms, Lisa A., 'Indivisible Rights and Intersectional Identities or, "What Do Women's Human Rights Have to do with the Race Convention?"' (1997) 40 *Howard Law Journal* 619

Cumper, Peter, 'The United Kingdom and the U.N. Declaration on the Elimination of Intolerance and Discrimination Based on Religious or Belief' (2007) 21:1 Emory Int'l L Rev 13

Darian-Smith, Eve, 'Re-reading W.E.B. Du Bois: The Global Dimensions of the US Civil Rights Struggle' (2012) 7 *Journal of Global History* 483

Das, Kamleshwar, 'Measures of Implementation of the International Convention on the Elimination of All Forms of Racial Discrimination with Special Reference to the Provisions Concerning Reports from States Parties to the Convention' (1971) 4 *Revue des Droits de l'Homme/Human Rights Journal* 213

David, Derek H., 'The Evolution of Religious Freedom as a Universal Human Right: Examining the Role of the 1981 United Nations Declaration on the Elimination of All Forms of Intolerance and of Discrimination Based on Religion or Belief' [2002] *Brigham Young University Law Review* 217

Davidson, Basil, *African Civilisation Revisited: From Antiquity to Modern Times*, Trenton, NJ: World Press, 1991

Davis, Uri, *Israel: An Apartheid State*, London: Zed Books, 1987

De Capello, H.H. Krill, 'The Creation of the United Nations Educational, Scientific and Cultural Organization' (1970) 24 *International Organization* 1

Debetz, Georghi F., 'Biology Looks at Race' (April 1965) *UNESCO Courier* 4–7

Decaux, Emmanuel, 'La décision du Comité pour l'élimination de la discrimination raciale relative à sa compétence adoptée le 12 décembre 2019 au regard de la communication interétatique déposée par l'État de Palestine contre Israël' (2021) 126 *Revue trimestrielle des droits de l'homme* 429

Dedering, Tilman, 'Petitioning Geneva: Transnational Aspects of Protest and Resistance in South West Africa/Namibia after the First World War' (2009) 35 *Journal of Southern African Studies* 785

BIBLIOGRAPHY 425

DeFalco, Randle C. and Frédéric Mégret, 'The Invisibility Of Race at the ICC: Lessons From the US Criminal Justice System' (2019) 7 *London Review of International Law* 55

Defeis, Elizabeth F., 'Freedom of Speech and International Norms: A Response to Hate Speech' (1992–1993) 29 *Stanford Journal of International Law* 57

Derrick, Jonathan, *Africa's 'Agitators': Militant Anti-Colonialism in Africa and the West, 1918–1939*, New York: Columbia University Press, 2008

Desautels-Stein, Justin, 'A Prolegomenon to the Study of Racial Ideology in the Era of International Human Rights' (2021) 67 *UCLA Law Review* 1536

Desautels-Stein, Justin, 'Race as a Legal Concept' (2012) 2 *Columbia Journal of Race and Law* 1

Dimier, Véronique, ' « L'internationalisation » du débat colonial: Rivalités franco-britanniques autour de la Commission permanente des Mandats' (2002) 89 *Outre Mers: Revue d'Histoire* 333

Donnelly, Jack, 'Human Rights and Human Dignity: An Analytic Critique of Non-Western Conceptions of Human Rights' (1982) 76 *American Political Science Review* 303

Dore, Isaak I., 'United Nations Measures to Combat Racial Discrimination: Progress and Problems in Retrospect' (1981) 10 *Denver Journal of International Law and Policy* 299

Douglass, Frederick, 'The Color Line' (1881) 132 *The North American Review* 567

Dover, Cedric, 'UNESCO on Race' (1950) 42 *Eugenics Review* 177

Du Bois, W.E.B., 'Inter-Racial Implications of the Ethiopian Crisis: A Negro View' (1935) 19 *Foreign Affairs* 82

Du Bois, W.E.B., 'Liberia, the League and the United States' (1933) 11 *Foreign Affairs* 682

Du Bois, W.E.B., 'Manifesto to the League of Nations' (1921) 23 *The Crisis* 18

Du Bois, W.E.B., 'Opinion' (1919) 18 *The Crisis* 7

Du Bois, W.E.B., 'Prospect of a World Without Race Conflict' (1944) 49 *American Review of Sociology* 450

Du Bois, W.E.B., 'The First Universal Races Congress. Presented in 1911 at a conference in London', in Phil Zuckerman, ed., *The Social Theory of W. E. B. Du Bois*, London: Sage, 2005, p. 26

Du Bois, W.E.B., 'The Pan-African Congress' (1919) 17 *The Crisis* 271

Du Bois, W.E.B., *The World and Africa and Color and Democracy*, Oxford: Oxford University Press, 2007

Du Bois, W.E.B., *Writings*, New York: New American Library, 1986

Du Plessis, Max, 'Historical Injustice and International Law: An Exploratory Discussion of Reparation for Slavery' (2003) 25 *Human Rights Quarterly* 624

Du Plessis, Max, 'International Criminal Law: The Crime of Apartheid Revisited' (2011) 24 *South African Journal of Criminal Justice* 423

Dubow, Saul, 'Smuts, the United Nations and the Rhetoric of Race and Rights' (2008) 43 *Journal of Contemporary History* 65

Dubow, Saul, 'The Commonwealth and South Africa: From Smuts to Mandela' (2017) 45 *Journal of Imperial and Commonwealth History* 281

Dubuy, Mélanie, '*Application de la convention internationale sur l'élimination de toutes les formes de discrimination raciale (Géorgie c. Fédération de Russie)*, exceptions préliminaires: un formalisme excessif au service du classicisme?' (2011) 57 *Annuaire français de droit international* 183

Dudziak, Mary L., 'Desegregation as a Cold War Imperative' (1988) 41 *Stanford Law Review* 61

426 BIBLIOGRAPHY

Dudziak, Mary L., 'Josephine Baker, Racial Protest, and the Cold War' (1994) 81 *Journal of American History* 543

Dudziak, Mary L., *Cold War Civil Rights: Race and the Image of American Democracy*, Princeton: Princeton University Press, 2000

Dugard, John and John Reynolds, 'Apartheid, International Law, and the Occupied Palestinian Territory' (2013) 24 *European Journal of International Law* 867

Dugard, John, '1966 and All That, the South West Africa Judgment Revisited in the East Timor Case' (1996) 8 *African Journal of International and Comparative Law* 549

Dugard, John, 'Apartheid, International Law, and the Occupied Palestinian Territory' (2013) 24 *European Journal of International Law* 869

Dugard, John, 'L'apartheid', in Hervé Ascensio, Emmanuel Decaux, and Alain Pellet, eds., *Droit international pénal*, 2nd rev. ed., Paris: Pedone, 2012, pp. 197–208

Dugard, John, 'Namibia (South West Africa): The Court's Opinion, South Africa's Response, and Prospects for the Future' (1972) 11 *Columbia Journal of Transnational Law* 14

Dugard, John, 'The South West Africa Cases, Second Phase, 1966' (1966) 83 *South African Law Journal* 429

Dugard, John, *The South West Africa/Namibia Dispute: Documents and Scholarly Writings on the Controversy Between South Africa and the United Nations*, Berkeley: University of California Press, 1973

Dunn, Leslie C., *Race and Biology*, Paris: UNESCO, 1951

Dunstan, Sarah Claire, 'Conflicts of Interest: The 1919 Pan African Congress and the Wilsonian Moment' (2016) 39 *Callaloo* 133

Eckel, Jan, 'The International League for the Rights of Man, Amnesty International, and the Changing Fate of Human Rights Activism from the 1940s Through the 1970s' (2013) 4 *Humanity* 183

Eden, Paul, 'The Practices of Apartheid as a War Crime: A Critical Analysis' (2013) 16 *Yearbook of International Humanitarian Law* 89

Eden, Paul, 'The Role of the Rome Statute in the Criminalization of Apartheid' (2014) 12 *Journal of International Criminal Justice* 171

Edmonds, James Edward and Lassa Oppenheim, *Land Warfare: An Exposition of the Laws and Usages of War on Land, for the Guidance of Officers of His Majesty's Army*, London: HMSO, 1914

Ehrlich, Howard J., 'The Swastika Epidemic of 1959–1960: Anti-Semitism and Community Characteristics' (1962) 9 *Social Problems* 264

Eiken, Jan and David Keane, 'Towards an Amicable Solution: The Inter-State Communications Procedure under ICERD' (2022) 21 *The Law and Practice of International Courts and Tribunals* 302

El-Ayouty, Yassin, *The United Nations and Decolonization: The Role of Afro-Asia*, The Hague: Martinus Nijhoff, 1971

El-Khawas, Mohamed, 'Third-World Stance on Apartheid: the U.N. Record' (1971) 9 *Journal of Modern African Studies* 443

Elkins, Caroline, *Legacy of Violence, A History of the British Empire*, London: Bodley Head, 2022

Eschen, Penny M. Von, *Race against Empire: Black Americans and Anticolonialism, 1937–1957*, Ithaca: Cornell University Press, 1997

Eslava, Luis, Michael Fakhri, and Vasuki Nesiah, eds., *Bandung, Global History, and International Law Critical Pasts and Pending Futures*, Cambridge: Cambridge University Press, 2017

Evans, Carolyn, 'Time for a Treaty? The Legal Sufficiency of the Declaration on the Elimination of All Forms of Intolerance and Discrimination' (2007) 3 *Brigham Young University Law Review* 617

Evans, Luther Harris, 'Are "C" Mandates Veiled Annexations?' (1927) 7 *Southwestern Political and Social Science Quarterly* 381

Evans, Malcolm D., *Religious Liberty and International Law in Europe*, Cambridge: Cambridge University Press, 1997

Falk, Richard and Virginia Tilley, *Israeli Practices towards the Palestinian People and the Question of Apartheid*, Beirut: Economic and Social Commission for Eastern Asia, 2017

Falk, Richard, 'The South West Africa Cases: An Appraisal' (1967) 21 *International Organization* 1

Fallah, Katherine and Ntina Tzouvala, 'Deploying Race, Employing Force: "African Mercenaries" and the 2011 NATO Intervention in Libya' (2021) 67 *UCLA Law Review* 1580

Farrior, Stephanie, 'Color in the Non-Discrimination Provisions of the Universal Declaration of Human Rights and the Two Covenants' (2015) 14 *Washington University Global Studies Law Review* 751

Farrior, Stephanie, 'Molding the Matrix: The Historical and Theoretical Foundations of International Law Concerning Hate Speech' (1996) 14 *Berkeley Journal of International Law* 1

Favoreu, Louis, 'L'arrêt de la Cour internationale de Justice dans les affaires du *Sud-Ouest africain*' (1966) 12 *Annuaire français de droit international* 123

Favoreu, Louis, 'Récusation et administration de la preuve devant la Cour internationale de Justice. À propos des affaires du *Sud-Ouest Africain* (Fond)' (1965) 11 *Annuaire français de droit international* 233

Felice, William F., 'The UN Committee on the Elimination of All Forms of Racial Discrimination: Race, and Economic and Social Human Rights' (2002) 24 *Human Rights Quarterly* 205

Ferguson, Clarence Clyde Jr., 'The United Nations Convention on Racial Discrimination: Civil Rights by Treaty' (1964) 1(2) *Law in Transition Quarterly* 61

Ferguson, Edwin E., 'The California Alien Land Law and the Fourteenth Amendment' (1947) 35 *California Law Review* 61

Ferrer Ortega, Luis Gabriel, *La Convención Internacional sobre la Eliminación de Todas las Formas de Discriminación Racial*, Mexico City: Comisión Nacional de los Derechos Humanos, 2015

Fink, Carole, *Defending the Rights of Others: The Great Powers, the Jews, and International Minority Protection*, Cambridge: Cambridge University Press, 2004

First, Ruth, *South West Africa*, Baltimore: Penguin, 1963

Fischer, Georges, 'Les réactions devant l'arrêt de la Cour internationale de justice concernant le *Sud-Ouest Africain*' (1966) *Annuaire français de droit international* 144

Fischer, Hugo, 'The Suppression of Slavery in International Law (II)' (1950) 3 *International Law Quarterly* 508

Fischer, Hugo, 'The Suppression of Slavery in International Law' (1950) 3 *International Law Quarterly* 28

Fishman, Joel, '"A Disaster of Another Kind": Zionism=Racism, Its Beginning, and the War of Delegitimization against Israel' (2011) 5 *Israel Journal of Foreign Affairs* 75

Flemming, Brian, 'South West Africa Cases – Ethiopia v. South Africa; Liberia v. South Africa Second Phase' (1967) 5 *Canadian Yearbook of International Law* 241

428 BIBLIOGRAPHY

Fogarty, Richard, *Race and War in France: Colonial Subjects in the French Army, 1914–1918*, Baltimore: Johns Hopkins University Press, 2008

Fokkens, Andries M., 'The Suppression of Internal Unrest in South West Africa (Namibia) 1921–1933' (2012) 40 *Scientia Militaria* 109

Foner, Eric and Henry Louis Gates Jr., eds., *W.E.B. Du Bois, Black Reconstruction and Other Writings*, New York: Library of America, 2021

Forrester, Katrina, 'Reparations, History and the Origins of Global Justice', in Duncan Bell, ed., *Empire, Race and Global Justice*, Cambridge: Cambridge University Press, 2019, pp. 22–51

Foster, Michelle and Timnah Rachel Baker, 'Racial Discrimination in Nationality Laws: A Doctrinal Blind Spot of International Law?' (2021) 11 *Columbia Journal of Race and Law* 83

Francis, Megan Ming and Leah Wright-Rigeur, 'Black Lives Matter in Historical Perspective' (2021) 17 *Annual Review of Law and Social Science* 441

Frankel, Philip H., *An Ordinary Atrocity: Sharpeville and Its Massacre*, New Haven: Yale University Press, 2001

Franklin, V.P., 'Commentary – Reparation as Development Strategy: The CARICOM Reparations Commission' (2013) 98 *Journal of African American History* 363

Fraser, Cary, 'An American Dilemma: Race and Realpolitik in the American Response to the Bandung Conference, 1955', in Brenda Gayle Plummer, ed., *Window on Freedom: Race, Civil Rights, and Foreign Affairs, 1945–1988*, Chapel Hill and London: University of North Carolina Press, 2003, pp. 116–40

Fraser, Cary, 'Crossing the Color Line in Little Rock: The Eisenhower Administration and the Dilemma of Race for U.S. Foreign Policy' (2000) 24 *Diplomatic History* 233

Frazão, Sergio Armanda, 'International Responsibility for Non-self-governing Peoples' (1954) 296 *Annals of the American Academy of Political and Social Science* 56

Frazier, E. Franklin, *Black Bourgeoisie*, New York: Macmillan, 1962

Frederickson, George M., 'The Rise and Fall of the Laboratory Racist' (September 2001) *UNESCO Courier* 21

Fredman, Sandra, ed., *Discrimination and Human Rights: The Case of Racism*, Oxford University Press, Oxford, 2001

Freeland, David, *American Hotel, The Waldorf-Astoria and the Making of a Century*, New Brunswick, NJ: Rutgers University Press, 2021

Friedmann, Wolfgang G., 'The Jurisprudential Implications of the South West Africa Case' (1967) 6 *Columbia Journal of Transnational Law* 1

Friesel, Ofra, 'Equating Zionism with Racism: The 1965 Precedent' (2013) 97 *American Jewish History* 283

Friesel, Ofra, 'Race versus Religion in the Making of the International Convention Against Racial Discrimination, 1965' (2014) 32 *Law and History Review* 351

Gaffield, Julia. 'The Racialization of International Law after the Haitian Revolution: The Holy See and National Sovereignty' (2020) 125 *American Historical Review* 841

Galonnier, Juliette and Patrick Simon, 'Le Comité pour l'élimination de la discrimination raciale: une approche pragmatique des statistiques ethniques (1970–2018)' (2020) 86 *Critique internationale* 67

Garson, Noel, 'Smuts and the Idea of Race' (2007) 57 *South African Historical Journal* 153

Garvey, Marcus, 'Declaration of Rights of the Negro Peoples of the World' (2021) 13 *Black Camera* 335

BIBLIOGRAPHY 429

Garvey, Marcus, 'Race Discrimination Must Go', *Negro World*, 30 November 1918, in Robert A. Hill, ed., *The Marcus Garvey and Universal Negro Improvement Association Papers*, Vol. I, Berkeley: University of California Press, 1983, p. 3

Gassama, Ibrahim J., 'Reaffirming Faith in the Dignity of Each Human Being: The United Nations, NGOs, and Apartheid' (1996) 19 *Fordham International Law Journal* 1464

Gastaut, Yvan, 'L'UNESCO, les « races » et le racisme', in *60 ans d'histoire de l'UNESCO*, Paris: UNESCO, 2007, pp. 197–210

Gathii, James T., 'Africa', in Bardo Fassbender and Ann Peters, eds., *The Oxford Handbook of the History of International Law*, Oxford: Oxford University Press, 2012, pp. 407–28

Gathii, James T., 'Henry J. Richardson III: The Father of Black Tradition of International Law' (2017) 31 *Temple International and Comparative Law Journal* 325

Gathii, James T., 'International Law and Eurocentricity' (1998) 9 *European Journal of International Law* 184

Gathii, James T., 'Studying Race in International Law Scholarship Using a Social Science Approach' (2021) 22 *Chicago Journal of International Law* 71

Gathii, James T., 'The Promise of International Law: A Third World View' (2021) *American University International Law Review* 377

Gathii, James T., 'TWAIL: A Brief History of Its Origins, Its Decentralized Network, and a Tentative Bibliography' (2011) 3 *Trade Law and Development* 26

Gathii, James T., 'Writing Race and Identity in a Global Context: What CRT and TWAIL Can Learn from Each Other' (2021) 67 *UCLA Law Review* 1610

Gayon, Jean, 'Commentaire', in *60 ans d'histoire de l'UNESCO*, Paris: UNESCO, 2007, pp. 223–7

Gayon, Jean, 'Do Biologists Need the Expression "Human Races"? UNESCO 1950–51', in Jacques J. Rozenberg, ed., *Bioethical and Ethical Issues Surrounding the Trials and Code of Nuremberg, Nuremberg Revisited*, Lewiston, NY: Edwin Mellen Press, 2004, pp. 23–47

Gayon, Jean, 'Faut-il proscrire en biologie l'expression: « races humaines »?, UNESCO 1950–51' (2002) 12 *L'Aventure humaine* 9

Gebhard, Julia, 'Apartheid', in Rüdiger Wolfrum, ed., *The Max Planck Encyclopaedia of Public International Law*, Vol. I, Oxford: Oxford University Press, 2012, pp. 462–8

Getachew, Adom, *Worldmaking after Empire, The Rise and Fall of Self-Determination*, Princeton: Princeton University Press, 2019

Gevers, Christopher, 'Africa and International Criminal Law', in Kevin J. Heller, Frederic Megret, Sarah Nouwen, Jens Ohlin, and Darryl Robinson, eds., *The Oxford Handbook of International Criminal Law*, Oxford: Oxford University Press, 2020, pp. 145–66

Gevers, Christopher, 'Prosecuting the Crime against Humanity of Apartheid: Never, Again' (2018) 1 *African Yearbook on International Humanitarian Law* 25

Gevers, Christopher, 'The "Africa Blue Books" at Versailles: World War I, Narrative and Unthinkable Histories of International Criminal Law', in Immi Tallgren and Thomas Skouteris, eds., *The New Histories of International Criminal Law, Retrials*, Oxford: Oxford University Press, 2019, pp. 145–66

Gevers, Christopher, 'Unwhitening the World, Rethinking Race and International Law' (2021) 67 *UCLA Law Review* 1652

Gil-Riaño, Sebastían, 'Relocating Anti-racist Science: the 1950 UNESCO Statement on Race and Economic Development in the Global South' (2018) 51 *British Journal for the History of Science* 281

430 BIBLIOGRAPHY

Giladi, Rotem, 'Negotiating Identity: Israel, Apartheid, and the United Nations, 1949–1952' (2017) 132 *English Historical Review* 1440

Giladi, Rotem, 'The Phoenix of Colonial War: Race, the Laws of War, and the "Horror on the Rhine"' (2017) 30 *Leiden Journal of International Law* 847

Gilchrist, Huntington, 'Colonial Questions at the San Francisco Conference' (1945) 39 *American Political Science Review* 982

Glendon, Mary Ann, 'The Forgotten Crucible: The Latin American Influence on the Universal Human Rights Idea' (2003) 16 *Harvard Human Rights Journal* 27

Gobineau, Arthur de, *Essai sur l'inégalité des races humaines*, Paris: Firmin Didot, 1853

Goldmann, Matthias and Mona Sonnen, 'Soft Authority against Hard Cases of Racially Discriminating Speech: Why the CERD Committee Needs a Margin of Appreciation Doctrine' (2016) 1 *Goettingen Journal of International Law* 131

Gong, Gerrit W., *The Standard of 'Civilization' in International Society*, Oxford: Oxford University Press, 1984

Gordon, Ruth, 'Critical Race Theory and International Law: Convergence and Divergence' (2000) 45 *Villanova Law Review* 827

Gortázar Rotaeche, Cristina J., 'Racial Discrimination and the European Convention on Human Rights' (1998) 24 *Journal of Ethnic and Migration Studies* 177

Gott, Gil, 'Critical Race Globalism?: Global Political Economy, and the Intersections of Race, Nation, and Class' (2000) 33 *UC Davis Law Review* 1503

Graf, Philipp, *Die Bernheim Petition 1933: Jüdische Politik in der Zwischenkriegzeit*, Götttingen: Vanderhoeck and Ruprecht, 2008

Grant, Colin, *Negro With a Hat. The Rise and Fall of Marcus Garvey*, Oxford: Oxford University Press, 2008

Gravett, Willem H., 'The Smutsian Concept of Human Rights' (2016) 32 *South African Journal of Human Rights* 538

Green, Leslie C., 'South West Africa and the World Court' (1966–1967) 22 *International Journal* 39

Gregg, Robert and Madhavi Kale, 'The Negro and the Dark Princess: Two Legacies of the Universal Races Congress' (2005) 92 *Radical History Review* 134

Grinberg, L.L., 'In Search of Language to Resist the Israeli "Thing Without a Name"' (2009) 22 *International Journal of Politics, Culture, and Society* 105

Gross, Ernest A., 'Legal and Political Strategies of the South West Africa Litigation' (1967) 4 *Law in Transition Quarterly* 8

Gross, Ernest A., 'The South West Africa Cases: On the Threshold of Decision' (1963) 3 *Columbia Journal of Transnational Law* 19

Grovogui, Siba N'Zatioula, *Sovereigns, Quasi Sovereigns, and Africans, Race and Self-Determination in International Law*, Minneapolis: University of Minnesota Press, 1996

Gualtieri, Claudia, 'Racism and Xenophobia' (2006) 77 *Revue internationale de droit pénal* 263

Guenther, Lisa, '"We Charge Genocide", Anti-Black Racism in the United States as Genocidal Structural Violence', in Anne O'Byrne and Martin Shuster, eds., *Logics of Genocide, The Structures of Violence and the Contemporary World*, New York: Routledge, 2020, pp. 134–51

Haines, Corrie Gerald, 'The United Nations Challenge to Racial Discrimination in South Africa 1946–1950' (2001) 60 *African Studies* 185

Halderman, John W., 'Some Legal Aspects of Sanctions in the Rhodesian Case' (1968) 17 *International and Comparative Law Quarterly* 672

BIBLIOGRAPHY 431

Hall, Christopher K., 'The Crime of Apartheid', in Otto Triffterer, ed., *Commentary on the Rome Statute of the International Criminal Court, Observers' Notes, Article by Article*, Baden-Baden: Nomos, 1999, pp. 167–70

Hall, Duncan H., *Mandates, Dependencies, and Trusteeships*, Washington: Carnegie Endowment for International Peace, 1948

Hall, William Edward, *A Treatise on International Law*, 3rd ed., Oxford: Clarendon Press, 1890

Hannikainen, Lauri, 'Dialogue Between States and International Human Rights Monitoring Organs – Especially the European Commission Against Racism and Intolerance', in Asbjørn Eide, Jakob Th. Möller, and Inete Ziemele, eds., *Making Peoples Heard: Essays on Human Rights in Honour of Gudmundur Alfredsson*, The Hague: Brill, 2011, pp. 323–40

Hannikainen, Lauri, 'Monitoring against Discrimination and Xenophobia – The European Commission against Racism and Intolerance (ECRI)', in Gudmundur Alfredsson, Jonas Grimheden, Bertrand G. Ramcharan and Alfred de Zayas, eds., *International Human Rights Monitoring Mechanisms, Essays in Honour of Jakob Th. Möller*, Leiden: Brill, 2009, pp. 541–6

Hargreaves, John D., 'Maurice Delafosse on the Pan-African Congress of 1919' (1968) 1 *African Historical Studies* 233

Harmon, Shawn H.E., 'The Significance of UNESCO's Universal Declaration on the Human Genome and Human Rights' (2005) 2 *SCRIPTed* 20

Harris, Cheryl I., 'Whiteness as Property' (1993) 106 *Harvard Law Review* 1707

Harris, Robert L. Jr., 'Racial Equality and the United Nations Charter', in Armstead L. Robinson and Patricia Sullivan, eds., *New Directions in Civil Rights Studies*, Charlottesville: University of Virginia Press, 1991, pp. 126–45

Harris, Susan, 'Tampering with the World Conference Against Racism' (2002) 21(3) *Social Alternatives* 20

Hart, Bradley W., 'Science, Politics, and Prejudice: The Dynamics and Significance of British Anthropology's Failure to Confront Nazi Racial Ideology' (2013) 43 *European History Quarterly* 301

Hart, Randle J., 'The Greatest Subversive Plot in History? The American Radical Right and Anti-UNESCO Campaigning' (2014) 48 *Sociology* 554

Hatuel-Radoshitzky, Michal, 'Israel and Apartheid in International Discourse Israel and Apartheid in International Discourse' (2015) 18 *Strategic Assessment* 105

Hauptman, Laurence M., *The Iroquois Struggle for Survival: World War II to Red Power*, Syracuse: Syracuse University Press, 1986

Hayden, Sherman S., 'The Trusteeship Council: Its First Three Years' (1951) 66 *Political Science Quarterly* 226

Hazard, Anthony Q., 'A Racialized Deconstruction? Ashley Montagu and the 1950 UNESCO Statement on Race' (2011) 19 *Transforming Anthropology: Journal of the Association of Black Anthropologists* 174

Hazard, Anthony Q., 'Ashley Montagu, the "Most Dangerous Myth," and the "Negro Question" during World War II' (2016) 72 *Journal of Anthropological Research* 289

Hazard, Anthony Q., 'Ashley Montagu: The Negro Question and the Myth of Race', in Anthony Q. Hazard, *Boasians at War*, New York: Palgrave Macmillan, 2020, pp. 59–100

Hazard, Anthony Q., *Boasians at War*, New York: Palgrave Macmillan, 2020

Hazard, Anthony Q., *Postwar Anti-racism, the United States, UNESCO and 'Race', 1945–1968*, New York: Palgrave Macmillan, 2012

432   BIBLIOGRAPHY

Heartfield, James, *The Aborigines' Protection Society, Humanitarian Imperialism in Australia, New Zealand, Fiji, Canada, South Africa, and the Congo, 1837–1909*, London: Hurst, 2011

Heartfield, James, *The British and Foreign Anti-Slavery Society, 1838–1956, A History*, London: Hurst, 2016

Helps, David, '"We Charge Genocide": Revisiting Black Radicals' Appeals to the World Community' (2018) 1 *Radical Americas* 3

Henderson, Errol A., *Hidden in Plain Sight: Racism in International Relations Theory*, London: Routledge, 2014

Henkel, Gerd, *Die Leipziger Prozesse: Deutsche Kriegsverbrechen und ihre strafrechtliche Verfolgung nach dem Ersten Weltkrieg*, Hamburg: Hamburger Institute, 2003

Henkel, Gerd, *The Leipzig Trials, German War Crimes and their Legal Consequences after 1921*, Dordrecht: Republic of Letters, 2014

Henry, Charles P. and Tunua Thrash, 'U.S. Human Rights Petitions Before the UN' (1996) 26 *The Black Scholar* 60

Herik, Larissa van den and Rafael Braga da Silva, 'The Crime of Apartheid', in Kai Ambos, ed., *The Rome Statute of the International Criminal Court, Article by Article Commentary*, 4th ed., Munich, Oxford and Baden-Baden: C.H. Beck, Hart, Nomos, 2021, pp. 241–4, 301–5

Hero, Alfred O. Jr., 'American Negroes and US Foreign Policy: 1937–1967' (1969) 13 *Journal of Conflict Resolution* 220

Heyns, Christof, 'The Preamble of the United Nations Charter: The Contribution of Jan Smuts' (1995) 7 *African Journal of International and Comparative Law* 329

Higgins, Rosalyn, 'The International Court and South West Africa: The Implications of the Judgment' (1966) 42 *International Affairs* 573

Higgins, Rosalyn, *Themes and Theories: Selected Essays, Speeches, and Writings in International Law*, Oxford: Oxford University Press, 2009

Hill, Robert A. and Edmond J. Keller, eds., *Trustee for the Human Community: Ralph J. Bunche, the United Nations, and the Decolonization of Africa*, Athens: Ohio University Press, 2010

Hill, Robert A., ed., *The Marcus Garvey and Universal Negro Improvement Association Papers*, Berkeley: University of California Press, 1983

Hinds, Lennox S., 'Apartheid in South Africa and the Universal Declaration of Human Rights' (1985) 24 *Crime and Social Justice* 5

Hivonnet, Joëlle, 'The European Union in the 2009 Durban Review Conference', in Jan Wouters, ed., *The European Union and Multilateral Governance*, London: Palgrave Macmillan, 2012, pp. 122–42

Hobbins, A.J., 'Eleanor Roosevelt, John Humphrey and Canadian Opposition to the Universal Declaration of Human Rights: Looking Back on the 50th Anniversary of the UNDHR' (1998) 52 *International Journal* 325

Hobbs, Steven H. and Frank H. Fitch II, 'The Marcus Garvey Case: A Law and Power Theory Analysis of Political Suppression of Human Dignity' (1991) 2 *George Mason University Civil Rights Law Journal* 15

Hobsbawm, Eric, *The Age of Empire, 1875–1914*, New York: Pantheon Books, 1987

Hochman, Adam, 'Against the New Racial Naturalism' (2013) 110 *Journal of Philosophy* 331

Hochschild, Adam, *King Leopold's Ghost: A Story of Greed, Terror, and Heroism in Colonial Africa*, Boston: Houghton Mifflin, 1998

Hollo, Lanna Yael, 'The European Commission against Racism and Intolerance', in Gauthier de Beco, ed., *Human Rights Monitoring Mechanisms of the Council of Europe*, London: Routledge, 2012, pp. 127–49

Hollo, Lanna Yael, *The European Commission against Racism and Intolerance (ECRI) – Its first 15 years*, Strasbourg: Council of Europe, 2009

Holton, Robert John, 'Cosmopolitanism or Cosmopolitanisms? The Universal Races Congress of 1911' (2002) 2 *Global Networks* 153

Hopkins, Kevin, 'Assessing the World's Response to Apartheid: A Historical Account of International Law and Its Part in the South African Transformation' (2001–2002) 10 *Miami International and Comparative Law Review* 241

Horne, Gerald, 'Race from Power: U.S. Foreign Policy and the General Crisis of "White Supremacy"' (1999) 23 *Diplomatic History* 457

Horne, Gerald, *Black and Red, W.E.B. Du Bois and the Afro-American Response to the Cold War, 1944–1963*, Albany: State University of New York Press, 1986

Horne, Gerald, *Black Revolutionary: William Patterson and the Globalization of the African American Freedom Struggle*, Urbana, Chicago and Springfield: University of Illinois Press, 2013

Horne, Gerald, *Communist Front? The Civil Rights Congress, 1946–1956*, Rutherford, NJ: Fairleigh Dickinson University Press, 1988

Hovet, Thomas Jr., 'The Role of Africa in the United Nations' (1964) 354 *Annals of the American Academy of Political and Social Science* 122

Howard-Hassmann, Rhoda E., 'Reparations for the Slave Trade: Rhetoric, Law, History and Political Realities' (2007) 41 *Canadian Journal of African Studies/Revue canadienne des études africaines* 427

Howard-Hassmann, Rhoda E., *Reparations to Africa*, Philadelphia: University of Pennsylvania Press, 2018

Howard, Erica, *The EU Race Directive, Developing the Protection against Racial Discrimination within the EU*, London: Routledge, 2009

Humphrey, John P., 'The UN Charter and the Universal Declaration of Human Rights', in Evan Luard, ed., *The International Protection of Human Rights*, London: Thames and Hudson, 1967, pp. 30–58

Humphrey, John P., 'The United Nations Sub-Commission on the Prevention of Discrimination and the Protection of Minorities' (1968) 62 *American Journal of International Law* 869

Humphrey, John P., *Human Rights and the United Nations: A Great Adventure*, Ardsley, NY: Transnational Publishers, 1984

Huxley, Julian S., 'America Revisited, III. The Negro Problem', *The Spectator*, 29 November 1924, p. 821

Hyam, Ronald and Peter Henshaw, *The Lion and the Springbok: Britain and South Africa since the Boer War*, Cambridge: Cambridge University Press, 2003

Iadarola, Antoinette, 'Ethiopia's Admission into the League of Nations: An Assessment of Motives' (1975) 8 *International Journal of African Historical Studies* 601

Ibhawoh, Bonny, 'Testing the Atlantic Charter: Linking Anticolonialism, Self-determination and Universal Human Rights' (2014) 18 *International Journal of Human Rights* 842

Ijere, Martin O., 'W.E.B. Du Bois and Marcus Garvey as Pan-Africanists: A Study in Contrast' (1974) 89 *Présence Africaine* 188

434 BIBLIOGRAPHY

Ingle, Dwight J., 'The 1964 UNESCO Proposals on the Biological Aspects of Race: A Critique' (1965) 8 *Perspectives in Biology and Medicine* 403

Irvin-Erickson, Douglas, *Raphael Lemkin and the Concept of Genocide*, Philadelphia: Penn, 2017

Irwin, Ryan, 'Apartheid on Trial: South West Africa and the International Court of Justice, 1960–66' (2010) 32 *International History Review* 619

Jacobs, Sean and Jon Soske, eds., *Apartheid Israel: The Politics of an Analogy*, Chicago: Haymarket, 2015

Jacobs, Stephen Leonard, '"We Charge Genocide": A Historical Petition All but Forgotten and Unknown', in Scott W. Murray, *Understanding Atrocities: Remembering, Representing, and Teaching Genocide*, Calgary: University of Calgary Press, 2017, pp. 125–43

Jackson, Miles, 'The Definition of Apartheid in Customary International Law and the International Convention on the Elimination of All Forms of Racial Discrimination' (2022) 71 *International and Comparative Law Quarterly* 831

Janken, Kenneth R., 'From Colonial Liberation to Cold War Liberalism: Walter White, the NAACP, and Foreign Affairs, 1941–1955' (1998) 21 *Ethnic and Racial Studies* 1074

Jennings, James, 'The International Convention on the Elimination of All Forms of Racial Discrimination: Implications for Challenging Racial Hierarchy' (1997) 40 *Howard Law Journal* 597

Jensen, Steven, *The Making of International Human Rights: The 1960s, Decolonization and the Reconstruction of Global Values*, Cambridge: Cambridge University Press, 2016

Jensen, Walter Jr., 'International Justice on Trial: The South West Africa Cases Phase Two' (1968) 6 *American Business Law Journal* 691

Jhabvala, Farrokh, 'The Drafting of the Human Rights Provisions of the UN Charter' (1997) 44 *Netherlands International Law Review* 1

Jobbins, David, 'Has the Commonwealth a Role to Play in the Row over Reparations for the Slave Trade?' (2014) 103 *The Round Table* 343

Johnson, David Lawther, 'Sanctions and South Africa' (1978) 19 *Harvard International Law Journal* 887

Johnson, Ernest, 'A Voice at the Peace Table?' (1944) 51 *The Crisis* 345

Jones, Dorothy V., 'The League of Nations Experiment in International Protection' (1994) 8 *Ethics and International Affairs* 7

Jones, Matthew, 'A "Segregated" Asia?: Race, the Bandung Conference, and Pan-Asianist Fears in American Thought and Policy, 1954–1955' (2005) 29 *Diplomatic History* 841

Joseph, Richard, 'The Royal Pretender: Prince Douala Manga Bell in Paris, 1919–1922' (1974) 54 *Cahiers d'études africaines* 339

Kaeckenbeeck, Georges, 'Upper Silesia Under the League of Nations' (1946) 243 *Annals of the American Academy of Political and Social Science* 129

Kaeckenbeeck, Georges, *The International Experiment of Upper Silesia: A Study in the Working of the Upper Silesian Settlement 1922–1937*, Oxford: Oxford University Press, 1942

Kaleck, Wolfgang. 'On Double Standards and Emerging European Custom on Acountability for Colonial Crimes', in Morten Bergsmo, Wolfgang Kaleck, and Kyaw Yin Hlaing, eds., *Colonial Wrongs and Access to International Law*, Brussels: Torkel Opsahl Academic EPublisher, 2020, pp. 1–40

Kang, Jerry, 'Trojan Horses of Race' (2005) 118 *Harvard Law Review* 1495

Karch, Brendan, 'A Jewish "Nature Preserve": League of Nations Minority Protections in Nazi Upper Silesia, 1933–1937' (2013) 46 *Central European History* 124

Kattan, Victor, 'Decolonizing the International Court of Justice: The Experience of Judge Sir Muhammad Zafrulla Khan in the South West Africa Cases' (2015) 5 *Asian Journal of International Law* 310

Kattan, Victor, 'There Was an Elephant in the Court Room: Reflections on the Role of Judge Sir Percy Spender (1897–1985) in the South West Africa Cases (1960–1966) after Half a Century' (2018) 31 *Leiden Journal of International Law* 147

Kaufmann, Chaim D. and Robert A. Pape, 'Explaining Costly International Moral Action: Britain's Sixty-year Campaign Against the Atlantic Slave Trade' (1999) 53 *International Organization* 631

Kawakami, Kiyoshi K., *Japan and World Peace*, New York: Macmillan, 1919

Kawamura, Noriko, 'Wilsonian Idealism and Japanese Claims at the Peace Conference' (1997) 66 *Pacific Historical Review* 503

Kawser Ahmed, 'The Domestic Jurisdiction Clause in the United Nations Charter: A Historical View' (2006) 10 *Singapore Yearbook of International Law* 175

Keane, David and Annapurna Waughray, eds., *Fifty years of the International Convention on the Elimination of All Forms of Racial Discrimination, A living instrument*, Manchester: Manchester University Press, 2017

Keane, David, 'Descent-based Discrimination in International Law: A Legal History' (2005) 11 *International Journal on Minority and Group Rights* 93

Keane, David, 'Mapping the International Convention on the Elimination of all Forms of Racial Discrimination as a Living Instrument' (2020) 20 *Human Rights Law Review* 236

Keane, David, *Caste-Based Discrimination in International Human Rights Law*, London and New York: Routledge, 2007

Keech, Marc and Barrie Houlihan, 'Sport and the End of Apartheid' (1999) 88 *The Round Table* 109

Keenleyside, T.A., 'The Indian Nationalist Movement and the League of Nations: Prologue to the United Nations' (1983) 39 *India Quarterly* 281

Kellogg, Charles Flint, *NAACP, A History of the National Association for the Advancement of Colored People*, Vol. I, 1909–1920, Baltimore and London: Johns Hopkins University Press, 1967

Kelly, Mark, *ECRI 10 Years of Combating Racism: A Review of the Work of the European Commission against Racism and Intolerance*, Strasbourg: Council of Europe, 2004

Kelsen, Hans, 'The Preamble of the Charter—A Critical Analysis' (1946) 8 *The Journal of Politics* 134

Kendi, Ibram X., 'Reigning Assimilationists and Defiant Black Power: The Struggle to Define and Regulate Racist Ideas', in Keisha N. Blain, Christopher Cameron, and Ashley D. Farmer, eds., *New Perspectives on the Black Intellectual Tradition*, Chicago: Northwestern University Press, 2018, pp. 157–73

King, Henry T. Jr., 'Origins of the Genocide Convention' (2008) 40 *Case Western Reserve Journal of International Law* 13

King, Martin Luther Jr., *Letter from Birmingham City Jail*, Stamford, CT: Overbrook Press, 1968

Klotz, Audie, 'Norms Reconstituting Interests: Global Racial Equality and U.S. Sanctions Against South Africa' (1995) 49 *International Organization* 451

Knop, Karen, 'Lorimer's Private Citizens of the World' (2016) 27 *European Journal of International Law* 415

436 BIBLIOGRAPHY

Knox, Robert and Ntina Tzouvala, 'Looking Eastwards, The Bolshevik Theory of Imperialism and International Law', in Kathryn Greenman, Anne Orford, and Anna Saunders, eds., *Revolutions in International Law, The Legacies of 1917*, Cambridge: Cambridge University Press, 2021, pp. 27–55

Knox, Robert, 'Civilizing Interventions? Race, War and International Law' (2013) 26 *Cambridge Review of International Affairs* 111

Knox, Robert, 'Haiti at the League of Nations: Racialisation, Accumulation and Representation' (2020) 21 *Melbourne Journal of International Law* 245

Knox, Robert, 'Race, Racialism and Rivalry in the International Legal Order', in Alexander Anievas, Nivi Manchanda, Robbie Shilliam, eds., *Race and Racism in International Relations: Confronting the Global Colour Line*, London: Routledge, 2014, pp. 179–92

Knox, Robert, 'Valuing Race? Stretched Marxism and the Logic of Imperialism' (2016) 4(1) *London Review of International Law* 81

Koller, Christian, 'The Recruitment of Colonial Troops in Africa and Asia and their Deployment in Europe during the First World War' (2008) 26 *Immigrants & Minorities* 111

Konstantinidis, Ioannis, ' "Know Thyself", Racial Discrimination before the ICJ – Recent Jurisprudential Developments', in Patrícia Galvão Teles and Manuel Almeida Ribeiro, eds., *Case Law and the Development of International Law*, The Hague: Brill Nijhoff, 2021, pp. 142–58

Korey, William, *An Epitaph for Raphael Lemkin*, New York: Jacob Blaustein Institute, 2001

Korey, William, *NGOs and the Universal Declaration of Human Rights*, New York: St. Martin's Press, 1998

Koskenniemi, Martti, 'Histories of International Law: Dealing with Eurocentrism' (2011) 19 *Rechtsgeschichte. Zeitschrift des Max-Planck-Instituts für europäische Rechtsgeschichte* 152

Koskenniemi, Martti, 'Race, Hierarchy and International Law: Lorimer's Legal Science' (2016) 27 *European Journal of International Law* 15

Koskenniemi, Martti, *The Gentle Civilizer of Nations: The Rise and Fall of International Law, 1870–1960*, New York: Cambridge University Press, 2001

Krebs, Edgardo C., 'Popularizing Anthropology, Combating Racism: Alfred Métraux at The UNESCO Courier', in Poul Duedahl, *The History of UNESCO, Global Actions and Impacts*, London: Palgrave Macmillan, 2016, pp. 29–48

Kress, Michael, 'African Diplomats in Washington', in Brenda Gayle Plummer, ed., *Window on Freedom: Race, Civil Rights, and Foreign Affairs, 1945–1988*, Chapel Hill and London: University of North Carolina Press, 2003, pp. 163–80

Kunz, Josef L., 'The Inter-American Conference on Problems of War and Peace at Mexico City and the Problem of the Reorganization of the Inter-American System' (1945) 39 *American Journal of International Law* 527

Kurz, Nathan A., *Jewish Internationalism and Human Rights after the Holocaust*, Cambridge: Cambridge University Press, 2021

La campagne allemande contre les troupes noirs, Rapport du Capitaine Bouriand surs ses missions en pays rhénans, Paris: Gauthier Villars, 1922

La lutte contre le racisme et la xénophobie, Paris: La Documentation française, 1990

Laing, Edward A., 'The Contribution of the Atlantic Charter to Human Rights Law and Humanitarian Universalism' (1989) 26 *Willamette Law Review* 113

Lake, Marilyn and Henry Reynolds, *Drawing the Global Colour Line, White Men's Countries and the International Challenge of Racial Equality*, Cambridge: Cambridge University Press, 2008

Lake, Marilyn, 'Chinese Colonists Assert their "Common Human Rights": Cosmopolitanism as Subject and Method of History' (2010) 21 *Journal of World History* 375

Lake, Marilyn, 'Universal Races Congress', in Akira Iriye and Pierre-Yves Saunier, eds., *Palgrave Dictionary of Transnational History*, Basingstoke: Palgrave, 2009, pp. 1079–80

Lake, Marilyn, 'Women's International Leadership', in Joy Damousi, Kim Rubenstein, and Mary Tomsic, eds., *Diversity in Leadership Australian Women, Past and Present*, Canberra: ANU Press, 2014, pp. 71–90

Landis, Elizabeth S., 'The South West Africa Cases: Remand to the United Nations' (1967) 52 *Cornell Law Quarterly* 627

Lane, William P., 'Keeping Good Faith in Diplomacy: Negotiations and Jurisdiction in the ICJ's Application of the CERD' (2013) 35 *Boston College International and Comparative Law Review* 33

Lantos, Tom, 'The Durban Debacle: An Insider's View of the UN World Conference Against Racism' (2002) 26 *Fletcher Forum of World Affairs* 31

Lappin, Richard, 'Should CERD Repudiate the Notion of Race?' (2016) 28 *Peace Review* 393

Lapradelle, Alfred Geouffre de, ed., *La Paix de Versailles, Responsabilité des auteurs de la guerre et des sanctions*, Vol. III, Paris: Éditions internationales, 1930, pp. 16–29

Laqua, Daniel, 'Transnational Intellectual Cooperation, the League of Nations, and the Problem of Order' (2011) 6 *Journal of Global History* 223

Lauren, Paul Gordon, 'First Principles of Racial Equality: History and the Politics and Diplomacy of Human Rights Provisions in the United Nations Charter' (1983) 5 *Human Rights Quarterly* 1

Lauren, Paul Gordon, 'Human Rights in History: Diplomacy and Racial Equality at the Paris Peace Conference' (1978) 2 *Diplomatic History* 257

Lauren, Paul Gordon, 'Seen from the Outside, The International Perspective on America's Dilemma', in Brenda Gayle Plummer, ed., *Window on Freedom: Race, Civil Rights, and Foreign Affairs, 1945–1988*, Chapel Hill and London: University of North Carolina Press, 2003, pp. 21–43

Lauren, Paul Gordon, *Power and Prejudice: The Politics and Diplomacy of Racial Discrimination*, Boulder: Westview Press, 1996

Lauren, Paul Gordon, *The Evolution of Human Rights, Visions Seen*, Philadelphia: University of Pennsylvania, 1998

Lawrance, Benjamin N., 'Bankoe v. Dome: Traditions and Petitions in the Ho-Asogli Amalgamation, British Mandated Togoland, 1919–1939' (2005) 46 *Journal of African History* 243

Le Melle, Tilden J., 'Race in International Relations' (2009) 10 *International Studies Perspectives* 77

Leaphart, Jerry V., 'The World Conference against Racism: What Was Really Achieved, The Durban Conference Revisited' (2002) 26 *Fletcher Forum of World Affairs* 153

Leiris, Michel, *Race and Culture*, Paris: UNESCO, 1951

Lennox, Corinne, 'Reviewing Durban: Examining the Outputs and Review of the 2001 World Conference against Racism' (2009) 27 *Netherlands Quarterly of Human Rights* 191

Lenoir, Noëlle, 'Universal Declaration on the Human Genome and Human Rights: The First Legal and Ethical Framework at the Global Level' (1999) 30 *Columbia Human Rights Law Review* 537

Leong, Nancy, 'Racial Capitalism' (2013) 126 *Harvard Law Review* 2152

438 BIBLIOGRAPHY

Lerner, Natan, 'Incitement in the Racial Convention: Reach and Shortcomings of Article 4' (1992) 22 *Israel Yearbook of Human Rights* 1

Lerner, Natan, 'New Concepts in the UNESCO Declaration on Race and Racial Prejudice' (1981) 3 *Human Rights Quarterly* 48

Lerner, Natan, 'The Convention on the Non-applicability of Statutory Limitations to War Crimes' (1969) 4 *Israel Law Review* 512

Lerner, Natan, 'The Final Text of the U.N. Declaration Against Intolerance and Discrimination Based on Religion or Belief' (1982) 12 *Israel Yearbook of Human Rights* 185

Lerner, Natan, 'Toward a Draft Declaration against Religious Intolerance and Discrimination' (1981) 11 *Israel Yearbook of Human Rights* 82

Lerner, Natan, *Group Rights and Discrimination in International Law*, The Hague: Martinus Nijhoff, 2003

Lerner, Natan, *U.N. Convention on the Elimination of All Forms of Racial Discrimination*, Alphen aan den Rijn: Sijthoff and Noordhoff, 1980

Lévi-Strauss, Claude, *Race and History*, Paris: UNESCO, 1952

Levitt, Jeremy, 'Black African Reparations: Making a Claim for Enslavement and Systematic De Jure Segregation and Racial Discrimination under American and International Law' (1997) 25 *Southern University Law Review* 1

Levitt, Jeremy, ed., *Africa: Mapping New Boundaries in International Law*, Oxford: Hart, 2008

Lewis, David Levering, *W.E.B. Du Bois, A Biography*, New York: Henry Holt, 2009

Lewis, David Levering, *W.E.B. Du Bois: The Fight for Equality and the American Century, 1919–1963*, New York: Henry Holt, 2000

Lewis, Hope, 'Reflections on Blackcrit Theory: Human Rights' (2000) 45 *Villanova Law Review* 1075

Lewis, Hope, 'Transnational Dimensions of Racial Identity: Reflecting on Race, the Global Economy, and the Human Rights Movement at 60' (2009) 24 *Maryland Journal of International Law* 296

Li, Darryl, 'Genres of Universalism: Reading Race into International Law, with Help from Sylvia Wynter' (2021) 67 *UCLA Law Review* 1686

Liberman, Peter, 'Israel and the South African bomb' (2004) 11 *Non-proliferation Review* 46

Lindgren Alves, José Augusto, 'The Durban Conference Against Racism and Everyone's Responsibilities' (2003) 21 *Netherlands Quarterly of Human Rights* 361

Lingaas, Carola, 'Imagined Identities: Defining the Racial Group in the Crime of Genocide' (2016) 10 *Genocide Studies and Prevention* 79

Lingaas, Carola, 'The Crime against Humanity of Apartheid in a Post-Apartheid World' (2015) 2 *Oslo Law Review* 86

Lingaas, Carola, 'The Elephant in the Room: The Uneasy Task of Defining "Racial" in International Criminal Law' (2015) 15 *International Criminal Law Review* 485

Lingaas, Carola, *The Concept of Race in International Criminal Law*, London: Routledge, 2019

Liskofsky, Sidney, 'The UN Declaration on the Elimination of Religious Intolerance and Discrimination: Historical and Legal Perspectives', in James E. Wood Jr., ed., *Religion and the State, Essays in Honor of Leo Pfeffer*, Waco, TX: Baylor University Press, 1985, pp. 441–76

Lloyd, Lorna, '"A Most Auspicious Beginning": The 1946 United Nations General Assembly and the Question of the Treatment of Indians in South Africa' (1990) 16 *Review of International Studies* 131

Lloyd, Lorna, 'A Family Quarrel: The Development of the Dispute over Indians in South Africa' (1991) 34 *Historical Journal* 703

Lockwood, Bert B. Jr., 'The United Nations Charter and United States Civil Rights Litigation: 1946–1955' (1984) 69 *Iowa Law Review* 901

Lodge, Tom, *Sharpeville: An Apartheid Massacre and its Consequences*, Oxford: Oxford University Press, 2011

Loeffler, James, *Rooted Cosmopolitans, Jews and Human Rights in the Twentieth Century*, New Haven and London: Yale University Press, 2018

Lollo, Stephanie, 'World Conference against Racism, Racial Discrimination, Xenophobia and Related Intolerance: Resolution amid Controversy' (2002) 18 *New York Law School Journal of Human Rights* 481

Lorca, Arnulf Becker, 'Petitioning the International: A "Pre-history" of Self-determination' (2014) 25 *European Journal of International Law* 497

Lorca, Arnulf Becker, *Mestizo International Law, A Global Intellectual History 1842–1933*, Cambridge: Cambridge University Press, 2015

Loschke, Angela, 'The United Nations Between "Old Boys' Club" and a Changing World Order, The South African-Indian Dispute at the United Nations, 1945–1955', in Nicole Eggers, Jessica Lynne Pearson, and Aurora Almada e Santos, eds., *The United Nations and Decolonization*, London: Routledge, 2020, pp. 83–104

Louis, William Roger, 'Roger Casement and the Congo' (1964) 5 *Journal of African History* 99

Louis, William Roger, 'The South West African Origins of the "Sacred Trust", 1914–1919' (1967) 66 *African Affairs* 262

Louis, William Roger, 'The United Kingdom and the Beginning of the Mandates System, 1919–1922' (1969) 23 *International Organisation* 73

Lovelace, H. Timothy Jr., 'Making the World in Atlanta's Image: The Student Nonviolent Coordinating Committee, Morris Abram, and the Legislative History of the United Nations Race Convention' (2014) 32 *Law and History Review* 385

Ltaief, Wassila, 'International Law, Mixed Marriage, and the Law of Succession in North Africa: " . . . but some are more equal than others"' (2005) 57 *International Social Science Journal* 331

Lucak, Natalia, 'Georgia v. Russian Federation: A Question of the Jurisdiction of the International Court of Justice' (2012) 27 *Maryland Journal of International Law* 323

Lugard, Frederick D., 'The Colour Problem', *The Edinburgh Review*, April 1921, p. 268

Lynn, Denise, 'Gender Violence as Genocide: The Rosa Lee Ingram Case and We Charge Genocide Petition' (2022) 7 *Radical Americas* 1

Lyons, David, 'Reparations for Slavery and Jim Crow, Its Assumptions and Implications', in Naomi Zack, ed., *The Oxford Handbook of Philosophy and* Race, New York: Oxford University Press, 2017, pp. 505–15

Lyons, Gene M., 'In Search of Racial Equality: The Elimination of Racial Discrimination', in Paul G. Taylor and A.J.R. Groom, eds., *Global Issues in the United Nations' Framework*, Basingstoke: Palgrave Macmillan, 1989, pp. 75–105

Lyons, Michelle E., 'World Conference against Racism: New Avenues for Slavery Reparations?' (2002) 35 *Vanderbilt Journal of Transnational Law* 1235

440   BIBLIOGRAPHY

Macdonell, John, 'International Law and Subject Races', in Gustav Spiller, ed., *Papers on Inter-Racial Problems Communicated to the First Universal Races Congress*, London: P.S. King, 1911, pp. 398–409

Mackay, Fergus, 'The ILO Convention No. 111: An Alternative Means of Protecting Indigenous Peoples' Rights?' (2020) 24 *International Journal of Human Rights* 144

MacQueen, Norrie, 'Belated Decolonization and UN Politics against the Backdrop of the Cold War: Portugal, Britain, and Guinea-Bissau's Proclamation of Independence, 1973–1974' (2006) 8 *Journal of Cold War Studies* 29

Mahalic, Drew and Joan Gambee Mahalic, 'The Limitation Provisions of the International Convention on the Elimination of All Forms of Racial Discrimination' (1987) 9 *Human Rights Quarterly* 74

Maio, Marcos Cho, 'Un programme contre le racisme au lendemain de la Seconde Guerre mondiale', in *60 ans d'histoire de l'UNESCO*, Paris: UNESCO, 2007, pp. 187–96

Maio, Marcos Chor and Ricardo Ventura Santos, 'Antiracism and the Uses of Science in the Post-World War II: An Analysis of UNESCO's First Statements on Race (1950 and 1951)' (2015) 12 *Vibrant: Virtual Brazilian Anthropology* 1

Maio, Marcos Chor and Rosemary Galli, 'Florestan Fernandes, Oracy Nogueira, and the UNESCO Project on Race Relations in São Paulo' (2011) 38 *Latin American Perspectives* 136

Maio, Marcos Chor, 'UNESCO and the Study of Race Relations in Brazil: Regional or National Issue?' (2001) 36 *Latin American Research Review* 118

Maisel, Peggy, 'Lessons from the World Conference against Racism: South Africa as a Case Study' (2002) 81 *Oregon Law Review* 739

Malhotra, Ram C., 'Apartheid and the United Nations' (1964) 354 *Annals of the American Academy of Political and Social Science* 135

Mandela, Nelson, *A Long Walk to Freedom*, Boston: Little Brown, 2000

Manning, Charles A.W., 'The South West Africa Cases, A Personal Analysis' (1966) 3 *International Relations* 98

Manning, Charles A.W., 'Those South West Africa Cases - A Second Look' (1970) 1 *Cambrian Law Review* 31

Maran, Rita, 'A Report from the United Nations World Conference Against Racism, Racial Discrimination, Xenophobia, and Related Intolerance, Durban, South Africa, 2001' (2002) 29 *Social Justice* 177

Marchuk, Iryna, 'Application of the International Convention for the Suppression of the Financing of Terrorism and of the International Convention on the Elimination of All Forms of Racial Discrimination (Ukraine v. Russia)' (2017) 18 *Melbourne Journal of International Law* 436

Marks, Sally, 'Black Watch on the Rhine. A Study in Propaganda, Prejudice and Prurience' (1983) 13 *European Studies Review* 297

Marks, Stephen, 'UNESCO and Human Rights: The Implementation of Rights Relating to Education, Science, Culture, and Communication' (1977) 13 *Texas International Law Journal* 35

Marshall, Peter, 'Smuts and The Preamble to The UN Charter' (2000) 90 *The Round Table, the Commonwealth Journal of International Affairs* 55

Martens, Fedor Fedorovič de, *Traité de droit international*, Vol. I, Paris: Maresq, 1883

Martin, Charles H., 'Internationalizing "The American Dilemma": The Civil Rights Congress and the 1951 Genocide Petition to the United Nations' (1997) 16 *Journal of American Ethnic History* 35

Martin, Michael and Marilyn Yaquinto, eds., *Redress for Historical Injustices in the United States: On Reparations for Slavery, Jim Crow and their Legacies*, Durham, NC: Duke University Press, 2007

Martínez Fernando, Valderrama, *A History of UNESCO*, Paris: UNESCO, 1995

Martinez, Jenny S., 'Antislavery Courts and the Dawn of International Human Rights Law' (2008) 117 *Yale Law Journal* 550

Martinez, Jenny S., *The Slave Trade and the Origins of International Human Rights Law*, Oxford: Oxford University Press, 2012

Mathiot, André, *Les Territoires non autonomes et la Charte des Nations Unies*, Paris: Librairie générale de droit et de jurisprudence, 1949

Matz, Nele, 'Civilization and the Mandate System under the League of Nations as Origin of Trusteeship' (2005) 9 *Max Planck Yearbook of United Nations Law* 47

Mazower, Mark, 'The Strange Triumph of Human Rights' (2004) 47 *The Historical Journal* 379

Mazower, Mark, *No Enchanted Palace: The End of Empire and the Ideological Origins of the United Nations*, Princeton, NJ: Princeton University Press, 2009

McCormack, Timothy L.H., 'Crimes Against Humanity', in Dominic McGoldrick, Peter Rowe, and Eric Donnelly, eds., *The Permanent International Criminal Court: Legal and Policy Issues*, Oxford: Hart 2004, pp. 179–202

McDougal, Myres S. and Michael Reisman, 'Rhodesia and the United Nations: The Lawfulness of International Concern' (1968) 62 *American Journal of International Law* 7

McDougall, Gay J., 'International Law, Human Rights, and Namibian Independence' (1986) 8 *Human Rights Quarterly* 445

McDougall, Gay J., 'The World Conference against Racism: Through a Wider Lens' (2002) 26 *Fletcher Forum of World Affairs* 135

McDougall, Gay J., 'Toward a Meaningful International Regime: The Domestic Relevance of International Efforts to Eliminate All Forms of Racial Discrimination' (1997) 40 *Howard Law Journal* 571

McDougall, Gay, 'The World Conference against Racism: Through a Wider Lens' (2002) 26 *Fletcher Forum of World Affairs* 135

McDuffie, Erik S., '"I Wanted a Communist Philosophy, but I Wanted Us to Have a Chance to Organize Our People": The Diasporic Radicalism of Queen Mother Audley Moore and the Origins of Black Power' (2010) 3 *African and Black Diaspora: An International Journal* 185

McKean, Warwick A., 'The South West Africa Cases (1966): Two Views: I. Legal Right or Interest in the South West Africa Cases: A Critical Comment' [1966] *Australian Yearbook of International Law* 135

McKean, Warwick A., *Equality and Discrimination under International Law*, Oxford: Clarendon Press, 1983

Mégret, Frédéric, 'From "Savages" to "Unlawful Combatants": A Postcolonial Look at International Law's "Other", in Anne Orford, ed., *International Law and its Others*, Cambridge: Cambridge University Press, 2009, pp. 265–317

Meiches, Benjamin, 'The Charge of Genocide: Racial Hierarchy, Political Discourse, and the Evolution of International Institutions' (2019) 13 *International Political Sociology* 20

Meillassoux, Claude, *Verrouillage ethnique en Afrique du Sud*, Addis Ababa: Organisation of African Unity, Paris: UNESCO, 1988

Meron, Theodor, 'The International Convention on the Elimination of All Forms of Racial Discrimination and the Golan Heights' (1978) 8 *Israel Yearbook on Human Rights* 222

442   BIBLIOGRAPHY

Meron, Theodor, 'The Meaning and Reach of the International Convention on the Elimination of All Forms of Racial Discrimination' (1985) 79 *American Journal of International Law* 283

Métraux, Albert, 'UNESCO and the Racial Problem' (1950) 2 *International Social Science Bulletin* 384

Métraux, Alfred, 'Race and Civilisation', 21 November 1950, UNESCO Archives 323.12 A 102

Métraux, Alfred, 'UNESCO and Anthropology' (1951) 53 (n.s.) *American Anthropologist* 294

Mettraux, Guénaël, *Crimes against Humanity*, Oxford: Oxford University Press, 2020

Meyers, B. Davic, 'African Voting in the United Nations General Assembly' (1966) 4 *Journal of Modern African Studies* 213

Mickelson, Karin, 'Rhetoric and Rage: Third World Voices in International Legal Discourse' (1998) 16 *Wisconsin International Law Journal* 353

Miers, Suzanne, 'Slavery and the Slave Trade as International Issues 1890–1939' (1998) 19 *Slavery and Abolition* 16

Mieville, China, *Between Equal Rights: A Marxist Theory of International Law*, Leiden: Brill, 2005

Millar, Thomas Bruce, ed., *Australian Foreign Minister: The Diaries of R.G. Casey, 1951–60*, London: Harper Collins, 1972

Miller, David Hunter, *The Drafting of the Covenant*, New York and London: G. P. Putnam's Sons, 1928

Miller, Jon and Rahul Kumar, *Reparations: Interdisciplinary Inquiries*, Oxford: Oxford University Press, 2007

Miller, Robert H., 'The Convention on the Non-Applicability of Statutory Limitations to War Crimes and Crimes Against Humanity' (1971) 65 *American Journal of International Law* 476

Momirov, Aleksandar, 'The Individual Right to Petition in Internationalized Territories: From Progressive Thought to an Abandoned Practice' (2007) 9 *Journal of the History of International Law* 203

Monar, Jörg, 'The EU's Role in the Fight Against Racism and Xenophobia: Evaluation and Prospects After Amsterdam and Tampere' (2000) 22 *Liverpool Law Review* 7

Montagu, Ashley, 'The Concept of Race' (1962) 64 (n.s.) *American Anthropologist* 919

Montagu, Ashley, 'The Genetical Theory of Race, and Anthropological Method' (1942) 44 (n.s.) *American Anthropologist* 369

Montagu, Ashley, 'UNESCO Statements on Race' (1961) 133 (n.s.) *Science* 1632

Montagu, Ashley, *Man's Most Dangerous Myth, The Fallacy of Race*, New York: Harper, 1942

Montagu, Ashley, *On Being Human*, New York: Henry Schuman, 1950

Montagu, Ashley, *Statement on Race: An Annotated Elaboration and Exposition of the Four Statements on Race issued by the United Nations Educational, Scientific, and Cultural Organization*, New York: Oxford University Press, 1972

Montagu, Ashley, *Statement on Race: An Extended Discussion in Plain Language of the UNESCO Statement by Experts on Race Problems*, New York: Henry Schuman, 1951

Morris, Lorenzo, 'Symptoms of Withdrawal—The U.N., The U.S., Racism and Reparations' (2003) 6 *Howard Scroll: The Social Justice Law Review* 49

Mouralis, Guillaume, 'Legal Imagination and Legal Realism, "Crimes against Humanity" and the US Racial Question in 1945', in Ornella Rovetta and Pieter Lagrou, ed., *Defeating*

Impunity: Attempts at International Justice in Europe since 1914, New York: Berghahn, 2022, pp. 109–32

Mouralis, Guillaume, 'Race et droit aux États-Unis: l'ombre de Nuremberg' (2021) 19 *Revue des droits de l'homme* 1

Mouralis, Guillaume, *Le moment Nuremberg, Le procès international, les lawyers et la question raciale*, Paris: SciencesPo, 2019

Müller-Meiningen, Ernest, '*Who are the Huns?*', *The Law of Nations and its Breakers*, Berlin: George Reimer, 1915

Müller-Wille, Staffan, 'Race et appartenance ethnique: la diversité humaine et l'UNESCO: déclarations sur la race (1950 et 1951)', in *60 ans d'histoire de l'UNESCO*, Paris: UNESCO, 2007, pp. 211–20

Munro, John, 'Ethiopia Stretches Forth Across the Atlantic: African American Anticolonialism during the Interwar Period' (2008) 13(2) *Left History* 37

Murray, James N. Jr., *The United Nations Trusteeship System*, Urbana: University of Illinois Press, 1957

Musselman, Tyler B., 'Skirfmishing for Information: The Flaws of the International Legal System as Evidenced by the Russian-Georgian Conflict of 2008' (2010) 19 *Transnational Law and Contemporary Problems* 317

Mutua, Makau, 'Critical Race Theory and International Law: The View of an Insider-Outsider' (2000) 54 *Villanova Law Review* 841

Mutua, Makau, 'What is TWAIL?' (2000) 94 *Proceedings of the American Society of International Law* 31

Mutua, Makau, 'Why Redraw the Map of Africa: A Moral and Legal Inquiry' (1995) 16 *Michigan Journal of International Law* 1113

Mutua, Makau, Book review of Jeremy I. Levitt, ed., *Africa: Mapping New Boundaries in International Law* (2010) 104 *American Journal of International Law* 514

Mylonas, Denis, *La Genèse de l'Unesco: La Conférence des Ministres Alliés de l'Éducation (1942–1945)*, Brussels: Bruylant, 1976

Myres, S.D. Jr., 'The Permanent Mandates Commission and the Administration of Mandates' (1930) 11 *Southwestern Political and Social Science Quarterly* 213

Namgalies, Clivia, 'Apartheid on Trial' (2004) 15 *Criminal Law Forum* 349

Nathanson, Nathaniel R. and Egon Schwelb, *The United States and the United Nations Treaty on Racial Discrimination*, Washington: West Publishing, 1975

Nault, Derrick M., *Africa and the Shaping of Human Rights*, Oxford: Oxford University Press, 2020

Neier, Aryeh, *The International Human Rights Movement, A History*, Princeton and Oxford: Princeton University Press, 2012

Nelson, Keith, 'The "Black Horror on the Rhine": Race as a Factor in Post-World War I Diplomacy' (1970) 42 *Journal of Modern History* 606

Nesiah, Vasuki, 'Crimes Against Humanity, Racialized Subjects and Deracialized Histories', in Immi Tallgren and Thomas Skouteris, eds., *The New Histories of International Criminal Law, Retrials*, Oxford: Oxford University Press, 2019, pp. 167–88

Nielsen, Henrik Karl, 'The Concept of Discrimination in ILO Convention no. 111' (1994) 43 *International and Comparative Law Quarterly* 827

Nier, Charles Lewis II, 'Guilty as Charged: Malcolm X and His Vision of Racial Justice for African Americans through Utilization of the United Nations International Human Rights Provisions and Institutions' (1997) 16 *Dickinson Journal of International Law* 149

444 BIBLIOGRAPHY

Niezen, Ronald, 'Recognizing Indigenism: Canadian Unity and the International Movement of Indigenous Peoples' (2000) 42 *Comparative Studies in Society and History* 119

Niezen, Ronald, *The Origins of Indigenism: Human Rights and the Politics of Identity*, Berkeley: University of California, 2003

Noer, Thomas J., *Cold War and Black Liberation: The United States and White Rule in Africa, 1948–68*, New York: Columbia, 1985

Normand, Roger and Sarah Zaidi, *Human Rights at the UN, The Political History of Universal Justice*, Bloomington and Indianapolis: Indiana University Press, 2008

Nothling, F.J., 'South Africa and the United Nations, 1945–66', in Thomas Wheeler, ed., *History of the South African Department of Foreign Affairs, 1927–1966*, Johannesburg: South African Institute of International Relations, 2005, pp. 337–64

O'Malley, Alanna, 'India, Apartheid and the New World Order at the UN, 1946–1962' (2020) 31 *Journal of World History* 195

O'Reilly, Kenneth, 'The Jim Crow Policies of Woodrow Wilson' (1997) 17 *Journal of Blacks in Higher Education* 117

Okafor, Obiora Chinedu, 'Critical Third World Approaches to International Law (TWAIL): Theory, Methodology, or Both?' (2008) 10 *International Community Law Review* 371

Okafor, Obiora Chinedu, 'Newness, Imperialism, and International Legal Reform in our Time: A TWAIL Perspective' (2005) 43 *Osgoode Hall Law Journal* 171

Okowa, Phoebe, 'The International Court of Justice and the Georgia/Russia Dispute' (2011) 11 *Human Rights Law Review* 739

Onishi, Yuichiro, 'The New Negro of the Pacific: How African Americans Forged Cross-Racial Solidarity with Japan, 1917–1922' (2007) 92 *Journal of African American History* 191

Oppenheim, Lassa, *International Law, Vol. I, Peace*, London: Longmans, Green, 1905

Osman-Hill, W.C., 'UNESCO on Race' (1951) 51 *Man* 16

Ozgur, Ozdemir A., *Apartheid, the United Nations, and Peaceful Change in South Africa*, Dobbs Ferry, NY: Transnational, 1982

Pachai, B., *The International Aspects of the South African Indian Question, 1860–1971*, Cape Town: C. Struik, 1971

Pahuja, Sundhya, *Decolonising International Law: Development, Economic Growth and the Politics of Universality*, Cambridge: Cambridge University Press, 2011

Pankhurst, Richard, 'Italian Fascist War Crimes in Ethiopia: A History of Their Discussion, from the League of Nations to the United Nations (1936–1949)' (1999) 6 n.s. *Northeast African Studies* 83

Partsch, Karl Josef, 'Die Strafbarkeit der Rassendiskriminierung nach dem Internationalen Abkommen und die Verwirklichung der Verpflichtungen in Nationalen Strafrechtsordnungen' (1977) 20 *German Yearbook of International Law* 119

Partsch, Karl Josef, 'Elimination of Racial Discrimination in the Enjoyment of Civil and Political Rights—A Study of Article 5, Subparagraphs (a)-(d), of the International Convention on the Elimination of All Forms of Racial Discrimination' (1979) 14 *Texas International Law Journal* 191

Patterson, William L., *The Man Who Cried Genocide: An Autobiography*, New York: International Publishers, 1971

Pearson, Jessica Lynne, 'Defending Empire at the United Nations: The Politics of International Colonial Oversight in the Era of Decolonisation' (2017) 45 *Journal of Imperial and Commonwealth History* 525

Pedersen, Susan, 'Back to the League of Nations' (2007) 112 *American Historical Review* 1091

Pedersen, Susan, 'Getting out of Iraq – In 1932: The League of Nations and the Road to Normative Statehood' (2010) 115 *American Historical Review* 975

Pedersen, Susan, 'Metaphors of the Schoolroom: Women Working the Mandates System of the League of Nations' (2008) 66 *History Workshop Journal* 188

Pedersen, Susan, 'Samoa on the World Stage: Petitions and Peoples before the Mandates Commission of the League of Nations' (2012) 40 *Journal of Imperial and Commonwealth History* 231

Pedersen, Susan, 'Settler Colonialism at the Bar of the League of Nations', in C. Elkins and S. Pedersen, eds., *Settler Colonialism in the Twentieth Century: Projects, Practices, Legacies*, New York, Routledge, 2005, pp. 113–34

Pedersen, Susan, *The Guardians, The League of Nations and the Crisis of Empire*, Oxford: Oxford University Press, 2017

Petitjean, Patrick, Vladimir Zharov, Gisbert Glaser, Jacques Richardson, Bruno de Padirac, and Gail Archibald, eds., *Sixty Years of Science at UNESCO 1945–2005*, Paris: UNESCO, 2006

Petrova, Dimitrina, ' "Smoke and Mirrors": The Durban Review Conference and Human Rights Politics at the United Nations' (2010) 10 *Human Rights Law Review* 129

Phillimore, George G., 'Some Suggestions for a Draft Code for the Treatment of Prisoners of War' (1920) 6 *Transactions of the Grotius Society* 25

Platt, Anthony M., *E. Franklin Frazier Reconsidered*, New Brunswick, N.J.: Rutgers, 1991

Plummer, Brenda Gayle, *Rising Wind: Black Americans and US Foreign Affairs 1935–1960*, Chapel Hill: University of North Carolina Press, 1996

Polakow-Suransky, Sasha, *The Unspoken Alliance: Israel's Secret Relationship with Apartheid South Africa*, New York: Vintage Books, 2013

Posner, Eric and Adrian Vermeule, 'Reparations for Slavery and Other Historical Injustices' (2003) 103 *Columbia Law Review* 689

Posner, Michael and Wade Henderson, 'A Response to Tom Lantos' "The Durban Debacle" ' (2003) 27 *Fletcher Forum for World Affairs* 6

Powell, Catherine, and Jennifer H. Lee, 'Recognizing the Interdependence of Rights in the Antidiscrimination Context through the World Conference against Racism' (2002) 34 *Columbia Human Rights Law Review* 235

Powell, Thomas Reed, 'Alien Land Cases in United States Supreme Court' (1924) 12 *California Law Review* 259

Prado, Jose L. Gomez del, 'United Nations Conventions on Human Rights: The Practice of the Human Rights Committee and the Committee on the Elimination of Racial Discrimination in Dealing with Reporting Obligations of States Parties' (1985) 7 *Human Rights Quarterly* 492

Prescott, Jody M., 'Litigating Genocide: A Consideration of the Criminal Court in Light of the German Jews' Legal Response to Nazi Persecution, 1933–1941' (1999) 51 *Maine Law Review* 297

Preux, Jean de, ed., *Commentary, Geneva Convention Relative to the Treatment of Prisoners of* War, Geneva: International Committee of the Red Cross, 1960

Prevost, Ann Marie, 'Race and War Crimes: The 1945 War Crimes Trial of General Tomoyuki Yamashita' (1992) 14 *Human Rights Quarterly* 303

Prins, Harald P. and Edgar Krebs, 'Vers un monde sans mal: Alfred Métraux, un anthropologue à l'UNESCO (1946–1962)', in *60 ans d'histoire de l'UNESCO*, Paris: UNESCO, 2007, pp. 115–25

446   BIBLIOGRAPHY

Proctor, Robert, 'Three Roots of Human Recency: Molecular Anthropology, the Refigured Acheulean, and the UNESCO Response to Auschwitz' (2003) 44 *Current Anthropology* 213

Prove, Peter, 'Caste at the World Conference Against Racism', in Sukhadeo Thorat, ed., *Caste, Race and Discrimination: Discourses in International Context*, Rawat Publications, New Delhi, 2004, pp. 322–5

Provine, William B., 'Geneticists and Race' (1986) 26 *American Zoologist* 857

Quigley, John, 'Apartheid Outside Africa: The Case of Israel' (1991) 2 *Indiana International and Comparative Law Review* 222

Rajagopal, Balakrishnan, *International Law from Below: Development, Social Movements, and Third World Resistance*, Cambridge: Cambridge University Press, 2003

Ramos, Arthur, 'The Question of Race and the Democratic World' (1949) 1(3–4) *International Social Science Bulletin* 1

Randall, Vernellia R., 'Racial Discrimination in Health Care in the United States as a Violation of the International Convention on the Elimination of All Forms of Racial Discrimination' (2002) 14 *University of Florida Journal of Law and Public Policy* 45

Rao, B. Shiva, 'The United Nations and Non-Self-Governing Territories' (1950) 6 *India Quarterly* 227

Reardon, Jenny, *Race to the Finish: Identity and Governance in an Age of Genomics*, Princeton: Princeton University Press, 2004

Rees, D.F.W. van, *Les Mandats internationaux*, Paris: Librairie Arthur Rousseau, 1927

Reif, Michelle, 'Thinking Locally, Acting Globally: The International Agenda of African American Clubwomen, 1880–1940' (2004) 89 *Journal of African American History* 203

Reinders, Robert, 'Racialism on the Left: E.D. Morel and the "Black Horror on the Rhine"' (1968) 13 *International Review of Social History* 1

Reis, Bruno Cardoso, 'Portugal and the UN: A Rogue State Resisting the Norm of Decolonization (1956–1974)' (2013) 29 *Portuguese Studies* 251

Reisman, William M., 'Revision of the South West Africa Cases' (1966) 7 *Virginia Journal of International Law* 1

Renoliet, Jean-Jacques, *L'UNESCO oubliée: la Société des Nations et la coopération intellectuelle (1919–1946)*, Paris, Publications de la Sorbonne, 1999

Reynolds, John, 'Empire, Emergency and International Law', Cambridge: Cambridge University Press, 2017

Reynolds, John, 'Third World Approaches to International Law and the Ghosts of Apartheid', in David Keane and Yvonne McDermott, eds., *The Challenge of Human Rights*, Cheltenham: Elgar 2012, pp. 194–218

Rich, Camille Gear, 'Marginal Whiteness' (2010) 98 *California Law Review* 1497

Rich, Paul B., '"The Baptism of a New Order": The 1911 Universal Races Congress and the Liberal Ideology of Race' (1984) 7 *Ethnic and Racial Studies* 534

Rich, Paul B., 'Philanthropic Racism in Britain: The Liverpool University Settlement, the Anti-slavery Society and the Issue of "Half-caste" Children, 1919–51' (1984) 3 *Immigrants & Minorities* 69

Richardson, Henry J. III, 'African Americans and International Law: For Professor Goler Teal Butcher, with Appreciation' (1984) 37 *Howard Journal of Law* 217

Richardson, Henry J. III, 'Constitutive Questions in the Negotiations for Namibian Independence' (1984) 78 *American Journal of International Law* 74

Richardson, Henry J. III, 'Excluding Race Strategies from International Legal History: The Self-Executing Treaty Doctrine and the Southern Africa Tripartite Agreement' (2000) 45 *Villanova Law Review* 1091

Richardson, Henry J. III, 'International Law and the Continuation of Sanctions Against South Africa' (1989) 3 *Temple International and Comparative Law Journal* 249

Richardson, Henry J. III, 'John Dugard's International Law: A South African Perspective' (1995) 89 *American Journal of International Law* 656

Richardson, Henry J. III, 'Reverend Leon Sullivan's Principles, Race, and International Law: A Comment' (2001) 15 *Temple International and Comparative Law Journal* 55

Richardson, Henry J. III, 'Self-Determination, International Law and the South African Bantustan Policy' (1978) 17 *Columbia Journal of Transnational Law* 185

Richardson, Henry J. III, 'Speculations on the Relevance of International Law to the Needs of Black Southern Africa' (1970) 1 *Ufahamu Journal of African Studies* 22

Richardson, Henry J. III, 'The Gulf Crisis and African-American Interests under International Law' (1993) 87 *American Journal of International Law* 4

Richardson, Henry J. III, 'U.S. Hegemony, Race, and Oil in Deciding United Nations Security Council Resolution 1441 on Iraq' (2003) 17 *Temple International and Comparative Law Journal* 27

Richardson, Henry J. III, *The Origins of African-American Interests in International Law*, Durham, NC: Carolina Academic Press, 2008

Rigney, Sophie, 'On Hearing Well and Being Well Heard: Indigenous International Law at the League of Nations' (2021) 2 *TWAIL Review* 122

Riles, Annelise, 'Aspiration and Control: International Legal Rhetoric and the Essentialization of Culture' (1993) 106 *Harvard Law Review* 723

Roberts, Christopher N.J., *The Contentious History of the International Bill of Human Rights*, New York: Cambridge University Press, 2014

Robins, Dorothy B., *Experiment in Democracy: The Story of U.S. Citizen Organizations in Forging the Charter of the United Nations*, New York: Parkside Press, 1971

Robinson, Cedric, 'The African Diaspora and the Italo-Ethiopian crisis' (1985) 27 *Race and Class* 51

Robinson, Jacob, Oscar Karbach, Max. M. Laserson, Nehemiah Robinson, and Marc Vichniak, *Were the Minorities Treaties a Failure?*, New York: Institute of Jewish Affairs, 1943

Rolin, Henri, 'La pratique des mandats internationaux' (1927) 19 *Recueil des cours de l'Académie de droit international de La Haye* 495

Roman, Ediberto, 'A Race Approach to International Law (RAIL): Is There a Need for Yet Another Critique of International Law?' (2000) 33 *U.C. Davis Law Review* 1519

Romano, Renee, 'No Diplomatic Immunity: African Diplomats, the State Department, and Civil Rights, 1961–1964' (2000) 87 *Journal of American History* 546

Romany, Celina and Katherine Culliton, 'The UN World Conference against Racism: A Race-Ethnic and Gender Perspective' (2002) 9 *Human Rights Brief* 14

Romany, Celina, 'Themes for a Conversation on Race and Gender in International Human Rights Law', in Adrien Katherine Wing ed., *Global Critical Race Feminism: An International Reader*, New York: NYU Press, 2000, pp. 53–66

Rose, Arnold, *Race and Prejudice*, Paris: UNESCO, 1951

Rostkowski, Joëlle, 'Deskaheh's Shadow: Indians on the International Scene' (1995) 9 *European Review of Native American Studies* 1

448 BIBLIOGRAPHY

Rostkowski, Joëlle, 'The Redman's Appeal for Justice: Deskaheh and the League of Nations', in Christian F. Feest, ed., *Indians and Europe: An Interdisciplinary Collection of Essays*, Lincoln: University of Nebraska Press, 1999, pp. 435–53

Rubin, Alfred P., 'International Law in the Age of Columbus' (1992) 39 *Netherlands International Law Review* 5

Saba, Hanna, 'La Convention et la Recommandation concernant la Lutte contre la Discrimination dans le Domaine de l'Enseignement' [1960] *Annuaire français de droit international* 646

Saito, Natsu Taylor, 'Critical Race Theory as International Human Rights Law' (1999) 93 *Proceedings of the American Society of International Law* 228

Saito, Natsu Taylor, 'From Slavery and Seminoles to AIDS in South Africa: An Essay on Race and Property in International Law' (2000) 45 *Villanova Law Review* 1135

Santa Cruz, Hernán, *Racial Discrimination*, New York: United Nations, 1977

Santos, Aurora Almada E., 'The Role of the Decolonization Committee of the United Nations Organization in the Struggle Against Portuguese Colonialism in Africa: 1961– 1974' (2012) 4 *Journal of Pan African Studies* 248

Sarkin, Jeremy, 'Reparation for Past Wrongs: Using Domestic Courts Around the World, Especially the United States, to Pursue African Human Rights Claims' (2004) 32 *International Journal of Legal Information* 426

Sarkin, Jeremy, 'The Coming of Age of Claims for Reparations for Human Rights Abuses Committed in the South' (2004) 1 *SUR, International Journal on Human Rights* 66

Sarraut, Albert, *La mise en valeur des Colonies françaises*, Paris: Payot, 1923

Schabas, William A., 'Canada and the Adoption of the *Universal Declaration of Human Rights*' (1998) 43 *McGill Law Journal* 403

Schabas, William A., *Introduction to the International Criminal Court*, 6th ed., Cambridge: Cambridge University Press, 2020

Schabas, William A., *The International Criminal Court: A Commentary on the Rome Statute*, 2nd ed., Oxford: Oxford University Press, 2016

Schabas, William A., *The UN International Criminal Tribunals: the former Yugoslavia, Rwanda and Sierra Leone*, Cambridge: Cambridge University Press, 2006

Schabas, William A., *Unimaginable Atrocities*, Oxford: Oxford University Press, 2011

Schabas, William, *The Trial of the Kaiser*, Oxford: Oxford University Press, 2018

Schifter, Richard, 'Human Rights at the United Nations: The South African Precedent' (1993) 8 *American University Journal of International Law and Policy* 368

Schifter, Richard, 'Racial Discrimination: The Soviet Record' (1981) 144 World Affairs 220

Schoenberg, Harris O., 'Demonization in Durban: The World Conference Against Racism' (2002) 102 *American Jewish Year Book* 85

Schokkenbroek, Jeroen, 'A New European Standard Against Discrimination: Negotiating Protocol No. 12 to the European Convention on Human Rights', in J. Niessen and Isabelle Chopin, eds., *European Anti-Discrimination Standards and National Legislation*, Leiden/Boston: Martinus Nijhoff, 2004, pp. 61–79

Schokkenbroek, Jeroen, 'Towards a Stronger European Protection against Discrimination: The Preparation of a New Additional Protocol to the European Convention on Human Rights', in Gay Moon, ed., *Race Discrimination: Developing and Using a New European Legal Framework*, Oxford: Oxford University Press, pp. 29–37

Schroer, Timothy L., 'Racial Mixing of Prisoners of War in the First World War', in James E. Kitchen, Alisa Miller, and Laura Rowe, eds., *Other Combatants, Other*

Fronts: Competing Histories of the First World War, Newcastle upon Tyne: Cambridge Scholars, 2011, pp. 177–98

Schroer, Timothy L., 'The Emergence and Early Demise of Codified Racial Segregation of Prisoners of War under the Geneva Conventions of 1929 and 1949' (2013) 15 *Journal of the History of International Law* 53

Schroth, Peter W. and Virginia S. Mueller, 'Racial Discrimination: The United States and the International Convention' (1975) 4 *Human Rights* 171

Schücking, Walther, 'International Law, Treaties, Conferences, and the Hague Tribunal', in Gustav Spiller, ed., *Papers on Inter-Racial Problems Communicated to the First Universal Races Congress*, London: P.S. King, 1911, pp. 387–98

Schwelb, Egon, 'The Implementation of the International Convention on the Elimination of All Forms of Racial Discrimination', in International Law Association, *Report of the Fifty-Fifth Conference (New York 1972)*, London: 1974, pp. 584–608

Schwelb, Egon, 'The International Convention on the Elimination of All Forms of Racial Discrimination' (1966) 15 *International and Comparative Law Quarterly* 996

Scott, Michael, *A Time to Speak*, New York: Doubleday, 1958

Scott, William Randolph, 'Black Nationalism and the Italo-Ethiopian Conflict, 1934–1936' (1978) 63 *Journal of Negro History* 118

Scott, William Randolph, *The Sons of Sheba's Race: African-Americans and the Italo-Ethiopian War, 1935–1941*, Bloomington: Indiana University Press, 1993

Sebeelo, Tebogo B., 'Hashtag Activism, Politics and Resistance in Africa: Examining #ThisFlag and #RhodesMustFall Online Movements' (2021) 13 *Insight on Africa* 95

Selcer, Perrin, 'Beyond the Cephalic Index, Negotiating Politics to Produce UNESCO's Scientific Statements on Race' (2012) 53 *Current Anthropology* S173

Sellars, Kirsten, 'Human Rights and the Colonies: Deceit, Deception and Discovery' (2004) 93 *The Round Table* 709

Semertzi, Aliki, 'Modernist Violence: Juxtaposing the League's Permanent Mandates Commission over the Bondelzwarts Rebellion and the US-Mexico Special Claims Commission over the Mexican Revolutions' (2020) 21 *Melbourne Journal of International Law* 275

Seymour, Charles, *The Intimate Papers of Colonel House, Vol. IV, The Ending of the War*, London: Ernest Benn, 1928

Shah, Samira, 'On the Road to Apartheid: The Bypass Road Network in the West Bank' (1997–1998) 29 *Columbia Human Rights Law Review* 221

Shahabuddin, Mohammad, *Ethnicity and International Law: Histories, Politics and Practices*, Cambridge: Cambridge University Press, 2016

Shahlaei, Faraz, 'Soccer Stadiums, Where International Law, Culture and Racism Collide' (2018) 7 *Arizona State University Sports and Entertainment Law Journal* 291

Shelton, Dinah, 'Righting Wrongs: Reparations in the Articles on State Responsibility' (2002) 96 *American Journal of International Law* 833

Shelton, Dinah, 'The World of Atonement: Reparations for Historical Injustices' (2004) 1 *Miskolc Journal of International Law* 259

Shenoy, Amritha V., 'The Centenary of the League of Nations: Colonial India and the Making of International Law' (2018) 24 *Asian Yearbook of International Law* 4

Sherwood, Marika ' "There is no New Deal for the Blackman in San Francisco": African Attempts to Influence the Founding Conference of the United Nations April–July 1945' (1996) 29 *International Journal of African Historical Studies* 71

450 BIBLIOGRAPHY

Sherwood, Marika, 'Diplomatic Platitudes': The Atlantic Charter, The United Nations and Colonial Independence' (1996) 15 *Immigrants and Minorities* 135

Shimazu, Naoko, 'A Cultural History of Diplomacy: Reassessing the Japanese "Performance" at the Paris Peace Conference', in Urs Mathias Zackmann, ed., *Asia after Versailles: Asian Perspectives on the Paris Peace Conference, 1919–33*, Edinburgh: Edinburgh University Press, 2017, pp. 101–23

Shimazu, Naoko, 'The Fallacies of Pragmatism: Israeli Foreign Policy towards South Africa' (1983) 82 *African Affairs* 169

Shimazu, Naoko, 'The Japanese Attempt to Secure Racial Equality in 1919' (1989) 1 *Japan Forum* 93

Shimazu, Naoko, *Japan, Race and Equality: The Racial Equality Proposal of 1919*, London: Routledge, 2009

Sicilianos, Linos Alexandre, 'L'actualité et les potentialités de la Convention sur l'élimination de la discrimination raciale' [2005] *Revue trimestrielle des droits de l'homme* 869

Sicilianos, Linos Alexandre, 'La dynamique de la Convention sur l'élimination de la discrimination raciale: évolutions récentes', in Alice Yotopoulos-Marangopoulos, ed., *L'état actuel des droits de l'homme dans le monde: défis et perspectives*, Paris: Pedone, 2006, pp. 193–235

Siegel, Mona L., *Peace on Our Terms, The Global Battle for Women's Rights After the First World War*, New York: Columbia University Press, 2020

Sierra, Maria Miguel, 'The World Conference against Racism and the Role of the European NGOs' (2002) 4 *European Journal of Migration and Law* 249

Sikkink, Kathryn, 'Latin American Countries as Norm Protagonists of the Idea of International Human Rights' (2014) 20 *Global Governance* 389

Silvester, Jeremy and Jan-Bart Gewald, *Words Cannot be Found. German Colonial Rule in Namibia: An Annotated Report of the 1918 Blue Book*, Leiden and Boston: Brill, 2003

Simpson, A.W. Brian, *Human Rights and the End of Empire, Britain and the Genesis of the European Convention*, Oxford: Oxford University Press, 2001

Singh, Kishore, 'UNESCO's Convention against Discrimination in Education (1960): Key Pillar of the Education for All' (2008) 4 *International Journal of Education Law and Policy* 70

Singh, Prabhakar, 'Indian International Law: From a Colonised Apologist to a Subaltern Protagonist' (2010) 23 *Leiden Journal of International Law* 79

Sitze, Adam, 'The Crime of Apartheid: Genealogy of a Successful Failure' (2019) 7 *London Review of International Law* 181

Skard, Torild, 'Getting Our History Right: How Were the Equal Rights of Women and Men Included in the Charter of the United Nations?' (2008) 35 *Forum for Development Studies* 37

Skrentny, John David, 'The Effect of the Cold War on African-American Civil Rights: America and the World Audience, 1945–1968' (1998) 27 *Theory and Society* 237

Sluga, Glenda, 'UNESCO and the (One) World of Julian Huxley' (2010) 21 *Journal of World History* 393

Slye, Ron, 'Apartheid as a Crime Against Humanity: A Submission to the South African Truth and Reconciliation Commission' (1991) 20 *Michigan Journal of International Law* 291

Smith, Andrea, *Indigenous Peoples and Boarding Schools: A Comparative Study*, New York: Secretariat of the United Nations Permanent Forum on Indigenous Issues, 2009

Snyder, Sarah B., *From Selma to Moscow: How Human Rights Activists Transformed U.S. Foreign Policy*, New York: Columbia University Press, 2018

Sohn, Louis B., 'How American International Lawyers Prepared for the San Francisco Bill of Rights' (1995) 89 *American Journal of International Law* 540

Solomon, Daniel E., 'The Black Freedom Movement and the Politics of the Anti-Genocide Norm in the United States, 1951–1967' (2019) 13 *Genocide Studies and Prevention* 130

Sow, Marisa Jackson, 'Ukrainian Refugees, Race and International Law's Choice Between Order and Justice' (2022) 116 *American Journal of International Law* 698

Spiller, Gustav, ed., *Papers on Inter-Racial Problems Communicated to the First Universal Races Congress*, London: P.S. King, 1911

Stalin, Joseph V., *On the Great Patriotic War of the Soviet Union*, Moscow: Foreign Languages Publishing House, 1954

Stefanelli, Justine N. and Erin Lovall, eds., *Reparations Under International Law for Enslavement of African Persons in the Americas and the Caribbean*, Washington: American Society of International Law, 2022

Stettinius, Edward R., 'Human Rights in the United Nations Charter' (1946) 243 *The Annals of the American Academy of Political and Social Science* 1

Stevens, Richard P. and Abdulwahab M. Elmessiri, eds., *Israel and South Africa: The Progression of a Relationship*, New Brunswick, NJ: North American, 1977

Stewart, James B., 'V.P. Franklin and the Case for Reparations' (2017) 102 *Journal of African American History* 341

Stewart, Thomas D., 'Scientific Responsibility' (1951) 9 (n.s.) *American Journal of Physical Anthropology* 1

Stewart, Thomas D., 'UNESCO Statements on Race' (1961) 133 (n.s.) *Science* 1634

Stoyanovski, Jacob, *La Théorie générale des mandats internationaux*, Paris: Presses Universitaires de France, 1925

Stultz, Newell M., 'Evolution of the United Nations Anti-Apartheid Regime' (1991) 13 *Human Rights Quarterly* 1

Stultz, Newell M., 'The Apartheid Issue at the General Assembly: Stalemate or Gathering Storm?' (1987) 86 *African Affairs* 25

Su, Anna, 'Woodrow Wilson and the Origins of the International Law of Religious Freedom' (2013) 15 *Journal of the History of International Law* 235

Sud, Usha, 'Committee on Information from Non-Self-Governing Territories: Its Role in the Promotion of Self-Determination of Colonial Peoples' (1965) 7 *International Studies* 311

Sud, Usha, *United Nations and Non-Self-Governing Territories*, Delhi: University Publishers, 1965

Sundberg, Ulrika, 'Durban: The Third World Conference against Racism, Racial Discrimination, Xenophobia and Related Intolerance' (2002) 73 *International Review of Penal Law* 301

Swaisland, Charles, 'The Aborigines Protection Society, 1837–1909' (2000) 21 *Slavery and Abolition* 265

Tamada, Dai, 'Inter-State Communication Under ICERD: From Ad Hoc Conciliation to Collective Enforcement?' (2021) 12 *Journal of International Dispute Settlement* 405

Tang, Kwong-leung, 'Combating Racial Discrimination: The Effectiveness of an International Legal Regime' (2003) 33 *British Journal of Social Work* 17

Tang, Kwong-leung, Ching Man Lam, and Mong Chow Lam, 'International Response to Racial Discrimination: Potentials and Limitations of the United Nations Race Convention' (2003) 6 *European Journal of Social Work* 283

Temperley, H.W.V., ed., *A History of the Peace Conference of Paris*, London: Henry Frowde and Hodder and Stoughton, 1924

Terretta, Meredith, '"We Had Been Fooled into Thinking That the UN Watches over the Entire World": Human Rights, UN Trust Territories, and Africa's Decolonization' (2012) 34 *Human Rights Quarterly* 329

Terretta, Meredith, '"Why Then Call it the Declaration of Human Rights?" The Failures of Universal Human Rights in Colonial Africa's Internationally Supervised Territories', in Jean H. Quataert and Lora Wildenthal, eds., *The Routledge History of Human Rights*, London and New York: Routledge, 2019, pp. 203–21

The Treatment of Natives and Other Populations in the Colonial Possessions of Germany and England: An Answer to the English Blue Book of August 1918: 'Report on the Natives of Southwest Africa and their Treatment by Germany', Berlin: German Colonial Office, 1919

Thésée, Gina and Paul R. Carr, 'The 2011 International Year for People of African Descent: The Paradox of Colonized Invisibility within the Promise of Mainstream Visibility' (2012) 1 *Decolonization: Indigeneity, Education and Society* 158

Thienel, Tobias, 'The Georgian Conflict, Racial Discrimination and the ICJ: The Order on Provisional Measures of 15 October 2008' (2009) 9 *Human Rights Law Review* 465

Thomas, Albert, 'The International Bureau of Labour of the League of Nations' (1921) 23 *The Crisis* 69

Thomas, Chantal, 'International Trade and African Heritage: The Cotton Story' (2017) 31 *Temple International and Comparative Law Journal* 225

Thompson, Andrew S., 'Tehran 1968 and Reform of the UN Human Rights System' (2015) 14 *Journal of Human Rights* 84

Thornberry, Patrick, 'Confronting Racial Discrimination: A CERD Perspective' (2005) 5 *Human Rights Law Review* 239

Thornberry, Patrick, *The International Convention on the Elimination of All Forms of Racial Discrimination, A Commentary*, Oxford: Oxford University Press, 2016

Tilley, Virginia, ed., *Beyond Occupation: Apartheid, Colonialism and International Law in the Occupied Palestinian Territories*, London: Pluto Press, 2012

Tinker, Hugh, *Race, Conflict and the International Order, From Empire to United Nations*, London: Macmillan, 1977

Torres, Jada Benn, '"Reparational" Genetics: Genomic Data and the Case for Reparations in the Caribbean' (2018) 2 *Genealogy* 7

Tourme-Jouannet, Emmanuelle, 'Des origines coloniales du droit international: A propos du droit des gens moderne au XVIIeme siècle', in Vincent Chetail and Pierre-Marie Dupuy, eds., *The Roots of International Law/Les fondements du droit international, Liber Amicorum Peter Haggenmacher*, Leiden: Brill, 2014, pp. 649–71

Troup, Freda, *In Face of Fear: Michael Scott's Challenge to South Africa*, London: Faber and Faber, 1950

Troy, Gil, *Moynihan's Moment, America's Fight against Zionism as Racism*, Oxford: Oxford University Press, 2012

Tuori, Taina, 'From League of Nations Mandates to Decolonization: A Brief History of Rights', in Pamela Slotte and Miia Halme-Tuomisaari, eds., *Revisiting the Origins of Human Rights*, Cambridge: Cambridge University Press, 2015, pp. 267–92

Turner, Oliver, 'Finishing the Job': the UN Special Committee on Decolonization and the Politics of Self-Governance' (2013) 34 *Third World Quarterly* 1193

Tzouvala, Ntina, 'These Ancient Arenas of Racial Struggles': International Law and the Balkans, 1878–1949' (2019) 29 *European Journal of International Law* 1149

Ulfstein, Geir, 'Qatar v. United Arab Emirates' (2022) *American Journal of International Law* 397

Umozurike, U.O., *International Law and Colonialism in Africa*, Enugu: Nwamife Publishing, 1979

Umozurike, U.O., *Introduction to International Law*, Ibadan: Spectrum Law, 1993

UNESCO, *The Race Concept: Results of an Inquiry*, Paris: UNESCO, 1952

UNESCO, *The Race Concept: Results of an Inquiry*, Paris: UNESCO, 1960

United Nations War Crimes Commission, *History of the United Nations War Crimes Commission and the Development of the Laws of War*, London: His Majesty's Stationery Office, 1948

Vallois, Henri Victor, 'UNESCO on Race' (1951) 51 *Man* 15

Van Dyke, Jon M., Carmen Di Amore-Siah, and Gerald W. Berkley-Coats, 'Self-Determination for Non-self-Governing Peoples and for Indigenous Peoples: The Cases of Guam and Hawai'i' (1996) 18 *University of Hawai'i Law Review* 623

Vandenhole, Wouter, *Non-Discrimination and Equality in the View of the UN Human Rights Treaty Bodies*, Antwerp and Oxford: Intersentia, 2005

Veatch, Richard, *Canada and the League of Nations*, Toronto: University of Toronto Press, 1975

Venkataramani, M.S., 'The United States, the Colonial Issue, and the Atlantic Charter Hoax' (1974) 13 *International Studies* 1

Verzijl, Jan Hendrik Willem, 'The South West Africa Cases (Second Phase)' (1966) 3 *International Relations* 87

Verzijl, Jan Hendrik Willem, 'Western European Influence on the Foundations of International Law' (1956) 1 *International Relations* 187

Vezzosi, Elisabetta, 'Una donna nera alla fondazione dell'ONU. Mary McLeod Bethune tra genere e "black global community"' (2011) 14 *Contemporenea* 681

Vik, Hanne Hagtvedt, 'Taming the States: The American Law Institute and the "Statement of Essential Human Rights"' (2012) 7 *Journal of Global History* 461

Vincent, Raymond J., 'Race in International Relations' (1982) 58 *International Affairs* 658

Vinson, Robert Trent, 'Up from Slavery and Down with Apartheid! African Americans and Black South Africans against the Global Color Line' (2018) 52 *Journal of American Studies* 297

Volpp, Leti, 'Talking "Culture": Gender, Race, Nation, and the Politics of Multiculturalism' (1996) 96 *Columbia Law Review* 1573

Vucetic, Srdjan, 'Black Banker, White Banker: Philosophies of the Global Colour Line' (2013) 26 *Cambridge Review of International Affairs* 27

Walden, Raphael, 'The Drafting of the Articles on the Middle East and Anti-Semitism at the Durban Conference against Racism', in Raphael Walden, ed., *Racism and Human Rights*, Leiden: Martinus Nijhoff, 2004, pp. 165–76

Waldon, Raphael, *Racism and Human Rights*, Dordrecht: Springer, 2004

Wallace, Marion and John Kinahan, *A History of Namibia, From the Beginning to 1990*, Oxford: Oxford University Press, 2011

Walters, Francis Paul, *A History of the League of Nations*, London: Oxford University Press, 1952

Wang Tieya, 'The Third World and International Law', in Ronald St. J. Macdonald and Douglas M. Johnston, eds., *The Structure and Process of International Law, Essays in Legal Philosophy Doctrine and Theory*, The Hague: Martinus Nijhoff, 1983, pp. 955–76

Weatherly, Ulysses G., 'The First Universal Races Congress' (1911) 17 *American Journal of Sociology* 315

Wedgewood, Ruth, 'Zionism and Racism, Again: Durban II' (2009) 171 *World Affairs* 84

Weichers, Marinus, 'South West Africa: The Decision of 16 July 1966 and Its Aftermath' (1968) 1 *Comparative and International Law Journal of South Africa* 408

Weil, Prosper, 'Towards Relative Normativity in International Law?' (1983) 77 *American Journal of International Law* 413

Weindling, Paul, 'Central Europe Confronts German Racial Hygiene: Friedrich Hertz, Hugo Iltis and Ignaz Zollschan as Critics of German Racial Hygiene', in M. Turda and P. Weindling, eds., *Blood and Homeland: Eugenics and Racial Nationalism in Central Europe 1900–1940*, Budapest: Central European University Press, 2006, pp. 263–80

Weindling, Paul, 'Julian Huxley and the Continuity of Eugenics in Twentieth-century Britain' (2012) 10 *Journal of Modern European History* 480

Weindling, Paul, 'The Evolution of Jewish Identity: Ignaz Zollschan between Jewish and Aryan Race Theories, 1910–1945', in Geoffrey Cantor and Marc Swetlitz, eds., *Jewish Tradition and the Challenge of Darwinism*, Chicago: University of Chicago Press, 2006, pp. 116–36

Weisbord, Robert G., 'British West Indian Reaction to the Italian-Ethiopian War: An Episode in Pan-Africanism' (1970) 10 *Caribbean Studies* 34

Weissbrodt, David and Georgina Mahoney, 'International Legal Action Against Apartheid' (1986) 4 *Law and Inequality* 485

Weissbrodt, David, 'The Approach of the Committee on the Elimination of Racial Discrimination to Interpreting and Applying International Humanitarian Law' (2010) 19 *Minnesota Journal of International Law* 327

Wells, Herbert G., *The Rights of Man, or, What are we Fighting for?*, Harmondsworth: Penguin Books, 1940

Wesley, Charles H., 'International Aspects of the Negro's Status in the United States' (1948) 11 *Negro History Bulletin* 108

Westlake, John, 'Native States of India' (1910) 24 *Law Quarterly Review* 312

Westlake, John, *Chapters on International Law*, Cambridge: Cambridge University Press, 1894

Westley, Robert, 'Many Billions Gone: Is it Time to Reconsider the Case for Black Reparations?' (1998) 19 *Third World Law Journal* 429

Wheaton, Henry, *Elements of International Law*, 6th ed., Boston: Little Brown, 1855

White, Walter, *A Rising Wind*, Garden City, NY: Doubleday, Doran, 1945

White, Walter, *How Far the Promised Land?*, New York: Viking Press, 1955

Whitton, John B., 'The United Nations Conference on Freedom of Information and the Movement against International Propaganda' (1949) 43 *American Journal of International Law* 73

Wigger, Iris, '"Against the Laws of Civilization": Race, Gender and Nation in the International Racist Campaign Against the "Black Shame"' (2002) 46 *Berkeley Journal of Sociology* 113

Wilde, Ralph, *International Territorial Administration: How Trusteeship and the Civilizing Mission Never Went Away*, Oxford: Oxford University Press, 2008

Willan, Brian, 'The Anti-Slavery and Aborigines' Protection Society and the South African Natives' Land Act of 1913' (1979) 20 *Journal of African History* 83

Williams, Eric, *Capitalism and Slavery*, Chappell Hill: University of North Carolina Press, 1943

Willis, James F., *Prologue to Nuremburg, The Politics and Diplomacy of Punishing War Criminals of the First World War*, Westport, CT and London: Greenwood Press, 1982

Wilson, Howard E., 'The Development of UNESCO' (1947) 25 *International Conciliation* 295

Wintemute, Robert, 'Israel-Palestine through the Lens of Racial Discrimination Law: Is the South African Apartheid Analogy Accurate, and What if the European Convention Applied?' (2017) 28 *King's Law Journal* 89

Wirth, Louis, 'Comments on the Resolution of the Economic and Social Council on the Prevention of Discrimination and the Protection of Minorities' (1949) (3-4) *International Social Science Bulletin* 137

Wolfrum, Rüdiger, 'International Convention on the Elimination of All Forms of Racial Discrimination', in Eckart Klein, ed., *The Monitoring System of Human Rights Treaty Obligations*, Berlin: Verlag Spitz, 1998, pp. 49-69

Wolfrum, Rüdiger, 'The Committee on the Elimination of Racial Discrimination' (1999) 3 *Max Planck UN Yearbook* 489

Wolpe, Harold, *Race, Class and the Apartheid State*, London: James Currey, Addis Ababa: Organisation of African Unity, Paris: UNESCO, 1988

Woo, Grace Li Xiu, 'Canada's Forgotten Founders: The Modern Significance of the Haudenosaunee (Iroquois) Application for Membership of the League of Nations' [2003] *Law, Social Justice and Global Development* 1

Wright, David, 'The Use of Race and Racial Perceptions among Asians and Blacks: The Case of the Japanese and African Americans' (1998) 30 *Hitotsubashi Journal of Social Studies* 135

Wright, Quincy, *Mandates under the League of Nations*, Chicago: University of Chicago Press, 1930

Wright, Richard, *The Color Curtain: A Report on the Bandung Conference*, New York: World, 1956

Wu, A., 'The World Conference against Racism, Racial Discrimination, Xenophobia and Related Intolerance' (2001) 17 *New York Law School Journal of Human Rights* 917

Yasuaki, Onuma, 'When Was the Law of International Society Born?: An Inquiry of the History of International Law from an Intercivilizational Perspective' (2000) 2 *Journal of the History of International Law* 1

Yates, Anne and Lewis Chester, *The Troublemaker, Michael Scott and his Lonely Struggle Against Injustice*, London: Aurum Press, 2006

Yellin, Eric S., *Racism in the Nation's Service: Government Workers and the Color Line in Woodrow Wilson's America*, Chapel Hill: University of North Carolina Press, 2013

Young, Stephen, 'Re-historicising Dissolved Identities: Deskaheh, the League of Nations, and International Legal Discourse on Indigenous Peoples' (2019) 7 *London Review of International Law* 377

Younis, Musab, 'Race, the World and Time: Haiti, Liberia and Ethiopia (1914-1945)' (2018) 46 *Millennium: Journal of International Studies* 352

Zahar, Alexander, 'Apartheid as an International Crime', in Antonio Cassese, ed., *The Oxford Companion to International Criminal Law*, Oxford: Oxford University Press, 2009, pp. 245-6

Zimmermann, Bruno, 'Article 85 – Repression of Breaches of this Protocol', in Yves Sandoz, Christophe Swinarski, Bruno Zimmermann, eds., Commentary on the Additional Protocols of 8 June 1977 to the Geneva Conventions of 12 August 1949, Geneva: Martinus Nijhoff, 1987, pp. 989-1004

Zollmann, Jakob, 'Affaire Naulilaa entre le Portugal et l'Allemagne, 1914–1933: Reflexions sur l'Histoire Politique d'une Sentence Arbitrale Internationale' (2013) 15 *Journal of the History of International Law* 201

Zollmann, Jakob, 'Unforeseen combat at Naulilaa. German South West Africa, Angola, and the First World War in 1914–1917' (2016) 20 *Journal of Namibian Studies* 79

Zollmann, Jakob, *Naulilaa 1914. World War I in Angola and International Law, A Study in (Post) Colonial Border Regimes and Interstate Arbitration*, Baden-Baden: Nomos, 2016

Zollschan, Ignaz, *Le role du facteur racial dans les questions fondamentales de la morphologie culturelle*, Paris: Arthur Rousseau, 1934

Zollschan, Ignaz, *The Significance of the Racial Factor as a Basis in Cultural Development*, London: Play House Press, 1934

Zuckerman, Phil, ed., *The Social Theory of W.E.B. Du Bois*, London: Sage, 2005

Index

For the benefit of digital users, indexed terms that span two pages (e.g., 52–53) may, on occasion, appear on only one of those pages.

Abi-Saab, Georges, 1–2
aboriginal children, 160–61
Aborigines Protection Society, 26–27, 57, 75
abortion, 339–40
Abraham, G.H.F., 60–61
Abram, Morris, 261–63, 272–73
Abyssinia, 2, 18–19, 55, 84–85
Accra, 253–54
Achiume, Tendayi, 10–11, 398–99, 402, 408
Addis Ababa, 195–96, 252–53
Administering Authority, 205–7, 210, 216–18
Advisory Committee of Experts on Slavery, 85
Afghanistan, 55, 145, 207, 249–50, 322, 353–54
African Association Mukindani, 215
African descent, 29–30, 55, 367–68, 380–81, 388–89, 399, 404–6, 408–9
African Group, 305–6, 310–11, 373–75, 377, 383, 404–5
African National Congress, 311–12
African troops, 52–54
African Union, 252–53
Afro-Asian group, 275, 321, 328
Afro-descendance, 394–95, 402
Afro-Peruvians, 388–89
Afrophobia, 390–91
Age of Discovery, 174–75
aggression, 88, 118–19, 342–43, 345–46, 400–1
Ago, Roberto, 259–60, 333–34
Ahmadinejad, Mahmoud, 386
Albania, 49, 267–68
Algeria, 52, 152, 247–48, 254, 261, 300–2, 310–11, 344–45, 353–54
Allain, Jean, 83
Alliance Israelite Universelle, 66–67
Alston, Philip, 15
American Anthropological Association, 174
American Association of Physical Anthropologists, 180–81
American Convention on Human Rights, 194–95
American Federation of Labor, 142–43, 145–46
American Jewish Committee, 99, 141

American Journal of International Law, 6–8, 278–79, 412–13
American Law Institute, 140–41, 142–43
American Sociological Association, 175–76
Amery, L.S., 70
Ammoun, Charles, 133–35
Ammoun, Fouad, 235–36, 259
Amnesty International, 349
An Appeal to the World, 123–24
Angell, Robert C., 177
Angelou, Maya, 247–48
Anghie, Antony, 7, 16
Anglo-Egyptian Sudan, 200
Anglo-Soviet-American coalition, 92
Angola, 40, 78–79, 152, 212–13, 237–38, 243, 316–17, 367
Anker, Peter, 61
Annan, Kofi, 24
Antelope, The, 7–8
anti-Arabism, 386
anti-colonialism, 201–2
anti-Semitism, 26, 33, 93, 114, 115, 188, 244–46, 249, 251, 254–55, 266–67, 272–75, 356, 371–72, 375–76, 379, 381–82, 386
Anti-Slavery and Aborigines' Protection Society, 75–76
Anti-Slavery Society, 75
apartheid, 20, 21–23, 73–74, 115–16, 136, 144, 167, 174–75, 191–93, 195–96, 198–99, 223–25, 227–28, 229–60, 262, 268–69, 272–75, 287–382, 400–1, 411–12
  crime against humanity, 235–36, 365
  definition, 331
  impact on women and children, 338
  jurisdiction of international criminal tribunal, 345–46
  relationship with genocide, 338
Apartheid Convention. *See* International Convention on the Suppression and Punishment of the Crime of Apartheid
apology, 375–78, 392–93, 399
Appeal to the World, 127

458 INDEX

Aptheker, Herbert, 122–23
Arab oil boycott, 357–58
Arab States, 250–51, 356, 359–60
Aragao, J.J. Moniz de, 171
Ardagh, John, 6–7
Argentina, 145, 147–48, 211, 257, 282, 289–90, 301–2
Arkansas National Guard, 133–34
Armenia, 19, 25, 42–43, 283, 313–14
Armenia v. Azerbaijan, 283
arms traffic, 73
Art against Apartheid Collection, 302–3
Aryan race, 169–70
Asahi, 31
Asian descent, 16–17, 380–81
Asiatic Land Tenure and Indian Representation Act, 111
assimilation, 160–61
asylum-seekers, 380–81, 385
Atlantic Charter, 90–93, 104, 138–39
Australia, 70, 160–61, 201–04, 209–10, 212, 219–20, 386
  Apartheid Convention, 329–30
  Code of Crimes, 332–33
  Convention on Racial Discrimination, 267
  Declaration on Racial Discrimination, 255
  education of aboriginal children, 160–61
  historical injustices, 396
  international criminal tribunal, 344–45
  Japanese migration, 69
  mandates, 68–69, 70
  Nauru, 219
  non-self-governing territories, 201–2, 206–7, 212–13
  Papua New Guinea, 220–21
  Paris Peace Conference, 35
  San Francisco Conference, 199
  Statutory Limitation Convention, 323, 324
  support for South Africa, 113–14, 222, 226, 287–90, 294, 300–1
  support for Southern Rhodesia, 239
  treatment of aborigines, 63, 160–61
  World Conferences on Racism, 361, 383, 386, 407
Australian Aborigines Progressive Association, 63
Austria, 43, 49–50, 64, 267, 280, 301–2, 305, 319, 328–29, 332–33, 365–67
Austrian Empire, 25, 69
Awad, Mohamed, 134–35
Axis Rule in Occupied Europe, 120
Azcárate, Pablo de, 66–67
Azerbaijan, 283, 331

Azerbaijan v. Armenia, 283
Azoulay, Audrey, 197

Bachelet, Michelle, 407
Badawi, Abdel Hamid, 225, 230–31
Bahamas, 364–65
Baker, Josephine, 109
Baker, Ray Stannard, 26–27
Baldwin, James, 247–48
Balfour, Lord, 33
Bandung Conference, 154–55, 200–2
Banton, Michael, 180, 353
Bantustans, 337–38
Barbados, 377
Barcelona Traction case, 235–36
Barclay's Bank, 302–3
Barkan, Elazar, 172–73, 179
Basic Principles and Guidelines on the Right to a Remedy, 395
Bassiouni, M. Cherif, 343–45
Batalha Reis, Jaime, 33
Baye, Ibrahima, 335
Bayer, 302–3
Beaglehold, Ernest, 175–76
Beccaria, Cesare, 313–14
Bedjaoui, Mohamed, 191
Begtrup, Bodil, 183–84
Being Black in the EU, 390–91
Beira pipeline, 241
Beirut, 340–41
Belafonte, Harry, 26
Belgian Congo, 87
Belgium, 2, 16, 40–41, 132, 143, 203–4, 216–17, 267, 296–97, 301–2, 356, 389–90
  African colonies and mandates, 26–27, 68–69, 87, 106, 134, 201–2, 204–5
  constitution, 145
  Declaration on Racial Discrimination, 255
  mission of Working Group, 388–89
  Permanent Mandates Commission, 70–71
  Statutory Limitation Convention, 323, 324
  Sub-Commission, 125–26
  support for South Africa, 112–14, 226, 287–88, 289–90, 294, 300–1
  universal jurisdiction, 329–30
Belize, 377
Bellegarde, Dantès, 58–59, 73–74, 85, 113–14, 287–88, 292, 409
Bemba, 210
Benedict, Ruth, 176–77
Beneš, Edvard, 172–73
Benin, 197, 237–38, 249–50, 306, 363. *See also* Dahomey

INDEX   459

Berg-Damara, 226
Bergman, R.A.M., 181–82
Bergson, Henri, 171–72
Berlin Conference, 16, 82–83, 221–22
Bernheim, Franz, 66–68, 87
Berthelot, Philippe, 44–45, 47–48
Besant, Annie, 18
Bethune, Mary McCleod, 98–100
Bienenfeld, Franz Rudolf, 159
Birmingham, 16th Street Baptist Church, 253–54, 274–75
birth control, 340
Birth of a Nation, The, 26
Bismarck, Otto von, 48
BlacKkKlansman, 26
Black Lives Matter, 22, 90, 403, 405
Black Pete, 388–89
Blue Book, 39–40
Boas, Franz, 18, 176–77
Bogomolov, Alexander E., 154
Bolivia, 115–16, 145, 207, 267, 289
Bolshevik revolution, 92
Bondelzwarts, 73–78
Bonn, Moritz, 41
Bonnet, Henri, 172–73
Borisov, Alexander P., 115–16, 125–26, 153–54
Bossuyt, Marc, 395–96
Bourquin, Maurice, 66–67
Bouteflika, Abdulaziz, 310–11
Boutros-Ghali, Boutros, 305–6
BP Mobil, 302–3
Branting, Hjalmar, 61–62
Brattain, Michelle, 176–77, 183–84
Brazil, 5–6, 30, 138, 145, 171, 184–85, 201–2, 249–50, 267, 273–75, 301–2, 353–54, 394–95, 405–6
Brazilian Society of Anthropologists, 174
British Guiana, 100
British Guiana Labour Union, 88
British Military Manual, 6–7
British Steel Corporation, 302–3
Brussels Conference, 16, 82–83, 85
Buchenwald, 119–20
Bujumbura, 213–14
Bulgaria, 43, 49, 163–64, 166–67, 249–50, 280, 282, 325–26, 328–29, 344–45
Bunche, Ralph, 107–8, 123, 132–33, 226–27, 292
Bureau international pour la défense des indigènes, 56–57, 83–85
Burma, 100, 200, 201, 209–10, 216–17, 218. *See also* Myanmar

Burundi, 26–27, 87, 357–58, 363
Bustamente y Rivero,
   Jo sé Luis, 230–31
Bydgoszcz, 64
Byrnes, James, 163–64

Cadet, Eleizer, 28
Cadogan, Alexander, 61–62, 95–96
Californian Alien Land Law, 31–32
Calmann-Lévy, Mme Paul, 28–29
Calvocoressi, Peter, 262–63
Cambodia, 267–68, 353–54
Cameroon, 39–40, 81–82, 214, 216–17, 310
   Declaration on Racial Discrimination, 249–50, 254
   French mandate, 78, 81–82
   International Year to Combat
      Racism, 353–54
   petitions, 214, 216
   South-West Africa judgment, 233–34
Campos Ortiz, Pablo, 164–65
Canada, 61–63, 75, 90, 92, 132, 203–4, 267, 291–92, 296–97, 306–8, 346–47, 386, 393–94
   Apartheid Convention, 326
   Convention on Racial
      Discrimination, 276–77
   crimes against humanity, 377–78, 397–98
   Declaration on Racial
      Discrimination, 255
   historical injustices, 396, 399
   International Year to Combat
      Racism, 353–54
   mission of Working Group, 388–89
   Organization for Security and Cooperation
      in Europe, 372–73
   other forms of discrimination, 356
   petitions to United Nations, 126–27
   reparations, 375–76, 381–82, 392
   Six Nations, 61–63
   Statutory Limitation Convention, 321–22, 323
   support for South Africa, 112–13, 226, 294, 300–1
   support for Southern Rhodesia, 239
   Universal Declaration, 281
   World Conferences on racism, 361, 366–67, 373–75, 377–78, 381–82, 383, 386, 397, 407
Canal Zone, 392
Candace, Gratien, 57
Cape Verde, 237–38, 243
capital punishment, 167–68, 326–27, 337, 339

460 INDEX

Capotorti, Francesco, 147–48
carding, 388–89
Caribbean, 29–30, 285, 392
Caribbean Community, Ten-Point Action Plan, 400
carnation revolution, 243
Cassese, Antonio, 324–25
Cassin, René, 5, 137, 148–49, 156–57, 158
Cecil, Robert, 30–31, 33, 34, 45–46, 74
Central African Empire, 364–65
Central African Republic, 249–50, 267–68, 326, 353–54, 359
Ceylon, 162–63, 200, 207–8, 301–2. *See also* Sri Lanka
Chad, 249–50, 254, 353–54
Chakravarty, Birendra N., 279–80
Chaney, James, 274–75
Chang, Peng Chun, 148–49
Chapultepec Conference, 96–97. *See also* Inter-American Conference on Problems of War and Peace
Charlottesville, 131, 403
Charter of the International Military Tribunal, 280, 314, 319–20, 329
Charter of the United Nations, 20, 90, 98–104, 113–15, 122, 138–39, 141–42, 144–46, 198–99, 213, 215, 222, 224–25, 227–35, 239–40, 242–43, 251–54, 256, 265–66, 289, 294, 298, 332, 351–53, 410
    Convention on Racial Discrimination, 268–69
    failure to address racism directly, 170
    human rights clauses, 30, 107, 291–92, 298–99
    purposes and principles, 331
    references to race, 98
    preamble, 90, 101–2
    art. 1, 241–42
    art. 1(2), 8–9
    art. 2(2), 293
    art. 2(7), 8–9, 90, 98, 111–14, 135–36, 289–90, 292–94, 296–97, 298–99, 312
    art. 35(1), 296–97
    art. 41, 241
    art. 73, 8–9, 203–4, 207–8, 237–38
    Chapter VII, 325–26
Chauvin, Derek, 403
Chiang Kai-shek, 94
Chicago Defender, 92, 103–4
Chile, 142–43, 145, 151–52, 159–60, 203–4, 222, 292, 322–23, 328–29
China, 2, 18–19, 26–27, 50–51, 92–94, 100–1, 104, 115, 117, 145, 153–54, 240, 255, 267, 290

Bandung Conference, 201
Commission on Human Rights, 143, 249–50
Dumbarton Oaks, 94–95
Japanese proposal on equality, 30, 34, 37, 50–51, 95–96, 231–32
League of Nations, 55
Paris Peace Conference, 34
San Francisco Conference, 99–100, 102–3, 138
Special Committee on Information, 201–2
Statutory Limitation Convention, 321–23,
Sub-Commission, 125–26
support for South Africa, 226
World Conferences on racism, 373–75
Chinda, Sutemi, 31–33, 35
Cho, Sumi, 9
Christianity, 16–17, 42
Christian Negro Republic of Liberia, 2
Christianophobia, 386
Christian States of Europe, 2, 14–15, 18–19
Chrzanowski, Paul, 67–68
Churchill, Winston, 91, 92, 104, 138–39
Ciba Geigy, 302–3
Cicero, Illinois, 151
cinema, 72
Citoyens nègres camerounais, 81–82
civilized nations, 1–8, 83
Civil Rights Congress, 122–23, 129–30
Claparède, René-Édouard, 57
Clarke, Ashley, 91
Clarke, Kevin, 405–6
Clemenceau, Georges, 26, 28–29, 47–50
climate change, 388–89
Code of Conduct for European firms operating in South Africa, 373
Code of Crimes Against the Peace and Security of Mankind, 314, 326–27, 332–33, 336, 345–46
Colby, Elbridge, 6–7
Cold War, 20, 110–11, 123, 129–30, 140, 273, 284–85, 359–60, 412
Cologne, 245–46
Colombia, 5–6, 145, 294, 405–6
Colonial Conference, 100
colonial domination, 311–12, 326, 333–34
colonialism, 1–2, 5–7, 9, 13–17, 20–24, 26, 39–40, 52–54, 71, 77–78, 82, 87, 90, 99–100, 127–28, 136, 189, 198–210, 212–14, 222–23, 236–37, 242–43, 246–48, 252, 262, 268–69, 273–75, 281, 291–92, 298–99, 302–3, 337, 358, 362–63, 367, 375–78, 386–413. *See also* non-self-governing territories

colonial powers, 56, 58–59, 199–202, 204–5, 207–8, 209–11, 216–17, 236–37, 242, 375–76, 392–93, 396
Colored Welfare Association, 88
colour line, 1–3, 7, 19, 21, 24, 77–78, 87, 149–50, 200–1, 243, 371, 382, 388, 390–91, 411–13
'colour', use of term, 9–10, 16–17, 64, 85–87, 144–49, 200–2, 213–14, 219, 251–52, 284–85, 339
Columbia University, 177, 182, 184–85
Columbus City Federation of Colored Women's Clubs, 88
Comas, Juan, 169–70, 175–76, 184–85
commemorative postage stamps, 353–54
Commission of Inquiry into Apartheid, 292
Commission on Apartheid in Sports, 303
Commission on Human Rights, 5, 98–99, 107–8, 123–26, 131–32, 136, 145, 184–85, 243, 249, 251–53, 256–57, 337, 338, 343–45, 353, 354–56, 366–67, 370, 383
  anti-Semitism, 246–47
  apartheid as genocide, 335
  Apartheid Convention, 326–29
  'colour', 146–47
  complementary international standards, 384
  composition of, 143
  Convention on Racial Discrimination, 264, 266–67, 270, 279–81
  crimes against humanity, 319
  Declaration on Racial Discrimination, 252
  draft convention on religious intolerance, 284–85
  election of Liberia, 253–54
  genocide issue, 340–41
  human rights Covenants, 143–44, 147–48, 151–52
  inadequate representation of Global South, 249–50, 411
  International Year to Combat Racism, 353–54
  nuclear commission, 107–8
  report of ad hoc Working Group, 335–36
  revision of Genocide Convention, 340
  Special rapporteur on contemporary forms of racism, 368–69, 370–71, 398–99
  Special rapporteur on minorities issues, 387–88
  Statutory Limitation Convention, 319–21
  Universal Declaration, 148–49, 152–54
  working group on crimes against humanity, 319–20

Working Group on People of African Descent, 388–89
World Conferences on racism, 373–75
Commission on the Racial Situation in South Africa, 290, 292–96
Commission on the Status of Women, 142–43, 157, 165, 166–67, 187–88
Commission to Study the Organisation of Peace, 93
Committee of Experts on Race Problems, 175–76
Committee of Experts on Slavery, 85
Committee of the Society of Friends, 53–54
Committee on Economic, Social and Cultural Rights, 167–68, 194–95
Committee on Information, 201–8, 210, 212, 237–38, 242–43
Committee on the Elimination of Discrimination Against Women, 402
Committee on the Elimination of Racial Discrimination, 10–11, 21–22, 167–68, 193–94, 219–21, 244, 272–73, 278, 349, 388, 403, 412–13
  cooperation with other United Nations bodies, 219
  Early Warning and Urgent Action Procedures, 403
  General Recommendation 30, 271
  inaugural session, 282
  interpretation of 'national origin', 271
  inter-State communications, 282
  Palestine v. Israel, 270
  petitions, 267–68, 282
  Qatar v. United Arab Emirates, 271
  situation in Papua New Guinea, 220–21
Commonwealth War Graves Commission, 52
Commonwealth, 52, 78, 102, 293–94, 361–62
Communism, 223–24, 392
Communist Party of the United States, 122–23, 129–30
complementary international standards, 384–85, 387
Conference for the Establishment of UNESCO, 170, 171
Conférence Internationale des Noires et des Arabes, 88
Conference of Allied Ministers of Education, 170
Conference of American States, Eighth International, 96–97
Conference of Independent African States, 227–28
Conference on Security and Cooperation in Europe, 372–73

462 INDEX

Congo (Brazzaville), 323
Congo Free State, 2
Congo River Basin, 82
Congo, Democratic Republic of the, 2, 16, 134, 297–98, 328–29, 335. *See also* Zaire, Belgian Congo
Congo, Republic of the, 323, 353–54
Congress of Berlin (1878), 48
Congress of Vienna (1815), 7–8
conspiracy, 326–27
contemporary forms of racism, 367–69, 399–400
Continuation Committee for All Harlem Independent Political Action, 88
Convention on equal remuneration, 157
Convention on discrimination in education, 260–61, 263
Convention against discrimination in employment, 259–60
Convention on the Elimination of All Forms of Discrimination Against Women, 400–1
Convention on Statutory Limitations, 319–25
Convention on the Prevention and Punishment of the Crime of Genocide. *See* Genocide Convention
Coomaraswamy, Radhika, 401
corporal punishment, 216
Costa Pinto, L.A., 175–76
Costa Rica, 145, 163–64, 279–80, 282, 301–2, 364–65
Costa, Afonso, 40–41
Côte d'Ivoire, 240–41, 249–50, 267, 353–54
Council of Europe, 229–30, 325, 353–54, 371–72, 391
Covenant of the League of Nations, 6–7, 19–20, 25–26, 43–44, 49–51, 55, 59–60, 94–95, 199, 231–32, 389–90
  mandate system, 61, 68–70
  proposed reference to racial equality, 27, 28, 30–38
  art. 17, 61–62
  art. 19, 29–30
  art. 22, 6–7, 55, 61, 68–69, 72–73, 228–30
  art. 227, 39
  art. 230, 43
COVID 19, 22, 388–89, 412–13
Crawford, James, 271–72
Credit Suisse, 302–3
Crenshaw, Kimberlé, 400–1
Crimean Tatars, discrimination against, 283
Crimes against Christianity, 42

crimes against humanity, 21, 39, 42, 117–21, 128–29, 191, 235–36, 313–27, 329–35, 337–38, 342–50, 377, 397, 400
criminal justice, 25, 120–21, 218–19, 313, 348–49, 387–88, 404–7, 411–12
Crisis, The, 28–29, 55, 57, 59–60, 94, 96
Critical race theory, 9, 22, 23
Crowe, Eyre, 70
Crusades, 42
Cuba, 13, 92, 96–97, 107, 117–18, 136, 142–43, 145, 226, 359–60
  calls Vietnam war 'genocidal', 352
  criticism of South Africa, 226–27
  Durban Conference, 373–75, 377
  education in colonies, 203–4
  First Session of General Assembly, 108
  genocide, 117
  Special Committee on Information, 201–2
  Statutory Limitation Convention, 322–23
  Universal Declaration, 148–49
  Zionism, 358
cultural genocide, 326–27
cultural relativism, 12–13
curfew, 216–17
Curie, Marie, 171–72
Curzon, George, 43
customary international law, 15, 229–30, 233, 235–36, 324–25, 346–48, 398
Cuthbert, Christy, 86
Cyprus, 314–15
Czech Academy, 172–73
Czechia, Durban commemoration, 407
Czechoslovakia, 145, 172–73, 186, 263
  Committee on the Elimination of Racial Discrimination, 282
  Convention on Racial Discrimination, 249–50, 260–61, 263
  Japanese proposal on equality, 30, 37
  minorities treaties, 10, 45, 49
  San Francisco Conference, 138

Dahlberg, Gunnar, 181–82
Dahomey, 249–50, 319–20, 322–23, 335, 353–54, 358. *See also* Benin
Dalits, 380–81
Daniels, Jonathan, 125–26, 145–46
Dannevig, Valentine, 71–72
Danzig, 65–66, 68–69
Dar-es-Salaam, 80–81
Dartiguenave, Philippe-Sudre, 58–59
d'Aspremont Lynden, Harold Charles, 291–92
Davidson, Basil, 16–17
death sentence, 339

Debetz, Georghi F., 186–87
Decades on racial discrimination, 21–22, 189, 354–56, 372, 373–75
Déclaration des droits de l'homme et du citoyen, 187–88
Declaration of Mexico on the Equality of Women, 358
Declaration of Rights of the Negro Peoples of the World, 390
Declaration of the United Nations, 92, 93–94
Declaration on Apartheid and its Destructive Consequences in Southern Africa, 311–12
Declaration on Race and Race Prejudice, 189–94
Declaration on the Elimination of All Forms of Intolerance and of Discrimination Based on Religion or Belief, 284–85, 369–70
Declaration on the Elimination of All Forms of Racial Discrimination, 1, 102–3, 135, 229–30, 251–52, 256–60, 268–69
Declaration on the Granting of Independence to Colonial Countries and Peoples, 12, 206–7, 211–13, 219, 246–47, 315–16
Declaration regarding non-self-governing territories, 199
Dedijer, Vladimir, 144
defamation of religions, 384
De Haller, Edouard, 61
Dehousse, Fernand, 156–57
Deir Yassein massacre, 251
De Klerk, F.W., 311–12
Delegation of Race Petitioners, 28, 49–50
Delson, Robert, 225
Denmark, 145, 178, 226, 255, 301–2, 322–23, 366–67
Dennis, Gabriel L., 106–7
DePaul University, 343
Der Stürmer, 67–68
Deskaheh, Levi General, 61–63
Deutscher Volksbund 'Rettet die ehre', 53
Deutsch-Südwestafrika, 221–22
Diagne, Blaise, 28–29, 409
diamond mines, 73
Dihigo, Ernesto, 117–18, 120–21
disabilities, persons with, 402
District of Columbia, 26
DNA, 196–97
Dobzhansky, Theodosius, 177, 181–82, 184
Dominican Republic, 289–90, 296–97
Donnedieu de Vabres, Henri, 10
Donnelly, Jack, 22–23

Douglass, Frederick, 388
draft articles on State responsibility, 333–34
Dreyfus, Alfred, 26
Drummond, Eric, 28, 49–50, 56–57, 60–62, 63, 66–67
Du Bois, W.E.B., 1, 2, 9–10, 16, 18, 19, 24, 50–51, 52, 58–61, 88, 100, 127, 131, 141, 253–54, 287–88, 388, 409, 412
  absence at Bandung Conference, 200–1
  complaints about Eleanor Roosevelt, 123–24
  Dumbarton Oaks Conference, 93–94, 96, 97
  International Labour Organization, 59–60
  League of Nations, 57–58
  nuclear Commission on Human Rights, 107–8
  Pan African Congress, 200–1
  Paris Peace Conference, 28–30, 50
  petition to United Nations, 123–25
  San Francisco Conference, 47–48, 98–99, 104, 115
  slavery in Liberia, 85–86
  tension with Garvey, 56–57
  United States Senate, 103–4
  We Charge Genocide, 130
Dugard, John, 222–23, 232–34, 349
Dulles, John Foster, 201–2
dum-dum bullets, 6–7, 88
Dumbarton Oaks Conference, 93–98, 101–3, 111–12, 115, 198–99
Dunn, Leslie C., 181–85
Durban Conference, 13–14, 21–22, 192, 193–94, 196, 360, 373–76, 381–82, 383, 385–86, 388, 395–96, 397, 401, 412–13
  crimes against humanity, 377, 378
  Final Act, 362–63
  NGO Forum, 379, 380
  preparatory regional meetings, 375–76, 388–89, 392–93
  reparations, 377, 395–96
Durban Declaration and Programme of Action, 16–17, 21–22, 365, 376–78, 380–86, 388, 397, 404–5, 407, 408–9
  anti-Semitism and Islamophobia, 379
  tenth anniversary, 387
Durban Review Conference, 386, 387, 408
Durkheim, Emile, 18

East Africa, 16, 26–27, 39–40, 80–81
Easterman, Alex, 154, 158
Economic and Social Council, 10, 98, 107–8, 119–26, 132, 136, 143, 249, 317, 338, 354–55
  crimes against humanity, 314–15

464 INDEX

Economic and Social Council (*cont.*)
Declaration on Racial Discrimination, 252
International Year to Combat
Racism, 353–54
mixed marriages, 164
review of Second Decade, 368–69
UNESCO race statements, 173, 174–75
Economist, 309
Ecuador, 125–26, 145, 156–57, 210, 267–68,
297, 325, 328–29, 388–89
education, 29–30, 65–66, 71–73, 80–82, 87,
123–24, 138, 141, 149, 158–64, 171, 190,
203–6, 210, 217–19, 228–29, 238, 260–61,
265–66, 272–73, 283, 293, 355–56, 387–
88, 390–91
Egypt, 13, 18–19, 60–61, 106, 143, 198, 296–97.
See also United Arab Republic
Apartheid Convention, 328–29
Bandung Conference, 200, 201
Commission on Human Rights, 143, 249–50
constitution, 145
Declaration on Racial Discrimination, 114
General Assembly resolution on
discrimination, 108, 114–17, 129, 136,
260–61, 287–89
League of Nations, 55
prohibitions on marriage, 165–66
Special Committee on Information, 201–2
Eichmann case, 340–41
Eide, Asbjørn, 16–17, 367–68, 371
Einstein, Albert, 171–72
Eisenhower, Dwight, 245–46
El Pacto de el Assiento de Negros, 14–15
El Salvador, 145, 216–17, 324
Encyclopaedia Universalis, 12
environment, 332, 388–89
*Epidemic of anti-Semitic Vandalism in America,
The*, 274–75
epidemics, 338
equal pay for equal work, 155–57
Estonia, 61–62, 130–31
Ethiopia, 2, 20–21, 85–86, 106, 109, 198, 227–
30, 231, 249
Bandung Conference, 200, 201
International Court of Justice, 115–16, 228–31
International Year to Combat
Racism, 353–54
Italian war crimes, 88–89
League of Nations, 85
resolution on racial discrimination in
colonies, 207
Security Council debate on
Sharpeville, 296–97

slavery, 84–85
ethnic cleansing, 371, 385
ethnic groups, 16–17, 50, 169, 178–79, 183
'ethnic origin', use of term, 251–52
eugenics, 173
Eugenics Review, 180
European Commission against Racism and
Intolerance, 371–72
European Commission of Human Rights, 372
European Community, 361–62, 363, 373
European Convention on Human Rights, 5, 372
European Convention on the Non-Applicability
of Statutory Limitation, 325
European Court of Human Rights, 45–46,
282, 372
European Fundamental Rights Agency,
373, 390–91
European Monitoring Centre on Racism and
Xenophobia, 373
European Parliament, 368–69, 371, 390–91
European Union, 192, 193–94, 368–69, 373,
377–78, 383, 385–87, 390–91, 404–5, 407
European Year Against Racism, 373
Évolution sociale camerounaise, 214
ex-nuptial children, 132–33
extradition, 167–68

Fagg, William B., 180
Falk, Richard, 233–34, 349
Federal Council of Churches of Christ, 99
feminists, 53
Ferguson, Clarence Clyde, 191, 261–62
Finland, 222–23, 255, 280, 296–97, 329–
30, 365–67
Firestone rubber company, 86
First World War, 6–7, 10, 19, 28–29, 39–40, 52,
55, 64, 68–69, 80, 229, 412
First, Ruth, 73
Fischer, Hugo, 15
Fitzmaurice, Gerald, 235
Flores Liera, Socorro, 347–48
Floyd, George, 22, 403–7, 412–13
Floyd, Philonese, 404
Fomin, Andrei Andronovich, 134–35
Food and Agriculture Organisation, 367–68
forced displacement, 337–38
forced labour, 39–40, 85–86, 331
Forced Labour Convention, 85
forcibly transferring children, 326–27
Foreign Affairs, 16, 66–67, 85–86, 109–10, 200
foreign occupation, 326, 358, 379, 385, 400–1
Forster, Isaac, 225
four freedoms, 91, 101, 138–39

France, 4–5, 40–41, 52, 145, 203–4, 227, 237–38, 291–92, 297, 357, 405–6
African troops in First World War, 52, 53
Assemblée nationale, 28–29, 193–94
Code pénal, 195
colonies, 29–30, 50, 68–69, 81–82, 106, 204–5, 212–13, 242
Convention on Racial Discrimination, 278
declaration on Ottoman atrocities, 42, 313–14
Declaration on Racial Discrimination, 255
denial of racial discrimination, 203, 205–7, 214, 216–17
Dreyfus case, 26
European Convention on Statutory Limitation, 325
historical injustice, 396
human rights Covenants, 151–52
legislation on hate speech, 278
London Conference, 118–19
mandates, 68–69, 81–82
memorandum on genocide, 121
opposition to Durban commemoration, 407
Paris Peace Conference, 25–26, 30, 37–38
Permanent Mandates Commission, 70–71
proposals for UNESCO constitution, 170–71
revolution, 412
San Francisco Conference, 102–3, 138
Statutory Limitation Convention, 319, 321–24
Sub-Commission, 125–26
support for South Africa, 113–14, 222–23, 226, 234, 236–37, 289–90, 294, 296–97, 300–1, 305–6, 312
support for Southern Rhodesia, 240–42
Universal Declaration of Human Rights, 137, 235–36, 265–66
use of veto, 13–14, 239–40, 306, 310
World Conferences on racism, 363, 366–67, 407
Frazier, E. Franklin, 175–76
Frederickson, George, 196
freedom of association, 256–57, 263, 276–80
freedom of expression, 12–13, 90–91, 103–4, 153–55, 162–63, 252, 256–57, 263, 276–79
Freire D'Andrade, Alfreido, 77
Friesel, Orla, 273

Gabon, 353–54, 364–65
Gambia, 267–68
Gandhi, Mohandas, 18, 92

García Palomino, Janner (Hanner), 405–6
Garvey, Marcus, 19, 28, 30–31, 56–57, 60–61, 390, 409
Gathii, James, 7, 22
Gaza, occupation of, 356
gender identity, 393–94, 402
General Act and Declaration of Brussels, 82–83
General Act of Berlin, 82–83, 199
General Assembly, 8–9, 13, 20, 21, 104–36, 139, 231–33, 237–38, 244–45
Ad Hoc Political Committee, 115–16, 289–92, 294–97, 299–300, 304–5, 316
Ad Hoc Working Group of Experts on the question of apartheid, 287–89, 326–27, 328–29, 335–45
Apartheid Convention, 325–31
changing composition, 140, 167, 198
Convention on Racial Discrimination, 260–61, 267–78, 281, 284
crimes against humanity, 117–21, 314–18
Declaration on Granting Independence, 246–47, 262, 268–69
Declaration on Racial Discrimination, 248–59
Egyptian resolution on discrimination, 114–16
Fourth Committee, 106–7, 115–16, 199–200, 203–12, 223–27, 237–38, 242–43, 314–17
genocide, 117–21, 336, 397
Indian diaspora in South Africa, 110–14
international criminal tribunal, 342–43, 345–47
International Decade to Combat Racism, 354–56
International Year for People of African Descent, 390
International Year to Combat Racism, 351–54
Namibia, 222–27, 234, 235–36
non-self-governing territories, 202–12
Nuremberg principles, 117–21
Portuguese colonies, 237–39
reparations, 396
Southern Rhodesia, 239–42
Statutory Limitation Convention, 319–25
Third Committee, 5–6, 127, 144, 146–49, 162–63, 250–51, 256–57, 268–69, 273–77, 280, 320–22, 328, 329–30, 356, 358, 362–63, 366–67
Universal Declaration, 139, 143–44, 148–50, 151–53, 154–55, 156, 159, 162–63, 166–67
World Conferences on racism, 363–67, 373–75, 383, 385–87, 407–8
Zionism, 190–91, 273–74, 356–60

466 INDEX

General Electric, 302–3
General Motors, 302–3
general principles of law, 5, 83
Geneva Convention III, 54
Geneva Convention IV, 337
Geneva Conventions, Additional Protocol
  I, 346–47
Geneva Prisoner of War Convention
  (1929), 10, 54
genocide, 3–4, 10, 13, 25, 41, 42, 67–68, 117–18,
  127–31, 136, 141, 152–53, 169, 221–22,
  260–61, 266–67, 313–14, 318–20, 326–28,
  329, 331–32, 334, 335–43, 345–46, 378,
  385, 397
Genocide Convention, 10–11, 13, 127–31, 314,
  325–26, 331, 335, 336, 340–43, 410
  definition, 128
  exclusion of political groups, 128–29
  interpretation, 338, 340
  proposed amendments, 326–27, 340
  South African accession, 336–37
  universal jurisdiction, 327–28
  art. 1, 329, 339
  art. 6, 327–28
Georgia, 331
Georgia v. Russia, 283
German League for the Protection
  of the Rights of Minorities in
  Poland, 64
German League of Upper Silesia, 64
German Settlers in Poland advisory
  opinion, 64–65
Germany, 6–7, 18–19, 40–41, 43–44, 46–50,
  58–59, 61, 63–64, 66–68, 103–4, 118,
  127–28, 158, 169, 172–73, 193–94, 223–24,
  274–75, 307–8
  African troops, 6–7, 53
  anti-Semitism, 245–46
  colonies in Africa, 19, 26–27, 39–40, 41,
    69, 221–22
  historical injustice, 396
  Naulilaa case, 40–41
  South West Africa, 75–76, 80
  statutory limitation, 320
  war crimes, 39–40
  World Conferences on
    racism, 386, 407
Germany, East, 344–45, 353–54
Germany, West, 307–9, 363, 366–67
Getachew, Adom, 85–86
Gevers, Christopher, 2–3, 22
Ghana, 134, 149–50, 200, 249, 363–65. *See also*
  Gold Coast

Convention on Racial Discrimination, 244,
  249–50, 261, 267–68, 275, 281
  critical of British colonialism, 208
  resolution on racial discrimination in
    colonies, 207
  Security Council debate on
    Sharpeville, 296–97
  Special Committee on apartheid, 301–2
  World Conferences on racism, 359,
    360, 364–65
Ghaoucy, Saadolah, 322
Ghetto Act, 111
Gibbs, Pearl, 63
Giladi, Rotem, 6–7, 331
Ginsberg, Morris, 175–76
Goa, 80–81, 237–38
Gobineau, Arthur de, 169–70
Goebbels, Joseph, 172–73
Gold Coast, 100, 134, 149, 200–1
Goodman, Andrew, 274–75
Gordon, Ruth, 9–10
Grand Hotel, Nuremberg, 120
grave breaches, 343, 346–47
Greece, 47–48, 145, 152, 203–4
  Convention on Racial Discrimination,
    267, 275
  Declaration on Racial Discrimination, 255
  human rights Covenants, 151–52, 162–63
  minorities treaties, 49
  Paris Peace Conference, 26, 30, 34
  prohibitions on marriage, 165–66
  status of Muslims, 45
  Statutory Limitations Convention, 322–23
  support for South Africa, 150, 222, 287–
    90, 294
  World Conferences on racism, 365–66
Green Book, 109
Green, Leslie, 233–34
Grimshaw, Harold A., 85–86
Gros, André, 235
Gross, Ernest A., 227–30
Grumbach, Salomon, 150
Guadeloupe, 57
Guatemala, 145, 216–17, 289, 331, 364–65
Guidance Note on Racial Discrimination and
  Protection of Minorities, 387–88
Guinea, 207–8, 237–38, 243, 249, 254
  Apartheid Convention, 325–28
  Convention on Racial Discrimination, 249–
    50, 261
  crimes against humanity, 316
  drafting of Declaration on Racial
    Discrimination, 249–50, 254

INDEX 467

International Year to Combat Racism, 353–54
Security Council debate on
Sharpeville, 296–97
Special Committee on apartheid, 301–2
Guterres, António, 90
Guyana, 377. *See also* British Guiana

Hague Conferences, 2, 6–7, 18–19
Hague Conventions, 3–4, 6–7
Haiti, 2, 18, 58–59, 73–74, 85, 92, 106, 109, 113–
15, 152, 204–5, 216–17, 287–88, 291–94
constitution, 145
Convention on Racial Discrimination,
244, 267–68
Durban Conference, 377
League of Nations, 55
Paris Peace Conference, 26
resolution on racism at
Chapultepec, 96–97
San Francisco Conference, 102–3
Special Committee on apartheid, 301–2
Sub-Commission, 125–26, 132
Haldane, J.B.S., 181–82
Halifax, Earl of, 95–96
Hall, William Edward, 4–5
Halpern, Philip, 133–35, 245–46
Hambro ruling, 310–11
Hammarskjöld, Dag, 247, 297–98
Harris, John H., 57, 75
Harris, Kamala, 24
hate speech, 154, 256–57, 261–62, 263, 275–76,
278, 385
Haudenosaunee, 61–62
Hazard, Anthony Q., 176–77, 187, 188
Headlam-Morley, James, 44–48
health care, 123–24, 215, 218–19, 388, 406
Hedjaz. *See* Saudi Arabia
Herbst, Major, 76–77
Herero, 39–40, 41, 63, 127–28, 221–27
Herriot, Edouard, 172–73
Hicks, James, 247
Higgins, Rosalyn, 228, 233–34
High Commissioner for Human Rights, 373–
76, 379, 389–90, 407, 411–12
Durban Conference, 383
experts on racism, 384, 385
report on systemic racism, 111, 399–400, 405,
406, 408–9
High Commissioner for Refugees, 25
Hindi, 210
Hindu, The, 110–11
Hiscocks, Richard, 134–35
historical injustices, 376–77, 386, 396, 399–400

Hitler, Adolf, 63, 100, 111–12, 118, 141, 158,
162, 169, 380
Hoare, Samuel, 5, 151, 161–62, 163, 265–
66, 279–80
Hobsbawm, Eric, 16, 412
Hobson, J.A., 18
Hoechst, 302–3
Hoffmann La-Roche, 302–3
Hofmann, Otto, 119–20
hollow tipped bullets, 6–7, 88
Honduras, 145, 289, 321–24, 331, 377
Hong Kong, 70–71
Horror on the Rhine, 53–54
Hotel Theresa, 109
Hottentot, 223–24
House, Edward M. ('Colonel'), 30, 32–35
housing, 123–24, 208, 254, 272–73, 388, 390–
91, 394–95
Houston, Charles Hamilton, 408–9
Howard University, 175–76, 261–62, 408–9
Huber, Max, 66–67
Hughes, Langston, 141
Hughes, William, 35
human dignity, 144, 149, 216–17, 228, 256,
268–69, 372
Human Rights Committee, 155, 167–68, 282
Human Rights Council, 22, 139–40, 385–86,
388–89, 403, 405–7
Ad Hoc Committee on the Elaboration of
Complementary Standards, 384, 387
Advisory Committee, 195
Durban Conference, 384, 407
George Floyd, 404
Universal Periodic Review, 139–40
human rights covenants. *See* International
Covenant on Civil and Political Rights;
International Covenant on Economic,
Social and Cultural Rights
Human Rights Watch, 349
Humphrey, John P., 98–99, 122–23, 124–25,
132–33, 145–46, 183, 281
Hungary, 43, 114, 267, 275, 280, 301–2, 315–16,
353–54, 407
Huxley, Julian, 173, 177–78, 182

Iceland, 145, 255
imperialism, 15, 16–17, 175, 357–58
incitement, 138, 152–55, 262–63
India, 5, 6–7, 13, 57–58, 60–61, 92, 100, 102–3,
114–15, 117–18, 145–47, 149–50, 152–53,
265–67, 276, 287–88, 290–92, 294, 298
306–8, 312
apartheid, 289

468 INDEX

India (*cont.*)
Apartheid Convention, 328–29
Bandung Conference, 200–1
colonialism, 207, 208, 216–17
Commission on Human Rights, 143, 249–50
Convention on Racial Discrimination, 270, 279–80, 282
crimes against humanity, 321
diaspora in South Africa, 110–13, 149
First Session of General Assembly, 108, 136
First World War, 52
genocide, 117, 120
International Court of Justice, 225
San Francisco Conference, 110–11
Security Council debate on Sharpeville, 296–97
South West Africa, 222
Special Committee on Information, 201–2
Sub-Commission, 125–26, 249
UNESCO founding conference, 171
Universal Declaration, 5
World Conferences, 373–75
indigenous peoples, 15, 17, 61–63, 160–61, 367–68, 370–71, 375–78, 385, 395, 400, 401, 402
Indochina, 52, 53, 100, 200–1, 204–6, 298–99
inhuman acts, 11, 319–24, 326–27, 331–32
Institut de droit international, 2–3, 82–83, 137
Inter-American Commission on Human Rights, 194–95, 388–89, 394–95, 402
Inter-American Conference on Problems of War and Peace, 96–97
Inter-American Convention against Racism, Racial Discrimination and Related Forms of Intolerance, 393–94
Inter-American Convention on the Elimination of All Forms of Discrimination and Intolerance, 393–94
Inter-American Court of Human Rights, 394–95, 402
Inter-American Juridical Committee, 142–43
Intergovernmental Group to Monitor the Supply and Shipping of Oil and Petroleum Products to South Africa, 302–3
Intergovernmental Working Group, 384
intermarriage, 164–67, 178, 182–83, 187
internally displaced persons, 380–81, 385
International Agreement for the Suppression of the White Slave Traffic, 83
International Bill of Rights, 13, 20, 107–8, 124–25, 135–39, 244–45
International Civil Aviation Organisation, 367–68

International Commission of Inquiry into slavery in Liberia, 86
International Committee of Intellectual Cooperation, 72, 171–72
International Committee of the Red Cross, 54, 346–47
International Compensation Scheme, 392–93
International Conference on White Slave Traffic, 83–84
International Congress on Anthropology, 172–73
International Convention against Apartheid in Sports, 303
International Convention for the Suppression of the White Slave Traffic, 83
International Convention for the Suppression of the White Slave Traffic, Protocol, 83
International Convention of Negroes, 56–57
International Convention of the Negro Peoples of the World, 390
International Convention on the Elimination of All Forms of Racial Discrimination, 5–6, 12, 13, 135, 152–53, 193, 198, 199–200, 229–30, 244, 261, 271–72, 285, 329, 334, 351–53, 356, 393–94, 408, 411
additional protocol, 326, 384, 387
compromissory clause, 283
entry into force, 219–20
exclusion of reference to anti-Semitism, 273
implementation, 281
petitions, 219
reference to apartheid, 272–73
reservations, 278–79
title, 268
preamble, 268–70
art. 1, 270, 283
art. 3, 272–73
art. 4, 275–76
art. 14, 282
art. 15, 267–68
International Convention on the Suppression and Punishment of the Crime of Apartheid, 11, 324–25, 329, 330, 332–33, 335, 340–50, 365, 411
concerns of Western States, 329
crimes against humanity, 21
entry into force, 331
Group of Three, 342
international criminal tribunal, 21, 342–43
opposition from United States, 346–47
periodic reports of States Parties, 342
universal jurisdiction, 21

INDEX   469

International Court of Justice, 5, 104–5, 112–13, 234–35, 271
International Covenant on Civil and Political Rights, 5, 137–38, 143–45, 147–48, 152–53, 166–68, 194–95, 244–45, 284
International Covenant on Economic, Social and Cultural Rights, 137–38, 143–45, 147–48, 155–59, 244–45, 284
International Criminal Court, 21, 39, 313, 344–50, 378, 411–12
international criminal jurisdiction, proposal for, 326–27
international criminal law, 21, 39, 117–19, 314, 326–29, 343, 355–56
International Criminal Tribunal for Rwanda, 11, 128–29, 155, 278, 313, 346
International Criminal Tribunal for the former Yugoslavia, 21, 313, 324–25, 346
International Day against Racial Discrimination, 381
International Day for People of African Descent, 381, 390
International Day for the Remembrance of the Slave Trade and its Abolition, 381
International Day of Remembrance of the Victims of Slavery and the Transatlantic Slave Trade, 381
International Decade of People of African Descent, 390
International Declaration against Apartheid in Sports, 303
International Federation of League of Nations Societies, 72
international humanitarian law, 346–47, 395
International Independent Expert Mechanism to Advance Racial Justice and Equality in the context of Law Enforcement, 406–7
International Institute for Higher Studies in Criminal Sciences, 344
International Institute of Intellectual Cooperation, 171–73
International Labour Office, 55, 59–60, 73
International Labour Organisation, 25, 55, 57, 85–86, 157, 229–30, 260–61, 263, 268–69, 353–54, 367–68
International Law Commission, 5, 121, 235, 259–60, 314, 318–19, 332–34, 336, 342–43, 346–47
International Law Quarterly, 15
International League for Darker People, 28
International League for the Rights of Man, 223–25, 245–46

International Military Tribunal, 10, 21, 117–20, 128, 169, 235–36, 318, 397. *See also* Charter of the International Military Tribunal
International Races Congress, 59–60
International Year for Action to Combat Racism and Racial Discrimination, 189, 351–53
International Year for Human Rights, 351–52
International Year of People of African Descent, 390
intersectionality, 214, 380–81, 398, 400–2
intertemporality, 397–98
'intolerance', use of term, 284–85, 369–70
IQ tests, 190, 193
Iran, 125–26, 128–29, 143, 145, 282, 335, 386. *See also* Persia
Iraq, 10, 55, 104, 145, 203–4, 207–10, 254, 329, 335, 353–54
Ireland, 60–62, 66–67, 255, 275, 278–79, 298–99, 300–1, 316–17, 318, 353–54
Iroquois, 61–62
Irvin-Erickson, Douglas, 130–31
Islamophobia, 379, 380, 386
Israel, 13–14, 21–22, 115–16, 203–4, 251, 273–74, 282, 287–88, 337, 352, 365
   allegations of apartheid, 349
   Convention on Racial Discrimination, 267
   historical injustice, 396
   occupied territories, 361, 375–76
   prohibitions on marriage, 165–66
   South Africa, 35, 226, 290, 309, 311, 356, 357–58, 361, 365–66
   Soviet Union, 266–67
   Statutory Limitation Convention, 319, 323–24
   World Conferences on racism, 360, 362–63, 364–65, 366–67, 376, 379, 383, 386, 407
Israel/Palestine issue, 363
Italy, 66–67, 147–48, 296–97, 301–2, 305, 316
   atrocities in Ethiopia, 88–89
   Declaration on Racial Discrimination, 255
   human rights Covenants, 147–48, 166–67
   mandates, 198–99
   Paris Peace Conference, 25–26, 30, 37, 44–45
   Second World War peace treaty, 280
   Statutory Limitation Convention, 322–23
   World Conferences on racism, 386
Ivanov, Boris S., 263, 273
Iwasawa, Yuji, 50–51

Jackson, Robert, 118–19
Jackson Sow, Marisa, 412–13
Jamaica, 100, 255, 316–17, 335, 377
Jankovic, Branimir, 335, 344

470 INDEX

Japan, 2, 4–5, 26, 37, 51, 55, 58–59, 69, 104,
126–27, 301–2
Apartheid Convention, 326
Bandung, 201
Convention on Racial
Discrimination, 278–79
equality proposal at Paris Peace Conference,
19–20, 25–26, 30–38, 50–51, 70, 93,
94–95, 101, 104, 231–32, 251, 389–90,
409, 412
mandates, 68–69, 70, 198–99
Permanent Mandates Commission, 70–71
support for South Africa, 300–1
support for Southern Rhodesia, 239
World Conferences on racism, 373–75
Japan Society, 35
Jessup, Philip, 230–31, 233
Jeunesses antiracistes, 88
Jews, 10, 109, 178, 188, 245–46, 251, 273,
349, 357
attacks in Eastern Europe, 114
discrimination in New York City, 109
genocide, 288–89, 314
Nazi persecution, 66–68, 118–20, 127–28
organizations, 167
population in Europe, 169
representatives at Paris Peace
Conference, 26–27
sabbath, 46
schools, 46
treatment in Poland, 19, 26–27, 44–47, 114
Jim Crow, 13–14, 24, 26–27, 109, 118–19, 129–
30, 174–75, 260–61, 411–12
Johannesburg, 223–24, 296–97, 306
Johnson, Ernest, 94
Jones, Leif, 57
Jordan, 251
Judgment at Nuremberg, 119–20
Junod, Edouard, 56–57, 83–85
jus cogens, 235, 334, 398

Kabir, Humayun, 175–76
Karch, Brendan, 67–68
Kattan, Victor, 224–25
Kaur, Rajkumari Amrit, 171
Keesee, Tracie, 406–7
Kelsen, Hans, 101–2
Kennedy, John F., 354–55
Kenya, 16, 134, 203, 207–8, 376–77
Kershaw, Anthony, 236–37
Ketrzynski, Wojciech, 263
Khan, Muhammad Zafrulla, 230–31, 234–35
Khrushchev, Nikita, 274–75

Kikujurō, Ishii, 35, 38
Kimbundu, 210
King, Charles D.B., 28
King, Henry, 120
King, Martin Luther, 248, 252–53
Kipling, Rudyard, 17
Kiwanis clubs, 98–99
Knesset, 357
Koo, Wellington, 34, 50–51, 94–95, 100,
115, 231–32
Korea, 2
Korea, North, 268, 359–60
Koskenniemi, Martti, 1–2
Kōtarō, Tanaka, 232–33
Kramer, Stanley, 119–20
Ku Klux Klan, 26, 131, 252–53, 263, 389–90
Kupreškić case, 324–25
Kutako, Hosea, 223–24, 226–27

Labéry, Henry, 238
Lachs, Manfred, 191
La Fontaine, Henri, 58–59
Lagos Observer, 16
Laleau, Léon, 106
Lange, E.J.H., 78–79
Lantos, Tom, 380
Larnaude, Ferdinand, 33, 37–38
Lasso, José Ayala, 373–75
Latvia, 49, 130–31
Laugier, Henri, 108, 113, 124–25, 292
Lauren, Paul Gordon, 14–15, 108
L'Aurore, 26
Lauterpacht, Hersch, 113, 141–42
laws and customs of war, 3–4, 6–7, 39, 42–
43, 345–46
Lawson, Edward, 176–77
League of Coloured Peoples, 88, 97
League of Nations, 19, 25, 30–31, 32, 35, 36,
52–74, 82, 84–87, 110–11, 113–14, 171–73,
213–14, 226, 227–28, 229–30, 231, 242,
253–54, 287–88, 409
Assembly, 38, 53–54, 56–59, 61, 71, 73–75,
78, 171–72
Committee of Jurists, 64
Conference on traffic in women and
children, 83–84
Council, 45–46, 78
Covenant (see Covenant of the League of
Nations)
mandates, 70, 82, 87, 98, 106–7, 198, 213,
221–22, 226, 229
Mandates Section, 56–57, 61, 84–85
Minorities Commission, 50

Permanent Mandates Commission (*see* Permanent Mandates Commission)
petitions, 55–64, 78–82
Secretary-General, 75
Sub-Committee on Mandates and Slavery, 74
League of Nations Union, 72, 75
Lebanon, 10, 133–34, 143, 145, 162, 165–66, 249–50, 254, 265–66
Lebar, Pierre, 158
Lee, Spike, 26
Légitime, François Denys, 18
Leiris, Michel, 184–85
Lemkin, Raphaël, 120–21, 128, 130–31, 352
Leopold II of Belgium, 2, 16, 389–90
Lerner, Natan, 189, 192–93
Lester, Seán, 66–68
Letter from Birmingham City Jail, 248
Levie, Michel, 83–84
Lévi-Strauss, Claude, 175–76, 184–85
LGBTQ persons, 402
liberation movements, 195–96, 355–56, 361–62
Liberia, 2, 18–21, 86, 106–7, 109, 145, 198, 207, 208, 227–31, 300
  apartheid, 289
  Bandung Conference, 200
  Commission on Human Rights, 249–50, 253–54
  Convention on Racial Discrimination, 249–50, 261
  International Court of Justice, 115–16, 228–31,
  League of Nations, 55
  Paris Peace Conference, 26
  Security Council, 296–97
  Security Council debate on Sharpeville, 296–97
  slavery, 85–86
Libya, 200, 254, 261, 306, 353–54, 358
Lie, Trygve, 109, 123
Liechtenstein, 373–75
Ligue haïtienne pour la défense du people éthiopien, 88
Lions clubs, 98–99
Lithuania, 49, 130–31
Little Rock Central High, 133–34
Lloyd George, David, 29–30, 44–45, 47–48, 53
London Conference, 118–19, 170, 171
London International Assembly, 140–41
London School of Economics, 2
Lorimer, James, 2–3, 4–5
Lotus case, 8
Louw, Eric, 300
Luganda, 210

Lugard, Frederick D., 70–71, 72, 77, 78–79, 80, 84–85
Lumumba, Patrice, 247
Luxembourg, 113–14, 132, 145, 255, 267, 287–88, 289–90, 296–97, 300–1, 323
lynching, 13–14, 24, 26, 118–20, 123–24, 131, 153–54, 247, 254

Macau, 237–38
MacBride, Seán, 191
Macdonald, Ronald St John, 276–77, 281
Macdonell, John, 18
Madagascar, 52, 53, 249–50, 261, 322–23, 326
Maho, Louis Joseph, 211
Malan, Daniël F., 160–61
malaria, 215
Malawi, 267–68, 359, 364–65
Malay, 210
Malaya, 301–2
Malaysia, 162–63, 268
Malcolm X, 201–2, 248
Mali, 115–16, 152, 249–50, 254, 261
Malik, Charles, 146–47
malnutrition, 338
Malta, 267–68
Man, 52, 61–62, 176–77, 180, 181–82
Mandela, Nelson, 24, 92, 110–11, 252–53, 287, 311–12
Mann, Thomas, 171–72
Mantoux, Paul, 63
Maori, 63, 210
March on Washington, 252–53
Marchand Stens, Luis, 335
marriage, right to, 164–67
Marshall Islands, 219, 386, 407
Marshall, John, 7–8
Martens, Fedor Fedorovič de, 4–5
Martens clause, 6–7
Marx, Karl, 15
Masani, Minocher A., 145–46
Mass, Heiko, 221–22
master race theory, 169
Matos Pinto, João Pedro, 405–6
Matzoh, 274–75
Maung, U Tin, 209–10
Mauritania, 249–50, 254, 261, 281, 299–300
Mauritius, 246–47, 306
Mazower, Mark, 68–69, 101–2, 113
Mbundu, 210
McCormack, Timothy, 347–48
Mead, Margaret, 180–81
Media case, 278
Mehta, Hansa, 146–47

472 INDEX

Meillassoux, Claude, 195–96
Mein Kampf, 169
Meir, Golda, 357
Memel, 68–69
Memmi, Albert, 12
Méndez, Juan, 406–7
Menon, Lakshmi, 149–50
mental harm, 326–27, 329, 331, 339–40
Meron, Theodor, 278–79
Métraux, Alfred, 16–17, 173–74, 180–85
Metropolitan Life Insurance Company, 109
Mexico, 96–97, 145, 147–48, 267–68, 292, 301–2, 323
Mexico City, 96–97
Micronesia, 219
Middle East, 42, 68–69, 78, 87, 251, 356, 363, 379, 384, 386
Middle Passage, 392
migrant workers, 31–32, 132–33, 316–18, 367–68, 370–71, 380–81, 385, 391
Miller, David Hunter, 33–34, 44–45
Millikan, Eugene, 103–4
Ministries case, 119–20
Minneapolis police, 22, 403, 404
minorities treaties, 43–50, 64–65, 229
Mixed Commission for Upper Silesia, 66, 67–68
mixed marriage. *See* intermarriage
Mokgoro, Yvonne, 406–7
Moldova, 331
Monaco, 278–79
Mongolia, 250–51, 353–54
Monroe Doctrine, 35
Monrovia, 86
Montagu, Ashley, 172–84, 188, 196–97
Montenegro, 331
Morehouse College, 71–72
Morocco, 18–19, 52, 151–52, 155, 163–64, 203–4, 207, 239–40, 296–97, 335
Morozov, Alexander P., 160–61
Morris, Roland, 31
mortality rates, 73, 406
Moslem children, 163–64
Mourant, A.E., 181–82
Mouvement de libération de la Guinée et du Cap-Vert, 238
Mouvement pour l'indépendence de la Guinée équatoriale, 211
Moyn, Samuel, 22–23
Mozambique, 77, 212–13, 237–38, 241, 243, 367
Murray, Gilbert, 58–59
Musée de l'Homme, 184–85
Mussolini, Benito, 88

Myanmar, 268. *See also* Burma
Myrdal, Alva, 184–85

Nachtscheim, Hans, 181–82
Nama, 73, 221–22, 223–24, 226
Namibia, 20–21, 73, 80, 87, 127–28, 195–96, 198–99, 221–23, 234–36, 243, 305, 311, 337, 357, 367
Nansen, Fridtjof, 78
narcotic drugs, 73, 345–46
Natal, 149
National Association for the Advancement of Colored People, 18, 26, 28–29, 41, 59–60, 97–100, 107–8, 123–26, 132–33, 167, 223–24, 226
petition to United Nations, 9–10, 123–24, 126, 149
San Francisco Conference, 100, 111–12, 115
National Coloured World Democracy Congress, 28
National Committee to Free the Ingram Family, 127
National Council of Negro Women, 97
national courts, 342–43, 348–49, 377
National Equal Rights League, 27, 49–50
National Negro Congress, 88, 122–23, 129–30
'national origin', use of term, 264, 270
Naulilaa case, 41
Nault, Derrick, 23
Nauru, 219, 411–12
navires négriers, 82–83
Nazi, 67–68, 93, 104, 120–21, 127–28, 169, 174, 179, 246, 268–69, 273–74, 304–5, 380, 397
anti-Semitism, 118, 245–46
atrocities, 118–19, 314, 350
demand to return colonies to Germany, 63
genocide, 141–42
racial doctrine, 20, 95–96, 119–20, 127–29, 137, 141, 147–48, 159, 169, 174, 265–66, 304–5
seizure of power, 66, 172–73
Negro Welfare and Cultural Association of Trinidad and Tobago, 88
Negro Welfare Association, 63
Negros of Panama, 88
Nehru, Jawaharlal, 112–13
Neier, Aryeh, 22–23
Nepal, 207, 301–2
Netherlands, 203–4, 255, 296–97, 388–89
Apartheid Convention, 326, 328–29
Convention on Racial Discrimination, 267, 275, 282
Declaration on Racial Discrimination, 255

defence of racial segregation, 291–92
denial of discrimination, 210–11, 259
historical injustice, 396
Kaiser Wilhelm II, 36
non-self-governing territories, 201–2
Special Committee on apartheid, 301–2
San Francisco Conference, 102–3
Six Nations petition, 61–62
Statutory Limitation Convention, 319, 321–24
Sub-Commission, 132
support for South Africa, 112–13, 222, 226, 289–90, 291–92, 294, 300–1
World Conferences on racism, 363–64, 366–67, 386
Netherlands Women's Association for the Improvement of Morals, 53
New York Age Defender, 201–2
New York Amsterdam News, 247
New York Herald, 35
New York Times, 27, 49–50, 124–25, 130–31, 179, 247–48, 254, 300
New York Times Magazine, 247–48
New Zealand, 92, 203–4, 323
   Declaration on Racial Discrimination, 255
   denial of discrimination, 210–11
   Japanese migration, 69
   mandates, 68–69
   Maori petition to League, 63
   non-self-governing territories, 201–2, 206–7, 212–13
   Statutory Limitation Convention, 319, 324
   Sub-Commission, 132
   support for South Africa, 112–13, 222, 226, 289–90, 294, 300–1
   support for Southern Rhodesia, 239
   World Conferences on racism, 361, 366–67
Nicaragua, 132, 145, 267–68, 364–65, 373–75
Nicholls, George Heaton, 106–7
Niger, 249–50, 254, 282, 353–54
Nigeria, 70–71, 98–99, 149, 207, 249–50, 254, 255, 261, 276–77, 301–2, 319–20, 326, 327–28, 335, 363, 364
Niuean, 210
Nobel Prize, 16–17, 58–59, 137, 292
Nobuaki, Makino, 31–37, 33–37
Nolde, O. Frederick, 99
non-governmental organizations, 13, 122, 137, 259, 292, 294, 373–75
non-self-governing territories, 8–9, 115–16, 199–200, 201–6, 208, 209–12, 237–38
Nordic States, 305, 327–30, 329–30
Northern Rhodesia, 207–8, 210–11

nuclear weapons, 308, 360–61, 366–67
Nuremberg laws, 118
Nuremberg Principles, 117–18, 121, 318
Nuremberg trial, 21, 117–21, 129, 313–14, 320, 321, 350, 397, 410
Nyanja, 210

Obama, Barack, 24
occupied territories, 53–54, 118, 337, 365–66
Office of the High Commissioner for Human Rights, Anti-Discrimination Unit, 385–86
O'Flaherty, Michael, 390–91
On Being Human, 179
Oppenheim, Lassa, 2
Orange Free State, 165–66
Organization for Security and Cooperation in Europe, 372–73, 390–91
Organization of African Unity, 252–53, 404–5
Organization of American States, 229–30, 392, 393–95
Ottoman Empire, 2, 25, 42–43, 55, 68–69, 313–14
outrages upon personal dignity, 346–47
Ovambo, 223–24
Oxford English Dictionary, 12

Pacelli, Eugenio, 172–73
Paderewski, Jan, 47–50
Padilla Nervo, Luis, 231–32, 235–36
Painlevé, Paul, 171–72
Pakistan, 113–14, 164–66, 200, 203–5, 221–22, 249–50, 291–92, 296–97, 326
Palais Wilson, 389–90
Palau, 219, 386
Palestine, 21–22, 60–61, 78, 251, 282, 325, 331, 340–41, 349, 357–58, 361, 363, 379
Pan African Congress, 28–30, 55–60, 200–1, 306
Panama, 13, 26, 61–62, 96–97, 108, 117–18, 120, 136, 142–43, 145, 207, 282, 392
pandemic, 22, 412–13
Pandit, Vijaya Lakshmi, 112–13, 289
Papua New Guinea, 219, 220–21, 278–79, 364–65
Paraguay, 145, 255, 331
Paris Peace Conference, 1, 12–13, 19, 25–51, 104, 198–99, 231–32, 251, 409, 412
   African American activists, 27–30
   Commission on Responsibilities, 42–43
   Commission on the League of Nations, 27, 28, 30, 33, 35, 36, 38, 69, 94–95
   Committee on New States, 43–50
   Council of Four, 26–27, 39–40, 44–48

474 INDEX

Paris Peace Conference (*cont.*)
   Council of Three, 44–45
   Japanese proposal for equality clause, 19–20, 30–38
   South West Africa, 221–22
Patterson, William, 122–23, 129–31
Pavlov, Alexey P., 149, 150, 200–1, 368
peace and security, 138, 199, 234, 237, 256, 259–60, 307–8, 315–16, 326–27, 331–32, 346–47, 360–61
Peace Palace, 64
Pearson, Lester B., 233–34
Pedersen, Susan, 58–59, 78
Pedroso, Manuel, 66–67
Pella, Vespasian, 120–21
penal sanctions, 217–18
Pérez-Cisneros, Guy, 226–27
Perlzweig, Maurice, 162
Permanent Court of Arbitration, 64
Permanent Court of International Justice, 8, 18–19, 49, 61–62, 64–66
Permanent Mandates Commission, 55, 57–59, 63, 71–78, 84–85, 100, 198–99, 213–14, 221–22, 229–30
   composition, 70–71
   education in Africa, 71–72
   petitions, 78–82
   proposal for Black member, 58–59
Persia, 2, 18–19, 55, 61–63. *See also* Iran
Peru, 26, 145, 226, 255, 289–90, 388–89
Philippines, 92, 102–3, 115–16, 145, 149–50, 265–66, 276
   Apartheid Convention, 328–29
   Bandung Conference, 201
   Commission on Human Rights, 143
   Convention on Racial Discrimination, 281
   International Court of Justice, 225
   San Francisco Conference, 102–3
   Security Council, 239–40
   Special Committee on apartheid, 301–2
   Special Committee on Information, 201–2
   Sub-Commission, 249–50
Phillimore, George G., 54
piracy, 330, 346–47
Pittsburgh Courier, 118–19
poison gas, 88
Poland, 10, 19, 25–26, 45, 47–50, 64–68, 114–15, 130–31, 211–12
   anti-Semitism, 26–27, 44–47, 114
   Convention on Racial Discrimination, 262, 282
   criticism of Hammarskjöld, 297–98
   Diet, 46–47

German-speaking minority, 47–48
human rights Covenants, 149–50, 163–64
International Court of Justice, 225
minorities treaties, 25–26, 45–49, 64–67
Nazi racism against Poles, 169
Paris Peace Conference, 30, 37
police profiling, 167–68
political prisoners, 201, 337
Politis, Nikolaos, 42–43
Pope Pius XII, 172–73
populist ideologies, 388–89
Portugal, 40–41, 77, 210, 238–43, 299, 318, 357–58
   Apartheid Convention, 326, 329–30
   colonies, 29–30, 201–2, 206–7, 212–13, 221, 237–38, 243, 252–53, 337, 357–58, 367
   Committee on Information, 237–38
   consortium of racist States, 237
   Convention on Racial Discrimination, 259
   crimes against humanity, 316–17
   massacres in Angola, 316–17
   Naulilaa case, 40–41
   second World Conference, 365–66
   Statutory Limitation Convention, 323, 324
   support for South Africa, 296–97, 300–1
Powell Jr., Adam Clayton, 201–2
pregnancy, 338, 406
Pretoria, 101–2, 236–37, 252–53, 297–98, 306, 357–58, 363, 365
Prevention of births, 326–27
prisoners, 10, 54, 326–27, 335
prisoners of conscience, 352
prisoners of war, 54
Programme of Action against Apartheid, 305–6
Propositions on the Biological Aspects of Race, 185–87
Proskauer, Joseph M., 99
Protocols of the elders of Zion, 380
Prussia, 64
Puerto Rico, 100
purposes and principles, 235, 289–90, 297–99, 331

Qatar, 245, 269–71, 282–83, 353–54
Qatar v. United Arab Emirates, 50–51, 245, 269–71, 283
Quebec City, 392–94

Race and Biology, 184–85
Race and Culture, 184–85
Race and History, 184–85
Race and Prejudice, 184–85

race conflict, 289, 290–91, 294, 296–97, 305–6, 368
'race conflict', use of term, 368
'race', use of term, 177, 178
'racial discrimination', use of term, 193–94
'racial group', use of term, 10–11, 128–29, 160, 169–70, 195
racial hatred, 65, 92, 137–38, 152–53, 162, 246–47, 248–49, 252, 256–57, 262–63, 273–77, 369–70, 372, 384, 385, 388–89
Racial Myths, 184–85
racial profiling, 167–68, 270, 388–91
racial segregation, 26, 75, 123–24, 163–64, 228–29, 236–37, 256, 272–73, 287–88, 291–92, 310–11, 331
racial superiority, 2–3, 101–3, 127–28, 160–61, 172–75, 193–94, 252, 256, 262, 268–69, 276–77, 360, 370, 392–93
'racialism', use of term, 12, 238–39, 368
'racism', use of term, 12, 187, 238–39, 353, 368, 370
racist organizations, 256–57, 261–63, 275–77, 279–80
Radhakrishnan, Sarvepalli, 171–72
Ramaphosa, Matamela Cyril, 407
Ramos, Arthur, 175
Randolph, A. Philip, 28
Rappard, William, 56–57, 61
Ratana, T.W., 63
Reading, Lord, 35
Reagan, Ronald, 311
Red Sea, 84–85
refugees, 107, 340–41, 351–52
Rehoboth, 80
'related intolerance', use of term, 368, 370
religious intolerance, 145–46, 193, 246–47, 249–51, 254–55, 268, 284–85, 369–70, 385
reparations, 21–22, 40–41, 375–78, 381–82, 395–400, 407, 412–13
responsibility to protect, 84–85
Reston, James, 247–48
retrospective application, 377–78
Rhineland, French occupation after First World War, 169
Rhodes, Cecil, 239
Rhodesia. *See* Southern Rhodesia, Northern Rhodesia
Richardson, Henry, 22, 408–9
right to be different, 192–93
right to vote, 124, 207
Rivonia trial, 252–53
Robeson, Paul, 122–23, 126–27, 130–31
Robinson, Mary, 375–76, 379–80

Roma, 169, 371, 375–76
Romania, 30, 45, 47–49, 114, 280, 353–54
Rome Statute of the International Criminal Court, 313, 347–48, 350, 378
Rómulo, Carlos, 92, 115
Roonstrasse synagogue, 245–46
Roosevelt, Eleanor, 123–24, 129–31, 138–39, 148–49, 151, 156–57, 159–60
Roosevelt, Franklin D., 90, 92, 94, 104, 125–26, 138–39
Rose, Arnold, 184–85
Royal Anthropological Institute, 180
Royal Anthropological Society, 174
Royal Canadian Mounted Police, 126–27
Royal Colonial Institute, 41
Ruanda-Urundi, 78, 134, 213–14, 216–19, . *See also* Rwanda
Ruhashanyiko, Nicodème, 342
Rukeba, Francis, 213–14
RuSHA case, 119–20
Russell, Bertrand, 273
Russia, 2, 19, 42, 313–14, 412–13
Rwanda, 26–27, 87, 353–54. *See also* Ruanda-Urundi

Saar, 68–69
Sabra and Shatilla, 340–41
sacred trust, 69, 199, 231–32, 234–35
Saint-Domingue, 1791 uprising, 381
Saint Vincent and the Grenadines, 377
Salisbury, Lord, 48
sanctions, 149, 235–36, 241–42, 298, 300–1, 303–9, 311–12, 360–62, 364–65, 373
San Francisco Conference, 1, 5, 20, 50–51, 92, 98, 101–2, 104, 110–11, 135–36, 142–43, 199, 289–90, 409
   adoption of domestic jurisdiction clause, 111–12
   consultants to American delegation, 99
   non-governmental organisations, 98–99
Santa Cruz Commission. *See* Commission on the Racial Situation in the Union of South Africa
Santa Cruz, Hernán, 16–17, 20, 292, 294
Santiago, 388–89, 392–93
Santiago Declaration, 392
Santos, Luana Barbosa dos Reis, 405–6
Sao Tome and Principe, 237–38, 243
Sartre, Jean-Paul, 352
Sastri, V.S. Srinavasa, 57–58
Saudi Arabia, 13, 26, 84–85, 114–15, 117, 138
Schreider, Eugène, 181–82
Schücking, Walther, 18–19

476   INDEX

Schwelb, Egon, 250–51, 271–74, 280
Schwerner, Michael, 274–75
'scientific' racism, 169–70
Scott, Michael, 223–27
Scott, William, 7–8
Second World War, 10, 21, 61–62, 88–89, 91,
    102, 140–41, 153–54, 159, 174, 176–77,
    188, 195–96, 215, 245–46, 280, 314, 319,
    320, 380, 412–13
Secretary-General, 28, 57, 60–61, 66–67, 84–85,
    109, 122–25, 132–33, 143–44, 197, 213–14,
    219–20, 223–25, 246, 254–55, 259, 278,
    297–98, 301–2, 307–9, 320, 362–63, 370–
    71, 387–88, 395–96
  crimes against humanity, 319
  draft convention on statutory
    limitation, 319
  International Year to Combat Racism,
    351–54,
  proposals for Third Decade, 373–75
  report on racial discrimination in
    colonies, 210–12
  Statutory Limitation Convention, 319, 321
  World Conferences on racism, 363–64, 383
Security Council, 13–14, 101, 219–20, 234,
    236–41, 243, 247, 259–60, 297–98, 300–2,
    304–6, 309, 310–12, 360–61, 405–6
  apartheid as crime against humanity, 332
  composition, 296–97
  condemnation of South Africa, 222–23
  embargo resolutions, 305–6, 308, 353–54
  international criminal tribunals, 346
  permanent members, 8–9, 242
  request for advisory opinion, 234–35
  resolutions condemning racial
    discrimination, 229–30
  Sharpeville, 296–97
  Southern Rhodesia, 239–42
  triple veto, 3–14, 310
Selcer, Perrin, 183–84
self-determination, 8–9, 12–13, 26–27, 93–94,
    152, 211–12, 355–56
Senegal, 5–6, 28–29, 207, 225, 233–34, 249–50,
    254, 319–20, 328–29, 335, 353–54
Serbia, 30, 47–48, 64, 331
sexual orientation, 393–94, 402
Shahabuddeen, Mohamed, 1–2
Shangugu Territory, 213–14
Shapiro, Harry, 181–82
Sharpeville, 73, 246–47, 274–75, 296–300, 381
Shell, 302–3
Shinyanga District, 213–14
Siam, 2, 18–19, 26, 55, 145

Sibeko, David, 306
Sierra Leone, 254, 299–300, 359
Simpson, Brian, 22–23
Singapore, 98, 267–68
Singh, Maharaj, 222
Singh, Prabhakar, 9–10
Sinti, 169
Six Nations, 61–63
slave labourers, 118
slavery, 3–4, 7–8, 13–17, 21–22, 73, 75, 82–86,
    174–75, 188, 254, 281, 334, 367–68,
    375–78, 382, 389–90, 394–92, 395–
    400, 412–13
Slavery Convention, 85–86
slavery-like practices, 326–27
slave trade, 1–4, 7–8, 14–17, 19, 69, 82–83,
    85–86, 127–28, 197, 334, 375–78, 381, 382,
    389–93, 395–99, 406–7, 410, 412–13
Slovakia, 114
Slovenia, 407
Smuts, Jan, 50–51, 69, 100, 101–2, 112–13,
    115, 138
Social Sciences, 175
Society for the Study of Social Issues, 174
Somalia, 207, 301–2, 358
Somali Coast, 52
Souls of Black Folk, The, 1
South Africa, 11, 13, 20–22, 50–51, 55, 57–59,
    61, 69, 73–79, 87, 92, 96–97, 100, 101–2,
    106, 110–11, 113–16, 134, 136, 141–44,
    149–50, 152, 174–75, 203–4, 209–10, 212–
    13, 221–37, 239, 240–43, 246–47, 252–54,
    256, 272–75, 316–17, 329, 335, 336–37,
    339–40, 347–48, 356–58, 360–61, 365–68,
    407, 411–12
  annexation of South West Africa, 106–
    7, 198–99
  apartheid, 136, 287–312, 331, 348–49
  arms embargo, 309, 353–54
  coercive measures, 304–5, 364
  consortium of racist States, 237
  Convention on Racial
    Discrimination, 267–68
  crimes against humanity, 315–16
  cultural boycott, 302–3
  domestic jurisdiction, 110–14, 224
  Durban Conference (*see* Durban
    Conference)
  education, 133–34, 160–61
  expulsion from General Assembly, 304–
    5, 310–11
  human rights Covenants, 149–50
  immigration, 145–46

Indian diaspora, 19, 108, 112–14, 149, 151–52
International Court of Justice, 224–36
Israel, 361
major trading partners, 305–6
mandates, 68–69
Michael Scott, 224
nuclear weapons, 360–61
prohibitions on marriage, 165–66
refusal to negotiate trusteeship agreement, 222–23
South West Africa, 73, 198–99, 221–22
sports boycott, 303
Statutory Limitation Convention, 321–24
UNESCO constitution, 170–71
Universal Declaration, 144
World Conferences on racism, 375–76, 378
South West Africa People's Organisation, 222–23
South West Africa, 39–41, 57–58, 63, 73, 78–80, 198–99, 212–13, 221–28, 231–32, 234, 243
annexation by South Africa, 106–7, 223–24
apartheid, 228–29
crimes against humanity, 315–16, 317
education, 133–34, 223–24, 228–29
German atrocities, 39–40, 127–28
mine workers, 73
right to food, 223–24
right to property, 223–24
right to vote, 228–29
South West Africa contentious cases, 20–21, 115–16, 227–34
South West Africa advisory opinions, 20–21, 222–27, 234–36, 259
Southern Rhodesia, 136, 145, 207–8, 212–13, 221, 237, 239–42, 252–53, 274–75, 314–15, 335–37, 360–61
crimes against humanity, 315–17
consortium of racist States, 237
end of racist regime, 367
unilateral declaration of independence, 240–41
Soviet Union, 5, 92, 98, 118, 149–52, 160–61, 184–85, 273–76, 290, 301–2
anti-colonialism, 204–5, 216–18, 220
anti-Semitism, 251, 266–67, 273–74
Apartheid Convention, 325–26, 327–29
collapse, 12–13, 412
Convention on Racial Discrimination, 260–61, 262
Dumbarton Oaks, 93–94
international criminal tribunal, 344–45

London Conference, 118–19
neutrality in war with Japan, 94
right to education, 162
San Francisco Conference, 99–100, 138
Special Committee on Information, 201–2
Sub-Commission, 125–26
Universal Declaration, 5
Yalta, 198–99
Soweto uprising, 307, 311
Spain Bradley, Anna, 22, 196–97
Spain, 126
colonies, 14–15, 29–30, 201–2, 212–13
Committee on the Elimination of Racial Discrimination, 282
denial of discrimination, 210–11
historical injustices, 396
Special Committee on apartheid, 301–2
support for South Africa, 300–1
World Conferences on racism, 365–66
Special rapporteur on contemporary forms of racism, racial discrimination, xenophobia, and related intolerance, 368–71, 398–99, 408
Special rapporteur on minorities issues, 387–88
Special rapporteur on the occupied Palestinian territories, 349
Special rapporteur on the rights of persons of African descent and against racial discrimination, 394–95
Special rapporteur on violence against women, 401
Special Standard Form, 202
Spectator, The, 172–73
Spiller, Gustav, 18–19, 59–60
Springarn, Arthur, 123
Stalin, Joseph, 92
stateless persons, 385
Statement on Race and Racial Prejudice, 187–88
State responsibility, 333–34
statutory limitation, 319, 322–23, 325
Statutory Limitation Convention. *See* Convention on Statutory Limitations
stereotyping, 53, 388–89, 391, 406
Stettinius, Edward, 95–96, 99
Stevenson, Adlai, 247–48, 254
Stone, I.F., 130
strikes, 339
Stuckart, Wilhelm, 119–20
Student Non-Violent Coordinating Committee, 263
Study Group on fragmentation of international law, 334

478 INDEX

Sub-Commission on the Prevention of
  Discrimination and the Protection of
  Minorities, 16–17, 20, 115–16, 132–36,
  142–43, 145–47, 153–54, 173, 189, 244–50,
  260–63, 265–66, 273, 275–76, 284–86, 342,
  355–56, 367–69, 370–71, 373–75, 411
anti-Semitism, 245–46, 254–55, 266–67
assessment of International
  Decades, 367–68
Convention on Racial Discrimination, 261,
  264, 266, 270, 272–73, 276, 279–80
Declaration on Racial
  Discrimination, 251–52
inadequate membership from Global South,
  249–50, 411
International Year to Combat
  Racism, 353–54
NAACP petition, 20–21, 132–33
proposal for third World Conference, 373–75
special rapporteur on genocide, 342
swastika epidemic, 135, 244–46
UNESCO race statements, 132–33, 173
Universal Declaration, 145–46
visit to Atlanta, 260–61
submarine warfare, 39–40
Sudan, 207, 249–50
Sukarno, 200–1
Sultanate of Zanzibar, 16
Summits of the Americas, 392–93
Sundberg, Ulrike, 368
Sun Pictorial, 160–61
supremacy, racial, 3–4, 26, 101–4, 169–70,
  200, 222, 243, 298–99, 310–11, 347–48,
  410, 412–13
Swahili, 210
swastika epidemic, 135, 184–85, 244, 274–75
Swaziland, 203–4, 364–65
Sweden, 10–11, 71, 125–26, 132, 203–4, 255,
  301–2, 365–66, 379
Switzerland, 16, 58–59, 278–79, 373–75
Syria, 78, 145, 216–17, 292, 325–26, 353–54,
  358, 379. See also United Arab Republic

Tadić case, 346
Tanga African Hospital, 215
Tanganyika, 78, 80–81, 213–15, 217–18, 253–
  54, 300–1
Tanzania, 281, 310–11, 316–17, 326
Task Force on Legal Aspects of
  Apartheid, 302–3
Task Force on Political Prisoners, 302–3
Task Force on Women and Children under
  Apartheid, 302–3

Taylor, Breonna, 405–6
Tehran Conference on Human Rights,
  322, 351–52
Tekoah, Yosef, 357–58
Temperley, H.W.V., 35
Temporary Slavery Commission, 85–86
Tenth Inter-American Conference, 392
Te Water, Charles, 144, 150
Thailand, 258
Thatcher, Margaret, 311
Theodoli, Alberto, 77–78
Thiam, Doudou, 332
Third World Approaches to International
  Law, 22
Third World, 9–10, 23, 299–300
third World Conference on Racism, 375 (see
  also Durban Conference)
Thomas, Albert, 59–60, 109–10
Thonga, 210
Thornberry, Patrick, 221, 272–73
Tilley, Virginia, 329–30
Times, The, 42, 73, 180
Timor, 237–38
Tintin in the Congo, 388–89
Tladi, Dire, 235, 334
Tobias, Channing, 226
Togney, J.E. Alfred, 214
Togo, 78, 207, 254, 299, 322–23
Tokyo trial, 314
Torres Bodet, Jaime, 180–81, 292
torture, 12–13, 63, 287–88, 331–32, 335, 339–
  40, 343
Total, 302–3
trade unions, 53, 98–99, 123, 302–3
traite des noirs, 82–83
transnational corporations, 302–3, 360, 363
Transvaal, 165–66
Traoré, Adama, 405–6
Treatment of Polish Nationals advisory
  opinion, 65–66
Treaty of Berlin, 25
Treaty of Sèvres, 43, 313–14
Treaty of St-Germain-en-Laye, 82–83, 85
Treaty of Utrecht, 14–15
Treaty of Versailles, 10, 25–26, 39, 40, 43–44,
  49–50, 53, 55, 59–61, 65–66, 110–11
Tree, Marietta, 273, 279–80
Trevor, J.C., 181–82
Trinidad and Tobago, 314–15, 377, 397
triple veto, 13–14, 310
Trotter, William Monroe, 27, 49–50
Truman, Harry S, 117–18, 125–26, 129–30, 138,
  142–43, 149

INDEX 479

Trump, Donald, 22, 403
Trusteeship Council, 104–5, 198–200, 213–14, 216–21, 242–43
Trust Territories, 71, 102–3, 106–7, 156, 198–99, 204–5, 213, 216–19, 224, 229–30, 367
Tunisia, 52, 152, 154–55, 296–97, 353–54
Turkey, 2, 18–19, 43, 69, 145, 201, 266, 289–90, 300–1, 313–14, 353–54
Tuskegee Institute, 71–72

Uganda, 100, 207–8, 254
Ukraine, 160, 204, 265–66, 283, 325–26, 412–13
Ukraine v. Russia, 283
UNESCO Courier, 184–87, 196
UNESCO, 10–11, 16–17, 72, 132–33, 169–97, 248–49, 263, 292
  Conference for the Establishment, 170, 171
  Constitution, 159, 170–71, 191–92, 196
  contribution to anti-apartheid struggle, 367–68
  Convention on discrimination in education (*see* Convention on discrimination in education)
  decline of anti-racism campaign, 184–85
  Department of Social Sciences, 184–85
  Director-General, 180–81, 185–86, 189, 190–92
  Division for the Study of Race Problems, 180–81
  Fact-Finding and Conciliation Committee, 189
  General Conference, 175, 189–92, 196, 259–60
  Global Forum against Racism and Discrimination, 197
  International Day for the Remembrance of the Slave Trade and its Abolition, 381
  International Year to Combat Racism, 353–54
  Slave Route Project, 197
  Social Sciences Department, 177
  statements on race, 20, 175–85
  Universal Declaration, 158
Union démocratique des femmes camerounaises, 214
United Arab Republic, 207, 335
United Kingdom, 5, 75–77, 83–84, 92, 98, 143–44, 152, 199, 212, 216, 226–27, 235, 237–38, 255, 262–63, 265–66, 279–80, 285–86, 297, 298–99, 311, 314–15, 340–41, 355–56, 399, 405–6
  apartheid, 294, 301–2

Apartheid Convention, 326, 330
  Code of Crimes, 332–33
  Colonial Office, 41, 70
  colonies, 29–30, 50, 134, 149, 201–2, 204–10, 212–13, 242
  Convention on Racial Discrimination, 262, 267, 279–80
  declaration on Armenian atrocities, 42, 313–14
  Declaration on Racial Discrimination, 255
  Dumbarton Oaks, 93–94
  Foreign Office, 38, 41, 50–51, 70, 82–83, 88–89, 91, 95–96
  historical injustices, 396
  House of Commons, 92, 236–37, 240
  London Conference, 118–19
  maternal mortality rates, 406
  Paris Peace Conference, 25–50
  Permanent Mandates Commission, 70–71
  racist language of bureaucrats, 70
  San Francisco Conference, 138
  Southern Rhodesia, 239–42
  Statutory Limitation Convention, 322–24
  support for South Africa, 8–9, 14–15, 112–13, 222–23, 226, 234, 236–37, 289–90, 296–97, 300–1, 305–6, 312
  Trust Territories, 217–18
  use of veto, 13–14, 239–40, 306, 310
  World Conferences on racism, 355–56
  Yalta, 198–99
United Nations
  anti-racism demonstration at headquarters, 247
  Charter (*see* Charter of the United Nations)
  Commission on Human Rights (*see* Commission on Human Rights)
  Conference of Non-governmental Organisations, 132–33
  Decolonisation Committee, 212
  Development Decade, 354–55
  Director of Human Rights, 122–23, 176–77, 329
  Economic and Social Commission for Eastern Asia, 349
  Economic and Social Council (*see* Economic and Social Council)
  founding members, 13
  General Assembly (*see* General Assembly)
  High Commissioner for Human Rights (*see* High Commissioner for Human Rights)
  host state agreement, 109–10
  Human Rights Council (*see* Human Rights Council)

480 INDEX

United Nations (*cont.*)
International Court of Justice (*see*
International Court of Justice)
nuclear Commission on Human
Rights, 107–8
Permanent Forum on Indigenous
Issues, 160–61
postal service, 353–54
Preparatory Commission, 107
Relief and Rehabilitation
Administration, 109
second World Conference on Racism, 365–67
Secretary-General (*see* Secretary-General)
Security Council (*see* Security Council)
Special Committee of Seventeen, 210–12
Special Committee of Six, 238
Special Committee of Twenty-four, 212–
13, 219
Special Committee on Apartheid, 300–3,
305–6, 311–12, 343, 357
Special Committee on Information, 201–4
Special Committee on the Situation
with regard to the Implementation
of the Declaration on the Granting of
Independence to Colonial Countries and
Peoples, 212
Special Political Committee, 298–99
Sub-Commission on Freedom of
Information and of the Press, 132
Sub-Commission on Prevention of
Discrimination and Protection of
Minorities (*see* Sub-Commission)
Sub-Commission on the Status of
Women, 132
World Conferences on racism, 13–14, 21–22,
244, 355–67, 373–81, 407
United Nations War Crimes
Commission, 88–89
United States, 13, 21–24, 53–54, 57, 60–61,
71–72, 86–87, 90, 92, 98–100, 104, 119–27,
129–33, 138–39, 141–44, 149–50, 170,
174–77, 180, 203–4, 212, 219–20, 223–24,
227, 239–40, 247–48, 251, 255, 261–63,
272–75, 285–86, 290–92, 305–6, 324,
346–47, 351–52, 380, 388–89, 392–94,
404–6, 411–12
African American troops, 52
anti-apartheid legislation vetoed by
President, 311
anti-colonial posture, 199
anti-Semitism, 245–46, 266–67, 273, 275
Apartheid Convention, 326–30
Congress, 91, 399

Constitution, 31–32, 137, 145, 261–
62, 277–78
Convention on Racial Discrimination,
262, 273
crimes against humanity, 315–16, 329
Declaration on Racial Discrimination, 255
denial of discrimination, 206–7, 210–11
Department of State, 27, 50–51, 98–99,
109–10, 122–24, 130, 170, 200–2, 227–28,
261–63
Dumbarton Oaks, 93–97
education system, 71, 133–35, 160–61,
162, 254
First World War, 25
genocide, 340–41
Genocide Convention, 129
historical injustice, 396
homelessness, 167–68
host state agreement with United
Nations, 109–10
House of Representatives, 201–2
human rights Covenants, 163–64, 262, 267,
277–80
immigration, 145–46
incitement, 154–55
International Court of Justice, 225
London Conference, 118–19
mission to United Nations, 254
non-self-governing territories, 201–
2, 212–13
opposition to oil embargo, 309
opposition to universal jurisdiction, 329
Organization for Security and Cooperation
in Europe, 372–73
Paris Peace Conference, 25–50
petitions against racial discrimination, 149
prohibition of mixed marriage, 165–67
racist legislation against Japanese, 31–32
refusal to issue passports, 27, 29–30, 200–1
reparations, 375–76, 381–82, 392
reservations to Convention on Racial
Discrimination, 278–79
right to work, 254
Rome Statute, 347–48
'scientific' racism, 196
Second World War, 91
Secret Service, 28–29
segregated schools, 87
Senate, 103–4
Special Committee on apartheid, 301–2
Statutory Limitation Convention,
319, 321–23
Sub-Commission, 125–26, 132

INDEX   481

support for South Africa, 112–14, 222–23, 226, 300–1, 310–12
support for Southern Rhodesia, 239, 241–42
Supreme Court, 7–8, 31–32, 118–19, 137
systemic racism, 403
Universal Declaration, 138–39, 142–43, 145, 149, 153–54
use of veto, 13–14, 306, 310
World Conferences on racism, 13–14, 103–4, 360, 376, 381–83, 386, 407
Yalta, 198–99
Uniting for Peace, 289
Universal Declaration of Human Rights, 5–6, 9, 10, 48–49, 115–16, 126–27, 137–39, 143–50, 152–54, 179, 202, 205–6, 226–30, 234, 235–36, 256, 265–66, 270, 276–77, 281, 287–88, 294, 298–99, 310, 332, 351–52, 355–56
adoption, 139, 143–44
French proposal on racism, 137
legal significance, 139–40
racial discrimination, 137–38
reference in Convention on Racial Discrimination, 268–69
preamble, 138–39, 289
art. 1 on equal rights, 144, 183–84
art. 2 on non-discrimination, 144–48, 251–52, 260–61, 284–85
art. 7 on equal protection, incitement, 148–50, 152–54
art. 16 on right to marry, 164–65
art. 20 on freedom of association, 279–80
art. 23(2) on equal pay, 155–57
art. 26 on education, 158–59
Universal Declaration on the Human Genome and on Human Rights, 196
universal jurisdiction, 21, 314, 326–30, 342, 348–49, 365, 411–12
Universal Negro Improvement Association, 60–61
Universal Postal Union, 18–19
Universal Races Congress, 18–19, 59–60, 171–72
Universidade da Bahia, 394–95
University of London, 19
University of Minnesota, 184–85
Upper Silesia, 64, 66–68, 87
Upper Volta, 249–50, 353–54, 364–65
Uruguay, 128–29, 143, 145, 201–2, 267, 331, 353–54, 365

Valdes, Francisco, 9
Vallois, Henri, 181–82

Vandeginste, Stef, 395–96
Vandenberg, Arthur, 103–4, 112
Vatican City, 353–54
Venezuela, 163, 166–67, 205–6, 281, 289–90
Venizelos, Eleftherios, 34
Verzijl, Jan Hendrik Willem, 4–5
Vienna Declaration and Programme of Action, 12–13, 385–86
Vietnam war, 352
Vietnam, 359–60
Vishinsky, Andrey, 120–21
Volkswagen, 302–3
Voltaire, 313–14

Waldheim, Kurt, 307–8
Waldorf-Astoria Hotel, 109
Waldron-Ramsey, Waldo Emerson, 281, 335
Walton, Edgar, 73–74
war crimes, 39–43, 107, 235–36, 313, 325, 330, 332, 347
Webb-Haney Act, 31–32
We Charge Genocide, 127–28
Weil, Prosper, 8
Wells, H.G., 18, 141
Wells, Ida B., 28
West Bank, occupation of, 356
Western European and Other Group, 404–5
Westlake, John, 4–5
What Is Race? Evidence from Scientists, 184–85
Wheaton, Henry, 15
Whitaker, Benjamin, 342
White Australia policy, 35
white slave trade, 83
white supremacy, 7, 19–22, 113, 138, 227–28, 236–37, 314–15, 388–89
White, Walter, 26, 98–100, 107–8, 124–25
Whitlam, Fred, 160–61
Wicksell, Anna, 71–72, 78
Widmark, Richard, 119–20
Wilhelm II of Germany, 39
Wilkins, Roy, 97, 98–99
Williams, Eric, 16–17
Wilson, J.V., 63
Wilson, Woodrow, 19–20, 26–38, 44, 47–48, 53, 93, 100, 199
Windhoek, 226–27
Witbooi, David, 223–24, 226
Wolpe, Harold, 195–96
Women's International League for Peace and Freedom, 53–54
Working Group of Experts on People of African Descent, 10–11, 193–94, 388–90, 399

482 INDEX

World Alliance for Promoting International Friendship, 49–50
World Confederation of Negroes, 56–57
World Conference of the International Women's Year, 358
World Health Organisation, contribution to anti-apartheid struggle, 367–68
World Jewish Congress, 154, 158–59, 162
Wright, Richard, 201

xenophobia, 16–17, 370–77, 383, 384, 385–86, 388–89, 390–93, 398–99, 402
'xenophobia', use of term, 368–69, 370
Xirau, Josep, 176

Yalta Conference, 198–99
Yemen, 205–6, 358
Yergan, Max, 122–23
Yom Kippur War, 357–58

Yugoslavia, 45, 49, 126, 144–45, 150, 159–60, 188, 314–15, 344–45

Zaire, 328–29, 364–65
Zambia, 208, 210–11, 359. *See also* Northern Rhodesia
Zanzibar, Sultanate of, 16
Ziauddin, Mian, 204
Zimbabwe, 149, 239, 243, 252–53, 360. *See also* Southern Rhodesia
Zionism, 190–91, 251, 273–75, 356, 357–60
Zola, Emile, 26
Zollman, Jakob, 40–41
Zollschan, Ignaz, 172–73
Zuckerman, Solly, 181–82
Zulu, 210
Zuma, Dlamini, 378
Zwarte Piet, 388–89